This, the fourth volume in the six-volume Commentary on the *Iliad* being prepared under the General Editorship of Professor G. S. Kirk, covers books 13–16, including the Battle for the Ships, the Deception of Zeus and the Death of Patroklos. Three introductory essays discuss the role of Homer's gods in his poetry; the origins and development of the epic diction; and the transmission of the text, from the bard's lips to our own manuscripts. It is now widely recognized that the first masterpiece of Western literature is an oral poem; Professor Janko's detailed commentary aims to show how this recognition can clarify many linguistic and textual problems, entailing a radical reassessment of the work of Homer's Alexandrian editors. The commentary also explores the poet's subtle creativity in adapting traditional materials, whether formulae, typical scenes, mythology or imagery, so as best to move, inspire and entertain his audience, ancient and modern alike. Discussion of the poem's literary qualities and structure is, where possible, kept separate from that of more technical matters.

This volume will be an essential reference work for all students of Greek literature and of oral epic poetry. Those who study and teach in a wide variety of related disciplines – mythology, ancient history and Aegean archaeology, humanities courses and Indo-European linguistics – will also find that it contains material of value to them.

The Iliad: a commentary

Volume IV: books 13–16

THE ILIAD:
A COMMENTARY

GENERAL EDITOR G. S. KIRK

Volume IV: books 13–16

RICHARD JANKO

PROFESSOR OF GREEK,
UNIVERSITY COLLEGE LONDON

CAMBRIDGE
UNIVERSITY PRESS

Published by the Press Syndicate of the University of Cambridge
The Pitt Building, Trumpington Street, Cambridge CB2 1RP
40 West 20th Street, New York, NY 10011-4211, USA
10 Stamford Road, Oakleigh, Melbourne 3166, Australia

First published 1992
Reprinted 1995

Printed in Great Britain by Athenaeum Press Ltd. Gateshead, Tyne & Wear

A catalogue record for this book is available from the British Library

Library of Congress cataloguing in publication data
Kirk, G. S. (Geoffrey Stephen)
The Iliad, a commentary.
Includes bibliographical references and indexes.
Contents: v. 1. Books 1–4   v. 4. Books 13–16 /
Richard Janko.
1. Homer. Iliad.   2. Achilles (Greek mythology) in
literature.   I. Trojan War in literature.   II. Janko,
Richard.   III. Homer. Iliad.
PA4037.K458   1985   883'.01   84-11330

ISBN 0 521 23712 2 hardback
ISBN 0 521 28174 1 paperback

This volume
is dedicated to

† Milman Parry
Albert Lord
† Michael Ventris
John Chadwick

founders of modern Homeric scholarship

and

to the memory of my father

Charles Arthur Janko

28 VII 1914 – 10 V 1991

τέρεν κατὰ δάκρυον εἴβω
χήτεϊ τοιοῦδ᾽ ἀνδρός, ἐπεί, πάτερ, ἤπιος ἦσθα.

CONTENTS

PREFACE

The aims of this commentary are laid down by its originator, Geoffrey Kirk, in vol. 1 (pp. ix–xi). I am grateful to him both for undertaking to fill this lacuna in classical scholarship and for asking me to share in his enterprise, which is all the more important at a time when bigotry worthy of Ptolemy Physcon has endangered the future of classical studies in my native land. Inspired by the late Sir Denys Page, I first began to investigate the diction of the Homeric poems in order to prove that they result from multiple authorship, but reached the opposite conclusion: that the *Iliad* and *Odyssey* were taken down by dictation, much as we have them, from the lips of a single eighth-century singer. In my view, one cannot do full justice to the songs of Homer without the benefit of many methods and approaches. These include Unitarianism, the view that each epic is a basically unified creation by a poetic genius; the proof by Parry and Lord that the epics belong to an oral tradition; the study of other such poems, both post-Homeric and from other traditional societies, especially in the Balkans; the recognition of Near Eastern influence on early Greece; the work of Burkert and the structuralists on myth; the work of Severyns and the Neo-Analysts on how Homer adapts traditional tales, especially those found in the post-Homeric Epic Cycle; Aristotelian and narratological literary theory; the decipherment of Linear B by Ventris and Chadwick; Greek dialectology and onomastics; Indo-European linguistics; Bronze and Iron-Age Aegean archaeology; the textual criticism of an oral-dictated poem, transmitted with oral and scribal variants in an open recension; van der Valk's work on Alexandrian scholarship; Erbse's edition of the scholia; and the recognition that our basic notions of 'literary' style have been decisively shaped by poems of oral origin. My vast debt to prior scholars and commentators will be plain to those who know.

A note on how to use this volume. I have tried to discuss more 'literary' questions in notes on whole blocks of text, and more technical items in notes on individual verses or small groups of verses, especially at the ends of notes. Thus, for example, the largest unit may be 14.153–353, then 153–9, and then 153–5. In this I have sought to help readers who know little or no Greek. At the same time I have not wished to stint on the full range of comment valuable to advanced students, particularly on the text and scholia; the radically oralist approach adopted here has revolutionary implications for Homeric textual criticism, and hence for the interpretation of many passages. I have not been able to note explicitly all my disagreements with the OCT, but these will usually be evident from my comments. Lack of space has demanded that I write with Aristotelian brevity (and, no doubt, obscurity), using many cross-references; exclude all later echoes or imitations, literary or pictorial, unless they clarify the text itself; erase numerous details, perhapses and scholarly debts; and adopt many short-hand conventions which may mislead the uninitiated. Readers will need to be attentive. When I write '*pace*' someone, I imply not only disagreement but also that that scholar offers useful arguments and/or references; lack of citation does not prove that I have not profited from a work. Other important conventions are explained after the list of abbreviations.

Lastly, I must thank the people and institutions that have assisted in this book's painfully slow and nomadic genesis. I am grateful above all to the John Simon Guggenheim Memorial Foundation for the Fellowship which gave me a year free of teaching. I thank my collaborators for commenting on my drafts and for their help, especially Mark Edwards. I am grateful to my teachers, colleagues and students, in Cambridge, New York and now the University of California at Los Angeles, for inspiration, advice and friendship; and to many others who have helped in ways of which they may well be unaware. Egbert Bakker, John Chadwick, Michael Haslam, Steve Reece and Keith Stanley read parts of the manuscript. With financial support from the UCLA Academic Senate Committee on Research, the following graduate students helped prepare the MS: Laurel Bowman, Todd Compton, Christine Ferris, Julie Laskaris, Leslie Myrick and Steve Reece. Caroline Alexander of Columbia and Fiona Wilson of Cambridge also aided me in this. Michael Cohen and David Blank resolved computer problems; Dana Sutton of UC Irvine gave me a copy of his database 'Homer in the papyri'. I am still indebted to John Dawson and his staff at the Literary and Linguistic Computing Centre, Cambridge, for helping me in 1977 to create an invaluable concordance to the entire epos. I also thank Susan Moore of the Press for her skilful and erudite copy-editing, and the staff of the university libraries at Cambridge, Columbia, UC Davis, the Ecole Normale Supérieure, Stanford and UCLA.

I shall always be grateful to the late Lord William Taylour for many summers of archaeological work in Greece; to John Leatham for fostering my early love of all things Greek; and to the memory of William Cowper, who rendered to both Homer and my native fields an equally inspiring homage. *Farewell, dear scenes, for ever closed to me.* It is a privilege to have sat at the feet of John Chadwick and, when passing through the other Cambridge, of Albert Lord; my dedication expresses my gratitude to them for their knowledge and example. Finally, I must thank my wife Michele for

Preface

reading the manuscript, for help with the index at a difficult time, and for her staunch support and companionship during this epic journey; she may not always have wished to hear whether Aristarchus read οὕτω or οὕτως.

Westwood, California, April 4 1990   R. J.

ABBREVIATIONS

Books

A   MS A of the *Iliad* (codex Venetus Graecus 822, 10th century)

AD   the A- and D-scholia to the *Iliad*; see D

Ahlberg, *Fighting*   G. Ahlberg, *Fighting on Land and Sea in Greek Geometric Art* (Stockholm 1971)

Albracht, *Kampfschilderung*   F. Albracht, *Kampf und Kampfschilderung bei Homer* (Naumberg 1886–95)

Allen, *Ilias*   T. W. Allen, ed., *Homeri Ilias* I–III (Oxford 1931, repr. New York 1979)

Allen, *Transmission*   T. W. Allen, *Homer: the Origins and the Transmission* (Oxford 1924, repr. 1969)

Ameis–Hentze   K. F. Ameis and C. Hentze, *Homers Ilias* (Leipzig 1913, repr. Amsterdam 1965)

ANET   J. B. Pritchard, ed., *Ancient Near Eastern Texts relating to the Old Testament* (3rd edn, Princeton 1969)

Ap. Rhod.   Apollonius Rhodius, *Argonautica*

Ap. Soph.   *Apollonii Sophistae Lexicon Homericum*, ed. I. Bekker (Berlin 1833)

Apthorp, *MS Evidence*   M. J. Apthorp, *The Manuscript Evidence for Interpolation in Homer* (Heidelberg 1980)

Arch. Hom.   *Archaeologia Homerica: Die Denkmäler und das frühgriechische Epos*, edd. F. Matz and H.-G. Buchholz (Göttingen 1967–)

Arend, *Scenen*   W. Arend, *Die typischen Scenen bei Homer* (Berlin 1933)

Arn   Aristonicus, Περὶ σημείων (in Erbse, *Scholia*)

Atchity, *Homer's 'Iliad'*   K. J. Atchity, *Homer's 'Iliad': the Shield of Memory* (Carbondale 1978)

B.   A. Bernabé, *Poetae Epici Graeci* (Leipzig 1987)

Bannert, *Formen des Wiederholens*   H. Bannert, *Formen des Wiederholens bei Homer* (Vienna 1988)

Barth, *Kallistratos*   H.-L. Barth, *Die Fragmente aus den Schriften des Grammatikers Kallistratos zu Homers Ilias und Odyssee* (Diss. Bonn 1984)

Beekes, *Laryngeals*   R. S. P. Beekes, *The Development of the Proto-Indo-European Laryngeals in Greek* (The Hague 1969)

Bolling, *External Evidence*   G. M. Bolling, *The External Evidence for Interpolation in Homer* (Oxford 1925, repr. 1968)

Bouzek, *Aegean*   J. Bouzek, *The Aegean, Anatolia and Europe: Cultural Interrelations in the Second Millennium B.C.* (Prague 1985)

Bowra, *Heroic Poetry*   C. M. Bowra, *Heroic Poetry* (Oxford 1952)

Bowra, *Tradition and Design*   C. M. Bowra, *Tradition and Design in the Iliad* (Oxford 1930, repr. Westport 1977)

Bremmer, *Soul*   J. Bremmer, *The Early Greek Concept of the Soul* (Princeton 1983)

Bryce, *The Lycians*   T. R. Bryce, *The Lycians* i (Copenhagen 1986)

bT   the bT-scholia to the *Iliad* (in Erbse, *Scholia*)

Buffière, *Mythes*   F. Buffière, *Les Mythes d'Homère et la pensée grecque* (Paris 1956)

Burkert, *Die orientalisierende Epoche*   W. Burkert, *Die orientalisierende Epoche der griechischen Religion und Literatur, SHAW* 1984, Abh. 1

Burkert, *Religion*   W. Burkert, *Greek Religion: Archaic and Classical* (Cambridge, Mass., and Oxford 1985); Engl. trans. by J. Raffan of *Griechische Religion der archaischen und klassischen Epoche* (Stuttgart 1977)

Calame   C. Calame, *Alcman* (Rome 1983)

Carlier, *Royauté*   P. Carlier, *La Royauté en Grèce avant Alexandre* (Strasbourg 1984)

Càssola, *Inni Omerici*   F. Càssola, *Inni Omerici* (Rome 1975)

Cat.   Hesiod, *Catalogue of Women* (fragments with numeration of M–W)

Chantraine, *Dict.*   P. Chantraine, *Dictionnaire étymologique de la langue grecque* (Paris 1968–80)

Chantraine, *Formation*   P. Chantraine, *La Formation des noms en grec ancien* (Paris 1933, repr. 1979)

Chantraine, *GH*   P. Chantraine, *Grammaire homérique* i–ii (Paris 1958–63)

Coldstream, *Geometric Greece*   J. N. Coldstream, *Geometric Greece* (London 1977)

Commentary   *A Commentary on Homer's Odyssey*, vol. i, A. Heubeck, S. West and J. B. Hainsworth (Oxford 1988); vol. ii, A. Heubeck and A. Hoekstra (Oxford 1989); [vol. iii to appear]; an Engl. version of *Odissea*

Companion   *A Companion to Homer*, edd. A. J. B. Wace and F. H. Stubbings (London 1962)

A. B. Cook, *Zeus*   A. B. Cook, *Zeus* (Cambridge 1914–40)

Cook, *Troad*   J. M. Cook, *The Troad: an Archaeological and Topographical Study* (Oxford 1973)

Crespo, *Prosodia*   E. Crespo, *Elementos antiguos y modernos en la prosodia homérica* (Salamanca 1977)

Crouwel, *Chariots*   J. H. Crouwel, *Chariots and Other Means of Land Transport in Bronze Age Greece* (Amsterdam 1981)

Cuillandre, *La Droite et la gauche*   J. Cuillandre, *La Droite et la gauche dans les poèmes homériques* (Paris 1944)

D   the D-scholia to the *Iliad*, in Σχόλια παλαιὰ τῶν πάνυ δοκίμων εἰς τὴν Ὁμήρου Ἰλιάδα, ed. J. Lascaris (Rome 1517)

D.   M. Davies, *Epicorum Graecorum Fragmenta* (Göttingen 1988) de Jong, *Narrators*   I. J. F. de Jong, *Narrators and Focalizers: the Presentation of the Story in the Iliad* (Amsterdam 1987)

Delebecque, *Cheval*   E. Delebecque, *Le Cheval dans l'Iliade* (Paris 1951)

Denniston, *Particles*   J. D. Denniston, *The Greek Particles* (2nd edn, Oxford 1954)

Did   Didymus, Περὶ τῆς Ἀρισταρχείου διορθώσεως (in Erbse, *Scholia*)

Dodds, *The Greeks and the Irrational*   E. R. Dodds, *The Greeks and the Irrational* (Berkeley and Los Angeles 1951)

Duckworth, *Foreshadowing*   G. E. Duckworth, *Foreshadowing and Suspense in the Epics of Homer, Apollonius and Vergil* (Princeton 1933)

Düntzer, *De Zenodoti studiis*   H. Düntzer, *De Zenodoti studiis Homericis* (Göttingen 1848, repr. Hildesheim 1981)

Dyck   A. R. Dyck, *The Fragments of Comanus of Naucratis* (Berlin and New York 1988)

Edwards, *HPI*   M. W. Edwards, *Homer, Poet of the Iliad* (Baltimore and London 1987)

G. P. Edwards, *The Language of Hesiod*   G. P. Edwards, *The Language of Hesiod in its Traditional Context* (Oxford 1971)

Erbse, *Ausgewählte Schriften*   H. Erbse, *Ausgewählte Schriften zur klassischen Philologie* (Berlin and New York 1979)

Erbse, *Götter*   H. Erbse, *Untersuchungen zur Funktion der Götter im homerischen Epos* (Berlin and New York 1986)

Erbse, *Scholia*   H. Erbse, *Scholia Graeca in Homeri Iliadem* I–VII (Berlin and New York 1969–88)

Erga   Hesiod, *Works and Days*

Eustathius   *Eustathii Commentarii ad Homeri Iliadem Pertinentes*, ed. M. van der Valk (Leiden 1971–87)

Fenik, *Homer and the Nibelungenlied*   B. Fenik, *Homer and the Nibelungenlied* (Cambridge, Mass., 1986)

Fenik, *TBS*   B. Fenik, *Typical Battle Scenes in the Iliad* (Wiesbaden 1968)

Fernández-Galiano   see *Odissea*

Ferrari, *Oralità*   F. Ferrari, *Oralità ed Espressione* (Pisa 1986)

Festschrift Risch   *O-o-pe-ro-si: Festschrift für Ernst Risch*, ed. A. Etter (Berlin and New York 1986)

FGH   F. Jacoby, *Fragmente der griechischen Historiker* (Berlin and Leiden 1923–58)

Fowler, *Lyric*   R. L. Fowler, *The Nature of Early Greek Lyric Poetry. Three Preliminary Studies* (Toronto 1987)

Foxhall and Davies, *The Trojan War*   L. Foxhall and J. K. Davies, edd., *The Trojan War: its Historicity and Context* (Bristol 1984)

Fränkel, *Gleichnisse*   H. Fränkel, *Die homerischen Gleichnisse* (Göttingen 1921, repr. 1977)

Fraser, *Ptolemaic Alexandria*   P. M. Fraser, *Ptolemaic Alexandria* (Oxford 1972)

Fraser and Matthews, *Names*   P. M. Fraser and E. Matthews, *A Lexicon of Greek Personal Names* I (Oxford 1987)

Frazer, *Apollodorus*   J. G. Frazer, ed., *Apollodorus: the Library* (Cambridge, Mass., 1921)

French and Wardle, *Prehistory*   E. B. French and K. A. Wardle, edd., *Problems in Greek Prehistory* (Bristol 1988)

P. Friedrich, *Trees*   P. Friedrich, *Proto-Indo-European Trees* (Chicago 1970)

W.-H. Friedrich, *Verwundung*   W.-H. Friedrich, *Verwundung und Tod in der Ilias* (Göttingen 1956)

Frisk   H. Frisk, *Griechisches etymologisches Wörterbuch* (Heidelberg 1954–72)

Frisk, *Kleine Schriften*   H. Frisk, *Kleine Schriften* (Göteborg 1966)

Gedenkschrift Güntert   *Antiquitates Indogermanicae: Gedenkschrift für H. Güntert*, edd. M. Mayerhofer and W. Meid (Innsbruck 1974)

The Greek Renaissance   *The Greek Renaissance*, ed. R. Hägg (Stockholm 1982)

Greenhalgh, *Warfare*   P. A. L. Greenhalgh, *Early Greek Warfare* (Cambridge 1973)

Griffin, *HLD*   J. Griffin, *Homer on Life and Death* (Oxford 1980)

h   the *h* family of MSS of the *Iliad* (see p. 21)

Hainsworth   see *Commentary*

Hdt.   Herodotus, *Histories*

Heubeck   see *Commentary*

Heubeck, *Kleine Schriften*   A. Heubeck, *Kleine Schriften* (Erlangen 1984)

Heyne   C. G. Heyne, ed., *Homeri Ilias* (London 1819)

Hoddinott, *The Thracians*   R. F. Hoddinott, *The Thracians* (London 1981)

Hoekstra   see *Commentary*

Hoekstra, *Modifications*   A. Hoekstra, *Homeric Modifications of Formulaic Prototypes* (2nd edn, Amsterdam 1969)

Hoekstra, *SES*   A. Hoekstra, *The Sub-Epic Stage of the Formulaic Tradition* (Amsterdam 1969)

Hoekstra, *Epic Verse before Homer*   A. Hoekstra, *Epic Verse before Homer* (Amsterdam 1979)

Hohendahl-Zoetelief, *Manners*   I. M. Hohendahl-Zoetelief, *Manners in the Homeric Epic* (Leiden 1980)

Horrocks, *Space and Time*   G. C. Horrocks, *Space and Time in Homer* (New York 1981)

Householder and Nagy, *Greek*   F. W. Householder and G. Nagy, *Greek: a Survey of Recent Work* (The Hague 1972)

Hrd   Herodian, Ἰλιακὴ προσῳδία (in Erbse, *Scholia*)

Hsch.   Hesychius Alexandrinus, *Lexicon*

Huxley, *GEP*　G. L. Huxley, *Greek Epic Poetry from Eumelos to Panyassis* (London 1969)

HyDem, HyAp, HyHerm, HyAphr　Homeric Hymns to Demeter, Apollo, Hermes, Aphrodite

Janko, *HHH*　R. Janko, *Homer, Hesiod and the Hymns* (Cambridge 1982)

Jouan, *Chants Cypriens*　F. Jouan, *Euripide et les légendes des Chants Cypriens* (Paris 1966)

Kakridis, *Researches*　J. T. Kakridis, *Homeric Researches* (Lund 1949)

Kakridis, *Homer Revisited*　J. T. Kakridis, *Homer Revisited* (Lund 1971)

King, *Achilles*　K. C. King, *Achilles* (Berkeley and Los Angeles 1987)

Kirk, *Songs*　G. S. Kirk, *The Songs of Homer* (Cambridge 1962)

KN　*The Knossos Tablets*, edd. J. T. Killen and J.-P. Olivier (5th edn, Salamanca 1989)

Krischer, *Konventionen*　T. Krischer, *Formale Konventionen der homerischen Epik* (Munich 1971)

Kullmann, *Quellen*　W. Kullmann, *Die Quellen der Ilias* (*Troische Sagenkreis*) (Wiesbaden 1960)

Kurt, *Fachausdrücke*　C. Kurt, *Seemännische Fachausdrücke bei Homer* (Göttingen 1979)

Lambert and Millard, *Atra-Ḫasīs*　W. G. Lambert and A. E. Millard, edd., *Atra-Ḫasīs* (Oxford 1969)

Language and Background　The Language and Background of Homer, ed. G. S. Kirk (Cambridge and New York 1964)

La Roche, *Textkritik*　J. La Roche, *Die homerische Textkritik im Alterthum* (Leipzig 1866)

Latacz, *Freude*　J. Latacz, *Zum Wortfeld 'Freude' in der Sprache Homers* (Heidelberg 1966)

Latacz, *Kampfdarstellung*　J. Latacz, *Kampfparänese, Kampfdarstellung und Kampfwirklichkeit in der Ilias, bei Kallinos und Tyrtaios* (Munich 1977)

Leaf　W. Leaf, *The Iliad* I–II (2nd edn, London 1900–2, repr. Amsterdam 1971)

Lehrs, *De Aristarchi studiis*　K. Lehrs, *De Aristarchi studiis Homericis* (3rd edn, Leipzig 1882)

Lesky, *Gesammelte Schriften*　A. Lesky, *Gesammelte Schriften* (Zurich 1966)

Leumann, *HW*　M. Leumann, *Homerische Wörter* (Basel 1950)

LfgrE　Lexikon des frühgriechischen Epos, edd. B. Snell and H. Erbse (Göttingen 1955–　)

LIMC　Lexicon Iconographicum Mythologiae Classicae, edd. H. C. Ackermann and J. R. Gisler (Zurich 1981–　)

Linear B　Linear B: a 1984 Survey, edd. A. M. Davies and Y. Duhoux (Louvain 1988)

Linke　K. Linke, *Die Fragmente des Grammatikers Dionysios Thrax* (Berlin and New York 1977)

Lloyd-Jones, *Justice of Zeus*   H. Lloyd-Jones, *The Justice of Zeus* (2nd edn, Berkeley and Los Angeles 1983)

Lohmann, *Reden*   D. Lohmann, *Die Komposition der Reden in der Ilias* (Berlin 1970)

Lord, *Singer*   A. B. Lord, *The Singer of Tales* (Cambridge, Mass., 1960)

Lorimer, *HM*   H. L. Lorimer, *Homer and the Monuments* (London 1950)

Lowenstam, *Death of Patroklos*   S. Lowenstam, *The Death of Patroklos* (Königstein 1981)

Ludwich, *AHT*   A. Ludwich, *Aristarchs Homerische Textkritik* I–II (Leipzig 1884–5)

LSJ   H. G. Liddell, R. Scott and H. S. Jones, *A Greek–English Lexicon* (9th edn, Oxford 1940)

MacCary, *Childlike Achilles*   W. T. MacCary, *Childlike Achilles* (New York 1982)

Macleod, *Iliad XXIV*   C. W. Macleod, *Homer, the Iliad, Book XXIV* (Cambridge 1982)

MacQueen, *The Hittites*   J. G. MacQueen, *The Hittites* (2nd edn, London 1986)

Maher, *Creation and Tradition*   J. P. Maher, *Creation and Tradition in Language* (Amsterdam 1977)

Mazon   P. Mazon, ed., *Homère, Iliade* (Paris 1937–8)

Meister, *Kunstsprache*   K. Meister, *Die homerische Kunstsprache* (Leipzig 1921)

Mélanges Delebecque   *Mélanges Edouard Delebecque* (Aix-en-Provence 1983)

Michel, *N*   C. Michel, *Erläuterungen zum N der Ilias* (Heidelberg 1971)

Montanari   F. Montanari, *I frammenti dei grammatici Agathokles, Hellanikos, Ptolemaios Epithetes* (Berlin and New York 1988)

Morris, *Burial*   I. M. Morris, *Burial and Ancient Society* (Cambridge 1987)

Moulton, *Similes*   C. Moulton, *Similes in the Homeric Poems* (Göttingen 1977)

Muellner, EYXOMAI   L. Muellner, *The Meaning of* EYXOMAI *through its Formulas* (Innsbruck 1976)

Mühlestein, *Namenstudien*   H. Mühlestein, *Homerische Namenstudien* (Frankfurt am Main 1987)

M–W   R. Merkelbach and M. L. West, *Fragmenta Hesiodea* (Oxford 1967); new fragments included in F. Solmsen, R. Merkelbach and M. L. West, edd., *Hesiodi Theogonia, Opera et Dies, Scutum, Fragmenta Selecta* (2nd edn, Oxford 1983)

MY   *The Mycenae Tablets IV. A Revised Transliteration*, ed. J.-P. Olivier (Leiden 1969)

Nagy, *BA*   G. Nagy, *The Best of the Achaeans* (Baltimore 1979)

Neitzel   S. Neitzel, *Apions Glossai Homerikai* (Berlin and New York 1977)

Nic   Nicanor, Περὶ τῆς Ὁμηρικῆς στιγμῆς (in Erbse, *Scholia*)

Nickau, *Zenodotos*   K. Nickau, *Untersuchungen zur textkritischen Methode des Zenodotos von Ephesos* (Berlin and New York 1977)

Niens, *Struktur*   C. Niens, *Struktur und Dynamik in den Kampfszenen der Ilias* (Heidelberg 1987)

Nussbaum, *Head and Horn*   A. Nussbaum, *Head and Horn in Indo-European* (Berlin and New York 1986)

OCT   Oxford Classical Texts: *Homeri Opera I–V*: I–II (*Iliad*) edd. D. B. Monro and T. W. Allen (3rd edn, Oxford 1920); III–IV (*Odyssey*) ed. T. W. Allen (2nd edn, Oxford 1917–19); V (*Hymns*, etc.) ed. T. W. Allen (Oxford 1912)

Odissea   Omero, *Odissea*, general editor, A. Heubeck (Rome 1981–6); see *Commentary*

Onians, *Origins*   R. B. Onians, *The Origins of European Thought* (Cambridge 1951)

Owen, *The Story of the Iliad*   E. T. Owen, *The Story of the Iliad* (Toronto 1946)

Page, *HHI*   D. L. Page, *History and the Homeric Iliad* (Berkeley and Los Angeles 1959)

Paley   F. A. Paley, ed., *The Iliad of Homer* (London 1866–71)

Palmer, *The Greek Language*   L. R. Palmer, *The Greek Language* (London 1980)

Parker, *Miasma*   R. Parker, *Miasma* (Oxford 1983)

Parry, *MHV*   Adam Parry, ed., *The Making of Homeric Verse: the Collected Papers of Milman Parry* (Oxford 1971)

A. A. Parry, *Blameless Aegisthus*   Anne Amory Parry, *Blameless Aegisthus* (Leiden 1973)

Peters, *Laryngale*   M. Peters, *Untersuchungen zur Vertretung der indogermanischen Laryngale im Griechischen* (Vienna 1980)

Pfeiffer, *Callimachus*   R. Pfeiffer, ed., *Callimachus* (Oxford 1949, repr. 1985)

Pfeiffer, *Scholarship*   R. Pfeiffer, *History of Classical Scholarship from the Beginnings to the End of the Hellenistic Age* (Oxford 1968)

PMG   *Poetae Melici Graeci*, ed. D. L. Page (Cambridge 1962)

Pokorny, *IEW*   J. Pokorny, *Indogermanisches etymologisches Wörterbuch* I (Bern 1959–69)

Pollard, *Birds*   J. Pollard, *Birds in Greek Life and Myth* (London 1977)

Porphyry   *Porphyrii Quaestionum Homericarum Reliquiae* I–II, ed. H. Schrader (Leipzig 1880–90)

Powell, *Lexicon to Herodotus*   J. E. Powell, *A Lexicon to Herodotus* (2nd edn, Cambridge 1938)

Prinz, *Gründungsmythen*   F. Prinz, *Gründungsmythen und Sagenchronologie* (Munich 1979)

Pritchett, *The Greek State at War*   W. K. Pritchett, *The Greek State at War* (Berkeley and Los Angeles 1971–   )

PY   *The Pylos Tablets Transcribed*, edd. E. L. Bennett and J.-P. Olivier (Rome 1973–6)

RE   *Paulys Real-Encyclopädie der classischen Altertumswissenschaft*, ed. G. Wissowa, W. Kroll, K. Mittelhaus and K. Ziegler (Stuttgart 1893–   )

Redfield, *Nature and Culture*   J. M. Redfield, *Nature and Culture in the Iliad* (Chicago 1975)

Reinhardt, *IuD*   K. Reinhardt, *Die Ilias und ihr Dichter*, ed. U. Hölscher (Göttingen 1961)

Res Mycenaeae   *Res Mycenaeae: Akten des VII. Internazionalen Mykenologischen Colloquiums*, edd. A. Heubeck and G. Neumann (Göttingen 1983)

Richardson   N. J. Richardson, *The Homeric Hymn to Demeter* (Oxford 1974)

Risch, *Kleine Schriften*   E. Risch, *Kleine Schriften* (Berlin 1981)

Risch, *Wortbildung*   E. Risch, *Wortbildung der homerischen Sprache* (2nd edn, Berlin and New York 1974)

Ruijgh, τε *épique*   C. J. Ruijgh, *Autour de 'τε épique'* (Amsterdam 1971)

Russo, *Scutum*   C. F. Russo, ed., *Hesiodi Scutum* (2nd edn, Florence 1965)

J. Russo   see *Odissea*

S   *Supplementum Lyricis Graecis*, ed. D. L. Page (Oxford 1974)

Sakellariou, *Migration*   M. B. Sakellariou, *La Migration grecque en Ionie* (Athens 1958)

Sandars, *Sea Peoples*   N. K. Sandars, *The Sea Peoples* (2nd edn, London 1985)

Schadewaldt, *Iliasstudien*   W. Schadewaldt, *Iliasstudien* (3rd edn, Darmstadt 1966)

Schadewaldt, *Welt*   W. Schadewaldt, *Von Homers Welt und Werk* (4th edn, Stuttgart 1965)

Scherer, 'Nichtgriechische Personennamen'   A. Scherer, 'Nichtgriechische Personennamen der Ilias', pp. 32–45 in *Studien zum antiken Epos*, edd. H. Görgemanns and E. A. Schmidt (Meisenheim 1976)

Schmidt, *Weltbild*   M. Schmidt, *Die Erklärungen zum Weltbild Homers und zur Kultur der Heroenzeit in den bT-scholien zur Ilias* (Munich 1976)

Schnapp-Gourbeillon, *Lions*   A. Schnapp-Gourbeillon, *Lions, héros, masques* (Paris 1981)

Schoeck, *Ilias und Aithiopis*   G. Schoeck, *Ilias und Aithiopis* (Zurich 1961)

Schwyzer, *Grammatik*   E. Schwyzer, *Griechische Grammatik* (Munich 1939–53)

Scott, *Simile*   W. C. Scott, *The Oral Nature of the Homeric Simile* (Leiden 1974)

Segal, *Mutilation*   C. Segal, *The Theme of the Mutilation of the Corpse in the Iliad* (Leiden 1971)

Severyns, *Cycle*   A. Severyns, *Le Cycle épique dans l'école d'Aristarque* (Paris 1928)

Severyns, *Homère*   A. Severyns, *Homère III: L'Artiste* (Brussels 1948)

SH   Supplementum Hellenisticum, edd. H. Lloyd-Jones and P. Parsons (Berlin and New York 1983)

Shipp, *Studies*   G. P. Shipp, *Studies in the Language of Homer* (2nd edn, Cambridge 1972)

Shipp, *Vocabulary*   G. P. Shipp, *Modern Greek Evidence for the Ancient Greek Vocabulary* (Sydney 1979)

SIG   Sylloge Inscriptionum Graecarum, edd. W. Dittenberger and F. Hiller von Gärtringen (3rd edn, Leipzig 1915–24)

Silk, *Interaction*   M. S. Silk, *Interaction in Poetic Imagery* (Cambridge 1974)

Slater, *Aristophanis Byzantii Fragmenta*   W. J. Slater, ed., *Aristophanis Byzantii Fragmenta* (Berlin and New York 1986)

Snodgrass, *Dark Age*   A. M. Snodgrass, *The Dark Age of Greece* (Edinburgh 1971)

Snodgrass, *EGA*   A.M. Snodgrass, *Early Greek Armour and Weapons* (Edinburgh 1964)

Sowa, *Themes*   C. A. Sowa, *Traditional Themes and the Homeric Hymns* (Chicago 1984)

Stella, *Tradizione micenea*   L. A. Stella, *Tradizione micenea e poesia dell'Iliade* (Rome 1978)

Steph. Byz.   Stephanus Byzantius, *Ethnica*, ed. A. Meineke (Berlin 1849)

Stith Thompson   Stith Thompson, *Motif-Index of Folk Literature* (2nd edn, Copenhagen 1955–8)

Strasburger, *Kämpfer*   G. Strasburger, *Die kleinen Kämpfer der Ilias* (Diss. Frankfurt 1954)

Studies Chadwick   Studies in Mycenaean and Classical Greek presented to John Chadwick, edd. J. T. Killen, J. L. Melena and J.-P. Olivier (Salamanca 1987)

Studies Palmer   Studies in Greek, Italic and Indo-European Linguistics offered to Leonard R. Palmer, edd. A. Morpurgo Davies and W. Meid (Innsbruck 1976)

SVF   Stoicorum Veterum Fragmenta, ed. H. von Arnim (Leipzig 1903–24, repr. Stuttgart 1964)

T   the T-scholia to the *Iliad* (in Erbse, *Scholia*)

TH   *The Thebes Tablets II*, edd. T. G. Spyropoulos and J. Chadwick (Salamanca 1975)

Thalmann, *Conventions*   W. G. Thalmann, *Conventions of Form and Thought in Early Greek Epic Poetry* (Baltimore 1984)

Thompson, *Birds*   D'A. W. Thompson, *A Glossary of Greek Birds* (2nd edn, London and Oxford 1936)

Thornton, *Supplication*   A. Thornton, *Homer's Iliad: its Composition and the Motif of Supplication* (Göttingen 1984)

Trümpy, *Fachausdrücke*   H. Trümpy, *Kriegerische Fachausdrücke im griechischen Epos* (Basel 1950)

Untermann, *Sprache*   J. Untermann, *Einführung in die Sprache Homers* (Heidelberg 1987)

van der Valk, *Researches*   M. van der Valk, *Researches on the Text and Scholia of the Iliad* I–II (Leiden 1963–4)

van der Valk, *TCO*   M. van der Valk, *Textual Criticism of the Odyssey* (Leiden 1949)

van Leeuwen, *Commentationes Homericae*   J. van Leeuwen, *Commentationes Homericae* (Leiden 1911)

Ventris and Chadwick, *Documents*   M. Ventris and J. Chadwick, *Documents in Mycenaean Greek* (2nd edn, Cambridge 1973)

Vermeule, *Death*   E. T. Vermeule, *Aspects of Death in Early Greek Art and Poetry* (Berkeley and Los Angeles 1979)

von Kamptz, *Personennamen*   H. von Kamptz, *Homerische Personennamen* (Göttingen 1982)

von Scheliha, *Patroklos*   R. von Scheliha, *Patroklos: Gedanken über Homers Dichtung und Gestalten* (Basel 1943)

Wackernagel, *SUH*   J. Wackernagel, *Sprachliche Untersuchungen zu Homer* (Göttingen 1916)

Wathelet, *Traits*   P. Wathelet, *Les Traits éoliens dans la langue de l'épopée grecque* (Rome 1970)

West, *Catalogue*   M. L. West, *The Hesiodic Catalogue of Women* (Oxford 1985)

West, *Orphic Poems*   M. L. West, *The Orphic Poems* (Oxford 1983)

West, *Theogony*   M. L. West, *Hesiod, Theogony* (Oxford 1966)

West, *Works and Days*   M. L. West, *Hesiod, Works and Days* (Oxford 1978)

S. West   see *Commentary*

S. West, *Ptolemaic Papyri*   S. West, *The Ptolemaic Papyri of Homer* (Cologne and Opladen 1967)

Westermann, *Genesis*   C. Westermann, *Genesis 1–11: A Commentary*, trans. J. J. Scullion (London 1984)

Whitman, *HHT*   C. H. Whitman, *Homer and the Heroic Tradition* (Cambridge, Mass., 1958)

Wilamowitz, *IuH*   U. von Wilamowitz-Moellendorff, *Die Ilias und Homer* (Berlin 1916)

Wilamowitz, *Kleine Schriften*   U. von Wilamowitz-Moellendorff, *Kleine Schriften* I–V (Berlin 1935–69)

Willcock   M. M. Willcock, *The Iliad of Homer* I–II (London 1978–84)

Winter, *MNO*   F. J. Winter, *Die Kampfszenen in den Gesängen MNO der Ilias* (Diss. Frankfurt 1956)

Wyatt, *ML*   W. F. Wyatt, Jr, *Metrical Lengthening in Homer* (Rome 1969)

Zgusta, *Ortsnamen*   L. Zgusta, *Kleinasiatische Ortsnamen* (Heidelberg 1984)

Journals

A&A	*Antike und Abendland*
AC	*L'Antiquité classique*
AJA	*American Journal of Archaeology*
AJP	*American Journal of Philology*
BCH	*Bulletin de correspondance hellénique*
BSA	*Annual of the British School at Athens*
CA	*Classical Antiquity*
CJ	*Classical Journal*
C&M	*Classica et Mediaevalia*
CPh	*Classsical Philology*
CQ	*Classical Quarterly*
CR	*Classical Review*
CRAI	*Comptes rendus de l'Académie des inscriptions et belles-lettres*
G&R	*Greece and Rome*
GRBS	*Greek, Roman and Byzantine Studies*
Gymn.	*Gymnasium*
HSCP	*Harvard Studies in Classical Philology*
JHS	*Journal of Hellenic Studies*
LCM	*Liverpool Classical Monthly*
MH	*Museum Helveticum*
Mnem.	*Mnemosyne*
MSS	*Münchener Studien zur Sprachwissenschaft*
PCPS	*Proceedings of the Cambridge Philological Society*
RA	*Revue archéologique*
REA	*Revue des études anciennes*
RFIC	*Rivista di filologia ed istruzione classica*
RhM	*Rheinisches Museum für Philologie*
RIL	*Rendiconti dell'Istituto Lombardo, Classe di lettere, scienze morali e storiche*
SBAW	*Sitzungsberichte der Bayerischen Akademie der Wissenschaften, Phil.-Hist. Klasse*
SHAW	*Sitzungsberichte der Heidelberger Akademie der Wissenschaften, Phil.-Hist. Klasse*
SMEA	*Studi micenei ed egeo-anatolici*
TAPA	*Transactions of the American Philological Association*

WS	*Wiener Studien*
YCS	*Yale Classical Studies*
ZPE	*Zeitschrift für Papyrologie und Epigraphik*
ZVS	*Zeitschrift für vergleichende Sprachforschung*

NOTE

My references to the narrator as 'the poet' or 'Homer' are narratologically imprecise, but save space. '*Il.*' means 'the *Iliad*', '*Od.*' 'the *Odyssey*', '*Hy.*' the Homeric Hymns, '*Cat.*' the Hesiodic *Catalogue of Women*, which is, I hold, genuinely by Hesiod (see p. 14 n. 21). The term 'epos' means all hexameter verse down to *c.* 500 B.C. Early epic fragments are cited from Bernabé *and* Davies, unless the numeration of these editions coincides. For the Hesiodic fragments, elegy and iambus I use (Merkelbach and) West's numeration; for lyric, Voigt and *PMG*; for the 'Orphica', Kern; for Pindar, Snell–Maehler; for the Presocratics, Diels–Kranz; for tragedy, Nauck and Radt; for comedy, Kassel–Austin; for Antimachus, Wyss; for Aristotle, Rose; for Callimachus, Pfeiffer and *SH*. Modern authors cited without initials appear in the bibliography.

Greek words found earlier in the same note are abbreviated to the first letter only, unless there is a risk of ambiguity. In discussions of formulae, the number of occurrences is given in the form '10× *Il.*, 6× *Od.*'; '10×' without qualification refers to the *Iliad*. The abbreviation 'etc.' in such references shows that the total includes all relevant terminations. Statements like '3/33×' mean 'thrice in a total of 33 instances'; the statistics are as accurate as I can make them. | marks the beginning or end of a verse. Greek names are transliterated following the rules laid down in vol. 1, x. Mycenaean (Myc.) reconstructed forms found in the tablets are given thus: /wanax/. Asterisks signal other reconstructed forms.

References to the scholia follow the system set out in vol. 1, 41f.; thus Arn/A means 'Aristonicus in MS A', Did/AT means 'Didymus in MSS A and T', Nic/A means 'Nicanor in MS A' and Hrd/AbT means 'Herodian in MS A and in the bT scholia'. Aristarchus is cited from Arn/A *ad loc.* unless stated. 'Papyri' are MS fragments down to *c.* 600 A.D.; 'codices' are medieval MSS; the 'good MSS' are the early minuscules (see pp. 20–2). Ancient works whose authorship is doubtful have the alleged author's name in quotation marks, e.g. 'Plut.'; spurious attributions are indicated by brackets, e.g. [Plut.].

The northern Aegean

INTRODUCTION

1. The gods in Homer: further considerations

In two vital aspects, early Greek epic poetry exactly reflects the nature of Greek religion as far back as it can be known. The system is polytheistic, as in nearly all other ancient societies, with Zeus as merely the mightiest member of the divine family; and the gods are regarded as anthropomorphic. Both facets of this system have important moral implications, which first appear in Homer but pervade all Greek literature. The pre-history of 'Homeric religion' was discussed above (vol. II, 1–14), where it was shown that the Greeks tended to elevate and humanize the Mesopotamian beliefs which they largely adopted. Here I will focus on the literary and moral dimensions of these beliefs, and how they are reshaped for the poetic purposes of the *Iliad*.[1]

(i) The literary and religious aims of Homer's innovations

Like any Greek poet, Homer had the right to adapt myths as he wished, within the wide limits of the traditions he inherited. As Griffin has shown,[2] he de-emphasizes their bizarre and magical aspects, plays up their potential for humour and tragedy, and above all stresses his gods' human nature: they are exactly like us save for their greater power and knowledge, and their freedom from age and death (they can still alter their location and shape at will, but Homer avoids vouching in his own *persona* for their more bizarre metamorphoses). He widens the gulf between mortal and immortal, which not even Herakles or Akhilleus can cross; even the more optimistic *Odyssey* vividly depicts the insubstantiality of the souls in Hades, barely alluding to tales that Menelaos and Herakles enjoyed a better afterlife. In the Cycle mortals became gods far more readily: Athene nearly immortalized Tudeus, Dawn gained immortality for her son Memnon and Thetis conveyed Akhil-

---

[1] For excellent treatments of this topic and bibliography see Whitman, *HHT* 221–48; Lesky, *RE* Suppl. XI (1968) s.v. *Homeros*, 725–40; Griffin, *HLD* 81ff.; Erbse, *Götter*. For background Burkert, *Religion* is indispensable.

[2] *JHS* 97 (1977) 39–53.

leus to the White Isle. But in Homer even Zeus can do no better than grant his own son Sarpedon a heroic burial and, it is implied, a lasting hero-cult. It is telling that at *Erga* 143ff. Hesiod blends both ideas: his race of bronze perishes in internecine strife and goes to Hades, whereas the 'heroes who are called demigods' perish likewise but go to the 'isles of the blessed' (i.e. 'of the gods'). Homer's dead live out an eternal death under the earth, thirsty for offerings of blood (just as the Olympians above relish the smoke of sacrifices), but devoid of even human powers. Ancient rituals known to Aeschylus, like the mutilation of a murdered man to keep him from taking revenge, or his kinsmen's summoning of aid from the underworld, confirm that other ideas of the afterlife were current. Again, Homer has clarified the world-view of his tradition, to stress that, when life is gone, it is gone for ever.

The paradoxical result is that, precisely by widening the chasm between mortal and immortal, Homer exalts the dignity and responsibility of human beings, placed between god and beast and potentially sharing the natures of both.[3] We may attain divine achievements, with the aid of the gods themselves, but not a divine existence. The here and now, for all the prevalence of adversity over happiness, is the only life we have, and we must make the best of it. Unlike the gods' moral choices, human ones are not trivial, since they can have results fatal for oneself or others, whereas gods cannot truly suffer. Again it is Griffin[4] who has shown how Homer exploits the gods' interactions with mortals as a metaphor for, and a guide to, the response of the human audience. Divine spectators may dignify the battle below by deeming it worth watching, and may glorify a warrior by aiding him: thus it enhances Akhilleus' victory when Athene helps him kill Hektor. Divine involvement is a major sign of the significance of an event and of how we should view it. Conversely, when the gods turn away, bored by the trivial squabbling of these ephemeral creatures, the bloodshed gains in pathos. The gods' unknowability to the characters creates irony, their irresistible power evokes fear, their frivolous irresponsibility arouses humour, their deliberations and plots excite suspense, and their effortless superiority yields a truly tragic pathos. The gods' actions are thus used to evoke the whole range of emotions which Aristotle has taught us to expect from great literature.

It was traditional to ascribe to divine agency any otherwise inexplicable event, like a spear missing its mark, a bowstring breaking, the amazing skill of a warrior, speaker, poet or artisan, and even a sudden feeling or thought. In everyday life one could rarely specify the god concerned, and thus spoke of a θεός, θεοί or δαίμων, just as someone who speaks or acts oddly is ad-

---

[3] Cf. Redfield, *Nature and Culture* 131–6.

[4] *CQ* 28 (1978) 1–22; *HLD* 179–204. The germ of this approach is in [Longinus], *On the Sublime* 9.7ff. See also J. M. Bremer in *Homer: Beyond Oral Poetry*, Amsterdam 1987, 31–46.

dressed as δαιμόνιε; only seers or other gifted persons could state which god was involved and what must be done in consequence. Homer's heroes can even doubt whether a god has intervened, and cannot recognize particular deities, whatever shape they take, unless they let themselves be perceived – Athene has to lift the mist from Diomedes' eyes so that he can tell men from gods (5.127f.). It takes a Kalkhas to diagnose Apollo's wrath at 1.93ff. But the bard claims a special vision, and can always say which deity is involved, showing us the world through the eyes of the gods themselves.

(ii) 'Double motivation' and human responsibility

Even aside from obvious favouritism, like Athene's dealings with Diomedes in the *Iliad* and with Odysseus in the *Odyssey*, many divine interventions in Homer appear artificial to modern readers. What is one to make of, for example, how Aphrodite forces Helen to go to bed with Paris even when Helen is disgusted by his conduct in the duel with Menelaos (3.383ff.)? Is this a mere externalization of normal human feeling – although enraged at Paris, Helen still finds him irresistibly attractive? When Athene appears to Akhilleus at 1.194ff., is this merely an objectification of prudent second thoughts? Such cases have led many to doubt the reality of the gods for the poet and his audience, and to deem them just a manner of speaking or a useful poetic convention.[5] The view, advanced by B. Snell[6] and prevalent until recently, that early epic has no concept of the whole personality, and objectifies mental processes as the *noos*, *thumos* and so forth, might seem to find a perfect parallel here; instead of a person's *thumos* or *phrenes*, passion or reason, taking the decision, a god decides. But it was always risky to base a complex psychological theory on the loose but conveniently extended set of overlapping terms by which the tradition described mental processes, as Lloyd-Jones[7] has shown; and the poet always makes clear that the god physically exists. When Aphrodite breaks Paris' chin-strap so that Menelaos cannot drag him off to his death, this could be ascribed to chance; but not so her next action, Paris' bodily removal to Helen's room in Troy. Athene, equally physically, tugs Akhilleus' hair; objectified prudence might well persuade, but could not pull hair. So why does Athene urge Akhilleus to do what, given his portrayal elsewhere in the poem, he would be likely

---

[5] Cf. Lloyd-Jones, *Justice of Zeus* 10; Griffin, *HLD* 144ff.

[6] *Die Entdeckung des Geistes*, 4th edn, Göttingen 1975; trans. T. G. Rosenmeyer, *The Discovery of the Mind in Early Greek Philosophy and Literature*, Cambridge, Mass. 1953. Cf. Erbse, *Götter*; H. Fränkel, *Early Greek Poetry and Philosophy*, trans. M. Hadas and J. Willis, Oxford 1975, 75–85; MacCary, *Childlike Achilles*; T. Jahn, *Zum Wortfeld 'Seele-Geist' in der Sprache Homers*, Munich 1987.

[7] *Justice of Zeus* 9; cf. Griffin, *HLD* 144ff.; Bremmer, *Soul*; Fowler, *Lyric* 4ff.

to do anyway, i.e. refrain from killing his commander-in-chief? And why is Aphrodite needed to make Helen yield to what is clearly a recurrent weakness for Paris?

The answer, formulated by Lesky,[8] lies in the idea of 'double motivation' or 'overdetermination'; gods and men cause the same actions and impulses simultaneously, and both can be held responsible. In his 'apology' Agamemnon saves face by stating that a like misfortune once befell Zeus himself; thereupon he offers full restitution, '*since* I suffered *atē* and Zeus took away my wits' (19.86ff., 137f.). On the same pattern, Aphrodite's coercion matches Helen's desires in a psychological framework that is all too familiar, Akhilleus is already debating inwardly whether to kill Agamemnon (1.188ff.), and we understand why he is loth to do so, despite the provocation he has received. It is a remarkable paradox that nearly every important event in the *Iliad* is the doing of a god, and that one can give a clear account of the poem's entire action with no reference to the gods at all.

Let Patroklos' death serve as a further example. Who is responsible? Patroklos himself, who was so swept away by his victory over Sarpedon that he ignored Akhilleus' warnings? Akhilleus, whose compromise of sending his deputy into battle in his place was a disaster? Nestor, who devised that compromise? Hektor, who strikes the death-blow? Euphorbos, the first Trojan to wound Patroklos? Apollo, who strips off his armour? Or Zeus, who cast fatal blindness into him (16.685ff.), and foretold the whole sequence to Here (15.63ff.)? If the latter, Zeus' prediction still includes something he would hardly want, the death of his son Sarpedon. So is it a power higher than Zeus? Or is it all of these? Or is nobody responsible at all? Only the last question demands a negative. Moral responsibility is one of Homer's major themes. Since the *Iliad* is in the tragic mode, the responsibility is never clear-cut, as it is in the morally simpler *Odyssey*, where the gods proclaim at the outset, and the plot affirms at the end, that we increase our miseries by our own misdeeds.

(iii) Free will, fate and the gods

By leaving an undefined area between free will and supernatural forces, Homer achieves two goals: his characters are seen to suffer for their own choices, which is clearly tragic, and yet the whole outcome seems beyond their individual control or even pre-ordained, which is tragic in another way. The same dualism which applies to the heroes also applies to the gods themselves, including Zeus, who performs several roles.[9] First, he is a per-

---

[8] 'Göttliche und menschliche Motivierung im homerischen Epos', *SHAW* 1961 Abh. 4; cf. Dodds, *The Greeks and the Irrational* 2ff.; Whitman, *HHT* 248.
[9] Cf. Erbse, *Götter* 209–56.

4

sonal god, the most powerful admittedly, who can be deceived and may use or threaten force to realize his wishes (Homer of course relegates this to reminiscences by the characters). He is concerned to punish perjurers and those who wrong suppliants and *xenoi* (strangers/hosts/guests); Paris' crime against Menelaos explains why he must ultimately back the Greeks against the Trojans. But there are signs that he cares about justice in a wider sense (16.384–93n.), and his will can be taken to represent that of his entire family, since the gods collectively are omniscient and omnipotent. One might expect that nothing could occur against his will; but he has to forgo saving even his own son Sarpedon, when he is reminded that this would be contrary to 'fate'.[10] This ancient idea is expressed by words for 'lot' or 'portion' – αἶσα, cf. Oscan *aeteis*, 'part', μοῖρα, μόρος, ἔμμορε, εἵμαρται, cf. μέρος, 'part'; πέπρωται, cf. Latin *pars*, 'portion'; κήρ, cf. κείρω, 'cut'. δαίμων, 'apportioner' (from δαίω), like 'kismet' (from Arabic *qasama*, 'divide'), reflects the same notion. The most universal aspect of one's lot is death, and so these words often connote death; indeed, μόρος has come to mean 'death', and βροτός (< *mr̥tos*) must come from the same root (this has eluded the etymologists).

The idea that everyone has an allotted portion in life is very old; a formular verse preserves an ancient metaphor for this, that someone suffers 'what fate spun into the thread as he was born' (20.127f. etc.). Such fatalism is an inevitable and necessary response to harsh circumstances, as is its opposite, the idea of free will (which Homer never formulated, but projects onto his gods). Without reflecting upon their inconsistency, we still tend to waver between these views, as life's changing situations affect us; the epic tradition itself was little different. Homer exploits the poetic advantages of both perspectives without bringing them into direct confrontation; the tangled relation between fate, human freedom and the gods was left for later thinkers to unravel.

Nothing ever happens contrary to fate in the *Iliad*, save for the extraordinary hyperbole at 16.780, when the Greeks prevail 'beyond destiny' (ὑπὲρ αἶσαν); normally we hear that events would have happened 'contrary to fate', had not someone intervened (e.g. 16.698ff.). 'Beyond fate' is even replaced by 'beyond god' at 17.327, when the god is Zeus (cf. 331). At 16.431ff. Zeus ponders whether to save his son Sarpedon; Here agrees that he could do so, but objects that it would set a precedent for other deities. The question of Zeus's power relative to fate lurks behind her words, but receives no answer. Instead, the scene reveals the depth of Zeus's grief, and shifts the emphasis to a theme central to the *Iliad*, the unbridgeable chasm between mortal and immortal: even the ruler of gods and men knows the limits to his power and exercises self-control for the sake of universal order

---

[10] See further *ibid.* 259–93; Bremer, *art. cit.* in n. 4.

– an example of the leadership Agamemnon ought to have displayed. But in the *Odyssey* mortals can suffer beyond what is fated, because of their own wickedness. Similarly, Zeus's interest in justice among men is confined in the *Iliad* to a simile at 16.384ff., but the *Odyssey* often mentions his concern to defend justice and punish wrongdoers (e.g. 3.132ff.). Neither difference between the epics should be explained by positing a historical evolution towards a Hesiodic theodicy – as we shall see, the linguistic data are fully compatible with the view that both epics are the work of a single poet. Instead, these differences exactly reflect each poem's divergent viewpoint – the *Iliad* stresses the tragic aspect of life, where suffering predominates, whereas the *Odyssey* offers a simpler, moralizing view, whereby the gods are concerned to ensure that we will eventually suffer beyond our due if we misbehave. Both views of the world were traditional; the first is more apt for war, the second for peace. Homer's art is shown by the consistency with which he has adopted the one appropriate to each epic and excluded the other.

In the *Iliad*, it is hardly too simplistic to regard fate as simply 'what happens', almost the needs of the tale or of the tradition, over which not even the poet has full control: nobody ever dared to deny, for instance, that Troy fell. If it happened, it must have been fated to happen. But fate and divine interference are also different ways of explaining the same event, depending on which one the character speaking finds more consoling or the poet more dramatic. Thus at 9.410ff. Akhilleus says that he has a choice of fates – a short and glorious life, or a long and inglorious one; at 18.96 Thetis tells him that, if he chooses to kill Hektor, his own death must soon follow. The literary effect is clear: nothing arouses more pathos than a hero going clear-eyed to his doom. If stress is placed on the inevitability of an event, its importance in a character's life-story or the need to endure it, then fate is invoked; if the emphasis falls on an action's power or strangeness, then it tends to be the work of a god. What is never suggested is that an odd or significant event is mere chance; Homer has no word for this, and does not know the idea either.

These ways of looking at events were clearly part of common belief, but Homer exploits them for literary effect; both ineluctable fate and unpredictable divine intervention reinforce the sense of man as a plaything at the mercy of mightier powers. But the conclusion drawn from this is far from a negative or passive one; we must win honour within the limits set for us by our existence within a cosmos which is basically well-ordered, however hard that order may be to discern. When Odysseus is reduced to beggary, he does not lower his moral standards; when Akhilleus faces the inevitability of death, he is still determined to die gloriously. Homer adapts for his own poetic and moral ends ways of thinking which are potentially contradictory,

6

refining the myths and world-view of his tradition. All his art is mobilized to stress the need for intelligence, courage and moral responsibility in the face of a dangerous universe, wherein mankind has an insignificant and yet paramount role. It is this attitude which makes the Homeric poems so sublimely and archetypally humane.[11]

[11] See further Simone Weil, *The Iliad, or The Poem of Force*, trans. M. McCarthy, Wallingford, Pa. 1956; Griffin, *HLD*.

2. The origins and evolution of the epic diction

The artificial diction of the Homeric poems ('*Kunstsprache*') is in essence identical to that of the other poems in the same tradition of oral narrative song in hexameters, i.e. the remnants of the Epic Cycle, the Hesiodic poems and 'Homeric' Hymns, which extend well into the sixth century.[1] Linguistic differences between these poems are barely discernible save by subtle statistical tests; the striking fact of the tradition's unity constitutes an impressive testimony to its panhellenic appeal and to the pre-eminence of that Ionic branch of it represented by Homer. Brief hexameter inscriptions from continental Greece have been held to show that local poets maintained epic traditions in local dialect, but this is doubtful. Some local influence is visible in Hesiod, e.g. in the Attic formula λαμπράν τε σελήνην;[2] but his diction is largely identical to Homer's, and he is fully heir to the Ionian epic tradition. Greek genres tended to adopt different regional styles of speech, according to where the finest practitioners of each originated. From Homer onward, wherever epic poets came from, they used the same basically Ionic diction, containing forms derived from different times and dialects, or from no time or place at all, but invented.

(i) The artificial nature of the epic diction

This diction was never spoken anywhere, only sung;[3] its origins were for centuries an insoluble puzzle. Aristarchus deemed it an archaic form of Ionic, spoken by the Ionians' ancestors before they left Attica (13.195–7n.). Once Bentley had realized that the metrical effects of the lost *w*-sound (digamma, Ϝ) were often detectable in the poems, editors tried to restore an 'original' text, assuming that copyists had modernized it; but even the most

---

[1] For basic accounts see Palmer in *Companion* 75–178; Ruijgh in *Linear B* 143–90; Hainsworth in *Commentary* 1 24–32; West, *JHS* 108 (1988) 151–72. The fundamental works are Chantraine, *GH*; Risch, *Wortbildung*. For the laryngeal theory, without which our understanding would be seriously incomplete, see Beekes, *Laryngeals*; H. Rix, *Historische Grammatik des Griechischen*, Darmstadt 1976; Peters, *Laryngale*.

[2] See G. P. Edwards, *The Language of Hesiod*, especially 102f.; Janko, *HHH* 223ff. For West Ionic forms see below n. 34. There is no Doric influence, *pace* West, *art. cit.* 167f.: for ἐσσεῖται, τύνη, see on 13.317f., 16.64f. The rare ἁμός (7× Hom.) and ὑμός (5× Hom., *Theog.* 662) must be pre-Aeolic archaisms (Householder and Nagy, *Greek* 66). τεοῖο, τεΐν, π(ρ)οτί and verbs in -άζω or -ίζω with futures and aorists in -ξ- are surely archaisms preserved from the Aeolic phase of the tradition.

[3] For speculation as to the music see West, *JHS* 101 (1981) 113–29.

traditional scenes are so full of 'recent' forms that attempts like Fick's reconstruction of an Aeolic 'Wrath of Akhilleus' never carried conviction, any more than does Shipp's theory, based on his discovery that 'recent' diction is concentrated in the similes, that these are post-Homeric additions. Further progress came from the proof by Witte and Meister[4] that metrical factors encouraged the use of both artificial forms, e.g. εὐρέα for εὐρύν in the fifth foot, and divergent dialectal forms of the same word, e.g. Aeolic ἄμμες beside Ionic ἡμεῖς.

The decisive step came with Parry, who saw that 'as the spoken language changes, the traditional diction of an oral poetry likewise changes, so long as there is no need of giving up any of the formulas'.[5] Parry surveyed the dialectal constituents of the diction, showing that it is the product of an Ionic oral tradition which has adopted with rather little change a traditional diction largely Aeolic in origin but including Arcado-Cypriot features; the Aeolic elements are generally retained only where they offer a metrically indispensable alternative to the Ionic forms. Confirmation that this diction mixes forms of different date came with the decipherment of Linear B, which has shed a flood of light on Homeric phonology, morphology, onomastics and vocabulary; and Hoekstra has shown how Homer and later bards introduced phonetic modifications, notably quantitative metathesis (e.g. -εω for -αο) and Ionic n-mobile (*nu ephelkustikon*), as they adapted old formulae.[6] But we still owe to Parry the explanation that such a linguistic mixture could only arise among many generations of poets, dependent to a greater or lesser degree on stereotyped phrasing to help them compose lengthy heroic narratives as they performed. Yet he was careful to insist that this diction was not just a matter of metrical utility; it also has the effect of distancing the tale from the everyday world, placing it more plausibly in the remote past and creating a suitably heroic tone.

(ii) The prehistoric origins of the *Kunstsprache*

The origins of the hexameter are obscure.[7] It was once thought to derive from the peoples who lived in Greece before Indo-Europeans arrived in

---

[4] K. Witte, *Zur homerischen Sprache*, Darmstadt 1972 (articles from *Glotta* 1–5, 1909–13); Meister, *Kunstsprache*. For studies antecedent to Parry's see Latacz (ed.), *Homer: Tradition und Neuerung*, Darmstadt 1979.

[5] *MHV* 331; his study occupies *MHV* 325–61.

[6] Thus a runover adjective or verb with movable nu before a consonant making the syllable heavy is often associated with modification (Hoekstra, *Modifications* 101–8). Statistics confirm that this is an innovation (Janko, *HHH* 64–8). For examples see 13.51, 13.78, 13.589, 13.705, 15.103, 15.280, 16.159.

[7] For recent surveys see M. Fantuzzi, *Materiali e discussioni* 12 (1984) 35–60, and Z. Ritoók, *Philologus* 131 (1987) 2–18; I refer below to Nagy, *Comparative Studies in Greek and Indic Meter*, Cambridge, Mass., 1974; West, *CQ* 23 (1973) 179–92; M. W. Haslam, *JHS* 96 (1976) 202; N. Berg, *MSS* 37 (1978) 11–36.

the late third millennium B.C. But the view has gained ground that, like other Greek verse-forms, it somehow descends from Proto-Indo-European verse, wherein the syllable-count was invariant (as it still is in 'Aeolic' verse-forms like the glyconic), but the scansion was fixed only towards the end of the verse; a relic of this is the freedom in syllabic weight seen in the opening syllables of many Aeolic rhythms. The hexameter arose from either the dactylic expansion of a single 'Aeolic' verse, the pherecratean (so Nagy), or, more probably, as a combination of two verses, whether hemiepes plus paroemiac, i.e. $- \cup \cup - \cup \cup - (\times)$ plus $\times - \cup \cup - \cup \cup - -$ (so West, Haslam), or choriambic dimeter B plus pherecratean, i.e. $\times \times \times \times - \cup \cup -$ plus $\times \times - \cup \cup - -$ (so Berg). Thus in tragedy and Corinna's poetry pherecrateans often end runs of glyconics. It is significant that some formulae with Vedic cognates, a sure sign of great antiquity, fit both Aeolic verses and hexameters. Phrases like ἱερὸν μένος (Sanskrit *iṣiréṇa ... mánasā*), κλέος ἄφθιτον (*ákṣiti śravaḥ, śrávo ... ákṣitam*) and ἀθάνατος καὶ ἀγήραος (*ajárā (a)mṛta*) prove that traditions of heroic song share a common Indo-European heritage, which is also represented in Indic and Slavic verse-forms.[8]

The oldest *Greek* epic we can reconstruct, via its formulae, was already in hexameters;[9] many old formulae straddle the main caesurae, and many old formular systems facilitate starting at the masculine or feminine caesura as the poet wishes. The hexameter has also innovated in allowing one heavy to equal two light syllables in the second half of each of the first five feet. Mycenaean had many more light open syllables than was the case once the weakening of intervocalic *h* (< *s* and *y*) and eventually *w* (ϝ) had led to vowel contraction. This more open structure would favour the regularization of the long line into a dactylic pattern, while contraction would reinforce the tendency to equate one heavy with two light syllables. We cannot exclude the possibility that the hexameter antedates Mycenaean times.

Several dactylic formulae prove archaeologically the Mycenaean contribution to the tradition; φάσγανον/ξίφος ἀργυρόηλον, ἀσπίδος ἀμφιβρότης and σάκος ἠΰτε πύργον all reflect *early* Mycenaean weaponry, and the existence of martial epic by this date accords with visual depictions of sieges of coastal towns on the Thera fresco and the silver rhyton from Shaft Grave IV at Mycenae. The popularity of boars' tusk helmets and figure-of-eight shields in art down to 1200 B.C. suggests that such equipment already had a heroic aura; the bard with a lyre on a fresco in the throne-room at Pylos may well be performing a heroic song. The formulae for a sword with silver rivets, the shield that surrounds a mortal and the hide like a tower show

---

[8] For bibliography see West, *JHS* 108 (1988) 152n.; M. Finkelberg, *CQ* 36 (1986) 1–5.
[9] So Hoekstra, *Epic Verse Before Homer* 33–53; Ruijgh, *op. cit.* in n. 1; West, *CQ* 23 (1973) 156–9.

that phrases containing two successive dactyls are as old as the objects themselves.[10]

This is supported by the diction. A whole set of formulae proves the survival of Bronze Age syllabic ṛ in the tradition's early stages.[11] ἀσπίδος ἀμφίβρότης does not scan unless we restore *amphĭmṛtās (cf. Sanskrit amṛtaḥ = ἄμβροτος); ἀνδροτῆτα (16.857, 22.363, 24.6) will not scan save as *ánṛtāta; ἀβρότη (14.78) represents *ámṛtā; ἀβροτάξομεν (10.65) is for ámṛt- (cf. ἤμβροτον = ἥμαρτον); Ἐνυαλίῳ ἀνδρειφόντῃ (7.166) scans only if we restore *anṛgʷhontāi – and this is half a hexameter. Again, in the old therio-morphic formula βοῶπις πότνια Ἥρη, h- is still felt as a consonant: cf. βέλος ἐχεπευκές (2×, < hekhe-),[12] ὑπείρεχε, συνεχές, ἀμφίεπον, ἐπιάλμενος, εἰνάλιος or εἰν Ἀΐδαο (< *smwid-), although some of these may be cases of metrical lengthening. Διὶ μῆτϊν ἀτάλαντος scans only if we restore Mycenaean *Διϝεὶ μῆτιν hατάλαντος (< sm-): this too is half a hexameter, and contains a spondee. Hermes' epithet ἐριούνης, 'good runner', is linked with Mycenaean by a cognate verb for 'run' in the dialects of Arcadia and Cyprus, whither many Mycenaeans fled after the catastrophe of c. 1200 B.C.;[13] epic vocabu-lary surviving as everyday words in these areas surely goes back to this era, e.g. ἀσκηθής, ἠπύω, ἰδέ. Still more telling is Horrocks' proof[14] that the 'tmesis' of those adverbs which were to become prepositions, a device basic to formular composition and modification and paralleled in Vedic, is out-moded in Mycenaean, where tmesis is rare; this implies that bards inherited from before that time one vital way in which the epic diction maintains its flexibility. Another was the optional use of the augment, which appears in Linear B.[15] Hoekstra must be right that what he calls the *amplitudo*, elaborate

[10] See S. P. Morris, *AJA* 93 (1989) 511–35; C. O. Pavese, *SMEA* 21 (1980) 341–52; C. Watkins in *Studies in Honor of M. Gimbutas*, Washington 1987, 286–97; West, *loc. cit.* in n. 9. The argument over whether forms specific to the Mycenaean dialect persist in Homer (the 'Achaean' stratum) continues: in favour see Householder and Nagy, *Greek* 62–6, and Ruijgh, in *Linear B* 148ff.; contrast Peters in *Festschrift Risch* 303–19.

[11] P. Wathelet, in Y. Lebrun (ed.), *Linguistic Research in Belgium*, Wetteren 1966, 145–73; see now West, *loc. cit.* in n. 9. Syllabic ṛ perhaps survived into Mycenaean, written -o-ro- or -o-, but this is hard to prove (Heubeck, *Kleine Schriften* 406–30; Mühlestein, *Namenstudien* 186f.). The vocalism ορ/ρο rather than αρ/ρα is Aeolic.

[12] Ruijgh, in *Linear B* 154–8; Crespo, *Prosodia* 72–4. Dissimilation of aspirates had not yet occurred in Mycenaean (Janko, *Glotta* 55 (1977) 1f.).

[13] Bowra, *JHS* 54 (1934) 54–74; Ruijgh, *L'Elément achéen dans la langue épique*, Assen 1957; Householder and Nagy, *Greek* 62–6. Note the possible Arcado-Cypriot forms (i.e. very late Myc.?) in 13.211–13, 16.173–5nn.

[14] *PCPS* 26 (1980) 1–11; *Space and Time in Homer*.

[15] Y. Duhoux (in *Studies Chadwick* 163–72) argues that use of the augment was typical of the Mycenaean lower classes – hence the presence of augments in 'special Mycenaean', gnomic aorists and usually in similes. L. Bottin (*SMEA* 10 (1969) 69–145) showed that its omission is an archaism, common in Aeolic forms like κάββαλε or duals. On the principle that poets make the *Kunstsprache* approximate to their vernacular, augments should be kept where our MSS have them, *pace* Aristarchus (see p. 25 n. 27).

formalized diction which can only have accompanied lengthy hexameter narratives, goes back to this era. Phrases like ἱερὸν μένος Ἀλκινόοιο do sound like Mycenaean courtly diction; compare 'His Royal Highness'.[16]

(iii) Trends of development in Homeric diction

The *Kunstsprache* was evolving before, during and after Homer's time; such development is a feature of all oral narrative poetry, since archaic phrases and forms which lose their original metrical shape tend to be replaced by an up-to-date metrical equivalent. Vernacular forms appear first in non-formular phrasing, then produce modified formulae and over time become fixed in set phraseology. In the extant poems, countless formulae are modified in line with recent developments. Thus μελιηδέα οἶνον (once *μελιϝᾱδέϝα ϝοῖνον) can become μελιηδέος οἴνου only after the loss of ϝ- and replacement of the genitive in -οιο by -ου; *μελιϝᾱδέϝος ϝοίνοιο will not scan. Similarly, phrases like *μειλιχίοισι ϝέπεσσι were changed to μειλιχίοις ἐπέεσσι; where there was no hiatus caused by the loss of ϝ-, bards did not innovate (e.g. χρυσέοισι νέφεσσι). Sound-changes led to the gradual replacement of old formulae, e.g. of (ϝ)ἑκάεργος Ἀπόλλων by Διὸς υἱὸς Ἀπόλλων or of (ϝ)εῖπέ τε μῦθον by φώνησέν τε. Obscure formulae like βοῶπις πότνια Ἥρη or νυκτὸς ἀμολγῷ came under pressure from intelligible equivalents, i.e. θεὰ λευκώλενος Ἥρη (with Aeolic θεᾱ) and νυκτὸς ἐν ὥρῃ.

The hexameter's complexity explains why Greek epic is more retentive of archaic diction than are similar traditions like Old English or South Slavic; if a bard needs to create phrases in so demanding a verse-form, he will more readily reuse or adapt pre-existing formulae than improvise from his vernacular. Even so, improvisation and adaptation were always vital to the tradition, which was clearly more fluid over a vast period than Parry thought, since he greatly overestimated the extent to which the poems consist of formulae. Not even the feeblest bards composed merely by stringing formulae together; poets always drew on their changing vernacular as they recreated and adapted the old tales, and their more striking or useful phrases entered the tradition, ultimately to become curious archaisms on the lips of singers hundreds of years younger.

In the complex blend of elements in Homeric diction, the most pervasive contribution is from the Ionic dialect spoken by the poet (η has replaced ᾱ in nearly every verse). Innovation is especially common in those parts of the poems, notably the extended similes, which we should associate with Homer himself. Attempts to assign different parts of the poems to different linguistic origins have never prospered; nor does the age of an object imply anything

---

[16] *Epic Verse before Homer* 81–9; cf. Ruijgh, in *Linear B* 158, and S. West on *Od.* 2.409.

about that of the scene where it is described – the boars' tusk helmet appears in a typically 'recent' passage (10.260ff.), and in fact its burglarious pedigree better befits an object looted from a tholos-tomb than an heirloom transmitted verbatim in a scrap of Mycenaean verse. Whereas neither context nor frequency can date a formula, the progress of archaeology and comparative philology enables us to assign relative or even absolute dates to many constituents of the amalgam; thus Κρόνου παῖς ἀγκυλομήτεω occurs 8× in Homer, εὐρύοπα Ζῆν only 3×, yet the former contains two 'recent' Ionian genitives, whereas the latter preserves the ancient accusative of Ζεύς and forms the basis for the modified formula εὐρύοπα Ζεύ(ς), which treats εὐρύοπα as a vocative or nominative and occurs 17×!

All agree that some elements are Mycenaean in origin, some Dark-Age and some Geometric; debate centres on how much each era contributed. On the *a priori* argument given above, one expects diction from the remotest epoch to survive to the smallest extent. Archaeologically provable Mycenaean phrases are rare; if Dark Age phrases (like ἀσπίδος ὀμφαλοέσσης) seem rarer, this is surely because the artifacts of this era are less distinctive, shield-bosses excepted (13.190–4n.). We cannot infer from the depressed culture of Dark Age Greece that poetry languished then – Kirk rightly argues the opposite.[17] But the Homeric poems are of Geometric date; not even the Catalogue of Ships is a Bronze Age survival or a Dark Age reconstruction, although it includes elements of both. The epics purport to recreate Mycenaean times, in a diction which seemed suitably archaic to bard and audience, but is largely post-Mycenaean.

This conclusion is confirmed by statistical study of the texts surviving from the tradition.[18] In a number of common features wherein younger forms replace older ones, as is proven by comparative philology, one can quantify the degree of change from one poem to the next. Whenever a bard has to use a given word or grammatical case, he may have to choose between a more recent form and an older one, seemingly unmetrical. He often keeps the older form, which is more convenient under the pressure of rapid composition; but to an increasing degree – even within the work of the same poet – newer forms enter the tradition. Thus pre-vocalic *w*- ceased to be sounded not long before Homer's time; its metrical effects are still felt 84% of the time in the *Iliad* (and almost always in the enclitic ἑ ἕο οἱ, where it survived longer: cf. on 13.163f., 561). Yet it was lost early enough for Homer to invent Ὀϊλεύς for Ϝιλεύς (13.66–7n.) and to misapply its metrical effects to ἑός (from *sewos) by analogy with ὅς (*swos): see 13.492–5n. Later

---

[17] *Songs* 105–56; *Homer and the Oral Tradition*, Cambridge 1976, 19–39.

[18] Janko, *HHH*, following Hoekstra and G. P. Edwards, *op. cit.* in n. 2; see also M. Cantilena, *RFIC* 114 (1986) 91–124. My figures for Ϝ- below are revised to exclude ἐρύκω.

poets increasingly ignore it, at least until the archaizing influence of far older texts fixed in writing begins to be felt in *c.* 600 B.C. Thus the *Odyssey* maintains the effect of ϝ- 83% of the time, the *Theogony* 66%, the *Erga* 62% and the *Hymn to Demeter* 54%; however, the *Shield of Herakles*, datable to *c.* 570 B.C., has a figure of 72%, which suggests that its poet learned much of his diction from hearing the Homeric and Hesiodic poems recited. So too Hellenistic poets archaize heavily, because they have acquired their diction from reading early epic. The same pattern of change appears in other equally common features.[19] My figures confirm the standard view that the *Iliad* is the oldest Greek poem we have, followed by the *Odyssey*, and then, after a gap, the *Theogony* and *Erga*.[20] Incidentally, the *Catalogue of Women* emerges as almost identical in diction to the *Theogony*, and must take its rightful place as a genuine early member of the tradition.[21]

It follows that the poems acquired fixed form at different stages in a single development; this has implications for how they came to be written down. The linguistic gap between the two Homeric epics is small, smaller than that between the two poems generally agreed to be by Hesiod; there is no linguistic evidence against the ancient view – and some in favour – that the *Iliad* and *Odyssey* are likewise the work of a single poet whose diction evolved with his years.[22] But what matters here is that the diction was evolving in

[19] It recurs in the tiniest details, e.g. the definite article (J. A. Scott, *The Unity of Homer*, Berkeley 1921, 90–2). Thus the old word τέκος, preserved mainly in formular phrases, is losing ground to τέκνον: its usage falls from 36/79× *Il.* (45%) to 15/49× *Od.* (31%), 2/23× in Hesiod (9%). θεῖος < θέϊος (cf. Myc. *te-i-ja* = |*thehiā*|) is irresolvably contracted 1/26× *Il.*, 12/47× *Od.*, 4/8× Hes. Compounds in ἐϋ- are irresolvably contracted to εὐ- 52/532× Hom., 27/43× Hes. (cf. 16.104–6n.); the adverb εὖ, less well-embedded in formulae, is contracted more often, but shows the same trend (80/211× Hom., 11/13× Hes.). Myc. *e-u-* thus stands for *ehu-* (cf. Hittite *aššus* 'good').

[20] The fashion for dating Homer after Hesiod owes much to Burkert (*WS* 89 (1976) 5ff.), who thinks the mention of 'hundred-gated' Egyptian Thebes at 9.381–4 must refer to that city's glory under the 'Ethiopian' dynasty, 715–663 B.C., and not the New Kingdom; but cf. Heubeck, *Gymn.* 89 (1982) 442f. The allegedly 'recent' scansion of Αἰγυπτίας proves nothing: it will not scan otherwise, |*Aiguptios*| is a Mycenaean name (KN Db 1105), and late language does not prove an object late. There is no reason why Egyptian Thebes cannot be a Mycenaean reminiscence, like Homer's references to the Sidonians (but these could also be Dark Age: see 23.740–9n.).

[21] West (*Catalogue* 130ff., 164ff.), ignoring the statistics, dates it to 580–520 B.C., but it certainly antedates the spurious *Aspis* of *c.* 570 B.C. (J. R. March, *The Creative Poet*, London 1987, 157–9). See further Janko, *HHH* 221–5, 248; *id.*, *CQ* 36 (1986) 42ff. M. Davies (*Glotta* 57 (1989) 89ff.) largely bases his sixth-century date for the Cycle on West's dating of *Cat.*, but the linguistic evidence is good enough only to give the Cycle a *terminus post quem* of around Hesiod's time.

[22] So [Longinus], *On the Sublime* 9.12–14. The greater frequency of abstract nouns in the *Odyssey* was once claimed to prove it the later poem, but Homer concentrates such nouns in speeches; as in Thucydides, most of the poems' moral commentary appears in speeches, of which the *Odyssey* has a higher proportion (cf. A. Shewan, *Homeric Essays*, Oxford 1935, 343ff.; Griffin, *JHS* 106 (1986) 36–57).

numerous ways of which bards cannot have been aware. On average, 13–20% of the diction was replaced or remodelled in the interval between the composition of the *Iliad* and that of the *Theogony*, which was at least a generation. If this rate of replacement applied throughout the period 1200–750 B.C., only 10–20% of the Mycenaean diction can have survived. But this is an unreliable yardstick. Formulae which will scan only when the Dark Age *o*-stem genitive singular in *-oo is restored, like ἀδελφειοῦ/ἀνεψῖοῦ κταμένοιο (for *ἀδελφεόο etc.), Ἰλίου προπάροιθεν or Αἰόλου κλυτὰ δώματα (5.21, 15.66, 554, *Od.* 10.60), are rare, although they are valuable signs of the topics of heroic poetry in that era.[23] The pace of change may have increased during that great burst of Ionian creativity which Homer represents.

(iv) The Aeolic phase of the epic tradition

The greatest area of current dispute is over the Aeolic element in the diction. To understand the issues, we must briefly survey another controversy, the origins of the Greek dialects. Much of their differentiation postdates 1200 B.C., but the basic distinction between 'East' and 'West' Greek goes deep into the Bronze Age.[24] The Mycenaean stratum in Homer is widely held to derive from the palatial centres in the Peloponnese, Crete, Boeotia, Aetolia and S.E. Thessaly, areas prominent in heroic saga. From several of them (save Greece north and west of Thebes) we have Linear B archives in the same type of 'East Greek', whose basic feature is the shift of τι to σι (e.g. δίδωσι < -τι). As we know from its shared choices and innovations, Mycenaean is related to the dialects of Arcadia, Cyprus, and, less closely, Attica and Ionia. These 'East Greek' dialects originated in Southern Greece in the later Bronze Age. But the Aeolic dialects of Eastern Thessaly, Boeotia and Asiatic Aeolis (the last two influenced by Doric and Ionic respectively) seem essentially cognate with the Doric and N.W. Greek whose basic 'West Greek' traits arose north of the Corinthian Gulf. Aeolic looks like a blend between Mycenaean, spoken perhaps by the upper classes in S.E. Thessaly, and a

[23] So too the phrases κακομηχάνου ὀκρυοέσσης or ἐπιδημίου ὀκρυόεντος (6.344, 9.64) reflect this genitive and the adjective κρυόεις, ie. *κακομηχάνοο κρ-, ἐπιδημίοο κρ-; but we must not restore *-οο or *-οου with a diectasis (cf. ὅου), since the MSS may reflect ancient traditions of pronunciation, and *-οο was contracted well before Homer's time (Janko, *HHH* 87–94). Cf. too 2.518n.

[24] For recent surveys see A. Bartoněk, *SMEA* 26 (1987) 7–22; Y. Duhoux, *Introduction aux dialectes grecs anciens* (Louvain 1983). Palmer brings proto-Aeolic as far down as Corinth and puts proto-Attic-Ionic in Attica and Euboea, deeming Aeolic part of 'East' Greek (*The Greek Language* 57–80); this neglects Risch's proof that Lesbian is heavily influenced by Ionic (in *Language and Background* 90–106). Arcado-Cypriot was once spoken in Rhodes (cf. Chantraine, *Dict.* s.v. ἴγνητες, the Arcado-Cypriot name of the indigenous inhabitants).

local 'West Greek' vernacular. After 1100 B.C. Aeolic speech was borne by migrants, with varying degrees of intermixture, to Asiatic Aeolis and Boeotia, Ionic was taken via Athens to Ionia, while pastoralists from N.W. Greece moved into the Peloponnese and Crete.[25]

The epic diction contains many forms deriving from Asiatic Aeolic, e.g. ὅππως, ὁππότερος etc., by analogy with ὅττι (< *yod-k^{w}id); ζα- from δια- in ζάθεος; or the vocalization of w in ἀπηύρα (for *ἀπ-έ-ϝρᾱ), εὔαδε for *ἔσϝαδε etc. (13.41–2n.). Other forms are shared with mainland Aeolic: the assimilation of original *σ to a following liquid or nasal, as in ἄμμες, ἔμμεν, ἔλλαβε, ἔμμορε or ἐρεβεννός, appears in Thessalian too; all three Aeolic dialects share the dative plural in -εσσι and the treatment of labiovelars (k^w, g^w) as labials even before e (e.g. Φῆρες for Θῆρες and perhaps πίσυρες for τέσσαρες, 15.680n.). Other shared Aeolisms are ἐρι- for ἀρι-, μάν for μήν, ἴα for μία, and the shift of *-ρι- to -ρε- seen in Νεστόρεος, Ἑκτόρεος, ἠνορέη (for *ἀνορία); indeed the last case, like metrically lengthened ἠνεμόεις for *ἀνεμόεις, shows that Ionic singers did not always recognize the Aeolic word, and therefore replaced ᾱ with η (contrast ἀθάνατος). Other Aeolisms are extended artificially, e.g. Ἀγαμεμνονέος for -ιος, αἰσχροῖσ' ἐπέεσσι for *-οῖσι ϝέπεσσι.

It might seem easiest to assume that Mycenaean singers crossed the Aegean direct from the Peloponnese and Athens to the new Ionian settlements of c. 1000 B.C., maintaining their poetic traditions unbroken through the disruption and depopulation at the start of the Dark Ages, and that the Aeolic elements are borrowed from a nearby tradition or vernacular, which supplied many metrically convenient alternative forms.[26] Yet recent studies[27] of the linguistic data uphold Parry's view that there was a radical discontinuity in the tradition, not long before the time of the Homeric poems, when a diction based on the vernacular of Asiatic Aeolis passed into the Ionian ambit, whether by the (historically documented) northward spread in c. 800 B.C. of Ionians into Chios and Smyrna (the places most strongly linked with Homer), or by a southward drift of poets from Lesbos

---

[25] Chadwick has disputed the idea of a movement of Doric-speakers into the Peloponnese, holding that they were present there as a substrate population. But this has not won acceptance (see the essays by Chadwick, Risch, S. Hiller and R. A. Crossland in D. Musti (ed.), *Le Origini dei Greci*, Rome 1986). I think the lower classes there spoke proto-Attic-Ionic. Archaeological evidence for a movement from N.W. Greece in LH IIIB2 onward now exists – the handmade burnished 'barbarian' ware (K. Kilian in French and Wardle, *Prehistory* 133).

[26] So Kirk, *Songs* 148–56; Wyatt, Ἐπιστημονικὴ Ἐπετηρὶς τῆς φιλοσοφικῆς Σχολῆς τοῦ Ἀριστοτελείου Πανεπιστημίου Θεσσαλονίκης 14 (1975) 133–47; D. G. Miller, *Homer and the Ionian Epic Tradition*, Innsbruck 1982. Horrocks, in *Studies Chadwick* 269–94, rejects an Aeolic phase only because he mistakes the infin. in -έμεν for a post-migration innovation.

[27] Parry, *MHV* 342–61; Hoekstra, *Modifications* 145–53; Wathelet, *Traits*; Householder and Nagy, *Greek* 67–9; Palmer in *Companion* 83ff.; Janko, *HHH* 89ff.; Ruijgh, in *Linear B* 145ff., 164ff.; West, *JHS* 108 (1988) 162–5.

and Aeolian Cyme (the birthplace of Hesiod's father) into the zone of Ionic speech. This matches the fact that Aeolic vocabulary, commonest in the *Iliad*, declines in frequency later.[28]

Now Parry held that oral poets use the most recent form which still keeps the same metrical shape. The clearest proof of this principle is diectasis. The bardic form ὁρόω preserves the shape of ὁράω while introducing the vocalism of contracted ὁρῶ; the latter was standard in the vernacular, as many contracted forms in the poems prove. Verbs like τρωπᾶσθε (15.666) are a different compromise, to the same end, between original *τροπάεσθε and contracted *τροπᾶσθε: the alternative with diectasis, τροπάασθε, is attested at 16.95.[29] So too φόως is a cross between φά(ϝ)ος and φῶς (cf. 16.249–52n.), ἐείκοσι between *ἐϝῑκοσι and contracted εἴκοσι, ἔην between ἔεν and ἦν, ἐήνδανε between *ἐ(ϝ)άνδανε and ἥνδανε, ὅου between Dark Age *ὅο and contracted οὖ (cf. ἕης, 16.207–9n.).

From Parry's principle it follows that any tradition which inherited Mycenaean speech should preserve the most recent form which maintains the metre. Thus the epic should have kept Mycenaean /posi/ (cf. Arcadian πός), but in fact uses the 'West Greek' form ποτί beside πρός; indeed πρός can be proved to have largely replaced ποτί, which must be proto-Aeolic. The same replacement apparently occurred in Lesbian, which has πρός under Ionic influence: the formula προτὶ Ἴλιον ἱρήν, with Lesbian ἱρός, confirms this.[30] The Aeolic infinitive in -έμεν is a similar case: -έμεναι is a Lesbian mixture of the inherited form with Ionic -ναι. Instead of retaining Mycenaean /-ehen/ as seen in e-ke-e /hekhehen/, the bards still use -έμεν.[31] Likewise the Aeolic perfect participle κεκλήγων is replaced by -ώς save when the scansion differs, as in κεκλήγοντες (cf. 16.430n.).

Again, Ἑρμείας is a compromise between the Ionian vernacular Ἑρμῆς or -έης (via *-ήης) and old *Ἑρμᾶας (cf. Mycenaean E-ma-a₂ = /Hermāhāi/). The Aeolic ending -ᾶς rather than -ης is inexplicable if the tradition ever contained *Ἑρμήης: the expected Ionism Ἑρμείης only appears later (2× Hes., 2× Hy.), when the Aeolic phase was far in the past. Likewise, the Ionic development of the a-stem genitives, nouns Ποσειδάων and λαός and

---

[28] ἰός, 'one', occurs 7× *Il.*, 2× *Od.*; μᾶν occurs 22× *Il.*, 2× *Od.*; τοίσδεσ(σ)ι occurs 1× *Il.*, 5× *Od.*; among cases of ἱρός/ἱερός, ἱρός occurs 30/83× *Il.* (36%), 17/77× *Od.* (22%). These Aeolisms vanish in post-Homeric epos. Wackernagel (*SUH* 17ff.) saw that the complementary distribution of μᾶν before vowels and Ionic μέν before consonants is another proof of an Aeolic phase (cf. Chantraine, *GH* I 15f.; Denniston, *Particles* 328f.).

[29] Note irresolvably contracted στρωφᾶτο, τρώχων (13.557, *Od.* 6.318). Chantraine (*GH* I 358) deems such verbs ancient, but all save νωμάω and πωτάομαι may be bardic creations.

[30] Beekes, *Mnem.* 26 (1973) 387–90; Janko, *Glotta* 57 (1979) 24–9; *contra*, Wyatt, *SMEA* 19 (1978) 89–124. Householder and Nagy (*Greek* 67–9) point out that βωτιάνειρα has both -τι- and an Aeolic treatment of metrical lengthening: cf. ὠλεσίκαρπος for οὐ-.

[31] Chantraine, *GH* I 492f.; Crespo, *Prosodia* 54f.

adverb ἕως was (i) -άο, -άων, λᾱϝός (as in Mycenaean), *ἅϝος (cf. Sanskrit *yāvat*); (ii) *-ηο, *-ήων, *ληϝός, *ἥϝος; (iii) after the loss of -ϝ-, *-ηο, *-ήων, ληός (in Hipponax and Herodotus), *ἥος; (iv) -εω͜, -έω͜ν, λεώς and ἕως with metathesis of quantity and synizesis. Instead of offering the vernacular forms (iv) beside the older forms (iii) with the original scansion, as we would expect in a continuous Ionic tradition, the epic offers primarily (i), the Mycenaean and early Aeolic forms (Sappho and Alcaeus have contracted -ᾱ, -ᾱν), with an admixture of (iv). Thus the Aeolism λαός was kept; λεώς appears in the invented name Ἀγέλεως (*Od.* 22.131) and in Λειώκριτος (17.344, 2× *Od.*), which represents the usual compromise between inherited Λᾱο- and spoken Λεω-, maintaining the scansion while modernizing the vowel-quality. Instead of *ἥος, our texts offer εἵως or ἕως scanned − − and − ∪ respectively, beside ἕως scanned − ; the Ionian bards for some reason avoided *ἅος and adapted their vernacular form to fit the original scansion – they never knew *ἥος, which editors wrongly restore.[32] The only convincing explanation for these phenomena is that the intermediate forms were no longer in the vernacular and were never part of the traditional diction. Thus there was no continuous Ionic tradition.

Now both formular usage and the statistics show that the genitives -εω͜ and -έω͜ν, and all other forms with quantitative metathesis, entered the tradition not long before Homer; they appear at about the same point in its prehistory as the short dative plurals of the *o*- and *a*-stems and the specifically East Ionic innovation Ζηνός.[33] The arrival of these Ionic forms in the diction, deduced by projecting back into prehistory the trends seen in the poems of Homer and Hesiod, marks the end of the Aeolic phase.[34] According

---

[32] So West, *Glotta* 44 (1966) 135–9; S. West and Hainsworth on *Od.* 4.90f., 5.123. As Parry says (*MHV* 353n.), 'the seeming vagaries of the manuscript tradition accord with the processes of oral poetry and thus bear witness to their faithfulness'. Cf. van der Valk, *TCO* 67ff.; *contra*, Hoekstra on *Od.* 13.315.

[33] This was identified by Wathelet, *Minos* 15 (1974) 195–225; genitives like Πηλέος are specifically Chian (15.339n.). These forms are missed by West (*JHS* 108 (1988)166), who thinks the poems lack East Ionic forms, and holds that in East Ionic we would expect κῶς etc. for πῶς etc.: the poems are in Central or West Ionic, with Euboea playing a central role in the Ionic phase. But forms like κῶς appear in inscriptions only at Erythrae, Asiatic Aegae and colonies of Phocaea (E. Sanmartí and R.A. Santiago, *ZPE* 68 (1987) 125); they were clearly not universal in East Ionic. There was certainly some Euboean influence, especially in the *Odyssey*; cf. Hesiod's performance at Chalcis (*Erga* 654ff.). See Wathelet, *AC* 50 (1981) 819–33, citing forms like μονωθείς and ξένος (for μουν-, ξείν- < ξένϝος); cf. too the rare ὤν for ἐών (14.271–4n.).

[34] Janko, *HHH* 87ff.; on the late date of quantitative metathesis cf. Crespo, *Cuadernos de Filología Clásica* 12 (1977) 188–219. Crespo, *Prosodia* 35–63, suggests that the prevalence of quantitative metathesis and contraction in the Ionic vernacular led to metrical anomalies like νηὸς (blending νηός and νεώς), κάνεὸν (blending κάνεον and κάνουν), Ἀλκίνοος (blending νόος and νοῦς), ἱπποῖιν (blending -οῖιν and -οιν), and even Ἀσκληπιοῦ δύο παῖδε (2.731) for * Ἀσκληπῑοο or -όου.

to my statistics, their appearance antedates the *Iliad* by a smaller interval than that which separates the *Iliad* from the *Theogony*, if the rate of linguistic change was constant. In absolute terms, if the *Theogony* dates to *c.* 700 and the *Iliad* to before 750 (a reasonable guess on the present evidence), the Ionic forms entered the tradition in *c.* 800 B.C. It is no obstacle to this theory that the statistics show that the loss of ϝ- goes slightly further back, since this also occurred in Asiatic Aeolic.[35]

Many forms found in Mycenaean, and often ascribed to an 'Achaean' substratum in the epics, are in fact archaisms shared by the ancestors of all later dialects, e.g. the genitives in -αο and -οιο, the demonstrative τοί, ταί or adjectives like Ποιάντιος, Τελαμώνιος. In the absence of evidence for the Bronze Age Greek of the mainland north of Thebes, it is risky to deny that these features were also in proto-Aeolic. Mycenaean diction and saga may have travelled direct from the Peloponnese to Asiatic Aeolis, especially if there is truth in the claims of the Penthilidai of Lesbos to descent from the house of Atreus. But much of the saga-material concerns northern and western Greece;[36] there are legends about Aetolia, Boeotia and Thessaly, as well as about Pylos with its Thessalian dynasty (the Neleids); Akhilleus is an Aeolian hero, the Catalogue of Ships gives Boeotia first place, and some of Homer's minor incidents and characters derive from the Theban Cycle (13.663–70n.). Phrases like προτὶ Ἴλιον ἱρήν or Ἑκτορέην ἄλοχον prove that Aeolic bards were already singing tales about a war at Troy. Local patriotism would give them good reason to develop old traditions of Mycenaean raids on the Asiatic coast; Lesbian ambitions on the Troad surely predated Pittacus' time. Contact with the indigenous inhabitants, or with local dynasts claiming descent from Bronze Age heroes, might encourage the portrayal of the Trojans as a worthy enemy. If anyone had good cause to glorify a panhellenic military enterprise in that area, it was the Aeolians. It cannot be coincidental that analysis of the epic diction points in the same direction.

[35] If the ϝ- was lost during the Aeolic phase, and Aeolic did not use *n*-mobile, this will also explain why the epos uses e.g. αἰσχροῖς ἐπέεσσι, not -οῖσιν ἔπεσσι, beside old datives like χρυσέοισι νέφεσσι or πολλοῖσι βέλεσσι (13.525, 555): cf. above p. 12 and 15.209–11n.

[36] So Hoekstra, *Modifications* 148ff.; Wathelet, *Traits* 375–9; West, *JHS* 108 (1988)159–62. Νηλεύς is an *Aeolic* form (A. Q. Moreschini, *SMEA* 27 (1989) 255–67). On the relation of oral tradition to history see H. M. Chadwick, *The Heroic Age*, Cambridge 1926; Bowra, *Heroic Poetry* 519–36; Hainsworth in Foxhall and Davies, *The Trojan War* 111–35; J. Vansina, *Oral Tradition as History*, London 1985; R. Thomas, *Oral Tradition and Written Record in Classical Athens*, Cambridge 1989.

3. The text and transmission of the *Iliad*

We know more about the textual history of the *Iliad* from *c.* 250 B.C. than of any other ancient work save the New Testament; yet the origin of our text and the nature of Alexandrian scholarship are still obscure and hotly disputed topics.[1] From the late sixth century B.C. the poem was the constant staple of Greek elementary education; this ensured its transmission, but also encouraged textual variation. The frequency and importance of memorized rhapsodic performances exacerbated this tendency; in its early stages the transmission was at least partly oral, whatever we conclude about how and when the poem was first written down. When we first encounter quotations (often from memory) in fourth-century Athenian authors, and scraps of manuscripts from third-century Egypt, the texts are often longer than ours and vary widely in wording. A medley of divergent MSS reached the Museum at Alexandria, where scholars worked to put them in order. Since we can follow the history of the text with confidence only from this point, we will begin there.

(i) The Roman and Byzantine vulgate

Fragments of over 600 MSS and myriads of quotations, not to mention the scholia and their lemmata, give us a clear view of the text which prevailed from about 150 B.C. to about A.D. 600.[2] This 'ancient vulgate' is close to that found in the 188 medieval codices of *c.* 900–1550.[3] Generally these preserve the text well; their variant readings and extra verses often go back to antiquity. But, although more carefully copied than most of the papyri, not all Byzantine MSS are of equal value. Without Allen's Herculean labours, we would know little about them, but the text he prints has serious faults.

---

[1] The best introductions are J. A. Davison, in *Companion* 215–33; Lesky, *RE* Suppl. XI (1968), s.v. *Homeros*, cols. 831–43; Chantraine, P. Collart and R. Langumier in Mazon, *Introduction à l'Iliade*, Paris 1943, 1–88. Bolling, *External Evidence*, van der Valk, *TCO* and *Researches*, Apthorp, *MS Evidence* and G. Pasquali, *Storia della tradizione e critica del testo*, 2nd edn, Florence 1952, 201–47, are basic; see also La Roche, *Textkritik*; Allen, *Transmission* 225–327; id., *Ilias* I 191–216; Erbse, *Gnomon* 37 (1965) 532–9; S. West, *Commentary* I 33–48; B. Gentili, *Poetry and its Public in Ancient Greece*, trans. A. T. Cole, Baltimore 1988, 3–23, 223–33. Fraser, *Ptolemaic Alexandria* 447–79, is excellent on Alexandrian scholarship.

[2] See H. J. Mette, *Lustrum* 19 (1976) 5ff., with earlier bibliography; Bolling, *External Evidence* 3–30; Apthorp, *MS Evidence* xif.; H. van Thiel, *ZPE* 79 (1989) 9–26.

[3] For details (and my sigla) see Allen's invaluable *editio maior*, *Ilias* I 11–55; Erbse, *Scholia* I xiii–xxxiii, describes those MSS with scholia. Allen's families of MSS, save *h*, do not survive Pasquali's criticism; cf. N. Tachinoslis, *Handschriften und Ausgaben der Odyssee*, Frankfurt 1984.

Pasquali stressed that the medieval tradition is almost totally contaminated; but he did not admit that, in such a tradition, the later codices are likely to be worse, as examination of their readings confirms. The twelfth-century and later MSS of the *h* family (U[4] etc.) derive many Alexandrian variants from a learned Byzantine recension.[4] The other late codices contain no otherwise unknown ancient readings; those which they do offer come from the scholia copied in their margins, as is obvious when (as often) such variants are added by another hand. Aristarchus' readings had more effect on the later medieval tradition than in antiquity, when commentaries were copied in separate rolls.[5] But Allen gave too much weight to the readings of the numerous late MSS and the post-Alexandrian plus-verses they contain.[6] Such late interpolations, usually limited to verses from elsewhere in Homer, often remedy what was felt to be a minor flaw, e.g. a missing verb, name, vocative or speech-introduction.[7] The extent of contamination is proved by how almost the whole medieval paradosis occasionally agrees in error against ancient sources.[8] Fewer learned marginal variants and minor additions have entered the early minuscule MSS, those of the tenth to twelfth centuries: in approximate order of date, Ve[1] A D B E[3] E[4] T Bm[1] C Et O[5] P[20] V[10] V[12] V[16]. But readings must be judged on their merits; the antiquity of a reading does not prove it correct – the papyri usually offer inferior texts. Many MSS, often with variants, survived the Iconoclastic period; the tradition was rich enough to ensure the survival, somewhere in the early codices, of all the readings and interpolations prevalent in later antiquity. In this volume, the 'good MSS' or 'good codices' means these sources, 'late MSS' are those of the fourteenth century onward, while 'the papyri' is shorthand for the ancient MSS, written for most of antiquity on papyrus-rolls.

[4] So Allen, *Ilias* I 128f., 210–16. K. Alpers dates *h* to the eleventh century (*Das attizistische Lexikon des Oros*, Berlin and New York 1981, 93n.); since the *h*-scholia draw on the lost archetype of the scholia in MS A, which was also used, under the name 'Apion and Herodorus', by Eustathius (Erbse, *Scholia* VII 267), the unique readings in *h* surely derive from lost scholia of Didymus and Aristonicus.

[5] So Allen, *Ilias* I 83–5; see I 200, 213–15 for how marginal variants enter the text in MS A.

[6] Thus he called the early minuscules 'barren of ancient readings' (*Ilias* I 216), by which he meant that they lack *Alexandrian* readings. Drawing on Bolling (*External Evidence*), Apthorp (*MS Evidence* xvii–xix) calculates that the OCT prints some 76 badly attested interpolations in the *Iliad*, and 94 in the *Odyssey*; he stresses the need for a new text. The other reason why one is urgently needed is van der Valk's radical re-evaluation of Alexandrian scholarship, which Allen had prized too highly. For the present, the best texts are those by Leaf and Mazon.

[7] See N. Wecklein, *SBAW* 1918, Abh. 7, 1–38. Thus books 13–16 contain post-Alexandrian interpolations to supply a verb or a name (13.316, 14.269, 16.129a, 16.381) or a speech-introduction (13.218a, 13.480), and concordance-interpolations from parallel passages at 13.422, 13.463a, 13.566a, 13.749, 14.70, 14.420, 15.481, 15.562, 15.578, 16.288a, 16.614f. and perhaps 16.689f. The risk that such interpolations have remained undocumented is higher in the *Odyssey*, where the evidence for the history of the text is vastly less.

[8] Thus at 13.745 only AE[4]T and a few late MSS avoid ἀπō̆τίσωνται; at 14.101 all early codices save O[5]V[10] read ἀποπτανέουσιν; at 14.172 only Ve[1] resists ἐδανῷ; at 16.766 all save E[3] read πολεμιζέμεν.

Whereas the Alexandrians' choice of readings had little effect on ancient MSS,[9] Aristarchus' determination of the length of each book affected copyists' practices from *c.* 150 B.C., when the longer 'wild' texts begin to disappear (they persist at second hand in quotations as late as Plutarch[10]). There is an obvious reason for this: few purchasers of book-rolls would know enough to worry about the quality of the text, whereas they could find out how many verses it should contain, especially since scribes were paid by the verse.[11]

(ii) The Alexandrian scholars: Zenodotus and Aristophanes

Well though we know the post-Alexandrian vulgate, it is harder to establish its origin. Its readings largely correspond to what the Alexandrians called the κοινή, εἰκαιότεραι, δημώδεις or φαυλότεραι, 'inferior' texts, in contrast to the χαριέστεραι or learned editions from known individuals or sources.[12] But did it exist before their time?[13] And did they base their texts on collation, or on conjecture?

It was the task of Zenodotus of Ephesus[14] to extract order from the chaos of MSS collected in the Museum. He evidently concluded that the then very numerous longer MSS were inferior: S. West, in her study of the extant Ptolemaic papyri, rightly agrees.[15] Unfortunately he left no written commentary; we depend mainly on Aristarchus' inferences (and our own) as to why he edited as he did.[16] But in this context one can easily see why he carried his principle so far that he omitted many lines accepted by his

---

[9] Allen (*Ilias* I 199ff.) calculated that, of 874 Aristarchean readings, only 80 are in all medieval MSS, 132 are in none, and 245 are in under ten; of 413 Zenodotean readings, 6 are in all MSS, 240 are in none, and 89 are in under ten. Alexandrian readings are even rarer in Roman papyri (*ibid.* I 83–5). Given the conditions of 'publishing' in the ancient world, such readings were diffused more by collation than copying; most readers cared little for scholarship anyway (K. McNamee, *GRBS* 22 (1981) 247–55).

[10] See van der Valk, *Researches* II 264–369; S. West, *Ptolemaic Papyri* 15n.

[11] See P. Collart, *Revue de philologie* 7 (1933) 52ff.

[12] Allen (*Transmission* 271–82) shows that, of 52 readings ascribed to the κοινή etc. in the scholia, 58% are in all or most medieval MSS.

[13] In favour: Ludwich, *Die Homervulgata als voralexandrinisch erwiesen*, Leipzig 1898; Allen, *Transmission* 302–27; van der Valk, *Researches* II 609. Against: Lesky, *loc. cit.* in n. 1; S. West, *Ptolemaic Papyri* 15–17, 26–8, *Commentary* I 33–48.

[14] For a general introduction see Nickau, *RE* XA (1972) s.v. *Zenodotos* (3); Pfeiffer, *Scholarship* 105–19.

[15] 'Our papyri are riddled with secondary variants and conjectures' (*Ptolemaic Papyri* 26); cf. van der Valk, *Researches* II 531–73. *Contra*: A. di Luzio, *Rivista di Cultura Classica e Medioevale* 11 (1969) 3–152.

[16] Unlike Aristophanes' pupil Callistratus, Aristarchus' followers had no direct knowledge of his predecessors' work (see Did/A on 2.111; 14.37n.; Barth, *Kallistratos*; Montanari 101–4). Aristarchus knew and attacked Zenodotus' monograph on the number of days in the *Iliad* (Nickau, *op. cit.* (n. 14) 36f.).

successors. His caution was salutary, given the abundance of interpolated texts; he certainly had MS authority for some omissions. Thus 21.195, which he omitted, was already absent in the text quoted by Megaclides (fourth century). He invented the first critical sign, the obelus, for verses which he could not omit with certainty, but 'athetized', i.e. left in the text with an indication of doubt. But many of his omissions and all his atheteses seem to rely on 'internal evidence' – intuited principles of the avoidance of repetition, inconsistency and impropriety, especially in religious matters, where (in my view) he was applying Plato's proposals for the censorship of the Homeric poems.[17] Aristotle in his *Homeric Questions* and *Poetics* had shown how to avoid such an approach, but it died hard.[18] Zenodotus apparently followed earlier practice in omitting verses he disliked or found difficult: thus, to restore zoological accuracy, he omitted 17.134–6, with the Chian text (presumably earlier); he also shortened the 'improper' 4.88f., with an early Ptolemaic papyrus, but the verses, accepted by Aristarchus, are in all our MSS. Such intuited principles now seem highly suspect.

It has been argued that some of Zenodotus' unique readings had better MS authority than Aristarchus' or the vulgate's.[19] The most plausible case is 1.5, where his οἰωνοῖσί τε δαῖτα instead of πᾶσι (in a verse which he athetized) must reflect the fifth-century Attic text because of parallels in the tragedians;[20] yet δαῖτα is surely an early emendation to remove the 'problem' that not all birds eat flesh.[21] Zenodotus' peculiar linguistic forms further undermine confidence. He read (or rather 'wrote', in ancient termi-

[17] With his atheteses of 1.225–33 and 16.432–58 cf. *Rep.* 389E, 388C–D. Nickau (*Zenodotos*) and Pfeiffer (*Scholarship* 105–19) hold that he relied on MS evidence, and that many of his changes are justified; cf. N. Wecklein, *SBAW* 1919, Abh. 7. See however Düntzer, *De Zenodoti studiis*; van der Valk, *TCO* 91ff., *Researches* II 1–83; and, on athetesis in general, R. Meijering, *Literary and Rhetorical Theories in Greek Scholia*, Groningen 1987, 171–6. For alterations to remove repetition see on 14.300–6, 15.263–8, 15.610 14, 16.89–96, 16.141–4; inconsistency, 14.376f., 16.431–61, 16.666–83; impropriety, 15.18–31, 15.31–3, 16.89–96, 16.97–100, 16.236–8, 16.666–83. The same motives can be seen in his conjectures (see n. 24).

[18] See A. R. Sodano, *Rendiconti dell'Accademia di Archeologia, Lettere e Belle Arti di Napoli* 40 (1965) 227–78; Huxley, *Proceedings of the Royal Irish Academy* C 79 (1979) 73–81, with bibliography; Janko, *Aristotle: Poetics*, Indianapolis 1987, 145–53. On Homeric scholarship before Aristotle's time see Richardson, *PCPS* 21 (1975) 65–81; on the importance of his approach for Alexandrian scholarship see Meijering *op. cit.* (n. 17), especially 176.

[19] West (*Commentary* I 43) thinks his readings at *Od.* 1.93 and 285 are so weird that they must be *lectiones difficiliores*, and that Aristarchus' explanation of them (in schol. *Od* 3.313) is a mere biased inference. But for similar changes in the *Iliad*, where Zenodotus' reasons are all too plain, see on 16.431–61, 16.666–83.

[20] So Pasquali, *op. cit.* (in n. 1) 236f.; Pfeiffer, *Scholarship* 111–14. Cf. especially Aeschylus, *Suppl.* 800f., κυσὶν δ' ἔπειθ' ἕλωρα κἀπιχωρίοις | ὄρνισι δεῖπνον. For δαῖς and δεῖπνον used of animals cf. 2.383, 24.43, *Erga* 209, Archilochus frags. 175.2,179. Zenodotus' text is known from Ath. *Epit.* 12E and Eustathius (19.45, 256.8), who knew a fuller version of *Epit.* (van der Valk in his edn of Eustathius, I lxxxivf.).

[21] So Eustathius; cf. Nicanor (in Eust. 19.42) and schol. b on 1.5. Differently van der Valk, *GRBS* 25 (1984) 46–9.

23

nology) a number of post-Homeric forms, often Ionisms like ἑωυτήν, ἐμεθίει or πεποιέαται.[22] These, and the artificial use of dual for plural (13.626–7n.), are all paralleled in Hesiod or the *Hymns*, unlike the Boeotian ἇας he inexplicably read at 8.470, Cretan Ἀριήδη (18.592), hyper-Ionic forms like κρητός for κρᾶτός (1.530), ξυνέηξε (13.165–8n.), ὀρῆτο (1.56, 198) and βουγήϊε (13.824), or the supposed imperative ἔειπε (*Od.* 4.379). He also read fourth-century forms like nominative singular comparatives in -ω, e.g. κρείσσω (16.688–90n.), οὐθέν (*Od.* 18.130) or οἶσθας (Eust. 1773.27). A few archaisms like δὲ (ϝ)εκάς (13.107–10n.) only reflect an effort at standardization, like his removal of the epic innovation μάρτυροι for -ες (14.271–4n.), replacement of Ὀϊλεύς with Ἰλεύς (13.66–7n.) and attempts to restore duals.[23] Such readings reveal a poor knowledge of Greek grammar and dialect; they could derive from sources which his successors distrusted (perhaps he had a patriot's preference for Ionian MSS).

Most of Zenodotus' other readings are best explained as conjectures meant to remove problems in the text. His motives are as mixed and varied as the text itself, but fall into the same categories as those of his atheteses: (i) failure to understand the grammar or syntax, (ii) the removal of repetition or (iii) of a supposed inconsistency or (iv) of impropriety, and (v) desire to standardize the text.[24] He extended some rare forms beyond their proper bounds: the analogist Aristarchus could err in the opposite way, removing oddities like φή (14.499, cf. 13.326–7n.). We can hardly know whether such conjectures are his own, or derive from the fourth-century λυτικοί who proposed solutions to problems raised by Zoïlus and other 'floggers of Homer'; what counts is that they *are* conjectures, and nearly all bad. In fact Aristophanes (frag. 378 Slater) tells us that Zenodotus emended Anacreon (frag. 408) to restore zoological accuracy: the same purpose will explain his text at 1.5, 13.198 and 17.134–6, and Aristophanes himself emended likewise (15.68on.)! I agree with van der Valk and Kirk

---

[22] See on 14.162–5, 15.716–17, 16.242–8.

[23] 6.121*, 8.290*, 12.127f.*, 12.342f.*, 13.198, 15.301, *Od.* 1.38*; an asterisk denotes that he is followed by Aristophanes, who also restores duals at 9.4, 11.103, 11.135, 13.613, 17.721, 18.526.

[24] In my commentary, for reasons of space, I may call such readings 'conjectures' without argument. In the following list, only those in bold type have any MS support; an asterisk denotes that Aristophanes adopted the reading. The categories are not clear-cut or mutually exclusive. For (i) see 13.148, 13.191, 13.229, **13.245***, 13.315, 13.374, **13.485**, 13.546, 13.627; 14.169, **14.208***, 14.229*, **14.236**, 14.349, 14.469; 15.134, **15.138**, 15.277, 15.347, 15.640; 16.150, **16.161**, 16.223*, 16.243, 16.281, 16.515; (ii) 14.177*, 14.394f. (transposed); 15.587; (iii) 13.198, **13.447**, 13.643; 14.37, 14.40 (ἑταίρων), 14.89, 14.366; 15.169, 15.225, 15.307, 15.356, **15.439**, **15.470**; 16.175, 16.233, 16.234, 16.748, 16.807; (iv) 13.237*; 14.340*, **14.351**; 15.192; (v) **13.107***, 13.246*, 13.351*, **13.551***, 13.610; **14.505***; 15.86, **15.377**, 15.716; 16.156, **16.710**.

(vol. 1, 43) that most readings where the Alexandrians lack support in the papyri and early codices are conjectures.

Aristophanes of Byzantium[25] had a better sense of older and younger diction, but began the persistent tendency of Homeric editors to assume that the older form must be better; thus for ἄαπτος, with diectasis, he read the older form ἄεπτος (from *ἄϝεπτος), which he found in archaic and tragic lyric (13.317–18n.). But the unanimity of the MSS and our understanding of how oral epic diction works guarantee ἄαπτος (cf. p. 17). In general his more conservative text prepared the way for his pupil Aristarchus; both avoid many of Zenodotus' omissions and atheteses. His work resulted in new critical signs, better punctuation, the invention of accents to distinguish between homonyms, and the refinement of grammatical terminology, which was to be developed by Aristarchus and codified by Dionysius Thrax.[26] Yet he too was far too ready to use athetesis or emendation to solve problems.[27]

(iii) The Alexandrian scholars: Aristarchus

Aristarchus' work is far better known than his predecessors'; building on their achievements, he made a great contribution to maintaining the quality of the text. Given the complexity of Homeric scholarship even then, it is not surprising that he sometimes changed his mind. We hear of different readings, a commentary on Aristophanes' text, revised commentaries and the monographs 'On Homer's homeland' and 'On the camp' (13.195–7, 13.681nn.); his pupil Ammonius wrote a book 'On the fact that there were not several editions of the Aristarchean recension', but another called 'On

---

[25] On Aristophanes see van der Valk, *TCO* 102–8; Pfeiffer, *Scholarship* 171–209; Slater, *Aristophanis Byzantii Fragmenta*; *id.*, *CQ* 32 (1982) 336–49, but also D. L. Blank and A. R. Dyck, *ZPE* 56 (1984) 17–24, and C. K. Callanan, *Die Sprachbeschreibung bei Aristophanes von Byzanz*, Göttingen 1987. Less is known of his text, because Aristarchus' frequent agreements with it tend not to be recorded.

[26] Aristonicus' abstracts suggest that Aristarchus already used Dionysius' system and terminology: cf. J. Pinborg, *Current Trends in Linguistics* 13 (The Hague 1975) 101–13; Erbse, *Glotta* 58 (1980) 236ff.; W. Ax, *Glotta* 60 (1982) 96ff. *Contra*: D. J. Taylor, *The History of Linguistics in the Classical Period*, Amsterdam and Philadelphia 1987, 1–14.

[27] So Slater, *Aristophanis Byzantii Fragmenta* 205–10. For examples of his atheteses see on 13.643–59; 14.95, 14.211–13, 14.313–28, 14.376f.; 15.56–77, 15.146–8, 15.231–5; 16.236–8, 16.261 (all followed by Aristarchus). His likely emendations fall into the following categories: (i) desire to improve the sense or diction, 13.12, 13.51, 13.443, 13.613; 14.58, 14.416; 15.680; 16.188, 16.634; (ii) removal of repetition, 13.733; (iii) removal of inconsistency, 13.502, 14.474, 15.451; (iv) removal of impropriety, 15.197; (v) standardization, 14.44; (vi) desire to introduce older linguistic forms, 13.92, 13.318; he removed augments, an archaic trait (1.598, 14.285, 15.601, 17.234), and 'restored' duals (see n. 23). He was perhaps the first to emend because he suspected 'metacharacterism' (see n. 62). He added or accepted from others a few extra verses (16.467–9n.).

the reissued recension'.[28] Apparently he first produced a commentary on Aristophanes' text, then a text of his own and then a commentary to go with it; finally his pupils made another text incorporating his last thoughts. All this was still available to Didymus.

The A-scholia often preserve Aristarchus' textual reasoning, and sometimes Didymus' reports of which MSS he cited; he classified these into two groups, the 'common', 'popular', 'inferior' or 'worse' MSS, and the 'more accurate' or 'more refined' ones. The latter class, which Didymus' epitomators often lump together with Aristarchus' own editions under the term πᾶσαι, included texts by his predecessors and by poets back to Antimachus, as well as the undated 'city' texts. But his 'better' MSS were, to judge by their reported readings, heavily emended; the 'common' texts are usually superior, since they preserve oddities which the others emend away, but which are now explained from comparative philology or oral composition.[29] Aristarchus is at his best when defending the paradosis against emendation, on the sound principle (whether or not he actually enunciated it) of 'explaining Homer from Homer'. Caution is his great virtue; many of his emendations entail minimal change and were merely diagnostic, being advanced in his commentaries but not his text. Thus at 9.222 he advanced two alternative readings to avoid having the ambassadors eat two dinners, but 'from excessive caution made no change, finding the reading thus in many texts' (Did/A). Neither conjecture is in our MSS, and neither matches standard formular usage.[30] Even emendations as good as γε μάσσεται for γαμέσσεται

---

[28] See Did/A on 2.111, 2.133, 2.192, 7.130, 10.397–9, 19.365. Cf. Erbse, *Hermes* 87 (1959) 275ff.; Pfeiffer, *Scholarship* 210ff.; Fraser, *Ptolemaic Alexandria* 464n. We need a collection of his fragments. The basic works are Lehrs, *De Aristarchi studiis*; Ludwich, *AHT*; Severyns, *Cycle*; van der Valk, *TCO* 108–57, *Researches* II 81–263; Pfeiffer, *loc. cit.* See also D. M. Schenkeveld, *Mnem.* 23 (1970) 162–78.

[29] *Pace* vol. I 43, αἱ πᾶσαι and πλείους mean 'all' or 'most' of the *named* MSS, not of the MSS in general: this is proved by πᾶσαι in Did/T on 1.123f., 1.435, 1.585, 1.598, 2.196, 2.436, 3.126 etc., where Did/A lists the learned editions meant, including Aristarchus' (Ludwich, *AHT* I 118–22). On the emended nature of the 'city-texts' see van der Valk, *TCO* 14–25, 157–66, *Researches* II 4–9; *contra*, V. Citti, *Vichiana* 3 (1966) 227–67. I doubt whether the Alexandrians had texts of Homer even as old as *c.* 450 B.C.; but an anecdote in Plutarch (*Alcib.* 7.1) shows that Alcibiades expected any decent schoolmaster to own at least a partial text (cf. S. West, *Commentary* I 41n.)

[30] His readings are often reported inaccurately, especially in T; this must apply even more strongly to his predecessors. Thus he *glossed* μετά and κατά in 1.423f. with ἐπί, as a verbatim quotation of his commentary proves (in Did/A), but Did/T say he *read* ἐπί both times; similarly Did/T on 9.222. Hence we probably gain a false impression of his work, but I lack the space to supply the necessary caveats. See further Slater in J. Grant (ed.), *Editing Greek and Latin Texts*, New York 1989, 37–61. For conjectures to remove inconsistency or impropriety see 13.423, 14.125, 15.197, 16.5, 16.50, 16.638. Other clear cases are 13.28, 13.191, 13.384, 13.449, 13.584, 13.599, 13.810, 14.72, 14.173, 14.235, 14.485, 15.82, 15.114, 15.252, 15.714, 16.35, 16.53, 16.106, 16.227, 16.252, 16.504, 16.522, 16.668, 16.775. On his removal of augments see van der Valk, *TCO* 140f.; L. Bottin, *SMEA* 10 (1969) 85–7; 16.207–9, 16.287–90, 16.402–6nn.

at 9.394 (which restores 'Hermann's Bridge' but is in no MS) look super-fluous once it is realised that oral poets cannot avoid metrical irregularities; often his analogical tendency restores regularity where it never existed, as do many literary editors of oral texts. Conjectures by lesser scholars like Callistratus or Demetrius Ixion are readily detected, whereas Aristarchus' are not; yet why should his method have differed from Bentley's, whose genius perpetrated a heavily emended text of Milton?

The reasons for Aristarchus' atheteses are usually given by Aristonicus and sometimes refuted by the bT scholia, which reflect post-Aristarchean scholarship (for a test-case see 15.56–77n.). Like his predecessors, Aristarchus reasoned like a good nineteenth-century scholar: verses are spurious because they are linguistically odd, repetitive, inconsistent, or improper.[31] He was keen to identify language and ideas proper to the Cyclic and post-Homeric poets (οἱ νεώτεροι), but his mistaken denial that Homer knew many of the legends narrated in the Cycle led him to some especially egregious atheteses (e.g. of 24.25–30, the reference to the judgement of Paris).[32] The ethical and probabilistic criteria he applies are not those of Homer's society; his knowledge of epic usage is less complete than ours (based on sophisticated indices and concordances); he was unaware of Indo-European and Near Eastern philology, archaeology, oral poetry, ring-composition and Linear B; and, as for literary insight, he is often outshone by the later scholarship seen in bT.[33]

Aristarchus' omissions have a firmer basis: he was on the watch for concordance-interpolations, verses added to supply a verb etc. As we saw, such interpolations are well attested, and continued to creep in after his time, whereas more extensive ones which materially alter the sense, always rare, disappear totally with the 'wild' texts.[34] Aristarchus' criterion for omission was clearly documentary: if a verse was soundly attested but suspect on internal grounds, he athetized it instead. Could he have omitted genuine verses in this process?[35] Since his omissions greatly influenced the later vulgate and are ignored in the scholia, evidence is meagre, but there is enough to arouse disquiet.

The most notorious case is 9.458–61, where Phoinix tells of how he

---

[31] He often follows Aristophanes (see n. 27) and rebuts Crates (Schmidt, *Weltbild* 189). Where no dependence on predecessors is recorded, his motives are: linguistic oddity, 14.500, 15.56–77; repetition, 15.265–8, 15.449–51; inconsistency, 15.56–77, 15.212–17, 15.449–51, 15.668–73, 15.712; suspected concordance-interpolation, 14.500, 15.166f. (as usual the categories overlap).

[32] Severyns, *Cycle*, is basic here.

[33] See Richardson, *CQ* 30 (1980) 265–87; K. Snipes, *AJP* 109 (1988) 196–222. For a systematic comparison of his views with those in bT see Schmidt, *Weltbild*.

[34] For a passage needlessly alleged to postdate 464 B.C. but present in all MSS see 7.334–5n.

[35] Apthorp, *MS Evidence* 47–101, is fundamental; he discusses 9.458–61 at 91–9.

contemplated killing his own father. Plutarch cites these verses, known from no other source, with the claim that Aristarchus removed them 'out of fear'.[36] They are good enough to be genuine. Similarly, Athenaeus[37] alleges that Aristarchus deprived the dancers of a musician by deleting a line at 18.604f. But the verse, in none of our MSS, is in fact interpolated precisely to give them a musician: a 'wild' papyrus which lacks this line adds a different one after 606, to the same purpose. Aristarchus rightly followed MS evidence here. The case of 23.92 supports this view of his method. This problematic verse, lacking ἐν πάσαις, was athetized by Aristarchus, who rightly deemed it an interpolation based on *Od.* 24.74 (Did/T); his arguments against it rely on consistency and propriety (Arn/A). Omitted in a citation by Aeschines and a Ptolemaic papyrus, it is present in all later MSS; Aeschines read two interpolated verses after 83 to the same effect. Aristarchus apparently felt obliged to retain 92 because most MSS already had it. But his atheteses hardly ever coincide with omissions in our quotations or MSS; for him, athetesis was largely based on *internal* evidence, whereas omission was not. Paradoxically enough, an athetesis proves that a verse was well attested in the MSS known to the Alexandrians.

Whether or not 9.458–61 are genuine, how did Plutarch know these verses? He had indirect access to pre-Alexandrian texts: thus in the same essay he cites 11.543, known also from Aristotle. His sources were perhaps Peripatetics like Aristoxenus or Stoics like Crates, who both knew texts of the *Iliad* with different proemia (1.1n.). Aristarchus' rival Crates was not above misrepresenting others: thus he claims that 'some' deleted 21.195 (schol. Ge *ad loc.*), but Megaclides at least merely omitted it and perhaps never knew it at all. The charge that Aristarchus 'removed' 9.458–61 means only that he left these lines out because they were absent in MSS whose authority he valued, probably the unreliable emended texts which he preferred. These sources surely deleted some recalcitrant verses, and formed the model for Zenodotus' practice. This passage chances to survive, but a very few genuine verses may have vanished entirely through the unscholarly habits of prudish schoolmasters and critics from Xenophanes' era down to Zenodotus'. Conversely, a pessimistic editor is entitled to suspect that some spurious lines permeated the whole paradosis so early that the Alexandrians could not detect them (they invented athetesis to express just such suspicions).[38] However, given the difficulty of finding linguistic or other means

[36] *Mor.* 26F; Porphyry 1.139.9 does not allude to them. A papyrus omits them (cf. S. West, *LCM* 7 (1982) 84–6).

[37] 5.181C–D: his source is either Diodorus of Tarsus 'the Aristophanean' (cited at 180E) or Seleucus, who both polemicized against Aristarchus (cf. the insults at 177E, 180C). See further van der Valk, *Researches* II 528; Apthorp, *MS Evidence* 160–5.

[38] So S. West, *Commentary* I 47f. Stesichorus frag. 209 may already reflect a text of the *Odyssey* with the interpolated verses 15.113–19, missing in some MSS (S. Reece, *Bulletin of the American Society of Papyrologists* 25 (1988) 1–8).

to verify undocumented interpolations, such suspicions must remain a last resort.

(iv) The Panathenaic rule and 'Pisistratean recension'

It remains to explain why the ancient and early medieval vulgate generally offers the best text of the *Iliad*. When we go back beyond the fourth century the picture becomes ever more obscure. Yet all our sources basically agree over matters of dialect, plot, episodes and so forth: other oral epics recorded in writing have a far wider range of textual variation, e.g. the *Nibelungenlied*, *Chanson de Roland*, *Mahabharata* or *Digenes Akrites*.[39] All our MSS somehow go back to a single origin, and have passed through a single channel; it is improbable that more than one 'original' of the *Iliad* ever existed, even if different rhapsodic performances and editorial interventions have led to the addition or (rarely) omission of verses here and there. This basic fixity needs to be explained. As shown above (pp. 13–15), linguistic data prove that the text acquired fixed form well before Hesiod's time; if the *Iliad* was first written down later, we must accept a long intervening period of reasonably accurate memorized transmission, which I find unlikely.[40] It is often held that it was in Pisistratid Athens that the Homeric poems were first dictated, or first edited into monumental form, or heavily reworked and revised. The superficial Attic features of the epic diction seem to support the idea of an Attic archetype for all our MSS, but other evidence proves that the text existed *before* Pisistratus' time.[41] The numerous testimonia form three groups, of which the first two date back to the fourth century.

(1) Aristotle says that 'the Athenians' adduced Homer to show that Salamis belonged to Athens (*Rhet.* 1.1375b30); around the same date Ephorus told the same story of Solon, and his wording implies that Solon interpolated 2.558, the verse concerned.[42] The Megarian local historian Dieuchidas (*c.* 330 B.C.?) perhaps alleged that Solon or Pisistratus inter-

---

[39] See Lord, *Singer* 202–20; S. West, *Commentary* 1 36n.

[40] For memorized transmission: Kirk, *Songs* 98ff., 301ff. (down to the seventh century); for an oral dictated text: Lord, *Singer* 148–57; M. S. Jensen, *The Homeric Question and the Oral-Formulaic Theory*, Copenhagen 1980, 81–95. Ruijgh (in *Linear B* 171f.) deems the *Iliad* an oral text dictated before 800 B.C.

[41] See for dictation in Athens: Jensen, *op. cit.* 128–71, with a fine collection of testimonia at 207–26; for monumental editing: R. Merkelbach, *Untersuchungen zur Odyssee*, 2nd edn Munich 1969, 239–62; for a Pisistratean archetype with reworking and revision: S. West, *Commentary* 1 36–40, and M. Finkelberg, *CQ* 38 (1988) 31–41; against any Pisistratean recension: Lesky, *op. cit.* in n. 1; J. A. Davison, *TAPA* 86 (1955) 1–21.

[42] Schol. b on 2.494–877, with Wilamowitz, *Kleine Schriften* IV 542–9: Σόλων τὴν Σαλαμῖνα Ἀθηναίοις ἀπένειμε διὰ τὸ "Αἴας ἐκ Σαλαμῖνος ἄγεν δυοκαίδεκα νῆας" (2.557), προσθεὶς τὸ "στῆσε δ' ἄγων ἵν' Ἀθηναίων ἵσταντο φάλαγγες", καίτοι Μεγαρέων ἀντεχομένων τῆς νήσου. Aristarchus read 'Solon's verse' in his first edition (Didymus in b on 2.558), but rejects it in Arn/A on 3.230, 4.273; papyri and some codices omit it, yet it seems genuine (13.681n.). It is parodied by Aristotle's contemporary Matro (*SH* 534.95–7).

polated 2.546ff. (meaning 2.558?), and Hereas, another Megarian (early third century), may have claimed that Solon interpolated 2.558.[43] This story implies that a fixed text already existed by the time of Athens' disputes with Megara over Salamis, which involved both Solon and the young Pisistratus.

(2) The orator Lycurgus in 330 B.C. told the Athenians that 'their fathers' instituted a rule that only Homer's poems could be performed at the Great Panathenaea (*In Leocr.* 102); his vagueness could be owed to reluctance to credit a Pisistratid with a good idea, since Plato (or a fourth-century imitator) says that Pisistratus' son Hipparchus was the first to 'introduce' the Homeric poems to Attica, and made the rhapsodes at the Panathenaea perform them in sequence, picking up where each left off.[44] Dieuchidas apparently ascribed the same rule to Solon and argued against crediting it to Pisistratus. According to a rival Spartan story in Aristotle,[45] the lawgiver Lycurgus first 'introduced' the Homeric poems to the Peloponnese from Samos, where he obtained them from the descendants of Creophylus. These versions must be secondary, since Lycurgus and Solon are obvious culture-heroes whereas Pisistratus and Hipparchus are not.

The incorporation of the Homeric poems into the Panathenaea was an Athenian attempt to claim the epics as their cultural heritage, and so to reassert their traditional leadership of the Ionians. The Panathenaic rule clearly aimed to prevent the rhapsodes from performing the same popular episodes too often and out of sequence; its operation depends on the idea of a fixed plot-structure, if not a written text. Apparently the festival included rhapsodic performances from its inception in 566/5, but these were eventually found to need regulation; the evidence of vase-painting suggests that the Panathenaic rule led to random extracts from the whole Epic Cycle

[43] For Hereas' claim see *FGH* 486 F 1, in Plut. *Solon* 10.3; he certainly held that Pisistratus interpolated *Od.* 11.631 and removed a verse from Hesiod (frag. 298), to the greater glory of Theseus (Plut. *Theseus* 20.1–2). According to a difficult passage (Diog. Laert. 1.57), Dieuchidas (*FGH* 485 F 6) said that Solon introduced the 'Panathenaic rule', and perhaps added that he interpolated 2.546ff. (= 558?). Solon τά τε Ὁμήρου ἐξ ὑποβολῆς γέγραφε ῥαψῳδεῖσθαι, οἶον ὅπου ὁ πρῶτος ἔληξεν, ἐκεῖθεν ἄρχεσθαι τὸν ἐχόμενον. μᾶλλον οὖν Σόλων Ὅμηρον ἐφώτισεν ἢ Πεισίστρατος, ὥς φησι Διευχίδας ἐν πέμπτῳ Μεγαρικῶν. ἦν δὲ μάλιστα τὰ ἔπη ταυτί· "οἳ δ' ἄρ' Ἀθήνας εἶχον" καὶ τὰ ἑξῆς. I suspect that ἦν ... ἑξῆς should be deleted as a gloss based on Diog. Laert. 1.48, in which case Dieuchidas did not mention interpolation at all (differently Leaf, I xviii). On his date see J. A. Davison, *CQ* 9 (1959) 216–22. Strabo (9.394) knew both sides of the controversy over 2.558 (see L. Piccirilli and M. Manfredini's n. on Plut. *Solon* 10.3); the Megarian version of 2.557f. which he cites seems old (K. J. Rigsby, *GRBS* 28 (1987) 100f.). Differently Finkelberg, *art. cit.* in n. 41.

[44] τὰ Ὁμήρου ἔπη πρῶτος ἐκόμισεν εἰς τὴν γῆν ταυτηνί, καὶ ἠνάγκασε τοὺς ῥαψῳδοὺς Παναθηναίοις ἐξ ὑπολήψεως ἐφεξῆς αὐτὰ διιέναι (*Hipparchus* 228B).

[45] Frag. 611.10, in the epitome of the *Lacedaemonian Constitution* made by Heraclides Lembus (*c.* 150 B.C.), ed. M. R. Dilts, *Greek, Roman and Byzantine Monograph* 5 (1971): Λυκοῦργος ἐν Σάμῳ ἐγένετο καὶ τὴν Ὁμήρου ποίησιν παρὰ τῶν ἀπογόνων Κρεωφύλου λαβὼν πρῶτος διεκόμισεν εἰς Πελοπόννησον. Ephorus made Lycurgus meet Homer on Chios (*FGH* 70 F 149.19).

being ousted in *c.* 520 by correct sequences from the *Iliad* and *Odyssey.*[46] The claim that Hipparchus 'introduced' the poems surely means that he imported a written text, hitherto monopolized by the rhapsodes, especially the guilds of the Homeridae on Chios and Creophylei on Samos.[47] Legends attest how vital such texts were to rhapsodes' livelihoods: Homer gave the *Cypria* as a dowry, and rewarded Creophylus for hospitality with the *Capture of Oechalia.*[48] Polycrates of Samos and Pisistratus are said to have assembled the first libraries; Onomacritus collected the oracles of Musaeus at Pisistratus' court until he was detected in a forgery.[49] The hostile tradition that the Homerid and rhapsode Cynaethus of Chios, active at Syracuse in 504–1 B.C., interpolated many verses into Homer's poetry, composed the *Hymn to Apollo* and ascribed it to Homer reflects more blatant editorial activity around this time.[50]

(3) Pisistratus was responsible for putting together the Homeric poems, previously scattered. In its simplest form this need mean no more than that he was the first to collect a full set of the separate book-rolls which made up the whole. The story first appears in Cicero[51] and in an anonymous epigram (*Anth. Pal.* 11.442) which may be imitated by his contemporary Artemidorus of Tarsus (*Anth. Pal.* 9.205); it is common later. Thus Pausanias (7.26.13) suggests that when Pisistratus and his assistants gathered Homer's scattered

---

[46] So H. A. Shapiro, *Art and Culture under the Tyrants in Athens*, Göttingen 1990, 43–6. See also K. Friis Johansen, *The Iliad in Early Greek Art*, Copenhagen 1967; R. Kannicht, *CA* 1 (1982) 70–86; and J. M. Hurwit, *The Art and Culture of Early Greece*, Ithaca 1985, 245f., 262–4, who conjectures that the Panathenaea were founded to celebrate Pisistratus' victory at Nisaea, which finally secured Salamis. The latter will have welcomed the chance to exploit the *Odyssey*'s allusions to Nestor and his son Pisistratus, from whom he claimed descent.

[47] Some think the division of each epic into twenty-four *rhapsodiai*, numbered with the letters of the Ionic alphabet, is related to his ordinance (so S. West, *Commentary* 1 39f., with further discussion). But it surely postdates Apollonius of Rhodes (see further Fowler, *Materiali e discussioni* 22 (1989) 104 n. 111); moreover [Plutarch], *Life of Homer* 11 4, ascribes the book-divisions to the school of Aristarchus, which accords with the first attestation of book-numbering, the title of Apollodorus of Athens' *Commentary on* Ξ, i.e. book 14 (Erbse, *Scholia* 111 557).

[48] Pindar frag. 265 in Aelian, *VH* 9.15; Strabo 14.638. On the Creophylei and Homeridae, see Burkert, *MH* 29 (1972) 74–85; *id.*, in *Papers on the Amasis Painter and his World*, Malibu 1987, 43–62.

[49] Athenaeus 1.3A; Herodotus 7.6.3.

[50] See schol. on Pindar, *Nem.* 2.1, from Hippostratus (*FGH* 568 F 5, third century B.C.). Burkert, in *Arktouros: Hellenic Studies presented to B. M. W. Knox*, Berlin and New York 1979, 53–62, and Janko, *HHH* 112–15, 258–62, argue (independently) from 'Hesiod' frag. 357 that, in his rivalry with Athens for leadership of the Ionians, Polycrates induced Cynaethus to put together the Delian and Pythian Hymns to Apollo for propaganda purposes at his Delian and Pythian festival on Delos (522 B.C.), an island which Pisistratus had just purified; see further A. Aloni, *L'Aedo e i tiranni*, Rome 1989. Aristotle's tale about Lycurgus could date from this time, since Sparta and Samos were then close allies.

[51] Pisistratus 'primus Homeri libros confusos antea sic disposuisse dicitur, ut nunc habemus' (*De Oratore* 3.34.137, 55 B.C.).

poems, he carelessly altered 2.573; T on 10.1 allege that the Doloneia was a separate composition by Homer, inserted into the *Iliad* by Pisistratus (but see 14.9–12n.); the scholia on *Od.* 11.602–4 claim that Onomacritus fabricated 602f. The tale that the latter and some Orphic poets put together the Homeric poems for Pisistratus can be traced back to Asclepiades of Myrlea, active at Rome in Pompey's time.[52] It has been held, plausibly enough, that Pergamene scholars developed the whole theory, basing it on the superficial Attic features of the epic diction and the old traditions about Athenian performances of Homer, in order to discredit the authority of Aristarchus' text.[53] In any case, a full-scale 'Pisistratean recension' is certainly a scholarly theory, not a genuine tradition; it was unknown in the heyday of Alexandrian scholarship. Had anyone had an official Pisistratid text, we would certainly have heard of it. The Athenians' poor showing in both epics proves that they altered the text little if at all.[54] I shall return below to the idea that a Pisistratean archetype is ancestral to all our MSS.

(v) The orthography of the earliest texts

Copies of the *Iliad* will have been rare until the later fifth century; much of the transmission was oral, by means of rhapsodes who memorized written texts by hearing or reading them. Performances of far older fixed texts like the Homeric epics can be seen to affect the diction of later poems like the *Hymn to Pythian Apollo* and the *Shield of Herakles* (see p. 14); this confirms what the Athenian traditions suggest – that the epics had already acquired a fixed form by then. Early texts were on wooden tablets and rolls of leather or papyrus: technical obstacles to the existence of such texts have

---

[52] John Tzetzes (*Prolegomenon Comoediae* xıaı 147, in W. J. W. Koster, *Scholia in Aristophanem* I, Fasc. ıA, Groningen 1975) says four men 'put Homer together in Pisistratus' time'; he names them as Zopyrus of Heraclea, Orpheus of Croton, Onomacritus and Epiconcylus (plainly corrupt for ἐπικὸν κύκλον!). Now the *Suda* (s.v. Ὀρφεὺς Κροτωνιάτης) cites Asclepiades (*FGH* 697 F 9) for the detail that this otherwise unknown Orpheus was a poet at Pisistratus' court. Tzetzes draws on Asclepiades via Proclus' *Chrestomathy* (so G. Kaibel, *Abhandlungen der königlichen Gesellschaft der Wissenschaften zu Göttingen, Phil.-Hist. Klasse* N.F. ıı 4 (Berlin 1898) 26). West (*Orphic Poems* 248–51) shows that this story is connected with the origin of the Orphic Rhapsodies; but his attempt to link it to Athenodorus Cordylion too is mistaken (Janko, *CPh* 81 (1986) 158). See also R. Böhme, *Peisistratos und sein homerischer Dichter*, Bern 1983.

[53] So Davison, *TAPA* 86 (1955) 18–21. Asclepiades criticizes both Crates and the Alexandrians (Pfeiffer, *Scholarship* 273), but his leanings are Pergamene. Aristarchus held that no poem older than Homer's existed, and that Homer was an Athenian from the time of the Ionian migration (13.195–7n.); his theory would explain the existence of both the Homeridae and the Attic features of the diction. He may also have held (with his pupil Ptolemy Pindarion) that the alphabet was invented in Athens: see schol. Dion. Thr. p. 192.8ff., 490.7ff. Hilgard, with Montanari, *Ricerche di Filologia Classica* ı (1981) 97–114.

[54] Cf. 13.689–91n. *Contra*: S. West, *Commentary* ı 38n.

been exaggerated.[55] But a more vital question is whether anything can be known of their orthography. In fact we know more, with a fair degree of certainty, than we might expect.

Our evidence is of two kinds: (i) external evidence from over 450 archaic verse-inscriptions like the Dipylon oenochoë – verses scratched on pots are one of the earliest uses of alphabetic script in Greece, which now goes back to *c.* 750 at Pithekoussai, Cumae and Lefkandi;[56] and (ii) internal evidence from oddities in the poems' text and spelling. This is harder to interpret, since we need to distinguish what bards actually sang from changes introduced by scribes, although the rhapsodes probably maintained traditions of pronunciation going back to the bards, especially in accentuation.[57] The poems' early form depends on where they were written down, since the East Ionians marked long *e* and *o*. Yet the following features apply regardless of the alphabet in which they were first recorded.

1. There was no convention of capital letters or accents, and punctuation and word-division were rare or non-existent; the dots separating words or word-groups on 'Nestor's cup' have few parallels in other archaic inscriptions. Internal evidence confirms this: thus the odd δηρινθήτην is really δῆριν θήτην, cf. δῆριν ἔθεντο (16.756n.).[58]

2. Words were written unelided (*scriptio plena*). Archaic inscriptions vary, but there is internal evidence that elided vowels were written out, leading to misinterpretation. Thus ἐντύνοντο ἄριστον | (24.124) has a peculiar hiatus and short α in ἄριστον, contracted from *ἀϝέριστον; it should be ἐντύνοντ' ἄριστον (cf. *Od.* 16.2). As in δηρινθήτην, the rare spondaic verse-ending encouraged misreading. So too κήρυκι Ἠπυτίδῃ should be κῆρῡκ' Ἠ., to maintain the proper vowel-length in κῆρῡξ (17.324).

3. Inherited *ĕ* and *ŏ* with compensatory lengthening were written E and O, e.g. εἰς < *ἔνς (written ΕΣ), τούς < τόνς (= ΤΟΣ); so were the contracted products of ĕ + ĕ and ŏ + ŏ, e.g. infinitives in -ειν (= -EN) or o-stem genitives in -ου (= -O). In both Attica and Ionia the spellings ει for ē and ου for ō appeared between 450 and 400 B.C., when these sounds had coalesced

---

[55] So Heubeck, *Arch. Hom.* x 150–6 (the basic discussion); see also Burkert in *The Greek Renaissance* 51–6. For wood cf. Solon's *axones* or the λεύκωμα in the temple of Artemis on Delos bearing the *Hymn to Apollo* (*Certamen* 316ff.). Homer mentions folding writing tablets of wood or ivory at 6.169; one is now known from the Levantine ship wrecked on its way to the Aegean at Ulu Burun, *c.* 1350 B.C. (G. F. Bass, *AJA* 93 (1989) 10f.). The early Ionians used leather rolls (Hdt. 5.58.3), like the Phoenicians and Hebrews. For surveys of early literacy see Ø. Andersen, *A&A* 33 (1987) 29–44; B. B. Powell, *CA* 8 (1989) 321–50.

[56] A. Johnston in *The Greek Renaissance* 63–8; Heubeck, *Arch. Hom.* x 73–126. For the corpus see P. A. Hansen, *Carmina Epigraphica Graeca Saeculorum VIII-V a. Chr. n.*, Berlin and New York 1983.

[57] Chantraine, *GH* 1 5ff., 189–92; Heubeck, *Arch. Hom.* x 161–9.

[58] But θειλόπεδον is not to be read θ' εἰλόπεδον at *Od.* 7.123 (Hainsworth *ad loc.*).

with the true diphthongs ει and ου; the new orthography was standard by 350 B.C.[59] E and O were also used for metrically lengthened ε̆ and ŏ, e.g. μαχειόμενος, οὔρεα (written ΜΑΧΕΟΜΕΝΟΣ, ΟΡΕΑ). Usually ē and ō were transcribed correctly, but at 11.686 some MSS still preserve ΧΡΕΟΣ for χρέος (χρεῖος), and Attic κρείσσων and μείζων have everywhere ousted Ionic κρέσσων and μέζων; this is how Attic scribes would naturally pronounce ΚΡΕΣΩΝ, ΜΕΖΩΝ. Similarly ἀνηρείψαντο may be an error for -ρεψ-, cf. ἀναρεψαμένη (*Theog.* 990) and Ἀρέπυια for ἅρπυια (cf. 13.143–4n.). Another fourth-century spelling is Ionic ευ for ε͜ο, which is frequent but not universal in our texts: occasionally ε͜ο has been replaced by Attic ου.[60]

4. Double letters are rarely noted in inscriptions before *c.* 525 B.C. Internal evidence proves that this was once the case in Homer; when combined with the preceding principles, some puzzling forms can be explained, notably καιροσέων (*Od.* 7.107). As Bergk saw, this stands for καιρουσσέων < *καιροϜεσσάων, 'closely woven', from the noun καῖρος, 'row of thrums'. The original text was ΚΑΙΡΟΣΕ-, with O for ō and -σσ- written singly: cf. ΤΕΙΧΙΟΣΗΣ for Τειχιούσσης in a sixth-century Milesian inscription (*SIG*[3] 3d). The fluctuation between ὀφείλω and ὀφέλλω, 'owe', must be similarly explained (11.686n.). At *Od.* 7.163 the imperative εἶσον from the aorist ἕσσα should be ἕσσον (original ΕΣΟΝ), and δεινόν at *Od.* 8.408 may be an error for δεννόν, 'abusive' (ΔΕΝΟΝ).[61]

(vi) The script of the earliest texts – Attic or Ionic?

These orthographic features of the earliest texts are beyond doubt, even if their implications for what editors should print are far from clear; to reconstruct even a fifth-century text requires dangerous guesswork. Further progress depends on whether we can establish if the poems were recorded in a script of Attic-Euboean, Central Ionic or East Ionic type. Alexandrian scholars held that the text underwent a 'metacharacterism' into the spelling they used themselves. They knew that 'ancient' copies used E and O for ē (ει) and ō (ου), whence Aristarchus' emendation ἐσλούς for -ός in Pindar (*Nem.* 1.24) or Crates' reconstruction ΜΕΛΔΟΜΕΝΟ for -ου (reported by Ammonius on 21.363). But they also held that the early script did not include η or ω, but used only E and O, as did Attic script. Thus the

---

[59] K. A. Garbrah, *A Grammar of the Ionic Inscriptions from Erythrae*, Meisenheim 1978, 26–30; L. Threatte, *The Grammar of Attic Inscriptions* I, Berlin and New York 1980, 172–90, 238–59.

[60] Chantraine, *GH* I 58–63.

[61] Even vowels were perhaps no exception. Πατρόκλεις may stand for -κλεες, written -ΚΛΕΣ (but see 16.20n.); the impossible forms δείους, σπείους, σπέσσι may represent *δέεος, *σπέεος, *σπέεσσι (written ΔΕΟΣ, ΣΠΕΟΣ, ΣΠΕΣΙ); δυσκλέα Ἄργος and κλέα ἀνδρῶν (2.115, 9.189) may represent -κλέε(α) from *κλέϜεhα. But for another explanation see Crespo, *Prosodia* 46ff.

scholia to *Od.* 1.52, 254 and 275 posit ΟΛΟΟΦΡΟΝ, ΔΕΥΕΙ and ΜΕΤΕΡ for ὀλοόφρων, δεύῃ and μήτηρ; this view is implied by Aristophanes' readings βοῦν for βῶν, ὅς for ὥς etc.[62] Aristarchus suspected that Zenodotus was misled by MSS in such a script: Arn/A on 11.104 reads Ζηνόδοτος γράφει 'ὅν ποτ' Ἀχιλλεύς'. μήποτε δὲ πεπλάνηται, γεγραμμένου τοῦ Ο ὑπ' ἀρχαϊκῆς σημασίας ἀντὶ τοῦ Ω, προσθεὶς τὸ Ν.

Our texts of early epic all have a uniform veneer of Attic dialect, with δέχομαι, μείζων, ἐνταῦθα, οὖν and χίλιοι, not δέκομαι, ἐνθαῦτα, μέζων, ὦν and χέλιοι (χείλιοι). Aspirated forms like ἀφικάνω have always ousted Ionic forms with psilosis like ἀπικάνω, unless the form was not recognized as Attic, as in cases like ἦμαρ, Ἐπάλτης or ἐπάλμενος; this general lack of psilosis goes well back into the fifth century, since Stesimbrotus based an argument on the anomalous form ἐπίστιον (15.189–93n.). Clearly our texts are Atticized in this respect; the adoption of the letter H (once named *hēta*) for the phoneme *ē* in East Ionic suggests that it had lost the phoneme h- before the alphabet reached the area.

However, there is little sign that η or ω were lacking in early texts.[63] The case of βῶν for βοῦν, '(oxhide) shield', at 7.238 strongly supports Ionic script. βῶν is in almost all MSS (βοῦν has entered a few late ones from the scholia); cf. εὔβων, 'rich in cattle', at *HyAp* 54. Didymus (in T) reports that Aristarchus read βῶν but Rhianus βῶ and Aristophanes βοῦν (obvious conjectures): he adds ἐν τοῖς παλαιοῖς ἐγέγραπτο ΒΟΝ, ὅπερ οὐκ ἐνόησαν οἱ διορθωταί. His supposition that correctors misread ΒΟΝ as βῶν may seem reasonable, given the rare sense 'shield' here. But this notable form continues Proto-Indo-European *$g^w\bar{o}m$ (cf. Sanskrit *gām*, Myc. *qo-o*), whereas βοῦν follows the analogy of the nominative (PIE *$g^w\bar{o}us$). βῶν, 'ox', is now attested for Simonides, who certainly used η and ω.[64] Had early texts offered (ΕΥ)ΒΟΝ, our MSS would surely read (εὔ)βουν. The same applies to the Aeolic archaism ὠλεσίκαρπος (for οὐ-).[65]

The other forms often adduced can go back to bardic convention or

[62] 7.238 (see below), 14.45, 21.127; cf. too his readings at 11.686, 13.92, 16.188, 17.264, 18.198, *Od.* 1.254, and Aristarchus' at 11.686 and Pindar, *Ol.* 2.97.

[63] In favour of Attic script: van der Valk, *Researches* II 629ff.; S. West, *Commentary* 39. *Contra*: G. P. Goold, *TAPA* 91 (1960) 272–91; Heubeck, *Arch. Hom.* x 165–7. Hesiod and some of the *Hymns* were probably recorded in mainland scripts (Janko, *HHH* 4f.).

[64] β 342 in C. Theodoridis, *Photii Patriarchae Lexicon* I, Berlin and New York 1982; cf. Wackernagel, *SUH* 12f., who suggested that βοῦν elsewhere is a later normalization. The scholia to Dionysius Thrax, p. 185.5 Hilgard, say Simonides invented η, ω, ξ and ψ (cf. Hyginus 277); does this mean he brought the Ionic alphabet to Athens, in texts of Homer?

[65] At 7.434 and 24.789 ἔγρετο comes from ἀγείρω and not ἐγείρω; it should be ἤγρετο (for ΕΓΡΕΤΟ?), but the bards could have confused the forms. It has been held that ει takes the place of η in δειδίσκομαι, 'greet', and ἀγκυλοχείλης, but these words are open to other explanations. See B. Forssman, *Die Sprache* 24 (1978) 3–24; Hoekstra on *Od.* 15.150; and 16.428n., opposing 4.4n. and Wackernagel, *SUH* 88.

learned reconstruction. Thus verb-stems in $\bar{e}$ normally have -ει- before *o*-vowels but -η- before *e*-vowels (δαμείω, δαμήης; βείω, στείομεν, τεθνειώς). This looks like a bardic convention; variants like βήομεν, στήωσι and τεθνηώς can often be traced to learned sources like Aristarchus.[66] The forms in -ει- result from the bards' usual desire to adapt their own vernacular vocalism to the inherited scansion; early texts clearly had E based on metathesis of quantity (e.g. τεθνεώς), and bards felt the *e*-vowel as a lengthened $\breve{e}$ rather than inherited η. So too ἀρνειός stands for *-ηός, cf. Attic ἀρνεώς, Lesbian ἀρνηάδες; ἐϋρρεῖος is the correct reflex of *ἐϋ-ηρέϝεhος, with $\bar{e}$ for contracted ε + ε (once written ΕΥΡΕΟΣ). An exception is probably owed to the bards, not the scribes. Names in -κλῆς retain η, e.g. Ἡρακλῆος where -εῖος is expected (< *-κλέϝεhος). The bards surely introduced these forms by analogy with the nominative, since adjectival forms have -ει- (-$\bar{e}$-), e.g. ἀκλειῶς.[67]

However, there certainly were MSS of Homer in Attic script or affected by it. The few book-rolls with legible texts depicted on Attic vases from *c.* 490 B.C. onward use Attic script or a mixture of Attic and Ionic: thus Ἑρμῆν ἀείδω, the opening of *Homeric Hymn* 18, appears on a vase of *c.* 470 as HERME⟨N⟩AEIΔO.[68] Some old variants must derive from misinterpretation of Attic script.[69] At 1.598 Antimachus, the Marseilles and Argive city-texts and the Alexandrians offer οἰνοχόει instead of ᾠνοχόει, from OIN- (but this is also the true Ionic form); at 3.10 the Chian and Marseilles texts had ἠΰτ᾽ ὄρευς instead of εὖτ᾽ ὄρεος, surely reinterpreting ΕΥΤΟΡΕΟΣ (note fourth-century -ευ- for -ερ-); ἐπίσχοιες for -οίης goes back to -ΟΙΕΣ, but the vulgate has the correct form (14.240–1n.); and the Chian text has μής for μείς at 19.117, perhaps misinterpreting ΜΕΣ (μ$\bar{e}$ς = μείς is the inherited form). The case of βῶν suggests that the transmission never depended wholly on Attic script, and the confusion between ζ and ξ, which often seems very early, goes back to Ionic Ι and Ɪ, not Attic Ι and ΧΣ.[70] Yet the Attic influence on the diction seems too pervasive to be owed to Athens' leading role in the later fifth-century book-trade; there was some early Athenian

---

[66] Cf. Chantraine, *GH* I 8ff.; R. Werner, η *und* ει *vor Vokal bei Homer*, Freiburg, Sw., 1948. τεθνηώς is recorded as Aristarchus' reading in 10/29 Iliadic examples: only at 16.16 does a clear majority of good MSS back him.

[67] Forms like Ὀδυσῆα persist because of the dative in -ῆϊ, but early papyri often decline nouns in -εύς as -εῖα -εῖος (S. West, *Ptolemaic Papyri* 116f.), by analogy with vernacular forms like βασιλέα.

[68] See J. D. Beazley, *AJA* 52 (1948) 336–40; E. G. Turner, *Athenian Books of the Fifth and Fourth Centuries B.C.*, London 1952; H. R. Immerwahr in *Studies B. L. Ullmann*, Rome 1964, 17–48 and *Antike Kunst* 16 (1973)143f.; Threatte, *op. cit.* (in n. 59) 34.

[69] But not the fluctuation of μαχήσομαι and μαχέσσομαι, which is affected by the aorist ἐμαχεσσάμην (cf. Chantraine in Mazon *op. cit.* (in n. 1) 136).

[70] The MSS are divided at 5.842, 5.844, 10.451, 13.644, 15.179, 20.85, 21.477, 22.310; at 16.830 κεραϊξέμεν is Bekker's indispensable emendation for -ΐζέμεν in all MSS.

predominance in the dissemination of Homer, and this was clearly owed to the Panathenaic festival. But the poems were not necessarily disseminated in Attic script. The gradual adoption of the Ionian alphabet at Athens during the latter half of the fifth century, culminating in its becoming the official script in 404/3 B.C., surely owes much to the widespread use in elementary education of Homeric texts in Ionic script; otherwise it is hard to explain.

In conclusion, the earliest texts of Homer were in East Ionic script, using η and ω. The poems followed the conventions of archaic texts – lack of word-division and elision, the use of E and O for ε̄ and ō (later written ει and ου), and the single writing of geminate letters; these have left more traces than any use of Attic script. Yet the superficial Attic traits in the epic diction do prove that Athens played a major role in the transmission, and this must be related to the Pisistratids' patronage of Homeric poetry. They probably procured the first complete set of rolls to cross the Aegean. That they tried to add a few verses is possible; that all later MSS derive exclusively from a copy they made is at best unlikely; and that they put the poems together from scattered lays, or altered them in any substantial way, is out of the question. As we saw, linguistic data prove that the Homeric epics had already acquired fixed form before Hesiod's time, and I do not see how this fixity can plausibly be divorced from writing, even though a song would acquire a certain degree of fixity on the lips of a mature singer who performed it often (and I regard the *Iliad* as such a poem).

(vii) The original recording of the Homeric poems: a hypothesis

It is risky to advance from these conclusions to the original circumstances of the Homeric poems' creation. My own conviction, which derives from A. B. Lord and which I will support in my commentary, is that we are dealing with two oral poems dictated by a single, no doubt illiterate, poet. Whether he knew how to write is essentially irrelevant; what matters is whether the existence of writing made any difference to the quality and scale of his poem. There are too many uncorrected blunders, like the dead man who is carried off groaning at 13.423, to allow us to suppose that the poet or his amanuensis used writing to revise his poem. In Homer, as in oral dictated texts generally, *nescit vox missa reverti*.

Many deem writing indispensable for the creation of a work of such grandeur, if only to produce drafts and summaries. But there is overwhelming modern evidence, from the Balkans, Central Asia and elsewhere, that vast epics can be created, given suitable conditions, without the use of writing; indeed the existence of a prestigious literate and literary culture presents a grave danger to the richness and continuity of traditions of large-

37

scale oral narrative. No such culture existed in Homeric Greece; without its harmful effects, in luring the best young singers toward other pursuits, we cannot set limits to the quality of a poet's work, especially when dealing with a genius like Homer. The idea that a poet needs writing to keep the structure clear in his mind is a fantasm based on our own inadequacy as literates; indeed I seek to show below how he builds up his own structure in his poem, e.g. by summarizing the larger background or by listing in advance those warriors whom he intends to kill off (e.g. 13.345–60, 13.478–8onn.). I concur, too, with Lord that the only way in which writing may affect such a poem's nature is this: once a poet has adjusted to the slower pace of dictation, he can take advantage of it to create a longer, finer and more elaborate song than he would have been able to sing.

A harder question is this: who had the inspired idea of writing the *Iliad* down, to create the first *text* in European literature? Here we can only guess, but, with Lord, I doubt that it was the poet himself. Whoever did so surely knew of the written epics of the Levant, as well as Phoenician writing and writing-materials; he also had great leisure and resources. This limits us to the courts of princes and nobles in places with good trading contacts. No long poem was ever taken down at a noisy public festival; Homer depicts his ideal audience in his vision of Alkinoos' palace. Questions of kingship loom large in both his epics: Agamemnon abuses his power in the *Iliad*, and Odysseus recovers his realm from aristocratic usurpers in the *Odyssey*. I suspect that the ideological support the poems could offer to traditional images of authority was a major reason why they were preserved, at exactly the time – the eighth century – when the weakly-rooted Dark Age monarchies were being successfully challenged by new aristocracies. It may not be chance that we still have shadowy knowledge of a King Hektor of Chios and a King Agamemnon of Aeolian Cyme:[71] these were major centres of Homeric poetry. But all this is beyond proof.

[71] Cf. 13.689–91n.; Carlier, *Royauté* 449, 463. On the ideological background see *ibid.* 195–214; Morris, *CA* 5 (1986) 81–138; L. Collins, *Studies in Characterization in the Iliad*, Frankfurt 1988, 69–89; Thalmann, *TAPA* 118 (1988) 1–28.

COMMENTARY

BOOK THIRTEEN

Books 13–16, some 2,970 verses long, form the fourth and largest of six units of four books each into which the *Iliad* naturally divides; such a unit would be suitable for oral performance on a single day as part of a six-day rendition of the whole (cf. Thornton, *Supplication* 46ff.). Like 5–8 and 9–12, books 13–15 open with a Greek success (from a weaker position each time), now led by the Aiantes and Idomeneus; but this is followed by losses even worse than those which closed 5–8 and 9–12. The ships are endangered, Protesilaos' is burned and, in a fourth recurrence of this same pattern of success and disaster, Patroklos, sent by Akhilleus to the rescue, is slain – all this in the single day that lasts from 11.1 to 18.239. Thus the Achaean defeat finally involves, in a most personal way, the hero who had done most to precipitate it. But this must not happen too fast: to delay it is a major function of book 13, anciently entitled ἡ ἐπὶ ναυσὶ μάχη, 'the battle at the ships'.

By the neat device of having Zeus avert his gaze, the poet gives the panic-stricken Greeks ample scope for valour. Poseidon inspires them to resist stubbornly, despite the absence of many leaders, who were wounded in book 11: he enters battle in person when Agamemnon proves to be completely defeatist in book 14. Once the Greeks have formed a line to defend the ships (126ff.), two brief scenes prepare for the division of the fighting into two sectors, left and centre, which gives the lesser hero Idomeneus a chance to shine. Meriones indecisively attacks Deïphobos, which prefigures how he later wounds him on the left (156–68, 527–39); then Hektor confronts Aias, as he will again at the centre (183–205, 674ff., 809–32). Homer splits the action by taking us behind the lines, where Idomeneus meets Meriones, whose spear was broken; sending him to his hut to fetch a new one is a deft expedient to achieve this meeting – he could have found one on the battlefield! The Cretans unjustly suspect each other of shirking; their embarrassed exchange culminates when Idomeneus excuses Meriones with a risqué joke about his lost spear. Their *aristeia* aptly prepared, they rejoin battle on the left (326), where we remain until 674. A summary (345–60) of the divine background, including Zeus's support for Thetis, recalls the start of the *Iliad* at its mid-point, just as *Od.* 13.90f. echoes

39

that poem's opening; it also explains, to any listener who is confused, why Zeus and Poseidon are now opposed.

Idomeneus, in the last Greek *aristeia* until Patroklos', now kills two sons-in-law of the Trojan royal house, and the allied leader Asios (361–454n.); but he has to retire before superior force, and other second-ranking leaders take over. Meriones, Antilokhos and Menelaos wound Deïphobos and Helenos, and kill Asios' son Adamas, the fool Peisandros and the coward Harpalion in ways gruesomely apt for each (455–539, 540–672nn.). Menelaos exclaims at Zeus's forbearance, as patron of *xenoi*, toward the Trojans' wrongdoing; Paris at once kills an unfortunate Greek, in anger at the death of a guest-friend of his! Such are the evil results of Akhilleus' wrath, which inverts Zeus's natural sympathies. The juxtaposition of these scenes re-emphasizes the moral ambiguity of the war, but moral certainty of Troy's final punishment (660–72n.); as usual, the moral commentary is muted, since Homer says little in his own *persona*. We return to the centre (673–837n.), where Hektor faces contingents whose unusual tactics threaten to break the Trojan line. Warned by Pouludamas, he finds the situation on the left critical, and unjustly blames the only leader still there, Paris; rallying the Trojans in general, he ends the distinction between the left and centre of battle. At the end of the book the armies are in much the same state as at its start, once the Greeks have rallied; their continued resistance is no less ominous for the Trojans than the eagle which appears when Aias boldly taunts Hektor with impending ruin. He replies with dire threats (824ff.), losing sight of the truth that his success depends on Zeus. We expect the two leaders to come into conflict directly, but the action is frozen while the Achaean chiefs debate what to do, and Here puts Zeus to sleep; they clash only at 14.402ff.

As a major 'retardation' of the wrath-story, book 13 invited attack by the Analysts. Leaf deems 136–672 inserted 'for the special honour of Cretan heroes', but Michel has shown that this section is no less tightly integrated into the rest than is the whole book into its larger context. Past attacks on 673–724 (or −794!) rely on misconceptions about Homeric narrative technique and conventions. In fact one must admire how deftly the poet has introduced and diversified this long stalemate (cf. 1–168n.). Poseidon's arrival is a fine elaboration of the standard divine journey by chariot; the overviews of armies in array at 126ff., 330ff. and 795ff., reinforced by powerful similes, are awesome. Idomeneus' dialogue with Meriones must be long for a reason, which can only be humour: this is not hard to find, and verges on the barrack-room variety (246–97n.). The fighting is 'vigorous and varied' (Leaf); the vignettes of dying warriors are detailed and pathetic; and the counterpoint between shifting types of character, encounter, wound and speech of challenge or triumph creates a fugue-like quality, even in the long stretch with no speeches (487–619). Like the death of Poseidon's grandson Amphimakhos (185ff.), that of Ares' son Askalaphos (518ff.) prepares for the deaths of other gods' offspring – Sarpedon and Akhilleus himself. Book 13 exemplifies both how well the poet handles traditional themes, motifs and narrative techniques, and how subtly he gives them the moral depth so plain to the ancients and so typical of both his epics. For analysis and bibliography Michel, *N*, is vital; see too Owen, *The Story of the Iliad* 126–33, and Reinhardt, *IuD* 278–99. For the battle-scenes in book 13 see Winter, *MNO* 56–119 and Fenik, *TBS* 115–58. For a recent Analytic approach to books 13–15 see H. van Thiel, *Iliaden und Ilias*, Basel 1982, 51–122; the Analysts' results are so mutually inconsistent that discussion of them will be kept to a minimum.

1–168 While Zeus is looking away, Poseidon crosses the sea by chariot and intervenes in the shape of Kalkhas to halt the Trojans before the ships. He encourages the Aiantes, and then the other Greeks, who stand firm and arrest the Trojans' charge; Meriones attacks Deïphobos, but breaks his spear and goes to fetch another from his hut

1–168 Fenik (*TBS* 119), by showing that the structure of 39–168 recurs on a larger scale in 169–539, has uncovered a major structural principle of much of book 13:

I	A	The Trojans charge (39–42)	II	A	Hard fighting (169–205)
	B	Poseidon exhorts the Aiantes (43–65)		B	Poseidon exhorts Idomeneus (206–45)
	C	The Aiantes converse (66–82) [Poseidon exhorts the Greeks (83–125)]		C	Idomeneus and Meriones converse (246–329) [Panorama and summary (330–60)]
	D	The Greeks repulse the Trojans (126–155)		D	Idomeneus' *aristeia* (361–525)
	E	Meriones fights Deïphobos (156–68)		E	Meriones wounds Deïphobos (526–39)

This pattern is obscured in the first case by Poseidon's arrival (1–38) and the reduplication of his exhortation (83–125), and in the second by vast elaboration in C and D; but the two conversations between warriors on the same side are unique, as they do not discuss immediate tactics. Leaf assigned Poseidon's intervention (1–125), with its 'romantic' elements, to the 'deception of Zeus'; its elaboration and neologisms seemed to Shipp a sign of 'lateness' (*Studies* 281). Homer certainly innovated here.

1–9 After the vivid picture of Hektor smashing down the gate of the camp with which book 12 ends, the action slows and we are carried far away. Zeus has been watching from Mt Ida since 11.182; now he is satisfied that the Trojans will win and Akhilleus will be aroused. His unconcern is in character; he is more usually an impartial arbiter than a partisan. His effortless ability to look away gives a pathetic emphasis to the gulf between mankind's struggles and divine serenity, while also providing a convenient occasion for Poseidon to intervene (Griffin, *HLD* 131, 197); the playfulness of the god's sea-creatures (27) reinforces this effect.

1–3 The prominence of Zeus's name stresses that the success is his more than Hektor's. The breach of the gate amounts to an attack on the ships themselves, the Greeks' last hope (cf. bT). τοὺς μέν denotes both sides, as 9 confirms, not just the Trojans. πάλιν means 'away', not 'back' (3.427, 5.836, 18.138). The second half of 3 recurs at 7, forming a frame (cf. 21.415); ὄσσε φαεινώ recurs 5×, only in books 13–21 (it is modified at 435).

4–7 The nations Zeus observes are to the N. (see Map, p. xxvi); the battle is to his N.W., as is Samothrakē. His gaze strays further and further away. The horse-herding Thracians are nearest (ἱπποπόλος recurs only at 14.227, in the same phrase). The Musoi are a branch of the race who stayed in Bulgaria when their kinsmen entered Anatolia (so Posidonius frag. 277a Edelstein–Kidd, in Strabo 7.295f.). Perhaps known to the Assyrians as the Muški (cf. MacQueen, *The Hittites* 154–7), they were later called Moesi, whence the Roman province of Moesia. In the Trojan Catalogue (2.858n.), the Musoi are settled S. of the Propontis. Their presence would be anachronistic, like that of the Phruges who crossed to Asia in the Early Iron Age; movements from Thrace into N.W. Anatolia after 1100 B.C. are archaeologically proven (Sandars, *Sea Peoples* 193). Herodotus (7.20) reverses the direction of the Mysians' movement and dates it before the Trojan War, perhaps to explain this passage. The epithet ἀγχέμαχοι may be formular (cf. 16.248, 17.165, *Aspis* 25, *Naupaktia* frag. 6 B. = 7 D.), like ἀγχιμαχηταί.

Further off are the 'Mare-milkers', Hippemolgoi, no doubt a nomadic Scythian tribe across the Danube, like the milk-drinking Massagetai (Hdt. 1.216). γλακτοφάγων explains their name (the milk was no doubt coagulated, like the Tartars' *koumiss*) and proves that ἀγαυῶν is an epithet, not a name (*pace* Steph. Byz. s.v. Ἄβιοι). Hesiod is first to mention the Danube (*Theog.* 339) and the Scythians, whom he calls 'mare-milkers' (*Cat.* 150.15); he also knows of 'milk-eaters who live in waggons' (*Cat.* 151). The form γλακτο- for γαλακτο- is related to γλάγος (16.641–4n.). These names, if not fictitious (so Apollodorus, *FGH* 244 F 157), rest on very vague knowledge: see J. D. P. Bolton, *Aristeas of Proconnesus*, Oxford 1962.

Homer derived the name 'Abioi' from ἀ-privative and βία, 'without violence', since he glosses them 'justest of men' (so van der Valk, *Researches* II 590–2; cf. *LfgrE* s.v.). Aristarchus (in Ap. Soph. 3.16) wrongly applied the whole of 6 to them, but rightly rejected the reading δικαιοτάτων τ', which made ἄβιοι mean 'with no (settled) livelihood', i.e. nomads. Nicanor (in A) favoured the present punctuation, but applied 'justest of men' to all the nations named. This is attractive: Zeus, weary of the squabble at Troy, gazes at peoples who live together with no violence or injustice (on his concern for justice see 16.384–93n.). Von Scheliha (*Patroklos* 148ff.) thinks it was Homer's own idea to exalt Zeus so far above the level of a local, partisan god that he respects even barbarian nations. This Utopia of the far North may be sheer invention, like Pindar's happy Hyperboreans (*Py.* 10). Assonance in -ων, overlengthening (i.e. syllables with long vowels closed by two or more consonants) and spondaic verse-endings seem to underline the duration and abstractedness of Zeus's reflections. Aeschylus' Gabioi (frag. 196), a δῆμος ἐνδικώτατος with a Utopian lifestyle and a mysterious *G-*, are based on Homer.

8–9 ἐέλπετο means 'expected' (the OCT wrongly reads ἔλπετο): this refers to Zeus's dire threats the day before against gods who aid either side (8.10ff.; with 9 cf. 8.11). Nobody has yet dared to defy him. Aristophanes' unsupported and unnecessary reading ἔτ' for ὅγ' (Did/AT) makes the reference more explicit.

10–38 Zeus's distraction lets Poseidon intervene, just as Poseidon's absence permits Odysseus to return to Ithake; cf. too how Hephaistos' withdrawal to Lemnos, his favourite place, permits his wife's adultery (with 10 cf. *Od.* 8.285, and 37 = 275). The god's intervention adapts a standard narrative pattern: cf. Apollo's at 10.515–18. Its basic elements are (*a*) catching sight of an event and reacting, (*b*) a journey, (*c*) intervention (exhortation, a rescue etc.) and (*d*) return (sometimes omitted). This pattern is vastly elaborated, since Poseidon only returns at 15.218. Inserted into it is a journey by divine chariot: cf. those at 5.364–9, 5.720–77, 8.41–50, 8.382–96 (Fenik, *TBS* 73, 115f.). The god steps across the sea from an island near Troy to Aigai, drives back to a submarine cave near Troy, where he leaves his horses, and then (by no stated method) goes to the camp (see Map, p. xxvi). Why, in such a crisis, does he deviate from the direct route for a stately entrance which only his sea-creatures notice? Leaf proposed deleting 11–16 to remove Samothrake. The description's brilliance has justly saved it from criticism: it majestically builds up his resolve and the importance of his arrival, arouses suspense and vividly expresses his three main attributes – earth-shaker, horse-god and sea-god (on his role in books 13–15 see Erbse, *Götter* 104–12). He arms like a hero for his *aristeia* (Reinhardt, *IuD* 279). bT and AD on 20–3 cite less cogent reasons: he arms so as to scare the Trojans, resist Zeus or give us a break from continuous battle-narrative. His intervention is prepared at 8.200ff., when Here fails to persuade him to do so, 8.397ff., when Zeus, watching from Ida, foils her own plan to drive to Troy, and 12.466, when we hear that nobody could stop Hektor 'except gods' (so

Winter, *MNO* 58). See further Kakridis in *Festschrift W. Kraus*, Vienna 1972, 188–97. On Poseidon's name, clearly 'lord of' something, probably 'earth', see Palmer in *Res Mycenaeae* 352–5; Hainsworth on *Od.* 8.322f. Cf. Myc. */Enesidaon/* (KN M 719), Ἐννοσίδας (lyric), beside ἐννοσίγαιος, 'earthshaker'.

10–12 The first half of 10 is formular (10.515, 14.135, *Od.* 8.285, *Theog.* 466). The picture of two gods watching from opposite mountain-tops is evocative; putting Poseidon on Samothrake distances him from restraint on Olumpos. The island's peak (5,250 ft) is visible N.W. from Troy above the isle of Imbros, which lies between. The poet who placed the god there had seen it from the plain of Troy himself; such a detail is hardly traditional. 'So Homer had appointed it, and so it was ... Thus vain and false are the mere human surmises and doubts which clash with Homeric writ' (A. W. Kinglake, *Eothen*, London 1844, 65). The island is called Samos at 24.78, a common pre-Greek name probably meaning 'hill'; its epithet 'Thracian' proves that Homer knew of Ionian Samos too (this distinction recurs at *HyAp* 34, 41). The variant Σάου (Did/AT) allegedly stood for Saoke, the mountain's name, but Aristarchus, who was born there, rightly equated the island with its peak (T). For ἀκροτάτης κορυφῆς Aristophanes read dat. plurals in -ῃς (Did/A), and good MSS have singulars in -ῃ, perhaps to avoid too many genitives; but corruption of -HIC K-/C- would be easy. For the variants see on 178–80, 16.141–4.

12–16 A concentric ring frames an account of how Poseidon came to be seated on Samothrake: thence he could see Mt Ida and the battle, which is why he had left the sea to sit there. Whereas Zeus gazes ever further away, Poseidon focuses with increasing precision on Ida, Troy and the ships; like Zeus's, his emotions are stirred by what he sees, but to contrary effect. Verse 16 = 353, recapitulating his intervention.

17–20 The forested slopes quake under the Earthshaker's feet, to suit his mood (cf. 20.57f.); contrast Herē's steps brushing the treetops of Ida (14.285). For his awesome strides over such a distance cf. 5.770–2 (of divine horses), Pindar, *Py.* 3.43 with schol.; deities step from one peak to the next, as in Leto's journey at *HyAp* 30ff., where summits are prominent among the places she visits. So too at 14.225ff. Herē quits Olumpos for the peaks of Thrace, darting from the summit of Athos to Lemnos (the shortest way to step over the N. Aegean); but, by a yet greater miracle, her feet never touch the earth. The pattern 'thrice ... and the fourth time' is traditional, cf. 16.702–6n., 21.177, *Erga* 596; it stresses the god's ease of movement. For παιπαλόεις see Càssola on *HyAp* 39.

21–2 Poseidon's cult at Aigai is mentioned at 8.203, *Od.* 5.381 and *Hy.* 22.3. Alcaeus (frag. 298.6) places the Greeks' shipwreck there; Huxley (*GRBS* 10 (1969) 5–11) convincingly equates this with a headland called Aiga opposite the S.E. corner of Lesbos (cf. Strabo 13.615). There were places called Aigai in Euboea, Achaea and Macedon (now Vergina): cf. C. Imber, *CQ* 29 (1979) 222; Fowler, *Phoenix* 42 (1988) 101n. Clearly it is not on the coast of Samothrake! The fact that the god's fairy-tale palace is under the sea suggests that we should not seek its location too seriously. The name may relate to his epithets Aigaios and Aigaion (Fowler, *art. cit.*). — Hephaistos' house and a chair he will make are 'imperishable' and of gold (18.370, 14.238); here the golden palace, manes, armour, whip-handle and hobbles stress the idea of imperishability and make the scene glitter. Such repetition of key words is a device typical of oral poetry: cf. 114–21, 14.175–7, 16.104f. and Kakridis, *Homeric Researches* 120ff. The hiatus in ἄφθιτα αἰεί | well illustrates how formular declension can cause prosodic irregularity: cf. ἄφθιτον αἰεί | (3×); Parry, *MHV* 199; M. Finkelberg, *CPh* 83 (1988) 206–11.

23–6 From ὑπ', 23–6 = 8.41–4, where see n. Just as Zeus drove to Ida to supervise the Greeks' defeat, so now Poseidon drives across the sea to save them.

27–31 The god's voyage is miraculous: he rides the waves, dolphins gambol about him, the sea herself gladly makes way to smooth his passage, and his chariot's axle is not even wet (contrast the bespattered axle of Hektor's speeding vehicle at 11.534f.). The god gave such a chariot to Pelops ('Apollodorus', *Epit.* 2.3). For parallels in folktale see Stith Thompson A170.0.1. So too Erikhthonios' horses run across the ears of the corn and the breakers (20.226ff.); the waves part for Thetis (18.66f., 24.96). Poseidon's team do not fly, despite τοί γε πέτοντο; the dactyls of 29f. reflect their speed. Their hooves (23) and the axle are bronze, for strength; Here's chariot boasts one of iron (5.723). For a moment we expect Poseidon to reach the camp with great pomp, such as might catch Zeus's eye! His triumph is premature; it is easier for him to work his will among his own creatures than among men, where, far from being greeted with joy, he must hide his identity (Reinhardt, *IuD* 279). His creatures' reaction is typical of divine epiphanies; cf. the beasts on Ida at *HyAphr* 69ff., who greet Aphrodite, or 14.347, *Theog.* 194f. (the growth of plants). κήτεα are not vague 'sea-monsters' but dolphins, Poseidon's horses of the sea (cf. Janko, *CQ* 30 (1979) 257–9). These are the only marine animals that play on the shimmering golden surface of the Aegean as they escort ships on a summer day; thus a dolphin, called μεγακήτης at 21.22, is a κῆτος at *Od.* 12.96f. The personification of the sea hardly goes further than at 14.17 or 392; for the 'laughter' of land or sea cf. 19.362, *HyDem* 14, *HyAp* 118, Theognis 9f., Semonides 7.28, 'Aesch.' *Pr.* 89f. and West on *Theog.* 40. The sympathy of nature is normal in the heroic world, and our awareness of it is fundamental to the beauty of that world. Such a belief is basic to Greek religion, which Christian polemicists perceived as worship of the creation rather than the creator. It is unjust to see it as only a poetic convention, a case of the 'pathetic fallacy': on Homeric 'animism' see further 444n.

βῆ δ' ἐλάαν uniquely blends the formulae μάστιξεν δ' ἐ. and βῆ δ' ἴμεν/δὲ θέειν: only here and at *HyDem* 431 is βαίνω used of going by chariot (*LfgrE* s.v.). ἄταλλε, 'skip', 'play', < ἀταλός, is transferred from children: cf. West on *Erga* 131; C. Moussy in *Mélanges Chantraine*, Paris 1972, 157–68; Shipp, *Vocabulary* 111, who shows that ἀταλός is no mere poetic invention (*pace* Leumann). The unique κευθμός is a rare case of an *e*-vowel ('e-grade') in nouns in -μός, cf. ῥυμός etc. (Chantraine, *Formation* 134–6); κευθμών and κεύθεα are the usual epic forms (6× and 8× each). It is surely an *ad hoc* creation by haplology for κευθμώνων, suggested by the pattern | παντόθεν ἐκ ‿‿ – (4× Hom.). For Aristarchus' reading ἠγνοίησαν see 616–19n. He took γηθοσύνη (-η) as a nom. adj., but Aristophanes recognized a dat. noun (Hrd/A); *Od.* 11.540 is also doubtful. The masc. adj. occurs 7× in epic, the noun at 21.390, *HyAp* 137, *HyDem* 437. The noun seems better (Latacz, *Freude* 152), since γηθόσυνος would have scanned here. Michel (*N* 31f.) rightly refers it to the bright surface of the calm summer sea. Ἀχαιῶν νῆας adapts the formula ν. Ἀ. | (29×). ἐΰσκαρθμος, from σκαίρω, 'skip', 'leap', is a Homeric *hapax legomenon* well suited to its context (it is equivalent to ἀερσίποδες -ων, 3×): cf. πολύσκαρθμος at 2.814, of an agile Amazon or nymph.

32–8 The 'topographical introduction', marked by the ancient usage 'there is…', breaks the narrative flow to fix attention on what follows: cf. 2.811, 11.711, 11.722, *Od.* 3.293 (with S. West's n.), 4.354, 4.844, 13.96, 15.403, 19.172, *Hy.* 1.8. The submarine cave between Tenedos and Imbros, the isles nearest Troy, is like that of Thetis between Samothrake and Imbros (with 33 cf. 24.78, *Od.* 4.845), which is simply 'in the depths of the sea' at 18.36. Poseidon's undersea palace and this cave frame his voyage: 32–6 repeat βένθεσι λίμνης (21), παιπαλόεις (17), ἐνοσίχθων (10) and ποσσί (19). The horses are unyoked, fed and hobbled to keep them from straying. All these elements are typical of this type-scene: for stopping and unyoking cf. the formular parallels at 5.368f., 5.775f., 8.49f. When the journey ends the horses may be hidden in mist (5.776, cf. 8.50) or fed (5.369, 5.777); both motifs occur here, as at 5.776f. At 8.434 they are tied to their mangers, which corresponds to the hobbling here. There are etymological plays in βαθείης βένθεσι, ποσσὶ πέδας … ἔμπεδον and εἶδαρ ἔδμεναι; ἔ. is from the obsolete *ἔδμι, cf. imperative ἔσθι (*Od.* 17.478?), Sanskrit *ádmi*.

37 = *Od.* 8.275 (of Hephaistos' net). αὖθι means 'here', 'on the spot', not 'again'. Formular with μένω, it interchanges with αὐτόθι, which therefore appears in 42; cf. *Od.* 12.161, ὄφρ' ἔμπεδον αὐτόθι μίμνω. The alliterative phrase ἀρρήκτους ἀλύτους, modified at 360, expresses the ideal tie, one that cannot break or come undone.

39–135 For the structure see 1–168n.; the god's intervention continues the type-scene discussed in 10–38n. For the double exhortation cf. 5.784ff., where Here takes human form to exhort the Greeks while Athene exhorts Diomedes. Both Here (5.788ff.) and Poseidon (105ff.) rebuke the Greeks by saying that the Trojans always cowered in fear while Akhilleus opposed them; both are likened to birds – Here and Athene arrive like doves (5.778) and Poseidon leaves like a hawk (62). Verses 39–42 revert to the end of book 12, when Hektor breached a gate and the Trojans poured over the rampart. We only now see their reaction to his success; this delay is matched on the other side, since we hear of the Greeks' despair only at 85–9, before the next exhortation. At the end of book 12 everything was happening too fast for reactions; delay is vital to the drama. Poseidon finds matters just as he left them, in accord with the rule that, when the epic presents simultaneous events, the action is 'frozen' as long as the parallel narrative lasts (14.1–152n.); so we must not ask how long his journey took. Verses 39–42, 85–9 and 125–35 frame his exhortations; the action is again 'frozen' for the god.

39–40 The brief comparisons φλογὶ ἶσοι ἀολλέες ἠὲ θυέλλῃ sketch the speed and din of the Trojan massed assault. φ. εἴκελος is the usual phrase in the sing.: so 53, 688 and 3× (of Hektor), 330 (of Idomeneus). An extended simile at 14.396–9 likens the din of battle to the βρόμος of the forest fire *or* gale. But *Od.* 12.68, πυρός ... θύελλαι, suggests that the image may be a hendiadys: gales whip up fires (cf. 17.737–9). With 40 cf. 80, 7.112; note the ancient word-play in ἄμοτον μεμαῶτες, literally 'striving for things hard to strive for' (etc., 6× Hom.). On the form ἄμοτον and this traditional idiom, as in ἄτλητα τλᾶσα, see B. Forssman in *Festschrift Risch* 329–39.

41–2 ἄβρομοι αὐΐαχοι is a unique but old alliterative phrase (cf. 37). Aristarchus rightly took ἄβρομος as 'shouting together', with ἀ-intensive < **sm̥*-, 'one' (cf. ἀολλέες) and psilosis. αὐΐαχος has the Lesbian doubling of intervocalic -ϝ- to replace metrical lengthening in a word originally shaped ∪∪∪ –, for *ἀϝίαχος; cf. ἔχευε < *ἔχε(ϝ)ϝε and ἀυάτα (*ἀϝάτᾱ) for ἄτη, scanned ∪∪ –, in Alcaeus (Chantraine, *GH* I 159). Less probably, it is from *ἀν(α)-ϝίϝαχος, cf. Aeolic αὐέρυον < *ἀν(α)ϝέρυον (12.261, a similar verse): ἀνιάχω (Ap. Rhod.) is based on the old variant ἀνίαχοι here. Apion (frag. 5 Neitzel) thought the epithets mean 'silent' with ἀ-privative (cf. Ap. Rhod. 4.153). The Trojans charge noisily elsewhere (3.2, 4.433–8), unlike the more disciplined and unilingual Greeks (3.8). Their imminent victory would hardly make them silent now (so bT); they were just likened to fire and wind, which are loud. ἔλποντο, 'expected', prepares for the ensuing *peripeteia* (cf. Zeus's equally false expectation at 8). The formular variant Ἀχαιούς (42) has papyri and good codices in its favour; ἀρίστους may come from a parallel at 10.273, removing an oral repetition. Van der Valk (*Researches* II 228n.) well observes that to say 'all the Greeks' heightens the danger (but cf. 117).

43–5 Poseidon takes Kalkhas' shape because he will criticize Agamemnon's attitude to Akhilleus at 111ff.; cf. the king's hostility to the seer at 1.68ff. (so bT), which was surely traditional (cf 1.108n.). As a seer (1.69f.), Kalkhas might be expected to know Hektor's thoughts, which he claims to report at 54; he was trusted by the army (so T on 14.136). The formula δέμας καὶ ἀτειρέα φωνήν describes anyone whose shape is taken by a god, cf. 17.555 (Phoinix), 22.227 (Deïphobos), neither of whom has a stentorian voice; when Here takes the form of the aptly named Stentor (5.785), his voice is described. More to the point, continuous ability to speak is a sign of life: cf. θαλερὴ δέ οἱ ἔσχετο φωνή (4× Hom.) or the endless babble of old Tithonos (*HyAphr* 237). γαιήοχος (Laconian γαιάϝοχος) is as obscure as αἰγίοχος. If neither is from ἔχω (see 15.308–11n.), we are left with 'who *rides* (on?) the earth' (or the 'storm'), from the old verb ϝέχω (326–7n.), or 'who *shakes* the earth' (or the 'aegis'), from the root of Latin *vexare*; but cf. γηοχέω 'possess lands' (Hdt.). See further S. West and Hainsworth on *Od.* 1.68, 8.322.

46 = 16.555, cf. 15.604; some papyri omit it from homoearchon. Asyndeton is normal in sentences stating who is 'first', cf. 91, 20.215, 24.710. Poseidon chooses to exhort those who show the most spirit, as is typical in divine interventions (cf. Idomeneus at 214ff.). Telamonian Aias, now the army's *de facto* leader, will score the greatest success of this battle by wounding Hektor (14.409ff.). Oïlean Aias was last seen in the central sector when the son of Telamon, followed by Teukros, left him to reinforce the right against Sarpedon (12.366ff., cf. 12.400); their departure let Hektor break through. But now the god exhorts the Aiantes together (cf. 66f.), and they are together in the centre at 312f. Must we suppose that they were reunited during the rout of 12.470f.? In fact this oddity was brilliantly explained by Wackernagel (*Kleine Schriften* 1, Göttingen 1953, 538–46; cf. 2.406, 7.164nn.). Following an old Indo-European usage, the dual Αἴαντε once meant Aias and his brother Teukros, not the two Aiantes who share nothing save the name; cf. Sanskrit *pitarau*, 'two fathers' = 'father and mother', Latin *Castores* = Castor and Pollux (J. Puhvel, *AJP* 98 (1977) 396–405). The sole Greek parallel is Μολίονε, 'Molion and his brother' (11.709); the weird dual led Homer, Hesiod and Geometric vase-painters to imagine them as Siamese twins (see 23.637–42n.)! Αἴαντε was reinterpreted to mean two men called Aias, but Teukros is always nearby; at 202ff. the same hypothesis explains Oïlean Aias' unexpected intrusion in a killing by Teukros and his brother (177–8n.). This verse originally denoted Teukros and Aias, who clearly derives from early Mycenaean epic (West, *JHS* 108 (1988) 158f.), but the dual led Homer to insert Oïlean Aias and then add Teukros (66f., 92). Teukros' name may be connected with the Teucri (Trojans) and Tjeker (one of the Sea Peoples): see F. Schachermeyr, *Die Ägäische Frühzeit*, Vienna 1976–82, v 93–122; Prinz, *Gründungsmythen* 56–77.

47–51 Shipp (*Studies* 281) deems σφώ an Atticism, since it cannot be for elided σφῶϊ (cf. 11.782); but bards may have reinterpreted σφῶ' as σφώ, by analogy with inherited νώ beside νῶϊ (cf. 326–7n.). σαώσετε, 'you must save', is a rare case of an aor. short-vowel subj. in an affirmative sentence; μή excludes a fut. (Chantraine, *GH* II 207). With κρυεροῖο φόβοιο cf. κ. γόοιο | (3× Hom.), φόβου κρυόεντος (9.2), κρυόεσσα 'Ιωκή (5.740). The storming of the rampart marks one limit, temporal and spatial, of the present battle; the burning of the ships, hinted at in 57, marks the other, which from now on is kept before our eyes as the rampart recedes from view. ἄλλῃ, 'elsewhere', i.e. where Hektor is not in command, is resumed by ᾗ in 53; for ἄαπτος see on 317–18. With 50 cf. 87. Aristophanes (Did/AT) read σχήσουσιν for ἕξ-, comparing 151; this is a conjecture on the ground that σχήσω is more usual for the sense 'hold at bay', but cf. 20.27. The runover verb with movable -ν before a consonant is innovative (p. 9 n. 6).

53 The metaphor of Hektor as a 'rabid' dog, λυσσώδης, and comparison of him to a flame, are key images in the poem, especially in this battle (Whitman, *HHT* 128–53): they culminate in his burning frenzy at 15.605–9 and the burning ship at 16.122ff. The flame image develops that of 39; it now singles out Hektor, exactly as Poseidon wishes the Aiantes to do. Hektor's foes already described him as 'rabid' at 8.299 (κύνα λυσσητῆρα), 9.238f. and 9.305; at 21.542 λύσσα grips Akhilleus himself as he routs the Trojans. This is also related to the major theme of dogs tearing warriors' corpses (see Segal, *Mutilation*; Redfield, *Nature and Culture* 201f.). λυσσώδης, a Homeric *hapax legomenon*, is from *λυκ-*ya* < λύκος, 'wolf', and -ώδης, 'smelling of', a suffix next used in this weakened sense at *HyHerm* 75.

54 Hektor 'claims to be the son of mighty Zeus'; this echoes his presumptuous words at 8.538–41, 'if only I were immortal and ageless for ever, and honoured as Athene and Apollo are honoured, as surely as this day brings the Greeks evil' (bT). He repeats these words to Aias, adding a reference to being the son of Zeus and Here, at 825–8; Aias can thus see the truth behind Poseidon's claim (for further parallels see 24.258–9n.). Odysseus juxtaposed Hektor's madness and his trust in Zeus at 9.237–9; so does the narrator at 15.605ff. Just as Odysseus' exaggeration was meant to spur Akhilleus to act, so Poseidon's is meant to provoke the Aiantes (cf. Eustathius 920.17); it also diverts attention from the depressing truth, hinted at in 58, that Hektor does now have Zeus's support. The god's hyperbole reminds us that Hektor overestimates this support (as the poet recalls at 347–50), and that he, like everyone save Akhilleus, is ignorant of its true motive. ἐρισθενής again describes Zeus at 19.355, 21.184, always with reference to a child of his; Hektor would presumably claim to inherit his huge strength, of which we heard at 8.19ff. Stesichorus and Ibycus made Hektor a son of Apollo (*PMG* 224, 295)! εὔχομαι here denotes a dubious boast, not a justified claim;

see on 1.90–1, 16.231–2, with Muellner, EYXOMAI, *LfgrE* s.v. and Hoekstra on *Od.* 14.199. The formula εὔχομαι εἶναι, here divided, is very ancient.

55–8 The irony in the god's wish that a god help the Aiantes is soon dissolved by its fulfilment; 'Kalkhas' is no prophet, but his words are true. 'To stand firm yourselves and exhort others' defines a good leader; Poseidon takes his own advice, encouraging leaders here and the ranks at 95ff. The forecast that the Aiantes would then repel Hektor, if even (εἰ καί) Zeus himself urged him on, is meant to sound like a hyperbole; they would win 'even beyond fate', as it were (Eustathius 920.23ff.). That Zeus urges him on is actually true; had Poseidon said καὶ εἰ, he would have granted as much. To the troops, of course, he gives no hint of this (95f.). ἐρωήσαιτε, usually 'draw back from', is trans., 'you may drive back', only here in Homer. The formula | νηῶν (τ’) ὠκυπόρων (5× Hom., 110 included) is split over the line-end, cf. ἵππων | ὠκυπόδων (8.128f.), νῆες . . . | ὠκύποροι (*Od.* 5.175f.).

59–61 With 59 cf. 24.247. A rod (ῥάβδος) is the usual symbol of magical power, like those of Hermes or Athene (24.343, *Od.* 10.238, 13.429, 16.172). With a tap of the wand, Athene alters Odysseus' age and Kirke turns his crew porcine. Poseidon wields it similarly; yet in appearance it is not a wand but the staff (σκῆπτρον, σκηπάνιον) borne by a seer, elder or speaker in the assembly, like Priam's at 24.247 or Teiresias' at *Od.* 11.91 (see 2.109n., S. West on *Od.* 2.37). This suits the god's disguise. Since 61 = 5.122 and 23.772, where Athene produces the same effect merely by divine will, Leaf assigns the motif of the staff to a later 'Odyssean' stratum; but Homer has largely suppressed magic wands, which were present in the background all along, as in Germanic folk-tales (so Hoekstra on *Od.* 13.429). — Antimachus and the Chian edition read κεκοπών (Did/AT), but these are emended texts (p. 26); Aristarchus wavered between the correct vulgate κεκοπώς (also at *Od.* 18.335) and κεκοφώς, which is Attic (Wackernagel, *SUH* 29). Chantraine (*GH* I 397) accepts κεκοπών, deeming it a strong aor. participle in origin (cf. van der Valk, *Researches* II 5–7), but it was surely taken as an Aeolic and Chian perfect participle in -ων (see 16.430n.), like the variant πεπλήγων at 2.264. The idea that μένος fills one is standard, but the phrasing is unique.

62–5 Poseidon leaves with the speed of a hawk, not in the shape of one, as is clear from 71f. So too Thetis leaves from Olumpos ἴρηξ ὥς at 18.616, where she has no reason for disguise. πέτεσθαι neatly introduces this image, because it is also used of men in a hurry (755; 21.247, before an eagle simile; 22.143, after a hawk simile). ἀΐσσω, too, appears in both contexts, cf. 21.254. This simile wryly likens 'Kalkhas' to the birds he interprets (70), and makes his 'prey' the Greeks; like the hawk, he has come to the plain from a great height, that of Samothrake. The old idea that gods could take avian shape lurks in the background but is far clearer elsewhere, e.g. *Od.* 22.240: see on

7.59–60, 15.237–8, S. West on *Od.* 3.372 and Bannert, *Formen des Wiederholens* 57–68.

ἴρηξ is the general term for smaller raptors (save owls). ὠκύπτερος is unique, but cf. ὠκυπέτης ἴρηξ τανυσίπτερος (*Erga* 212); ὦρτο πέτεσθαι plays on its sound. On αἰγίλιπος πέτρης see on 9.15 (= 16.4, also a simile). περιμήκης, 'very high', glosses the obscure αἰγίλιψ, which recurs outside this phrase only as a place-name on Ithake, qualified as τρηχεῖα (2.633); this is surely invented, since our Ionian bard knew little of Ithake but that it is αἰγίβοτος and τρηχεῖα (*Od.* 4.606, 13.242). The late but Ionic contraction across -F- in ἀρθείς, from *ἀϝέργω, recurs at 17.724, 2× *Od.* πεδίοιο διώκειν means 'chase over the plain', as at 21.602; the gen. is partitive in origin (Chantraine, *GH* II 58f.). Aristarchus, lacking our knowledge of Indo-European syntax, often noted difficult case usages (e.g. 110, 217, 403); here he supplied διά, adding that ἄλλο stands for ἕτερον, since hawks do not prey on their own kind (cf. bT).

66–7 bT think Oïlean Aias recognizes divine aid first because Telamonian Aias is too stolid, or stronger and hence slower to do so. The latter never receives such help elsewhere, and in reply here comments only on his own feelings (cf. T on 77). Oïlean Aias' remark is also in character (72n.). Ὀϊλεύς is a problematic form. Ἰλεύς, wrongly deemed a later misspelling by Aristarchus (Arn/A on 2.527), appears in the *Sack of Troy* (in Proclus), Hesiod and Stesichorus; Zenodotus emended it into Homer, usually by reading ὁ Ἰλῆος ταχὺς Αἴας or the like, although he had to rewrite 203, 712 and 12.365 (see Nickau, *Zenodotos* 36–42). Dialect-inscriptions have ϜΙΛΕΎΣ (von Kamptz, *Personennamen* 295–8); cf. Etruscan *Aivas Vilatas*. Ὀϊλεύς is an attempt to maintain the *w*-, which the Ionians no longer pronounced; it is Homeric, since ϜΙΛΕΎΣ cannot always be restored, and *w*- was lost in Ionia before Homer's time (Hoekstra, *Modifications* 42–5). A similar prefixing of Ὀ- to express Ϝ- is seen in Ὄαξος for Cretan ϜΑΞΟΣ in Herodotus. 'Aias', still Αἴϝας in Corinthian, is hypocoristic for αἰ(ϝ)όλος, 'swift', 'dappled'; *Ai-wa* is the name of an ox at Knossos (C 973)! Mühlestein (*Namenstudien* 12–23) thinks the existence of two Aiantes reflects this, since one is *swift*, the other has a *dappled* oxhide shield (cf. 16.107). The formula Ὀϊλῆος ταχὺς Αἴας (7×) is odd, since the only other phrase using the father's name in the gen. without 'son of' is the improvised Διὸς δ' ἐριούνιος Ἑρμῆς (*HyHerm* 145). It remodels Ὄ. τ. υἱός (701, 14.520), unless Ὄ. has replaced an adj. *Ὀϊλήϊος. With 67, omitted by some scribes because of the homoearchon Αἰ-, cf. 11.464, 12.342; προσέφη Τελαμώνιον υἱόν blends (Αἴαντα) μέγαν Τ. υ. (3×) with π. Τελαμώνιος Αἴας (76, 7.283). Since such adjectives were not originally limited to use as patronymics, υἱός is not pleonastic: cf. Νηληΐῳ υἷι (2.20) and von Kamptz, *Personennamen* 116.

68–75 Not unnaturally, Locrian Aias loses the thread, saying 'since a god has bidden us fight – for he is not Kalkhas – gods are easily recognized, and my heart is more eager for the fray'. Nicanor (in A), wishing to remove the inconsequence, thought καὶ δέ (73) resumes ἐπεί, but lack of resumption after ἐπεί is not rare; cf. 3.59 and Bolling, *Glotta* 38 (1959) 27ff.

70–2 θεοπρόπος is a synonym of μάντις (1.85n.); as Kalkhas specializes in bird-omens (see on 1.69–70), Aias adds that he is an οἰωνιστής (cf. 2.858). — Gods are often recognized only as they depart (24.460–7n.), but Aias' recognition of a god from the ἴχνια of his 'feet and shins' is odd. If he is known from his 'footprints', why mention his shins? Pollard (*Birds* 158) thinks he left bird-tracks, but in the swirl of battle his speed, which the poet indicates at 65 and 90, would be far more obvious! ποδῶν ἠδὲ κνημάων is paralleled at 17.386, κνῆμαί τε πόδες θ'; this suggests that the 'shins' are merely a redundant formular usage, perhaps meaning 'feet' (cf. the Old Irish cognate *cnáim*, 'foot'), as in synonymic phrases like πόδας καὶ γούνατ' ἔνωμα (cf. 16.335–6n.). For other recognitions from feet or footprints cf. *Od.* 4.149, 19.381, 19.467ff., *HyHerm* 220–5, Aesch. *Cho.* 205–10 and Sowa, *Themes* 247–9. Zenodotus and Aristophanes read ἴχματα, others ἴθματα, 'movements' (Did/AT), which comes from 5.778, where goddesses go πελειάσιν ἴθμαθ' ὁμοῖαι. Both readings look like conjectures to show that the god was recognized from his gait. bT wish to take ῥεῖα with ἀπιόντος, to the same end; but it must go with ἔγνων, since Aias justifies his rash statement by adding 'even gods are easily recognized'. ῥεῖα . . . ἀρίγνωτοι is a formula modified by separation, cf. | ῥ. δ' ἀρίγνωτος (etc.) at 15.490, 4× *Od.*

72 Oïlean Aias is boastful (cf. 23.448–98n.). It is hard to penetrate gods' disguises, if they do not wish to be known (22.9f., *Od.* 13.299f., 13.312f., *HyDem* 111); they do not appear to all mortals, and nobody can identify a god who is incognito (*Od.* 10.573f., 16.161, 17.485–7). But Poseidon wants to be detected, so as to hearten the Aiantes (so T on 65). Divine aid is similarly recognized at 17.322–41 and 15.488–93, where Hektor says ῥεῖα δ' ἀρίγνωτος Διὸς ἀνδράσι γίγνεται ἀλκή; but he fails to identify Athene until too late (22.297ff.)! So too Aias will fail to recognize that Poseidon saved him from shipwreck, boasting that he escaped ἀέκητι θεῶν, for which the god destroys him (*Od.* 4.500–11); Homer certainly knew of his foul rape of Kassandre (S. West on *Od.* 1.325–7). So there may be irony in how he detects the god here.

73–5 We know from 60f. that a god did cause Aias' renewed zest for battle. καὶ δέ virtually equals καὶ γάρ (Denniston, *Particles* 199f.). The epic use of φίλος with parts of the body is surely an extension of its normal use to denote members of the same group (J. T. Hooker, *Glotta* 65 (1987) 44–65). πόδες καὶ χεῖρες ὕπερθε is nom. only here; it is acc. 8× Hom. (61 included). The prefixed ἔνερθε creates a neat chiasmus.

77–80 Telamonian Aias echoes 75 in reverse order, referring to his arms and then his legs; but he proceeds to a bold climax, saying he feels ready for a duel with Hektor. This prepares for his clashes with him at 188ff., 802ff., 14.402ff. and 15.415ff.; he wins all save the last. περὶ δούρατι uniquely adapts π. δουρί | (4× Hom.). | μαιμῶσῖν, contracted beside | μαιμώωσι (75), is innovative (47–51n.). ὤρορε is intrans., as at *Od.* 8.539, 24.62 – an abnormal use of a reduplicated aor. of this type; Heubeck (*ZVS* 97 (1984) 88–95) deems it trans. It is felt as equivalent to the perf. ὄρωρε (Eustathius 921.13, cf. Chantraine, *GH* 1 397f.). Verse 80 recalls 40; ἄμοτον μεμαῶτι μάχεσθαι blends ἄ. μεμαώς etc. with μεμαῶτε μάχεσθαι (both 5×), which is also dat. at 317. Aias' words are full of μένος, since μαιμάω, μενοινάω, ἄμοτον and μεμαώς are all from that root; on μένος see Bremmer, *Soul* 57–60.

81–2 Verse 81, a standard line marking a shift to a simultaneous scene elsewhere (24× Hom.), precedes τόφρα at *Od.* 23.288 also; as at *Od.* 24.203, a second line is added to sum up this scene's effect. γηθόσυνος, conjoined, uniquely, with χάρμη, alludes to the noun's original sense of 'desire (for combat)', < χαίρω. See on 7.217–18; Hoekstra, *Modifications* 151n.

83–125 Poseidon rushes from the Aiantes, close to the enemy, to exhort the routed Greeks. This scene, about as long as 46–82, is framed by an echo of 83 at 125; a mention of the Aiantes at 126 recalls the previous scene, to signal that the action may now advance.

83–90 Verses 83 and 89f. frame a vignette of the Greeks' utter exhaustion, bodily and mental. We see, from their viewpoint, first, their physical weariness, then, as they recover enough to notice the Trojans swarming over the rampart, their tears and despair. δερκομένοισι and εἰσορόωντες stress their shock at what they see (so bT); their helplessness in the face of ruin stirs our emotions. Apart from 125, the use of γαιήοχος unsupported by another epithet is unique in 23 epic uses; cf. ἐνοσίχθων used alone at 89, 20.13, 20.405 and 4× *Od.* in 46 epic uses. νηυσὶ θοῆσιν (12× epos) exemplifies how fixed epithets need not suit their contexts; the ships are static, like the men by them. With the rest of 84 cf. 10.575. With 85 cf. καμάτῳ δ' ὑπὸ γυῖα λέλυνται (7.6), φίλα γ. λ. (2× *Od.*); φίλα follows the formula φίλον ἦτορ despite the repetition. Editors may be wrong to alter the γίνομαι and γινώσκω of the MSS: such forms were used in Ionia by the fifth century (Chantraine, *GH* 1 12f.). With 87 cf. 50. For εἰσορόωντες in this position cf. 5.418, *Od.* 8.327; the rest of 88 is formular. With 89 cf. 15.700, *Od.* 12.107 and ὑπὲκ κακότητα φύγοιμεν (3× *Od.*). φημί is often extended to mean 'say to oneself', 'think', especially in the imperf. or opt.: cf. 100, 15.167, 15.251, 15.697, 16.61, 16.830 (LSJ s.v., IIb).

90 Poseidon hurries about, urging the Greeks to build a strong formation: κρατερὰς ... φάλαγγας is proleptic, cf. κρατεραὶ στίχες at 4.90 = 201 (cf. also 4.254). φάλαγγες are the same as στίχες (Latacz, *Kampfdarstellung* 45ff.). It is hard to move about a battlefield save with divine help (cf. 4.539–42), but for a god anything is easy: for this topos see 3.381, 15.490–3, 562–4, 16.688–90, 846 and West on *Erga* 5ff. μετεισάμενος is the aor. of (ϝ)ίεμαι, 'hasten', with ϝ 'neglected' as in 17.285 (Chantraine, *GH* 1 293f.).

91–4 Poseidon exhorts men in the centre, facing Hektor's breakthrough, and the left (for the order of battle cf. 681n.). The leaders of the units he visits are listed before his speech (with ὤτρυνε at 90 cf. ἐποτρύνων at 94). Teukros is now with the Aiantes (46n.), Leïtos and Peneleos in the centre of the line, with the Locrians and Boeotians (681ff.); Thoas is chief of the Aetolians (T claim he is next to Peneleos because he married the latter's daughter); the unknown Deïpuros, also seen with Meriones and Aphareus at 478f. and 9.83, is slain on the left at 576 (T report guesses that he is a Pylian or brother of Meriones); Meriones, on the left, leads the Cretans (249–50n.); another junior warrior, Antilokhos, helps lead the Pylians, a unit in the centre. All take part in the fighting to come. Such bare lists may contain six names, as at 5.705, seven (21.209), eight (8.274) or nine (11.301, 16.415, 16.694) – the most audiences might tolerate. From Δηΐπυρον, 92f. = 478f., when Idomeneus calls for help. For μήστωρας ἀϋτῆς see 4.328n. Verse 94 may be spurious like 480, 17.219, cf. *Od.* 15.208: on 'winged words' cf. Parry, *MHV* 414–18, and Hoekstra on *Od.* 13.165.

92 Peneleos is prominent in this battle only (14.487ff., 16.335ff., 17.597ff.). His name may come from the obscure root *πηνελο- seen in 'Penelope' and πηνέλ-οψ, 'duck' (S. West on *Od.* 1.223). Its original form, Πηνέλεος, survives in the vulgate Πηνελέοιο at 14.489, whence Aristophanes wrongly restored it here (Did/A); Ionian bards have assimilated the ending to names in -λεως like Ἀγέλεως (*Od.* 22.131). Cf. Hoekstra, *Modifications* 32n.

95–124 In a desperate situation, Poseidon needs to sound all possible registers of feeling; in Kalkhas' guise he can do so with real authority. Thus he appeals to the Greeks' sense of shame (95), his own trust in them (95f.), their fear of defeat (96f.), his shock at what has happened (99f.) and their disgrace in being beaten by so cowardly a foe (101ff.). It is shameful that, as he avers, they are unwilling to defend the ships out of pique at how Agamemnon treated Akhilleus (107–14); this acknowledges but also deflects the army's anger at its leader for the disaster, deftly avoiding any hint that the Greeks are now too badly mauled to resist. He plays on their pride in their valour, his anger at them if they betray it and their fear that worse may happen, as it will if they let it (115–22); Hektor is now by the ships (123f.)! The rehearsal of events known to all is usual in exhortations (cf. 2.796ff., Callinus frag. 1); it is meant to jolt the troops into awareness and hence action. The god hammers home six times his central theme of slackness, typical of exhortations: cf. his speech at 14.364 and Callinus frag. 1.3, Tyrtaeus frag. 12.44. He mentions the ships five times. His speech falls into two parts, with ring-composition and ἀλλά at 111 lightly marking the middle. The first half, after an initial appeal, states the facts of the disaster, the second, full of reproaches, ends with a reprise of the appeal:

I. A   Appeal to *aidōs* (95f.).
   B   Defeat will follow from *slackness* (97f.).
   C   The Trojans, once *cowards*, are now at our ships (99–107)
   D   because of our *leader's error* and the army's *slackness* (108–10).
II. D' But our *leader's error* is no excuse for your *slackness* (111–17).
   C' I would not reproach a *coward*, but I reproach you (117–19).
   B' Disaster will follow from *slackness* (120f.).
   A' Appeal to *aidōs* and *nemesis* (121–4).

bT admire this exhortation, but Leaf calls it 'so long and so tautological as to be ill suited for its position'; the Analysts tried to distinguish the two or more speeches allegedly combined herein. It is typical of their divergent results that Leaf held that 99–107 + 116–24 were added after the interpolation of the Embassy, whereas Wilamowitz (*IuH* 220) deemed 99–114 the younger part. For defences of the speech see Eustathius (921.55–922.43, 923.8–23), Schadewaldt (*Iliasstudien* 123), Winter (*MNO* 58f.), Reinhardt (*IuD* 282), Fenik (*TBS* 120–2), Michel (*N* 38–47) and Latacz (*Kampfdarstellung* 153n., 214f.).

95–6 With the opening reproach 'For shame!' cf. 5.787 = 8.228, αἰδώς, Ἀργεῖοι, κάκ' ἐλέγχεα; 15.502, 16.422 (on αἰδώς see 120–3n.). κοῦροι νέοι is a respectful address from an older person; either term alone can mean 'warriors'. Thus Tyrtaeus calls his men ὦ νέοι (frags. 10.15, 11.10). Nicanor (in A) rightly separated κοῦροι from νέοι, by a comma as it were; Homer 'does well to mention their valour, which leaves no excuse for cowardice – hence he repeats the word twice' (bT). The Greeks are in such straits that to call them 'young boys' (Leaf), like παῖδες νεαροί at 2.289, would be bad psychology. 'Kalkhas' trusts in their ability, *if they fight*, to save the ships (cf. 47f., to the Aiantes); it would be shameful to disappoint his mantic expectation. μαρναμένοισι and ἔγωγε (repeated at 100) are emphatic; this observer's opinion should be taken seriously. With 96 cf. *Od.* 16.98 = 116. σαωσέμεναι is aor., not fut. (Chantraine, *GH* I 418), but does not convey scorn, *pace* Leaf. νέας is late but Homeric (e.g. 101, 620); for ἁμός see p. 8 n. 2.

97–8 By calling the war λευγαλέος, Poseidon acknowledges the men's exhaustion. λ., used nowhere else of πόλεμος, describes δάϊς at 14.387 and θάνατος (both dat.) at 21.281, 2× *Od.* 'War' and 'death' share the epithets δυσηλεγής, δυσηχής, κακός and στυγερός; their formular systems are akin, like their natures. With πολέμοιο μεθήσετε cf. 118, 4.351, and μεθιέντα(ς) ἴδοι(ς) στυγεροῦ π. (4.240, 6.330). εἴδεται has its original sense 'is seen', not 'seems' (cf. 8.559, 24.319). ὑπὸ Τρώεσσι δαμῆναι recurs at 668 only: it is striking how often a phrase clusters in a limited portion of the epic and then vanishes, as if the poet recalled it for a while and then forgot it. See Hainsworth in *Studies Palmer* 83–6; Janko, *Mnem.* 34 (1981) 251–64.

99–101 Verse 99 = 15.286, 20.344, 21.54, *HyHerm* 219, cf. 7.124, *Od.* 19.36. The exclamation ὢ πόποι (53× epos) usually opens a speech, but occurs near the end of one at 14.49, as second line at 17.171, half-way through at *Od.* 13.209 and as third verse at *HyHerm* 309. Likewise (ὢ) πέπον(ες) does not begin the speech in 11/22 epic uses, including 120. The exclamations, five verses from the beginning and end of the speech, take their place in the ring-structure (95–124n.). With ὢ πόποι cf. the (πο)ποπό with which Greeks still voice surprise or dismay. The hiatus in ὃ οὔ ποτ' has a basis in formular usage (ὅ is for *yod*), since at 5.303, 20.286 and *Od.* 3.275 we find hiatus in μέγα ἔργον, ὃ οὔ (ποτε); cf. 20.466. Here the formula μ. θαῦμα evoked this phrase, but it is displaced to an unusual position in the next verse. ἔφασκον is the sole iterative imperf. in -σκον to receive the augment, since φάσκω was felt to equal φημί (Chantraine, *GH* I 319f.). ἡμετέρας conveys an understatement: Greeks are being attacked by barbarians, brave men by cowards, a greater number by a lesser – all of this shameful (bT).

102–4 Full similes do occur in speeches, often in reproach or denigration of the enemy (2.337f., 3.60–3, 4.243–5, 9.323f., 12.167–70, 16.746–8, 20.252–5, 24.41–3); see Scott, *Simile* 50. φυζακινός is a *hapax* from φύζα, 'panic'. The deer, a common victim, connotes cowardice: cf. 4.243, 21.29, 22.1, *Od.* 4.334ff. Akhilleus says his foe has the 'heart of a deer' at 1.225. Poseidon counterposes to its timidity three carnivores. θῶες are jackals, the *canis aureus*, still a pest in rural Greece and Anatolia; they are tawny and resemble large dogs. At 11.474–81 they feed on a deer's carcass but flee when a lion appears. The ancients drew no clear distinction between leopards and panthers; they still roamed Cilicia in Cicero's day (*Ad Fam.* 2.11.2, 8.9.3). Thus we do not know which species is meant. πόρδαλις may be an Atticism (Shipp, *Studies* 18); παρδ- is in Semonides and Hdt. The MSS often vary when this feline appears (*Od.* 4.457, *HyAphr* 71); Aristarchus standardized to παρδ- (Did/A on 17.20, 21.573), yet the papyri and lexicographers keep πορδ-, save in παρδαλέη at 3.17, 10.29 (van der Valk, *Researches* II 177f.). ἤϊα, here simply 'food', usually means 'provisions for a voyage' (6× *Od.*); at *Od.* 5.368 ἦα means 'chaff', which may be a different word (Chantraine, *Dict.* s.v.), but J. Puhvel cites a Hittite term with both senses (*AJP* 104 (1983) 223f.). The ι, again long at *Od.* 2.289, 410, is elsewhere short (2×) or contracted with the η. ἔπι = ἔπεστι, as at 1.515, 3.45: 'there is no fight in them'. Cf. οὐδ' ἔπι φειδώ, *Od.* 14.92.

105–6 Poseidon again notes the Trojans' boldness in Akhilleus' absence in his exhortation at 14.364ff., cf. 139ff.; so does Here in her exhortation after her parallel chariot-journey (5.788–91). Akhilleus mentions this him-

self at 9.352–5, cf. 16.69f. and 15.718–25n. μένος καὶ χεῖρας, found 9×
Hom., also precedes Ἀχαιῶν at 6.502; for οὐδ᾽ ἠβαιόν, 6× Hom., see on
2.379f.

107–14 When Agamemnon proposes to abandon the war, he assumes
that the men are angry at him, and hence loth to defend the ships (14.49–
51): cf. also 19.85f. Anger over his leadership would be natural in such a
crisis; yet Homer never shows the men shirking battle for this reason, but
confines such unworthy conduct to suppositions by his speakers. This leaves
Akhilleus' withdrawal all the more isolated, although anger and withdrawal
formed a traditional topos (459–61n.). Like Odysseus at 2.284ff., Poseidon
distracts attention from Agamemnon's bungling by accusing the army itself
of disloyalty, when despondency is a natural reaction; and, like Odysseus
halting the rush to the ships, he is harsher to the men than to their leaders
(2.180n.). By saying that the troops are unwilling, he makes each think that
he aims his reproach at the others (cf. bT); but he soon makes his rebukes
more forceful, with first 'us' (114) and then 'you' (116–19).

107–10 Verse 107 = 5.791, where Here made a rhetorical overstate-
ment; now it is literally true. The MSS and Aristarchus read δ᾽ ἕκαθεν, but
his predecessors (Did/A) and a papyrus read δὲ ἑκάς as at 5.791, whence this
reading surely derives, in an attempt to harmonize the text (cf. van der Valk,
op. cit. II 54f., who observes that ἑκάς but not ἕκαθεν takes a gen. in later
Greek). δ᾽ ἕκαθεν is better, although it entails a 'neglected' ϝ- like that in
ἑκάς at 20.422 (cf. 178–80n.). The divergence looks like oral variation; in
one verse the poet modernized, in the other he did not. Redactors have often
erased such oral variants; for some cases where they survive see Janko, *HHH*
2f. κοῖλος is from *κόϝιλος: cf. Myc. *ko-wi-ro-* (KN B 101), κόϊλος (Alcaeus,
Anacreon). In its 73 epic occurrences, the uncontracted form can always be
read save at *Od.* 22.385, *Cypria* frag. 15.5 B. = 13.5 D. The epithet may stress
the ships' capacity or their lack of a deck. With the chiastic 108 cf. 2.368.
κακότης can mean 'cowardice' as much as wickedness: cf. 15.721. μεθ-
ημοσύνη recurs in Greek only at 121; it was perhaps created for this passage,
like συνημοσύνη at 22.261, since the suffix -(μο)σύνη was productive in
Ionic (Chantraine, *Formation* 210–13). νηῶν is an abl.-gen. with ἀμύνειν,
i.e. 'ward (the Trojans) off from', as at 15.731, Τρῶας ἄμυνε νεῶν: see
16.521–6n. and Chantraine, *GH* II 56, 64.

111–13 Agamemnon privately admits that he is αἴτιος (9.116), but denies
it in public (19.86). Poseidon's criticism is respectfully phrased: the king may
not be totally responsible. The honorific verse 112 helps uphold his dignity
(= 1.102, 7.322; cf. Akhilleus' words at 1 .355f.!). The formulae in 112f.
reflect the substance of the quarrel: Agamemnon is defined by his authority, Akhilleus by martial virtue. ἀπατιμάω, unique beside ἀτιμάζω (17×
Hom.), intensifies ἀτιμάω: cf. ἀπομηνίω, ἀπεχθαίρω.

115–17 Verse 115 means simply 'let us correct (our slackness)'. ἀκέομαι is also metaphorical at 22.2, where it describes thirst, *Od.* 10.69 (*atē*), 14.383 (ships), Hdt. 1.167 (error); see LSJ s.v. I 3. The Homeric *hapax* ἀκεστός with φρένες is parallel to another metaphorical usage at 15.203, the end of Poseidon's intervention, when Iris asks him to relent: ἦ τι μεταστρέψεις; στρεπταὶ μέν τε φ. ἐσθλῶν (cf. 9.497, 24.40f.). The repetition is typical of maxims (e.g. 7.282, 11.793, 24.354, *Erga* 352, 369). φ. ἐ. flatters the troops, as in 117, where they are called πάντες ἄριστοι; the best men have a duty to fight (cf. 11.408ff.). Verse 115 states positively what is stated negatively in 114 and 116f., and is an indirect reminder of Akhilleus' obduracy. 'Some' in bT deemed it an oblique appeal for an embassy to him: 'let us heal (the rift) quickly; the minds of good men can be healed'. φ. ἐ. is based on φ. ἐσθλαί (etc.) at 17.470, 3× *Od.* 'Some commentaries' offered τε for τοι (Did/A), perhaps by analogy with 15.203, but see Ruijgh, τε *épique* 793f. οὐκέτι = 'no longer' makes no sense; it was no more right before that the Greeks slacken their efforts than it is now. The idiom here is best understood if we divide the word into οὐκ and ἔτι (cognate with Latin *et*); the sense is 'not the further, and perhaps expected, step', i.e. 'your anger may be right, but that does not justify slackening your efforts'. Cf. 9.598, *Erga* 34 and Dawe on Soph. *O.T.* 115; differently J. R. Wilson, *Glotta* 65 (1987) 194–8. οὐκέτι καλά recurs 2× *Od.*, μεθίετε θούριδος ἀλκῆς at 4.234, 12.409. | πάντες ἄριστοι is at the verse-end 5× Hom. (also acc. 11×); its displacement from 116 by the formula θ. ἀ. has caused a clumsy trochaic caesura in the second foot, suggestive of a misplaced verse-ending.

118–19 μαχεσσαίμην means 'quarrel', as at 1.8, 2.377, 5.875, 9.32; cf. 6.329f. (Hektor to Paris found at home during the battle), σὺ δ' ἂν μαχέσαιο καὶ ἄλλῳ, | ὅν τινά που μεθιέντα ἴδοις στυγεροῦ πολέμοιο. Normally poor fighting ability was no excuse for shirking (4.299f., 12.270f., in an exhortation); nor is it here, since Poseidon rhetorically assumes his hearers to be 'all the best'. λυγρός again describes persons at 237, *Od.* 9.454, 18.107 and in tragedy. περὶ κῆρι, often at the main caesura (as in 206), participates here in the substitution-system of ἀπέχθωνται/αἰδέομαι π. κ. | (4.53, 24.435): cf. 4.46n.

120–3 The plur. ὦ πέπονες recurs only at 2.235, when Thersites calls the Greeks cowards for not going home. In the sing. it is a polite and friendly address, as bT take it here, since Poseidon is 'comforting' the men; but the idea that they may suffer a yet worse disaster is not reassuring. From meaning 'ripe', of fruit, πέπων evolved to 'over-ripe', 'soft' (Chantraine, *Dict.* s.v.): see also 99–101n. ἐν(ὶ) φρεσὶ θέσθε ἕκαστος | recurs (in the fem.) at *Od.* 4.729, cf. *HyAphr* 15; its equivalent in the sing. is (σύ δ') ἐνὶ φ. βάλλεο σῇσι. It is adapted from the formula ἐν(ὶ) φ. θείω | (etc.) by the addition of a word shaped ∪ – –, a common device. — αἰδώς and νέμεσις are paired at *Cypria* frag. 9.5f. B. = 7.5f. D., *Erga* 200, *Cat.* 204.82: cf. αἰδοῖος νεμεσητός (11.649n.), νέμεσίν τε καὶ αἴσχεα (6.351). One should feel αἰδώς, 'a sense of shame', before one's comrades (15.661f.) or the gods (*Od.* 9.269–71), when acting wrongly, against one's nature or below one's best; αἶσχος must be cognate, although this has never been proposed. So too Aias appeals to the Greeks' αἰδώς at 15.561–4: they again close ranks in response. νέμεσις is the proper indignation felt by others at one's misconduct (3.156n.); cf. Agamemnon's specious plea at 14.80, 'there is no *nemesis* in escaping from evil', i.e. 'nobody can object if we give up the war', and *Od.* 2.136, 22.40. αἰδώς is thus the subjective counterpart of νέμεσις; Aristotle juxtaposed these emotions (*Eth. Nic.* 2.1108a32ff.). He who has no shame will have no honour either. See further Macleod on 24.435; S. West on *Od.* 2.64–6. These concepts still persist in Greece: see Lloyd-Jones, *A&A* 33 (1987) 1ff., with bibliography. The rest of 122 recurs at 15.400, cf. 17.384, 3× *Od.*, *Theog.* 87. The original sense of νεῖκος, 'quarrel', is often extended; cf. μάχεσθαι in 118. Poseidon is not indulging in understatement.

124–5 βοὴν ἀγαθός describes Hektor at 15.671 also (acc.); save at 15.249, 17.102 and 24.250 (Aias, Polites), this generic epithet is restricted to Diomedes and Menelaos. It is adapted for this unusual separated phrase (cf. Hoekstra, *Modifications* 95). At 12.455 and 460 the gate had double bolts; here it has only one, as at 12.291 (a similar verse). So too at 24.446 and 566 a gate has first two bars, then one. Both discrepancies are owed to adaptation of formulae: verbs often precede ὀχῆας | (4×), but when an adj. is substituted no plur. fits the space. Thus beside πύλας καὶ ἀπῶσεν (-αν) ὀχῆας (2×) we find πύλας/σανίδας καὶ μακρὸν ὀχῆα (3×). The 'double bolts' of 12.455 were surely invented on the spur of the moment to magnify Hektor's achievement in breaking through. With the innovative use of n-mobile in ἔρρηξεν δέ cf. οὐδ' ἔ. χαλκός (3×) and p. 9 n. 6. Verse 125 echoes 83; for κελευτιόων, also at 12.265, see Risch, *Wortbildung* 321.

126–35 These verses are often seen as an interpolated or at best problematic depiction of hoplite-tactics, in which, in contrast to the scattered duels of the champions, organized formations fight at close range (e.g. Kirk, *Songs* 186–8). There is a like passage at 16.211–17 (215–17 = 131–3 here). But Latacz (*Kampfdarstellung* 63–6) shows that these depict not a hoplite phalanx, but a specially dense formation, used for weight in massed offence or, as here, to halt an enemy charge; the poet takes for granted the normal looser deployment of the mass formations which fight Homeric battles. Poseidon urges that the ranks be κρατεραί (90, cf. 126f., 5.591f.); Hektor and his men are halted by the πυκιναὶ φάλαγγες (145), into which the Greeks have fitted themselves 'like a tower' (152). This image is clarified at 16.212f. by that of building a wall, stone next to stone. At 15.567f. and 17.354f., dense formations 'fence' the enemy off (φράσσω): the lines of spearmen evoke a fence like Eumaios', of stones laid close with thorns on top and stakes in front (*Od.* 14.10–12). Classical tacticians termed such a closing of ranks *synaspismos*, 'putting shields together' (so T): cf. Polybius 12.21.3, 18.29.6, and Diodorus 16.3.2. On mass fighting as the basis of Homeric battles see, in addition to Latacz, Pritchett, *The Greek State at War* IV 1–44; Morris, *Burial* 196ff.; H. van Wees, *CQ* 38 (1988) 1–24.

126–8 Αἴαντας δοιούς uniquely varies Αἴαντε δύω (5×), δ. Α. (2×), cf. δυ' Αἴαντες (2×); the nom. and acc. plur. (6×) is itself an innovation for the dual (18×), cf. 46n. The emphatically placed | καρτεραί is the Greek answer to the fact that Hektor is | καρτερός at 124. The density of the ranks would impress even Ares or Athene, the war-gods of the opposing sides (4.439, cf. 18.516). This develops the traditional idea of an observer who could safely view the fighting, as at 343f., 4.539–42 (cf. 4.539, ἀνὴρ ὀνόσαιτο μετελθών), and guides our reactions. It is further heightened at 17.398f., when the fighting is so fierce that οὐδέ κ' Ἄρης λαοσσόος οὐδέ κ' Ἀθήνη | τόν γε ἰδοῦσ' ὀνόσαιτο; cf. too 20.358f. λ., often mistranslated 'saviour of the people', is for *λαϝο-σσόϝος, from σεύομαι, 'drive', 'chase', cf. ἐσσύμην, ἔκιον, Sanskrit *syávate*, 'move'; it means 'who drives the army' (into battle *or* flight). Cf. δορυσσόος (*Aspis* 54), βοοσσόος, 'drover' (Callimachus). Though linked with Athene (*Od.* 22.20), the epithet is generic: cf. 17.398, 20.48 (of Ares and Eris, with Athene's name following), 20.79 (Apollo), *Od.* 15.244, *Aspis* 3, 37 (various heroes). The rare use of ἄν and κε together is protected by parallels like 24.437, *Od.* 9.334 (*pace* Chantraine, *GH* II 345). ἄν and κεν may both derive from an enclitic *ken/kṇ; Aeolic adopted κε(ν), but Arcadian and Attic-Ionic first blended it with κα < *kṇ as *καν, and then misdivided *οὐ καν as οὐκ ἄν (cf. Arcadian εικ αν): see Chantraine, *Dict.* s.v. ἄν.

129 The warriors were 'picked' for the expedition from the whole people. Verse 129 blends Ἕκτορα δῖον | (19×) with Τρῶάς τε καὶ Ἕ., found mainly in these books (1, 15.42, 16.654; dat. 347, 720, 10.318; nom. at verse-end 8.158, 15.589). Cf. Τρωσίν τε καὶ Ἕκτορι δίῳ | (17.719), and, for the addition of ἔμιμνον at the verse-end, ἦω (*ἦοα) δῖαν ἔμιμνεν | (9.662, *Od.* 19.50) and 120–3n.

130–1 These lines vividly depict the density of the formation; cf. Tyrtaeus frag. 11.31–3, where similar verses express the closeness of two hostile forces. φράξαντες ... σάκος σάκεϊ means much the same as ἀσπὶς ἄρ' ἀσπίδ' ἔρειδε (Eustathius 924.21–6). A like interaction of meaning and word-order appears at *Od.* 7.120f. (Alkinoos' orchard): ὄγχνη ἐπ' ὄγχνη γηράσκει, μῆλον δ' ἐπὶ μήλῳ, | αὐτὰρ ἐπὶ σταφύλη σταφύλη, σῦκον δ' ἐπὶ σύκῳ. Both couplets have chiasmus in the second verse; but the Odyssean lines are less dense, since they avoid asyndeton, contain eight nouns, not ten, and interleave the fruits with ἐπί. Verse 130 fences paired nouns with φράξαντες and προθελύμνῳ; 131 presses ἔρειδε towards the middle, like γηράσκει. Other cases of multiple polyptoton in one verse are 2.363, 14.382, *Erga* 25f. (see further West on *Erga* 23); polyptoton often expresses reciprocity (S. West on *Od.* 1.311).

προθέλυμνος here means 'one upon another'. In origin θέλυμνα were 'foundations' or 'roots', θεμέλια (Janko, *CPh* 81 (1986) 308f.); trees and hair are torn out προθέλυμνα, 'by the roots' (9.541, 10.15). Homer glosses the archaism with αὐτῇσιν ῥίζῃσι at 9.542 (cf. πρόρριζος). But earlier bards had misunderstood '(trees torn out) by the roots' as '(fallen) upon one another, overlapping', so a second sense evolved. Aristarchus wrongly saw this as primary (see his n. on Aristoph. *Peace* 1210, in Erbse, *Scholia* II 516), adducing σάκος θέτο τετραθέλυμνον, 'with four overlapping layers' (15.479f. = *Od.* 22.122f.). But, *pace* Hoekstra, *Modifications* 94f., the latter phrase, found in two abnormal arming-scenes, is surely a late and fanciful expansion of σ. ἑπταβόειον, by analogy with κυνέην θ. τετραφάληρον (5.743 = 11.41, in standard arming-scenes); τετραθέλυμνον replaced ἑ. after the insertion of θ., to avoid hiatus, and the separation of the phrase prevents the restoration of *τϝ- in σάκος, '(shield made of) hide', cf. φερεσσακής (*Aspis* 13), Sanskrit *tvác-*, 'skin', Hittite *tuekka-*, 'body'. Chantraine too deems τετραθέλυμνος original, and takes προθέλυμνος as 'with surface facing forward', which is then applied to uprooted trees (*Dict.* s.v. -θέλυμνος)! He relies on τριθέλυμνος in Eustathius 849.5, a form invented by the archbishop (who says ὡς εἰπεῖν). Nor is προ- an Aeolic reflex of *qetr̥-, 'four', *pace* Fernández-Galiano on *Od.* 22.122; cf. 132–3n. σάκος, originally the old body-shield, came to be used interchangeably with the circular ἀσπίς (Trümpy, *Fachausdrücke* 20–36). — κόρυν for -υθα (9×), unique in early Greek, was created by analogy with νέκυν, βαρύν (etc.), to fit the word in without elision at the end of the fourth foot; the converse licence, εὐρέα for εὐρύν, avoids a spondee in the fifth (Chantraine, *GH* I 97, 208).

132–3 'The crested helmets touched with their shining plates (φάλοι) when the men nodded.' Helmets have four φάλοι (12.384, 22.314f.): cf. their epithet τετραφάληρος (5.743, 11.41); their φάλαρα (16.106); and τρυφάλεια, 'helmet', probably from *(qe)tru- 'four', like Latin *quadru-* and τρά-πεζα, '(four-legged) table'. φάλοι are made of polished metal: a leather helmet worn at night is ἄφαλος (10.258), no doubt so that its wearer gives off no glint of light. Swords break on them (3.362, 16.338); spears pierce through them to the forehead (4.459 = 6.9); the top of a φάλος (or the top φ.) is pierced near the crest (614f.). The sense 'plate (of metal)' suits these passages. Myc. helmets had four plates, called /opikorusia opaworta/ (Ventris and Chadwick, *Documents* 376–8, 524); no such helmet has yet been found, but J. Borchhardt compares some Myc. depictions (*Arch. Hom.* E 73; *Homerische Helme*, Mainz 1972, 82f.). φάλος is from the root *bhel-, 'shining', seen in English 'bald'; φάλαρα, later 'metal discs'; φαλός, 'shining', 'white'; φαλύνει, 'brightens', φάλκη, 'dandruff' (Hsch.); φάλ-ακρος, -ανθος, 'shiny-topped', 'bald'; φαληριόωντα, 'white-foaming' (795–9n.).

Many scholars, doubting that the men could be packed so tightly that *plates* would touch, think some projection is meant. Aristarchus deemed φάλοι to be studs (Arn/A on 10.258, cf. 3.362n.); Leaf thought of horns like those seen on the LHIIIC Warrior Vase, but these are double, not quadruple. Hoekstra (*op. cit.* 96–9) thinks φάλοι are here reinterpreted as the 'crest-holders', running from the front of the helmet to the nape, seen in Late Geometric art and the Argive panoply of *c.* 720 b.c. (cf. Coldstream, *Geometric Greece* 147f.): hence the allusion to crests (but Myc. helmets had crests too).

134–5 ἐπτύσσοντο and its origin *πτύξ mean 'fold' or 'layer'. Albracht (*Kampfschilderung* I 37f.) explains that it refers to the phalanx, where the first rows hold out one *layer* of spears behind another (cf. bT); the battle 'bristles' with spears (ἔφριξεν) at 339. θρασειάων ἀπὸ χειρῶν (7× Hom.) elsewhere describes spears being cast, e.g. at 11.571. σείομεν' also hints at throwing; σείω is used of brandishing spears before casting them, e.g. at 3.345, 22.133. Homer surely adapted verses from the start of battle, when spears fly thick and fast, to suit the line of thrusting spears wanted here (cf. 147). μέμασαν δὲ μάχεσθαι explains ἰθὺς φρόνεον; cf. 12.124 and the formula ἰ. μεμαώς etc. (5×). The men's minds are fixed on what is before them: ἀντικρὺ μ. (137) is a unique variation for the opposing side.

136–42 These vv. create a dynamic contrast with the static picture of the Greek ranks that preceded. A simple comparison expands into a grand image which both expresses Hektor's onrush and itself moves the action on (cf. 17.722ff. and Moulton, *Similes* 75f.). What will happen when the unstoppable force meets the immovable object? At first the boulder, dislodged from the heights by a downpour, crashes down irresistibly; but it stops when it reaches level ground, as will Hektor and his men when they pass beyond the rampart, with the advantage of height it may confer, to clash with the foe. The comparison of Hektor to an inanimate entity, the rock, is telling, but not only because it recalls the boulder with which he smashed open the gate at 12.445ff. Once likened to a torrent (5.597ff.), he now moves not under his own impetus but by Zeus's will, as he proudly avers at 153f.; likewise rain, which made the boulder slide, comes from Zeus. Personification reinforces this point: the rock 'flies', 'runs' and is still 'eager' when it stops. The simile thus presages the failure not of this attack only, but of Hektor's entire drive to the sea.

136–8 Verse 136 = 15.306, 17.262; προτύπτω, 'advance', is intrans., like προκόπτω (cf. *Od.* 24.319). ὀλοοίτροχος, 'roller', is from ϜολοϜο- (cf. εἰλέω, 'roll', ὅλμος, 'mortar' < the root 'roll', Latin *volvo*) compounded with τρέχω, on which Homer plays in θέει (141): so Chantraine, *Dict.* s.v. Some derived it from ὀλοός, 'ruinous' (cf. Comanus frag. 7 Dyck). Herodotus (8.52) uses contracted ὀλοίτροχος to mean 'cylinder': cf. Democritus frag. 162. The unexplained ι recurs in ὀλοοίτροπα, '(rolled) cakes' (Hsch.). — στεφάνη reappears in the sense 'crown (of a hill)' in Hellenistic prose. Aristarchus took it as 'summit', others, more plausibly, as a flat 'brim' of a plateau over which the torrent pours (cf. Comanus frag. 8 Dyck). ποταμὸς χειμάρροος recurs, but with *-ροϝος contracted, at 4.452, 5.88 and 11.493 (similes), split over the verse-end in the last two cases. At 11.493, as here, rain causes the flood, which sweeps away trees in its path to the sea. ὥση is a subj. of general statement, soon followed by indicatives; this is common in similes (Chantraine, *GH* II 253; Ruijgh, τε *épique* 399ff.).

139 The rain loosens the boulder by creating the torrent, but the torrent comes first as immediate cause. With the 'shameless' rock cf. the λᾶας ἀναιδής of 4.521, *Od.* 11.598, and 'pitiless bronze'. There is wit in the simultaneous personification of the rock and denial that it has human feelings of shame at its own destructiveness. ἔχματα are small stones that support it, like the ἔ. πύργων at 12.260 or the ἔ. νηῶν at 14.410. πέτρη means 'boulder' here, like πέτρος, not 'cliff' as elsewhere, e.g. at 137 (see Maher, *Creation and Tradition* 127–41). This 'late' usage recurs 3× *Od.*, 3× *Theog.*, *HyAp* 383; cf. *Aspis* 374ff., 437ff., similes influenced by this one. With ἀσπέτῳ ὄμβρῳ cf. ἀθέσφατον ὄμβρον in similes at 3.4, 10.6 (reversed).

141–2 There is more wit in ἀσφαλέως θέει ἔμπεδον, since both adverbs mean 'steadily'; unsteadiness caused the boulder's entire career, and it is hardly ἔμπεδον until it reaches the ἰσόπεδον. The phrase comes from contexts like 15.683, a man leaping between the backs of running horses (ἔ. ἀσφαλὲς αἰεί), 22.192, a hunting dog (θ. ἔ), or *Od.* 13.86, a ship's rapid but steady motion. The unusual enjambments may echo the boulder's onrush. Some good MSS have εἵως or ἕως, which do not scan: the vulgate ὄφρ' ἄν is surely a correction for metrical reasons (cf. the variants at *Od.* 23.151). For the false restoration ἦος see p. 18. ἰσόπεδον is next in Xenophon. ἐσσύμενός περ | recurs only at 11.554 = 17.663 (similes); cf. 57, a related context. κυλίνδεται describes Hektor himself at 11.347.

143–4 Hektor threatens to pass through the ships to the sea, cutting off any hope of retreat. ἀπειλέω rarely expresses non-verbal threats. εἵως = τέως, 'for a while'; cf. 12.141, 15.277f. Aristarchus read ῥέα διελεύσεσθαι as at 20.263 (Did/T), cf. 10.492; each time most MSS have nonsensical ῥεῖα δ' ἐλεύσεσθαι. Both forms come from *ϝρᾶα via Ionic *ῥῆα; ῥέα is already Homeric, as at 20.101 and 8× (cf. 14.203–4n.). The mistaken transliteration of PEA prompted copyists to alter δι- to δ' (van der Valk, *Researches* II 197). μέχρι(ς) recurs in the epos only at 24.128, but cf. ἄχρι(ς) < *mkhri(s).

146–8 Hektor comes so close that he brushes against the Greeks (μάλ' ἐγχριμφθείς); he stops (στῆ) and is pushed back. His failure to break the Greek line stands for that of the Trojans *en masse* (ἀολλέες, 136): see Latacz, *Kampfdarstellung* 201–5. Verse 147 recurs 3× (and 2× with νυσσο-μένων); the use of n-mobile in ξίφεσῖν is recent. ἔγχεσιν ἀμφιγύοισι (8× Hom.) occurs 6× in books 13–17, a clear case of 'phrase-clustering' (97–8n.). ἀμφίγυος, obscure to Aristarchus, is from *γυ-, 'curved (hand)', as in γυῖα, γύαλον, ἀμφιγυήεις (cf. 15.490–3n.), and surely means 'curved on both sides', of a leaf-shaped blade; cf. the exaggerated curves of the LHIIIB-C 'type B' spear in Snodgrass, *EGA* 119; Bouzek, *Aegean* 135–42. See also H. Humbach in *Studi V. Pisani* (Brescia 1969) 569–78.

148 = 4.535, 5.626. Zenodotus read ὁ δὲ χάσσατο πολλὸν ὀπίσσω, based on 193 and 16.710; Aristarchus says he emended because 'he did not know that upon withdrawal they shake the spears that have stuck in their shields, so that they fall out'. The phrase is usually taken as 'he was shaken', i.e. 'rebuffed' (4.535n.), and then 'retreated', with a *hysteron proteron*. Aristarchus' view also survives in Arn/A on 4.535, 11.572 and D on 5.626. He is right; a warrior would have to retreat before he could risk shaking his shield and exposing his body to attack (bT on 4.535). Thus at 11.572 Aias, retreating under pressure, cannot do this and is impeded by the spears stuck in his shield; Hektor's would be sure to have spears stuck in it, after he had come so close to the enemy line.

149–54 After this setback, Hektor encourages his men with the hope that he will be able to break through; cf. Sarpedon's speech after his failure at 12.409–12. Verse 149 = 12.439 (in an exhortation by Hektor); for δια-πρύσιον see on 8.227. Verse 150, found 6×, elsewhere follows ἐκέκλετο μακρὸν ἀΰσας and precedes ἀνέρες ἔστε, φίλοι, μνήσασθε δὲ θούριδος ἀλκῆς (save at 15.425). παρμένετ' means 'stay by me', i.e. in order. πυργηδὸν σφέας αὐτοὺς ἀρτύναντες is found at 12.43 (cf. 12.86), of hunters forming dense lines (στίχες) against a lion; on the tower-image see 126–35n. — ὀΐω, 'I suspect', is common in understatements; Hektor is more confident than he admits (54n.). εἰ ἐτεόν με/γε/περ | is found 6× Hom., and εἰ ἐ. begins the verse at 375, 7× *Od*. The statements it introduces are almost always true: Zeus himself sent a message to Hektor at 11.185ff., urging him to attack. But Pandaros rashly brags that Diomedes will not long withstand his wound, εἰ ἐτεόν με | ὦρσεν ἄναξ Διὸς υἱός (5.104f.). θεῶν ὥριστος recurs at 19.413; cf. ἀνὴρ (δ') ὤ., 5×. The old phrase ἐρίγδουπος πόσις Ἥρης (7× Hom.), with Aeolic ἐρι- for ἀρι-, is metrically equivalent to Ὀλύμπιος ἀστεροπητής (3× *Il.*, *Theog.* 390) and Ὀ. εὐρύοπα Ζεύς (*Od.* 4.173, *Cat.* 211.8); but Parry showed that it is confined to prayers or wishes save here and at 16.88, where the speakers have wishes in mind (*MHV* 181f.).

156–68 Meriones, who opens the stalemate that lasts until 14.506, was, like Teukros, among Poseidon's addressees at 91–3; the battle soon escalates to involve Teukros and the Aiantes, whose valour is also a result of the god's exhortations. This scene motivates Meriones' meeting with Idomeneus behind the lines (246ff.), where he had gone to fetch a new spear, and thus the Cretans' glittering return to battle. It also prefigures his defeat of Deïphobos (527–39), just as Hektor will twice face Akhilleus; for its place in the larger structure of book 13 see 1–168n. The Analysts excised it because at 402ff. Deïphobos is fighting on the left; here he is in the centre, if 'among them' at 156 means specifically Hektor's contingent. But it means only that this clash is chosen from a range of incidents as fighting begins along the entire line (Winter, *MNO* 63): Deïphobos can be on the left here too. He was introduced at 12.94 as a leader of the third Trojan division; prominent in this battle until his wounding, he reappears only at 22.227 (Athene in his shape), 24.251. There was a tradition that he led the Trojans after Hektor's death (so T and schol. on *Od*. 8.517), but he was not eminent enough to have his own set of epithets. Aristarchus deemed the tale that he married Helen after Paris' death a Cyclic invention (schol. on *Od*. 4.276; Severyns, *Cycle* 334–7). But it is implicit at *Od*. 4.276 and 8.517f., and levirate marriage was an Anatolian custom (C. Watkins in M. J. Mellink (ed.), *Troy and the Trojan War*, Bryn Mawr 1986, 50).

156–8 Deïphobos advances, protected by his round shield (he is called λεύκασπις at 22.294, where see n.). A *promakhos* may either dart forward from the ranks, exposed but only briefly, or advance slowly as here, offering his shield as an obvious target, confident that the enemy will draw back in fear before him (cf. μέγα φρονέων). But a single warrior rarely breaks a well-formed enemy line (cf. 17.352ff.). Hektor uses the same tactic, with no more success, at 802–8 (803 resembles 157): cf. 16.609. κοῦφα ποσὶ προβιβάς uniquely varies κραιπνὰ π. π. (18, *Od*. 17.27) or μακρὰ βιβάς, of confident strides: κοῦφος is an Iliadic *hapax*. Deïphobos may step lightly because he advances half-crouched to keep his legs behind his shield (so bT); had he darted forward we would expect κραιπνά instead. Conversely ὕψι βιβάντα at 371 denotes the incautious swagger of a Trojan who advances relying on his corslet alone. Since προβιβάς preceded, ὑπασπίδια προποδίζων (cf. 806) replaces ὑ. προβιβῶντι -ος (807, 16.609); the formula once accompanied not the later round shield, but the Myc. body-shield that protected the legs completely (Lorimer, *HM* 134–46). The poet, blending traditional phrases devised for different types of shield, has been led to imagine Deïphobos as half-crouched for protection.

159–61 From δ' to βάλεν, 159f. = 370f., with Idomeneus replacing Meriones: αὐτοῖο has its weak sense 'him'. Cf. 21.582 and ἀκόντισε δουρὶ φαεινῷ

| καὶ βάλεν (3×). 'He hit, and did not miss, his – shield' briefly arouses suspense, as at 11.350; cf. καὶ β. – ‿‿ – ‿ κατ' ἀσπίδα (6×) and 22.290. Then follows a further instant of suspense until we learn that the spear did not pierce it. | ταυρείην, a runover adj. as at 10.258 (of a helmet), leads up to the phrase | ἀ. τ. at 163 (also 16.360, dat.); this is surely an under-represented formula from the same system as | ἀσπίδος εὐκύκλου etc. (5×), ἀ. ἀμφι-βρότης (3×, cf. 11.32–9n.). Leather was the ancient material for shields; bronze facing entered the tradition relatively late (D. Gray in *Language and Background* 65; Snodgrass, *Dark Age* 272: *contra*, H. Borchhardt, *Arch. Hom.* E 49). See also on 7.220, 222.

162 The spear 'broke at its socket', as at 17.607, where δ' obviates the hiatus before ἐάγη; cf. ἄξαντ' ἐν πρώτῳ ῥυμῷ (6.40). The junction with the shaft was a spear's weak point. καυλός is properly a stem or stalk, e.g. of a plant (Chantraine, *Dict.* s.v.; van der Valk, *Researches* I 499). D and bT deem it the tip of the shaft that fits into the socket, or, better, the socket itself (T on 608, D on 17.607): see on 16.114–18, where it certainly means 'socket' (it is a *lectio falsa* at 16.338). LSJ wrongly take it as 'shaft'.

163–4 Deïphobos thrusts his shield away lest the spear pierce it (cf. 20.261, 278). This implies a round shield with central handle, which could be held at arm's length if need be – the usual type from 1200 to 700 B.C. (Snodgrass, *EGA* 49–51; Borchhardt, *loc. cit.*). σχέθε is aor., not imperf. (Chantraine, *GH* I 329). The scansion ἀπὸ ἕο δεῖσε typifies how the epic diction mixes old and new: the shape of *σϜέο is kept, but the Ϝ in *δϜεῖσε is lost. Ϝ- lasted longest in the enclitic ἑ, as is seen in Lesbian Aeolic (Hoekstra, *Modifications* 44n.). The generic epithet δαΐφρων is probably from δάϊς, 'battle' (5.181n.).

165–8 For the pattern of combat where A hits B's shield but breaks or loses his spear and withdraws frustrated cf. 14.402ff., 22.289ff.; 165 blends the formular verse 14.408 (7×) with the ending χώσατο δ' – – seen at 14.406 (cf. 531–3n.). The genitives are causal with χ., 'angered both ways, at the victory (that he missed) and the spear that he shattered' (Chantraine, *GH* II 65). Zenodotus (Did/A), unaware that ἄγνυμι once began with Ϝ, read ξυνέηξε; he introduced this double augment everywhere, perhaps thinking it a kind of diectasis for -ῆξε (Düntzer, *De Zenodoti studiis* 61). Verse 167 = 208, 8.220; cf. 11.617 (βῆ δὲ θέειν). κλισίηφι is a unique form; cf. the pattern of ἔγχος ὅ οἱ παλάμηφιν ἀρήρει (3.338).

169–245 The Greeks have the upper hand in indecisive fighting, but Poseidon's grandson Amphimakhos is slain. Angered by his death, the god exhorts Idomeneus, who arms and heads for battle

169–205 This sequence of killings, or *androktasia*, foreshadows Aias' eventual defeat of Hektor (14.402ff.) and shows us who the main fighters are, before we shift to Idomeneus and Aineias (Winter, *MNO* 70ff.). It merges two set patterns (Fenik, *TBS* 125–7, 138):

A. P kills Q and tries to strip his corpse (Teukros kills Imbrios)
B. R aims at P but misses (Hektor misses Teukros)
C. R hits S instead (Hektor hits Amphimakhos)
D. R tries to strip S (Hektor tries to strip Amphimakhos)
E. R is thwarted (Hektor is driven off by Aias)
F. The Greeks win both corpses (much developed here).

A–C and D–E occur separately (A–B at 361ff.), and the whole recurs with varied elaborations: at 506–33 F is only implicit; D–E is replaced at 4.473–506, 17.293–318. These scenes have parallel elements: Imbrios' life-story resembles those of Othruoneus and Simoeisios (363ff., 4.474ff.); all three passages liken the fallen to a tree, although at 389ff. the simile describes Asios, killed at stage C (here there is a second simile at stage F). Like Imbrios, Othruoneus came to Troy to marry a daughter of Priam. Askalaphos, the Greek victim at 518, is Ares' son, just as Amphimakhos is Poseidon's grandson here: each passage refers to the god hearing of his offspring's death. The parallelism is also verbal: 184 = 404, 503, 17.305; 187 = 17.311; with 207 cf. 522.

169 This transitional verse reminds us of the fighting going on all round; it changes the scene at 540 also, instead of ὡς οἱ μὲν μάρναντο (δέμας πυρὸς αἰθομένοιο), 5×. The formula βοὴ δ' ἄσβεστος ὄρωρει (5×) was perhaps suggested here by recollection of δ. π., since ἄ. too evokes fire. For another variation involving noise cf. 17.424f.

170–81 The first killing of this battle is expansively narrated in the poet's best style. As usual, the description has three parts: the naming of slayer and victim (170f.), the latter's biography (172–6) and an account of the blow (177f.), here preceding a simile, as often. C. R. Beye, who discovered this tripartite structure, compares the structure of entries in catalogues (*HSCP* 68 (1964) 345–73). The details are vivid, moving and traditional (Fenik, *TBS* 125f.). (*a*) The victim's origin: Imbrios lived at Pedaios *until the Greeks came* (cf. 9.403, 22.156). This recalls his once tranquil existence; he was not obliged to return to Troy to fight. (*b*) His marriage to Priam's daughter by a concubine. The topos of the young husband slain recurs at 365 and 428, cf. 11.226–8; we are meant to think of his widow's grief (Griffin, *HLD* 131–4). (*c*) Priam honoured him like his own sons, although Medesikaste was not his daughter by Hekabe: so he is a loss to Priam too. The bereaved father is a leitmotif of the entire poem, from Khruses in book 1 to Priam in book 24. The idea of grieving for someone as for one's own child arouses pathos: thus Theano reared Antenor's bastard Pedáios like her own sons, to please her spouse, but now Pedaios is slain; the Trojans honour Deïkoon like one of Priam's own sons, but now he is fallen (5.70f., 534–6). Medesikaste is the only bastard daughter mentioned in the epos; this varies the topos of bastard sons begotten by kings or nobles (see Fenik, *TBS* 18). Such sons of Priam are slain elsewhere (4.499, 11.102, 490, 16.738); Imbrios is almost one of them.

170 = 12.378 (with Αἴας). πρῶτος often marks the start of an *androktasia*, to focus the picture, e.g. π. ... ἕλεν ἄνδρα, 4.457, cf. 5.38, 6.5, 11.91f., 14.509, 16.284, 16.307 (de Jong, *Narrators* 49–51). The formula ἄ. κατακτάς/ κτείνας etc. (8× Hom.) normally describes manslaughter in civilian life; it appears here because of the space filled by the split name–epithet phrase.

171–3 Imbrios is named after the isle of Imbros. Cf. Imbrian Eëtion (21.43) and the patronymic Imbrasides (4.520), based on Imbrasos, another toponym; also the shepherd /*Imrios*/ in Knossos tablet Db 1186. His father's name is Greek; despite their Odyssean prominence, both Mentor and Mentes are names of barbarians in the *Iliad*. His epithet πολυίππου, unique in the epos beside its generic equivalent μεγαθύμου (e.g. 5.25), hints at another pathetic element of such vignettes – Mentor's loss of the son to whom he was to leave his wealth (cf. 14.489–91n.); this is more explicit at 5.153f., 612f., where πολυκτήμων and πολυλήϊος are similar *hapax legomena*. — For ναῖε δέ Zenodotus read ὃς ναῖε here (with some MS support) and at 6.34; for the scansion cf. 275–8n. Aristarchus, calling it an emendation 'to make the sentence continuous by enjambment', rejects it, but his text may be a standardization here. Pēdaios (or -on) is unknown (for guesses as to its location see T); Pedaios is a man's name at 5.69. The root is Anatolian: cf. Carian Πήδασος -σα, Hittite *Pitassa* (L. Zgusta, *Kleinasiatische Ortsnamen*, Prague 1984, 489f.). Priam's name too may be Luwian: cf. *Paris*, Hittite *Pari-*, *Pariyamuwa* (composed from a toponym or adverb plus -*muwa*, 'strong'), Lycian *Prijenuba* = Πριανοβας, Anatolian *Teutamos*, *Pigramos* (Scherer, 'Nichtgriechische Personennamen' 36–8). /*Priameias*/ is attested at Pylos (An 39). A *sister* of Priam called Medesikaste appears in 'Apollodorus', *Epit.* 6.15c.

174–6 = 15.549–51, describing Hektor's cousin Melanippos. νέες −∪∪ ἀμφιέλισσαι, also at *Od.* 7.9, is part of a formular system using the late Ionic forms νέες -ας: see Hoekstra, *Modifications* 124–30, and for the epithet 2.165n. ἄψ implies that Imbrios had already been to Troy to fetch his bride (so T). We may imagine that he occupies one of the dozen chambers Priam built for his sons-in-law (6.247–50).

177–8 The 'son of Telamon' kills Imbrios with a spear-thrust, as is clear from νύξε, 'stabbed', and the fact that he pulls the spear out. This is odd, because Teukros was using his bow (12.372, 388, 400), has it in his hand at 15.443, and dons his panoply only at 15.478ff. Moreover such close combat is unexpected at this stage in the battle, unless Imbrios is thought of as having run out almost as far as the Greek line; but at 182 Teukros rushes forth to strip his body, as if he had hit him at long range, and Hektor replies with a javelin. The poet has momentarily confused Teukros with Aias 'son of Telamon', because he was unsure who was meant by 'the two Aiantes' (46n.). Another lapse at 202–5 confirms this: Aias son of Oïleus lops off Imbrios' head and hurls it at Hektor as an insult, as if he had slain the Trojan himself. The slip is made easier by Teukros' virtuosity with both bow and panoply: cf. Meriones and Helenos, also heroes of lesser rank (249f., 581–600n.). The first half of 178 appears only at 12.395, just before.

178–80 The swift and rigid fall of warriors hit in the head or chest, who therefore lose consciousness at once, is often likened to that of trees; those hit lower down crumple up, like Harpalion at 653ff. (Strasburger, *Kämpfer* 38–40). The simile describing Simoeisios' fall is a famous example (4.482–7); like this one, it extends a brief comparison, 'like a poplar'. Asios too is compared to a tree felled in the mountains (389–91), but without the explicit pathos of the other two similes, here intimated by the 'tender' foliage (cf. D, bT); 389–91 develop the image at greater length, because Asios is a greater figure (Moulton, *Similes* 23). The details are apt. Springy ash-wood was used for spears, often called μελίαι in the epic – and a spear kills Imbrios; cf. the poplar at 4.482ff. destined for a chariot-wheel or the pine at 390f. for a ship-timber. The tree falls on a high mountain, not because Imbrios is tall (we have not heard this), but because he stands in high honour at Troy, and his fall is conspicuous and audible – hence Hektor's intervention. Another tree-simile precedes a lion-simile at 16.482–9, Sarpedon's death.

Aristarchus (Did/A) reads κορυφῇ, as do some good MSS: 'others' and the vulgate read -ῆς, which is a late but Homeric ending. If it is elided for -ῃσι, it entails a 'neglect' of ϝ- in ἕκαθεν, as in οὔρεος ἐν κορυφῇς, ἕ. δέ τε φαίνεται αὐγή (2.456) or οὔ. ἐν βήσσῃς, ἕ. ... (16.634). The plur. is well-attested in ὄρεος κορυφῇσι (4×, in similes); for the variants cf. 10–12n. It is uncertain whether the sing. with its hiatus is the *lectio difficilior*, or merely a pedantic correction because a tree can stand on only *one* peak! χαλκῷ ταμνομένη recalls χ. | τάμνον (3× Hom.); leaves are 'tender' at *Od.* 12.357 also, flesh elsewhere (830–2n.).

181 This verse recurs, with a different first foot, at 12.396, 14.420 (spurious); τεύχεα ποικίλα χαλκῷ is also at 6.504. Such death-formulae exclude any hint of prolonged suffering, and are deftly varied to avoid monotony (M. Mueller, *The Iliad*, London 1984, 86–9).

182–94 Imbrios' death starts a chain-reaction which engages the leaders (169–205n.). The action is symmetrical: Teukros advances to strip the body, but Hektor aims at him; Hektor advances to strip *his* victim, but Aias drives him off. The unique repetition of ὁρμήθη/-θέντος stresses this (182f., 188–90). The Greeks' retrieval of both corpses proves their superiority.

183–4 ὁρμηθέντος is a gen. with verbs of aiming; the harsh omission of Teukros' name or a pronoun standing for him (cf. 14.461) reflects the poet's desire for symmetry. ὁ μέν is Teukros, ὁ δέ Hektor. ἀκόντισε δουρὶ φαεινῷ (4×) follows ἀπιόντος twice, μεμαῶτος once; it precedes 'he avoided the brazen spear' at 403,17.304 (with τυτθόν), 17.525. This whole-line formula occurs 6× between 184 and 17.526, but nowhere else – another case of 'phrase-clustering' (97–8n.): the spear is 'brazen', not 'ashen', because we wish to avoid the bronze point, not the wooden shaft (597n.). The slaying of someone at whom one did not aim is common, e.g. 402–12, 516–18, 4.91, 15.430, 17.304ff.

185–7 Amphimakhos is one of four Epean leaders (2.620–3nn.); as often, Homer also gives the name to a barbarian (2.870f.). His father is Kteatos, son of Poseidon or Aktor (11.750, 23.637–42nn.); at 206f. it is assumed we know that he is the god's grandson. Wilamowitz (*IuH* 221n.) thinks Nestor's descendants took such unobvious details to Colophon and Smyrna, which is less unlikely than it sounds (689–91n.). With the double parentage of the (Siamese) twins Kteatos and Eurutos cf. how Zeus and Amphitruon beget their opponent Herakles and his half-brother Iphikles. νίσομαι is surely from the root *nes- in νέομαι, νόστος, despite phonetic difficulties (Peters, *Laryngale* 37f.); the spelling with one σ seems better (West on *Theog.* 71, but cf. Chantraine, *Dict.* s.v. νέομαι). υἷα, like υἱέα (350 only), is rare (8× Hom.); both replace υἱύν, beside υἱόν (170×). See Chantraine, *GH* i 227f. Verse 186 resembles 15.577, which ends βάλε στῆθος παρὰ μαζόν; from κατὰ το πεσών, 186f. = 15.420f. (cf. 16.593–9n.). The sequential (but not syntactical) *hysteron proteron* δούπησεν δὲ πεσών conveys the rapidity of the warrior's fall.

190–4 ὀρέξατο δουρὶ φαεινῷ is a unique variation of ἀκόντισε δ. φ., as at 183, whence the reading ἀ. But ὀ. is right; Aias comes so close that he smites Hektor's shield and pushes him back physically (192f., where ὁ δ' ἄρ' is Aias, ὁ δέ Hektor). The poet could extend the symmetry no further (183–4n.), since a spear-throw, even one so formidable as Meriones', would not have sufficed to repel Hektor. Aias thrust Sarpedon back likewise at 12.404–6. — The ὀμφαλός or central shield-boss, unknown to the Mycenaeans, was standard from the twelfth to the mid-eighth century; hence the formula ἀσπίδες ὀμφαλόεσσαι etc. (12× Hom.) is of Dark Age origin. A boss consisted of a flat, circular bronze disk with a central breast-shaped protrusion, often culminating in a thick blunt spit (Snodgrass, *EGA* 37–49). Doubts as to the identity of such objects have been settled by the excavation in the Kerameikos of one with leather still adhering to the back (Snodgrass, *Dark Age* 288). Aias, meaning only to thrust Hektor back, purposely hits that part of his shield which must take his full force without giving way. Verses 191–4 contain three phrases found just before and never again: πᾶς δ' ἄρα χαλκῷ 11.65, χ. | σμερδαλέῳ 12.464f., σθένεϊ μεγάλῳ 12.224. For σμερδάλεος see 5.302–4n.

191 χροός is a partitive gen. implying its own nom. as the subject of εἴσατο, 'not (an inch of) his flesh could be seen'. Chantraine (*GH* II 50f.) compares 22.324f., φαίνετο δ', ᾗ κληῖδες ἀπ' ὤμων αὐχέν' ἔχουσι, λαυκανίης, 'part of his neck was visible, where...', when Akhilleus scans Hektor for a weak spot. Zenodotus and Aristarchus, rightly deriving εἴσατο from εἴδομαι not ἵεμαι (*pace* D) and understanding 'his flesh was nowhere visible', thought a nom. was needed: the former read χρώς; the latter, truer to the paradosis, altered the accent to χρόος, which he supposed to stand for χρώς by a diectasis (Arn, Did, *pace* Alexion in Hrd/A).

195–205 The retrieval of the corpses is elaborated: contrast e.g. 4.506. We learn the names of the Greeks who bear each body; a lion-simile and the hurling of Imbrios' head at Hektor, equivalent to a taunting-speech, emphasize their success.

195–7 Menestheus had just called the Aiantes and Teukros to his aid (12.331–77); the Athenians' proximity to the Aiantes in the regrouping of forces after the rout at 12.470f. is natural enough. On this controversial association, and on Menestheus, see on 681, 689–91. Stikhios, whose name means 'Ranker' and may appear as Myc. *ti-ki-jo* (PY An 129), is in Menestheus' entourage at 691; slain by Hektor at 15.329, he remains a mere name. — Aristarchus noted the profusion of duals here, referring to his hitherto unnoticed monograph 'On Homer's homeland': ἡ δὲ ἀναφορὰ πρὸς τὰ Περὶ τῆς πατρίδος· Ἀθηναίων γὰρ ἴδιον, i.e. the duals are an Attic idiom. He deemed Homer an Athenian, contemporary with the Ionian migration (OCT v, pp. 101, 244, 247); no doubt these details derive from this same work (and, perhaps, the arguments for an Athenian Homer in T on 827, D on 2.371). The Athenians' obscurity in the *Iliad* was notorious: thus T's note, 'some mock Stikhios and Menestheus as corpse-bearers', is polemic against Aristarchus, not Zoïlus (*pace* Wilamowitz, *IuH* 221n.). – We must place a comma after 196 with a stop after 197, and supply κόμισαν from 196; this produces a simple parataxis. To put a stop after 196 and a comma after 197 creates a nasty anacoluthon and delays the verb until 202. The scansion μεμαῶτε, by metrical lengthening, is paralleled at 2.818 (cf. 16.754n.).

198–200 Imbrios' corpse is aptly likened to a goat carried by two lions away from dogs, who stand for the Trojans (cf. 53). Paired warriors are compared to pairs of lions at 5.554–8, 10.297, 15.324; goats are their victims at 3.23–6, 11.383. The lions may have snatched the goat from dogs who have hunted it down, as at 3.23ff., or raided a flock guarded by dogs, as at

18.579ff. On the lions see on 15.586–8 and Schnapp-Gourbeillon, *Lions* 77–9. Since Zenodotus knew that lions do not co-operate in hunting, he read αἶγε to give each lion a goat (Did/T): cf. how lions duel over a deer at 16.757f., no less false zoologically. He emended for similar reasons elsewhere (p. 23f.). This conjecture ruins the image. bT (from Aristarchus?), admitting that it is not true to life, cite as a parallel Aesch. frag. 39. As usual, the diction is paralleled in other similes: καρχαρόδους describes dogs or a sickle (10.360, 5× Hes.). ῥωπήϊα πυκνά is formular (23.122, *Od.* 14.473, *Hy.* 19.8); ὑψοῦ ὑπὲρ γαίης recurs only at *Erga* 551.

201–3 Cutting off an enemy's head is rare. Agamemnon and Peneleos do so in unusual circumstances (11.146, 11.261, 14.496f., cf. 14.465–8, 20.481f.); Hektor wished to decapitate Patroklos' corpse (17.126, 18.176f.); Akhilleus thought of doing the same to Hektor's (18.334f.). As bT note, this atrocity is ascribed to Locrian Aias, not to his namesake, and a motive – anger at Amphimakhos' death – is added to palliate it, just as Akhilleus' anger over Patroklos palliates his treatment of Hektor. Oïlean Aias is a nasty character (72, 2.527nn.); on why he appears here see on 46, 177f.

δύω Αἴαντε κορυστά recurs at 18.163: cf. Α. δ. (5×), ἄνδρα κορυστήν (4.457n.). The imperf. συλήτην is unexpected, but συλησάτην would not scan. Chantraine (*GH* I 306) deems it an old athematic pres. dual, like προσαυδήτην (2×) beside -ηύδα. But the pull of traditional phrasing has caused a minor anomaly: cf. | τεύχεα συλήσας -σων -σειε -σωσι (7×). Usually two warriors carry a body, but only one strips it: cf. only 5.48, 15.544f. ἁπαλῆς ἀπὸ δειρῆς recurs in a like context at 18.177 (also 2× acc. and 2× dat. in epos); cf. ἁπαλοῖο δι᾽ αὐχένος (3× Hom.). For Zenodotus' text ἄρ᾽ Ἰλιάδης (Arn/A) see 66–7n.

204–5 The unique σφαιρηδόν evokes the vastly different world of ball-games (cf. *Od.* 6.100 etc.). The comparison is as grotesque as when Agamemnon rolls a headless trunk down the battlefield like a cylinder, Aias makes Hektor spin like a top or Peneleos holds up a head on his spear like a poppy (11.147, 14.413, 14.499). ἑλιξάμενος means that Aias reaches back, half-turning his body so as to put more force into the throw: cf. 12.408 and 12.467, κέκλετο ... ἑ., of shouting to the troops behind, and also 23.840n. ῥῖψ᾽ ἐπιδινήσας at 3.378 describes a different motion, twirling a helmet by its broken chin-strap. bT discern a happy accident in how the head lands before Hektor, as if to mock him for his loss (making up for the helmet he failed to gain at 188f., I would add); but perhaps Aias was aiming at him. We are left to guess Hektor's feelings upon seeing his brother-in-law's head. προπάροιθε ποδῶν (5×) again precedes πέσεν at 20.441.

206–45 For Poseidon, grandfather of the slain Amphimakhos (185–7n.), the revenge-killing of Imbrios is not enough. His own revenge consists of stirring up Idomeneus to an *aristeia*, which leads to severe Trojan losses

(Michel, *N* 48f.); but the dialogue with Meriones delays this until 361ff. On this scene's place in the structure of book 13 see 1–168n. Fenik (*TBS* 128f.) shows that it embodies a typical pattern where X chides Y for not fighting, Y explains and X persuades him to enter battle; such exchanges often provoke *aristeiai*. As Reinhardt says (*IuD* 294ff.), the arousal of the hero, his arming, and his mention of past victories in his dialogue with Meriones, all typical elements in *aristeiai*, are apt here (further references to his armament and his birth are at 405ff., 449ff.). The *aristeia* of Patroklos and the Myrmidons also starts with an exhortation to them to remember their ἀπειλαί (16.200). The three speeches at 20.79–111 are the best parallel: Apollo, disguised as Lukaon, chides Aineias with the words Αἰνεία Τρώων βουληφόρε, ποῦ τοι ἀπειλαί... Cf. also 5.170–239, where Aineias rebukes Pandaros, who replies twice; note the parallels ποῦ τοι τόξον (171), βουληφόρε (180), Τρώων ἀγὸς ἀντίον ηὔδα (217, cf. 221 here). Cf. too 5.800–34 (Athene and Diomedes, three speeches following Here's general exhortation to αἰδώς), 15.440–1n. and 17.553–66, when Athene, disguised as Phoinix, exhorts Menelaos; the third speech is dropped, and the deity fills him with strength instead. Leaf held that this scene has replaced an explanation of how Idomeneus came to be unarmed (see 210n.); but this tiny problem, and the obscure allusion to Amphimakhos in 207, are weak grounds for suspicion.

206–9 Poseidon's anger over Amphimakhos' death is delayed until the account of it is complete, like Paris' anger over Harpalion's (660). For περὶ κῆρι see on 118f. Verse 207 adapts and moves the formular expression κασιγνήτοιο/ Ἀλεξάνδροιο πεσόντος | (3×), as in | Πατρόκλοιο π. (17.10) or | υἱὸς ἑοῖο π. ἐνὶ κρατερῇ ὑσμίνῃ (522), with a doublet of ἐν αἰνῇ δηϊοτῆτι. The doublets arose because these formulae have different metrical properties when used in other cases; they are equally frequent (11× epos). Line 208 = 167, 8.220. Verse 209 has a neat chiasmus. κήδε' ἔτευχεν | is part of a large substitution-system, cf. κ. ἔτευξαν (*Od.* 1.244), Τρώεσσι δὲ κ. ἐφῆπται (3×), ἄλγεα τεύχει, ἄλγε' ἔδωκε/ἔθηκε/ἔπασχον etc.

210 Idomeneus, last seen at 11.510, is abruptly introduced: Poseidon finds him at the ships as if by chance, and his presence is only explained after the fact (211ff.). A tough warrior, with the third-largest contingent (2.645ff.), he is already greying (361); only Nestor is more senior (2.404–9n.). The wounding of the leaders now lets him show his valour in his own *aristeia*, with a properly emphatic opening. Since he cannot receive a full arming-scene during a continuous battle, the poet brings him behind the lines and quickly arms him (241), adding a divine exhortation, dialogue with Meriones and similes, to gloss over this problem. The contrast between his apparent cowardice now and the heights to which he will rise enhances the success of this scene. Since he is Zeus's descendant (449), it is ironic that

Poseidon employs him to avenge Amphimakhos, in opposition to Zeus's plan. δουρικλυτός is a generic epithet (19×) given 6× to Idomeneus: only here is the formula separated. The structure of 210 recurs at 246, where see n.; Idomeneus' meeting with Meriones humorously echoes Poseidon's meeting with Idomeneus, as parallels between 214f. and 247f. confirm.

211–13 bT think Idomeneus' injured comrade is unnamed for the sake of realism; the rare anonymity suggests improvisation (cf. 422n.). Idomeneus' concern for the wounded was prepared at 11.510ff., when he persuades Nestor to save the healer Makhaon. ἰγνύη, unique in Homer, means the back of the knee; it is from ἐν and the root of γόνυ, with Arcado-Cypriot ἰν for ἐν as in ἴγνητες (cf. p. 15 n. 24). A wound there must have been received in the rout that just ended. With the rest of 212 cf. 16.819, *Od.* 11.535. 'His comrades carried him' explains 'he came', showing how the casualty reached the hut with such a wound.

214–15 Idomeneus was going to his shack to arm; T's variant ἦν ἴεν ἐς κλισίην for ἤιεν ἐς κ. was meant to make clear that he was not going to his comrade's. The vulgate ἐκ κλισίης (contradicted by a papyrus, a few good MSS and 240 below) reflects a misunderstanding – if he wants to fight, why *enter* the hut? The runover infin. ἀντιάαν, which is not needed to complete πολέμοιο μένοινα, makes 215 a rising threefolder, a rare shape in lines of address with προσέφη (244× epos). Cf. 248, οἰσόμενος, τὸν δὲ π., again with a runover verb-form not needed for the sense of the previous verse (contrast 168, 257); *Od.* 15.110; and ὣς φάτο, τὸν/τὴν δ' οὔ τι π. (7× Hom.).

216–18 Thoas was among those whom Poseidon exhorted (92). As Reinhardt says (*IuD* 296), the god selects a suitable mask: Thoas is a warrior and counsellor (15.281–5n.), whose large realm precedes Crete in the Catalogue (2.638–44). Thus he can question Idomeneus as an equal, not a superior, and avoid resentment; contrast Agamemnon's address to the latter at 4.257ff. With 216 cf. 2.791 and 43–5n.; Ἀνδραίμονος υἷϊ Θόαντι is modified from Θόας Ἀ. υἱός (4× epos). For Pleuron and Kaludon see on 2.639–40; Aetolia was perhaps the destination of the ship on the Pylos tablet headed /eretai Pleurōnade iontes/ (Ventris and Chadwick, *Documents* 185f.). Save for ὃς πάσῃ, 217 = 14.116. ἀνάσσω usually takes the gen. of the place ruled, not a dat., which is used for the people governed: cf. *HyAphr* 112, | ὃς πάσης Φρυγίης ... ἀνάσσει, and *Cat.* 23.32, ὃς π. Τεγέης ... ἤνασσε, beside ὃς πᾶσιν ... ἀνάσσει (12.242 etc.). But Πλευρῶνι and Καλυδῶνι can be taken as locatives. With 218 cf. 10.33, Ἀργείων ἤνασσε, θεὸς δ' ὣς τίετο δήμῳ (with a rare gen.), and *Od.* 7.10f. The phrase 'he was honoured like a god by the people' is ancient, as is shown by the old postpositive *Ϝώς; it suggests the Myc. attitude to kingship. After 218, *h* and T interpolate different verses to show that Poseidon begins to speak (cf. 478–80n.). But a verse or more can follow a speech-introduction, e.g 4.357, 19.405–7, 21.213 (προσέφη ... ἀνέρι εἰσάμενος).

219-20 For parallels with this brief speech see 206-45n. Poseidon's question is hardly felt as a rebuke, since he generalizes it to include the other Greeks; nor does Idomeneus take it personally. βουληφόρε is no idle compliment, but implies that Idomeneus should live up to his responsibilities; cf. 463, 2.24, 5.633, 20.83. At 255 and 5.180 it is used by the person reproached, as if to acknowledge the value of the advice received. Κρητῶν β. is part of a formular system including Τρώων (4×) and Λυκίων (5.633); these ethnica are also used with ἀγὸς ἀντίον ηὔδα (221 and 7×). It may be a result of formular patterning that many of these rebukes are aimed at those whom these formulae describe – Aineias, Sarpedon and Idomeneus. For references to boasts in rebukes cf. 8.229ff., 16.200f., 20.83ff.

222-30 Idomeneus' reply is in two parts, of which the second is a call to action marked as usual by | ἀλλά (228). As in his reply to Agamemnon at 4.266ff., he deflects criticism by bidding his interlocutor exhort others, thus showing his character as a 'counsellor' (Michel, *N* 50).

222-5 'Now' admits that the Greeks were to blame when they fled, but are no longer. After νῦν Aristarchus read γ', Aristophanes δ' (Did/T); the vulgate has no particle, and none is needed. ἐπιστάμεθα amounts to 'we can', just as Akhilleus 'understood' how to wield his spear, or Hektor 'knows' how to fight (16.142, 7.237ff.). Poseidon resumes Idomeneus' phrase at 238; since the god echoes at 234 his reference to shirking, the speeches form a chiasmus. Idomeneus excludes all the reasons why men shirk battle. With 224f. cf. 5.812, 5.817, οὔτε τί με δέος ἴσχει ἀκήριον οὔτε τις ὄκνος, which is blended with | οὔτ' ὄκνῳ εἴκων (10.122). ἀνδύεται (= ἀνα-) 'back off from' (cf. 7.217, *Od.* 9.377), is a metaphor from animals refusing the yoke (so T); T's variant ἀδδύεται, based on καδδῦσαι = κατα-, breaks the rules of apocope (cf. 14.442-8n.).

226-30 There is irony in Idomeneus' correct guess at the truth and telling of it to Poseidon, who knows far more; and pathos in the inglorious end, far from Argos, that threatens the Greeks. For the thought that a brave leader stands firm and exhorts others see 55-8n. Verses 225f., like 224f., split set phrasing across a verse-end, in this case Agamemnon's glum words οὕτω που Διὶ μέλλει ὑπερμενέϊ φίλον εἶναι (14.69 and 2×), blended with ὑ. Κρονίωνι (6× epos); 227 = 12.70. μενεδήϊος is only at 12.247. With the end of 229 cf. 4.516, whence perhaps the variant ὅθι (the vulgate is ὅτε). Zenodotus read ὅτις μεθίῃσι πόνοιο (Did/AT), no doubt to give the verb an object, as at e.g. 4.240; the reading μ. π. at 234, ascribed by T to Aristarchus, is an error based on this. With 230 cf. 20.353, which introduces a speech.

232-8 Poseidon's reply again falls into two parts separated by ἀλλά: three verses answer Idomeneus' last three lines, then four respond to the first part of his speech. Verbal parallels stress the chiasmus (222-5n.).

232-4 Poseidon counters Idomeneus' fear that the Greeks will perish ingloriously – it is the slackers who merit this fate. Similar threats against slackers are uttered at 2.391-3 (Nestor), 12.248-50, 15.348-51 (Hektor), 16.721-3 (Apollo); Menelaos and Iris exhort others by saying that Patroklos may 'become a plaything for the dogs' (17.255, 18.179). For the grisly metaphor in μέλπηθρα (636-9n.) cf. σφαιρηδόν (204-5n.); D and bT helpfully note that dogs do play with balls of flesh. ἑκών is emphatic – it makes shirking even worse; for the phrase cf. 6.523, 23.434, *Od.* 4.372. The subj. μεθίῃσι is unparalleled; the indic. μεθίησι may be better (Chantraine, *GH* I 457, II 246).

237–8 From saying that even two men may be useful, Poseidon shifts to a variant of the maxim that two heads are better than one (cf. σύν τε δύ' ἐρχομένω, 10.224): literally 'there is a joint valour of men, even of very poor ones', i.e. 'together, even the worst fighters can show valour; ⟨how much more should⟩ we two, ⟨who⟩ can fight even the brave' (so Aristarchus in Nic/A). The god's self-inclusion softens the rebuke. I doubt whether 237 is a pre-fabricated maxim. Rhymes in -τη and -ρων give it a proverbial ring: Zenodotus and Aristophanes (Did/AT) read συμφερτὴ δὲ βίη, which removes one rhyme and is a conjecture intended to deny poor fighters any valour at all. Aristarchus' paraphrase, as given by Ap. Soph. 146.25, wrongly suggested to Ludwich that he read συμφερτῶν (see Dyck on Comanus frag. 9). This adj. is unique, but πέλει ἀνδρῶν recurs at 9.134, *HyAp* 458, and imperf. 2×; μάλα λυγρός recurs 2×. ἐπιστάίμεσθα μάχεσθαι varies ἐπιστάμεθα πτολεμίζειν (223, cf. 2.611): not only do all we Greeks know how to fight, as Idomeneus said, but *we* two know how to fight even the brave, who certainly have ἀρετή.

239–41 Warriors often pair up, as at 5.576ff. or 11.314, when Odysseus urges Diomedes to join him: hence δεῦρο and ἅμα in 235 and the maxim in 237. Yet the god does not wait for Idomeneus to arm, since his sole aim was to stir him up for battle; Meriones soon joins him, as if in Thoas' stead. Verse 239 = 16.726, 17.82. The poet hurries past Idomeneus' arming, for reasons given above (210n.); 241 condenses into one verse the standard arming-scene of e.g. 3.330-8 (see *ad loc.*). The sole detail which persists is that he takes his spears last. As at 16.129, | δύσετο τεύχεα (καλά) is moved from the line-end (contrast 7.103, 2× *Od.*). Like ἐΰτυκτον (cf. 26 above, of a whip!), περὶ χροΐ γέντο comes from the theme of divine arming and chariot-journey: cf. χρυσὸν ... ἔδυνε π. χ., γ. δ' ἱμάσθλην (25 = 8.43). The poet recasts his previous description, displacing the epithet onto a different noun; κλισίην ἐΰτυκτον recurs at 10.566 (with ἵκοντο), *Od.* 4.123. Only here does δοῦρε follow a verb at the line-end; only here and at 16.139 is it found without δύο (in 13 occurrences).

242–5 Idomeneus' hasty arming is counterbalanced by a fine simile likening him to Zeus brandishing a lightning-bolt. His speed and flashing armour are the main points of comparison (bT); but the rare detail that

Zeus holds the bolt in his hand recalls Idomeneus holding his spears. Yet, of course, his intervention is against Zeus's will. The depiction of Zeus on Olumpos also makes us compare Idomeneus' entry into battle to that of Poseidon from the top of Samothrake, of which it is a result. Idomeneus moves *away* from battle in order to return armed, as had Poseidon (Michel, *N* 72). It is thus no accident that 24of. resembles 25f. — We expect Idomeneus to enter battle at once, since similes often describe this moment, but the poet again thwarts our expectation. Two parallels are especially close. At 11.61–6 Hektor leads a Trojan attack like a baneful star: he shines with bronze 'like the lightning of father Zeus'. At 22.26–32 Akhilleus is like the dog-star, 'an evil sign', and there are unique verbal parallels: ἀρίζηλοι δέ οἱ αὐγαί recurs, and 32 = 245. Signs from Zeus may be benign (2.353, 8.170f., 9.236f.) or sinister (4.381, 7.478f.). The parallels, as well as the action, evoke a sinister sign here. Zenodotus and Aristophanes read ἐνὶ στήθεσσι (Did/AT), but this is normally used of feeling emotions.

246–360 Returning to battle, Idomeneus meets his subordinate Meriones, who explains that he is behind the lines to fetch a new spear. Idomeneus offers him one, and both defensively assert their courage. They decide to fight on the left, and re-enter battle together; both sides are fiercely engaged at close quarters, because the wills of Zeus and Poseidon are at odds

246–97 This dialogue has been attacked as irrelevant and tedious, and rejected as an interpolation. Fenik (*TBS* 129) calls it 'one of the longest sections of untypical narrative in the poem'; Shipp (*Studies* 282) points to 'late' linguistic elements. Since Idomeneus is neither so old nor so garrulous as Nestor, his verbosity is not a misplaced attempt to depict an aged windbag. Willcock well remarks the humour of the situation: each warrior, unexpectedly found behind the lines in such a crisis, is aware of what the other must be thinking, and so, with no overt apology or accusation, asserts his heroic credentials. Idomeneus relieves their mutual embarrassment with a ribald joke about Meriones and his spear (290f.), which he broke at 156ff. Their meeting amusingly echoes that of 'Thoas' and Idomeneus. Also, as Reinhardt says (*IuD* 297), this scene introduces their joint *aristeia* and enhances our expectations of their courage; we await with increased suspense their return to battle.

The five speeches are less odd than Fenik thought. The last is almost a speech of exhortation, like Sarpedon's address to Glaukos (12.310–28) or the end of Akhilleus' speech to Patroklos (16.83–100), which includes a discussion of tactics like 307–27 below. Cf. too Herakles' three-speech exchange with his squire Iolaos at *Aspis* 78–121. Glaukos' verbosity when he faces Diomedes or Aineias' to Akhilleus (6.145–211, 20.200–58) is certainly humorous, but they have more reason to fear, and their speeches replace an *aristeia* rather than introduce one. Lohmann (*Reden* 133n.) shows that this dialogue develops a limited number of topics (italicized below) with *variatio* and changes of perspective, common Homeric techniques:

1. Idomeneus: Meriones' *absence from battle* (249f.)
   [tacit query about Meriones' *bravery*, hence]
   possible *reasons* for his absence (251f.)
   [tacit query about *absence* of Idomeneus, hence]
   bravery of Idomeneus (252f.)
2. Meriones: true *reason* for his absence – his *spear* (255–8)
3. Idomeneus: Meriones can have a *spear* from Idomeneus' *trophies* (260–2),
   resulting from his *bravery* (262f.),
   which produces *trophies* (264f.).
4. Meriones: Meriones has *trophies* too (267f.),
   resulting from his *bravery*, as Idomeneus knows (269–73).
5. Idomeneus: Yes, Meriones' *bravery* is outstanding (275–91).
   But they should *return to battle*: let Meriones fetch a *spear* (292–4).

The topics of speeches 1–2 are resumed in 5, and each is dealt with from the viewpoint of both men. The pattern is completed when Idomeneus graciously attests to Meriones' valour, and turns his opening questions into a call for action.

246–8 These verses are an amusing echo of 210 + 214f.: Meriones is now in the same embarrassing position vis-à-vis Idomeneus which Idomeneus occupied vis-à-vis 'Thoas'. Idomeneus is still by his hut, but Meriones' is further off, surprisingly: this is surely an improvisation so that Idomeneus can oblige him with a spear. Meriones is called θεράπων ἐΰς Ἰδομενῆος 3×, but δουρικλυτός only at 16.619. Zenodotus and Aristophanes (Did/AT) read δ. here, perhaps to enhance the parallel with 210ff. But θ. ἐ. stresses Meriones' subordinate status, which is why Idomeneus can ask him directly why he is off duty, and not vice versa. δόρυ χάλκεον (7× Hom.) recurs in this position only at 16.608. σθένος Ἰδομενῆος belongs to a formular pattern: cf. σ. Ὠρίωνος (18.486, 2× *Erga*), μέγα σ. Ἠετίωνος/Ὠκεανοῖο/Ἰδομενῆος (23.827, 2× *Il.*, *Cat.* 204.56), or the heroic periphrases βίη Ἡρακληείη (15.639–43n.), ἱερὸν μένος Ἀλκινόοιο (see p. 11f.).

249–50 Meriones is not only Idomeneus' retainer (θεράπων), but his second-in-command (2.650f., 4.253f.), like Patroklos or Sthenelos (2.563f., 4.365–7); on the status of the θεράπων see Greenhalgh, *Bulletin of the Institute of Classical Studies* 29 (1982) 81–90. To judge by the archaisms ἀτάλαντος Ἐνυαλίῳ ἀνδρειφόντῃ (p. 11), θεράπων ἐΰς and ὀπάων, all applied to him alone, Meriones traditionally performed both functions, and had long been an important figure, resembling Odysseus (J. S. Clay, *The Wrath of Athena*, Princeton 1983, 84ff.); on his early Myc. origins see West, *JHS* 108 (1988) 159. A fierce fighter, he excels in the games with bow and javelin, traditional Cretan weapons (23.86off., 888ff.), but fails in the chariot-race (23.528ff.). His name, like his father's (also mentioned at 10.269, see 16.692–7n.), is linked with running (from μηρόν + ὀνίνημι) by Mühlestein, *Namenstudien* 43n. If Molos was Deukalion's bastard son or brother, Idomeneus is Meriones' uncle or cousin (so 'Apollodoros' 3.3.1, Diod. 5.79); cf. Herakles' relation to Iolaos. bT note that in one verse Idomeneus reminds Meriones of his kinship, vigour and amity with him. For πόδας ταχύς -ύν (8×), voc. only here, see 18.1–2n.; we next hear of Meriones' speed at 295f., 16.342. φίλταθ' ἑταίρων recurs at 19.315 (of Patroklos), *Od.* 24.517. πόλεμόν τε λιπὼν καὶ δηϊοτῆτα expands π. καὶ δ. (etc.), 6×; cf. πολέμοιο καὶ αἰνῆς δηϊοτῆτος (3×).

251–3 Idomeneus generously offers reasons why Meriones is not fighting. Aristarchus took ἀγγελίης as a nom. masc. noun, 'messenger', supposedly also found at 4.384, 11.140, 15.640, and not as gen. of ἀγγελίη, 'message'. Leumann (*HW* 168–72) argued that bards created the new noun by misunderstanding verses like 3.206 (σεῦ ἕνεκ' ἀγγελίης). At 4.384 or 11.140 ἀγγελίην is an acc. of respect, 'on a message-bearing mission' (cf. ἐξεσίην ἐλθεῖν, 24.235, *Od.* 21.20), but is open to the same misunderstanding (see 3.206n.; B. Forssman, *MSS* 32 (1974) 41–64; C. Saerens, *MSS* 34 (1976) 165–8). But here and at 15.640 Aristarchus must be right. ἀγγελίης persisted as a metrically useful variant of ἄγγελος (Erbse, *Ausgewählte Schriften* 73-80). ἧσθαι means 'sit idle' as at 1.134 etc.

254 = 266. πεπνυμένος adorns names shaped −∪∪−: Antenor, Antilokhos, Laertes, Telemakhos (47× Hom.). For its sense see Hoekstra on *Od.* 15.86. The equivalent generic epithet δουρικλυτός is used in other contexts; π. always precedes ἀντίον ηὔδα, ἦρχ' ἀγορεύειν or ἤρχετο μύθων save at 16.619, Μηριόνης δ. ἀ. η., *Od.* 15.544 (Πειραῖος...). δ. is Idomeneus' usual epithet (5×).

255 = 219, save for χαλκοχιτώνων. Verse 255 is not read by Aristarchus (cf. T on 254), the papyri or most early codices; it was interpolated because it was thought impolite that Meriones leaves unanswered the honorific address of 249, especially since Idomeneus is his lord and senior. But no such address is needed (*pace* van der Valk, *Researches* II 497–9, and Michel, *N* 74): found in some exchanges of superiors with inferiors, e.g. at 8.5–31, 281–93 or 9.673–6, such reciprocity is lacking in others, e.g. 8.352–8, 9.17–32, 10.234–42.

256–8 At 168 Meriones went οἰσόμενος δόρυ μακρόν, ὅ οἱ κλισίηφι λέλειπτο; now he wants a spear of Idomeneus' (τοι), if he has any. His change of intent is natural – he did not expect to meet Idomeneus, and his own hut is further on, as he explains (268). Idomeneus seizes on his tentative expression as a chance to remind Meriones of his own trophies and thus obviate his own embarrassment. The odd shift from sing. to plur. (κατεάξαμεν) and back to the sing. is not the mock-modesty of a leader associating his men with himself, which is not apt for Meriones (*pace* Chantraine, *GH* II 33f.); in fact the plur. refers to Meriones *and* Deïphobos, since 'both broke the weapon, Meriones who cast it and Deïphobos who held the shield in which the spear broke' (Eustathius 930.4). Hence 258 is needed to explain this plural (Michel, *N* 75). For Zenodotus' text κατεήξαμεν (Did/A) see 165–8n. ὑπερηνορέων is sing. here only in Homer, but plur. at 4.176 (where see n.), 12× *Od.* To have faced so proud a foe reflects well on Meriones.

260–1 ἓν καὶ εἴκοσι means 'one *or* twenty, as many as you want'. Greeks still say ἕνα καὶ δύο for 'one or two'; Idomeneus multiplies by ten to stress his valour. It would be comical if he knew exactly how many spears he had; for twenty expressing any large number cf. 16.810, 847, 24.765 (with n.), *Od.* 9.241 ('two *or* twenty waggons'), 12.78. For the 'observed' Ϝ- in καὶ εἴκοσι cf. 2.510, 748 etc.: it is odd that our texts do not offer καὶ ἐείκοσι instead (see Beekes, *Laryngeals* 60–2). ἐνώπια παμφανόωντα are façades of white plaster to protect from wear the mud-bricks by an entrance (Lorimer, *HM* 428). This formula is used of leaning chariots against a yard-wall or propping a bow against the wall near the door-post (8.435, *Od.* 4.42, 22.121); its usual link with κλίνω is maintained by the presence of κλισίη. Nicanor (in A, cf. Aristarchus on 23.509) took 'shining' with 'spears', no doubt thinking huts would be too badly built to have ἐνώπια!

262–5 Owning Trojan spears is no proof of valour – Idomeneus could have found them on the battlefield; so he adds that he strips them from the slain, because he fights at close range, and therefore has complete trophies, i.e. not spears only. *Qui s'excuse, s'accuse!* His understatement οὐ γὰρ ὀΐω is echoed more strongly by Meriones at 269 (οὐδ' ἐμέ φημι). Chantraine (*GH* II 307) thinks ὀΐω expresses intention, but Idomeneus is explaining how he wins his trophies. With 264f. cf. 19.359–61, κόρυθες λαμπρὸν γανόωσαι | ... καὶ ἀσπίδες ὀμφαλόεσσαι | θώρηκές τε ... καὶ μείλινα δοῦρα; Alcaeus frag. 140. There is no fixed sequence for describing trophies, unlike arming, where the order of items is set. Omitted in a papyrus, 265 could be spurious. Only the participle of γανάω, 'gleam', related to γάνος, γάνυμαι and γαίω, is found in epic (*Od.* 7.128, *HyDem* 10): see Latacz, *Freude* 157f.

267–8 Meriones deflates Idomeneus' boasts – he too has many trophies, but they are too distant to fetch; this signals that he accepts Idomeneus' offer, and is loth to be away from battle any longer than need be. The latter half of 267 is formular (4×); each unit's huts were by its ships (15.406–9n.). Leaf discerned a hendiadys, '*in* my hut *by* my ship'.

269–71 Whereas Idomeneus dilated on his trophies, Meriones speaks directly of his own bravery. οὐδὲ γὰρ οὐδέ (5× Hom.) is emphatic; the first οὐδέ picks up Idomeneus' negative at 262, the second stresses ἐμέ (Denniston, *Particles* 197). Eustathius (930.51–3) notes that 'to forget one's valour' is an elevated way of saying 'to be a coward'. The periphrastic perf. λελασμένον ἔμμεναι ἀλκῆς is a rare but distinctive feature of epic diction: see 14.194–7n., and Lehrs, *De Aristarchi studiis* 361–3; W. J. Aerts, *Periphrastica*, Amsterdam 1965. It can be middle (6.488, 14.172, 23.343) or even active (5.873). Here it adapts e.g. λελάσμεθα θούριδος ἀ. (11.313, cf. 15.322, 16.357); cf. λελασμένος εἷς/ἔπλευ (16.538, 23.69). Verse 270 melds μετὰ πρώτοισι μάχεσθαι | (etc., 4×) with μάχην (ἀνὰ) κυδιάνειραν | (etc., 8×). ὀρώρηται is a perf. middle subj. based on the indic. ὀρώρεται (*Od.* 19.377, 524), itself odd (cf. Shipp, *Studies* 117); this formular modification blends (πόλεμος καὶ) νεῖκος ὄρωρε | (8×), ν. ὀρεῖται (etc., 4× Hom.), ν. ὁμοιίου πολέμοιο (2× *Od.*).

272–3 Since Idomeneus exhorted Meriones with his own example, the latter pays him back by calling on him to attest to his deputy's bravery in battle, as he is uniquely qualified to do. λήθω μαρνάμενος picks up λελασμένος ἀλκῆς with an etymological play: not only has Meriones' bravery not deserted him, but if it escapes others, his lord must have seen it! The understatement ὀίω parries ὀίω at 262; Meriones' repartee is effective.

275–94 This speech is the climax to the whole exchange (246–97n.). Its first section, where Idomeneus affirms Meriones' bravery, and by his tone reveals his friendly trust in his subordinate, is framed by 275 (τί σε χρὴ ταῦτα λέγεσθαι;) and 292 (μηκέτι ταῦτα λεγώμεθα); this calls attention to the length of the dialogue, exactly what commentators have disliked. If Homer felt it was too long, he would hardly have thus told his audience to yawn. The speech surely has a literary aim, which can only be humour. In fact this section culminates in a mildly ribald *double entendre* at the expense of Meriones, who has lost his spear (290f.). The second section, a call to action opened as usual by ἀλλά (292), is suitably brief.

275–8 The scansion ὅιος recurs at 18.105, *Od.* 7.312, 20.89 in the phrase | τοῖος ἐὼν οἷός ἐσσι (etc.); it must have been pronounced *hŏyos*. Cf. υἱός scanned ∪ − (16.21n.); Chantraine, *GH* 1 168; West on *Theog.* 15. For the rest of 275 cf. *Od.* 24.407. λέγεσθαι, 'discuss', recurs only in the formula ἀλλ' ἄγε, μηκέτι ταῦτα λεγώμεθα (see on 292–4, 2.435); but the sense 'enumerate (your trophies)' is possible. In 276 it means 'be gathered', not 'be counted', *pace* Aristarchus; cf. 21.27, *Od.* 24.108. With ἀρετὴ διαείδεται cf. 8.535. Leaf thought 278 a 'terribly flat' gloss on 277: δειλός has a definite article and always means 'wretched' in Homer, not 'cowardly' (Shipp, *Studies* 282). But 278 is needed to introduce the antithesis between timidity and bravery. The 'article' is in fact a relative pronoun beside ὅς, despite the structural similarity to ὅ τ' ἀεργὸς ἀνὴρ ὅ τε πολλὰ ἐοργώς (9.320), ὅ τε δειλὸς ἀνὴρ ὅ τε πολλὸν ἀμείνων | φαίνεται ('Theognis' 393f.). The 'neglect' of ϝ in *δϝειλός is common (Janko, *HHH* 154); its original sense 'cowardly' (from δέος, 'fear') is found in Ionic from Archilochus onward. (ἐξε)φαάνθην (6× Hom.) is an aor. of φαείνω, with diectasis after the contraction of *φαένθην and the same sense as ἐφάνην (Chantraine, *GH* 1 81).

279–87 The apodosis to 276f. is delayed until 287; the intervening parenthesis, framed by repetition of ἔνθα, contrasts the conduct of the timid and the brave in ambush, the sternest test of courage, moving each time from their complexions to their posture and their thoughts. The tension of waiting to attack is unbearable (cf. *Od.* 4.270ff., 11.523ff., 14.217ff.); Akhilleus taunts Agamemnon for not daring to take part (1.226f.). One is aware of foes in battle, but friends when waiting in ambush; since Meriones complained that his courage in battle goes unnoticed, Idomeneus replies that he would be conspicuous at an ambush. On ambushes in Homer see A. T. Edwards, *Achilles in the Odyssey*, Königstein 1985, 18ff. The 'late' forms cited by Shipp (*loc. cit.*) are as usual a bad reason for excision; this 'vivid and vigorous passage … does not look like the work of an interpolator' (Leaf), and recalls similes in its unusual details and diction.

279–81 τρέπεται χρώς (etc.) is used of blanching in fear at 284, 17.733, *Od.* 21.412f. (split over a verse-end); cf. *Erga* 416. ἄλλυδις ἄλλη, 'this way and that' (etc., 13× Hom.), sits uncomfortably beside it. Leaf renders this 'all sorts of colours', but it is used with verbs of dispersing or fleeing; Homer surely had in mind the coward's wish to escape. With ἀτρέμας ἧσθαι cf. 2.200; with the rest of 280 cf. 9.462 (cf. 635). μετοκλάζω, 'fidget', almost a *hapax* in Greek, is based on ὀκλάζω, 'squat'; it was obscure enough for the poet to gloss it ἐπ' ἀμφοτέρους πόδας ἵζει, i.e. 'shifts his weight from one leg to the other' (cf. Frisk, *Kleine Schriften* 289f.).

282–3 Beating heart and trembling limbs are signs of fear (7.215f.); Agamemnon's heart leaps from his chest and Dolon's teeth chatter (10.94f., 10.375). Note the etymological play on πατάσσω and πάταγος, elsewhere of trees breaking or warriors colliding (3×). Verse 283 belongs to a surprisingly large formular system for noises made by teeth: κόμπος ὀδόντων | γίνεται (11.417f. = 12.149f., similes), cf. περί τ' ἀφρὸς ὀδόντας | γ. (20.168f., simile); ἄραβος θ' ἅμα γίνετ' ὀδόντων | (*Aspis* 404, simile); ἄ. δὲ διὰ στόμα γ. ὀ. | (10.375). For the sense and etymology of κήρ see p. 5; ὀίομαι next governs a direct acc. at *Od.* 20.349.

284–7 With 284f. cf. οὐδέ τι θυμῷ | ταρβεῖ(ς) (21.574f., 2× *Od.*), μήτ' ἄρ τι λίην τρέε μήτε τι τάρβει (21.288), μήτε τι θ. | τ. (*Od.* 7.50f.). ταρβεῖ scanned − ∪ is 'late', but it is also irresolvably contracted at 4.388. ἐπειδάν, unlike ἐπειδή (ἐπεὶ δή) and ἐπήν from ἐπεὶ ἄν, is unique in the epos. It is not Attic only, *pace* Shipp (*Studies* 141); Herodotus uses it. ἐπὴν δή, made up of the same elements, is likewise recent: a variant at 16.453, it occurs 7× *Od.*, 2× *Erga*. πρῶτον, for πρῶτα or τὰ πρῶτα after ἐπεί, 'when once', is simply a

convenient variation: cf. ἐπὴν δὴ πρῶτον, 3× *HyAphr*. The pres. ἐσίζηται
means 'he is seated (in the ambush)', with proleptic ἐσ-. With 286 cf.
9.240; ἐν δαῖ λυγρῇ is a rare but current formula (14.383–7n.). In 287 supply
either 'a brave man' or τις with ὄνοιτο, '*nobody* would criticize': cf. οὔ τις ὅ.
(*Od.* 8.239), and the omission of τις at 22.199. The formula μένος καὶ χεῖρας
perhaps squeezed it out.

288–9 Were Meriones wounded, it would not be from behind; for the
shame of such wounds cf. T and Tyrtaeus frags. 11.17–20, 12.25f. References
to wounds here and at 251 frame the whole dialogue (246–97n.).

Aristarchus (Arn/A) noted that βάλλω is contrasted with τύπτω, as is
casting with stabbing (οὐτάζω) elsewhere: cf. 570–3, 16.102–8nn., 11.191,
15.495. βλεῖο is aor. opt. middle for *βλῆο; cf. p. 35f. and the subj. βλήεται
(*Od.* 17.472). πονεύμενος denotes the *toil* of battle (cf. 239). With 289 cf.
5.147. The context requires 'from behind', since a brave man too can be hit
in the neck, just as 'charging ahead' (291) shows that he is not struck down
while standing idle. Aristarchus (Did/A) and the MSS read οὐκ ἄν, the
'common' texts (αἱ κοιναί) and a papyrus οὔ κεν, the rarer combination
(10/71× Hom.); yet he preferred the latter, against our MSS, at 12.465. At
14.91 and 15.228 οὔ κεν avoids the sequence ἄν ἀν-, and οὐκ ἄν never
precedes α-; here οὐκ ἄν avoids κεν ἐν. The MSS thus preserve a bardic
system of euphony, whereby Ionic ἄν is preferred unless α- follows. See
further 126–8n.; Chantraine, *GH* II 345f. Verse 289 should end with a
comma, not a stop.

290–1 Only here in Homer does ἀντιάζω, 'seek out', 'meet', describe
an inanimate object: so the spear is personified. ὀαριστύς, metaphorically
'battle', originally meant 'courting', 'amorous encounter' (cf. on 14.216f.),
from ὄαρ, 'wife' (Chantraine, *Dict.* s.v.). For the metaphor cf. πολέμου
ὀαριστύς (17.228) and ὁμιλέω, properly of friendly association, in martial
contexts at 5.86, 5.834, 11.502; it thus continues the distinctly erotic image
of seeking a breast or belly. At 22.124f. Hektor realizes that Akhilleus would
kill him 'like a woman' if he went to him unarmed – a clearly sexual idea,
since he adds that they cannot hold converse (ὀαρίζω) like a youth and a
maiden. The spear seeks its victim like a man his lover; for spears' demonic
vitality see 444n. πρόσσω ἱεμένη describes an eager spear at 15.543. In fact
the *double entendre* began with μιγήμεναι (286), as the archbishop saw (Eust.
932.40); τύπτω is ambiguous too (J. Henderson, *The Maculate Muse*, New
Haven 1975, 172). For the coarse but playful imagery cf. 'Theognis' 1286f.
(a lover to his boy): νικήσας γὰρ ἔχεις τὸ πλέον ἐξοπίσω, | ἀλλά σ' ἐγὼ
τρώσω φεύγοντά με. On erotic imagery for war in Homer see MacCary,
Childlike Achilles 137–48; H. Monsacré, *Les Larmes d'Achille*, Paris 1984,
63–72.

292–4 Idomeneus moves from sex to its result – they are talking 'like infants'. Verse 292 = 20.244, when Aineias interrupts his long speech to Akhilleus, again with | ἑσταότε following; cf. too *Od.* 13.296. A verse for breaking off is needed, like ἀλλὰ τίη μοι ταῦτα φίλος διελέξατο θυμός in Hektor's monologue (22.122) or ἀ. τ. μ. τ. περὶ δρῦν ἢ περὶ πέτρην in Hesiod's (*Theog.* 35); 292 may be the verse used for dialogues, but Hoekstra (on *Od.* 13.296) thinks that, given the sense 'enumerate' latent in λέγομαι (275–8n.), it was used to end lists and genealogies. νηπύτιος is otherwise confined to books 20–1 (8×), a clear case of 'clustering' (97–8n.); found as a name in Myc., it means 'infant', one who 'cannot speak' (ἠπύω: see Hoekstra on *Od.* 14.264). For the second half of 293 cf. *Od.* 17.481 = 21.285. ὑπερφιάλως, 'excessively' (18.300, 6× *Od.*), lacks the adjective's nuance of pride; it may derive from ὑπὲρ φιάλην 'overflowing the cup' (Chantraine, *Dict.* s.v.). On νέμεσις see 120–3n. With 294 cf. 10.148. The usual formula for taking a spear is εἵλετο δ' (ἄλκιμον) ἔγχος, 10× Hom. (cf. 296). ὄβριμον ἔ. | is nowhere else exchanged with ἀ. ἔ. in Homer (contrast *Aspis* 135): it is used in contexts of fear or wounding (12×). The poet already had Ares in mind (cf. 295ff.), and unconsciously substituted the god's standard epithet ὄβριμος (6×, cf. 518–20n.).

295–7 Meriones grabs a spear and follows his lord, whose exhortation has had its effect. Verse 295 = 328, cf. 528. The ancient formula ἀτάλαντος Ἐνυαλίῳ ἀνδρειφόντῃ (p. 11) is limited to Meriones, but θοῷ ἀτάλαντος Ἄρηϊ also describes Hektor, Patroklos and Automedon. A. A. Parry lists brief comparisons with gods (*Blameless Aegisthus* 218–23). This one leads into a simile likening Idomeneus to Ares and Meriones to Ares' son Phobos, lest Meriones' banter and grand epithet have let us forget that he is Idomeneus' junior (cf. bT on 299f.). Verse 297 = 469, cf. 5.708, μέγα πλούτοιο μεμηλώς: elsewhere the construction differs, e.g. σφι ... ἔργα μεμήλει (2.614).

298–303 A warrior starting his *aristeia* is often briefly likened to Ares (e.g. 20.46, 22.132): as after the simile at 242–4, we expect the action to begin, but the poet is a master at drawing suspense from what is foreseen. By a common technique, he amplifies the comparison of 295 into a six-line image (Moulton, *Similes* 21f.). Full-blown similes comparing men to gods are the rarest type in Homer: cf. 2.478f., Agamemnon likened to Zeus, Ares and Poseidon; 7.208–10, Aias entering battle like Ares going to fight among men; *Od.* 6.102–8. The image suggests the indecisive fighting to come, and the importance of divine intervention for its course.

298–300 Phobos, 'Rout', with Deimos, 'Terror', is Ares' son by Aphrodite at *Theog.* 934 (see West's n.). He appears with his brother at 4.440 and 15.119, where he acts as Ares' retainer: so too at *Aspis* 195, 463. To scare the foe, he appears on armour beside a Gorgon at 5.739,11.37, cf. *Aspis* 144. He had cults at Selinus (apparently instead of Ares) and Sparta; cf. Aesch. *Seven* 45 with Hutchinson's n. With the etymological play in 300 cf. the use of 'Ares' for 'war'. βροτολοιγός, 'ruinous to men', describes Ares and Eris (13× Hom.). For the redundancy in πόλεμόνδε μέτεισι cf. the parallel simile at 7.209 (εῖσιν π. μετ' ἀνέρας) and πόλινδε μετέρχεο (6.86). Verse 299, from φίλος, = Od. 3.111, of Antilokhos. ἅμα... | ἕσπετο is a formula split over the verse-end, cf. ἅμ' ἕ. before the diaeresis 7× epos, ἅμ' ἕποντο | 10×. ταλάφρων is unique for ταλασίφρων, cf. 4.421, ταλασίφρονά περ δέος εῖλεν: cf. Ares' formula ταλαύρινον πολεμιστήν (3×). ἀταλάφρων is of different origin (6.400–1n.). For the gnomic aor. ἐφόβησε cf. 16.583 (a hawk-simile).

301–3 Ares' Thracian origin is traditional: at *Od.* 8.361 he goes to Thrace after being caught with Aphrodite. It need not follow that, like the Paphian goddess, he really was an alien (Erbse, *Götter* 164f.). The Greeks often perceived violent emotions as coming from outside themselves, and deities who embody such forces, e.g. Dionusos, as from outside their society – hence, perhaps, their readiness to adopt alien gods like Adonis or Sabazios. Ares' name may be Greek (14.484–5n.). Like Enualios and Dionusos, he is already attested in Myc. as *A-re* (KN Fp 14), cf. the name /Areimenes/ (TH Z 849).

The Ephuroi and Phleguai are enemies in one conflict, not alternatives from separate ones. Vv. 302f. explain why the war-gods join *either* the Ephuroi *or* the Phleguai (for this use of μετά cf. 20.329): 'they do not listen to ⟨the prayers of⟩ both, but give glory to one side' (ἑτέροισι), cf. δώῃ δ' ἕ. γε νίκην 'give victory to one side or the other' (7.292 and 2×). The aorists are gnomic, since the pres. θωρήσσεσθον indicates a repeated event: so these are traditional foes. The Phleguai were in fact Lapiths: their eponym Phleguas, a son of Ares, begat the Lapith Ixion, and has many links with Thessaly (J. Fontenrose, *Python*, Berkeley 1959, 25–7, 46ff.). This was surely their first imagined home, whence they were moved to Phocis when the Boeotians migrated south (so F. Vian in *Hommages à G. Dumézil*, Brussels 1960, 221). Aristarchus thought Homer called only two cities Ephure – Corinth and Kikhuros in Thesprotis (15.531n.); here he favoured the latter, and is followed by Paus. 9.36.1–3, who puts the Phleguai in Phocis (cf. *HyAp* 278–80; Pherecydes, *FGH* 3 F 41, in ADT; *P.Oxy.* 3003). But neither location of Ephure suits the local warfare meant here. Aristarchus' predecessor Comanus (frag. 21 Dyck) and pupil Apollodorus of Athens (*FGH* 244 F 179, in AD) equated this Ephure with Krannon in Thessaly (cf. Pindar, *Py.* 10.55 with schol.; Steph. Byz. s.v.). Apollodorus is followed by Strabo (7 frags. 14, 16, 9.442), who places the Phleguai nearby at Gurton, Homeric Gurtone (2.738). Thus Homer draws on Thessalian saga, as often (see p. 19). The generic epithet μεγαλήτορας, acc. plur. only here (cf. 8.523n.), does not state that the Phleguai were godless and brutal, but fits both that tradition and their name, from φλέγω, 'burn' (Chantraine, *Dict.* s.v.).

304–5 ἀγοὶ ἀνδρῶν (cf. Κρητῶν ἀγός) and κεκορυθμένοι αἴθοπι χαλκῷ are adapted formulae (sing. 3× and 9× each). Ἰδομενεύς (38×) never recurs in this *locus*.

306–29 Meriones tentatively proposes reinforcing the Greek left; after weighing the needs of the centre, his lord agrees. This device lets the poet give their *aristeia* the limelight until 673, avoiding direct comparison with Aias and Teukros or conflict with Hektor. Idomeneus again takes the lead, though Meriones understands the needs of the hour; we now see that they will fight together, and that their meeting by the huts was a preparation for this. Idomeneus' comparison of Aias to Akhilleus (324) keeps the latter in our minds.

306 This v. recurs at 5.632 and 2× *Od.*, with other names shaped − ∪∪ −; Hoekstra on *Od.* 16.460 explains the clumsy καί. With Idomeneus' patronymic cf. 'Anthemides' for 'son of Anthemion' (4.488); 'Deukalionides' will not scan (Janko, *Glotta* 65 (1987) 71). For his genealogy see 449–54n.

308–10 Meriones offers three choices – right, centre or left. The left is often mentioned, but we hear of the right only here; Idomeneus ignores it, which implies there is no risk there. For an explanation see on 675, 681. Homer usually says ἐπ' ἀριστερά, ἐπὶ δεξιά (5.355, 12.239); Shipp (*Studies* 69f.) objects to δεξιόφιν etc., as no other adj. ends in -οφι in Homer, but cf. αὐτόφι and fourteen o-stem nouns in -οφι. This innovation, based on old instrumentals of other declensions like παλάμηφι or ναῦφι, already appears in the Knossos tablets, e.g. in the adj. /elephanteiophi/: see Ventris and Chadwick, *Documents* 85, 401–3; Risch, *Wortbildung* 361f. Verses 309f. mean 'for nowhere do I think them so deficient in battle ⟨as on the left⟩' (so T). With δεύεσθαι πολέμοιο, 'be unequal to the contest', cf. μάχης ἐδεύεο (17.142, cf. 23.670, 24.385). For 'long-haired Achaeans' see 3.43n.

312–27 Idomeneus' reply is in ring-form:

a   the centre has other defenders,
b   the Aiantes and Teukros, who is good in the *stadiē*;
c   they will hold off Hektor, who will not burn the ships, unless Zeus himself does it;
b′ but to no human would Aias yield, not even to Akhilleus in the *stadiē*;
a′ so we should defend the left.

312–14 The picture of the fighting recalls 170–94, when Teukros and Aias repelled Hektor. On Teukros' versatility cf. 177–8n.; Idomeneus calls him the best archer, yet Meriones beats him in the games (23.859ff.). So too Thoas is 'best of the Aetolians, deft with a javelin, good in the *stadiē*', i.e. close-range fighting (15.282f.). The contrast between the *stadiē* and pursuit in a rout (325) also appears at 7.240f. (where see n.). Idomeneus refers to the three stages of a Homeric battle – long-range fighting with missiles, σταδίη and rout. He himself is best in the σταδίη; he is less good at a distance (ἀποσταδόν) or in flight (514f.). Conversely, the Locrian bowmen avoid the *stadiē* but are effective at long range (713–18). With ἀμύνειν εἰσί cf. 814, *Od.* 22.116.

315–16 The idiom in οἵ μιν ἅδην ἐλόωσι ... πολέμοιο, 'they will drive him to tire of war', recurs at 19.423, Τρῶας ἅ. ἐλάσαι π., and *Od.* 5.290, ἅ. ἐλάαν κακότητος (cf. Tyrtaeus frag. 11.10, ἀμφοτέρων ἐς κόρον ἡλάσατε). ἅδην, perhaps better written with Ionic psilosis (*LfgrE* s.v.), is a fossilized acc. of *ἅδη, 'satiety', cognate with Latin *satis*: cf. Aesch. *Ag.* 828, ἅδην ἔλειξεν αἵματος. Thus πολέμοιο goes with ἅδην not ἐσσύμενον, although this may govern a gen., e.g. ἐσσυμένους πολέμου (24.404); cf. ἐσσύμενον πολεμίζειν (787, cf. 11.717), which Zenodotus read here because he did not understand the sense (so Aristarchus). 'Some commentaries' (Did/A) had ἑάσουσι, supposedly 'will sate': cf. ἑᾶν at *Od.* 5.290, and T's conjecture ἀάσωσι. This may depend on miscopying ΕΛΟѠϹΙ as ΕΑϹѠϹΙ; Mühlestein wrongly reverses the process (*Studies Chadwick* 469–72). Van der Valk ascribes ἑάσουσι to Aristarchus (*Researches* II 145f.), but see Erbse, *Hermes* 87 (1959) 278. — Verse 316 is in only one early codex and the two latest of six papyri (with εἰ καί for the feeble καὶ εἰ of later MSS). Concocted from standard phrases (cf. 80, 5.410, *Od.* 22.13), it is needlessly interpolated to identify μιν as Hektor, last named at 205; Apthorp (*MS Evidence* 145–7) compares τῆς at 19.176, where Briseis has not been alluded to.

317–18 The adv. αἰπύ here alone has the metaphorical sense 'difficult', but cf. πόνος αἰπύς etc. (769–73n.). ἔσσειται has metrical lengthening to avoid − ∪ −, a useful adaptation beside ἔσσεται, ἔσεται and ἔσται: cf. 2.393, *Od.* 19.302, equally non-traditional contexts (see Hoekstra, *SES* 15, for parallels). West (on *Erga* 503), accepting Herodian's accentuation ἐσσεῖται, deems it a Doric contracted fut. For the rest of 317 see 15.601–4n. — The bards perhaps understood ἄαπτος, found only with χεῖρες -ας in the epos (18×), as 'untouchable', from ἅπτομαι; but then we would expect **ἄναπτος. In fact ἄεπτος, in Aesch. *Suppl.* 908 and frag. 213, is the original form, from *ἀ-ϝεπτος, 'unspeakable'; contracted to *ἄπτος after loss of -ϝ-, its metrical shape was kept by diectasis. Cf. | Ἥρη ἀπτοεπές, 'speaking the unspeakable', from *ἀϝεπτοϝεπής (8.209); for the sense cf. ἀθέσφατος, ἄφατος (H. Neitzel, *Glotta* 56 (1977) 212–20). Did/A says Aristarchus read ἀέπτους, but his name may have replaced 'Aristophanes' (cf. Hrd/A on 1.567); this happened easily, especially when they were abbreviated (16.467–9n.). Aristophanes (frag. 418 Slater) surely found ἄεπτος in other archaic poets and proposed it without MS support; πᾶσαι read it at 1.567.

319–20 Idomeneus still distrusts Zeus's intentions towards the Greeks (cf. 225–7). Poseidon more confidently had told the Aiantes that they could stop Hektor if even Zeus was behind him (57f.). ὅτε μή means 'unless' (cf. 14.248), like εἰ for 'when'. With αἰθόμενον δᾱλόν cf. αἰ. πῦρ (etc.), 17× in epos, and αἰθομένας δαΐδας (etc.), 6× Hom.: *δἄϝελός (cf. δαίω, 'burn') can always be restored, but must not be (4× Hom.). For the modified formula νήεσσι θοῇσι see 15.601–4n.

322–5 ἀκτή, 'food', is fossilized in the formulae ἀλφίτου (ἱεροῦ) ἀ. (11.631, cf. *Od.* 2.355) and Δημήτερος (ἱερὸν) ἀκτήν (also 21.76, 5× Hes.). Gods can adopt mortal shape but never eat mortal food; hence this addition (so bT). For a different qualification cf. 24.58, 'Hektor is mortal and sucked a woman's breast' (also *HyAphr* 145). The mention of stones after bronze weapons (cf. 11.265 = 541) may not be random: Aias finally disables Hektor with one (14.409ff.). It is common to maim one's foe with a stone and dispatch him with a weapon (e.g. 4.517ff., 5.580ff.). Akhilleus' fearsome epithet ῥηξήνωρ (also dat. at 16.575, 2× acc., gen. *Od.* 4.5) also serves as a name at *Od.* 7.63; Ap. Soph. derives it from breaking the enemy *ranks* (138.24). ῥηκτός perhaps reminded the poet of it. αὐτοσταδίη is unique for σταδίη, '(battle) standing in the *same* place' (313–14n.): cf. αὐτοσχεδίη (15.510) beside αὐτοσχεδόν.

326–7 νῶϊν is an acc. dual for expected νῶϊ or νώ. Aristarchus took it as a gen., 'on our left', like μάχης ἐπ' ἀριστερά. But νῶϊν is nom. or acc. at 8.377, 8.428, 11.767, 16.99, *Od.* 23.211; Zenodotus kept it, and even introduced it at 22.216. Similarly σφῶϊν is acc. at 15.155 and perhaps 8.452, nom. at *Od.* 23.52, as if with n-mobile added. Cumulatively, Aristarchus' efforts to expel these forms fail to convince (van der Valk, *TCO* 139f.). Duals, being obsolete in Ionic, were liable to artificial alteration by bards (cf. on 47–51, 346–8). ὧδ' means either 'thus, as we are doing' or 'in this direction' (cf. 10.537, 12.346); Aristarchus wrongly denied that the local sense is Homeric (Ap. Soph. 170.21).

ἔχε is the imperative of the old verb ϝέχω, 'drive', attested in Cypriot and Pamphylian: cf. Latin *veho*, Myc. /wokhā/, 'chariot', at Pylos, and 43–5n. Traces survive in the formula ἔχε μώνυχας ἵππους (8×) and absolutely, e.g. 679, 16.378, 23.422. So the Cretans are suddenly in a chariot. It is not surprising that Homer made this slip when a hero is telling his squire where to go in the battle: cf. 5.241–73, Diomedes telling Sthenelos where to drive. Homer perhaps meant to say 'let us keep on the left', cf. *Od.* 3.171, (νῆσον) ἐπ' ἀριστέρ' ἔχοντες; cf. his slips over the use of chariots in the gap between the rampart and ships (657n.). The sentiment 'let us enter battle to see who will win glory' traditionally ends exhortations to a comrade (e.g. 5.273, 8.532–4, 22.243–6). This version of it (cf. 12.328) may adapt an independent clause: cf. 22.130 and Hoekstra, *Modifications* 104f.

330–60 The tension is increased by a panorama and a recapitulation of the opposing attitudes of Zeus and Poseidon, corresponding to the conflict on the human level; Idomeneus does not kill until 363.

330–44 The battle evolves from individual combats by *promachoi*, typified by 156–205, to a general engagement at close quarters by the ships' sterns (so near has the danger come!); as often, comparisons and the reaction of an imagined observer make it vivid. As convention requires, we have missed nothing important: only now, when the Cretans arrive, do the armies clash. The Greeks' new vigour upon seeing them augments the pair's stature and shows that Poseidon's plan is proceeding, as we are soon reminded. The panorama, including the bristling battle and wind-simile, develops passages like 7.62, (στίχες) ἀσπίσι καὶ κορύθεσσι καὶ ἔγχεσι πεφρικυῖαι, which precedes a simile about a φρίξ of wind, or 4.282, (φάλαγγες) σάκεσίν τε καὶ ἔ. π., which follows a simile of a shepherd alarmed by a squall. There Agamemnon delights in the bristling ranks (γήθησεν ἰδών): cf. 344. Many details are typical (Fenik, *TBS* 130): Idomeneus is 'like a flame', an image often used of warriors joining battle (39–40n.); a wind-simile depicts the violence and dust of the conflict; the glare from the weaponry resembles e.g. 2.455–8, and a hypothetical onlooker enters three similar descriptions (126–8n.).

330–3 The brief comparison of Idomeneus to fire recalls his simile at 242–4, just as that of Meriones to Ares (328) echoed 298ff. Idomeneus is the greater figure, but 331 adds that both were conspicuous in their armour (A's variant μαρμαίροντας is from 16.279, a verse otherwise identical). Verse 332 = 11.460. Like νεῖκος ὁμοίιον (4.444), ὁμὸν ἵστατο ν. is one of several phrases for the mingling of hostile front lines indicated by ὁμόσ' ἦλθε μάχη and ἐρχομένων ἄμυδις (337, 343): see Latacz, *Kampfdarstellung* 191f.

334–7 Wind-similes describe armies raising dust at 3.10ff., 5.499ff. (the wind pours mist on the mountains or scatters chaff). The speed of the gusts suggests that of the front lines colliding; the mingled dust-swirls evoke the two sides' confusion and the dust-clouds that are the usual atmosphere of battle (e.g. 11.163). Hesiod (*Theog.* 878ff.) complains of winds that choke the fields with dust; dirt roads are yet dustier in summer when the meltemi blows. The narrative shares with the simile ἄμυδις and ἵσταμαι, the *mot juste* for dust hanging in the air (2.150f.).

339–44 The effect on an observer is implied throughout this panorama. Massed spears bristle like hair standing on end from terror, and the armour's glare is blinding. The metaphor ἔφριξεν and compounds φθισίμβροτος and ταμεσίχρως are grand and sinister. Each piece of armour rhymes with its dazzling epithet amid the harsh consonants: αὐγὴ χαλκείη κορύθων ἀπὸ λαμπομενάων | θωρήκων τε νεοσμήκτων σακέων τε φαεινῶν. The picture ends with a reminder that this is the two sides joining battle (343, picking up 337), and with an observer's grief at the sight. His emotion deepens our impression of the violence; if we were really watching it, we could not enjoy it as we enjoy this description. This observer, imagined as a god elsewhere (126–8n.), provides a smooth transition to that other audience, the gods, who are stirring up all this suffering. Cf. Ap. Rhod. 3.1354–8, influenced by Eumelus (frag. 19 B. = 4 D.).

The diction is powerfully innovative. For ἔφριξεν cf. Ap. Rhod. *loc. cit.* and p. 9 n. 6. φθισίμβροτος describes the aegis at *Od.* 22.297, Ares in Ap. Rhod. *loc. cit.*; cf. πόλεμον φθισήνορα (5×), νὺξ φθῖτ' ἄμβροτος (*Od.* 11.330). ἐγχείῃσι | μακρῆς is a split formula: cf. 782, 3.137, 3.254. For ταμεσίχρως see 4.511, 23.803. ὄσσε δ' ἄμερδε, 'blinded the eyes' (also at *Theog.* 698), modifies the original sense 'deprive' in e.g. ὀφθαλμῶν . . . ἄμερσε (*Od.* 8.64), cf. τὸν ὁμοῖον . . . ἀμέρσαι, 'rob one's fellow' (16.53); thus at *Od.* 19.18, ἔντεα . . . καπνὸς ἀμέρδει, the smoke does not just tarnish the weapons but blinds them, as if bronze shines with its own eye, not with reflected light (light was held to come from the eye: 837n.). Here, in a bold image, the bronze's eye glares so brightly that it blinds the onlooker, as the sun's eye can. νεόσμηκτος is a *hapax*, metrically equal to κραταιγύαλος (19.361). θρασυκάρδιος is in a like hemistich at 10.41, cf. *Aspis* 448. A papyrus reads λάων for ἰδών in 344: cf. *Od.* 19.229f. with J. Russo's n.

345–60 What Leaf calls 'a lengthy and superfluous recapitulation' is typical and suited to its context. Summaries of the divine background occur elsewhere, from the briefest at 5.508–11 to the longest at 15.592ff., when Homer both expounds the present state of battle in terms of Zeus's will and charts the future (Fenik, *TBS* 54f., 130). The poet often recalls Zeus's plan by saying that the god is giving the Trojans glory (11.300, 12.37, 12.174, 12.255, 12.437, 15.567, 15.596ff., 15.694f.). The most similar summary, 11.73–83, also marks a shift from massed fighting to a Greek's *aristeia*: the other gods blamed Zeus because he wished to give the Trojans glory, but he sat heedless, watching the slaughter. This summary clarifies the gods' motives for any hearer who, excusably, risks getting confused, or missed the start of the poem. Verses 345f. and 358–60 also set the tone for the heavy but indecisive fighting that continues until 14.506; another summary soon follows (15.54ff.). That gods direct the conflict increases its importance (so T) and gives it pathos; it may comfort a partisan audience to be reminded that both gods are really on the Greek side (so bT on 348)! The structure is well analysed by Heubeck (*Kleine Schriften* 121–5):

345–6   *Summary*: Kronos' two sons are at odds, causing suffering for the heroes.

347–50   *Zeus's will*: to help the Trojans; *his motive*: to honour Akhilleus; *his limitation*: he does not wish the Greeks' total ruin, but honours Thetis and her son.

351–7   *Poseidon's will*: to help the Greeks secretly; *his motive*: grief at their suffering and anger at Zeus; *his limitation*: as Zeus is senior, he cannot help openly but arouses the army secretly.

358–60   *Summary*: the two gods hold fast the rope of war, and many fall.

The middle sections are framed by repetition in 348 and 350 (κυδαίνω), 351f. and 357 (λάθρη). Zeus's refusal to permit the Greeks' total ruin prepares for the Trojans' eventual repulse; Poseidon's reluctance to challenge his brother openly, prefigured when he refused to help Here against him (8.210f.), adumbrates 15.175ff., when he yields to Zeus's insistence on the elder's right to command. The summary presupposes Zeus's promise to Thetis, prohibition of the other gods from battle and message to Hektor (1.495ff., 8.5ff., 11.186ff.); it is also consistent with 13.1 ff., when Zeus looks away, confident that nobody will interfere in the battle. Verse 352 recalls 32–8, when Poseidon arrives unseen; his motives are the same (353 = 16). Verse 357 implies that he took human shape to avoid Zeus's notice: this hardly contradicts his adoption of human form to hide his identity *among men*. He makes a virtue of necessity, choosing identities suited to his aims, and revealing his godhead when he wishes (66ff.); once Zeus is safely dormant his disguise is no longer mentioned (14.361ff., 15.8). See further Michel, *N* 51–62.

'Late' diction is even more plentiful than Shipp realized (*Studies* 282); as usual this betrays the poet's creativity. κραταιός (also at 11.119 (simile), 2× *Od.*, 2× *HyHerm*) is based on fem. *κραταιά (16.330–4n.). | ἀνδράσιν ἡρώεσσι recurs in the gen. 3× *Od.*, 4× Hes., but cf. the runover phrase ἀνδρῶν | ἡρώων (3× Hom.). τετεύχατον is odd (346–8n.). The separated phrase λαὸν ... Ἀχαιικόν is unmodified at 9.521, 15.218. Ἰλιόθι πρό (4× Hom.) oddly combines a loc. with πρό. In 350 υἱέα is artificial (cf. 185–7n.); it adapts υἱέϊ καρτεροθύμῳ (*Theog.* 476), like εὐρέα (πόντον) for εὐρύν by analogy with εὐρέϊ πόντῳ. For Τρωσῖν see p. 9 n. 6. Verse 354 is archaic: both μάν and ἴα 'one' are Aeolic (see p. 17 n. 28). Willcock well explains ὁμὸν γένος ἠδ' ἴα πάτρη as an old misapplied formula, since π. usually means 'homeland' (17×), not 'ancestry'; otherwise 'ancestry' is another archaism, cf. the sense 'clan' in Pindar (LSJ s.v.).

346–8 Most good MSS have τετεύχατον, not -ετον, which Aristarchus accepted as a perf., noting that a preterite is really needed. -τον has replaced a preterite third person dual in -την for metrical convenience, as at 10.361, 10.364, 18.583 (cf. Zenodotus' text at 8.448, 10.245, 11.782). Since duals were obsolete in Ionic, it is probably an artificial pluperf.: cf. the weird duals at 3.279, 5.487, 8.74, 8.378, 8.455, 9.182ff., *HyAp* 456, 487, 501. The *lectio facilior* ἐτεύχετον, a variant in A, makes the past tense explicit (contrast van der Valk, *Researches* II 207).

350–5 Aristarchus athetized 350 as redundant after 348; but it adds Zeus's promise to Thetis, mentioned in other summaries (15.76f., 598) and frames the account of Zeus's aims (Michel, *N* 52f.). His predecessors (Did/A) read ὤτρυνε in 351 (from 5.461?). The construction ἤχθετο ... δαμναμένους is paralleled later (LSJ s.v.; Chantraine, *GH* II 328). Respect for one's elders' superior knowledge is normal in Homer; with 355 cf. πρότερος γενόμην καὶ πλείονα οἶδα (19.219, 21.440). Although respect, not Zeus's greater force (which Poseidon had cited at 8.210), constrains the latter, this cannot wholly dignify his covert action (so bT). For Zeus's seniority see 15.165–7n.

358–60 'Alternately, they pulled taut the rope of violent strife and equal war over both sides – unbreakable, not to be undone, that undid the knees of many', i.e. the two gods made the armies fight a fierce and indecisive battle. Since the structure of the passage shows that the gods' discord is still the topic (cf. 345f.), we can exclude Crates' view (in bT) that the two *armies* engage in a metaphorical tug-of-war. The rope-metaphor signals divine interference in battle: cf. ἔριδα πτολέμοιο τάνυσσαν (14.389, Poseidon and Hektor), ἔ. κρατερὴν ἐτάνυσσε Κρονίων (16.662, where see n.), κατὰ ἶσα μάχην ἐ. Κ. (11.336), Ζεύς ... ἐ. κακὸν πόνον (17.400f.), θεός περ | ἶσον τείνειεν πολέμου τέλος (20.101). ὣς μὲν τῶν ἐπὶ ἶσα μάχη τέτατο (12.436 = 15.413) follows similes describing a deadlock, in the latter case a carpenter stretching a guide-line; cf. 17.543, ἐπὶ Πατρόκλῳ τ. κρατερὴ ὑσμίνη. The image is of a rope stretched by the rival gods over the two sides, symbolizing that they are locked in stalemate.

The original sense of πεῖραρ, as its Sanskrit and Avestan cognates reveal, is 'the point where something ends (and another begins)', 'limit', 'determinant' or 'bond', since the end of one thing and start of the next can be seen as the link between them. As at *Od.* 12.51, 162, 179 and *HyAp* 129, it means 'rope', since it is 'unbreakable, not to be untied' (cf. the divine bonds at 37, *Od.* 8.275). Heubeck rightly thinks this sense arose from a misinterpretation of traditional phrases where it once meant 'end' (*Kleine Schriften* 88–93). So too ἀρχή came to mean 'rope' in Hellenistic slang (Diod. 1.35.10, Acts 10.11, 11.5): 'throw me the end' became 'throw me the rope'. Aristarchus (Did, Arn/A), taking πεῖραρ as 'rope-end' and ἐπαλλάξαντες as 'cross over' (in tying a knot), thought the gods tied the 'end' of strife to that of battle, and drew the rope tight round the armies, forcing them together as with a noose; hence in one edition he read ἀλλήλοισι, describing the ends, for ἀμφοτέροισι. But 358 is merely a grand phrase for 'war', cf. 18.242. ἐπαλλάσσω later means 'alternate', which suits a battle where each side is alternately victorious. See 6.143n.; Onians, *Origins* 310–42; van der Valk, *Researches* II 97–9; W. Northdurft, *Glotta* 56 (1978) 25–40.

358 Aristophanes (Did/AT) and the vulgate offer the odd reading | τοί. When possible, bards have replaced inherited (Aeolic) τοί with Ionic οἱ (Janko, *HHH* 118n.). τοί persists after a naturally heavy syllable only 11× *Il.*, 5× *Od.*, and at *Cat.* 204.84, *Aspis* 276 (see 7.54–6n.). It opens a verse here only in the *Iliad*, at *Od.* 22.271, 281 and 304 (a curious cluster) and several times in Hesiod, slips by a poet who used it in his vernacular (the poet of the *Aspis* favours it). Here, *pace* van der Valk (*Researches* II 71), it is surely corrupt for τῷ, read by Aristarchus and MS Ve[1]: cf. the frame at 345. οἱ, attested by Did/A, papyri but few good codices, does not explain why τοί exists. For the formula ὁμοιῖου πτολέμοιο (once *ὁμοιῖοο πτ-) see 4.315n., S. West on *Od.* 3.236. The ancients equated this epithet of old age, death, strife and war with ὁμοῖος, 'common to all', 'impartial'. They may even be right: at *Erga* 182 it is used for ὁμοῖος; cf. too ξυνὸς ᾽Ενυάλιος and the forms γελοίιος, κοίιλος for κοϊ- (Mimnermus frag. 12.6).

361–454 Idomeneus kills Othruoneus and Asios; Antilokhos slays Asios' charioteer. Deïphobos kills a certain Hypsenor, but Idomeneus slays Alkathoos and mocks the Trojans' lack of success

361–454 Idomeneus kills three major victims in his *aristeia*, which ends, as it begins, with a reference to his advancing years (511–15). There is symmetry in his victims (Michel, *N* 91): Othruoneus is betrothed to Priam's daughter and Alkathoos is married to Ankhises' (rivalry between the Trojan royal houses is mentioned at 460f.); family feeling thus rouses first Deïphobos and then Aineias. The first two casualties are boastful fools (bT on 384); the first and third provoke speeches of triumph – Idomeneus has the last word, capping Deïphobos' counter-vaunt. Alkathoos provides the tragic climax of the *aristeia*, but he and Othruoneus were surely invented to frame Asios (cf. Michel, *N* 87).

361–82 Othruoneus' fall is typical (Fenik, *TBS* 130f.), but enlivened by grim humour at his expense. It follows the tripartite pattern of basic statement (363), life-story of the slain (364–9) and account of the blow (370–2), with a fine taunting-speech. His foolish pride undercuts the usual pathos. As a late-comer to the war, he resembles other allies at 792ff. and Rhesos, Euphorbos, Lukaon and Asteropaios (10.434, 16.810f., 21.80f., 155f.); only here is this detail in an 'epitaph'. Marriage is a favourite motif (170–81n.). But Othruoneus' terms for Kassandre's hand forfeit our sympathy: it is greedy to offer no gifts, but only a promise to repel the Greeks. Her other suitor, Koroibos, was no less stupid (Virgil, *Aen.* 2.341ff.). Priam shows his desperation by accepting such terms; hence the Trojans' alarm at Othruoneus' fall. Like Dolon, he is ruined by undertaking for an exorbitant price a task wholly beyond his powers; Pandaros and Asios also perish by over-reaching themselves. We need not pity him, *pace* Griffin (*HLD* 131): he gets his deserts according to the *mores* of his time.

361 Idomeneus' years are more than a match for a raw recruit. His age is not invented for this moment, *pace* Reinhardt (*IuD* 298f.), nor to motivate his withdrawal at 512ff.; his role as counsellor, his appearance with Nestor and Phoinix at 19.311 and Oïlean Aias' insult at 23.476 prove it traditional (Michel, *N* 82). Odysseus, slightly younger, is ὠμογέρων (23.791, cf. bT *ad* *loc.*). The unique μεσαιπόλιος, 'half-grey', contains an old locative (Risch, *Wortbildung* 220), or (better) displays metrical lengthening by analogy with μεσαίτερος (Chantraine, *Dict.* s.v. μέσος). With 362 cf. 11.489.

363 Othruoneus' name may be based on ὄθρυς, 'mountain' (cf. Mt Othrus in Thessaly), glossed as Cretan by Hsch.; cf. the toponym *O-du-ru, /*Odrus*/, on the Knossos tablets (Chantraine, *Dict.* s.v.). For the formation cf. ᾿Ιλιονεύς and the Spartan warrior Othruadas. Does Othruoneus' slaying by Idomeneus reflect Cretan saga, like the Phaistos slain by Idomeneus at 5.43, or even Asios, whose home, Arisbe, is named after a Cretan girl (so Steph. Byz. s.v.) – cf. Arisbas, father of a Cretan at 17.345? Cf. too 16.603–7n. Asios' patronym Hurtakides recalls the Cretan city Hurtakos or Hurtakine (von Kamptz, *Personennamen* 313), but also Lycian Ορτακια = *urtaqijahñ* (Scherer, 'Nichtgriechische Personennamen' 37). — The ancients identified the unique toponym Kabesos with various places with similar Anatolian-sounding names, in the Hellespontine area, Thrace, Cappadocia or Lycia (cf. T, Steph. Byz. s.v. Καβασσός and Zgusta, *Ortsnamen* 207f.). As bT note, ἔνδον ἐόντα (21× Hom.) often means 'who was present', but only when he is indoors. Here it is a misused formula, cf. ὃν νῶϊ Κυθηρόθεν ἔ. ἐ. | ... ἐτίομεν ἐν μεγάροισι (15.438f.): Homer was thinking of Othruoneus joining Priam's household from Kabesos, but he is not literally 'inside' here (cf. *HyAp* 92!). To solve the 'problem' the Argolic 'city' MS read ῾Εκάβης νόθον υἱὸν ἐόντα, making him a half-brother of his bride-to-be (Did/AT)!

365–7 Kassandre's beauty is mentioned at 24.699, cf. *Od.* 11.421f. Homer probably knew of her prophetic madness, as the *Cypria* did, but ignores it, save when he rationalizes her second sight as keen vision (see 24.703–6n.). It is in character for Othruoneus to desire such a girl. (Πριάμοιο) θυγατρῶν εἶδος ἀρίστην also describes Laodike at 3.124 and 6.252, but, *pace* Nagy (*BA* 26ff.), epic is more gallant than pedantic in bestowing compliments (cf. on 427–33, 15.281–5); θ. εἶ. ἀ. is a formula (5×). 'Kassandre', like 'Medesikaste' her sister (173), may be from *kas-, 'excel' (Chantraine, *Dict.* s.v.); cf. Kastianeira (8.305). Several Mycenaeans were called /*Kessandros*/ or -/*ra*/.

Suitors frequently offer gifts to secure a bride (e.g. 16.178, 190): see Snodgrass, *JHS* 94 (1974) 114–25; Morris, *CA* 5 (1986) 105–15. As a mark of honour Agamemnon offers Akhilleus his daughter ἀνάεδνον (9.146): on the form see Beekes, *Laryngeals* 58f. The provision of a dowry, which is what ἕδνα means in about half its uses, no doubt reflects a later, eighth-century, practice, when, with a rising population, it became harder to marry off one's daughters (dowries are the classical custom). Zenodotus altered ἀπωσέμεν, which he perhaps deemed too bold, to ἀνωσέμεν (Did/AT with Schmidt, *Weltbild* 143f.). Another effort to palliate Othruoneus' rash promise was the addition of 367a, φοίτων ἔνθα καὶ ἔνθα θοὰς ἐπὶ νῆας ᾿Αχαιῶν (in T), supposed to mean that he would attack at various points (van der Valk, *Researches* II 479); it feebly combines 2.779 with 1.12 etc.

368–9 Cf. ὑπέσχετο καὶ κατένευσε (etc.), 7×, preceding | δωσέμεναι at *Od.* 4.6 also. ὑποσχεσίη is a *hapax*: Othruoneus fought 'trusting Priam's promise', not 'obeying his own'.

370–3 With 370f. cf. 159f., where Meriones is subject; for Othruoneus' swagger see 156–8n. Idomeneus duly drags him by the leg (383). From οὐδ', 371f. = 397f. The repetition links these killings, which lends them irony, since there is a difference: Othruoneus should not be prancing about with no shield, whereas Asios' driver, with the reins in his hands, must rely on his corslet for protection. With 373 cf. 11.449, 20.388, where a name and epithet fill the last two feet. Since 'Idomeneus' will not fit, φώνησέν τε is substituted: Homer did not say μακρὸν ἀῦσας, as at 413, 445 and 2×, since this is tied to ἔκπαγλον ἐπεύξατο.

374–82 These verses comprise the first of three vaunts, all on the theme of recompense (414–16, 446–54): cf. the set of four at 14.453–505. Idomeneus is assumed to know of Othruoneus' folly, and mocks him for it. Agamemnon can offer better terms than Priam: far from defeating the Greeks single-handed, he need only join them and sack Troy! Let him follow to the ships, to arrange a betrothal! Follow he must, since Idomeneus drags him by the leg. The joke is in character: Idomeneus made a coarser one at 288ff.

374–6 'I compliment you above all men, if you are really going to fulfil all you promised . . .': cf. *Od.* 8.487 (the sole other use of αἰνίζομαι). Since 'astonishment, rather than praise, seems to be in order if the mortally wounded Othryoneus can accomplish his promises' (Dyck), Zenodotus and Comanus (frag. 10 Dyck) read αἰνίσσομαι, supposedly 'am amazed', others -ίξομαι (Did/A). Δαρδανίδη Πριάμῳ is dat. only here (7× in other cases).

378–82 Verse 378 echoes 365. The old verb ὀπυίω survives in Cretan: it means 'be married' rather than 'get married' (G. P. Edwards in *Studies Chadwick* 173–81). Verse 380 = 2.133, cf. 21.433. ἐπὶ νηυσὶ συνώμεθα ποντοπόροισιν is based on e.g. 16.205, σὺν ν. νεώμεθα π.; συνώμεθα is aor. subj. of συνίεμαι, cf. συνημοσύναι, 'agreements' (22.261). The *hapax* ἐεδνωτής means an 'in-law' who has received ἔεδνα (cf. 365–7n.): cf. ἐεδνόομαι, 'receive/give gifts in exchange for a daughter/wife' at *Od.* 2.53 (with S. West's n.), *Cat.* 190.5, 200.7. Leaf suggests 'match-maker', but Idomeneus speaks loosely of his own side as one family, which the Trojans actually are.

383–401 Asios is Idomeneus' greatest victim, being one of the leaders of the Trojan attack (12.95ff.); on his connexions see 363n. His name is Asiatic in the fullest sense; it once meant 'man of Assuwa', i.e. 'the good land' (from Anatolian *aššuš*). We know of several Mycenaeans called /*Aswios*/. He disobeyed Pouludamas' advice that the Trojans leave their chariots behind the ditch (12.110ff.); the poet called him a fool for doing so, and foretold his death by Idomeneus' spear. His extra speed gave him initial success – he entered a gate that was still open but met stiff resistance inside, since the Greeks still held the rampart. We last saw him in frustration calling Zeus a liar (12.164ff.). Like Othruoneus', his pretensions obtain their just deserts: the very horses and chariot of which he was so proud (12.96f., 114), and which he unwisely kept with him, fatally impede his movements. Worse, his driver is so astounded by his sudden fall that he too is slain, and the Greeks seize his precious steeds. Pandaros was ruined by excessive love for his horses in the opposite way: he left them behind, afraid they would suffer in the war (5.192ff.).

The scene belongs to a recurrent pattern which extends to 423 (169–205n.), but is less typical than Fenik thinks (*TBS* 131). (i) It is common to attack a warrior who is hauling a body away, but only here and at 15.524ff. is the attacker slain. (ii) It shows exceptional anxiety on Asios' part that his driver keeps his horses so close behind him that they breathe on his shoulders (385); Automedon, facing overwhelming odds, bids his charioteer do the same (ἐμπνείοντε μεταφρένῳ), so they can escape if need be (17.501f., cf. 23.380f.). Drivers must stay fairly close, but it is not 'dangerous *not* to fight with one's horses breathing down one's neck' (Fenik, *TBS* 29, cf. on 4.229–30, 17.501–2). (iii) Asios dies the same death, with the same simile, as another important ally, Sarpedon (389–93n.); on the parallels see Schoeck, *Ilias und Aithiopis* 61–4. (iv) Fenik (*TBS* 61f.) compares how, after Menelaos has slain a warrior, Antilokhos kills his charioteer as he tries to turn, and captures his horses (5.578ff.); Patroklos kills a driver who panics and falls from his vehicle (16.401ff.).

383–8 Asios' death is almost as startling to us as to him, so swiftly is it told in concise, enjambed sentences with rapid shifts of subject. It is apt that a boaster is hit in the throat – cf. 5.292f. (Pandaros), 17.47 (Euphorbos), *Od.* 22.15 (Antinoos); but it is hard to see significance in the similar killing at 542.

383–5 With 383 cf. 17.289, whence comes the variant κατά for διά; corpses dragged by the leg form a topos (10.490, 11.258, 14.477, 16.763, 17.289, 18.155, 18.537). πούς means leg *and* foot rather than foot only, just as χείρ can mean arm *and* hand, in Greek ancient and modern (cf. 531–3n.). | ἥρως Ἰδομενεύς recurs at 439, cf. 575. The vulgate is ἦλθεν ἀμύντωρ, as at 14.449, 15.540; Aristarchus' reading (Did/AT) ἦλθ' ἐπαμύντωρ, also reported at 15.540, may be based on *Od.* 16.263. It should be rejected, cf. ἧεν ἀ. (15.610); the word is clustered in books 13–15 (cf. 97–8n.). πρόσθ' ἵππων forms a ring with 392.

386 No other victim is nameless (cf. 211–13n.). ἡνίοχος θεράπων is nom. only here, but acc. 3× at the verse-end (12.111 included, of this same person). Perhaps Ἡνίοχος or Θεράπων was meant as his name in both places – an improvisation based on a common formula, cf. Ἀρηΐθοον θεράποντα, or ἀ. Θ., at 20.487 (but at 394 ἡνίοχος is not a name). So too Tekton may be a carpenter's name at 5.59 (cf. *Od.* 8.114); another ἡνίοχος θεράπων is called 'Ηνιοπεύς, 'rein-handler', at 8.120, where Homer also seems to have had trouble inventing a name. Heniokhos was a name later, e.g. the comic poet.

389–93 This fine tree-simile and grim picture of a dying man's last moments also describe Sarpedon (16.482–6). They stress Asios' importance, which the suddenness of his fate might have led us to forget; the woodmen select this tree because it is loftier than the rest, just as is Asios in another way (cf. 178–80n.). The verses were perhaps reserved for the fall of a major figure, especially 392f.: so too 16.855–7 = 22.361–3 describe the deaths of Patroklos and Hektor only. Eight full similes recur in Homer (15.263–8n.).

389–91 The repeated verb, and arboreal alternatives, suggest that we hear the tree fall more than once. For other tree-similes see 178–80n.; in them we can watch ship-timbers progress from being felled on the slopes (3.6off.) and hauled down by mule (17.744) to being worked by a shipwright (15.41of., *Od.* 5.243ff., 9.384). The ἀχερωΐς is the white poplar, later λευκή. The obscure archaism βλωθρός surely means 'tall', since such similes often mention height, e.g. 437 (Strasburger, *Kämpfer* 38). It describes a pear-tree at *Od.* 24.234, and trees, in the form γλωθρός, at *Cat.* 204.124 (Janko, *HHH* 225). νεήκης, 'newly whetted', is unique but correctly formed (Chantraine, *Dict.* s.v. ἀκ-).

392–3 Verse 392 blends the formular system ἵππους καὶ δίφρον, ἵ. τε καὶ ἄρματα, ἵπποιιν καὶ ὄχεσφιν (etc.) with κεῖτο τανυσθείς | (20.483), cf. τ. | κ. (18.26f.), | κ. ταθείς (655 = 21.119). That the victim lies before his horses and chariot seems more pointed here than at 16.485. Verse 393 blends familiar motifs: a dying Trojan's groan (5.68, 20.403 etc.), falling in the dust and grasping it in handfuls (508 and 4×), bloodying it (4.451) and lying in blood and dust (15.118, 16.775). The dust is no doubt soaked with his own blood (bT). βεβρυχώς describes the roar of lions, bulls or the sea; here it suggests the gurgle of air passing through the gash in Asios' throat (see 16.481n.). D think he gnashed his teeth.

394–401 Antilokhos, like Meriones, was among Poseidon's addressees (93); his appearance in Meriones' stead shows that he too was heartened by the god's words. He has a large role in the sequel (545–65, 14.513, 15.568ff.). Killing a charioteer is a favourite exploit for a junior hero (e.g. 5.58of.). In the parallel scene at 16.403 (where see n.), the driver ἐκ ... πλήγη φρένας; cf. also 18.225. The poet implies that he might have escaped had he not been too terrified to turn his vehicle; his cowardice recalls Asios'. With 'the wits which he had before' cf. 24.201f.; as Macleod comments, such expressions stress present folly, not past sense. In turning, one's flank was dangerously exposed; this is how Antilokhos slew a driver at 5.58of. (585 = 399), and Akhilleus another ἂψ ἵππους στρέψαντα (20.487–9). But Antilokhos pierces his corslet anyway. — Standard diction slows the pace after the shock of Asios' death. Antilokhos is μενεχάρμης 3× (the epithet is generic, not particular) and μεγαθύμου Νέστορος υἱόν 4×; the vivid metaphor περόνησε, 'pinned', is at 7.145; 397f. echo 371f. For 399 cf. 16.740–4n.; hiatus after | αὐτὰρ ὁ occurs 15× Hom., but Aristarchus inserted γ' (Did/A). Verse 401 = 5.324.

402–23 Deïphobos, angry over Asios, his fellow-officer (12.94f.), aims at Idomeneus but kills Hupsenor instead, a standard pair of motifs (with 403f. cf. 183f.); despite his vaunt, the Greeks rescue Hupsenor's body, which 'groans' (423), a slip by the poet. Hupsenor's death is proved by Idomeneus' retort that he has slain three men in exchange for one (447); moreover γούνατ' ἔλυσε (412) always denotes killing, *pace* Schadewaldt, *Iliasstudien* 103n. Had Deïphobos' vaunt been premature, as Michel thinks (*N* 89), Homer would have made this clear.

404–10 The unique description of Idomeneus' round shield, framed by his crouching at 405 and 408, interrupts the common pattern 'he avoided his spear | ... which flew over', seen at 22.274f. (cf. 404, 408); with 403ff. cf. 16.610ff. Aineias crouches likewise at 20.278, but *after* his shield resounds, pierced at its edge. Here Homer appends a variation on this, the noise when the spear grazes the shield-rim, evidently of bronze (409f.). A 'dry' grating sound is paralleled in Greek only by αὖον ἄϋσεν (441), when a spear pierces a bronze corslet, and αὖον ἀΰτευν (12.160), of helmets and shields under missile attack. αὐονή, usually 'dryness', means 'din' at Semonides frag. 7.20. Leumann (*MH* 14 (1957) 50f.) thinks popular etymology linked αὖον with ἀϋτέω, via αὔω, 'call': if so, καρφαλέον here is an adaptation. The spear 'runs over' into the next verse (410), which comes from scenes where spears do or do not fly in vain: with 403 and 410 cf. 4.496–8 = 15.573–5; with 404 and 410 cf. 503–5; with 410 cf. 5.18, 16.480, 21.590.

406–7 The basic construction of this shield – oxhides adorned or faced with bronze – is often presupposed (e.g. 804, 12.295ff., 20.275f.). A bed is δινωτός at 3.391 (where see n.); cf. the 'inlaid' chair at *Od.* 19.56 (δινωτὴν ἐλέφαντι καὶ ἀργύρῳ). The cognate Myc. forms *qe-qi-no-me-no* and *qe-qi-no-to* describe luxury furniture decorated with figures (Pylos, Ta series). Heubeck (*Kleine Schriften* 435–43) proposed as origin a verb meaning 'enliven (with figures)', from *$g^w i$- as in βίος; cf. the semantic evolution of ζωγραφέω. Here δινωτός probably means 'adorned' or 'faced' with leather and bronze, like the shield with bronze bosses and rim from Kaloriziki in Cyprus (*c.* 1100), or the eighth-century bronze-faced, single-grip round shield (Snodgrass, *EGA* 53 with pl. 19); but it may have been reinterpreted as 'decorated with concentric circles', like many eighth-century round shields (cf. the Introduction to the Shield of Akhilleus), or as 'turned (on the lathe)', cf. δῖνος, 'lathe' (so bT). — Its two 'rods' differ from the gold ῥάβδοι ('staples') round the rim of Sarpedon's circular shield, which is constructed likewise

(12.294–7). Nestor's shield has gold κανόνες at 8.193, but that is all we hear of them. A scholium on 8.193 (Porphyry/E⁴) suggests rods crossed in an X; a Geometric clay model of a Dipylon shield shows two double struts inside in an X-shape (Lorimer, *HM* pl. vii). The Myc. figure-of-eight shield, of which the Dipylon type is a dim recollection, had two struts crossed in a +, one vertical and one horizontal; the round single-grip type, standard from 1200–700 B.C., must have had two cross-struts (Snodgrass, *op. cit.* 46). As Idomeneus' shield is round and fitted with bronze, this type must be meant. We can exclude the arm-band and hand-grip of the hoplite shield, unknown until *c.* 700 (Snodgrass, *op. cit.* 65), or bars holding a wicker shield in shape (cf. Lorimer, *HM* 192–4). On ῥινοῖσι βοῶν see 16.635–7n.

411–12 Hupsenor son of Hippasos is surely pure invention in a context of proud warriors and charioteers. A Trojan Hupsenor dies at 5.76. Hippasos, whose name appears in inscriptions, begets other cannon-fodder – two Trojans and a Paeonian called Apisaon (11.426f., 17.348). Since 411f. = 17.348f. (but with καὶ βάλεν ... Ἀπισάονα), and, from ποιμένα, recur at 11.578f., of another Apisaon, the improvisation is palpable. Hoekstra (*Epic Verse before Homer* 63–6) argues that, like the Sikuonian horse-breeder Ekhepolos son of Ankhises (23.296–9), these figures derive from pre-migration tales of the N.E. Peloponnese, cf. Mt Apesas by Nemea; Ankhises' tomb was near Arcadian Orkhomenos (Paus. 8.12.8f.)! But Hupsenor, as Antilokhos' 'comrade' (419), may be a Pylian. πραπίδες = φρένες, 'lungs' (16.481n.).

413–16 Verse 413 = 445, 14.453, 14.478 (with different names); the latter cases, where verses equivalent to 417f. follow the boast, again belong to the pattern 'A kills B, C aims at A but kills D instead' (14.458–9n.). For ἔκπαγλος see 1.145–6n.; it is for *ἔκπλαγλος, cf. ἐκπλήσσω. The idea of a dead warrior going 'without recompense' recurs at 14.483f.; note Deïphobos' pun Asios–ἄτιτος. With 415 cf. εἰς Ἀΐδαο πυλάρταο (κρατεροῖο) at 8.367, *Od.* 11.277; πυλάρτης means 'gate-keeper', and is a name at 11.491, 16.696, cf. Myc. *Pu-ra-ta* (PY Jn 605). The usual escort of the dead was Hermes (*Od.* 24.1ff.).

419–23 Verse 419 expands ἀχνύμενός περ ἑταίρου (3×); cf. 8.330, 17.9f. It is standard to protect a body with one's shield. Verses 420–3 = 8.331–4 (where see n.), when the injured Teukros is taken away 'groaning heavily'; this phrase occurs in like contexts at 538, 14.432. Since Hupsenor is stone dead (402–23n.), his groans troubled the ancients. Aristarchus altered στενάχοντα (read by Zenodotus and the vulgate) to -οντε, so that the bearers groan instead (Arn, Did/A); a papyrus and some codices adopt this solution. Leaf excises 417–26. In fact, as Fenik says (*TBS* 132), the poet has been led astray by the type-scene he had in mind (perhaps anticipating 538), which does not quite fit its context; for similar resurrections see 643–59n. Such blunders decisively support Lord's view that the *Iliad* is an oral dictated text (see pp. 37–8 and D. M. Gunn, *AJP* 91 (1970) 192ff.); had Homer used writing to better his poem, he would surely have erased this error.

422 Omitted in MS A, 422 may well be a concordance-interpolation from 8.333; for another anonymous 'comrade' cf. 211–13n. If genuine, it prepares for these victims' deaths at 15.339 (cf. 478–80n.). Mekisteus and Alastor would be Pylians (cf. 4.295, *Cat.* 33.9); at 8.333 they were Aias' comrades, i.e. Salaminians. That they are mere pawns, manipulated to suit the poet, is proved by 15.339, where Mekisteus and Ekhios, the former's *father* here, are both slain (for a like discrepancy see 14.511–22n.). Another Ekhios is a Trojan (16.416); another Mekisteus is Adrestos' brother (2.565–6n.). An *E-ki-wo* is on Pylos tablet Jn 320. These names have sinister chthonic overtones; Mekisteus, 'giant', is from μήκιστος.

424–54 The fall of Alkathoos, Ankhises' son-in-law, parallels that of Othruoneus, son-in-law *manqué* of Priam, giving Idomeneus the last word in the series of vaunts (361–454n.). Since Alkathoos helped lead a Trojan column at 12.93, he is almost as important as Asios; both receive tree-similes (cf. 388). His obituary (428ff.) and the vivid account of his death (434ff.) follow Beye's tripartite structure, but 424–6 replace the initial death-notice (cf. 15.429–35n.). His 'biography' concerns his marriage, as often (170–81n.). After the bathos of Othruoneus' débâcle his fall restores this theme to its usual tragic level; his fearsome death increases the emotional impact.

424–6 That Idomeneus 'did not cease' from his *aristeia* prepares us for his retirement (512ff.); his resolve contrasts with Deïphobos' doubts (455–7). Readiness to do or die is normally asserted by characters at the end of speeches (326–7n.), not said of them by the poet. Linguistic oddities confirm that these verses are untraditional. The Aeolic formula ἐρεβεννῇ νυκτὶ καλύψαι (etc., 3×) is unique for 'kill' (cf. 12.116f.). δουπέω, 'die', recurs in δεδουπότος Οἰδιπόδαο | ἐς τάφον (23.679f.), *pace* Aristarchus, who held, against the Glossographoi, that it means 'crash ⟨and so die⟩', i.e. fall in war (on the Glossographers see Dyck, *HSCP* 91 (1987) 119–60, especially 138f.). Leumann deems it an epic adaptation of δούπησεν δὲ πεσών, misunderstood as 'he fell and died' (*HW* 215–17); but, as D suggest, it could be colloquial, like modern ψοφῶ, 'die', from 'thud', cited by D and first in Soph. *Ichn.* 168 (for semantic parallels see Shipp, *Vocabulary* 581f.). Note too the short dat. Ἀχαιοῖς | (Janko, *HHH* 54–7). λήγω, allegedly trans. as in the similar 21.305 and *Od.* 22.63, governs μένος as an *internal* acc. and is thus intrans. as usual.

427–33 There is pathos in the broken ties between the young man of promise, his talented bride and her doting parents; her virtues are canonical (cf. 1.115). A married daughter who is mentioned is always the eldest

(11.740, 21.142f.); it is still a Greek custom to marry off one's daughters in order of seniority (cf. Genesis 29.26). As often, Homer has taken minor figures from another cycle of legend; his invention glosses over the old tale of Ankhises' affair with Aphrodite (Severyns, *Homère* 76). One Alkathoos, son of Porthaon, was among the suitors of Hippodameia slain by Oinomaos (Hesiod frag. 259); another was Pelops' son ('Theognis' 774). Our Alkathoos' wife is a Hippodameia, and an Oinomaos is the next victim (506)! Thus Homer knew of the legend of Pelops. Hippodameia, supposedly daughter of an Eriopis here (T), has a common heroic name, e.g. 2.742; Briseis bears it in later sources (D on 1.392, Dictys of Crete etc.). But Aisuetes is of Asiatic origin. An Aisumnos is a Greek at 11.303, but Aisume is a town in the Troad (8.304) and the tomb of 'old Aisuetes' is a Trojan landmark (2.793); cf. αἰσυητήρ, 'prince' (24.347), no doubt an Anatolian loan-word like αἰσυμνήτης and other terms for 'ruler' (789–94n.; O. Szemerényi, *SMEA* 20 (1979) 217–20). — ἔνθ' and the accusatives of 427f. are resumed by τὸν τότε at 434 (Nic/A); cf. the oral anacoluthon at 16.401ff. With 427 cf. 12.355. Verses 428f. are curiously like 11.739f., another reminiscence of Elis! After 433 someone (in T) added

433a πρὶν Ἀντηνορίδας τραφέμεν καὶ Πανθόου υἷας
433b Πριαμίδας θ', οἳ Τρωσὶ μετέπρεπον ἱπποδάμοισιν
433c ἕως ἔθ' ἥβην εἶχεν, ὄφελλε δὲ κούριον ἄνθος.

The interpolator, disliking the praise of Alkathoos, explained that his superiority only lasted until the rest grew up; but Homer uses compliments freely, to heighten the pathos or heroic tone (cf. 365–7n.). The diction has late features. Πριαμίδης is never plur. (33× Hom.), the rest of 433b is a unique adaptation and κούριον ἄνθος is a post-Homeric phrase: cf. 481–4n. and κουρήϊον ἄ. (*HyDem* 108).

434–44 Of two fantastic events – Poseidon stupefies Alkathoos, whose heart's dying palpitations make Idomeneus' spear quiver along its length – the first is paralleled at 16.791ff. (Apollo stuns Patroklos), the second adapts the image of a spear quivering in the ground. Nobody has linked them, but surely Alkathoos' terrifying paralysis, stressed by the elaboration and imagery of 436f., has its equal and opposite reaction, obeying some supernatural law of physics, in the spear's bizarre motion.

434–6 Poseidon's sudden intervention, coming at the climax of Idomeneus' exploits, reminds us that the god's initiative caused his *aristeia* (see 206–45n. and Michel, *N* 62f.); it is not meant to obviate the implausibility that the middle-aged warrior achieves so much (*pace* bT). Like Athene's aid to Akhilleus (22.214ff.), this in no way lessens his valour, but confers on him divine approval, while Alkathoos' helplessness in the face of divine power arouses pathos (Michel, *N* 91). Poseidon is fully capable of 'magical' intervention: cf. his encouragement of the Aiantes or rescue of Aineias (59ff., 20.318ff.). That he bewitches Alkathoos' eyes means that he put him into a trance: cf. Patroklos' trance or Hermes who ὄμματα θέλγει (16.792ff., 24.3). So too Zeus 'bewitches' the Greeks' *thumos* (12.255, 15.594); Apollo uses the aegis to do the same (15.321f.). Alkathoos is not simply terrified like the driver at 394, to whom he is often likened (Fenik, *TBS* 133). His paralysis is prolonged, as if shown in slow motion, by the elaboration and enjambment of 436–9: for such slow-motion effects see on 16.114–18, 16.791ff. ὄσσε φαεινά is modified by declension and transposition from ὅ. φαεινώ | (6×): cf. ἄλκιμα δοῦρε (11.43). For the redundant phrasing in 436 cf. 12.327, *Od.* 20.368.

437 Alkathoos is fixed to the spot like a grave-stone or tree: cf. how warriors stand firm like trees, or horses stand ὥς τε στήλη (12.132ff., 17.434f.). Grave-stones on burial-mounds appear at 11.371, 16.457, 16.675, 23.329–31, *Od.* 12.14 (see M. Andronikos, *Arch. Hom.* w 32–4); Homer reflects Dark Age custom here (Morris, *Burial* 151–4). The double comparison is common (e.g. 39); its inclusion within the syntax of 438 is unusual. δένδρεον ὑψιπέτηλον (etc.) recurs at *Od.* 4.458, 11.588; the η is Ionicized from ᾱ after metrical lengthening, cf. πέτᾰλον.

438–41 Perhaps Alkathoos unwisely relied on his corslet alone, like Othruoneus and Asios' driver; we hear nothing of his shield. His cuirass is a χιτῶνα | χάλκεον, a unique and perhaps late remodelling of χαλκοχίτωνες, which is no doubt a Myc. epithet; the corslet may be of linen reinforced with bronze, or simply of bronze (see on 4.135f., 5.112f.). ἀπὸ χροὸς ἤρκει ὄλεθρον recurs in the aor. at 15.534 with the original sense of ἀρκέω, 'keep ⟨off⟩' (C. Watkins, *HSCP* 74 (1970) 66ff.); but 440 also varies 371f. and 397f., οὐδ' ἤρκεσε θώρηξ | χάλκεος. For αὖον ἄϋσεν cf. 404–10n.; ἐρείκω, 'shatter', 'split', rare in epos (17.295, *Aspis* 287), appears in tragedy and Ionic prose. περὶ δουρί means 'with the spear in it' (570–3n.).

442–3 This weird event is based on the typical detail of a spear thrown wide, which sticks in the ground so the butt-spike vibrates (cf. 502–5n.): thus at 16.610–13 = 17.526–9 the spear οὔδει ἐνισκίμφθη, ἐπὶ δ' οὐρίαχος πελεμίχθη, and the same verse as 444 follows. Cf. too 17.523f., when a spear quivers in a victim's entrails; but that is less odd than a heart in its death-throes (ἀσπαίρουσα, cf. 573) making the shaft palpitate, as if giving it its vital force. The butt-spike is called a σαυρωτήρ at 10.153; for finds of such objects see Snodgrass, *EGA* 133. πελέμιζεν, read by Aristophanes, Aristarchus (Did/A) and two good MSS, makes the miracle last longer than does the aor. -ιξεν; the variant is very old (p. 36 n. 70).

444 The μένος which Ares takes away is not Alkathoos' but the spear's; cf. Poseidon's action at 562f. Spears are imagined to have wills of their own and to be loth to stop; they 'long to be glutted with flesh' (11.574).

Griffin cites parallels from Near Eastern texts (*HLD* 33f.): weapons with strong characters appear in several epic traditions (Bowra, *Heroic Poetry* 149–54). We may dub this personification (Aristotle, *Rhet.* 3.1411b31ff.), but it amounts to animism: cf. the sword so carved as to seem driven into the living rock in the Hittite shrine at Yazılıkaya (MacQueen, *The Hittites* 130), and further Frazer on Paus. 9.40.11. Hoekstra (*Epic Verse before Homer* 68n.) rightly deems formulae entailing such beliefs highly archaic. See on 27–31, 502–5, 11.574, 14.402–8, 14.454–7, 15.313–17, 15.539–45; Stith Thompson D 1084; M. Kokolakis, *Museum Philologicum Londinense* 4 (1981) 89–113. Ares is treated here as an impersonal spirit of war, of which he is in origin a personification: see on 14.484f. and Erbse, *Götter* 166–8.

445 This verse echoes 413, but is not part of the larger pattern discussed *ad loc.* The repetition is deliberate: Idomeneus answers Deïphobos' boast (414ff.).

446–54 Idomeneus' vaunt is the climax of its series (361–454n.), a forceful retort and a further provocation, as his foe's reaction proves. His greater verbosity befits his importance, but may also characterize him as a trifle garrulous (246–97n.); he relates his genealogy unasked (so Eustathius 941.43). His speech consists of familiar motifs (Fenik, *TBS* 135): (i) a fair exchange of casualties: cf. 14.471f., ἦ ῥ' οὐχ οὗτος ἀνὴρ Προθοήνορος ἀντὶ πεφάσθαι | ἄξιος, or 17.538 – this answers 414; (ii) a challenge, cf. e.g. 810f., 6.143; (iii) declaring one's ancestry to the foe: cf. Glaukos and Aineias at 6.150ff., 20.213ff., responding to their opponents. Idomeneus is briefer, like Asteropaios or Akhilleus (21.153–60, 21.187–9), without the repeated verses used by Glaukos and Aineias. Diomedes tells the leaders his genealogy to bolster his authority (14.113–25); Idomeneus intends to make Deïphobos accept his challenge, but simultaneously to overawe him. (iv) The idea that one is an evil to the enemy also ends speeches at 3.160, 10.453, 22.288. Motifs (ii) and (iv) frame (iii), marked by ἐνθάδ' ἱκάνω and ἐνθάδε νῆες ἔνεικαν (449, 453), with (i) as an introduction (cf. Lohmann, *Reden* 13n.).

446–7 'Do we suppose that it is at all sufficient to have slain three in exchange for one? – since you boast in this way.' The three are Othruoneus, Asios and Alkathoos, in exchange for Hupsenor: Asios' driver, killed by Antilokhos, is conveniently ignored. Let Deïphobos now present himself as a fourth! Aristarchus (Did/A) rightly rejects the variant τί σ(οι) ἐΐσκομεν (from *Od.* 11.363?), which removes the hiatus before *ϝεϝίκ-σκω (Chantraine, *Dict.* s.v. ἔοικα). Its sense 'suppose' evolved from 'liken', 'think *p* like *q*', cf. *Od.* 11.363f. With ἄξιος cf. 8.234, οὐδ' ἑνὸς ἄξιοί εἰμεν, 'we are not even a match for one man', and 14.471f. (quoted above). Aristarchus and the vulgate read οὕτως, Zenodotus αὕτως, 'vainly' (Did/A), with a papyrus: cf. εὔχεαι αὔ., 11.388. The variation is common (*LfgrE* s.v. αὕτως D); Aristarchus follows the vulgate save at 810, Zenodotus does not (18.584, *Od.*

12.284). αὖ. is an alteration to evade the problem over Hupsenor – he was really only wounded, and Deïphobos' boast is vain (cf. 419–23n.).

448–9 δαιμόνιος, 'possessed by a *daimon*', is so weakened that anyone who acts oddly is thus addressed, e.g. even Here at 4.31; it often retains a trace of irony, as here or at 810 (*LfgrE* s.v.). All good MSS save A keep ἐναντίος, cf. ἀντίος ἵστασ' ἐμεῖο (17.31 = 20.197), ἐναντίοι ἔσταν Ἀχαιῶν (4×); the variant ἐναντίον is common (*LfgrE* s.v.). Zenodotus reads ἴδης, Aristarchus (Did/T) ἴδῃ, which is elided for, or contracted from, ἴδηαι (Chantraine, *GH* ɪ 57); this divergence is often recorded when ὄφρα ἴδῃ(ς) appears (7× Hom.). The best MSS have ἴδῃς save at 1.203; the Alexandrians wrongly standardize one way or the other.

449–54 When Idomeneus claims to be Zeus's γόνος, it sounds as if he is his son (cf. 5.635, Διὸς γόνον, of Sarpedon); he hastens to explain. For his genealogy cf. *Od.* 19.178ff., *Cat.* 204.56f. Minos was Zeus's son (14.322, *Od.* 11.568, *Cat.* 140f.); his weird kingship and family (already in Hesiod) somehow relate to the Minoan, and then Greek, rulers of Bronze Age Knossos. His son Deukalion has the same name as Prometheus' son, the first man, variously located in N. and central Greece (West on *Erga* 81); on this name, also borne by a Mycenaean soldier (PY An 654) and a Trojan, see 20.478n. So little is told of him in myth that he surely existed only to link the dimly remembered Minoan lords of Knossos with Idomeneus, its sole Greek king who entered legend: the fem. |Idomeneia| is attested at Pylos (Eb 498). His name derives from 'Ida', which never had a ϝ-.

Genealogy formed the basis of a whole epic genre, which Homer knew well (14.313–28n.). Hence the archaism ἐπίουρος, 'guardian' (also 2× *Od.*), may derive from it; cf. Myc. |opi ... (h)oromenos| (PY Ae 134), ἐπὶ ... ὄρονται (*Od.* 14.104), οὖρος Ἀχαιῶν (5× Hom.) and Chantraine, *Dict.* s.v. ὁράω. The resumption of Deukalion's name in 452 is also traditional: cf. 20.236f., Ἶλος δ' αὖ τέκεθ' υἱὸν ἀμύμονα Λαομέδοντα· | Λαομέδων ..., and 6.22f. But Ζηνός is an innovation (p. 18 n. 33). With 452 cf. 17.308, *Od.* 19.181 (cf. *Cat.* 144, of Minos); the novel πολέσσι, also at 17.236, replaces πολέ(ϝ)εσσι (as at 5.546), to allow its use after a fem. caesura (Hoekstra, *Modifications* 117f.). | Κρήτῃ ἐν εὐρείῃ is at *Theog.* 480, cf. *Od.* 13.256, 260. The ugly phrase καὶ πατρὶ καὶ ἄλλοισῖ Τρώεσσιν resembles Διὶ π. κ. ἄλλοις ἀθανάτοισι (818, 6.259), which Homer probably had in mind in this context.

455–539 Deïphobos obtains Aineias' help against Idomeneus; fierce fighting erupts over Alkathoos' body. Idomeneus retires exhausted; Deïphobos kills Ares' son Askalaphos but is wounded by Meriones and has to withdraw

455–539 Having given Idomeneus his glory, Homer arranges that he retire with honour. He now faces an enemy of equal rank, who has the advantage of youth; Hektor excepted, Aineias is the toughest foe he could meet. Even so, Deïphobos loses the spoils. His cast at the retreating Idomeneus (516f.) ends the second half of the latter's *aristeia*, which the Trojan had begun by going behind the lines to fetch Aineias; so too, by wounding Deïphobos, Meriones concludes their indecisive duel (156ff.), after which, by going behind the lines, he set in train his lord's entry into battle (Winter, *MNO* 83f.). This wounding also completes a ring-pattern among the Cretans' victims – Othruoneus (Priam's family), Asios, Alkathoos (Aineias' family), Oinomaos (Asios' follower), Deïphobos (Priam's family). Idomeneus' duel with Aineias also opens the indecisive fighting announced at 358–60, and waged by the warriors listed at 478f. and 490; his *aristeia* is so well integrated into its context that one cannot say whether it ends at 515, 525 or 539 (Michel, *N* 113–15). — This scene belongs to a set pattern (Fenik, *TBS* 24–6). (i) A Trojan gets help against a Greek, 455ff.; cf. 5.166–238, 12.310ff., 16.538ff., 17.483ff. (Hektor seeks Aineias). (ii) The Greek calls for help, 469ff.; cf. 5.239–74, 12.331ff., 16.553ff., 17.498ff. Only here are Trojan reinforcements gathered in response. (iii) The Trojans are beaten off, 489ff.; cf. 5.275ff., 12.370ff., 16.563ff., 17.516ff. On 502–39 see also 502–75n.

455–68 This passage consists of typical elements (Fenik, *TBS* 135). (i) Deïphobos ponders what to do; (ii) he finds Aineias, withdrawn from battle in anger at Priam; (iii) he spurs him to fight by telling him that his brother-in-law Alkathoos is dead.

455–8 There are set formulae for pondering (Arend, *Scenen* 106ff.; C. Voigt, *Überlegung und Entscheidung*, Berlin 1934). διάνδιχα μερμήριξεν also precedes a choice between two options at 1.189, cf. 8.167; 458 = 14.23, 16.652 (also 5× *Od.*). The old verb δοάσσετο, 'seemed', occurs outside this verse only at 23.339; cf. δέατο (*Od.* 6.242 and Arcadian dialect), δῆλος (Chantraine, *Dict.* s.v. δέατο). Only here is the first option chosen. When the choices are not stated, but someone decides how to proceed, we find instead ἥδε δέ οἱ (μοι) κατὰ θυμὸν ἀρίστη φαίνετο βουλή (8× epos; *Od.* 15.204 blurs the distinction). On the well-supported variant εἰ in 456 see on 2.299f.; Aristarchus read ἤ (Did/A). ἑτα(ι)ρίζομαι, here 'take as one's comrade', is rare (24.335, *HyAphr* 96); ἑταρ- is the older yet rarer form of this root in Homer (Chantraine, *Dict.* s.v.).

459–61 Aineias, leader of a Trojan column at 12.98f., has not appeared since; now that he is needed, his absence is explained – he was sulking over Priam's failure to show him due respect. Since we are not told how Priam is at fault, this must be an improvisation to explain why Aineias is behind the lines, like Idomeneus' wounded comrade at 211f. In fact it balances that scene, as Michel saw (*N* 93); thus 463 resembles 219, and 469 = 297. Cf. Poseidon's assumption that the Greeks are slacking from anger at Agamemnon, or Hektor's that Paris left battle in a huff (108ff., 6.325ff.), and of course the wrath of Akhilleus: Πριάμῳ ἐπεμήνιε δίῳ is like Ἀγαμέμνονι μήνιε δ. (18.257). Here too the hero returns when his φίλος is slain. A hero's angry withdrawal and return was a traditional topic; cf. Meleagros, or Demeter in the *Homeric Hymn* (M. L. Lord, *CJ* 62 (1967) 241–8; Erbse, *Hermes* 111 (1983) 3; Sowa, *Themes* 98ff.). Homer blends this with a tradition of two rival branches of the Trojan royal house (20.178ff., 302ff.). He portrays Aineias' family in a better light than Priam's. The contrast between Othruoneus and Alkathoos reflects upon the families admitting them as members by marriage; Aineias, not Deïphobos, saves the Trojans from disgrace.

Aineias' name may relate to the Thracian Αἰνειεῖς (Hipponax frag. 72.7), cf. the town Ainos and the northerners who took over Troy VIIb (West, *JHS* 108 (1988) 164); but it is common in inscriptions, and a derivative of αἰνέω is likelier (Nagy, *BA* 274f.; cf. too 481–4n.). On run-over ἑσταότα see 4.201–2n. The application of (ἐπι)μηνίω to Aineias and a beggar (*Od.* 17.14) weakens C. Watkins' idea (*Bulletin de la Société Linguistique de Paris* 72 (1977) 187–209) that μῆνις denotes *divine* wrath, and is used pointedly of the demigod Akhilleus (cf. Nagy, *BA* 73f.). Yet some modern survivals of the word keep this nuance, e.g. θεομηνία: cf. P. Considine in *Studies in Honour of T. B. L. Webster*, Bristol 1986, 1 53–64; Shipp, *Vocabulary* 388. μετ' ἀνδράσιν goes with ἐσθλὸν ἐόντα, not with τίεσκεν: cf. 15.611f., 16.492–501n.

463–7 Deïphobos' message, formulated for maximum effect, falls into two parts, with a call for action introduced by ἀλλά. Aineias, reminded of his responsibilities by the compliment βουληφόρε (219–20n.), hears that his brother-in-law needs to be defended, which could mean he is alive but in peril; εἴ πέρ τί σε κῆδος ἱκάνει hints at bad news, and κῆδος, elsewhere 'grief' (as in the same phrase at 15.245, 16.516), may play on the sense 'in-law', otherwise unattested before Aesch. and Hdt. Deïphobos reminds Aineias that Alkathoos reared him as a child – a further spur to action; he delays the news of his death to his last word.

ἐπαμύνομεν is a short-vowel subj.: the old variant -έμεν surely began as a copyist's error after ἀμυνέμεναι. Deïphobos tactfully includes himself in the exhortation (so bT). Ankhises' son-in-law lived at his house, like Priam's (174–6n.). Like Alkathoos himself, the detail that he reared Aineias was surely invented for its effect on the latter. Willcock thinks Alkathoos' role implies that Ankhises, who is oddly absent from the *Iliad*, is dead or disabled, no doubt because he divulged his liaison with Aphrodite, as she foresees at *HyAphr* 286–8 (differently P. Smith, *HSCP* 85 (1981) 49ff.); but a grandfather 'looks after' his grandson in the similar verse 11.223, although the boy's father is still alive. Perhaps Alkathoos merely took an avuncular interest in Aineias, as did Phoinix in Akhilleus (9.486ff.): for this weak sense of τρέφω cf. *Od.* 7.256. γαμβρός means 'brother-in-law', as at 5.474, *Cat.* 197.4f.: it originally denoted a sister's or daughter's spouse, just as Proto-Indo-European *nepots once meant a sister's or daughter's son (cf. *nephew*, Latin *nepos* and Chantraine, *Dict.* s.v. ἀνεψιός).

468 = 4.208, 11.804, followed by | βῆ ... | ἀλλ'; 469 = 297.

470–95 The build-up to Aineias' duel with Idomeneus is neatly structured:

A Idomeneus stands firm; simile of a boar at bay (470ff.)
B He calls for supporters; list of their names (477ff.)
C His speech asking for help (481ff.)
B' Aineias calls for supporters; list of their names (489ff.)
A' He leads on; simile of a ram and flock (492ff.).

'The similes at the start and finish establish antithesis, with the violence of the boar hunt set against the closing pastorale' (Fenik, *Homer and the Nibelungenlied* 37).

470 Some wondered how φόβος does not seize Idomeneus, when he admits to fear at 481; but it means 'flight' not 'fear' in Homer (so Aristarchus). He does not flee 'like a spoilt child'; such children are often timid (AbT). τηλύγετος (11× epos), used alone only here, must mean some such thing: see S. West on *Od.* 4.11; Richardson on *HyDem* 164; M. Janda, *Glotta* 66 (1988) 20–5. For other comparisons of warriors to children see 15.362–4n.

471–5 This simile resembles 11.414–18, 12.146–50, *Aspis* 386–91. As Fränkel saw (*Gleichnisse* 64), the crowd which the boar faces anticipates the comrades whom Aineias will summon; their presence in the simile makes Idomeneus' refusal to budge yet more impressive (note thrice-repeated μένω). The image of the boar, less fierce than the lion but brave in self-defence, is apt (so bT on 514f.); a lone warrior facing an enemy charge is often likened to a beast facing hunters (Fenik, *TBS* 99f.). The crowd of men frames the description of the boar; he prepares to resist by bristling up his neck and flashing his eyes (cf. *Od.* 19.446), but also by whetting his tusks, as boars were thought to do (Aelian, *NA* 6.1). — The monosyllable σῦς ending the third foot in 471 causes an extraordinary break, as if the boar crashes into the verse (cf. *Od.* 19.393 and 2×); Virgil recreates this effect at *Geo.* 4.407. As usual, several phrases appear in other similes; these are surely formulae which happen to be rare in the extant epos. κύνας ἠδὲ (τε) καὶ ἄνδρας (etc.) appears 4× in similes, as does ἀλκὶ πεποιθώς: one expects this to be useful in war, but it recurs only at 18.158, yet μεῖναι ἐπερχόμενον (etc.) occurs 4× in battles only. χώρῳ ἐν οἰοπόλῳ reappears at 17.54 (simile), but belongs to a larger system: cf. χ. ἐνὶ προαλεῖ (21.262, simile) and περισκέπτῳ ἐνὶ χ. (4× *Od.*). On the old words κολοσυρτός and οἰόπολος, 'lonely', see

Chantraine, *Dict.* s.vv. φρίσσει is intrans., νῶτον an internal acc. The dual ὀφθαλμώ recurs at 9.503 only. λάμπετον is unique; for the bold metaphor cf. ὄσσε δέ οἱ πυρὶ λαμπετόωντι ἔϊκτην (1.104 = *Od.* 4.662). ἀλέξασθαι, younger than ἄλαλκον, is older than ἀλεξῆσαι (*LfgrE* s.v.).

476–7 Eustathius (942.58) saw word-play in μένεν Ἰδομενεύς. The contraction in οὐδ᾽ ὑπεχώρει recurs at 22.96, after a simile; the phrase turns out to be parenthetical, since μένεν governs Αἰνείαν. T think πόδας ταχύν, in the similar 482, paraphrases βοηθόον, but this must be pointed, 'coming to ⟨Deïphobos'⟩ rescue'. Derived from ἐπὶ βοὴν θεῖν, 'run to the cry for help' (Chantraine, *Dict.* s.v. βοή), its rarity suggests a recent creation; it recurs at 17.481, where Aristarchus (Did/T) rejected the reading βοῇ θοόν.

478–80 This list of warriors blends the captains of the guard at 9.82f., Ἀσκάλαφον καὶ ... | ... Μηριόνην Ἀφαρῆά τε Δηΐπυρόν τε, with Poseidon's audience at 92–4 (=478–80, from Δ.). Ares' son Askalaphos, with his brother Ialmenos, leads the Orkhomenians (2.512n.). His name means 'owl', his brother's perhaps 'pouncer'; cf. Otos, 'long-eared owl', and his brother Eph*ial*tes, who bind Ares at 5.385 (von Kamptz, *Personennamen* 273f.). Sinister nocturnal predators might well be linked with the war-god! Another Askalaphos was a demon whom Demeter turned into an ὦτος ('Apollodorus' 2.5.12; Ovid, *Met.* 5.538–50). Since later sources say Askalaphos did not die at Troy (Kullmann, *Quellen* 70f., cf. p. 371 below), Homer has innovated to stress his cardinal theme of the gulf between mortals and gods. Aphareus is Kaletor's son (541); T *ad loc.* claim he is akin to Nestor. His name occurs on Knossos tablet B 804. On Deïpuros see 91–4n. All three are introduced to provide cannon-fodder for the next hundred verses, and are slain in the order in which they are listed; Meriones and Antilokhos are reintroduced to replace Idomeneus. Such lists often adumbrate the narrative structure, and were surely a device to help the bard create and recall it; thus most of the Trojan leaders catalogued at 12.91ff. are slain in books 13–16. ἐσορῶν, with Ionic ἐσ- and contraction, recurs at 490, 3× *Od.*; contrast εἰσορόων (49×). — Verse 480 = 94. Absent in two early papyri, it is present in three later ones and all codices; T say many texts lacked it. It is a concordance-interpolation from 94 to supply a speech-introduction that is not needed, like 218a, 10.191, 17.219 or 21.73 (Apthorp, *MS Evidence* 150–2).

481–6 For parallels to this call for help see 455–539n.; cf. too 11.461ff., when Odysseus αὖε δ᾽ ἑταίρους and is likened to a lone beast at bay, or 17.110–22, when Menelaos, recipient of a like comparison, seeks help to rescue a body. Idomeneus is realistic about his foe's superiority and the reason for it; the end of his speech reverts to its beginning – the idea of fighting alone.

481–4 δείδια δ᾽ αἰνῶς | Αἰνείαν plays on the name's folk-etymology, as is proved by *HyAphr* 198f., Αἰνείας ὄνομ᾽ ἔσσεται οὕνεκά μ᾽ αἰνὸν | ἔσχεν ἄχος (for its true origin see 459–61n.). The generic formula πόδας ταχύν (249–50n.), applied to Aineias here only, is apt; Idomeneus calls him 'swift of foot' because he himself is not (cf. 515) and cannot escape, as his urgent repetition ἐπιόντα... ἔπεισιν stresses (Eustathius 943.6f.). With 483 cf. 1.178. ἔχει ἥβης ἄνθος, a metaphor that was formular later, was perhaps a cliché of erotic poetry: cf. ἄ. ἔχοντ᾽ ἐρικυδέος ἥ. (*Theog.* 988, cf. *HyHerm* 375); ἥ. ἀγλαὸν ἄ. ἔχῃ (Tyrtaeus frag. 10.28, cf. Theognis 1007f., Simonides frag. 8.6 West); and ἥ. ἄ., 7× in elegy and early verse-inscriptions (cf. 427–33n.). The reading ὅτε, 'youth, *when* one's might is greatest', is refuted by the parallel at 9.39, 'valour, *which* (ὅ τε) is the greatest might'; the relative agrees with its complement, not its antecedent (cf. 15.37). Nestor too equates youth and strength (7.157).

485–6 'Were we the same age with our feelings as they are, at once ⟨we would fight, and⟩ one of us would win': for the ellipse cf. 18.307f. The nom. ὁμηλικίη stands for ὁμήλικες, just as we say A is 'the same age' as B: cf. *Od.* 3.49, 3.364, 6.23, 22.209. The idiom was badly understood. Zenodotus and a papyrus read -ίην; Aristarchus, with a papyrus and some MSS, apparently read -ίη (Did/AT), and *Od.* 3.364 has the same variants. For ἐνί he, πᾶσαι and MS A offer ἐπί (cf. *Od.* 16.99, 24.511), but this expresses cumulation, cf. σοί γ᾽ ἐπὶ εἴδεϊ καὶ φρένες (*Od.* 17.454); the vulgate always has ἐνί (cf. van der Valk, *Researches* II 104–6).

487–90 Like *Theog.* 239, 487 blends ἕνα θυμὸν ἔχοντες (etc., 4×) with ἐνὶ φρεσὶ θυμός (etc., 5× Hom.). Verse 488 = 11.593, where see n.; this defensive posture forms a firm front line. With 489 cf. 15.501. Deïphobos, who asked Aineias for help at 463, is now called on by him in turn; bT detect a reproach for his backwardness. Paris and Agenor led the same column as Alkathoos (12.93), whose body they are defending; on them see on 3.16, 3.122–4 and I. Espermann, *Antenor, Theano, Antenoriden*, Meisenheim 1980.

492–5 Aineias leads his men as a ram leads its flock to drink after feeding, but he then becomes a shepherd who is glad at the sight (Fränkel, *Gleichnisse* 6f.); this shift makes him leader of the leaders (bT), a 'shepherd of the people'. The peaceful simile reflects the two sides' equilibrium, complementing the preceding violent simile where one opponent faces many (470–95n.). A κτίλος, originally 'tame (animal)' from κτι- (Chantraine, *Dict.* s.v.), is a bell-wether, the ram trained to lead his flock: cf. Quint. Smyrn. 1.175; Thompson, *CR* 46 (1932) 53f. The Kuklops' ram is such a beast, first to crop the grass or reach the river (*Od.* 9.449ff.); getting the flock to water after grazing is important. Priam likens the reliable Odysseus to a κτίλος (3.196); cf. 2.480f., Agamemnon as bull of the herd. No doubt the Trojans also resemble sheep because of their noise, as at 4.433ff. ἕσπετο μῆλα is at 4.476; with πιόμεν᾽ ἐκ βοτάνης, 'from pasture to drink', cf. *Od.* 10.159f. Aristarchus took ἐκ as 'after', adducing the idiom ἐξ ἀρίστου παρέσομαι, but in Homer this usage is limited to the weather (16.364–5n.). With the rest of 493 cf. γέγηθε δέ τε φρένα ποιμήν (8.559, simile). λαῶν ἔθνος is unique: cf. ἔ. ἑταίρων or ἔθνεα πεζῶν (11.724). ἑοῖ for οἷ, an epic creation by analogy with (ἐ)μοι and (ἑ)ός (Shipp, *Studies* 77), is confined to this phrase: cf. *Od.* 4.38, σπέσθαι ἑοῖ αὐτῷ; 643f., ἕποντο ... ἑ. α.; and ἑέ (20.171, 24.134). The scansion ἐπισπόμενόν ἑοῖ, as if ἑοῖ once began with ϝ- as οἷ did, is amply paralleled in ἑός (p. 13).

496–501 The battle has escalated to a mass combat at close quarters (for αὐτοσχεδόν see 322–5n.); against this background Aineias and Idomeneus are highlighted. The phrase α. ὡρμήθησαν (dual at 17.530) opens the fight over the next body at 526, and the ensuing scene too (559, σχεδὸν ὁρμηθῆναι; with 560 cf. 498). ξυστόν (6×) is a metrically useful synonym for δόρυ; both terms describe the spear's shaft of polished wood. κονάβιζε (4×) and κονάβησε are epicisms fossilized with σμερδαλέον (13× epos).

499–501 Just as ἀλλήλων, repeated at 501, evoked ἔξοχον ἄλλων (9× Hom.), so the unique ἄνδρες ἀρήϊοι suggested the comparison with Ares. Both warriors have received similes; now both are equated with a god, so superior are they to the rest. Cf. 16.751–61, where Hektor and Patroklos, each with a lion-simile, are δύω μήστωρες ἀϋτῆς; 761 = 501, introducing their duel. ἀτάλαντοι Ἄρηϊ, sing. elsewhere (10×), displaces Ἰδομενεύς from his usual positions, so that 500 is a rising threefolder. πᾶσαι (Did/AT) rejected the well-supported 'improvement' ἔξοχοι (cf. *Od.* 21.266).

502–75 The massed battle, which continues throughout (cf. 540), forms the setting of two similar combats; 506–39 follow the pattern of 169–205, where see n. (cf. Fenik, *TBS* 136–44). The Greeks keep the advantage (Trojans are italicized):

A 1. *Aineias* casts at Idomeneus but misses (502–5).
   2. Idomeneus kills *Oinomaos*, but fails to strip him and retreats (506–15).
   3. *Deïphobos* casts at Idomeneus but kills Askalaphos instead (516–25).
   4. Meriones wounds *Deïphobos*, advances and plucks out his spear (526–39).
B 1. *Aineias* slays Aphareus (541–4).
   2. Antilokhos kills *Thoon*, strips him and retreats (545–59).
   3. *Adamas* casts at Antilokhos, but his spear fails to penetrate (560–6).
   4. Meriones slays *Adamas*, advances and plucks out his spear (567–75).

The three Trojan dead, listed at 12.140 as followers of Asios, die in the reverse order. The language is traditional, as one expects given the lack of speeches in 487–725 (620–39 excepted); as Aristotle tells us (*Poet.* 1460a5ff.), speeches were Homer's greatest glory *vis-à-vis* the Cycle (see further vol. II, 28–33).

502–5 The pattern 'A throws at B but misses, and B kills C' is standard (e.g. 17.304–13, where 305 = 503 and 314f. = 507f.). Aristophanes (Did/ AT) conjectured πρόσθεν, no doubt claiming that to be πρῶτος you cannot be one of two; but π. ἀκόντισε recurs at 14.402, 16.284. For 503 see 183– 4n. The motif of a stray spear sticking in the ground recurs at 16.608–13 (Aineias misses Meriones: 503 = 16.610), and at 17.525–9, 22.273–6 (cf. 21.171f.); for weird variations see 442–3n. κατὰ γαίης means 'down into the earth' (cf. 11.358). That the spear 'leapt from his hand' is more than 'personification' (444n.).

506–9 Idomeneus missed Aineias (cf. 501); to stress the Greek success, the poet leaves this unsaid, yet states that Aineias missed *him* (cf. 16.462– 75n.). On Oinomaos see 427–33n.; a Greek so named dies at 5.706 with an Orestes, the name of another follower of Asios (12.139)! For γύαλον see 15.530–4n. With 'the bronze made the entrails gush through' cf. 14.517, *Od.* 19.450: ἀφύσσω is used of drawing wine from a cask. The rest of 508 (5×) describes the next victim (520), who is slain to avenge this one. Fallen warriors grasp at the soil (392–3n.); for ἀγοστός and the 'long-shadowed' spear see on 11.425, 3.346–7.

510–15 Idomeneus' growing exhaustion is conveyed by the declining scale of actions he can perform – strip a corpse, charge, fetch his spear or avoid another's; this arouses our sympathy. But he can still defend himself in the *stadiē* (312–14n.): his feet, no longer swift in flight (which saves him from that disgrace), carry him back step by step as if of their own will (cf. 15.405n.). All this preserves his dignity in retreat. Verses 510f. = 5.621f. The periphrasis γυῖα ποδῶν looks like a survival of the original sense of γυῖα, 'joints', inferred from its root γυ- (cf. 146–8n.). At 23.627, οὐ γὰρ ἔτ' ἔμπεδα γυῖα, φίλος, πόδες (Nestor speaking) is even odder. τρέσσαι means, as usual, 'flee in fear', e.g. 5.256 (so Aristarchus).

516–17 Deïphobos, still smarting from Idomeneus' taunt (446ff.), takes advantage of his retreat to have another try (cf. 650, 14.409, 14.461). Even so, he misses again, as at 404, the incident to which 'even then' refers (518). As is shown by ἔμμενες αἰεί (5× Hom.), a κότος is a grudge, more lasting than χόλος, but its cause lies within the present battle. βάδην, a Homeric *hapax*, was current later (LSJ s.v.); the rest of 516 = 14.461.

518–20 With 518 cf. 8.311. Verses 519f. = 14.451f., where Areïlukos replaces Enualios; cf. 508 and 4.481f., δι' ὤμου χάλκεον ἔγχος | ἦλθεν· ὁ δ' ἐν κονίῃσι χαμαὶ πέσεν. Wounds in the shoulder are usually fatal, unrealistically (5.46n., with parallels). Verbal associations are important in oral composition. Here Enualios evoked ὄβριμον ἔγχος (292–4n.) via ὄβριμος Ἄρης, which soon appears at 521: next, Meriones is compared to Ares (527); then ὄβριμον ἔ. recurs (532)! For Askalaphos see 478–80n.

521–5 The picture of Ares on Olumpos, ignorant of his son's demise, prepares for 15.110–42, when he learns of it from Here, but is dissuaded from intervening against Zeus; it also contrasts with Poseidon's vigorous reaction to his grandson's death (with 522 cf. 207). bT note the irony that Ares' son is slain by the Trojans, whom Ares supports. Verses 521–5 presuppose Zeus's prohibition of the other gods from battle (8.10ff.). ἐελμένος means only that fear of Zeus kept Ares there, as at 15.110ff. (Michel, *N* 63f.). The motif of a god detained on Olumpos is traditional: cf. *HyAp* 97ff., οὐκ ἐπέπυστο μογοστόκος Εἰλείθυια. | ἦστο γὰρ ἄκρῳ Ὀλύμπῳ ὑπὸ χρυσέοισι νέφεσσιν, | Ἥρης φραδμοσύνης ... The clouds explain why Ares cannot see, as at 5.344–6, 14.343–51 (another golden one: cf. 18.205f.). Short summaries of the divine situation are typical, providing a useful reminder of the background (345–6on.); typical too is the glimpse of characters who are absent and unknowing but deeply affected by the action, cf. 674–6, 1.488–92, 11.497f., 17.377–83n., 17.401ff., 22.437–65.

βριήπυος ὄβριμος Ἄρης is a unique expansion of ὄ. Ἄ. (6×), cf. β. οὔλιος Ἄ. (*Cat.* 10a.69), the other instance of β. in Greek. This alliterative formula belongs to Ares' rather undeveloped epithet-system, with the same shape as Ἄ. ἆτος πολέμοιο, which starts with a vowel (Parry, *MHV* 55); it embodies the archaism ἠπύω, 'call' (p. 11), but also the recent scansion ∪ βρι-. On Ares' 'heavy' voice, which echoes the din of war, cf. 5.859–61n. For the retention of old datives like χρυσέοισι νέφεσσι see p. 19 n. 35. ἄλλοι | ἀθάνατοι θεοί adapts ἀ. θ. ἄλλοι | (9× Hom.), as is betrayed by the bouncing word-end after the second foot.

526–39 The rapid formular narrative emphasizes Deïphobos' withdrawal, which is no less sudden and poetically just than Idomeneus' was gradual and dignified; two short comparisons build Meriones up. Deïphobos' wounding is typical (Fenik, *TBS* 40, 139f.). Trying to strip an enemy (cf. 4.467ff. etc.), he grabs at the helmet, like Hektor at 188f., but drops it, as others drop the body they are dragging (4.493, 16.577, 17.298f.); this stresses his failure. His removal by chariot to Troy is like Hektor's (536–8 = 14.430–32); his groans contrast with his swaggering entry at 156–8. Fenik compares the wounding of Aphrodite (5.330ff.).

526–30 Verse 526 echoes 496. With πήληκα φαεινήν cf. 802–5n.; with ἀτάλαντος Ἄρηϊ cf. 295–7n. αὐλῶπις τρυφάλεια is an odd formula too, cf. 16.795, 5.182 (dat. with τε), 11.352f. (separated): see on 132–3, 5.182–3. For the rest of 530 cf. 16.118, *Od.* 18.397; fallen objects rolling noisily on the battlefield are a topos (579, 11.147, 14.411, 16.117f., 16.794).

531–3 Meriones is like an αἰγυπιός because of his speed in darting after his spear; cf. 'like *swift* Ares' (528). This bird, distinct from the vulture proper (γύψ), is closer to the eagle in its habits. The bearded vulture or 'Lämmergeier', largest of all Mediterranean raptors, is the best identification (cf. 7.59–6on. and Pollard, *Birds* 79f.). J. M. Boraston, *JHS* 31 (1911) 229–34, compares 'lamb-vulture' with 'goat-vulture' – it eats ovicaprids;

on the form cf. J. Manessy-Guiton, *Annales de la Faculté des lettres et sciences humaines de Nice* 50 (1985) 139–47. Hawks or eagles are usual in similes describing speed in attack, but cf. 17.460, *Od.* 22.302–6; αἰγυπιοί appear in a different context at 16.428f. It seems odd that Meriones darts forward twice, and does not simply puncture his foe, extract his spear and retreat; the poet reran the action to include this second comparison, which implicitly likens Deïphobos to the bird's prey. πρυμνοῖο βραχίονος means the upper arm by the shoulder, as at 16.323 (acc.); hence at 539 χείρ means arm, not hand – a clear case of that sense (cf. 383–5n.). ἂψ (δ᾿) ἑτάρων εἰς ἔθνος ἐχάζετο occurs 7× with κῆρ᾿ ἀλεείνων, including 566, 596 and 648, but without it only at 165, also of Meriones; it is used of warriors who are injured or will be slain (Fenik, *TBS* 140). That Meriones is the exception confirms that this scene evokes 156ff.

533–9 The pace slows as Deïphobos is carted back to Troy. The more dignified withdrawal of Odysseus, with perhaps a worse wound, is narrated in only two verses; even Agamemnon does not groan (11.487f., 280ff.). Cf. 419–23n. and Michel, *N* 106f. This is Polites' début, 2.791 excepted, when Iris takes his shape. He is again fighting on foot at 15.339, and reappears with Deïphobos at 24.250. His name, 'Townsman', recurs at *Od.* 10.224. For ἐξῆγεν πολέμοιο Homer could have said -ε πτ-, but the Ionic remedy came to mind more readily (p. 9 n. 6). For δυσηχής see 2.686n. From ὄφρα, 535–8 = 14.429–32. These verses end with formulae but are not wholly traditional: note ἵππους | ὠκέας beside ὠ. ἵ. | (20× Hom.), and the rare νεούτατος (18.536, 2× *Aspis*). ἅρματα denotes a single chariot, as often; since /harmo/ meant 'wheel' in Myc., its plur. once meant 'wheels', i.e. *one* chariot (Ventris and Chadwick, *Documents* 372).

540–672 Indecisive and bloody warfare, in which the Greeks keep the upper hand

540–672 The brief Trojan victories of Aineias, Helenos and Paris (541–4, 576–80 and 660–72) articulate this apparently amorphous fighting. The Trojans are now on the attack, but their inferiority even against minor Greek warriors is shown by the lesser number and elaboration of their successes and their failure to strip any corpses. Yet Menelaos' passionate denunciation of their persistence (framed by Greek victories) dispels any impression that the Achaeans are having an easy time, and the scene ends with the death of the most important Greek to fall, Eukhenor. Menelaos stops the Trojan attack less definitively than Aineias had halted Idomeneus' (Winter, *MNO* 100). On the structure of 540–75 see 502–75n.; for 540 cf. 169n.

541–4 Aphareus (478–80n.) is slain facing Aineias, unlike Thoon who turns to flee, presumably in fright at the casualty by his side (on neck-wounds see 383–8n.). The diction is unusual. Aristarchus (Did/AT) and several good MSS read ἔνθ' Αἰνέας for the unmetrical vulgate ἔ. Αἰνείας; others (a papyrus included) read Αἰνείας (δ'), but a like Ionic innovation is seen in Ἑρμέᾳ (5.390). The variants go back to a misreading of ΑΙΝΕΑΣ (p. 34). ἐκλίνθη δ' ἑτέρωσε κάρη blends ἐ. δ' ἐ. (*Od.* 22.17, of Antinoos' head, cf. 19.470) with ἐ. κ. βάλε, 8.306. Here ἐ. means 'backwards', in the opposite direction to the origin of the blow (cf. 14.18). From ἀσπίς to οἱ, 543f. = 14.419f. (but 420 is spurious). The chilling θάνατος χύτο θυμοραϊστής recurs at 16.414, 16.580, cf. 16.591, 18.220: for the adj. cf. Chantraine, *Dict.* s.v. ῥαίω. ἐάφθη, unique save for 14.419, is obscure (*LfgrE* s.v. αφθῆναι); the context suggests 'fell'. Meister (*Kunstsprache* 110n.) derives it from ἰάπτω, 'throw'; cf. Peters, *Laryngale* 101n.

545-7 Antilokhos, reintroduced at 479, continues the massacre of Asios' followers (502-75n.). Thoon is a common heroic name: cf. 5.152, 11.422 (Trojans), *Od.* 8.113. φλέψ is unique in the epos. Since no blood-vessel runs straight up the back through the neck, this 'vein' is usually deemed a Homeric fantasy (Friedrich, *Verwundung* 43); but it reflects ancient belief. 'Hippocrates' mentions veins running from the nape down the spine (6.58, 6.282, 9.186-90 Littré); some thought veins ran down the spinal marrow (Aristotle, *Hist. An.* 3.512b2). Aristotle (*ibid.* 3.513b26) and bT identify this vessel as the *vena cava*, but it is surely the spinal chord; for another problem with the spinal column cf. 20.482f., where it spurts marrow when the head is cut off. See A. Kerkhoff, *RhM* 124 (1981) 193-5. For ἀπό, in all sources including Aristotle and a papyrus, Zenodotus read διά (Did/AT): this is conjecture – cf. 548 and λαιμὸν ἀπαμήσειε (18.34), of cutting one's throat.

548-9 Thoon lands on his back with his feet towards his comrades. Aristarchus often noted whether victims fall into the blow or away from it, depending on whether they fall because of the blow's force or its bodily results (Arn/A on 4.108, 4.463, 5.58, 5.68, 11.144); here he said that Thoon fell in the direction whence the blow came, because, with the 'vein in his back' severed, his νεῦρον (spinal cord?) no longer supported him. Fenik (*TBS* 142) wrongly judges his fall impossible. His pathetic despairing gesture is typical (cf. 4.522n., 14.495f., 21.115f.).

550-9 The slow retreat of the lone Antilokhos to safety, assailed by Trojans on three sides, is a topos (Fenik, *TBS* 98, 232): we never see the reverse, a lone Trojan retreating from many Greeks, nor is the Greek ever slain; he often receives a simile or utters a monologue. Here Homer refers instead to Poseidon's protection of his descendant, which reminds us of the god's role in sustaining the Achaeans (cf. 434, 563).

550-3 With 550 cf. 11.580; the imperf. αἴνυτο is used like an aor. (cf. 4.531). Hoekstra (*Epic Verse before Homer* 21f.) shows that the various phrases for stripping armour form a system admirably useful for oral verse-making.

περισταδόν is an epic *hapax* (cf. περίσταιεν of an ambush, *Od.* 20.50); Zenodotus and Aristophanes (Did/A) read παρασταδόν, no doubt from 15.22, but this is used of standing near someone to address him (3× *Od.*). For σάκος εὐρύ cf. 608, 17.132, *Od.* 22.184. Only here and at *Aspis* 139 is a shield παναίολον (but cf. 11.374): this epithet describes a ζωστήρ 4×. εἴσω means 'within' his shield. For τερένα χρόα (3× *Il.*, 2× Hes.) cf. 830–2n.

554–5 Antilokhos is called Nestor's son to show that Poseidon is protecting his great-grandson, since the god begat Neleus (*Od.* 11.254, *Cat.* 30–3). Hence Poseidon taught him horsemanship and is honoured at Pylos (23.306f., *Od.* 3.5f.), where the tablets confirm his special status in Mycenaean times. The formula Νέστορος υἱός (etc.) is transposed from the second foot (4× Hom.) or verse-end (10×), causing an ugly break after the second trochee. T think καὶ ἐν πολλοῖσι βέλεσσιν refers to other battles, since this one is at close quarters: but the Trojans are also hurling spears, as Antilokhos considers doing at 559.

556–9 ἄνευ δηΐων means simply 'without enemies', not 'away from' like ἄνευθεν (*LfgrE* s.v.); the struggle is seen through Antilokhos' eyes. For the contraction in στρωφᾶτο see p. 17 n. 29. ἔχε is intrans. – 'his spear held steady'. ἐλέλικτο is here correctly from ἐλελίζω, 'shake': contrast 11.39. τιτύσκομαι, supposedly 'think' here and at *Od.* 8.556 (Chantraine, *Dict.* s.v.), surely means 'aim' metaphorically in both verses; it has its literal sense in 560. For 559f. cf. 496–501n.

560–75 As Fenik saw (*TBS* 143f.), the killing of Asios' son Adamas, which resembles how Meriones wounded Deïphobos (502–75n.), itself sets the pattern for his dispatch of Harpalion (643–55). Antilokhos and Menelaos have each slain an enemy; a would-be avenger vainly hits the Greek's shield (with 561f. cf. 646f.) and retreats (566 = 648, cf. 14.408); Meriones then casts or shoots (with 567 cf. 650, 14.409), fatally wounding his foe below the belt. Similes adorn both combats. Meriones' reappearances bind the narrative together.

561 ὅ οἱ is Bentley's emendation, supported by a papyrus, of the vulgate ὅς οἱ (cf. Aristarchus' text at *Od.* 1.300). Neglect of ϝ- in the enclitic οἱ is rare (163–5n.), but is paralleled after ὅς in our MSS at 6.90, 4× *Od.*: see further Chantraine, *GH* 1 147f.; West on *Erga* 526. μέσον σάκος (6×) thrice precedes οὔτασε δουρί (cf. especially 15.528f.), whence the variant δ. here; ὀξέϊ δ. (11×) is often equivalent to ὁ. χαλκῷ (25×), but the latter can also describe swords.

562–3 ἀμενήνωσεν is a *hapax* based on ἀμενηνός; like Ares at 444 (where see n.), Poseidon took away the spear's μένος. This varies the standard ἀνεγνάμφθη δέ οἱ αἰχμή (3×), to stress that he is still concerned with the battle. Gods ward off blows at 4.130 (Athene), 8.311, 15.521 (Apollo). κυανοχαῖτα, also nom. at 14.390, was originally voc., as at 15.174, 15.201,

Od. 9.528, *Hy.* 22.6; such ancient epithets often came to be felt as nominatives, cf. μητίετα, νεφεληγερέτα, ἀκάκητα. Risch (*Wortbildung* 37f.) adduces Latin *Iuppiter*, but the phenomenon extends beyond divine epithets, and a metrically convenient voc. often replaces a nom. in South Slavic epic (cf. 16.20n.). This adj. also describes horses (20.224, *Thebaid* frag. 7 B. = 6 D.) and the god Hades (*HyDem* 347). No doubt it once meant 'dark-*maned*', with reference to Poseidon's hippomorphic tendencies: cf. the implications of βοῶπις and γλαυκῶπις for Here and Athene. κύανος, 'blue glass' in Myc., is a Levantine loan-word (R. Halleux, *SMEA* 9 (1969) 46–66). βιότοιο μεγήρας means 'grudged (him Antilokhos') life': μεγαίρω also takes a gen. at 4.54.

564–6 Part of Adamas' spear pierces the shield and hangs there (αὐτοῦ); the rest drags on the ground. In the parallel death of Harpalion, the spear simply fails to penetrate (647). A σκῶλος (a *hapax*) is that most primitive weapon, a spike with one end charred to harden it, cf. σκόλοψ and the 'fire-sharpened' stake which blinds the Kuklops (see Heubeck on *Od.* 9.328); rustics used them as spears (AbT). With ὥς τε σκῶλος ... | ... ἐπὶ γαίης | cf. 654, ὥς τε σκώληξ ἐ. γαίη; the echo proves that its sound and syntax persisted in the bard's mind for 90 verses (Ruijgh, τε *épique* 575n.). πυρίκαυστος is also a *hapax*. For 566 cf. 531–3n.

567–9 Meriones is accused of perpetrating the worst wounds in the *Iliad*; of four injuries in the groin, at 4.492, 5.66, here and 651, he inflicts the last three. But, as Michel says (*N* 108–10), wounds usually reflect on the victim, not the victor: boasters like Asios are struck in the throat, and the fool Peisandros loses his eyes (383–8, 609–10nn.). By the laws of heroic society, Asios' son should pay for his father's misdeeds (although 569 adds pathos): thus Phereklos, whom Meriones slays at 5.66, is doomed as the son of the man who built Paris' fateful ships, and Harpalion is Paris' guest-friend (661). Also, both Adamas and Harpalion are cowards: note ἀπιόντα in 567 (cf. 649). ὀϊζυροῖσι βροτοῖσι recurs at *Od.* 4.197 in an equally grim context, but whether it is pointed or the standard formula for 'men' is not clear. Its sole equivalent is ἐπιχθονίοισι β. in *Homeric Epigram* 10, but the existence of μερόπεσσι β. beside δειλοῖσι β. in the *Iliad* suggests that bards had alternative formulae for 'men', one neutral, the other tinged with sorrow.

570–3 Adamas, who was followed (μετασπόμενος) by Meriones, now struggles as he *follows* his foe's tugs on the spear, just as a bull struggles as it *is led* by the cowherds who have hobbled it. περὶ δουρί means 'with the spear inside him': cf. 441, 8.86, *Od.* 11.424. At 12.395 ὁ δ' ἑσπόμενος πέσε δ. is simpler, as the spear is pulled out. The old variant δὲ σχόμενος, 'held', emends the 'problem' away. ἑσπόμενος is an old reduplicated form, < *se-sk^w- (Chantraine, *GH* 1 395). The bull is wild, as οὔρεσι shows (bT); cf. the scenes on the gold cups from Vapheio. For the end of 571 cf. 390;

Book Thirteen

βουκόλος is already in Myc. as /g^woukolos/. ἱλλάς, 'rope', a *hapax* in Greek, is from εἰλέω, 'twist' (Chantraine, *Dict.* s.v. 2). τυπείς is odd after βάλε (so T): Meriones is clearly at a distance (cf. the odd use of οὐτάζω at 16.467). Aristarchus held that τύπτω, 'strike', is used at short range (288–9n.). Was the poet thinking of sacrifice? Dying warriors are likened to sacrificed bulls at 17.520ff. and 20.403ff. Verse 573 ends in an old polar formula with *δϝήν (1.416, *Od.* 22.473, where ἀσπαίρω reappears); even here the poet plays down the agony of the dying.

574–5 Adamas dies when Meriones pulls out his spear: cf. 14.518f., 16.505. ἥρως Μηριόνης resembles ἥ. Ἰδομενεύς (384, 439). A name–epithet phrase only here precedes τὸν δὲ σκότος ὄσσε κάλυψε (11×).

576–80 The shift to Helenos killing Deïpuros (91–4n.) is abrupt, like that to Aineias at 541; these are the only disconnected duels in book 13. Winter (*MNO* 91, 100) deems it a sign that the Trojans still have the initiative. Helenos shared with Deïphobos the command of a division (12.94), and now takes over from him. This killing expends the last of the Greeks listed at 478. Helenos' success is typical and briskly told: his sword hits Deïpuros' temple, cutting the strap of his helmet and sending it flying, to be lost to an Achaean in the dense mêlée. Again a Trojan is cheated of armour he might have expected to win! But the emphasis falls on the Greek's death (note μέν ... δέ). With 576 cf. 5.584, ξίφεΐ ἤλασε κόρσην; ξίφος occurs with μέγα (etc.) 5×; with 579 cf. 14.411 and 526–30n.; 580 = 5.659, 22.466 (fem.), and is adapted at 425 above.

577 A Thracian sword won from a Paeonian is offered as a prize at 23.807f. Such swords were clearly of superior quality (others are called 'big'). In the years before 1200 B.C. the Mycenaeans adopted a new type of slashing-sword from the Danube basin, the flange-hilted 'Naue II' type, which may be meant (H.-G. Buchholz, *Arch. Hom.* E 258ff., 271; Bouzek, *Aegean* 119–32). AbT compare the large swords of later Thracians. They were long famous for metalwork (10.438f., 24.234): cf. Hoddinott, *The Thracians* 62. Further rare weapons, the sling and battle-axe, soon follow.

581–600 Deïpuros' fall provokes Menelaos, last seen at 11.487. The opponents attack simultaneously, as at 613, 5.656f. and 8.321ff., where Teukros tries to shoot Hektor but is not fast enough. Helenos' wounding, like Teukros', shows the inferiority of the bow. He has to leave the field (cf. 781), like Deïphobos; they even have similar injuries. The narrative maintains balance and suspense. At first, honorific formulae equate the opponents, and their different methods of attack are stated (581–3); each looses his missile simultaneously (584f.). We hear of Helenos' failure before Menelaos' success. Details convey the force of each missile: Helenos' arrow ricochets like a bean; Menelaos' spear passes through Helenos' hand into the bow he holds. Helenos was just using a sword; he seems equally deft with the bow, like Teukros or Meriones (177–8n.). Lorimer deems his long sword incompatible with his bow (*HM* 295f.), but a sword was a vital part of an archer's gear, in case he was assailed at close range; Paris has a bow *and* a sword at 3.17f.

582–3 With βῆ δ' ἐπαπειλήσας ('threateningly') cf. 20.161. Ἑλένῳ ἥρωϊ ἄνακτι | is a unique and clumsy adaptation of (βίη θ') Ἑλένοιο ἄνακτος | (756–9n.). Helenos is called ἄναξ because of the shape of his name, but also his status; in historical Cyprus the sons and brothers of βασιλεῖς were still called ἄνακτες (Aristotle frag. 526). A /g^{w}asileus/ was a lesser official in Mycenaean times; this is reflected in the formulae, which prove βασιλεύς an innovation (Hoekstra, *Epic Verse before Homer* 97–9). The πῆχυς is the centrepiece by which the bow is held (cf. *Od.* 21.419, τόν ῥ' ἐπὶ πήχει ἑλὼν εἷλκεν νευρήν); strictly speaking, Helenos retracts the bowstring, not the πῆχυς. So some took it as 'bowstring', supposedly a Dorian usage (AbT, cf. Hsch.). Both halves of 583 recur (20.423, 11.375).

584–5 These verses form a chiasmus with what follows, since Helenos' shot is described first. All papyri and codices read ὁμαρτήτην (or ἁμ-), which yields a clumsy asyndeton in ὁ μέν. The poet has mixed τὼ δ' ἄρ' ὁμαρτήτην, ὁ μὲν ἔγχεϊ ἱέμενος ἀκοντίσσαι, ὁ δέ ..., with τὼ δ' ἄρ' ὁμάρτῃ, ὁ μὲν ἔ. ἵετ' ἀ., ὁ δέ ...; cf. τὼ δὲ διακρινθέντε ὁ μὲν ... ἤϊε, ὁ δέ ... (7.306). Aristarchus read an adv. ὁμαρτήδην, a *hapax* in Greek (Did/AT); this is a conjecture to avoid having two main verbs. ὀξυόεις, in this formula 11× Hom., looks like a derivative of ὀξύς, cf. ὀξὺ δόρυ in 583 and 5.48–50n.; but it is probably from ὀξύη, 'beech', 'spear', at Archilochus frag. 229. This once meant 'ash', the best wood for spears; it is cognate with Norse *askr*, 'ash', 'spear' (Friedrich, *Trees* 96). With ἵετ' ἀκοντίσσαι cf. 16.359; ἀπὸ νευρῆφιν ὀϊστῷ | (etc.) occurs 4× Hom., cf. | ἰῷ ἀ. νευρῆς (2x).

586–7 As if we are watching in slow motion, Helenos 'next' hits Menelaos; κατὰ στῆθος βάλεν ἰῷ (also 8.303, cf. 186) makes us think for an instant that he is slain. Verse 587 = 5.99, but with ἀπό for διά, whence the blunder διά here. The scansion γύαλον suggests that the verse usually had διά; piercing the corslet would be the more frequent incident (cf. Shipp, *Studies* 283). For the ricochet cf. 21.591–4n.

588–90 A fine simile, full of assonance and alliteration, transports us to the peasant's humble round, like that of winnowing grain at 5.499ff. or threshing it at 20.495ff. The legumes are separated from their husks by tossing them against the breeze from one side of the circular threshing-floor to the other, using a winnowing-fan (πτύον), a flat wooden shovel. Beans are more easily winnowed than grain (cf. Columella 2.10.12ff.). Leaf took 590 as a hendiadys – the wind is produced by the fan's action. But nature's help is needed for this task: cf. bT, 5.499 and Xenophon, *Oec.* 18.6–8. Hesiod and others say the threshing-floor should be in a windy place (see West on *Erga* 599), and modern ones are always at a breezy spot down wind from the village.

Repetition of 'the bitter arrow flew' frames the image, which is especially apt because beans and lentils, being round, bounce further than grain (so AbT). The menial task is dignified by epithets (πλατύς, μέγας, μελανόχρως, λιγυρός) and the epic *hapax legomena* πτύον, ἐρέβινθος, λικμητήρ and μελανόχρως; cf. ἐϋχροής, μελαγχροίης and innovatory μελανόχροος (*Od.* 19.246). For θρῴσκωσῖν κ- cf. p. 9 n. 6; πτυόφιν, gen. sing., is also relatively recent (Chantraine, *GH* I 238). The instrumental in -φι, already syncretized with the abl. in Myc., was rare in *o*-stems and originally plur. (Horrocks, *Space and Time* 131ff.; A. M. Davies, in *Linear B* 99f.; R. Coleman, in *Studies Chadwick* 113–25). πνοιῇ ὑπὸ λιγυρῇ recurs at 23.215; ὑπό means 'with the effect of' (Chantraine, *GH* II 140), and does not mean that the beans go *with* the breeze, *pace* Fränkel, *Gleichnisse* 43f.

591–6 The danger to Menelaos past, the tempo slows, with repeated formulae (581, 593; 591, 601, 607, formerly with *Μενελάϝοο). By poetic justice, Helenos is hurt in the hand with which he had shot at Menelaos (Winter, *MNO* 103n.). Instead of ἦ, 'hit that arm *which* held the bow', Aristarchus (Did/A), with MS support, rightly reads ᾗ, but he took it as 'hit his arm *where* he held the bow', when it means '⟨that hand⟩ with which', explaining the demonstrative τήν. τόξον ἔϋξοον occurs 9× Hom.; for 596 see 531–3n.

597 For μείλινον ἔγχος a few MSS import χάλκεον ἔ. from 595 (cf. the variants at 20.272). The former phrase, with metrical lengthening for μέλινον, is obsolescent: it is rarer (6/29×), and not in *Od.* As in the case of δόρυ μ./δ. χ., these formulae are not fully equivalent: E. Cosset (*REA* 85 (1983) 196–8) has proved that a spear is usually 'brazen' when stress falls on its bronze point, 'ashen' when it falls on its wooden shaft (cf. R. Schmiel, *LCM* 9 (1984) 34–8). Thus the point wounds Helenos, but he drags the shaft.

598–600 Agenor, leader of the second Trojan column, succours a leader of the third (12.93f.): cf. Polites' care for Deïphobos (533ff.), and the removal of arrows at 4.210ff., 5.112, 11.397f. For a retainer carrying a hero's weapon cf. 708–10n. Slings recur at 716 only, where the Locrians use bows also. The epic *hapax* σφενδόνη later means 'surgical sling' too, but is clearly military here; its use as a bandage is a swift improvisation, but bandages were a traditional remedy (S. Laser, *Arch. Hom.* s 113ff.). Verse 600 explains that ἐϋστρόφῳ οἰὸς ἀώτῳ means a sling, and how Agenor came by it: there is no reason to expel the verse as a gloss. ϝ- is 'observed' in ἔρυσεν although the phrase is not formular. With μεγάθυμος Ἀγήνωρ (also 4.467) cf. the frequent θυμὸς ἀγήνωρ. Leaf is suspicious because Agenor's retainer is nameless, but cf. 11.341; ποιμένι λαῶν often replaces a hero's name (e.g. 14.423, 15.262).

599 The wool is twisted into a sling; later Greeks used sinews instead. As at 716, all MSS offer ἐϋστρόφῳ. Aristarchus read ἐϋστρεφεῖ (Did/A), found at 15.463 and 3× *Od.*, but ἐϋστροφος is equally well-formed, as in Ἀγά-, Ἐπί- or νεό-στροφος (of a bowstring at 15.469); cf. ἐϋρρής/-ροος. He is conjecturing to impose homogeneity. ἄωτον is often likened to ἄνθος, 'that which comes to the surface', the 'pile', evolving to mean 'best' (so E. K. Borthwick, *JHS* 96 (1976) 1–7). But J. L. Melena has shown that ἄωτον once meant 'plucked wool', which is finer than sheared wool; wool was originally gathered by plucking (*Studies Chadwick* 404n.). Cf. οἰὸς ἄ. of a woolly blanket (*Od.* 1.443).

601–42 Peisandros seeks to finish what Helenos began. This elaborate duel is linked with those either side solely by Menelaos' presence; its importance is also signalled by his long speech, in which he sets this battle in the context of the whole war and its eventual outcome. It cannot be chance that Agamemnon slew another Peisandros, the aptly named son of the man Paris bribed to urge the Trojans to kill Menelaos during his embassy to Troy (11.122ff.). A. Parry (*HSCP* 76 (1972) 19f.) brilliantly suggests that, in another version, Menelaos slew this latter Peisandros; but Homer, recalling that he had already made Agamemnon do so, and wishing to avoid slaying the same man twice (cf. Pulaimenes below), puts in Peisandros without identifying him, yet leaves Menelaos' fine speech. Moreover 610 = 3.361, where Menelaos hits the helmet of another personal foe, Paris! This duel combines standard elements – a fruitless exchange of spears and a second round at close quarters (see 16.462–75n.); cf. 16.335ff., with another blow to the helmet and fantastic wound (Fenik, *TBS* 145f.), and 11.231–40, when the victim's spear bends and Agamemnon kills him with a sword (232f. = 604f.). The blows are in chiastic order, Menelaos–Peisandros–Peisandros–Menelaos.

602–3 For evil fate leading a man to his death, a motif which reassures us that Menelaos will win, cf. 5.613f., 5.628f. (Tlepolemos), 22.5 (Hektor). The emotional apostrophe or direct address is applied to Menelaos 7×, to Patroklos 8×, and to other heroes too: see 7.104, 16.20nn.; Hoekstra, *Modifications* 139; E. Block, *TAPA* 112 (1982) 7–22. As A. Parry showed (*art. cit.*), it is used more to build up sympathetic characters than from metrical utility. μοῖρα κακή is equivalent to μοῖρ' ὀλοή (7× Hom.); cf. κῆρα κακήν/ὀλοήν (16.684–7n.). With θανάτοιο τέλοσδε (also 9.411) cf. τέλος θ., 7× Hom. (reversed at 3.309). δαμῆναι is displaced from the verse-end (11× Hom.) by the formula ἐν αἰνῇ δηϊοτῆτι (206–9n.).

608 'The shield stopped it', not 'he held his shield' as at 163: cf. 12.184, κόρυς ἔσχεθεν. The blunder ἔσχετο is already in one of two papyri and bT. The force of the thrust is such that the spear snaps at the socket (καυλός, cf. 162n.).

609–10 Peisandros is pleased at his hit on Menelaos' shield and anticipates victory. Of the other Trojans who display premature optimism – Pandaros, Paris and Hektor (5.101ff., 5.283ff., 11.378ff., 22.279ff.) – the first two have wounded their opponents, not utterly failed as he has; Eustathius saw the irony (949.25). Peisandros' misperception makes it almost comically apt that his eyeballs pop out. T refer ὁ δ' to Menelaos, which is impossible before Ἀτρεΐδης δέ. A few good MSS read καὶ ἐέλπετο, which leaves the ϝ- moot; it is 'observed' in the *lectio difficilior* καὶ ἔλπετο, the vulgate. Zenodotus (Did/AT) offered μέγα δ' ἤλπετο, which makes the characterization more explicit. He also read χείρεσσι μάχαιραν, whereby 610 = 3.271, 19.252, and not 3.361; but, as Aristarchus objected, μάχαιρα means 'knife' not 'sword' in Homer, even if its etymology shows it was once used for fighting (cf. S. Foltiny, *Arch. Hom.* E 240–2). The single-edged μ., which became the standard sword, only appeared in *c.* 500 B.C. (Snodgrass, *Arms and Armour of the Greeks*, London 1967, 97). For ἀργυρόηλος see 2.45n.

611–12 Peisandros' bronze battle-axe, which he produces from behind his shield, is a foreign weapon archaic in form and material. ἀξίνη is of Semitic origin (cf. Akkadian ḫaṣṣinnu, Aramaic ḫaṣṣīnā): see O. Szemerényi, *Gnomon* 43 (1971) 656. πέλεκυς is a loan-word too. The Hittites and Syrians used such axes in the second millennium; a Syrian axe from Vapheio, a mould for an Italian type from Mycenae and a Balkan specimen from Dodonē are mere strays. The Hittites eventually relegated axes to sacred status as an attribute of Teshup, like the *labrys* of Carian Zeus or the Minoan and Geometric double-axe (see H. Bonnet, *Die Waffen der Völker des alten Orients*, Leipzig 1926, 18–23, 33; H.-G. Buchholz, *Arch. Hom.* E pl. XXVI; Bouzek, *Aegean* 142, 151f.). The legend that the Amazons used axes may reflect their early prevalence in Anatolia. One of the Sea Peoples has one in a hunting-scene from Enkomi (Sandars, *Sea Peoples* 200); the Thracians long used them (Hoddinott, *The Thracians* 62). Two iron double-axes were found with the famous Late Geometric panoply at Argos (Snodgrass, *EGA* 166), but battle-axes were rare later and aroused comment (Hdt. 7.64, cf. 135).

In Homer axes reappear at 15.711, when the two sides fight around the ships πελέκεσσι καὶ ἀξίνῃσι (see *ad loc.*). Axes were also used as targets or prizes at games (23.851n., *Od.* 19.572ff.; P. Walcot, *SMEA* 25 (1984) 357–69). It is unclear whether an ἀξίνη had one blade or two; two blades saved the woodman from having to sharpen his tool so often. A πέλεκυς had two (cf. Plut., *Mor.* 302A), ἡμιπέλεκκα one (23.851). Some took the πέλεκκος or -ον (*hapax*) as the axe-head or the ensemble (bT); Aristarchus rightly glossed it 'haft' (Hsch. s.v. ἀμφὶ πελέκκῳ). It is for *πέλεκϝος (Risch, *Wortbildung* 168). Odysseus' bronze double-axe for woodcutting likewise has an olive-wood haft (*Od.* 5.236); this especially tough wood was used for hammer-hafts and cudgels (Theophrastus, *Hist. Plant.* 5.7.8; Aristoph., *Lys.* 255).

For the rare 'violent' enjambment καλὴν | ἀξίνην, cf. 3.44f. (καλὸν | εἶδος),

16.338f. (κ. | φάσγανον), 104f., *HyAp* 91f., *HyDem* 83f. Usually a numerical or partitive adj. is involved, e.g. πᾶς, πολύς, ἄλλος, θαμύς, ἄμφω, ἄκρος (cf. 6.498–9n.). Many cases are caused by the play of formulae; here 'axe' will not fit after εἵλετο, and ἀξίνην εὔχαλκον (also in *Alcmaeonis* frag. 1, cf. 20.322) was available to begin the next verse. We must expect some such enjambments even in fully oral composition.

613–14 μακρῷ ἐϋξέστῳ may be an under-represented formula (cf. 18.276, describing panels on gates). Aristarchus, the κοινή and the MSS rightly read ἐφίκοντο, a verb unique in epic but common later, and used with the gen. Aristophanes probably read ἐφικέσθην, falsely restoring a dual (cf. p. 24 n. 23); others had ἀφίκεσθον (Did/AT) or -οντο (some MSS). For odd dual endings cf. 346–8, 626–7nn. and the old but weak variants at 16.218, 23.506; ἀφικνέομαι never takes a gen. See van der Valk, *Researches* II 199f. The formula κόρυθος φάλον (3.362) recurs with ἤλασεν (16.338) and ἱπποδασείης (4.459, 6.9); on φάλος see 132–3n.

616–19 The grisly excussion of Peisandros' eyes by a thrust above the bridge of his nose is paralleled at 14.493f., when a spear expels an eyeball; at 16.741f. χαμαὶ πέσον ἐν κονίῃσι recurs and the victim's eyes, knocked out by a rock that smashes his forehead, fall at his feet as here. But these incidents are terrifying, not poetically just, as this one is (609–10n.). In reality one blow could not make both eyes pop out; but the scholia do not protest, which suggests that Homer's audience would not have objected either. Had the poet deemed this unnatural, he would surely have used divine intervention to expedite it, as at 434–42. Aristarchus kept the vulgate πέσον instead of -εν (in a papyrus), adducing 12.159, βέλεα ῥέον (Did/A); the same rule led him to alter ἠγνοίησεν at 28 and πέσεν at 15.714 (see La Roche, *Textkritik* 383f.). But it is wrong to normalize an oral dictated text; Homer's verbal usage with neuter plurals varies (Chantraine, *GH* II 17f.). λάκε is best rendered 'shrieked'. With ἰδνώθη δὲ πεσών cf. *Od.* 22.85; with the rest of 618 cf. 6.65, 16.503 (for λάξ see 5.620n.). Verse 619 = 17.537, 21.183.

620–39 Menelaos' speech, the only one in 487–725, gains weight from its isolation as well as its content. Ranging far beyond his present triumph, he recalls Zeus's duty as protector of host and guest to ensure that Troy falls, which we know will finally occur; he cannot know that Zeus is showing favour to Thetis, not to the Trojans. His faith in Zeus will eventually be vindicated (cf. Lloyd-Jones, *Justice of Zeus* 7f.). For the use of speeches to remind the audience of the larger situation cf. 95–124, especially 111–13. Menelaos' theme of Trojan persistence underlines the ferocity and indecisiveness of the battle. His speech is full not of 'hatred and bitterness' against the Trojans (Willcock), but of grief and indignation based on his sense of injustice. He is also bewildered that, far from making reparations, they are compounding their offence by fighting on, and – stranger yet – that they enjoy the apparent connivance of Zeus, who has already ignored Menelaos' prayer at 3.351–4 (cf. 17.24–8n.; Michel, $\mathcal{N}$ 110–13; Hohendahl-Zoetelief, *Manners* 152f.). This is just what Homer's Menelaos would say in the circumstances; his perplexity lends him sympathy even more than does his justified indignation.

Most critics misjudge this speech. Leaf deems 631–9 or 634–9 interpolated, since 'to be unwearied in war is not a reproach which is likely to touch an enemy, nor is success in battle a sign of ὕβρις' (but see 633–5n.). Fenik (*TBS* 147) deems 636f. an 'inept list', and the whole a bad example of the 'expansion technique' seen at 95ff.; in *Homer and the Nibelungenlied* 42 he calls it 'sanctimonious moralizing' at odds with the brutal killings that follow. In fact it weaves several motifs into an integrated whole; see the fine analysis of its rhetoric by Eustathius (950.22–46) and of its structure by Michel (*loc. cit.*), which yields the following pattern:

A   You Trojans *will* leave the *ships* (620),
B   though you are *insatiable* in battle (621).
C   You showed great disrespect for *Zeus* god of *xenoi* (622–5),
D   who will destroy Troy one day (625),
C' when, although you were my *xenoi*, you took my wife and property (626f.).
A' Now you are eager to burn the *ships* too, but *will* fail (628–30).
C" *Zeus* almighty, you show these sinners favour (631–3),
B' the Trojans who cannot be *sated* of war (634f.).
b   There is *satiety* in things far better than war (636–9);
B" yet the Trojans are *insatiable* in battle (639).

The passage 620–30 is structured to stress the Trojans' offence and the penalty Zeus will exact. Menelaos ends on a pensive note; his theme of the Trojans' insatiability picks up the opening and close of 620–30. This theme is deftly varied thrice, as if in a mimesis of Trojan persistence. To shift from rebuking persons to chiding Zeus is common. Agamemnon criticizes the Greeks' weakness and then Zeus's ingratitude, ending with a prayer (8.228–44); Aias tells his comrades that Zeus must be against them, exhorts them and asks Zeus to lift the mist (17.629–47). Conversely, a reproach to Zeus may open a speech: cf. 3.365ff. (Menelaos), 12.164ff., 19.270ff., 21.273ff. and 17.19ff., where Menelaos continues with a threat based on his recent triumph (29, cf. 620 here). These all begin with the solemn address 'father Zeus', as here.

620–5 Shipp (*Studies* 282) would expel 622–39 because of linguistic oddities, which in fact cluster here. The ironic particle θήν, 'surely' (13× *Il.*, 3× *Od.*), otherwise limited to Archilochus frag. 23.21 (restored), Sicilian Doric and 'Aesch.' *Pr.* 928, must be an archaism, since a Dorism is excluded.

νέας is recent Ionic for νῆας. οὐκ ἐπιδευεῖς | for -έες is paralleled at 9.225, where Aristarchus emends it away; ἐστέ must be supplied. Ζηνὸς ἐριβρεμέτεω is trebly novel: -εω and Z. (p. 18 n. 33) are recent Ionisms, and the phrase is a unique variation on Ζεὺς ὑψιβρεμέτης (6× Hom.), duplicating Ζηνὸς ἐριγδούπου (15.286–93n.). The formula πόλιν αἰπήν | for αἰπεῖαν, probably denoting fortifications rather than site, recurs 4× *Od.* (separated), always referring to the sack of Troy; αἰπὰ ῥέεθρα | (2× *Il.*, *Cat.* 150.23) is a like innovation *metri gratia* (Chantraine, *GH* 1 252f.). The rest is standard: note Δαναῶν ταχυπώλων, 9× *Il.* only; Τρῶες ὑπερφίαλοι 21.459, 414 (dat.); μόθου/πολέμου/μάχης ἀκόρητος (etc.), 7.117, 12.335, 20.2 (cf. ἀ. ἀϋτῆς, 621, 3× *Aspis*); λώβην τε καὶ αἴσχεα, *Od.* 19.373, cf. 18.225; χαλεπὴ ... μῆνις |, 5.178; Διὸς – – ∪∪ μῆνιν | ξεινίου, *Od.* 14.283f., cf. 9.270f. The runover epithet ξ. is emphatic, especially after the thunderous ἐριβρεμέτεω.

622–3 As the Trojans' persistence in battle can hardly be blamed, Menelaos turns to their real crime. μέν is picked up by νῦν αὖτ' at 628. There is no parallel for 'bitches', although enemies are called 'dog' 7× Hom. (plur. at *Od.* 22.35); Ἀχαιίδες οὐκέτ' Ἀχαιοί implies cowardice (2.235), but 'dogs' connotes shamelessness (1.225n.), because the Trojans continue to fight when they are so clearly wrong. See M. Faust, *Glotta* 48 (1970) 26f.; S. Lilja, *Dogs in Ancient Greek Poetry*, Helsinki 1976, 21–3.

624–5 This forecast of Troy's fall is one of a series whose frequency will increase: see next 815f. Zeus first receives the title Xenios here (the adj. /xenwios/ is Myc.); but his responsibility for *xenoi* is implied by Menelaos' prayer at 3.351ff., and is a major theme of the *Odyssey* (as well as the above references see 6.207f., 14.158, 389). The rarity of such allusions in the *Iliad* is no disproof that Zeus had this title from an early date. The root $*k^w s(e)nw$- is Indo-European, cf. Avestan *xšnu-*, 'reciprocate', Hittite *kuššan-*, 'requital' (M. Schwartz in *Papers in Honour of M. Boyce*, Leiden 1985, II 495).

626–7 There is irony in 'you went away taking my wife for no reason (μάψ), *since* she gave you hospitality'. Aristarchus deduced from the formula κουριδίην ἄλοχον, 'virgin bride', that Homer did not know of Helen's abduction by Theseus (so too at 3.140, 7.392); cf. his denial that Homer knew of the judgement of Paris (24.23–30n.). But Menelaos would not allude to any prior dalliance on Helen's part! A's variant κτήμαθ' ἄμ' αὐτῇ is from 3.458 etc. Zenodotus read οἴχεσθον ἄγοντες (Arn/A), introducing an abnormal dual for plur. as at 1.567, 3.459, 6.112, 8.503, 15.347, 18.287, 23.753, *Od.* 1.38, 8.251; like Eratosthenes and Crates, he held that Homer used the two interchangeably, but this is a post-Homeric innovation (see N. Wecklein, *SBAW* 1919, Abh. 7, 36–9; Chantraine, *GH* II 28f.; Hoekstra, *SES* 28f.). He probably objected to ἀνάγω, which merely means 'bring with' (Schmidt, *Weltbild* 143–5; *LfgrE* s.v. ἄγω IV).

628–30 The epithets suggest the enormity of the Trojans' aims. ἥρωες

Ἀχαιοί (15.219, *Od.* 24.68 and acc. 8×, mostly in these books) was not originally interchangeable with (ϝ)ἑλικῶπες Ἀ. (3× nom., 3× acc.). Ἄρηος probably goes with σχήσεσθε, not with ἐσσύμενοι (315–16n.).

631–2 Menelaos' tone is tactful but aggrieved; he simply notes that Zeus caused 'all this', without impugning his intelligence (cf. bT). Praise likewise softens rebuke at 17.171, ἦ τ' ἐφάμην σὲ περὶ φρένας ἔμμεναι ἄλλων …; but Menelaos leaves praise of Zeus's wisdom to others, as does Agamemnon at 19.96f. (τόν περ ἄριστον | ἀνδρῶν ἠδὲ θεῶν φάσ' ἔμμεναι).

633–5 οἶον δή explains the reproach, as at 17.587, 21.57: it is 'hubristic' to continue to fight when one is plainly wrong (so T on 638f.). *Hubris* is a violent manifestation of wantonness (ἀτασθαλίη): cf. *Od.* 24.282 and the formulae ὑβρίζοντες ἀτάσθαλα μηχανόωνται (etc., 11.695, 4× *Od.*), ἀτάσθαλον ὕβριν (2× *Od.*). ὑβριστής (11× epos) is unique in the *Iliad*; on the link between *hubris* and satiety cf. A. Michelini, *HSCP* 82 (1978) 35–44. φύλοπις (28× epos) is never an adj. Its common pairing with πόλεμος (4× epos) shows that 635 is a singer's error for φυλόπιδος κορέσασθαι ⟨καὶ⟩ ὁμοιίου πτολέμοιο; cf. 18.242, φ. κρατερῆς καὶ ὁ. π., and 14.216–17n.

636–9 Menelaos emphasizes his frustration with a priamel (note the agitated asyndeton); one tires even of things far better than war, yet the Trojans go on fighting! The basic structure is seen in *Od.* 12.341f., 'all deaths are hateful to mortals, but it is worst to die of hunger' (W. H. Race, *The Classical Priamel from Homer to Boethius*, Leiden 1982, 32f.). Verse 637 = *Od.* 23.145; some thought it redundant (bT). μολπή ('song') and dance are also paired at *Od.* 1.152, cf. ὀρχηστυῖ (-θμῷ) καὶ ἀοιδῇ, 4× epos, and 731 below. The bard reminds his hearers of their delight in his performance. Aristarchus rightly held that μέλπεσθαι and μολπή denote play generally and music specifically, but music alone in later poets (οἱ νεώτεροι): see K. Bielohlawek, *WS* 44 (1924/5) 1ff., 125ff. ἐξ ἔρον εἶναι, i.e. to have one's fill, is based on the Aeolism ἐξ ἕ. ἔντο (24× epos); cf. ἐξίης πόθον (Sappho frag. 94.23). The active replaces the middle, as in the similar adaptation at 24.227.

641–2 A. A. Parry (*Blameless Aegisthus* 39ff.) rightly denies that Menelaos is called ἀμύμων because of what he says, but the etymological basis for the ancient rendering 'blameless' is better than she allows: cf. μῦμαρ, 'blame' (Hsch.); Chantraine, *Dict.* s.v.; F. M. Combellack, *AJP* 103 (1982) 361ff. Heubeck's derivation from ἀμύνω is implausible (*Glotta* 65 (1987) 37–44). Μενέλαος ἀμύμων is a unique phrase: ξανθὸς Μ. (27× Hom.) would have fitted. Since Menelaos has no formula shaped ∪∪ – ∪∪ – – | and starting with a single consonant, this fills a gap in his system; yet it is surely improvised after ἀ. in 637, like ἀγαθὸν Μενέλαον at 4.181. His name is rare in this position (4×, versus 72× at the verse-end). From ἐξαῦτις, 642 = 5.134, cf. 15.457; note the assonance in -αυτ-.

643–59 Harpalion's demise resembles Adamas' (cf. 560–75n.), with pathetic elaborations: foreshadowing at 645, his unique collapse into his comrades' arms (cf. 6.81–2n.), the worm-simile, and his conveyance back to Troy by chariot, followed by his weeping father (cf. Griffin, *HLD* 113, 123–5). Other father–son pairs at Troy are Asios + Adamas, Nestor + Antilokhos. His father is Pulaimenes, king of the Paphlagonians (cf. 2.851); this is odd because Menelaos slew a Pulaimenes, king of the Paphlagonians, at 5.576–9. The verses about the weeping father following the son's body are simply traditional; as Pulaimenes is not named in them, Homer overlooked their implications (so Bowra, *Heroic Poetry* 300). The discrepancy is less glaring than that of Schedios slain twice or Melanippos thrice (15.515–17, 547–51nn.), or indeed the groaning corpse of 423. The ancients disbelieved in Pulaimenes' resurrection. Zenodotus emended 643 to rename him 'Kulaimenes' (so Arn/A in Erbse, *Scholia* I lxv); Aristophanes athetized 658f.; Aristarchus doubted whether to athetize or posit two men of the same name (Did/T *ad loc.*). Others squeezed a negative into 658 (so D)! Cf. O. Tsagarakis, *Hermes* 104 (1976) 1–12. Harpalion and Pulaimenes both bear Greek names: with the former cf. ἁρπαλέος, Harpalos.

644–5 For the foreshadowing in 645 cf. 602f.; the adaptation of this verse to Protesilaos at 15.706 arouses similar pathos. The only deaths prefigured in book 13 are those of the Trojans either side of Menelaos' prophetic speech (Winter, *MNO* 94). On the minority variant πτολεμίξων for the correct -ίζων (omitted by the OCT's *apparatus criticus*) see p. 36 n. 70.

646–9 Harpalion's blow is ignoble, his retreat craven; hence his shameful wound in the buttock (cf. 567–9n.) and his likeness to a worm (Eustathius 952.25–31, 43–5). Verse 649 conveys his fear, but that he had turned to flee is first shown by his wound – a subtle touch which Friedrich (*Verwundung* 97f.) misinterprets as an inconsistency. The diction resumes the description of previous Trojan victims: 646f. recalls 561f., 647 varies 607, 648 = 566 and 596, 650 resembles 567. The first half of 649 recurs at 17.674 and, modified, 2× *Od.*; the second half varies χρόα λευκὸν ἐπαυρεῖν (11.573 = 15.316).

650–2 Meriones, last seen using a spear (567), is equally deft with the bow (249n., cf. 177–8n.). At 5.66f. he inflicts the same injury in almost the same words, unparalleled elsewhere: on his reputation for nasty wounds see 567–9n. The arrow's course is described with startling precision, as A. R. Thompson observed (*Proc. Royal Soc. of Medicine*, June 1952, 23, cited by Willcock): 'the weapon would enter through the middle of the right buttock and pass through the great sacrosciatic notch, enter the pelvis, pass through the base of the bladder, and come out under the pubic arch' (but see 5.66–7n.). χαλκήρε' ὀϊστόν recurs at 662 only; cf. χαλκήρεϊ δουρί (5× Hom., and 2× acc. plur.).

654–5 A dying worm is contorted, but when dead stretches out (Strasburger, *Kämpfer* 40). The image is even less flattering if we recall that σκώληξ also means 'maggot'. As worms are bloodless, the poet adds that Harpalion's blood soaks into the earth. For θυμὸν ἀποπνείων see 15.252–3n.; for κεῖτο ταθείς cf. 392–3n. The words ἐπὶ γαίῃ | ... γαῖαν (cf. 564–6n.) recur at 21.118f.

657 bT report that someone athetized 657 because only the wounded are removed by chariot, which is true (cf. 535–8 = 14.429–32). The objection goes back to Zenodotus, since Apollonius Rhodius in his *Against Zenodotus* tried to defend 657 by altering ἀνέσαντες, 'sitting him in the chariot' (from ἕζω, cf. *Od.* 14.280), to ἀναθέντες 'putting', which better suits a corpse (Did/A). But we have yet to hear that Harpalion is dead; his men 'tend' him as if he still lives. He is borne away dying; the poet delays his death until the last word of the scene (659), although ἀχνύμενοι· μετὰ δέ σφι has funereal connotations (cf. 18.234, 23.14). Cf. how long Meriones' last victim took to die (570–3n.). For the Aeolic formula (προτὶ) Ἴλιον ἱρήν see p. 17. The Trojans' use of a chariot between the rampart and ships is surprising, since all save Asios left their vehicles beyond the ditch (12.76ff.); this is recalled at 15.3. Homer tends to forget about this breach of the norms of heroic warfare: Trojans use chariots at 679 and perhaps 684 (749 is spurious).

658–9 As son once followed father into battle (644f.), so father follows son out of it. The *Iliad*, from Khruses to Priam, is full of bereaved fathers, the hideous result of that ghastly phenomenon, war (Griffin, *HLD* 123–5); 'in peace sons bury fathers, but in war fathers bury sons' (Hdt. 1.87.4). Aristarchus thought the reversal of 644 supported his athetesis (cf. 643–59n.)! Just as Harpalion's bereaved father prefigures Hektor's, so the next victim, Eukhenor, recalls Akhilleus in being slain by Paris with an arrow and in facing the choice of an early death or an inglorious one (cf. 9.410ff.), as Aristarchus saw (Arn/A on 663, cf. Fenik, *TBS* 148f.). To the son's disgrace and his father's grief is added the fact that there is no revenge on his killer; Paris only manages to kill another Greek (so D; Michel, *N* 103f.). ποινή means 'compensation' generally, not only for manslaughter (18.498); cf. 9.633 (ποινήν ... οὗ παιδὸς ἐδέξατο τεθνηῶτος), 14.483 (revenge for a brother slain in battle), 21.28 (Trojans sacrificed as ποινή for Patroklos' death). On τεθνειώς see p. 36 with n. 66.

660–72 Paris, last seen with Aineias (490), is angered by the fall of his guest-friend (with 660 cf. 4.494) and shoots poor Eukhenor. At last his arrow is fatal (he only wounded Diomedes, Eurupulos and Makhaon). It is ironic that he acts to defend *xenia* just after Menelaos reminds us of his fateful crime against it (624–7). Harpalion would still be alive had Paris not stolen Helen in the first place; the criticism of his morality is muted but unmistakable. Eukhenor's death is briefly told (671f.); the stress falls on his life-story

(665–70). The introduction ἦν δέ τις, with no initial announcement of his death, arouses suspense and makes his presence here seem almost as tragic an accident as the mischance that he is the one to fall; cf. the introductions of other wealthy but doomed characters at 5.9 (the sons of a priest), 10.314 (Dolon), 17.575, *Od.* 20.287.

663–70 Eukhenor's fall is typical in several ways. He is the son of a priest or seer (cf. 5.9ff., 5.76–8, 5.149, 11.329, 16.604f.); there is pathos in the idea that his family's wealth could not avert his death (cf. 5.9, 6.14, 16.596, 17.576). The motif of a seer's prediction about his son is neatly varied. One seer foresees his sons' fate and tries to stop them enlisting (11.330f.); another fails to predict it (5.148–51). Poluïdos foretells that his son must die either at Troy, or at home of a painful disease; it is to the son's credit that he decides to go, to the father's that he does not stop him (bT). This choice of fates resembles Akhilleus' (658–9n.). ἀφνειός τ' ἀγαθός τε (also at 17.576) means 'wealthy and well-born', but ἀγαθός connotes 'brave'; Corinth was a rich town (2.570–5n.). Eukhenor's avoidance of the Greeks' hefty fine by serving is not miserly in the Homeric view; he protects his family's property and his honour by a single action. The poet does not criticize even Eukhenor's neighbour Ekhepolos of Sikuon, who bought an exemption so he could enjoy his wealth at home (23.296ff.). The fine is invented to contrast Eukhenor with Harpalion, whose father received no recompense for his son (as Poluïdos in effect did).

Eukhenor and Poluïdos (from *-ϝιδϝος) are both apt names for seers: cf. Teiresias from τείρεα (von Kamptz, *Personennamen* 29). But neither is created *ex nihilo*. Like Alkathoos (427–33n.), Eukhenor comes from Peloponnesian saga (see E. Bernert in *RE* 21 (1952) 1647ff.). His father is really the noted seer Poluïdos son of Koiranos (of Melampous' clan), linked by Pindar with Corinth (*Ol.* 13.75). Pherecydes, no doubt harmonizing the Trojan and Theban cycles, says Poluïdos married Eurudameia, who bore him Eukhenor and Kleitos; his sons took Thebes with the Epigonoi and went on to Troy, where Paris slew Eukhenor (*FGH* 3 f 115). Pausanias (1.43.5) mentions a Megarian Eukhenor, son of a Koiranos and *grandson* of Poluïdos. Hesiod perhaps made Eukhenor and Theoklumenos sons of Koiranos, and had Poluïdos warn Eukhenor that he would die at Troy (frag. 136; cf. West, *Catalogue* 79–81). Poluïdos reappears as the Melampodid seer *Polu*pheides, Theoklumenos' father (*Od.* 15.250ff.); he has a *brother* called Kleitos and lives near Corinth. Poluïdos even turns into a Trojan at 5.148f., son of a seer Eurudamas (cf. Eurudameia) and brother of Abas; Abas is Poluïdos' grandfather in Paus. *loc. cit.*! For the *Iliad*'s adaptation of material from the Theban cycle cf. 2.830–4, where the Trojans Amphios and Adrestos, who go to war despite their father's prophecy, are based on Amphiaraos and Adrastos, leaders of the ill-omened attack on Thebes: on the Myc. origin of this tale see Vermeule, *PCPS* 33 (1987) 122–52. Polupheides is linked with his cousin Amphiaraos at *Od.* 15.253, and Poluïdos with Adrastos at Ath. 11.459A.

666 γέρων ἀγαθὸς Πολύϊδος is an improvised blend between the types of βοὴν ἀ. Μενέλαος and γ. ἱππήλατα Πηλεύς, inspired by ἀ. at 664: the *Odyssey* has γ. ἥρως ∪∪ – – | instead (4×). ἀγαθός is rarely used as an epithet unless it has a qualification, e.g. πύξ (*LfgrE* s.v., 1 6).

667–72 The chiasmus disease–Achaeans–Achaeans–disease is entwined with the chiastic antitheses disease–at home–by the ships–Trojans. The synonyms ἀργαλέος and στυγερός stress Eukhenor's painful choice; ἀ. is for *ἀλγαλέος from ἄλγος, used at 670. His death is hardly preferable; the darkness that seizes him is 'hateful', like the disease. Both epithets describe illness elsewhere (*Od.* 15.408, *Erga* 92, *Aspis* 43). With 667 cf. 22.61, *Od.* 15.354. θωή, 'impost' (from τίθημι), next appears at *Od.* 2.192: a θωή is paid to the community, a ποινή to a family (cf. C. Vatin, *Ktèma* 7 (1982) 275–80). We should read θωήν, with a few of the best MSS; cf. θωϊή in Ionic inscriptions and Callim. frag. 195.22, Attic θωά for θωϊά (attested at Argos), ἀθῷος. Verses 671f. = 16.606f., of a priest's son; cf. 5.47, 17.617, 23.880. The asyndeton seems to increase the pathos.

673–837 Hektor, unaware of the Greek successes on the left, fights in the centre, where the Trojans are in disarray from the Achaeans' missiles. Pouludamas advises him to consult his officers. Hektor agrees, only to find that most of those on the left are dead or injured; so he rallies the whole line, but the Greeks stand firm, led by Aias

673–837 In contrast to the preceding sets of duels (361–672), this scene depicts the battle in mass terms. After summarizing the Trojan losses on the left, it shifts to Hektor and his opponents in the centre, who are dignified with a miniature catalogue; it culminates with their leaders, the Aiantes, and their successful tactic of missile warfare. By 723 the Trojans are in trouble all along the line; only Pouludamas' intervention averts a rout. For lack of officers on the left, Hektor cannot consult them as Pouludamas proposed; instead he rallies his men and trades threats with Aias, raising expectations of a duel (as at 183ff.), which finally occurs at 14.402ff. This passage has been much maligned: 'from 673 to 794 all is confusion' (Leaf). The Analysts' heaviest attack was against 679–724. Allegedly, the account of the fighting in the centre (681ff.) implies that the battle there was not described before; the arrangement of ships contradicts the rest of the *Iliad*; the list of contingents is an unmotivated and post-Homeric 'mainland' expansion; the Locrian slingers are 'not epic' and at odds with 4.280–2; and the Greeks' inability to repel Hektor at 687f. contradicts their near-success at 723f. Shipp (*Studies* 282f.) has dug up the usual trove of linguistic oddities, which adorn all Homer's best passages. On these questions see Michel, *N* 116–33; I shall discuss them *ad loc.*

Fenik (*TBS* 106–8) shows that this scene is an elaborated version of a pattern seen at 11.497–542, where Hektor is on the left of battle:

1. Hektor is unaware of a Trojan defeat elsewhere (673–684, 11.497–503)
2. Intervening catalogue/battle-description (685–722, 11.504–20)
3. He is rebuked for not being where needed (723–53, 11.521–30)
4. He rallies his men to attack (754–808, 11.531–42)
5. Aias leads the Achaean reaction (809ff., 11.544ff.).

Paris and Kebriones appear in both places (765–88, 790; 11.505–7, 11.521–30). Hektor's ignorance is introduced at once, to build suspense while we learn of the peril of which he is unaware. Part of this pattern appears elsewhere (cf. Fenik, *TBS* 154f.):

3. Hektor is rebuked by Pouludamas/Glaukos (725–47, 12.60–79, 17.140–68)
4. He (dis)agrees and rallies his men (748–57, 12.80–7, 17.169–87)
4a. Intervening activity of Hektor (758–88, 17.188–214)
4b. Catalogue of Trojans (789–94, 12.88–104, 17.215–18 (before an exhortation))
5. Trojan attack, Achaean resistance (795ff., 12.105ff., 17.233ff.)

673 = 11.596, 18.1; on such markers of a scene-change cf. 169n. δέμας, used as an adverbial acc. in this formula only, evolved from 'body' to 'like', just as 'like' is from Old English *gelic*, 'of the same body'.

674–8 For the motif of a character unaware of important events see 521–5n. The two sides may have seemed well-matched on the left, but the Greeks in fact had the best of it (540–672n.). The retrospect stresses this, in case any hearer missed the point, and also reminds us of how Poseidon exhorted them and gave material help (434, 554, 562f.). Although he does not lead their attack until 14.363ff., he is already practising unobtrusively the kind of leadership he preached at 56. The statement that the Greeks could have won is resumed by 723f. For Διῒ φίλος read διΐφιλος, which is based on the old dat. seen in Myc. /Diwei/; cf. Cypriot ΔιϜείφιλος. The epithet is Iliadic only (17×); cf. διϊπετής (16.173–5n.), but also contracted σθένεϊˇ (678, 20.361) beside σθένεϊ 13× (for *-εει). κῦδος Ἀχαιῶν (10× Hom.) lacks μέγα only here. τοῖος stands for an adv. like οὕτω, cf. οἷος at 7.211. πρός is adverbial, 'in addition'.

675 The 'left of the ships' is the same as the 'left of the battle'; the viewpoint is always the Greeks'. This was Aristarchus' view (Arn/A on 765; see 681n.). It was proved anew by W. Ribbeck (*RhM* 35 (1880) 610ff.) and

Cuillandre, *La Droite et la gauche* 37–41. The Greek camp is imagined as in the 'wide mouth between the headlands' (14.36), i.e. along the deep bay on the Hellespont that still existed in Strabo's time, but has since been silted up by the Skamandros and Simoeis, a process already noted by Herodotus (2.10). The plain must have been wider than geologists posit (cf. vol. II, 48), since by Homer's time the Simoeis had joined the Skamandros below Troy (5.774, cf. 6.4). Thus the 'left' is the E. side by later Rhoiteion, where (as the name proves) the Skamandros flowed and Telamonian Aias had his ships; the 'right' is the W. towards the Sigeion headland, where Akhilleus was stationed (11.5–9, 498f., cf. Hdt. 5.94). Tumuli at each point were probably linked with these warriors by the fifth century B.C. (Cook, *Troad* 88f., 180f.). This is consistent with Asios' attack on the left, where he faced Idomeneus (12.118), and with the battle-plan presupposed at 312–26 and 765–83. The stereotyped references to the left (with 765 cf. 17.116 = 682), and lack of formulae for the right, do not prove that there is no larger coherent picture (*pace* 5.355n. and Michel, *N* 117); as Cuillandre saw (*op. cit.* 51–7), the Trojans avoid attacking on the right for fear of provoking Akhilleus. On the idea that the original bay was Besika Bay see vol. II, 49f.; the excavations there may bolster this view but do not prove that *Homer* held it.

679–80 Willcock takes ἔχεν as 'kept going', but it is surely from *Fέχω, 'drive', as at 326: Homer again slips into the easy error that the Trojans are using chariots in the space between rampart and ships (657n.). Hektor has stayed near the gate he smashed open (12.445ff.), although that was not precisely located. With 680 cf. κρατεραὶ στίχες ἀσπιστάων (4.90 = 201), σ. — ∪∪ ἀ. (2×).

681 'Aias' with no epithet usually means Telamonian Aias, but denotes the Locrian here, as Aristarchus explained in his book Περὶ τοῦ ναυστάθμου (Arn/A), wherein he established the order in which Homer imagined the fleet to be drawn up, even supplying a diagram: cf. B. J. Goedhardt, *De Aristarchi commentatione Π. τ. v. instauranda*, Utrecht 1879; Lehrs, *De Aristarchi studiis* 221–4. The order differed greatly from that of the *Catalogue of Ships*. At 10.109–13, the ships of Meges and Locrian Aias are near Odysseus', but those of Idomeneus and the other Aias lie further off; at 11.7–9 Odysseus' ships are in the centre of the camp, Telamonian Aias' at its left edge (675n.). The order is roughly as follows (some units were behind others):

Right (West)		Centre		Left (East)
Akhilleus	Menestheus	Meges Oïl. Aias	Odysseus Agam.	Idom. Telamon. Aias
	Boeotians	Podarkes	Diomedes Nestor	Menelaos

But here the Athenians, Meges and *both* Aiantes' men are stationed together: cf. 195–7, where the Aiantes and Athenians fight together, and the controversial 2.558, where Telamonian Aias' ships are next to the Athenians. The contradiction over the Aiantes' position surely derives from Homer's pervasive and creative misunderstanding of Αἴαντε, originally 'Aias and Teukros' (46n.). It is apt that the battle will rage round Protesilaos' ship (15.704–6n.); it is hauled furthest inland since he was first ashore (2.701f., cf. 14.31–6n.). His vessel first appears now because the fighting only now nears the fleet itself. His name arose by analogy with names based on verbs, e.g. Ἀρκεσί-λαος.

682–4 The rampart 'above', i.e. inland from, Protesilaos' ship must be the one built at 7.436ff. and breached in book 12, not, as Willcock holds, that which Thucydides deduced that the Greeks built when they landed (14.31–2n.). It is lowest at this point not because Sarpedon had wrecked its battlements (*pace* AbT), but because it was built that way. Less bravery was needed at the centre than on the wings (so 11.8f.), since units whose ships were on both sides and behind could come to the rescue; hence it could be lowest here. ἔνθα ... ἵπποι confirms that the Greeks were strongest in this sector. ζαχρηεῖς, from χραύω, 'attack', means 'powerful' as at 5.525, 12.347, 360, not 'deficient' (*pace* Hsch.). αὐτοί τε καὶ ἵπποι most naturally denotes the Greeks, as at 17.644; some apply it to the Trojans, who should not be using chariots here (cf. 657n.).

685–722 This small roster of units from the N. and W. edges of Myc. Greece faces both Hektor and an army of Analysts. For some it is unmotivated and belongs earlier; but the fighting in this sector has barely been described (170–205), and the passage clarifies what is happening, magnifies its importance and makes the Greek near-success more credible. As at 478, the names listed provide the poet with cannon-fodder, expended this time at 15.328–42. The catalogue varies in its constructions and order: the initial list of Boeotians, Ionians, Locrians, Phthians and Epeans is expanded by the roster of leaders at 689–700, in the order Athenians (= Ionians), Epeans, Phthians and Boeotians (a brief mention at 700), to focus on the Locrians led by Oïlean Aias in collaboration with his namesake. A few personalities are otherwise unknown, but how else can poets fill out catalogues? The rest occupy the same positions as elsewhere. Thus the Epeans were near the Aiantes and Athenians at 195, where the Athenians Stikhios and Menestheus rescued the body of the Epean Amphimakhos; the pair recurs, with Medon, Ekhios and Mekisteus (422n.), at 15.329ff. Podarkes and Medon lead the Phthians, replacing Protesilaos (694–8nn.). Medon, Oïleus' bastard son, provides a neat transition to his half-brother's Locrians.

685–8 The Ionians and Phthians, both otherwise absent from Homer, are listed next to their neighbours. That the Ionians are equated with the Athenians (689) matches the tradition, first attested in Solon (frag. 4a.2) and verified by archaeology and linguistics, that the Ionians colonized

Asia Minor from Athens (but not all Ionians were of Athenian origin: see Sakellariou, *Migration*). The name 'Ionians' entered Assyrian, Hebrew and Egyptian while it was still *'Ιᾱϝονες (*Yamanu* < *Yawanu, Yawan, Ywn(n)a*); /*Iawones*/ also appear on Knossos tablet B 164, probably as mercenaries (J. Driessen, *BSA* 79 (1984) 49–56). The Aeolic vocalism 'Ιάονες instead of *'Ιήονες is another proof that there was an Aeolic phase in the prehistory of the tradition (see pp. 15–19). A later Homerid applies the phrase 'Ιάονες ἑλκεχίτωνες to the festive Ionians gathered on Delos (*HyAp* 147). The epithet must be traditional, since it ill suits this martial context (cf. 16.419–21n.). The Ionians were still famous later for trailing robes (Asius frag. 13, Thuc. 1.6.3). Cf. ἑλκεσίπεπλοι, used of women, Trojan (3×) or Theban (*Cat.* 193.2).

Phthia is Akhilleus' land, but his men are always Myrmidons, Achaeans or Hellenes; here the Phthioi are ruled by Podarkes, Akhilleus' epithet (694–7n.). Phthia was clearly the name of a large area (so Strabo 9.432); it even extends to the Peneios in Hesiod, *Cat.* 215. The tetrad of Phthiotis later covered much of S. Thessaly; Achaea Phthiotis and Phthiotic Thebes certainly belonged to Podarkes (2.695–7n.). Tribal movements from 1200 b.c. onward have no doubt blurred the picture. The Epeans elsewhere inhabit Elis (2.615ff.); here they are led by Meges (692), who rules Doulikhion opposite (2.627–30). When his father migrated thither from Elis (2.627–30n., cf. 23.637), he obviously took Epeans with him (so Aristarchus in T, cf. 15.518–19n.). They are thus a people split into two kingdoms (cf. Hoekstra on *Od.* 13.275). This may be a memory of the colonization of the Ionian isles from Elis in LHIIIB–C (V. R. d'A. Desborough, *The Greek Dark Ages*, London 1972, 85–91). Neither 'discrepancy' with the Catalogue of Ships is serious, *pace* Page (*HHI* 133). — φαιδιμόεις, unique in Greek, is a *metri gratia* adaptation of φαίδιμος: cf. λειριόεις for λείριος (830–2n.) and Risch, *Wortbildung* 152–4. νεῶν goes with ἔχον, 'they kept him from the ships', not with ἐπαΐσσοντα, 'springing forward', which is used absolutely as at e.g. 546; all its alleged uses with the gen. (5.263, 5.323) are illusory, *pace* LSJ. With 688 cf. ὥσαν ἀπὸ σφείων (3×, 148 included); 'like a flame' is a stereotyped image (6×), effective because it reminds us how the ships are at risk. It seems more natural to put a stop after 688, with an asyndeton in 689, than to place a comma after 688 (so Leaf).

689–91 Like the other Greeks (129n.), the Athenians are picked men; προλέγω is unique in Homer. Menestheus is often deemed an Athenian insertion linked with the alleged 'Pisistratean recension'; whatever this was (see pp. 29ff.), it caused no major interpolations, as the poor showing of Homer's Athenians proves (cf. 2.552n.). Winter (*MNO* 178–92) well argues that Menestheus derives from Asiatic, not Athenian, tradition; thus Peteos founded Elaia in Aeolis (Strabo 13.622). Menestheus once had no place in the Athenian king-list, but was added because Ionian bards had elevated this minor character (Heubeck, *Kleine Schriften* 60n.). So too Nestor's role may owe more to the likelihood that Colophon and Neleid-ruled Miletos were important locales of epic performance than to the passage of Neleidai through Attica en route from Pylos (for this old tradition see Mimnermus frag. 9; Hdt. 1.147; Mühlestein, *Namenstudien* 1–11; Carlier, *Royauté* 432–9). For other cases where bards could honour local ruling families without making the poetry too topical see on 16.173–8, 16.317ff., 16.419ff., 16.593–9, 20.75ff. Menestheus' aides, except Stikhios (195–7n.), are unknown and no doubt invented; another one, Iasos, dies at 15.337. Other Biases are at 4.296, 20.460, *Cat.* 37. Shipp's discussion (*Studies* 55–7) of the isolated form Πετέωο is vitiated by reliance on the *lectio falsa* Πηνελέωο (14.489–91n.). If the ending is Attic, cf. the post-Homeric formula λαμπρά τε σελήνη (p. 8 n. 2).

692 The variant Μέγης τ᾽, rejected by Aristarchus (Did/A), arose from ignorance of Meges' pedigree (cf. Zenodotus' blunder at 19.239): his father Phuleus married Helen's sister Timandre (*Cat.* 176). His officers are unknown.

694–7 = 15.333–6, when Medon is slain by Aineias. His name, 'Ruler', is suspiciously common, like the motif of the bastard son (170–81n.). Why does he live at Phulake, *Protesilaos*' capital (2.695, *Cat.* 199.4), when at 2.727 he is substitute commander for *Philoktetes*? Willcock implausibly supposes he did not need to live in the area whence his troops came. So odd is it that a stranger should inherit Philoktetes' command that Homer must have improvised this detail at 2.727 (cf. the similar case in 698n.). Here he re-invented Medon to help replace Protesilaos instead, bringing him to Phulake by the easy device of having him be exiled for murdering his stepmother's brother (γνωτός, cf. 22.234). This traditional topos often involves uncles or stepmothers (e.g. 2.661ff., 9.447ff.): it frequently seems invented, as also in the cases of Patroklos or Phoinix (see pp. 313, 387). On this motif see 23.85–90n.; Strasburger, *Kämpfer* 29f.; R. Schlunk, *AJP* 97 (1976) 199ff.; Apthorp, *MS Evidence* 96; M. Gagarin, *Drakon and Early Athenian Homicide Law*, New Haven 1981, 6–19. Now in one tradition Oïlean Aias' mother Alkimakhe was a daughter of Phulakos, Podarkes' grandfather (Porphyry/T on 15.333). This must be why Homer linked Oïleus with this dynasty. But it would be illogical for Medon to flee to Alkimakhe's father after killing her brother (for a similar illogicality in a fictitious tale of exile see 16.570–4n.). So Homer suppresses the stepmother's relationship to Phulakos and renames her Eriopis, later known as Eriope (T on 15.336); cf. how he renamed Sarpedon's mother (p. 371). The *Naupaktia* (frag. 1) harmonizes both versions by making Eriope and Alkimakhe the same woman.

698 Podarkes is named for his father Iphiklos, a noted runner (23.636, *Cat.* 62). In Hesiod, Protesilaos is Aktor's son and thus Podarkes' cousin (*Cat.*

199.6), not his elder brother, as he is emphatically stated to be at 2.704–8; the Catalogue of Ships has again departed from tradition in improvising a substitute commander (cf. 694–7n.). This confirms that the Catalogue was not designed for the tenth year of the war. Iphiklos' name, like *his* father's, fits his role as 'warder' of Melampous and the cows at Phulake, a tale that was evidently well-known. The seer won his release and the cattle by magical means (see Hes. frag. 261, 'Apollodorus' 1.9.12 with Frazer's Appendix IV, and Hoekstra on *Od.* 15.231–6); Homer suppresses the magic, as usual. Save for the article τοῦ, 698 seems old, with *Ϝιϕίκλοιο and *πάϝις for παῖς (Hoekstra, *Epic Verse before Homer* 47f.); cf. 'Ιϕίκλου υἱὸς πολυμήλου Φυλακίδαο (2.705), υἱ. τ᾿ 'Ιϕίκλοιο Ποδάρκης Φ. (*Cat.* 199.5). Such verses helped poets recall genealogical links.

700 ναῦϕιν, an abl.-gen., goes with ἀμύνομαι; like παρὰ ν., 'from the ships' (5× Hom.), it reflects the Myc. abl. plur. in -ϕι (see 588–90n.). μετά plus the gen., meaning 'with', is a rare innovation (5× Hom.): cf. Chantraine, *GH* II 119f.

701–22 The poet moves from a brief mention of Locrian to Telamonian Aias; next, forming the centre of a ring, he depicts both in a simile; he then describes the men of Telamonian and, lastly, of Locrian Aias, with their unique tactics. An overview (719–22) leads into the next scene.

702 Zenodotus' text χάζετ᾿ for ἵστατ᾿ (Did/AT), based on 12.406f. or 18.160, ill suits the ensuing comparison (cf. ἕστασαν, 708). Αἴαντος Τελαμωνίου is a unique formular modification.

703–7 A fine ploughing-simile illustrates the Aiantes' single-mindedness, physical closeness (only the yoke separates the toiling oxen, 706), effort (the oxen sweat, cf. 711) and success (they reach the end of the furrow). Cf. 17.742ff., when the Aiantes bear a body as two sweating mules haul a beam, or *Od.* 13.31ff., when Odysseus is like a man who has ploughed a fallow field all day (the latter half of 13.32 = 703). Fallow land, ploughed longest ago, is the hardest to work (see West on *Erga* 462f.); oxen are less apt for this task than mules (10.352f.). Leaf thinks sweat oozes from the base of their horns because they are yoked by the horns, but this practice, rarely depicted (A. S. F. Gow, *JHS* 34 (1914) 249ff.), was discouraged (Columella 2.2.22f.).

The usual linguistic tangle covers this field (see Beekes, *Laryngeals* 275–7). πρυμνοῖσῑν κ- is recent, like τόξοισῑν (716). The 'neglected' ϝ- in ἱδρώς, cognate with *sweat*, and scansion πολῦς show that 705 adapts π. δ᾿ ἀνακήκιεν ἱ. (23.507), whence come the false readings avoided by Aristarchus and πᾶσαι (Did/AT) but found in a papyrus (differently van der Valk, *Researches* II 196). Yet archaisms burgeon. (ϝ)οἶνοψ, 'dark-faced', used mainly of the sea in Homer, occurs among Myc. names for oxen (KN Ch 897,1015). κατὰ ὦλκα (also *Od.* 18.375) is misdivided for κατ᾿ ἄωλκα, from *κατ᾿ ἄϝολκα, with a diectasis after the vernacular contracted it to ὦλκα (cf. αὖλαξ); but ὦλκα is already certain at *Od.* 18.375. τέλσον means the 'turning-point', 'headland' at the end of the furrow, seen only in τ. ἀρούρης (also at 18.544, cf. 18.547); its root is *qel-, 'turn', cf. τέλος, πολέω, 'plough', τέλσας· στροφάς (Hsch.). Chantraine (*GH* I 309) rightly relates the unique τέμει to the antiquated aor. ἔτετμον, 'met'; Aristarchus (with Ap. Rhod. 3.412) adduced τέμνω, i.e. 'it cuts the headland', which is always ploughed last. Its subject is ἄροτρον, supplied from 703. πηκτὸν ἄ. is formular (10.353, *Od.* 13.32); π. could be a generic epithet like τυκτός or ποιητός, but the composite plough is the more advanced type (West on *Erga* 427–34).

708–10 ἀλλήλοισιν, in some papyri and codices, is from ἐφέστασαν ἄ. (133, 15.703); -οιιν matches the simile better. μάλα intensifies παρ- in παρβεβαῶτε, 'very close beside'. Retainers carry a man's weapons at 600 (a sling), 12.372 (a bow); a shield-bearer is unique. Near Eastern analogies come to mind, but the verses are surely meant to suggest the great weight of Aias' body-shield, as at 16.106ff.; Aias always has a σάκος, not a round ἀσπίς (Trümpy, *Fachausdrücke* 30f.). ἕταροι forms an odd expansion of λαοὶ ἕπονθ' (3×); contrast how Oïlean Aias' followers do not 'follow' him.

712–18 It sounds shameful that his Locrians do *not* follow Oïlean Aias, worse yet that they do not stand firm in close combat, until we hear how their guerrilla tactics break the Trojan ranks from behind the armoured screen of the other units. The variant σταδίης ὑσμίνης ἔργα μέμηλε (Strabo 10.449, cf. T) emends the amusing paradox away. Note the fourfold anaphora of οὐ and the ring formed by ἕποντο; the conventional weapons heavy with epithets are balanced by the light arms of these hill-men. Helenos too used the bow and sling (598–600n.). Unlike Rhodian slingers or Cretan archers, the Locrians were not known as skirmishers later; even at *Aspis* 25 they bear the generic epithet ἀγχέμαχοι (cf. 4–7n.). But these tactics are attested both on the Siege Rhyton from Shaft Grave IV at Mycenae and in seventh-century warfare. Archilochus distinguishes fighting with slings and bows from that with swords, and Strabo (*loc. cit.*) knew an inscription barring the parties in the Lelantine War from using long-range weapons (see 15.709–12n.). Tyrtaeus (frag. 11.35–8) urges the light-armed to lurk behind the shields of the heavy-armed and hurl stones; vase-paintings from Corinth and Sparta show unarmoured slingers behind a screen of hoplites (Snodgrass, *EGA* 167, 203f.). Thus there is no reason to reject this passage, whether it depicts an ancient or a novel tactic; it is not of Dark Age origin, since the sole area with an unbroken tradition of archery was Crete (*ibid.* 142–4). There is no discrepancy with 2.529, where Oïlean Aias wears light armour (λινοθώρηξ), or 4.273ff., where the Aiantes leading a heavy-armed unit are surely Aias and Teukros.

For Zenodotus' text in 712 see 66–7n. With 714 cf. *Od.* 22.111, 22.145, κυνέας χαλκήρεας ἱπποδασείας; κόρυθος has one or both of these epithets at

614, 3.369, 4.459 = 6.9, 15.535 (κόρυς was no longer distinct from κυνέη, once 'dog-skin cap'). ἀσπίδας (-ος) εὐκύκλους (-ου) recurs 4× at the start of the verse; the contraction of ἐΰ- proves this formula relatively recent (p. 14 n. 19), as we would expect of round shields (163–5n.). μείλινα δοῦρα recurs only at 19.361, but cf. μείλινον ἔγχος (597n.). The second half of 716 = 599 (where see n.); with the first half of 717 cf. *Od.* 11.372, 24.117. ἔπειτα means 'after their arrival'. ταρφέα, 'thick and fast', is always an adv. in Homer (5×).

720–2 Verse 720 blends Τρωσίν τε καὶ Ἕκτορι (2×) with Ἕ. (-α) χαλκο-κορυστῇ (-ήν), 7×; cf. 16.654. There is further wit in the contrast between ἐλάνθανον and μιμνήσκοντο; cf. μνήσαντο δὲ χάρμης | (etc.), 7× Hom., split over the verse-end only here, and λήθετο χ. | (etc., 3×). λανθάνω is a 'recent' form, next at *Od.* 12.227, *Thebaid* frag. 2.8, *Hy.* 18.9 (Risch, *Wortbildung* 271f.).

723–5 Crises are often narrowly averted when someone intervenes; on the function of such contrafactual statements see de Jong, *Narrators* 68–81. Thus Patroklos just misses taking Troy at 16.698ff., or the Trojans avoid a rout at 8.130–2 and 6.73–5 (... εἰ μὴ ... Ἕκτορι εἶπε παραστάς ...). This crisis makes us take Pouludamas' speech more seriously; the contrast between λευγαλέως νηῶν ἄπο and πὰρ ν. ... ἀπήμονες (744) proves him right. ν. ἄπο καὶ κλισιάων is a unique variation of νεῶν ἄ. κ. κ. (7×). This is surprising, since νεῶν is the more recent form: for an explanation see Hoekstra, *Modifications* 126–8. For 'windy Troy' see 3.305n. The same verse as 725 (but with | δή τότε) introduced Pouludamas' previous advice to Hektor (12.60 = 12.210). θρασὺν Ἕκτορα is formular (22.455, 24.72, 24.786, cf. 8.312), and imaginable alternatives like μέγαν or κλυτὸν Ἕ. never appear; yet the reference to Hektor's over-confidence is apt. His formular system makes boldness essential to his nature (cf. 6.407).

726–47 On the place of Pouludamas' speech in larger patterns see 673–837n. Lohmann (*Reden* 178–81) well compares it to his other warnings to Hektor (12.61–79, 12.211–29, 18.254–83). Its first half (726–34) closely follows the first half of his *previous* speech (12.211–14: with 215 cf. 735); his warning about Akhilleus at 744–7 recurs in the first half of his *next* speech (18.256–65). Hektor's reactions chart his increasing (and misplaced) confidence: he acts on the first and third speeches, with beneficial results (12.80 = 13.748), but rejects the second and fourth, in the latter case disastrously. Some find Pouludamas verbose. Fenik (*TBS* 121) dislikes 730–4, but the priamel softens the rebuke by granting that one cannot be good at everything, including taking advice (and 731 is spurious). He also objects to the veiled warning that Akhilleus might return to battle, the first time this possibility has entered Trojan counsels. But this gives Pouluda-mas good reason to propose consulting the others, reminds us again that Akhilleus looms over the action (cf. 113, 324, 348), especially as his name is too terrible for Pouludamas to utter (as also at 18.257), and builds up our respect for the latter's advice, since we know that the hero will eventually fight.

726–9 At 12.216 Pouludamas vainly warned Hektor not to attack the ships; now that the attack seems about to fail, he argues that he was right and tactfully suggests withdrawal, turning Hektor's bravery, which is implicitly praised, into the reason why he will not take advice (cf. bT). The ring-structure in 727–30 stresses that gifts like courage are from a god and not in one's own power, a common idea (15.440–1n.). Hektor needs this reminder both now and later (cf. on 54, 825–9). For the maxim that one cannot excel at everything cf. 4.320, 23.670f., *Od.* 8.167f. The usual antithesis between valour and wisdom, fighter and counsellor (e.g. 1.258, 4.322ff., 18.105f.), is applied to Hektor and Pouludamas by the poet at 18.252. Some warriors are also wise in council, like Odysseus, Diomedes, Idomeneus or Thoas (15.281–4), but none is the best at both, although this is the ideal in Homer and other heroic poetry too (M. Schofield, *CQ* 36 (1986) 6–31).

726–8 ἀμήχανος describes someone incorrigible, cf. 10.167, 15.14, 16.29; παραρρητός, 'persuasive', means 'able to be persuaded' at 9.526, its other occurrence. Verse 726 should end with a stop, 727 with a comma (*pace* Leaf); for οὕνεκα ... τούνεκα see 3.403–5, *Cat.* 30.26–9 (restored), *Theog.* 88 (reversed). Nicanor (in A) made 727f. a question, like 3.405, but this would be too scornful here.

731 Copyists could easily omit 731 by homoearchon, but it is surely spurious: it has weak MS support and the priamel invites expansion (Apthorp, *MS Evidence* 36f.). Aristarchus did not read it, since Arn/A on 4.320 quotes 730–2 without it. T say Crates' disciple Zenodotus of Mallos added it (Nickau in *RE* xA (1972) 45–7); perhaps he complained that Aristarchus left it out. It is absent in one of four quotations, one of three papyri and most early codices. Later MSS reintroduce it from the scholia; van der Valk's defence of it neglects its weak attestation (*Researches* II 499–502). But it looks like a rhapsodic elaboration, not a Pergamene invention; like Crates' text of 1.1ff., it surely came from sources that Aristarchus did not know or did not like. Thus κίθαριν καὶ ἀοιδήν recurs in the nom. at *Od.* 1.159, *HyAp* 188; cf. ὀρχηστύν τε καὶ ἱμερόεσσαν ἀ. (*Od.* 1.421 = 18.304, which is how Lucian quotes 731). Verse 731 obscures the antithesis between warrior and counsellor, as Eustathius saw (957.10–14), but that between war and the dance is also traditional (15.508–10n.). The *variatio* ἑτέρῳ for ἄλλῳ, and the topos of poetry as a divine gift with its self-referential flattery of the bard's craft (cf. 637), made this an attractive expansion, like the interpolations to include a bard at 18.604–6 (see p. 28). Michel accepts it (*N* 124f.); contrast F. Solmsen, *TAPA* 85 (1954) 3f.

732–5 For τιθεῖ and πολέας see Chantraine, *GH* I 298f., 220f. As often, πολεῖς is read by all MSS, papyri included: Aristarchus rejected this probable Atticism (Did/A on 21.131). πόλεις, 'cities' (bT), is a bad attempt to avoid repeating 'many', like Aristophanes' πολλόν for πολλοί (Did/A). But the climax 'many *benefit* … it *saves* many' excuses the repetition. The point that he who gives wise advice most realizes it himself (because he is vindicated) is best made if κ'(αἱ) αὐτός not κ'(ε) is read; Aristarchus assumed a redundant κε (Arn/A on 20.311). For the sense cf. μάλιστα δέ τ' ἔκλυον αὐτοί (*Od.* 6.185). Verse 735 = 9.103, 9.314, *Od.* 23.130. Pouludamas was no less diffident at 12.215: he could have ended σύ δὲ σύνθεο καί μευ ἄκουσον, or σὺ δ' ἐνὶ φρεσὶ βάλλεο σῇσι, or ὡς τετελεσμένον ἔσται (the superior variant at 9.314).

736–9 Pouludamas puts first the reason for his advice (hence γάρ), and within this a reminder of Hektor's success, before making his proposal. He says that the Trojans standing aloof are 'in their armour' to show that they could easily rejoin battle and aid their outnumbered comrades. στέφανος is close to its original sense 'circle', 'something that surrounds thickly' (Chantraine, *Dict.* s.v. στέφω): Aristarchus' predecessor Comanus (frag. 12 Dyck) first saw that its developed sense 'garland' is post-Homeric (*Theog.* 576, *Erga* 75, *Cypria* frag. 5, *Hy.* 7.42). The metaphor δέδηε, 'burn', also describes battle at 12.35, 17.253, 20.18; the Τρῶες are also μεγάθυμοι at 5.27, 11.459 and 5× gen. κατὰ τεῖχος ἔβησαν means 'came *over* the wall', as at 15.384. The Ionic poet prefers ἀφεστᾶσῖν σύν to -σι ξύν (cf. 533–9n.); the older form ξύν, attested in Myc., has been largely ousted by σύν in the epos (Janko, *HHH* 236f.; differently G. Dunkel, *Glotta* 60 (1982) 55–61).

742–4 Pouludamas' presentation of the Trojans' options subtly reveals his desire that the attack be called off: 'we *may* fall at the .. ships (ἐν νήεσσι … πέσωμεν) – *if* the god is willing to grant us victory – or … we *might* return (ἔλθοιμεν) unscathed from the ships'. ἐν … πέσωμεν is ambiguous (Eustathius 958.10–13): its surface meaning is 'fall upon the ships' as at 9.235, but ἐν νηῦσι … πέσωσι means 'fall (dead) among the ships' at 15.63. ἤ κεν ἔπειτα can mean 'or otherwise' (cf. 24.356, *Od.* 20.63, Alcaeus frag. 129.19), but in its temporal sense ἔ. hints at a further warning: we might not return safely *after an attack*. The opt. ἔλθοιμεν makes the idea of a safe return more remote than that of falling at the ships; cf. the shift of mood at 18.308. Only a papyrus, A and two late MSS offer the *lectio facilior* ἔλθωμεν.

745–6 'I fear lest the Greeks repay yesterday's debt …' Pouludamas raises the unpleasant topic of Akhilleus with a flattering allusion to Hektor's victory the day before. ἀφίστημι means 'weigh out' here only in epos, whence the coin called a στατήρ; in Homer's day trade was still by weight alone. Few sources preserve ἀποστήσωνται: most have the unmetrical gloss ἀπο- τίσωνται (p. 21 n. 8). ἀνήρ ἄτος πολέμοιο is based, perhaps with sinister effect, on Ἄρης ἄ. π. (3×, cf. *Theog.* 714, *Aspis* 59). ἆτος is from ἄατος, 'insatiable'; the uncontracted form, used by Hesiod, lingers as a variant elsewhere (see West on *Theog.* 714).

748–9 = 12.80f. (ἀπήμων echoes 744); but 749, omitted by a papyrus and some codices, is clearly a concordance-interpolation thence (cf. 657n.).

751–88 The scene-change, needed so that the different sectors of battle can be reunified, is deft: Hektor's speech shifts from Pouludamas to Hektor himself (752f.), then the poet narrates Hektor's actions and the rally around Pouludamas (756f.), before a final shift to Hektor, who visits the left (765) and returns to the centre (789); thereafter we hear no more of different sectors.

752–3 = 12.368f., with ἐπιτείλω for ἐπαμύνω. Leaf deems this 'careless borrowing' thence, since κεῖσε has no reference; but none is needed, and Homer avoids having a Trojan use the terms 'left' and 'right', which are seen from the Greek viewpoint (675n.). ἐπιτείλω means 'tell them (to rally)', as the Trojans' reaction proves (757); the half-line is also at 10.63.

754–5 Hektor strides off 'like a snowy mountain'. The image has two points of comparison: (i) his huge size (a giant is 'like a mountain' at *Od.* 9.190ff., cf. 10.113, 11.243); (ii) the flash of his armour, likened to dazzling snowflakes at 19.357f. (so Fränkel, *Gleichnisse* 21). The 'savage and fearsome' effect (bT) is enhanced, not spoilt, by the fact that mountains do not move. 'Snowy' is vital to this; the metrically equivalent epithet 'shady' would have had a pastoral nuance. ὄρεα are νιφόεντα at 14.227, 20.385, *Od.* 19.338 (cf. 18.616, 20.385), but σκιόεντα at 1.157, 2× *Od.*, 4× *Hy.* See also E. M. Bradley, *TAPA* 98 (1967) 37–41. κεκληγώς, 'screaming', which can apply to men or birds, introduces the metaphor πέτετο, 'he flew' (Eustathius 958.55–7); the double image conveys his terrifying speed. The κεκληγώς of the MSS is the correct form, not -ων (16.430n.). The rest of 755 is formular: cf. Τρώων ἀγοὶ ἠδ' ἐπικούρων 2×, Τ. κλειτῶν (τ') ἐ. 3×, etc. Since the Mycenaeans probably used mercenaries (685–8n.), *e-pi-ko-wo* surely stands for /epikorwoi/, 'the extra lads', in KN As 4493, PY An 657.

756–9 Pouludamas is a son of Panthoos, Priam's counsellor (3.146), and so brother of Euphorbos and Huperenor (17.24f.). All share a minor formular system. With 756 cf. 16.535 (reversed); cf. too | — — Πάνθου υἱὸν (etc.) ἐϋμμελίην ('Εὔφορβον) |, 15.522, 17.9, 23, 59; | (Πουλυδάμαντος ∪ — ∪) ἀγαυοῦ Πανθοΐδαο |, 15.446; μεγαθύμου Π. |, 14.454. ἀγαπήνορα describes Laodamas, another name shaped — ∪∪ — and starting with a consonant (*Od.* 7.170), in parallel with μεγαλήτορα: it occurs 3× gen. with vowel-initial names shaped — ∪∪ — — | (also 1× nom.). It is thus part of the normal epithet-system for minor heroes, and means 'hospitable', not 'loved by men' or 'loving valour'. Hektor adapts 758f. to the nom. at 770f. (cf. 781). The first pair he names are injured Trojans (527ff., 593ff.), the second, dead allies (560ff., 384ff.); Aineias is left out because he is unscathed. With the periphrasis βίην θ' Ἑλένοιο ἄνακτος cf. βίη Τεύκροιο ἅ. (23.859) and 246–8, 582–3nn.

761–4 In the understatement οὐκέτι πάμπαν ἀπήμονας οὐδ' ἀνολέθρους each word is worse than the preceding, as if to mirror Hektor's growing alarm. ἀπήμων actualizes Pouludamas' warning (cf. 744, 748), while ἀνόλεθρος anticipates 763 and 773. Aristarchus notes that the adjectives describe the whole group, whereas only some are dead and others are injured, as we are told in chiastic order. βεβλημένοι οὐτάμενοί τε reinforces the effect; Helenos βέβληται (594), Deïphobos οὔτασται (529). ἀνόλεθρος, unique in Greek, adapts ἀνώλεθρος. Verse 763 = 24.168, cf. 8.359; with 764 cf. 11.659 = 826 = 16.24. The 'wall' is surely that of Troy, whither Deïphobos was taken (538), not the Greek rampart behind which wounded Trojans could now shelter.

765–87 Hektor, himself just chided by Pouludamas, rebukes the hapless Paris. His tirade is unjust, as he should have realized when he found Paris exhorting his men. We may read into it his alarm, vexation and guilt that he caused these losses by plunging on regardless of whether others were keeping their formation (so bT on 768–73); nowhere in the *Iliad* are two rebukes so close together. Hektor abused Paris before (3.39ff., 6.326ff.); being to blame for the war and often otherwise irresponsible, he is an easy target. Each time he admitted his fault; now he does not, but placates Hektor by putting himself under his command (Michel, *N* 129). Their exchange fits into larger patterns (673–837n.). Just as the battle on the left began with the appearance of Idomeneus and Meriones (330ff.), after Poseidon's exhortation and their mutual chaffing, so this battle begins with the appearance of Hektor and Paris, after Pouludamas' exhortation and Hektor's rebuke. Each time there is a further delay before the combat begins: the summary of the gods' attitudes at 345–60 corresponds to the council and the deception of Zeus in book 14.

765–9 Verses 765 + 767 resemble 17.116f. = 682f., which begin τὸν δὲ μάλ' αἶψ' ἐνόησε μάχης ἐπ' ἀριστερὰ πάσης; 17.684 continues ἀγχοῦ δ' ἱστάμενος προσέφη, cf. 768. δακρυόεσσης, found 4× with ἰῶκα or πόλεμον -ῳ, is suited to what Hektor feels: it is equally apt at 16.436. Verse 766, needed to supply Paris' name, is traditional (it occurs 3× nom., and 2× without δῖος); but its reference to Helen reminds us, especially after Menelaos' words at 626f., that Hektor has a right to be critical. Spartan inscriptions confirm that Ἑλένη once began with ϝ- (S. West on *Od.* 4.121). αἰσχροῖς ἐπέεσσι is limited to 3.38 = 6.325 (cf. 24.238, where (ϝ)έπεσσι is maintained); these verses introduce Hektor's other rebukes of Paris, and 769 = 3.39 (where see n.). It is usual to call someone accused of cowardice or weakness 'handsome', e.g. 5.787 = 8.228, 17.142 (Ἕκτορ εἶδος ἄριστε).

γυναιμανής and ἠπεροπευτής recur at *Hy.* 1.17, *HyHerm* 282 (of Dionusos and Hermes respectively).

769–73 Hektor's speech is neatly symmetrical despite his passion. After four abusive epithets (see above), he uses two urgent descending dicola with anaphora of first ποῦ τοι, then νῦν. He names two of their brothers, a whole friendly dynasty (Asios'), and the hope of Priam's house, Othruoneus (361–82n.), whose name is the more emphatic for being omitted earlier (758f.), as if Hektor thinks of him only now. The list lends support to his hyperbole about the ruin of all Troy. 'Now your ruin is *safe*' (σῶς), i.e. 'certain', emphasizes that this means Paris' ruin too; the oxymoron recurs at *Od.* 5.305, 22.28. The repeated τοι points to Paris' role in the disaster; the adjacent formulae in αἰπύς may hint that his ruin will be as headlong as if he fell from the walls he has ruined 'from the top down' (κατ' ἄκρης, sc. πόλιος). The figurative sense of αἰπύς, 'steep', 'hard to overcome' (S. West on *Od.* 1.11), is confined to direct speech or the poet's expression of a hero's thought (de Jong, *Narrators* 142n.): cf. 17.364–5n.

775–87 Paris gently rejects the rebuke, admitting to slackness at other times; he lets 'but not now' be inferred from 'since my mother did not bear me an utter coward'. That he alone remains proves his valour, but again he does not say this. His ellipses and his admission are both in character (cf. 3.59). Since Hektor stirred up battle by the ships (Paris refers to his speech at 150–4), everyone has stood fast – alive or dead! Hektor, he hints, is at fault for ordering the attack. ἀναίτιον αἰτιάασθαι (etc.) recurs at 11.654 (of Akhilleus), *Od.* 20.135. The synizesis ἐπεὶ οὐδ' (777) is Odyssean (4.352, 11.249 (?), 19.314, 20.227), as is 784 (6×, with variants). On the modified formula μακρῇσι ... ἐγχείῃσιν (782) see 339–44n. Verses 785f. = *Od.* 23.127f. (spurious). Aristarchus (Did/A) rightly read δ' ἐμμεμαῶτες against δὲ (μ)μεμ.; cf. the spelling ἐνὶ μμεγάροισι favoured by Aristophanes (schol. *Od.* 2.338) and common in papyri. The same doubt arises at 17.735, 746, 22.143. ἐμμεμαώς is certain 11×; Leumann (*HW* 52) thinks it evolved by misdivision in cases like this, but see H. Seiler, *ZVS* 75 (1957) 19f. ἀλκή (786) picks up ἄναλκις (777), again in an understatement. πὰρ δύναμιν (787) is the sole case of παρά 'beyond' in the *Iliad*, but cf. *Od.* 14.509 (Chantraine, *GH* II 123); πὰρ δ. δ' οὐκ ἔστι plays wittily on δύναμίς γε πάρεστι. πολεμίζειν goes with ἔστι, not ἐσσύμενον: cf. 315–16n.

788 = 7.120, cf. 6.61. ἀδελφειοῦ reflects the Dark Age gen. *ἀδελφεόο (see p. 15).

789–94 We now return to the centre, where Pouludamas and Hektor's brother and driver Kebriones have obeyed Hektor's orders and gathered others about them. These prefigure the next casualty-list (cf. 478–80n.): Phalkes, Morus and Hippotion all die at 14.513–15, with a *Peri*phetes, who is *Polu*phetes here. Hippotion's death is another slip; here he is only a warrior's father, so he should not be slain along with his son (cf. 422n. for a like error)! Otherwise we would have another case of father and son at war together (cf. 643–59n.).

The names are interesting. 'Kebriones' may derive from Kebren, a Cymaean colony in the Troad with a native name (*Homeric Epigram* 9, with G. Markwald, *Die homerischen Epigramme*, Königstein 1986, 182). A Phalkes was one of the Temenidai: cf. φάλκη, 'dandruff' (132–3n.). Read Φάλκην τ' (so a papyrus). The unknown 'Orthaios' recalls Orthe, a Thessalian town (2.739). 'Poluphetes' is the apt name of Laios' herald (schol. Eur. *Phoen.* 39), cf. Periphetes, son of a herald 15.638–40. But 791 has an Asiatic tone. 'Palmus', otherwise unknown, meant 'king' in Lydian, as in Hipponax (Scherer, 'Nichtgriechische Personennamen' 39); but it belongs to a Phrygian, perhaps in a misremembering of the Phrygian king Phorkus (2.862). Borrowing of Anatolian words for 'king' is not limited to post-Homeric τύραννος, cf. Hittite *tarḫunt-*, Etruscan *Tarχunies*; note too the Lycian Prutanis (5.678, with Chantraine, *Dict.* s.v.), Rhesos (Thracian for 'king', cf. Latin *rēx*) and 427–33n. The Phrygian leader Askanios (2.862f.), eponym of Askaniē in Phrygia, is the supposed founder of many cities in the Troad; he has been linked with Ashkenaz, ancestor of the Scythians at Genesis 10.3 (von Kamptz, *Personennamen* 287). He first becomes Aineias' son in Hellanicus, *FGH* 4 F 31; Homer had already turned Skamandrios, co-founder of these cities, into Hektor's son by the easy device of giving Astuanax another name (cf. P. Smith, *HSCP* 85 (1981) 57f.). 'Morus' could be Asiatic: cf. Phorkus, Kapus (2.862, 20.239). Lycian and Lydian have many short names in -ις and -υς (Heubeck, *Kleine Schriften* 520). A Hippotion is known ·from eighth-century Chios (Fraser and Matthews, *Names* I s.v.).

792–4 υἷ' is for υἷε not υἷα, as the ensuing plurals show. After 792 Strabo (12.565) read Μυσῶν ἀγχεμάχων ἡγήτορα ⟨καρτεροθύμων⟩; this is based on 5 and 14.512–14, whence the interpolator wrongly deduced that these were Mysians. The statement that they came the day before, because Zeus sent them only then (a lame explanation), causes a discrepancy: they must have arrived some days ago for Askanios to be listed at 2.862f. (see G. Jachmann, *Der homerische Schiffskatalog und die Ilias*, Cologne 1958, 134–42)! Homer already had their sad fate in mind – arrived yesterday, they will die today: for the pathetic motif of latecomers to war see 361–82n. The idea of continual Trojan reinforcements is more creditable to the Greeks, who receive none (bT). ἀμοιβός is an epic *hapax* formed like ἀοιδός.

795–9 The Trojans finally begin the attack; a full-blown simile describes their massed advance before attention focuses on Hektor. The image has more points of comparison than are explicit; for behind the ships is the beach, at which Hektor aims. Diction which suits both squalls and battle enhances its effect. The initial similarity is between the Trojans' speed and a gale's

(795), an image applied to attackers in brief comparisons at 12.40, 12.375 (11.297 has a one-line extension). But the mention of Zeus in 794 evokes other resemblances: the squall comes with Zeus's thunder, just as the Trojans now enjoy his backing; it heads for the shore, like the Trojans (but they come from landward). But in the simile sea and sky are working together, unlike Poseidon and Zeus. The squall's 'din' is like the din of battle, often called ὅμαδος (cf. 16.295); the waves crashing on the beach one after another suggest the army's serried ranks, as the repetition of 799 outside the simile in 800 proves. bT saw much of this, adding that the white-capped waves evoke the men's flashing helmets (cf. 805). This is likelier than it seems, because in a similar comparison at 4.422–6 the wave κορύσσεται and κορυφοῦται; it is also κυρτός, as here (cf. too *Od.* 11.244, *Cat.* 32). bT also note that 798f., admired as vivid by Aristotle (*Rhet.* 3.1412a9f.), contain alliteration in *l*, *p* and *z* (to convey the crashing of the waves), quadruple assonance in -τα and epithets referring to different aspects of the waves – παφλάζοντα to sound, κυρτά to shape, φαληριόωντα to colour. The very rare fourth-foot elision in πρὸ μέν τ' ἄλλ', αὐτὰρ ἐπ' ἄλλα, suggests how the many waves come one upon another. The Trojan rows fit closely together like stones in a wall, as ἀρηρότες indicates (800, cf. 15.618, 16.211–17n.).

The simile belongs to two pairs. Like the storm-image at 11.297f., it is paired with βροτολοιγῷ ἶσος Ἄρηϊ, used of Hektor at 802f., 11.295. It is also resumed at 14.16–19, when Nestor's mounting disquiet is likened to the swell presaging a storm; that simile too mentions a wind from Zeus (Moulton, *Similes* 23f.). ἀτάλαντος is used to liken a hero to Ares in a set of ancient formulae (295–7n.); cf. too νυκτὶ θοῇ ἀ. (12.463). ὑπὸ βροντῆς means 'with thunder' (Chantraine, *GH* II 143); the thunder does not *send* the squall. παφλάζω, 'boil', 'seethe', of the sea, appears in Alcaeus and is colloquial in Attic; κῦμα πολυφλοίσβοιο θαλάσσης (4× epos) is separated here. φαληριόωντα, 'white-capped', a *hapax* in epos, is from *bhel- (132–3n.); cf. Hesychius' glosses φάληρα· λευκά, ἀφρίζοντα and φαλίσσεται· λευκαίνεται, ἀφρίζει. Its opposite is ἀκροκελαινιόων (21.249, of a river).

802–5 For the description of Hektor's shield as he charges cf. those at 12.294–7, 17.492f. With 802 cf. 11.295; 803 = 157. Herodian (in A), with some good MSS, has a *lectio difficilior* πρὸ ἕθεν instead of πρόσθεν (read by all MSS at 157). ΠΡΟΣΘΕΝ, easily confused with ΠΡΟΕΘΕΝ, has ousted it in a few MSS at 5.96. Homer used both phrases (and cf. πρόσθεν ἕθεν, 3×). ῥινοῖσιν and πολλός are recent; standard in Ionic prose, π. is rarer than πολύς in the epos (19/90×, counting the nom. and acc. masc. sing.). Here it allows a masc. caesura, adapting πολὺς δ' ἐπελήλατο χαλκός (17.493). The top layer was bronze, over leather. Verse 805 splits the phrase πήληκα φαεινήν (527), cf. κροτάφοισι φαεινὴ | πήληξ (16.104f.).

806–8 On Hektor's tactics see 156–8n. As if to draw a parallel between him and Deïphobos, 806f. resembles 158, just as 803 resembles 157. Zenodotus' extra verse, λίην γάρ σφιν πᾶσιν ἐκέκριτο θάρσεϊ πολλῷ, is nonsensical after 808 where the scholia place it (Arn, Did/AT). Friedländer put it after 807, '(Hektor tested the ranks), for he was very distinguished among them all for his great courage'; but it could follow 809. Its phrasing is unepic, its statement redundant (van der Valk, *Researches* II 41).

809–32 Aias confidently challenges Hektor, striding forward in contrast to his foe's cautious steps; Hektor's reply shows that, far from heeding Pouludamas' warning, Aias' threats or the ensuing omen, he is surer than ever of victory. Both speech-introductions are unique (Edwards, *HSCP* 74 (1970) 24).

809 μακρά βιβάσθων, also at 15.676, 16.534, artificially adapts μ. βιβάς (4×, 1× fem., 1× acc.) to fit the verse-end (Shipp, *Studies* 97); a papyrus has φώνησέν τε instead, perhaps from 24.193. On how this stride differs from κοῦφα (or ὕψι) β. see 158n.

810–20 Aias' challenge is in ring-form; he is a fine orator (17.626–55n.). σχεδὸν ἐλθέ is resumed by σ. ἔμμεναι (817) – far from Hektor daring to draw nigh, the time is nigh when he will flee. Zeus's lash has subdued the Greeks (812), but Hektor will soon beg Zeus to make his horses faster than hawks (818f.), i.e. he will lash them in flight. The Greeks have arms to keep him from the ships (χεῖρες ... ἡμῖν, 814), arms with which they will sack Troy (χερσὶν ὑφ' ἡμετέρῃσιν, 816). bT note that Aias draws the danger onto himself ('come near'), but shares the valour with all (in 811); they add that his confidence is based on knowledge of Akhilleus' threat to halt Hektor if the fighting reaches his own ships (9.654f.).

810 δαιμόνιε is sarcastic (448–9n.). Aristarchus, followed by the OCT, read αὔτως (Did/A), i.e. 'why do you *vainly* try to scare ...'; a papyrus and the good codices have οὔτως, i.e. 'why are you so afraid of ...', with δειδίσσομαι in its passive sense (cf. 2.190). This is supported by τίη δὲ σὺ κήδεαι οὔ. and τ. ὀλοφύρεαι οὔ. (6.55, 21.106), where there can be no doubt over the text (cf. 446–7n.).

812–16 'Zeus's whip' is a vivid traditional metaphor, cf. Διὸς μάστιγι δαμέντες (12.37). His whip is the thunderbolt (so D, cf. bT on 12.37, 15.17). Thus at 2.781f. he 'lashes' the Earth around Tuphōeus, with lightning, surely; at 15.17 he threatens to 'lash' the gods with 'blows', i.e. thunderbolts (cf. too *Theog.* 857). Aeschylus uses the metaphor more loosely (*Ag.* 642, *Seven* 608, *Pr.* 682). It may reflect a belief that thunder was the rumble of Zeus's chariot (A. B. Cook, *Zeus* II 830–3), just as it was the rumble of Thor's (H. R. Ellis Davidson, *Gods and Myths of Northern Europe*, London 1964, 76); the Sun's horses were called 'Thunder' and 'Lightning' (*Titanomachy* frag. 7 B. = 4 D.). Cf. Stith Thompson A 1141.4. West (*Works and Days* 366–8) thinks goats once drew Zeus's chariot, like Thor's (whence *αἰγίϝοχος); see

15.308–11n. — For ἐέλπεται a few MSS read ἐέλδεται: but Aias mocks the Trojans' expectations, not their wishes. φθαίη gives the sense 'Troy will fall long before you can destroy our ships'. ἐῢ ναιομένη πόλις ὑμή, acc. at 5.489, adapts ἐῢ ναιόμενον πτολίεθρον to show whose city will fall; for ὑμός see p. 8 n. 2. Verse 816 = 2.374, 4.291.

818–20 The contraction in ἀρήσῃ for -εαι is certain 3× *Il.*, 8× *Od.* (Chantraine, *GH* I 57); the rest of 818 = 6.259, with innovative adaptations at 2.49, *Thebaid* frag. 3.3, *Hy.* 19.44. The hawk is the fastest bird (*Od.* 13.86f.); its speed is traditional in comparisons (62–5, 15.237–8nn.). This image evoked the formula which ends 820 and thrice appears as πέτοντο κονίοντες πεδίοιο! — καλλίθριξ describes sheep as well as horses, and refers to coats, not manes (Hoekstra on *Od.* 15.215).

821–3 Just as Aias' metaphor of Zeus's whip led up to Hektor's real chariot, so his hawk-metaphor introduces a real bird, Zeus's eagle (24.310ff.). No other omen follows a challenge. To maintain suspense about Zeus's attentiveness, we are not told that he sent it: contrast the eagle at 12.200–9, when this is at least implied. That omen prompted Pouludamas' first warning to Hektor, of which we were just reminded. There Hektor scoffed (237ff.), but the army understood (209); here too he takes no notice, but the men comprehend (823). Cf. the only other bird-omen during the fighting (8.247–50); each portent is more favourable to the Greeks than the last (Thornton, *Supplication* 53f.). Bird-omens always come true in Homer: scoffers like Hektor or Eurumakhos (*Od.* 2.181f.) are doomed to a bad end. Verse 821 = *Od.* 15.160, 15.525; αἰετὸς ὑψιπετήεις is at 12.201, 12.219, but need not of itself evoke that scene, since it is a formula (*Od.* 20.243, cf. 22.308, *Od.* 24.538). θάρσυνος recurs in Greek only at 16.70 (see Risch, *Wortbildung* 150f.).

824–32 As at 769, Hektor opens with abuse. He answers Aias' reference to 'father Zeus' and the other gods, and his promise to defend the ships, with the presumptuous words 'I wish I were as surely the son of Zeus, and honoured like the other gods, as this day will bring evil to all the Argives'. To Aias' forecast that he will flee to Troy by chariot, and to the bird-omen, he replies that Aias will glut the Trojan dogs and birds. In fact it is Hektor who nearly becomes carrion and raises dust on the plain, not fleeing but dragged behind Akhilleus' chariot (22.354, 22.399ff.).

824 Cf. Ἥρη ἀπτοεπές, ποῖον τὸν μῦθον ἔειπες (8.209); ἀφαμαρτοεπής (3.215). The idea is of accurate speech: cf. οὐχ ἡμάρτανε μύθων (*Od.* 11.511). βουγάϊε means 'you oaf' or 'you ox', as at *Od.* 18.79 (Antinoos to the gluttonous braggart Iros). Ap. Soph. (52.11ff.) rightly derived it from βου-, 'big', like βούπαις or '*horse*-chestnut', plus the root of γαίω, 'exult', which yields 'big fool' or the like; with the (Aeolic) ᾱ cf. Doric γᾱθέω, Latin *gāvisus* (cf. Chantraine, *Dict.* s.v.). A link between βου- and Aias' oxhide shield ill suits Iros. Ap. Soph. also records an interpretation 'plough-ox' (cf. the simile at 703ff.). The second element could come from γαῖα/γῆ, both from *gāya* (Janko, *HHH* 234–6): cf. γάϊος, 'plough-ox' (Hsch.). Hence, no doubt, Zenodotus read βουγήϊε (Did/AT). AbT's variant βουκάϊε resembles βουκαῖος, 'rustic', in Nicander (cf. Gow on Theocritus 10.1); βουκάκιε in the OCT's *app. crit.* is a misprint.

825–9 Were Hektor the son of Zeus and Here, he would be immortal; εἴην ἤματα πάντα is equivalent to ε. ἀθάνατος καὶ ἀγήρως ἦ. π. in his parallel wish at 8.539 (827f. = 540f.). It is fine to call another 'honoured like a god', but to refer it to oneself, adding that one would be equal to Athene and Apollo, smacks of presumption; it confirms Poseidon's words to Aias that Hektor Διὸς εὔχετ' ἐρισθενέος πάϊς εἶναι (54n.). Verse 827 adapts the ancient introduction to impossible wishes, αἲ γὰρ Ζεῦ τε πάτερ καὶ Ἀθηναίη καὶ Ἄπολλον (9× Hom., e.g. 16.97). For the syntax of the impossible wish αἲ γάρ . . . ὡς, 'if only . . . as surely as', cf. 18.464–6n.; αἲ is far better supported than εἰ. πεφήσομαι (also 15.140, *Od.* 22.217) is a fut. based on the perf. πέφαμαι of θείνω, 'slay', cf. φόνος, from *gʷhen-, 'smite': at 17.155 the same form is from φαίνω. ταλάσσῃς, from *τλᾱ-, is also rare (15.164, 17.166).

830–2 δάπτω, used literally of predators, is extended to the spear, which 'feasts' on flesh as at 5.858; for animated spears see 444n. Warriors' flesh is called 'tender' and 'white' at 553, 11.573 = 15.316 and 14.406 (of Aias!) and 'soft' at *Meropis* frag. 3.3 B.; such epithets contrast their flesh with the spear that hungers for it, just as their necks are regularly 'soft' in the same situation. λειρόεις is surely a poetic derivative of λείριος, 'bright', found at Bacchylides 17.95 (so van Leeuwen, *Commentationes Homericae* 233–5): cf. φαιδιμόεις for φαίδιμος (685–8n.). λείριον, 'lily', will mean 'bright (flower)'; with Ποδα-λείριος, 'with flashing feet', cf. πόδαργος, ἀργίπους. Cf. λείρως, 'slender and pale', in Hesychius (read -ιος). Bards took it as 'fine', 'delicate', or 'white', and perhaps already linked it with the Madonna lily native to Greece. Like λεπταλέος, it is transferred to the 'clear' sound of cicadas at 3.152 (where see n.), and of the Muses at *Theog.* 41: cf. W. B. Stanford, *Phoenix* 23 (1969) 3–8; differently R. B. Egan, *Glotta* 63 (1985) 14–24. From ἀτάρ, 831f., like 825ff., is repeated from book 8 (379f.), when Athene and Here decide to intervene against Hektor's 'madness' (355).

833–7 Book 13 ends with the battle much as it was at 126ff., when the armies first clashed before the ships. The shouts on both sides betoken equal zest; we still cannot see who will win. With a masterly touch, the poet has the sound drift skyward, leaving in suspense whether Zeus hears it – but at least Nestor does . . .! As usual, the transition between books is smooth, with no sense of closure. The repeated motif of the din of battle articulates the entire narrative (see on 14.1ff.); on why Hektor's duel with Aias is delayed until 14.402ff. see n. there. To ἐπί, 833f. = 12.251f., the end of Hektor's

riposte to Pouludamas' warning about the eagle-omen (833 also occurs 3×
Od.). The rest of 834 echoes 822 (cf. too 17.723), and brings the Trojans'
cheering into balance with the Greeks'; note the chiasmus ἠχῇ – ἐπὶ δ'
ἴαχε – ἐπίαχον – ἠχή. λάθοντο | ἀλκῆς adapts λ. δὲ θούριδος ἀ. (2×, cf.
720–2n.).

837 This v. means more than ἀϋτὴ δ' οὐρανὸν ἵκει (14.60). The unique
expression Διὸς αὐγάς reverts to the theme of Zeus's eyes, as at 13.3ff.
αὐγή is properly a 'ray' from a fire or the sun. Since vision by reflected light
was not understood, Helios was thought to see with his rays (cf. 339–44n.,
14.342–5n., *Od.* 11.16), and everyone else with invisible rays coming from
the eyes: see *HyHerm* 45; Empedocles frag. 84; Plato, *Tim.* 45B–C; Onians,
Origins 76–8. This is a very old idea: cf. αὐγάζομαι, 'see' (23.458), from
αὐγή, and λεύσσω, 'see', from λευκός, once 'shining'. Hence Zeus's eyes are
φαεινώ (3), and φάεα means 'eyes' 3× *Od.* The concept of hearing was
analogous (16.633–4n.). αὐγαί, 'eyes', is next attested at *HyHerm* 361; cf.
Pindar, *Py.* 9.62. Someone conjectured αὐλάς (T), because of the 'court' of
Zeus that Telemakhos imagines (*Od.* 4.74, cf. 'Aesch.' *Pr.* 122). But the idea
of an all-seeing god is ancient (Griffin, *HLD* 179f.), and is aptly evoked here.
But we are still in suspense: the din has only reached his *eyes*, not his ears!

BOOK FOURTEEN

The structure of book 14 is delightfully clear, consisting of a concentric ring:

A 1–134   the Greek leaders' council: the prospect of failure
B 135–152   Poseidon's renewed intervention
C 153–353   the seduction of Zeus by Here
B′ 354–401   Poseidon leads the Greeks into battle
A′ 402–522   the Greeks rout the Trojans: the prospect of success.

The 'deception of Zeus', discussed in detail in my n. on 153ff., gave book 14 its ancient name (Διὸς ἀπάτη); save for its sequel at 15.4ff., it could be thought of as a brilliant yet detachable episode. But it performs the same ultimate function as the rest of book 14, by retarding the relentless Trojan advance; even without Akhilleus the Greeks can hold their own, so long as Zeus is not actively hostile. The narrative presents both 1–152 and 153–353 as simultaneous with the fighting in book 13, so that Aias' duel with Hektor picks up at 402 exactly where it left off at 13.836. On how this is achieved while the impression of sequential narration is preserved, see below; on why the duel is interrupted see on 402ff. Thus book 14 forms a natural unit, although a ring-structure at 14.506–15.4 overlaps its boundary. It is a paradigm of Homer's virtuosity in diverse types of traditional composition – debate, exhortation, genealogical and hymnic narration, and taut, symmetrically constructed battle-narrative with vaunts of stinging sarcasm. But above all it is the humour of the deception of Zeus, all the more unquenchable because it flickers against so dark a background, that makes book 14 a masterpiece.

1–152 Nestor, roused by the din while tending Makhaon in his hut, goes out to investigate. He meets the wounded leaders Diomedes, Odysseus and Agamemnon, who proposes to save the ships by launching them. Odysseus objects, and Diomedes persuades them to exhort those men who are holding back; Poseidon, in disguise, heartens Agamemnon with a speech and the Greeks with a great shout

1–152 Leaf thought the leaders' council 'in no way advances the action'; worse still, the situation Nestor sees (14f.) – the Greeks in disorder, the Trojans advancing, the rampart breached – reflects the situation at the end of book 12, *before* Poseidon inspired the Achaean rally, even though the din that rouses Nestor must be the same as that at 13.834ff. Thus Leaf saw book 14 as an alternative sequel to book 12. The solution to the chronological problem lies in Homeric narrative technique, and is best explained by C. H. Whitman and R. Scodel, *HSCP* 85 (1981) 1–15, especially 4f. (cf. Krischer, *Konventionen* 114–17, and B. Hellwig, *Raum und Zeit im homerischen Epos*, Hildesheim 1964, 58ff.). It was discovered by T. Zielinski (*Philologus* Suppl. 8 (1901) 419ff.) that Homer presents simultaneous actions as occurring one after the other, as in Zeus's dispatch of Iris and then of Apollo at 15.154–261. A scene which the poet sets aside is frozen into immobility, to be picked up later exactly where it left off; thus Poseidon's intervention (13.10–38) seems to happen almost instantaneously, since the battle is frozen at just the same point. This is why Nestor, who began to drink in his hut at 11.624ff., is still drinking at 14.1; his long carouse embarrassed the scholiasts, although D on 1 already has the true explanation. Two simultaneous yet sequential scenes likewise interrupt the battle at the ships. Both the council of war and the deception of Zeus break into (and thus augment in importance and suspense) Aias' duel with Hektor; heralded by the taunts of 13.809ff., this only starts at 14.402, where it has no preliminaries. Homer uses a simple but effective motif to separate these scenes, which at the same time makes them seem sequential: the shout or din of battle. The outline below adapts Whitman and Scodel (*art. cit.* 10), with 'simultaneous' scenes indented:

Breach of the rampart (to 12.470); shout (12.471)
    Arrival of Poseidon (13.1–40); shout (13.41)
Battle, leading up to Hektor's duel with Aias (13.42–833); shout (13.834–7)
    Council of leaders (14.1–146); shout (14.147–52)
    Deception of Zeus and its aftermath (14.153–392); shout (14.393–401)
Hektor's duel with Aias (14.402ff.)

That these shouts are not merely random is clear from the elaborate descriptions of the last three, which frame far larger units of narrative than does that at 13.41. Moreover, it is the din of battle that rouses Patroklos from Eurupulos' hut at 15.390ff., when Zeus has awakened and reversed the effect of the Greek rally. Patroklos has been with Eurupulos even longer than Nestor was with Makhaon, yet emerges to find the situation the same as at the end of book 12, with the Trojans swarming over the rampart, and the Greeks in flight!

Nestor was last seen persuading Patroklos to urge Akhilleus into battle (11.642–805); Patroklos, however, stops *en route* to tend Eurupulos (11.806–48). By reintroducing Nestor, the poet ties up one of the two loose ends left in book 11, and also reminds us of that book by reintroducing the leaders who were wounded then. Although they cannot fight, their decision to exhort the others reinvolves them in the battle; their debate reveals the seriousness of the crisis, showing Agamemnon's defeatism, Odysseus' practicality and Diomedes' energetic decisiveness. The latter display the same attitude toward Akhilleus as they had the previous night, after the Embassy failed (9.676ff.); neither suggests approaching him again (as Akhilleus expects), although he had in fact shown signs of yielding, by deciding not to return home (16.1–100n.). Their firmness, admirable as it is, contributes to the disaster. As R. M. Frazer saw (*Hermes* 113 (1985) 1–8), the Greeks' leadership-crisis requires Poseidon's renewed intervention for its full resolution; moreover his encouragement of the army with a yell leads naturally to Here's intervention. The allusions to Akhilleus at 50 and 139f., as again at 366, keep the latter in our minds; Agamemnon's awareness of Achaean anger with him over the quarrel picks up 13.111f. and helps explain his conduct. On this scene see also Schadewaldt, *Iliasstudien* 119–26; M. Schofield, *CQ* 16 (1986) 22–5.

1–26 Even this smaller scene is framed by the din of battle – shouting in 1, the clash of weapons at 25f. Nestor's short speech precedes a brief version of the arming type-scene (9–12); another type-scene follows, that of pondering what to do (13.455–8n.), with a fine simile. Cf. 10.1ff., when Agamemnon lies awake and ponders (simile), decides to fetch Nestor, and then arms.

1–8 After 13.837 (where see n.), it comes as a surprise that Nestor, not Zeus, notices the din. Essential details remind us why Nestor is in his hut – Makhaon's wound, the wine they are drinking and busy Hekamede. Nestor gives him a reviving drink *before* his wound is bathed, because of his weakness (so bT). There is no discrepancy with 11.642, where they are said only to have slaked their thirst, not to have finished drinking. Nestor's words of comfort resemble Patroklos' speech to Eurupulos (15.399–404), which likewise opens with two verses noting the increased din, and then has ἀλλὰ σὺ (σὲ) μέν ... αὐτὰρ ἐγών, but transfers the two extra verses, here about Hekamede, to the end.

1 A compliment to Nestor is meant: although drinking and talking, he still hears the noise (bT). Nicanor (in A) rejected efforts to curtail Nestor's carouse by punctuating after ἰαχή and so making Makhaon the boozer. Others (in T) made Makhaon abstain by rewriting 5 as μίμνε καθήμενος ἐν κλισίῃσι! For the scansion ἔλαθεν ἰαχή cf. 11.463, ἄϊεν (ϝ)ι(ϝ)άχοντος.

3–7 For Asklepios' son Makhaon see 2.731–2n. His name is an Aeolism: cf. Thasian Μαχέων (Fraser and Matthews, *Names* s.v.). δῖε is a polite mode of address (6× Hom.). ὅπως ἔσται τάδε ἔργα occurs 7×, thrice after φραζώμεθ' (notably at 61): cf. φράζεο here, and also 20.115f. θαλερῶν αἰζηῶν is another formula (also nom. and acc. with τ', 5× in all). πῖνε καθήμενος, 'sit and drink' recurs at *Od.* 20.136. ἐϋπλόκαμος (ϝ)Εκαμήδη is at 11.624, where her tale is told. In θερμὰ λοετρά (22.444, Pisander frag. 7 B. = 9 D., *HyHerm* 268), θ. must be proleptic; θερμήνῃ καὶ λούσῃ plays on this phrase (note contracted λου-). λ. ἀπὸ βρότον αἱματόεντα (cf. 7.425, 18.345, 23.41) is based on an old formula, since βρότος, 'clot', found only once elsewhere, may be an Aeolic form (Chantraine, *Dict.* s.v.).

8 Nestor expects to have to climb to a viewpoint (περιωπή), e.g. a ship's stern, to see the fighting beyond the rampart. Aristarchus thought he actually did so (Arn/A on 13); but it is all the worse that he can see the battle from outside his hut, so near has it come (cf. bT). ἐλθών goes with ἐς περιωπήν, τάχα with εἴσομαι (from οἶδα, not ἵεμαι): this is echoed by τ. εἴσιδεν at 13, when he finds out even sooner than he wished! περιωπή recurs 2× Hom. and in prose.

9–12 Nestor need only snatch a shield and spear to be as fully armed as when he quit the field (11.517ff.); but he has to borrow the shield of his son Thrasumedes, who is using his father's. The motif anticipates how Patroklos borrows Akhilleus' panoply. Thrasumedes lent his own shield to Diomedes the night before, since the latter had left his shield behind (10.255f.). Such lifelike details need no deeper explanation, *pace* the scholia; this curious parallel also helps to prove the Doloneia genuine (Thornton, *Supplication* 166). Nestor's shield was described at 8.192f.; Thrasumedes has not yet appeared in the actual fighting (see 9.81,16.321). — τετυγμένος describes armour nowhere else, cf. e.g. 66 below. Oddly, epithets like τ., ποιητός or τυκτός do not specify that an object is '*well* made'; the same idiom is seen in Myc. /tetukhwoha/, 'finished', of wheels or cloth. Verses 9–11 rhyme because of the balanced formulae υἱὸς ἑοῖο and πατρὸς ἑ., with the generic epithet ἱπποδάμοιο between. Unless 12 is omitted in a papyrus and a good codex by accident, it must be an interpolation from 10.135, to emend away the oddity that Nestor has no spear (cf. 15.479–82n.).

13–15 The picture is confused at first, as we do not know to whom τοὺς μέν and τοὺς δέ refer; it is then made horribly clear by the breached rampart in the background, framed by Τρῶας ... Ἀχαιῶν (Eustathius 964.24–8). Nestor himself remarks how hard it is to tell where the lines are, so confused is the battle (58ff.). Apart from this echo, 14 reappears at 15.7, when Zeus beholds the roles reversed. ἔργον ἀεικές shows us Nestor's viewpoint, subtly guiding our sympathies. The Trojans are ὑπέρθυμοι, in an apt use of the formula (5× nom., acc. also 15.135). The language does not distinguish the rampart's present ruin from its utter destruction by Apollo at 15.361 (ἔρειπε δὲ τεῖχος Ἀχαιῶν), but we are free to infer that only part of it is ruined (cf. bT); the motif is used with more attention to emotional effect than to consistency (see pp. 226–7). ἐρέριπτο, from ἐρείπω, is an odd pluperf. for expected *ἐρήριπτο; cf. the perf. with passive force κατερήριπε (55). It is surely a form improvised at the caesura (cf. Beekes, *Laryngeals* 115, 118), and need not be Attic (*pace* Shipp, *Studies* 284n.).

16–19 Similes are rare in a type-scene of pondering; a monologue is more

usual (Fenik, *TBS* 96f.). V. di Benedetto (*RFIC* 115 (1987) 272f.) adduces
9.4ff., when the Greeks' anxiety is compared to the sea whipped up by two
winds, in the introduction to a like debate involving Agamemnon, Diomedes
and Nestor. The similes at *Od.* 4.791, 19.518 or 20.25 are less comparable,
as these ponderings produce no decisions. This image is paired with
13.795–9 (where see n.), as if the squall there causes the ominous swell here,
as indeed in the narrative it does. — The sea is personified with diction that
fits a human decision: thus πορφύρω recurs only in the metaphor πολλὰ δέ
μοι κραδίη πόρφυρε (κίοντι), 21.551 and 3× *Od.* Here it denotes the water's
turbid eddying, its literal sense (Chantraine, *Dict.* s.v. φύρω). It connotes
'dark' like πορφύρεος, an epithet for waves or the sea (16.391), which
matches dark thoughts (cf. 1.103) as well as the hue of the wave. The swell
is silent, not splashing as it does before a wind: note the assonance in π,
μ and κ. κωφός means 'neither heard nor hearing', just as τυφλός and
caecus mean 'unseen' *and* 'unseeing'; it may already have been used of
persons, although this is first attested at *HyHerm* 92, when it means 'deaf'
(cf. 24.54). It means 'blunt' at 11.390 (15.388–9n.); Alcman applies it to a
wave (frag. 14c). ὀσσόμενον, 'foreseeing', 'foreboding', and αὔτως, 'vainly',
strengthen the personification (cf. 1.105 etc.). Moreover the sea awaits a
'decided' wind from Zeus (κεκριμένον); cf. *Erga* 670, εὐκρινέες τ' αὖραι, of the
steady Etesians.

λιγέων ἀνέμων recurs at 13.334 (simile), *Od.* 3.289 and, with λαιψηρὰ
κέλευθα, at 15.620 (simile). The alliteration in λ perhaps contributed to the
remodelling of αἰψηρός (from αἶψα) into λαιψηρός: cf. Chantraine, *Dict.* s.v.,
and the compound αἰψηροκέλευθος (*Theog.* 379). πέλαγος μέγα recurs 2×
Od.; Διὸς οὖρον is dat. 2× *Od.*, 1× *Hy.* 'Zeus' here expresses 'the sky'; but we
of course perceive the irony that Zeus, as an individual god, is not paying
attention – yet! Did/AT reports that Zenodotus, no doubt objecting to the
syntax, read πορφύρει; that 'some' replaced κωφῷ with πηγῷ (from *Od.*
5.388, 23.235); and that Aristarchus upheld the generalizing epic τε in 18
– a papyrus has the *lectio falsa* τι.

20–6 In a chiasmus, Nestor ponders whether to enter *battle* or seek
Agamemnon; he decides to seek *Agamemnon*; meanwhile the *battle* goes on. Verse
20 is a unique variation of εἷος ὁ ταῦθ' ὥρμαινε κατὰ φρένα καὶ κατὰ θυμόν
(7× Hom.), which follows monologues (e.g. 18.15) more often than silent
thought (1.193, cf. 10.507); ἐδαΐζετο θυμός follows the storm-simile at 9.8.
διχθάδια is an adj. at 9.411, its sole recurrence in the epos. The standard 23
precedes βῆναι ἐπ' Αἰνείαν at 13.458 (where see n.). ἀλλήλους ἐνάριζον
marks a change of scene, as at 11.337, 17.413; it would be odd to show Nestor
going about asking for Agamemnon. The din of clashing armour shows how
close the fighting is (with 25 cf. 19.233). Verse 26 again describes close
combat at 16.637; cf. 13.146–8n. νυσσομένων follows a different case (σφι);

the usage anticipates the gen. absolute (Chantraine, *GH* II 322f.). The middle is reciprocal, like βαλλομένων at 12.289.

27–40 Nestor's meeting with the injured leaders frames a digression which neatly explains why they took so long to hear the din: other rows of ships separate theirs from the rampart. Now that the fleet is in peril, we see it more vividly. The leaders are coming inland (ἀνιόντες, 28) to see what is going on (37) when they meet Nestor: they must not be seen to be inactive in this crisis. The account of the camp is surely an *ad hoc* invention (Leaf), but the topography of the bay matches other indications in Homer and the geological evidence (13.675n.).

29 = 380. All three were wounded in book 11: Agamemnon at 252, Diomedes at 376, Odysseus at 437. Strictly speaking, only Diomedes βέβληται, as the others were stabbed (so Aristarchus): cf. 11.66of. and βεβλημένον at 63 below.

31–2 Depending on the accentuation, 31f. means either 'they had hauled up those [the leaders'] ships first on shore, but had built the rampart by the *last* (πρυμνῆσιν) ships', i.e. those furthest inland, or 'they had hauled the first ships [to be beached] towards the plain, and built the rampart by their *sterns* (πρύμνησιν)', with τάς as the article. πρῶται νῆες is ambiguous too: at 75 the 'first ships' are those nearest the sea, but at 15.654–6 this phrase denotes those furthest inland – it depends on the perspective. Crates held the former view, reading πρυμνῆσιν (15.656n.); but Herodian (in A), rightly objecting that πρυμνός never means 'last (of a series)' but only 'end (of an object)', e.g. 13.532, 13.705, read πρύμνησιν, 'sterns', a 'late' but Homeric usage. Indeed, if Homer meant 'last', he could have used πυματός instead; and πεδίονδε means 'onto the plain', not 'onto the shore' – as Heyne saw, this is decisive. Willcock thinks the wall at the sterns is the one posited by Thucydides (1.11.1, cf. 7.327–43n.), not that at 15 above. But Homer makes no use of any inner wall in the narrative; the attack on the rampart and that on the sterns are separate phases in the battle. ἐπί is vague enough to allow plenty of room between sterns and rampart.

33–6 Since the beach (αἰγιαλός) could not hold all the ships, they were drawn up in rows in a curve round the entire shore (ἠϊών) of the deep bay (στόμα μακρόν) which existed between the two headlands, i.e. those of Rhoiteion to the East and Sigeion to the West, some two and a half miles apart as the crow flies (13.675n.). The bay at *Od.* 10.90 has a narrower 'mouth'. Aristarchus called the rows of ships round the bay 'like a theatre' in plan. πρόκροσσαι clearly means 'in rows' when Herodotus describes ships moored eight deep at Artemisium (7.188.1); it is from κρόσσαι, whose original sense must be 'echelon' or 'zig-zag' (see 12.258–6on.). Zenodotus and Aristophanes read πολλόν, Aristarchus wavered (Did/A), but the MSS have μακρόν. On the aor. συνεέργαθον see Chantraine, *GH* I 328.

37 ὀψείοντες, 'wishing to see', the earliest known desiderative in -σείω, naturally takes a gen. (Chantraine, *GH* II 54). Zenodotus' reading ὄψ' ἀΐοντες imports a more explicit excuse for the leaders' late arrival. Aristarchus' unjust suspicion that he meant ὀψὰ ἰόντες, with 'barbarous' ὀψά for ὀψέ, shows that his text had no elision-marks or written commentary. Ptolemy Epithetes (frag. 3 Montanari), so named for his attacks on Aristarchus, defended Zenodotus by ascribing to him the yet worse conjecture οὐ ψαύοντες (Did/A), supposed to mean 'not taking part (in the battle)'; Aristarchus' successors, driven into exile, lacked access to his predecessors' work (p. 22 n. 16).

38–9 Diomedes and Odysseus are still limping and 'leaning on a spear' at the assembly next day; Agamemnon speaks from his chair (19.47–9, 76–84n.). The rest of 38 comes from the same context of assembly: cf. *Od.* 16.361, 24.420. θυμὸς ἐνὶ στήθεσσι rarely begins a verse (4/37× epos).

40 Meeting with Nestor alarms his comrades because they see that he too has quit the battle, as Agamemnon at once remarks. But 40 is so odd that Aristarchus athetized it, since the 'old man' in 39 is clearly Nestor, and πτῆξε means 'cower' not 'frighten' (at Theognis 1015 and Soph. *O.C.* 1466 it takes an internal acc.). Others emended: some read πλῆξε, Zenodotus πῆξε, 'froze' (T), which is in a papyrus. He also changed Ἀχαιῶν to ἑταίρων, surely because Nestor is an Achaean too; but this yields an untraditional phrase, whereas θυμὸν ... Ἀ. |, clumsy as it is (especially before 42), occurs at 13.808, *Od.* 2.90, and nom. at 9.8 = 15.629. None of this helps: 40 repeats a phrase from 39, and is ugly even if we emend to θυμός. Either Homer nodded, or this is an early interpolation to bring in Nestor's name, or (better) Homer meant to say θυμός, i.e. 'the leaders' hearts cowered'.

42–132 The leaders' debate consists of six balanced and varied speeches (see Lohmann, *Reden* 138ff.). Even their lengths are symmetrical: the first two are of 10 and 11 verses, the third and fourth are of 17 and 20, the fifth is shortest, the last longest (23 lines). Other patterns intersect. Agamemnon makes the first, third and fifth speeches; the second and third correspond structurally (65–81n.), the third and fourth represent a false start, while the sixth, by Diomedes, the youngest present, adapts a remark of Nestor, the eldest (with 128–30 cf. 62f.). Diomedes counters Agamemnon's fear of Hektor's future success (in the first speech) with his own family's past glory; both speeches end with allusions to the troops hanging back (49–51, 131f.). His implicit reminder of the leaders' duty, no less than Odysseus' attack on Agamemnon's defeatism as unfitting and impractical, persuades them to exhort those still able to fight.

42–52 Agamemnon does not wait for Nestor to speak, but – after a respectful whole-line voc. – blurts out his question (cf. bT), and answers it himself; Nestor implicitly rebuts him at 62f. As usual, he despairs and rails against others and himself; he distrusts even Nestor, seeing in everyone yet another Akhilleus. His speech is in ring-form (Lohmann, *Reden* 19f.):

A   Nestor, why have you left the battle (42f.)?
B   I fear Hektor's threats may come true (44).
C   He threatened to burn the ships (45–7).
B' It is all coming true (48).
A' Like Akhilleus, the Greeks will not fight, angry at me (49–51).

43–8 With 43 cf. 6.254. In 44 Aristophanes (Did/AT) read δείδια, which derives by analogy from the plural δείδιμεν; it occurs 6× Hom., but only once in the first foot (21.536), where original δείδω (from *δεδϝογα) survives 11× – a weird distribution (the MSS vary likewise at *Od.* 5.473). He also read ὅς in 45, perhaps suspecting metacharacterism (p. 35 n. 62); but 45 repeats hemistichs from 8.148 and 8.150, which supports ὥς. Hektor made his threats (or rather promises) the day before. Verse 47 picks up 8.182 (cf. 15.702), part of his exhortation, not his address to the assembly (497ff.); since *we* heard this, we need not ask how Agamemnon did, any more than in Odysseus' case at 9.241ff. For the odd scansion ἀπονέεσθαι see 17.415n. For the usage of αὐτούς cf. 7.338, 24.499. Verse 48 = 2.330, *Od.* 18.271, where the MSS have θ' ὥς, τόσ(σ)' or δ' ὥς; as at 2.330, Aristarchus no doubt read θ' ὥς with most MSS. Ptolemy of Ascalon (Hrd/A) rightly read the old demonstrative τώς, found at 3.415, *Od.* 19.234, *Theog.* 892 and 4× *Aspis* (!); cf. A's variant γ' ὥς.

49–51 For ὦ πόποι in the middle of a speech see on 13.99ff. With Agamemnon's concern cf. Poseidon's claim that the men are loth to fight from anger at the king's treatment of Akhilleus (13.109f.), and the latter's acknowledgement of the Myrmidons' resentment against himself (16.203ff.). For Nestor's hoary epithets 'Gerenian horseman' see S. West on *Od.* 3.68.

53–63 By saying that not even Zeus could alter what has occurred, Nestor means only that what is done cannot be undone (Eustathius 966.47). For us there are the ironies that Zeus has caused it all, and that this at once follows Akhilleus' name; cf. 69–73, when Agamemnon blames Zeus more justly than he can know. Nestor's account of the fighting by the ships soothes Agamemnon's fear that the Greeks are refusing to fight (65 shows that the king noticed this); its conclusion 'the shouting reaches the sky' takes us back to Zeus (cf. 13.833–7n.). Nestor calls for a debate; Leaf took 62 as a rhetorical suggestion that intelligence can do nothing, but bT do better to praise the example Nestor sets. By saying 'I do not bid us enter the battle' the old man includes himself among the disabled, as is reasonable; this tactfully refutes Agamemnon's insinuation (42–52n.).

53–6 ἑτοῖμα τετεύχαται means 'have come about' – the rampart *has* fallen and Greeks are dying (60), cf. *Od.* 8.384: ἑτοῖμος means 'to hand' of present possibilities, 'certain' of future ones (e.g. 9.425, 18.96). παρατεκταίνομαι is a metaphor from carpentry: cf. σὺν μῆτιν ... τεκτήναιτο (10.19), ἔπος παρατεκτήναιο (*Od.* 14.131). It leads up to the mention of the half-timbered rampart (cf. 12.29), for which Nestor may well feel regret, since building it was his idea (7.327ff.). Verse 56 = 68; cf. εἶλαρ νηῶν τε καὶ αὐτῶν (7.338, 437). Here ἄρρηκτον ... εἶ. encloses the ships and men; the weak medial caesura enhances this effect. Since the 'unbreakable' rampart *is* broken, a pedant in T read ἄρρατον, 'strong'; but this odd word, limited to Plato and Euphorion, is not Ionic in vocalism.

57–63 ἀλίαστον once meant 'inescapable', < λιάζομαι; but its conjunction with νωλεμές in passages like this led to its acquiring the sense 'continual', which is already Homeric (*LfgrE* s.v.). Thus v. may be a gloss on it. σκοπιάζω refers back to 8; found in the epos only at 10.40, it forms another link between the start of book 14 and that of book 10 (cf. on 1–26, 9–12). For the confused rout cf. 14 above; 11.525f., Τρῶες ὀρίνονται ἐπιμίξ ... | Αἴας δὲ κλονέει; 5.85, Τυδεΐδην δ' οὐκ ἂν γνοίης ποτέροισι μετείη. Aristophanes read γνοίη (Did/AT), not recognizing the generalized second person sing., which Aristarchus often noted. For the second half of 60 cf. 2.153, 12.338. Verse 61 = 4.14, cf. *Od.* 13.365, 17.274, 23.117; see 3–7n.

65–81 Agamemnon wishes to save at least some of the ships by ordering them to be launched, despite the fact (soon stated forcefully by Odysseus) that to do so while under attack would court total disaster. As usual, he miscalculates. At 2.110ff., leaning on his sceptre instead of a spear, he tried the army's mettle by falsely announcing a withdrawal, which was halted by Odysseus; at 9.17ff., after the defeat of book 8, he proposed to the elders a real withdrawal, but a vigorous speech by Diomedes saved the day. Now his audience is yet smaller, the crisis is yet worse and both heroes intervene. His three speeches have similar structures, and are articulated by the same verses: 69 = 2.116, 9.23; 74 = 2.139, 9.26, but also occurs 4× elsewhere. But his account of Zeus's will and the details of his proposal differ. His speech also parallels Nestor's (Lohmann, *Reden* 139f.). Its first half responds to the first half of his, but in reverse order: fighting at the ships, the rampart (given a regretful emphasis: 68 = 56!) and Zeus's attitude to the Greeks. In its second half, introduced by ἀλλά, he proposes that they launch the ships by the sea now, and the rest at night; he omits the next shameful step, sailing away in the dark, but hints at it in the two gnomic verses about escaping from evil with which he uneasily closes. These counterbalance Nestor's apologetic maxim at 63.

Winter (*MNO* 120) holds that, in the face of such peril, withdrawal was the wiser course (cf. Odysseus and the Kikones, *Od.* 9.43ff.); the audience would not have tolerated so long and risky a battle with no mention of this option. But even if Agamemnon's proposal owes something to the needs of the plot, it is telling that it comes from him, not Nestor or Odysseus. bT and D think he means to test the leaders, preferring the odium of withdrawal to that of destroying the army; the men will fight better if they stay of their own volition. Aristotle (frag. 142) offered a like extenuation of his conduct at 2.73; but Homer would have signalled such a deception, as in book 2. Perhaps the poet adapted the idea of sailing away by night from the Greeks' feigned departure before the fall of Troy (related in the *Little Iliad*, cf. 'Apollodorus', *Epit.* 5.15).

67–70 Cf. (Troy) ἧς πέρι πολλὰ πάθον Δαναοί (*Little Iliad* frag. 28 B. = 1 D.). In one edition Aristarchus altered ἧ to οἷς, to include the rampart in their toil (Did/AT), but ditch and rampart are felt as a unit, like a Roman *vallum*; the mention of both heightens the sense of disaster. Verse 70, absent in a papyrus, most early codices and *h*, is interpolated from 13.227 (where it follows a variation of 69) to specify what Zeus wants: but οὕτω in 69 refers backwards, as at 2.116 = 9.23.

71–3 'I knew (it) *when* he willingly aided the Danaans, but I know now *that* he is giving honour' to the Trojans. Aristarchus' ὅτε for ὅτι in 72 (Did/AT) tidies up the syntax without altering the sense; this needless conjecture has weak MS support. ὅτε is purely temporal, as at 8.406, *Od.* 16.424 (Chantraine, *GH* II 290). The ὅτι-clause should not be taken as object of both ἤδεα and οἶδα, i.e. 'I knew (even) when ... , and I know now, that ...' Such cynicism may suit the king's character but is belied by πρόφρων, which implies real and not just apparent aid: cf. 357, π. νῦν Δαναοῖσι ... ἐπάμυνε; *Erga* 667. We find ironic his hyperbole that Zeus honours the Trojans like gods (contrast Nestor's understatement at 54): in fact Hektor longs for such honour (13.825ff.), but Zeus only aids the Trojans for Akhilleus' sake, and is not now helping them at all. Agamemnon feels the Greeks' hands are tied, but Odysseus thinks of them as winding up wars like long skeins of wool (86): for the metaphor of binding, just before the proposal to launch the ships, no doubt with ropes, cf. *Od.* 4.380. κυδάνω beside -αίνω is probably an archaism like οἰδάνω (Risch, *Wortbildung* 271, *pace* Shipp, *Studies* 85f.); it is intrans. at 20.42. Verse 73 also resembles 12.166.

75–7 The 'first ships' are those nearest the sea (31–2n.). πάσας means 'all these': contrast ἀπάσας, 'the whole fleet', at 79. νῆες is more idiomatic than the variant νῆας: cf. 371. ἕλκωμεν, 'drag down', is opposed to ἐρύσσομεν, 'launch', but means 'launch' elsewhere (e.g. *Od.* 3.153); the second half of 76 is formular (1.141, *Od.* 8.34, and 2× with the indic. instead of short-vowel subj.). In ἅλα/αἰθέρα δῖαν, the epithet retains the sense of the root *dei-*, 'shine', elsewhere weakened to 'glorious': it means 'of Zeus', god of the bright sky, at 9.538 and in Myc. *di-u-ja* = /*Diwya*/ (Hainsworth on *Od.* 5.20). ὕψι means only 'afloat', not 'out to sea' (cf. ὑψοῦ at *Od.* 4.785, 8.55); the sea is 'up', cf. ἀνάγω, 'put to sea'. Ships were moored with anchor-stones (εὐναί); the Ulu Burun wreck yielded at least twelve. See O. Szemerényi in *Festschrift Risch* 425–34; G. F. Bass, *AJA* 93 (1989) 12.

Book Fourteen

78–9 Agamemnon is so nervous that he thinks the Trojans may even press their attack after dark; ἔπειτα and the opt. ἐρυσαίμεθα show that he thinks the fate of the remaining ships hinges upon this. νὺξ ἀβρότη is for ν. ἀμβρότη: cf. ν. φθῖτ' ἄμβροτος (*Od.* 11.330), the formulae ἀμβροσίη ν. (3× *Od.*), νύκτα δι' ἀμβροσίην (5× Hom.), and also 2.57, 18.267f. νὺξ ὀλοή (*Od.* 11.19, 2× *Theog.*) has the same scansion. E. Tichy (*Glotta* 59 (1981) 35ff.) deems ἀβρότη a late analogical form based on ἀμφιβρότη, and points to late Ionic ἤν next to it (for εἴ κεν: Chantraine, *GH* II 281f.). But context cannot date a formula, and this one is very old, since its scansion is among those which prove that syllabic *r* (as in Sanskrit *amŕtaḥ* = ἄμβροτος) existed in early stages of the tradition (see p. 11). τῇ is not a dat. of the demonstrative pronoun, i.e. 'by reason of it (night)', but the demonstrative adv. 'at that point'. With ἀπόσχωνται πολέμοιο | Τρῶες cf. 11.799f. = 16.41f., 18.199f.

80–1 To avoid the shame of saying that they should flee from battle, Agamemnon says 'flee from evil' instead, but adds 'not even by night', which shows that even this disgrace has not escaped him (bT). οὐ νέμεσις was a stock excuse for a shameful act: cf. 3.156, and οὐ ν. καὶ ψεῦδος ὑπὲρ ψυχῆς ἀγορεύειν (Pisander frag. 8 B. = frag. dub. 1 D.). For νέμεσις cf. 13.120–3n. Speeches often end with maxims (e.g. 12.412). φυγέειν κακόν is elaborated in a second gnomic-sounding verse, where προφύγῃ, 'escapes', justifies φεύγων alliteratively: on repetition and alliteration in proverbs see Silk, *Interaction* 224ff. Cf. 'he who fights and runs away, lives to fight another day', 'well fight, well flight', ἀνὴρ ὁ φεύγων καὶ πάλιν μαχήσεται (Menander, *Monost.* 56), and for the syntax 7.401, 15.511–2n., *Od.* 15.72f., *Erga* 327, Ps.-Phocylides 130, 142.

83–102 Odysseus reacts vigorously to Agamemnon's loss of nerve; cf. his effective reply to the king's harsh rebuke at 4.350ff. (82f. = 4.349f.). He is well placed to do so, as the most practical and loyal of the leaders (cf. Agamemnon at 4.360f.), and the one best aware of the right conduct for a king and the importance of leadership (cf. 2.203ff.). Eustathius' analysis (968.4–24) is better than Lohmann's (*Reden* 33–6):

A What a *saying* (ποῖον ἔπος) (83)!
B Ruinous *king*, if only you ruled another army, not one as tenacious as this (84–7)!
C Are you so keen to leave Troy (88f.)?
B′ Let nobody else hear such words, unfit for a *king* (90–4)!
A′ I blame you for what you *said* (οἷον ἔειπες) (95).
c You propose to launch the ships (96f.),
b so that the Trojans will win, while the Greeks stop fighting and are ruined (98–101).
a Your plan will cause ruin, ruler of men (102)!

159

Verse 83 is picked up at 95, but also at 91; ὄλεθρος (99) echoes οὐλόμενε (84). The sarcastic 'ruler of men' reverts to the criticism of Agamemnon's leadership, but avoids any mention of cowardice, thus leaving his honour unhurt. Such tactful yet forceful persuasion is typical of the man who prevents the Greeks from going home (2.188ff.) and makes Akhilleus let them eat (19.155ff.); on his tact see Hohendahl-Zoetelief, *Manners* 42–5.

83–5 See 4.350n.; the formula is brilliantly apt, since talk of *escape* escaped the king's fence of teeth (Eustathius 968.61–3). One's mouth can be too small to let out a dreadful saying, cf. 91 and *HyAphr* 252f., οὐκέτι μοι στόμα χείσεται ἐξονομῆναι | τοῦτο. But henceforth Odysseus avoids that shameful word φεύγειν, substituting καλλείπειν (89). Some thought it too harsh that he calls Agamemnon 'ruinous'; Aristarchus replied that he does so for the king's own good and the army's. οὐλόμενε means 'accursed', someone to whom one would say ὄλοιο, since he causes ὄλεθρος. The voc. recurs at *Od.* 17.484; the epithet also describes the Wrath and Atē (1.2, 19.92). ἀεικέλιος is next in the *Od.* (12×); its context is innovatory, like much in this speech. σημαίνειν takes a gen. here only (Chantraine, *GH* II 57).

85–7 Odysseus picks up the previous speakers' references to Zeus. Does he mean 'Zeus has granted that we wind up wars *until* (ὄφρα) we all perish', i.e. we are dogged fighters, unlikely to flee at a time like this; or '... *so that* we all perish', echoing Agamemnon's cynicism? This accords less well with his heroic resolve to fight till he falls (11.408ff.); in any case it would not be a jibe at Agamemnon, but a hit at Zeus to mollify a king too quick to blame the gods. Contrast 97, where ὄφρα sarcastically implies that Agamemnon wants the Trojans to win. R. Scodel (*HSCP* 86 (1982) 47f.) cogently detects an allusion to the tale that Zeus brought the heroic age to a tragic end with the Theban and Trojan Wars (*Cypria* frag. 1, *Erga* 143–65, *Cat.* 204.95ff., with Thalmann, *Conventions* 104–6); cf. Diomedes' mention of Tudeus' death at Thebes (114). νεότης is rare (23.445, *Cat.* 1.13). τολυπεύω, also at 24.7, occurs 4× *Od.* in the formula πόλεμον τολύπευσε (-α) |, here split over the verse-end. It denoted winding spun yarn into a ball (Chantraine, *Dict.* s.v. τολύπη); connoting length, the metaphor is dead save at *Od.* 19.137, where Penelope 'winds' tricks by weaving Laertes' shroud. In this context it evokes the thread that symbolizes one's fate (20.127–8n.). With 87 cf. *Erga* 229.

88–90 Verse 88 unites Τρώων πόλιν (6× Hom.) and π. εὐρυάγυιαν (5× Hom.): cf. 2.12f. Zenodotus (Did/AT) read ἐκπέρσειν for καλλείψειν, but Odysseus is already sarcastic enough. The first half of 90 = *Od.* 19.486. Verses 90f. uniquely split the verse-end formula μῦθον ἀκούσας etc. (27× epos, and 3× in other positions), displacing ἄλλος Ἀχαιῶν (5× at the verse end) as at 17.586, 20.339.

91–4 Such a thing should not be voiced by a *man* (ἀνήρ is pointed), let alone one of sense, let alone a king, let alone one with an obedient people, let alone one with a people as numerous as Agamemnon's (Eustathius 968.13–18)! The ascending scale climaxes at 94, which lays stress on his responsibilities: the second half of 93, used elsewhere for seers not kings (1.79, 12.229), contributes to this effect. Verse 92 = *Od.* 8.240. Aristarchus (Did/A) rightly read ἐπίσταιτο, which is subordinate to ἄγοιτο (Chantraine, *GH* II 248); most MSS have unmetrical ἐπίσταται. ἄρτια seems equivalent to αἴσιμα; both are used with οἶδα (*LfgrE* s.v.).

95 = 17.173, where νῦν δέ follows a reference to Glaukos' former good sense. Since there is no such reference here, Aristophanes and Aristarchus athetized (Arn, Did/AT); Zenodotus did not, reading σε – or more likely σε'(ο) – in both places. It is easy to supply 'but as it is ⟨you said this, and⟩ I blame your wits'; the verse picks up 83, and is needed for the structure of the speech (83–102n.). ὠνοσάμην refers to Odysseus' reaction at the instant he heard the proposal (cf. καθίκεο, 104); we use a present tense. The idiom is common (Chantraine, *GH* II 184).

96–100 Innovative phrasing. ὅς κέλεαι is equally scornful at 12.235, 18.286 (Hektor to Pouludamas). πολέμοιο συνεσταότος καὶ ἀϋτῆς reverses and separates ἀ. κ. π. (37), which in turn declines the formula ἀϋτή τε πτόλεμός τε (etc., 4× epos); συνίσταμαι next means 'join battle' in Hdt. νῆας (ἐϋσσέλμους) ἅλαδ' ἑλκέμεν (97, 106, 9.683) is declined at 100; for ἑ. see Hoekstra on *Od.* 13.101. With the periphrasis εὐκτὰ γένηται cf. 194–7n. and φυκτά/ἀνεκτὰ πέλονται (etc.) at 16.128, 3× *Od.* ἔμπης conveys the nuance 'though the Trojans are already winning, you will give them what they most want'. For αἰπὺς ὄλεθρος, normally at the verse-end (24×, including acc.), see 13.769–73n. ἐπιρρέπῃ is a metaphor from weighing (balls of wool?); cf. 86 and Zeus's scales at 8.72, ῥέπε δ' αἴσιμον ἦμαρ Ἀχαιῶν. Common later, the metaphor next occurs in Alcman frag. 41.

101–2 Were the ships launched, the men would look to their own safety: cf. πάπτηνεν δὲ ἕκαστος ὅπῃ φύγοι αἰπὺν ὄλεθρον (16.283). παπταίνω can connote 'be distracted' (*Erga* 444): see S. Lonsdale, *CJ* 84 (1989) 325–33. The correct form is given by Plato (*Laws* 4.706E), Hsch., the scholia and MS O[5]. The other MSS have the unmetrical haplology ἀποπτανέουσιν, a nonsense-word already in D and Ap. Soph. Plato's other departures from the vulgate here are owed to lapses of memory or wilful misquotation (G. Lohse, *Helikon* 7 (1967) 225). δηλήσεται is aor. subj. (Chantraine, *GH* II 225) or, better, a fut. with κε, 'in that case' (Willcock); as at *HyDem* 228 (where see Richardson's n.), it is intrans., 'will bring harm'. ὄρχαμος, fossilized in the formula ὄ. ἀνδρῶν with its voc. form ὄρχαμε λαῶν, is cognate with *o-ka* (/orkhā/, = ἀρχή) in the Pylos An tablets.

104–8 Agamemnon is shocked into retracting with graceful brevity, stating that he would not have the Greeks launch the ships against their will; he evades the practical difficulties which Odysseus just cited as decisive. καθίκεο θυμὸν ἐνιπῇ blends ἵκετο θ. | (3× epos) and θ. ἔνιπτε | (3.438, cf. *Od.* 20.266); καθικάνω recurs in Homer only at *Od.* 1.342, when it describes grief reaching the heart. Later usage shows that its literal sense is of hitting someone with a stick or lash (LSJ). εἴη ὅς means 'may there be someone who', cf. εἴη δ' ὅς ... ἀπαγγείλειε (17.640). Diomedes' reply ἐγγὺς ἀνήρ supplies the missing noun (this phrase also opens a speech at 20.425). With 108 cf. νέοι ἠδὲ παλαιοί | (also fem., 4× *Od.*); this gives the youthful warrior his cue. ἄσμενος recurs at 20.350 and 3× *Od.* in the phrase ἄ. (-οι) ἐκ θανάτοιο, where it means 'saved', from νέομαι; but it clearly means 'glad' here (cf. Heubeck in *Studies Chadwick* 227–38). The idiom is the same as classical ἐμοὶ βουλομένῳ εἴη, cf. *Od.* 3.227f., 21.115f.

110–32 Diomedes, the sole hero yet to speak, answers Nestor's call for opinions at 61, and even contradicts him over the wounded entering battle (62f., cf. 128); injured himself, he is better placed to propose that they exhort the men while staying out of range (ἐκ βελέων). Eustathius (970.8–20) saw that this reverses the situation at 9.32ff., when Diomedes rebukes Agamemnon for proposing to withdraw, as Odysseus does here, but is then chided by Nestor for making no positive proposal to replace Agamemnon's – a failure which Nestor ascribes to his youth (57ff.). Here Diomedes argues that his lineage and valour (126) make up for his juniority; cf. his banter with Nestor about his age at 10.164ff. An allusion to book 9 is probable, since at 9.34f., in a speech no less brave but more optimistic in tone, he explicitly alludes to Agamemnon's rebuke at 4.370ff. For verbal parallels see 110–12n. Nor is a reminiscence of book 4 excluded, where Agamemnon cited Tudeus' exploits to impugn Diomedes' valour; Diomedes now uses his genealogy to do the reverse, in opposition to a less than brave Agamemnon (cf. Ø. Andersen, *Der Diomedesgestalt in der Ilias*, Oslo 1978, 139–41). Diomedes' tact in dealing with him, seen at 4.412ff., reappears in his omission of his own exploits. But he hints that Tudeus set a good example: rather than retreat, *he* died besieging Thebes (114); exiled to Argos, no doubt by Zeus's will (120), he won glory there. So may Agamemnon yet! Diomedes' reference to Zeus is more positive than the others' (53f., 69, 85ff.).

Willcock's complaint that Diomedes' proposal 'falls somewhat flat after the long genealogical build-up' misses the debate's formal structure (42–132n.); as N. Austin says (*GRBS* 7 (1966) 306), 'in paradigmatic digressions the length of the anecdote is in direct proportion to the necessity for persuasion'. The poet could not have Diomedes review the military situation yet again (Lohmann, *Reden* 140f.); his genealogy lends variety to the debate, and is brief and purposeful, like Idomeneus' at 13.449–54. It could have been vastly inflated, as at 6.145–211 or 20.208–41; Diomedes misses his chance to rehearse Oineus' deeds! The speech is bipartite, like the second and third speeches, but also in ring-form, like the first (cf. Lohmann, *Reden* 93f.):

I   A   Do not scorn my advice because of my youth (110–12).
    B   I am of good family, as I am Tudeus' son (113f.).
    C   My lineage – Portheus, Oineus, Tudeus (115–25).
    B′ So do not say I am of low birth (126),
    A′ and disregard my words (127).
II A   We should enter battle,
    B   although we are injured (128).
    B′ As we are wounded, we should keep out of range (129f.),
    A′ but exhort reluctant warriors to fight (131f.).

110–12 ματεύω, 'search', is next in Pindar; cf. ματέω, with Chantraine, *Dict.* s.v. The variant ἐξείπω for πείθεσθαι (in Ap. Soph.) may come from 9.61, where Nestor chides Diomedes. Other parallels are γενεῆφι, εὔχομαι εἶναι and μῦθον ἀτιμήσειε (9.58–62), cf. 127 below (this phrase does not recur); κακὸν καὶ ἀνάλκιδα φάντες (126) resembles 9.35, φὰς ἔμεν ἀπτόλεμον καὶ ἀ. (Diomedes alluding to Agamemnon's rebuke), cf. 8.153 (Nestor excusing Diomedes). Aristarchus, πᾶσαι (Did/AT) and the vulgate oppose the trivializing variant νεώτερος, derived from 21.439.

114 This v. was suspected in antiquity, probably because, according to an Attic tradition first found in Aeschylus' *Eleusinians*, Tudeus was buried at Eleusis, where some Middle Helladic cist-graves were enclosed as a heroon, no doubt already dedicated to the Seven against Thebes, in Late Geometric times (Coldstream, *Geometric Greece* 351). But he died at Thebes (6.222f.). Homer knew the story of this war (4.376–98, 5.801–8, 13.663–70n.), but avoids telling how Tudeus, frenzied and dying, sucked out the brain of his foe Melanippos, so that Athene decided not to immortalize him. This grim tale was in the *Thebaid*, which perhaps ended with the funerals of the Seven outside Thebes: see D on 5.126 = *Thebaid* frag. 9 B. = 5 D.; Pherecydes, *FGH* 3 F 97; Severyns, *Cycle* 219–24; Vermeule, *PCPS* 33 (1987) 138ff. — Verse 114 is needed to introduce the genealogy and give Tudeus' name. Athetized by Zenodotus, Aristophanes omitted it entirely (Did/AT); he was not always the more lenient critic (cf. 95n.). Aristarchus athetized, if we can trust A's obelus; as he deemed Homer an Athenian, he might prefer the Attic version. Three papyri and most codices read κάλυψε not καλύπτει; cf. κατὰ γαῖα κάλυψε (3× *Erga*), χυτὴ κατὰ γ. καλύπτοι (6.464). χ. γ. means a 'tumulus' (23.256n.).

115–20 The statement that Tudeus 'wandered' to Argos veils a bloody Aetolian saga. Hesiod (*Cat.* 10a.50ff.) gives a similar genealogy, starting from Porthaon, the usual form of Portheus' name, 'sacker' (cf. *Po-te-u*, PY An 519); this comes from a noun *πορθή, like Makhaon from μάχη (Ruijgh,

Minos 9 (1968) 112–15). Porthaon begets Oineus, Alkathoos, Agrios, Melas and Pulos; Oineus' son Tudeus kills his uncle to protect his father's rights, in a doublet of the tale that Meleagros, also Oineus' son, slew his uncle (9.566f.). In later variants Tudeus kills his usurping cousins, Melas' sons (*Alcmaeonis* frag. 4), or slays Agrios' sons and his own brother or uncle by mistake (Pherecydes *FGH* 3 F 122, in D, cf. T on 114). The result is always exile in Argos.

Homer knew some such story, but makes Diomedes ignore it (*pace* Ø. Andersen, *Symbolae Osloenses* 57 (1982) 7–15): 120 proves this, for nobody 'wanders' save perforce, and 'by the gods' will', a euphemism for 'by necessity', arouses sympathy for a victim (cf. *Od.* 16.64). The son exiled for bloodshed and richly rewarded in his new home is a common epic motif, explaining the mobility of royal families between states (13.694–7n.) – here, Diomedes' control of Argos. Homer differs from Hesiod in that the brothers are fewer and Oineus is the youngest, which is why his pre-eminence over the others is stressed (for the use of τρίτατος cf. 15.188); this is surely an *ad hoc* invention to support Diomedes' claim that his valour makes up for his youth. Mythological *exempla* are rife with such inventions (Willcock, *CQ* 14 (1964) 141–54). Oineus' staying in Aetolia is contrasted with Tudeus' exile to make the latter's fate more pitiable, but he finally followed Tudeus to Argos, since Diomedes left him there (6.221). The tale also explains why Thoas now rules Aetolia, a succession left obscure at 2.641–3; Thoas' father Andraimon married Oineus' daughter ('Apollodorus' 1.8.6). Oineus had to lose two sets of sons – Althaia's, including Meleagros, who is really Ares' son (*Cat.* 25), and is thus mentioned separately at 2.642, and Periboia's, Tudeus included. Oineus blends two distinct figures: the son of Phutios who discovers the *vine* and is linked with the hunters Artemis and Meleagros (cf. his brothers Agrios and Melas!), resembling *Oino*pion with his son Melas and opposition to the hunter Orion; and the son of Porthaon, who *sacks* Olenos to win Periboia, and is a scion of *furious* Ares (cf. Ares' son *Oino*maos).

ἐξεγένοντο (17× epos) governs the dat. only here, because the poet has mixed up two expressions, Πορθέϊ γὰρ τρεῖς παῖδες (ἔσαν) and Πορθῆος ... τ. π. ἀμύμονες ἐξεγένοντο; cf. Τρωὸς δ' αὖ τ. π. ἀ. ἐ. (20.231, cf. *Od.* 8.118, 419), beside κοῦραι Πορθάονος ἐ. | τ. (*Cat.* 26.5f.). For the form Πορθέϊ see 15.339n. With 116 cf. 13.217 with n.; Oineus ruled Kaludon, his brothers Pleuron (bT). πατρὸς ἐμοῖο πατήρ recurs at *Od.* 19.180 (a genealogy); with the rest of 118, where two papyri read ἄλλων from 120, cf. ἀρετῇ δ' ἔσαν ἔξοχ' ἄριστοι (*Od.* 4.629 = 21.187). With 119 cf. *Od.* 4.508.

121 Adrastos is a central figure of the Theban cycle: cf. vol. i, 180, 211 and 13.663–70, 23.346–7nn. Pherecydes (*loc. cit.*) calls his daughter, whom Tudeus married, Deïpule. It is rather incestuous, though good for the legitimacy of Diomedes' rule, that he too married a daughter of Adrastos, his own aunt Aigialeia (5.412–15, cf. Arn/A on 11.226). Adrastos married his own niece ('Apollodorus' 1.9.13), but such a union is less odd (Hainsworth on *Od.* 7.54–66). In Pisander, Oineus wed his own daughter to beget Tudeus (*FGH* 16 F 1, not in B. or D.)! ἔγημε θυγατρῶν, 'he wed (one) of the daughters', adapts traditional phrasing like πρεσβυτάτην δ' ὤπυιε θ.

122–5 Tudeus' demesne consisted of three parts: arable fields (ἄρουραι), orchards of olive-trees, fig-trees or vines (φυτά) and grazing for animals (πρόβατα). Heroes' estates often consist of the first two, e.g. Meleagros' is half vineyard and half arable (9.579f.); cf. the formula τέμενος ... | καλὸν φυταλιῆς καὶ ἀρούρης at 6.195, 12.314, 20.185. It is unclear whether the royal *temenos* at 18.550 extends as far as 589, to include vines, cattle and sheep as well as ploughland. The Mycenaean *temenos*, which underlies the epic institution, was similar; the Pylian king's holding (not his *temenos*) at Sarapeda produced wheat, wine, figs and animal products (Ventris and Chadwick, *Documents* 266f., 282f.). See further Hainsworth on *Od.* 6.293. For ἀφνειὸν βιότοιο cf. 5.544, 6.14. ἄρουραι | πυροφόροι is a split formula, cf. ἀρούρης πυροφόροιο (12.314), πεδίοιο ... π. (21.602), and also *Erga* 549, *Cat.* 180.3: πυρηφόρος (*Od.* 3.495) alters the adj. *metri gratia*. Willcock thinks ἀμφίς means that the orchards surrounded the fields, but it may merely stress the sense of ὄρχατος, 'enclosure' (cf. ἔρχατος· φραγμός in Hsch., the toponym E/Orkhomenos and Chantraine, *Dict.* s.v. ὄρχος). πρόβατα means 'cattle' of all sorts (property which *walks*): cf. *Erga* 558, *HyHerm* 571. The term is not limited to 'sheep' until Attic comedy (so Aristophanes frag. 122ff. Slater); cf. Schmidt, *Glotta* 57 (1979) 174–82. Aristarchus, followed by the OCT, read εἰ in 125, but the δημώδεις (Did/A), papyri and codices offer ὡς, rightly. εἰ makes Diomedes more modest ('you have probably heard *whether* it is true'), and ἐτεόν follows εἰ elsewhere (21×); but ὡς is common after ἀκούω.

127–8 One 'shows forth' a word by saying it, cf. φαῖνε δ' ἀοιδήν (*Od.* 8.499); φαίνω and φημί, from the same root, preserve a close semantic relation (Chantraine, *Dict.* s.v.). πεφασμένον has an odd, unetymological -σ- (cf. the third person sing. πέφανται); see Schwyzer, *Grammatik* I 773. δεῦτε, the 'plur.' of δεῦρο, is used simply to urge action, like ἄγε, rather than to call someone 'hither': cf. 7.350, *Erga* 2.

130–2 With the phrasing ἐφ' ἕλκεϊ ἕλκος cf. 13.130–1n. and ἐπὶ κέρδεϊ κέρδος, ἔργον ἐπ' ἔργῳ (*Erga* 644, 382). For ἐνήσομεν, 'send into (battle)', AbT report a *lectio facilior* ἀνήσομεν, 'excite', which is pleonastic after ὀτρύνοντες. The phrase θυμῷ ἦρα φέροντες (1.578n.) contains the petrified acc. of a root-noun *ϝηρ-, 'favour': cf. the old formula ἐρίηρες ἑταῖροι; the Myc. name *E-ri-we-ro* (PY Vn 130); Latin *vērus*, German *wahr*, Hittite *warri*- 'help' (R. Gusmani, *SMEA* 6 (1968) 17–22). The noun must have meant 'loyal service', 'favour' (related senses, *pace* J. Russo on *Od.* 18.56).

134–5 Agamemnon 'lord of men' now leads the way. βὰν δ' (ῥ') ἴμεν,
ἦρχε δ' ἄρα σφι(ν) recurs only at 384, when the chiefs marshall the army and
Poseidon leads them into battle. The god's reappearance links their debate
with the divine scenes to follow. The first half of 135 comes from the
type-scene of a god's intervention (13.10–38n.). At 13.10 the verse ends with
κρείων ἐνοσίχθων (8× Hom.) not κλυτὸς ἐννοσίγαιος (7×); these equivalent
formulae persisted because the first can be extended by prefixing εὐρύ
(11.751), but the second can be declined (acc. 15.173, *Od.* 9.518).

136–7 Poseidon appears as an unnamed old man: so too Aphrodite takes
the guise of 'an old woman' at 3.386, and Athene is merely a 'man' at *Od.*
8.194. He does not take Kalkhas' shape, as at 13.45, because Agamemnon
distrusted the seer at 1.105ff. (all the more, no doubt, because of his persuas-
iveness with the army); he does not turn into Thoas, as at 13.216, because
Thoas is not senior enough for his words to carry weight (so bT). His age
balances Diomedes' youth, and he offers assurances that Nestor could not
give. To supply a name, Zenodotus (Arn/A) added 136a, ἀντιθέῳ Φοίνικι
ὀπάονι Πηλείωνος; this is surely based on 23.360 (... ὀπάονα πατρὸς ἑοῖο)
and Athene's adoption of Phoinix' shape at 17.555. Aristarchus rightly
objects that abuse of Akhilleus comes ill from Phoinix. Reinhardt (*IuD* 284)
thinks the god appears as an old man to make his ensuing epiphany more
striking, but cf. 147–52n. Taking one's right hand was a gesture of welcome
(*Od.* 1.121) or consolation, as here (cf. 7.108, 24.361, 24.671f., *Od.* 18.258);
see H. N. Couch, *TAPA* 68 (1937) 129–40.

139–46 Poseidon, rebutting Agamemnon's fears at 42ff., cheers him with
the *ad hominem* sentiment that Akhilleus must be glad at the disaster. Contrast
13.111ff., where, exhorting the army, the god hints that the king is to blame.
In fact Akhilleus showed concern for Makhaon at least (11.599ff.); otherwise, we are not allowed to glimpse his feelings until 16.17ff. Poseidon adds
that the gods are not totally hostile, another half-truth; it is ironic that
Agamemnon is unaware that a god is speaking. The speech falls into two
chiastic halves, each of four verses: Akhilleus' attitude to the Greek defeat,
the gods' attitude towards him, their attitude to Agamemnon, and the
Trojan defeat to come.

140–2 Contracted γηθεῖ scanned − ∪ makes the opening of 140 more
innovative than *Theog.* 611, ζώει ἐν στήθεσσι; alliteration makes its second
half more vigorous than 21.134, φόνον καὶ λοιγὸν Ἀχαιῶν. With 141 cf. *Od.*
18.355, 21.288. Verse 142 is vital to the balance of the speech, but someone
in T (Aristarchus?) deemed it redundant (because too impolite?), and called
σιφλόω post-Homeric (τῶν νεωτέρων). ὥς, 'if only', introduces ἀπόλοιτο to
strengthen the curse, as at 18.107, *Od.* 1.47; cf. Chantraine, *GH* II 214. It
should not be accented ὥς, i.e. 'thus', *pace* bT and Leaf. σιφλόω is unique
in Greek (cf. van der Valk, *Researches* I 491–3). σιφλός meant 'infirm' in some

way: cf. πόδε σ. (Ap. Rhod. 1.204) and the σιφλὸν γένος of fish, 'blind' or 'dumb' rather than 'greedy' (Oppian, *Hal.* 3.183). Callimachus applies it to Glaukos the Lycian, 'stupid' to swap gold armour for bronze (*SH* frag. 276.2). Since Eustathius (972.36) says σιφλός is *Lycian* for 'lazy' or 'inert', this theory must go back to Callimachus at least; many words in σι- are of alien origin. The interpretation 'blind' may depend on its likeness to τυφλός (-όω), but a possible cognate σιπαλός could mean 'blind' rather than 'deformed' (Callim. frag. 289), and blindness would be an apt punishment for Akhilleus' crime – watching the Greeks' ruin (so Ameis–Hentze).

143–6 οὔ πω means 'not yet' (cf. ἔτι below), not 'by no means'. From Τρώων, 144 = 10.301. κονίσουσῖν πεδίον varies κονίειν πεδίοιο, i.e. 'they will make the plain dusty' in flight, instead of 'raise dust across the plain' (the usual construction resurfaces in 147, cf. 22.26): κονίειν is also trans. at 21.407, 22.405. The n-mobile is innovative, as is νεῶν (13.723–5n.). αὐτός, far superior to the *lectio facilior* αὐτούς, hardly outlives the early codices (both readings are in papyri).

147–52 Poseidon's great yell to hearten the army is typical: cf. Eris' or Akhilleus' (11.10ff., 18.217ff.); 5.859ff., Ares' bellowing when injured (86of. = 148f. here); and 20.48ff. A shout like nine or ten thousand men's lifts morale like reinforcements of that strength. From Ἀχαιοῖσιν, 151f. = 11.11f.; cf. 2.451f., Athene rousing the men. As R. M. Frazer saw (*Hermes* 113 (1985) 7), the couplet that follows elsewhere ('war became sweeter to them than going home') is omitted, as it would dispel the spirit of defeatism too fast: Poseidon's exhortation at 364ff. continues the build-up towards victory. This is one of the series of shouts that articulate the narrative (1–152n.); the leaders pass from sight, and the effect is of a panorama of the battle (cf. 394–401). The shout also arouses suspense, as at 13.837, lest Zeus hear it; in fact Here does. The poet pays a price for these effects: how can Poseidon stay incognito when he yells so loudly? Reinhardt thinks the god wants the Greeks to recognise his epiphany, just as at 13.66ff. (*IuD* 283, cf. bT, D and Nic/T); but Homer does not signal this, perhaps because it would make the problem too obvious. Aristarchus (in T) tried to evade it by reading ἐννεά- and δεκάχειλοι, supposedly 'with nine or ten mouths', from χεῖλος, 'lip': the god yells like nine or ten men only. Eustathius (972.61–4) rightly found this unimpressive: even the mortal Stentor yelled like fifty (5.785f.)! It is also linguistically impossible. Perhaps Aristarchus found a spelling -ΧΕΛ- (= -χε͂λ-) in old MSS, since this is correct in Ionic, whereas -χῑλ- is an Atticism (see p. 35).

Verses 148f. = 5.860f., where they continue a sentence; but here a stop is needed after πεδίοιο and a comma after Ἄρηος, not the converse (*pace* Ruijgh, τε *épique* 552f.). The comparison is drawn from its martial context: cf. 16.589ff., when the Trojans retreat 'as far as a spear-cast in battle'. On repeated similes see 15.263–8n. Aristophanes read δ' (Did/A); Aristarchus rightly kept τ', cf. *Od.* 5.400, ὅσσον τε γέγωνε βοήσας etc. (Chantraine, *GH* II 242). Verse 151 has an innovative n-mobile and 'neglects' ϝ- in blending ἔμβαλε θυμῷ (9× epic) with e.g. σθένος ὦρσεν ἑκάστῳ (2.451): see Hoekstra, *Modifications* 54.

153–353 To keep Zeus from noticing Poseidon's intervention, Here arrays herself in all her beauty, tricks Aphrodite into lending her an irresistible love-charm and bribes Sleep to go with her to Mt Ida. Zeus is seized with passion, and the divine couple sleep together beneath a golden cloud

153–353 The Deception of Zeus is a bold, brilliant, graceful, sensuous and above all amusing virtuoso performance, wherein Homer parades his mastery of the other types of epic composition in his repertoire. Its merits have made this episode all the more offensive to those, from Xenophanes and Plato (*Rep.* 3.390c) onward, who do not expect gods to take part in a bedroom farce. Many of the ancients tried to explain it as an allegory: see 'Heraclitus', *Homeric Problems* 39; Buffière, *Mythes* 110–15; H. Clarke, *Homer's Readers*, Newark 1981, 6off.; R. D. Lamberton, *Homer the Theologian*, Berkeley 1986. Modern scholars have often seen it as the product of a 'late' and sophisticated 'Ionian' sensibility which had (like many of themselves) discarded traditional religious belief. But there is no good reason to think it a later insertion (Reinhardt, *IuD* 289ff.). Here's intervention is not vital to the plot, since the poet could have left Zeus blissfully unaware for as long as he wished (Edwards, *HPI* 247); but it entirely fulfils its aim – to retard further Zeus's plan, while the ships' fate hangs in the balance. Its merits, and the fact that Zeus must not be worsted too easily, amply justify its length. The plausibility and charm of its circumstantial details enhance our wonder at the sudden shift to a different plane of existence; subtle characterization reveals the gods' human weaknesses without alienating our sympathies from them.

This episode continues the themes and tone of earlier divine scenes. Zeus's quarrel with Here, which begins at 1.536ff. and is shown to have deadly implications for Troy and Greece alike (4.5ff.), was far from settled by his threat of force at 8.5ff. Angry at the Achaean defeat, Here asks Poseidon to intervene, but he refuses (8.198ff.); Zeus halts her own intervention (350–484). But now, far from obediently stabling Zeus's horses (8.440ff.), Poseidon has driven out in perilous defiance (13.23ff.). Here's new intrigue is parallel to Poseidon's, but more subtle and effective. Whereas he takes the disguise of others, she goes as herself; every jewel she dons assists her end, unlike Poseidon's golden chariot, which had to be left out at sea (she lies to

Zeus that she has left her own nearby, 307f.). Her renewed resistance to her husband is all the more dangerous because it is founded on hatred, but clothed in love and achieved through submission; she perverts her function as protector of married love precisely by performing her conjugal duty. Before we deduce from this salacious tale that (as is likely enough) the poem's audience was largely male and all too ready to laugh at the schemes of the fair sex, we should note that Zeus too, by cataloguing his past amours (317ff.), appears in none too dignified a light, and ends up cocooned in one of the clouds that normally manifest his power. This episode undermines the proper order of the cosmos on all levels, the highest included; the poet confirms this by frequent allusions to trouble among the gods – Okeanos' cosmogonic quarrel with Tethus (200–7n.) and Zeus's near-overthrow by the Titans and Giants, which was related to Here's opposition to him (see on 250–61, 271–9, 295f., 330–40, 15.18–31, 15.87f., 15.185–93, 15.224f.). This material comes from an early Titanomachy; Homer also derived inspiration from the judgement of Paris (214–17n.). The list of Zeus's liaisons proves that he knew many other tales which cast the supreme deity as a seducer and Here as his vengeful wife. On the episode's cosmic paradoxes see Atchity, *Homer's 'Iliad'* 102–10; L. Golden, *Mnem.* 42 (1989) 1–11.

The generic origins of humorous narratives like this or 21.385–514 lie near at hand. The divine burlesques of Epicharmus and Middle Comedy (whence Plautus' *Amphitruo*) are merely later stages in a tradition attested as far back as the Hittites and as far north as Iceland; it is wrong to posit an evolution from crude brutality to playful comedy (Burkert, *RhM* 103 (1960) 132f.). Hesiod's tales of Prometheus' deception of Zeus and the creation of Pandora, and the Hymns to Hermes and Aphrodite, show that traditional hexameter poetry, Boeotian and Aeolic as well as Ionian, could portray the gods humorously without making light of them. The levity of tone is usually counterbalanced by the serious issues on which these tales touch, e.g. work in Hesiod or mortality in *HyAphr*. Demodokos' similar tale of Aphrodite's adultery with Ares (*Od.* 8.266–366) has thematic relevance for its hearer Odysseus himself, should his own wife turn out to have been untrue.

If this episode seems to lack serious issues, it is surely because it is embedded in a narrative of the utmost seriousness, rather than recounted in a separate 'Homeric Hymn': when Zeus awakens, Hektor is injured and the Greeks are heading for Troy; a little later, and they might even have sacked it without Akhilleus' help (see Erbse, *Ausgewählte Schriften* 47–72). The allusions to myths about threats to Zeus's rule also counterbalance the humour. The gods' frivolity is, for Homer, the inevitable concomitant of their immortality. Even if, as seems likely, he turned some cruder details into burlesque, adumbrating the 'expurgation' of myth practised by Ste-sichorus and Pindar, he did not invent this flippant tone, which must go as far back into oral literature as do ritual abuse and obscenity in cults like that of Demeter at Eleusis; iambic verses like Archilochus' were the poetic counterpart of such rituals, as Iambe's role at Eleusis proves. Indeed, like the Romans, the Samians celebrated weddings with abuse, supposedly because of Zeus's pre-marital relations with Here (bT on 296)! Few Greeks ever took their gods wholly seriously; this is, perhaps, the Greeks' greatest gift to civilization. Yet Homer depicts the wrath of an Apollo with no sign of disrespect; prophecies in his poems always come true, and those who scoff at them meet a bad end. In no sense can his poetry be termed impious, nor would his audience have applauded an irreligious tone.

The episode contains four scenes of increasing length, linked by Here's motion: 153–86, her toilette; 187–223, her interview with Aphrodite; 224–82, her persuasion of Sleep; 283–353, her seduction of Zeus. Seduction is a traditional story-pattern with a well-defined series of incidents: the epos contains several examples (Sowa, *Themes* 67–94). The pattern appears in embryonic form in Poseidon's seduction of Turo (*Od.* 11.235–57). She loves the Enipeus and roams by his banks; Poseidon takes the river's shape, wraps her in a wave, seduces her and reveals who he is when she awakes. Pandora and Epimetheus form an interesting variant (*Erga* 47–89). More complex cases are Aphrodite and Ankhises, Ares and Aphrodite, Odysseus and Penelope, and Paris and Helen; these share the following elements with the deception of Zeus:

1. Motivation: Here's hate (153–8, with her plan, 159–65); Aphrodite's desire (*HyAphr* 56f.); Ares' lust (*Od.* 8.288).
2. Preparation: Here's toilette (166–86, with two extra scenes – her decep-tion of Aphrodite and bribery of Sleep); Aphrodite's toilette (*HyAphr* 58–65, elaborated in the description at 86–90); Odysseus' bath (*Od.* 23.153–63); cf. Hephaistos' preparations (*Od.* 8.272ff.) and Aphrodite's toilette (*Od.* 8.362–6, shifted to the end); Paris' beauty (*Il.* 3.391–4).
3. Physical approach: 225–30, 281–93; *HyAphr* 66–83; *Od.* 8.285–91; cf. *Od.* 23.164–72 (Odysseus asks to go to bed); *Il* 3.383–94 (Aphrodite fetches Helen).
4. Reaction of the seduced: Zeus's desire (294–6); Ankhises' wonder and desire (*HyAphr* 84, 91); cf. Helen's wonder at Aphrodite but rejection of Paris (*Il.* 3.396–412).
5. The seducer's false tale: 297–311; *HyAphr* 92–142; cf. *Od.* 8.292–4 (Ares thinks Hephaistos is away); *Od.* 23.177–80 (Penelope lies about the bed).
6. The other party's desire: 312–28; *HyAphr* 143–54; *Od.* 8.295; *Il.* 3.395, 3.441–6.

7. The removal of obstacles: 329–45 (Zeus provides a cloud); *HyAphr* 155–66 (Aphrodite undresses); *Od.* 8.293f. (Hephaistos' absence); *Od.* 23.181–204 (Odysseus reveals the secret of the bed); *Il.* 3.413–20 (Aphrodite coerces Helen).
8. Intercourse and sleep: 346–53; *HyAphr.* 166f.; *Od.* 8.296; *Od.* 23.205–343 (expanded with conversation); *Il.* 3.447.
9. The rude awakening: 15.4ff.; *HyAphr* 168ff.; *Od.* 8.296ff.; cf. *Od.* 23.344ff.

Archilochus' seduction-epode (frag. 196a) includes only elements 7–8, but may reflect the same pattern; with 196a.3f. cf. 337f. below, and the cloak with which he covers the girl resembles Zeus's cloud. The most similar narrative is the *Hymn to Aphrodite*, with much shared language; but it is more likely that both poets are elaborating the same traditional type-scenes, than that one imitates the other. The Hymn is more advanced in diction and may come from seventh-century Aeolis (Janko, *HHH* 151–80): see further A. Dihle, *Homer-Probleme*, Opladen 1970, 83–93; L. H. Lenz, *Die homerische Aphroditehymnus und die Aristie des Aineias in der Ilias*, Bonn 1975, 84ff.; P. Smith, *Nursling of Mortality*, Frankfurt 1981, 3.

One may detect behind this episode Zeus's 'holy wedding' with Here (*LIMC* IV.1 682f.; C. Kerényi, *Zeus and Hera*, London 1976, 55–113, 122–7). Their tryst took place on a mountain-top in the Argolid or Euboea (schol. Aristoph. *Peace* 1126, Steph. Byz. s.v. Κάρυστος), or in the garden of the gods near Okeanos (Pherecydes *FGH* 3 F 16, Eur. *Hipp.* 742ff. with Barrett's n.); see also G. Crane, *Calypso*, Frankfurt 1988, 144f. According to an archaic story in Aristocles (*FGH* 33 F 3), Zeus took the shape of a cuckoo to seduce the maiden Here during a storm on Mt Thornax near Hermione; this was an *aition* for the cults of Zeus and Here there (Paus. 2.36.1f.). Their wedding was re-enacted yearly at Knossos and Samos (Diodorus 5.72.4, Varro in Lact. *Div. Inst.* 1.17.8); cf. the Athenian *Theogamia*. Such festivals, in which tales like this could have played a part, go back to Mycenaean times, since Zeus's association with Here on Pylos tablet Tn 316.9 shows that they had already married by then; cf. the /*lekhestrōtērion*/, 'spreading of couches', at Pylos (Fr 343, with Palmer, *The Interpretation of Mycenaean Greek Texts*, Oxford 1963, 251f.). F. Robert (*CRAI* 1941, 293–7) held that the detail of Sleep taking the shape of a bird (290f.) derives from a story like Aristocles', and that the whole episode is inspired by the clouds with fertilizing dew that often sit on mountain-tops, the cloud-gatherer's epiphany. This formed part of Aeschylus' thought; he describes the fertilizing marriage of Sky and Earth, in which Aphrodite is instrumental (*Danaides* frag. 44, with Radt's parallels *ad loc.*; cf. Virgil, *Aen.* 4.160ff.). Ida was the most impressive mountain for the Aeolians to the S., who would consider it the haunt of their weather-god (Wilamowitz, *IuH* 140n.). Zeus's promiscuity (317–27) has its cultic counterpart in the bevy of local goddesses with whom he was linked in the easiest manner; some cults tried to reconcile such alliances with his marriage to Here, whose jealousy was thus explained (W. D. Furley, *Studies in the Use of Fire in Ancient Greek Religion*, New York 1981, 201ff., on the Daidala at Plataea). But such ideas are well in the background here (cf. 346–53n.).

153–8 Like Poseidon's intervention (13.10ff.), Here's is caused by what she sees from her own mountain-top and the feelings the sight arouses; the contrast between Zeus's aloof immobility and the bustling Poseidon below, and the repetition of εἰσεῖδε and θυμῷ, give 158 a particular air of finality. She 'of the golden throne' stands rather than sits, no doubt because it is harder to see Ida from Olumpos than from Samothrake; Ida is some 220 miles away, far beyond the vision of those mortals who now presume to scale these peaks. Homer stresses that she is bound to Poseidon by the closest ties, as his sister and sister-in-law (156), yet leaves unstated the fact that she is even more closely bound to Zeus, as if that fact is too horrid for Here herself to contemplate. For such touches of 'subjective narrative' see on 162–5, 15.422–5, 16.650f.

153–5 The split formula Ἥρη ... χρυσόθρονος recurs at *Hy.* 12.1 (acc.), cf. 15.4–8n.; the epithet usually describes Eos (for whom such split formulae are common) but never male gods, who also sit on thrones. The bards no doubt derived it from 'throne', but it surely originated in θρόνον, 'flower' (Càssola on *HyAphr* 218; Hainsworth on *Od.* 5.123). στᾶσ' ἐξ Οὐλύμποιο ἀπὸ ῥίου (cf. 225) goes closely with εἰσεῖδε; ἐξ and ἀπό are used with verbs denoting position when an action is done *from* that position. The second phrase defines where she is more exactly than the first (differently Jebb on Soph. *Ant.* 411). ποιπνύω, 'bustle', once meant 'pant', from the root of πνέ(ϝ)ω (Chantraine, *Dict.* s.v.).

157–8 Ζῆνα, unique in the *Iliad*, is an East Ionic innovation based on the original acc. Ζῆν (4× Hom.), which was usually replaced by Δία; it entered the diction just before Homer's time, along with the analogical forms Ζηνός -ί (Janko, *HHH* 62f.). Mt Ida's special epithet πολυπῖδαξ recurs 4× acc. (e.g. 283) and 7× gen., the latter in two forms: πολυπίδακος is the vulgate here and at 23.117, and is in papyri at 307, but an *o*-stem form in -ου predominates at 307, 20.59, 20.218, and is sole reading at *HyAphr* 54, *Cypria* frag. 5.5. Aristarchus, knowing its derivation from πῖδαξ, 'spring' (16.825n.), called the form in -ου 'utterly stupid' (Did/AT), but it is known to Plato (*Laws* 3.681E) and dates back to at least the seventh century. Even the pre-Homeric tradition tended to transfer nouns and adjectives to the *o*-stem declension, e.g. χρυσάορος for -άωρ (15.254–9n.), δάκρυον for δάκρυ (Leumann, *HW* 157ff.), πολυδάκρυου for -υος (17.192), χέρνιβον for -α, φύλακος for -αξ (24.304, 566), διάκτορος for -τωρ (cf. the variant at *Od.* 12.390), μάρτυρος for -τυς (271–4n.). See schol. pap. on 7.76 and Janko, *Glotta* 56 (1978) 192–5; perhaps Homer himself wavered. The locals recognized the epithet's suitability for Ida (Strabo 13.602, cf. Cook, *Troad* 306); it is likewise called πιδήεσσα at 11.183 (cf. πιδακόεις in 'Hegesinus' frag. 1). στυγερὸς δέ οἱ ἔπλετο θυμῷ uniquely adapts (καί τοι) φίλον ἔ. θ. (16.450–5n.); T's variant ἔπλετ' ἰδούσῃ removes the repetition of θυμῷ, but spoils the symmetry *vis-à-vis* 156. Another T-scholium rejects 158, no doubt on moral grounds, but it is impossible to supply the verb from 154.

159–61 The poet outlines Here's plan to ensure that we can enjoy its execution undistracted by doubt as to her aim. The standard verses on pondering are introduced into the larger story-pattern of seduction (153–353n.). Surprisingly, the first half of 159 (5× Hom.) precedes 161 nowhere else; 2.3–5 is the closest parallel (cf. 13.455–8n.). Verse 160 blends the formulae Διὸς νόος and Δ. αἰγιόχοιο: cf. Δ. νόον ἐξαπαφίσκων (*Theog.* 537).

162–5 These verses show signs of clumsiness, perhaps embarrassment, but are succinct and vital to the story. Note the hiatus after εὖ and rare 'neglect' of ϝ- in ἕ (13.561n.). Zenodotus read ἑωυτήν (Arn/A), like ἐμωυτόν at 1.271 (cf. p. 24), perhaps an error for ἐμεωυτόν (van der Valk, *Researches* II 51f.). These Ionic forms are based on the contraction of ἕο αὐτοῦ: the gen. and dat. in ἑωυ- are Hesiodic (*Theog.* 126, *Cat.* 45.4), but the closest parallel in Homer is ὡὑτός = ὁ αὐτός at 5.396. With παραδραθέειν φιλότητι cf. καθεύδειν (ἐν) φ. and *Od.* 20.88. χροιή, unique in Homer, means 'skin' and so 'flesh', as at *Cat.* 43.73, Mimnermus frag. 5.1; like χρώς, it came to mean 'colour' via 'complexion'. ἢ χροιῇ is awkward after φ., as is ἀπήμονά τε λιαρόν τε applied to Zeus's far from harmless sleep; this phrase describes a breeze at *Od.* 5.268 = 7.266. Sleep is poured into his φρένες, i.e. lungs (16.481n.), like a liquid: for parallels cf. Onians, *Origins* 31ff. The subj. χεύῃ looks odd after the opt. ἱμείραιτο, since Here will only be able to put Zeus to sleep if he desires her, and the subj. should express the likelier contingency (cf. 18.308, 22.245f., 24.586, 24.654f., *Od.* 4.692, 6.286ff.); but it surely conveys that the idea of Zeus's desire is less vivid *to Here* than is that of attaining her ends (cf. 153–8n.). πευκάλιμος, 'sharp' (cf. Chantraine, *Dict.* s.v. πεύκη), is fossilized in this usage with φρεσί; cf. 20.34–5n.

166–86 The type-scene of adornment, here much expanded, hardly occurs outside the context of seduction; its closest cognates are *Od.* 8.362–6 and *HyAphr* 58–66, where, as here, the goddess first takes a bath. Here's plan is so secret that she has no divine beauticians to help her: contrast Aphrodite in the above passages and *Cypria* frags. 4f., *Hy.* 6.5–13; Penelope at *Od.* 18.192–7; Pandora at *Theog.* 573ff., *Erga* 63ff. But this scene is also related, in purpose and even expression, to the arming of a warrior, especially a goddess. Thus ἀμβροσίη μὲν πρῶτον, first item in the list of beauty-aids, corresponds to κνημῖδας μὲν πρῶτα (hence Zenodotus in Arn/A is wrong to emend away the asyndeton by reading ἐπιθεῖσα in 169); an adaptation of 187 appears in a summary arming-scene (187n.); and Athene's arming (5.733–44) draws on standard verses for men getting dressed and going out (e.g. 2.42–4), from which come also 186 (7× Hom.) and the first half of 188 (cf. *Od.* 2.4f. = 4.309f.), whereas sandals are omitted in brief scenes of women dressing like *Od.* 5.230–2 (robe, girdle, wimple). In this case Aphrodite's love-charm corresponds to the warrior's special weapon, like Athene's aegis or Akhilleus' spear (19.387ff.); Here's '*aristeia*' follows (so H. Schwabl, *WS* 16 (1982) 15f.). On dressing-scenes see Arend, *Scenen* 97f.

166–9 Like Aphrodite (*HyAphr* 60), Here prefers to titivate herself behind closed doors. This detail has extra point here: the account of her boudoir, which no other god can unlock, stresses her skulduggery and prepares for her crafty proposal that Zeus escort her to this chamber (330–40n.). Save at 339, doors are not πυκιναί, but (θαλάμοιο θύραι) πυκινῶς ἀραρυῖαι (etc., 9.475, 21.535, 7× *Od.*): cf. the adaptation at *Od.* 23.229, θύρας πυκινοῦ θαλάμοιο. A κληΐς is a bolt or bar, as at 24.455, where it is the same as the ἐπιβλής, or *Od.* 1.442; when it lost this sense, τήν was 'corrected' in bT to τόν (sc. θάλαμον) or τάς (sc. θύρας). At *Od.* 4.838 the keyhole is in the door-jamb, which may explain why the jambs are mentioned here: on Homeric locks see R. F. Willetts, *Selected Papers*, Amsterdam 1986, 181ff. θύρας ἐπέθηκε φαεινάς is formular (etc., 6× *Od.*); T's reading πύλας is from 4.34.

170–1 Aristarchus insisted that ambrosia is a solid, but the basic idea is simply of a substance that prevents death and decay (5.339–42n.), like.the *amṛta* consumed by the gods of Indic myth; it is used as an unguent to embalm (16.670, 19.38) or immortalize (*Cat.* 23a.22f., *HyDem* 237). It hardly differs from the κάλλεϊ ... ἀμβροσίῳ with which Athene wipes Penelope's face, and which Aphrodite uses herself (*Od.* 18.192–4). Mortals cleaned themselves with olive oil; this is the divine equivalent (cf. *HyAphr* 61f.), just as nectar is analogous to wine (Onians, *Origins* 292–9). At *Od.* 4.445f. ambrosia carries its own fragrance, the sweet scent natural to the gods (see S. West *ad loc.*); here the goddess uses a special perfumed oil. The two are really the same: at 23.186f. Aphrodite protects Hektor's corpse with ῥοδόεντι ... ἐλαίῳ | ἀμβροσίῳ. Here's skin is 'lovely', like Aphrodite's *décolleté* at 3.397. ἱμερόεις elsewhere describes dance, clothes, scent, song or marriage, not the body; Homer coyly avoids saying that Here is naked. λύματα recur in the epos only at 1.314 (where see n.). For the etymological play in ἀλείψατο δὲ λίπ' ἐλαίῳ, which forms a ring with 175, see Chantraine, *Dict.* s.v. λίπα.

172–4 The unique ἑδανῷ was already obscure in antiquity: some linked it with ἡδύς, others opted for 'fragrant' (D). Now this passage is paralleled at *HyAphr* 6off.:

ἔνθ' ἥ γ' εἰσελθοῦσα θύρας ἐπέθηκε φαεινάς (= 169).
ἔνθα δέ μιν Χάριτες λοῦσαν καὶ χρῖσαν ἐλαίῳ (= *Od.* 8.364f.)
ἀμβρότῳ, οἷα θεοὺς ἐπενήνοθεν αἰὲν ἐόντας,
ἀμβροσίῳ ἑανῷ [*sic*], τό ῥά οἱ τεθυωμένον ἦεν (= 172).

The reading ἑανῷ also appears in two quotations, Hesychius (glossed 'fragrant, or fine clothing') and a papyrus; a later one has ἑδανδῷ altered to ἑδανῷ (inserting δ twice), and the good MS Ve¹ has ἑανῶ with δ added above. Erbse (*Scholia* III 597) thinks ἑανῷ has been erroneously introduced from 178. But 172 does contain the noun (ϝ)ε(h)ᾶνός, 'dress' (cf. (ϝ)έννυμι), as A. Hurst proved (*Živa Antika* 26 (1976) 23–5, cf. I. K. Probonas, Μυκηναϊκή ἐπική ποίηση, Athens 1980, 56–65). At Pylos, oil was used in making perfume and treating clothes: thus on Fr 1225 Potnia is allotted oil as *we-a₂-no-i a-ro-pa*, 'ointment for dresses' (= ἑανοῖσιν ἀλοιφή). In the *Cypria* (frag. 4), when Aphrodite prepares for the judgement of Paris, her attendants dip her clothes 'in spring flowers', so that she 'wore scented clothes'. Therefore, argues Hurst, the true reading is ἀμβροσίῳ ἑανῷ, '(oil) ... scented for her immortal dress'. The formula ἀμβρόσιος (ϝ)εανός recurs in the acc. at 178 and nom. at 21.507; cf. νεκταρέου ἑανοῦ (3.385), ἀμβροσίου διὰ πέπλου (5.338). *we-a₂-no* is glossed 'fine linen' at Pylos (Un 1322); linen treated with oil 'becomes, not greasy, but supple and shining, and it remains so after washing' (C. W. Shelmerdine, *The Perfume Industry of Mycenaean Pylos*, Göteborg 1985, 128ff.). This Myc. practice also explains phrases like ἑανῷ ἀργῆτι φαεινῷ (3.419) or tunics 'gleaming with oil' (18.595f., cf. *Od.* 7.107). θυόω, 'make fragrant', is from the Myc. word for perfume, θύος (PY Un 219).

However, it seems odd to say that, when the *oil* was 'moved' in Zeus's house, its scent filled heaven and earth alike (ἔμπης); do the gods run a *parfumerie*, stirring vats of oil? But to say that fragrance pervades the world when Here's *dress* moves as she walks vividly expresses the perfume's potency. Moreover, 'for her immortal *dress*, which was scented' flows more easily. The phrase surely described clothing originally, as in ἄμβροτα εἵματ' ἔχων τεθυωμένα (*HyAp* 184) and τ. εἵματα ἕστο (*Cypria* frag. 4.7), the sole other uses of this participle; cf. θυώδης/-ήεις (*Od.* 5.564, 21.52, *HyDem* 231, 277, *HyHerm* 237). Since the masc. nom. ἑανός is attested only at 21.507, we must surely accept here a *neuter* ἑανόν, exact cognate of the Sanskrit neuter *vásanam*. ἑδανῷ, then, is an error (EAN- > EΔAN-) that was no doubt already standard in Alexandria. Athenaeus' quotation with ἑανῷ (15.688E) comes from a pre-Alexandrian 'wild' text with χρόα λευκήν for λίπ' ἐλαίῳ in 171.

173 The MSS (four papyri included) read ποτί, Aristarchus (Nic/A) κατά. It seems far better to say of Here's dress that it is *in* Zeus's house rather than *to* it; but Aristarchus' alteration is unjustified, since we are dealing with a misused formula. (Διὸς) ποτὶ χαλκοβατὲς δῶ recurs 5× Hom., always with ποτί; it was triggered here by κινυμένοιο and the thought of fragrance reaching heaven. δῶ is an old root-noun *δωμ, as is proved by Myc. *do-de*, 'to the house' (cf. Heubeck on *Od.* 24.115).

175-7 These vv. are full of alliteration and assonance, reinforced by word-play in πλοκάμους ἔπλεξε and *variatio* in ἀμβροσίους ... ἀθανάτοιο; etymological plays continue in ἑανὸν ἕσαθ', ζώσατο δὲ ζώνη (178, 181). ἀμβρόσιος appears 4× (170, 172, 177f.), too often for the taste of Zenodotus and Aristophanes: both read καὶ μεγάλους in 177 (Did/A), but cf. the repetition of καλός (175, 177, 185) or of 'golden' in Poseidon's voyage (13.21-2n.). χαίτας is governed by ἀλειψαμένη and is supplied with πεξαμένη: Herē oils her hair, like Hestiē in *Hy.* 24 – her locks are 'gleaming'. The custom is Eastern (Shelmerdine, *loc. cit.*). πλόκαμος is unique in Homer, but its compounds are common. κράατος, paralleled at 19.93 and *Od.* 22.218, is an ancient form with Aeolic ᾱ, older than καρήατος and κρατός; the latter appears in an adaptation of the same phrase at 1.530 = *Hy* 1.15, and dat. at *Hy.* 6.7, in Aphrodite's toilette. Cf. Nussbaum, *Head and Horn* 177: differently Wyatt, *ML* 100; Shipp, *Studies* 287.

178-9 By weaving Here's dress even the virgin Athene aids her plot, with which she would sympathize (cf. 8.350ff.); she made her own dress too (5.735). Her skill was traditionally contrasted with Here's beauty (*Od.* 20.70-2). She 'finishes' the dress (ἀσκεῖν, cf. Myc. *a-ke-ti-ri-ja* = /askētriai/, 'finishers'); the last stage stands for the whole process. She does so by scraping the cloth, either to smooth it or to make a nap (so AbT); cf. the Attic garment called a ξυστίς. Lorimer (*HM* 378) thinks she may have woven figures into the cloth like Helen at 3.125-8, with a Homeric *hysteron proteron* in 179, but she surely smoothed and embroidered it, since the ἑανός was of linen (172-4n.); making a nap and weaving figures implies wool.

180 The fact that Here pins her dress more than once 'at her chest' is a doubtful clue as to its type. Leaf rightly deems κατὰ στῆθος compatible with 'Doric' *peploi* fastened with long straight pins, whose heads lie in front of the shoulder below the collar-bone; cf. Soph. *Trach.* 924ff. Such dress-pins with unprotected projecting tips are implied at 5.424f. and perhaps 734, where Athene need only unpin her *peplos* for it to slip to the ground. Lorimer (*HM* 378ff.) thinks Here dons an 'Ionic' chiton with a wide V-shaped aperture for the head, like the later σχιστὸς χιτών, since she plaits her hair first; she fastens the opening down the front with brooches of Anatolian (Carian?) origin. But this requires that 180 postdate *c.* 600 B.C.! In fact we cannot tell whether ἐνεταί are straight pins or fibulae: the word recurs only in

Callimachus (*SH* frag. 285.11), and means merely something 'stuck in' (ἐνίημι). περόνη means 'dress-pin' at 5.425, 'fibula' at *Od.* 18.293f., 19.226f.

S. Marinatos (*Arch. Hom.* A 19–21) holds that 180 recalls Myc. dresses sewn at the shoulders with V-shaped apertures for the head, and that these are shown in the Linear B ideogram *146, a rectangle with a V-shaped notch at the top centre and tassels on the bottom, which stands for a textile and is surcharged *we*, perhaps short for /wehanos/ (ἑανός). Presumably the opening could be narrowed with a pin or fibula once the dress was put on. Small pins are known throughout the Bronze Age; large ones were found on some women's chests in the Shaft Graves (E. Bielefeld, *Arch. Hom.* C 38f.). Fibulae appear late in LHIIIB, long dress-pins worn at the shoulders during LHIIIC (Snodgrass, *Dark Age* 226); the latter signal the change from Myc. sewn dresses, seen on the figurines (Minoan fashions prevail in the frescoes), to the woollen *peplos* that is little more than a folded blanket pinned at the shoulders ('folded' is all πέπλος means: Chantraine, *Dict.* s.v.). Bards equate πέπλος and ἑανός (so Aristarchus and Snodgrass, *Gnomon* 41 (1969) 390ff.), but the Myc. evidence suggests that they were once different garments. The short dat. in -ης is recent, but late diction can describe ancient objects (e.g. 10.261ff., the boar's-tusk helmet).

181 Herē's belt is adorned with tassels, no doubt golden like those on the aegis (2.448f., cf. Hdt. 4.189). It is mismatched with the *peplos*, whose ample folds would hide it. The only parallel is the Myc. princess buried wearing a girdle edged with gold, from which dangled 35 spiral pendants in sheet gold decorated *en repoussé* (A. W. Persson, *The Royal Tombs at Dendra* I, Lund 1931, 14, 40; Bielefeld, *Arch. Hom.* C 33). The fringes on the leather tunics of LHIIIC soldiers, e.g. on the Warrior Vase, are different. Gold-adorned belts reappear, under Oriental influence and seemingly with no fringes, in *c.* 800 B.C. (Coldstream, *Geometric Greece* 125f.). Aristarchus (Did/AT), with a few MSS, preferred ζώνη … ἀραρυίη to the acc.; the MSS oppose his similar preference at 5.857. Both constructions of ζώννυμι are known (dat. at 10.78, *Od.* 18.67, acc. at 23.130).

182–3 Neither Mycenaeans nor Minoans wore earrings (Bielefeld, *Arch. Hom.* C 36f.); Herē's are indubitably Geometric. τρίγληνος, from γλήνη, 'eyeball' (8.164–6n.), is a title of Hekate (Ath. 8.325A); cf. γλήνεα, 'jewels' (24.191–2n.), and the necklaces the Athenians called τριόττιδες, 'with three eyes' (bT). μορόεις means 'like mulberries' (μόρα). It is not from μόρος, 'death', nor, *pace* Hrd/A, from μορέω, 'toil', a verb of Hellenistic invention; nor does it mean 'gleaming', *pace* P. G. Maxwell-Stewart (*AJP* 108 (1987) 411–15). Like blackberries, mulberries have a number of separate seeds in a cluster; clearly the earrings had three protuberances somehow resembling mulberries.

C. Kardara (*AJA* 65 (1961) 62–4) compared Assyrian earrings with three oval projections from the hoop, as seen on a Syrian ivory of Late Geometric date from Ialysos; this type was popular in Greece down to 500 B.C. But she reports S. Marinatos' insight that μορόεις refers to granulation in gold, a technique reintroduced from Phoenicia in *c.* 850 B.C. Earrings with three projections, each shaped like a mulberry by means of granulation, have now been found at Lefkandi in an Early Geometric II grave (M. R. Popham, L. H. Sackett and P. G. Themelis, *Lefkandi* I, London 1980, 221, pl. 231d); a contemporary imitation from the same site uses three cones of coiled gold wire (*BSA* 77 (1982) pl. 30b). G. S. Korres (*Platon* 31–2 (1964) 246–58) compared Geometric earrings from Eleusis with three electrum lumps set in an arc, granulated decoration and dangling gold beads (Coldstream, *Geometric Greece* fig. 25b, cf. fig. 13e; *id.* in H. G. Niemeyer, *Phönizier im Westen*, Mainz 1982, 261–72). Penelope wears earrings like Here's at *Od.* 18.297f. (298 = 183 here, cf. the variant at *Theog.* 583); in her own toilette, Aphrodite puts a pair shaped like rosettes, made of orichalc and gold, in her τρητοῖσι λόβοισι (*Hy.* 6.8f.). But ἕρμα, ἐΰτρητος, τρίγληνος and μορόεις recur nowhere else, and the double hiatus in 182 suggests improvisation.

184 A κρήδεμνον, as the word indicates (from κάρα + δέω, 'bind'), is a kerchief or wimple covering the head and shoulders but leaving the face open, like the μαντίλα still worn by Greek countrywomen; the rendering 'veil' is wrong. When Penelope holds it before her cheeks (e.g. *Od.* 21.65), this shows that it does not usually hide the face. Homer also calls it καλύπτρη or κάλυμμα; as the following description suggests, and ὀθόναι (3.141) and λιπαρὰ κρήδεμνα (5× *Od.*) confirm, it was made of fine linen. Like its military equivalent the helmet, it is donned last (*Od.* 5.232). Hoekstra on *Od.* 13.388 well suggests that it once meant a kind of ribbon worn by ladies in Myc. frescoes. M. N. Nagler, *Spontaneity and Tradition*, Berkeley 1974, 44–60, explores its simultaneous connotations of chastity and allure, and its metaphorical application to the battlements of a city (cf. 16.97–100n.). Andromakhe's headgear at 22.468ff. is elaborated to stress her anguish in tearing it off.

185–6 νηγάτεος describes a tunic (καλὸν νηγάτεον, 2.43) and a blanket (*HyAp* 122). The ancients guessed 'newly-made' or 'fine', but νη- suggests 'not', and modern Macedonian ἀνήγατος, 'unworn', 'new', is our best clue (Frisk s.v.). The simile ἠέλιος ὥς was perhaps traditional in toilette-scenes: cf. *Od.* 19.234 (whence the variant λαμπρόν here), *HyAphr* 89. λευκός means 'bright' as well as 'white', cf. *Od.* 6.45 λευκὴ ... αἴγλη. Sandals were tied with laces passed under the instep (Fernández-Galiano on *Od.* 21.340f.).

187–223 With a minimal preamble, we find ourselves in the first of two unheralded developments, all the funnier for their unexpectedness – Here's request for Aphrodite's magic love-charm. Metaphorically, she needs Aphrodite's aid if Zeus is to desire her, just as she needs Sleep's if he is to slumber; but this is imagined, as usual, in anthropomorphic terms. Neither scene is strictly essential for Here's success; but, as often, the poet seizes his chance to poke fun at Aphrodite, who is tricked into helping the side she opposes (Edwards, *HPI* 248). To further her request Here relies on her seniority, addressing Aphrodite as 'dear child'; Aphrodite acknowledges this, replying 'august goddess, daughter of Kronos' (194). After a disarming mention of their disagreement over the war, Here picks up this reference to Kronos, lying that she wishes to reconcile the yet more august deities Okeanos and Tethus. Her story is an *ad hoc* invention, like the gods' journeys to Ocean at 1.423f., 23.205ff.; but it is also a favourite trick of Homer's to make his characters allude to other stories he knows (200–7nn.). That we never hear of the love-charm again is typical: it is enough that Here carry it, like Ino's magic kerchief or Hermes' herb (*Od.* 5.346ff., 10.287ff). Zeus need only look at her to desire her (294); bT think the charm also arouses Sleep's desire for Pasitheē (276)! But, although this scene is dispensable, we would be sad to lose it. Its five speeches are formally symmetrical, like those at 301–45: Here's preamble and Aphrodite's reply fill three verses each; Here's lengthier request is matched by how Aphrodite's brief speeches frame a description of the charm (it might have seemed too precious to lend if she had described it herself). Her aim achieved, Here smiles (222f.); she has the last laugh in her meeting with 'smile-loving Aphrodite' (211)!

187 The same verse ends Aphrodite's toilette at *Hy* 6.14 (with κόσμον ἔθηκαν): cf. *Erga* 76, πάντα δέ οἱ χροΐ κ.; *Aphr.* 64, 172; *Hy* 27.17. In structure it resembles αὐτὰρ ἐπεὶ ῥ᾽ ἕσσαντο περὶ χ. νώροπα χαλκόν (383, 2× *Od.*) and is adapted to arming at 7.207, α. ἐ. δὴ πάντα π. χ. ἕσσατο τεύχεα, cf. π. χ. εἵματα ἕστο (5× Hom.). Verses 186 and 188 come from the type-scene of dressing (166–86n.). θήκατο, also at 10.31, is a recent replacement of θέτο (Shipp, *Studies* 105).

190–3 ἦ ῥά νύ μοί τι πίθοιο opens polite requests (4.93, 7.48); the opt. is half-way between a wish and a potential, as ἦέ κεν ἀρνήσαιο shows (Chantraine, *GH* II 216). 'Dear child' is a common affectionate address to a younger person, e.g. Priam to Helen or Phoinix to Akhilleus (3.162, 9.437); Aphrodite's parents are actually Dionē and Zeus (5.370–2n.), as the formula 'daughter of Zeus' reminds us. She is called Διὸς θυγάτηρ again at 224, rather than φιλομμειδής as at 211; the effect is to stress how badly she misjudges her stepmother's motives and the importance of her various relationships. Homer's divergence from Hesiod over her parentage accords with the likelihood that he knew a cosmogony with no castration of Ouranos (cf. 200–7n. and Huxley, *GEP* 28f.).

194–7 Sleep repeats 194 at 243, but it is used with nom. θυγάτηρ at 5.721 (where see n.). πρέσβα, here still an ancient voc. of a fem. in *-ya, is nom. and means 'eldest' at 19.91, *Od.* 3.452. Verses 195f. = 18.426f., *Od.* 5.89f., ending speeches where an unexpected visitor is welcomed (cf. 208–10n.); the play on τελέω is attractive. τετελεσμένον ἐστί means 'it can be accomplished', with a participle replacing a verbal adj.: cf. ἐ. πεφυγμένον, 'it can be escaped' (22.219 etc.), and 96–100, 13.269–71nn. Verse 197 = 300, 329, 19.106 (Herē beguiling Zeus); δολοφρονέουσα is especially neat here, as it introduces a devious reply to Aphrodite's αὔδα ὅ τι φρονέεις.

198–210 Every detail in Here's speech is calculated to trap Aphrodite, as bT saw. Her direct request falsely suggests that her explanation is equally direct. After a flattering reference to Aphrodite's power (198f.), she lies that she is going to the end of the world (where she could scarcely harm the Greek cause), to reconcile a husband and wife – just what the patroness of marriage should be doing. Nobody could refuse to help, especially when she implies that she acts out of gratitude for the kindness Okeanos and Tethus once showed her (202f.); Aphrodite may well infer that Here will not forget her own kindness either. Verses 203f. also remind Aphrodite that Zeus worsted Kronos; 213 confirms that she does not miss this hint of his superior force (which seems not to worry Here). At 301–6, when Here repeats her tale to Zeus but needs to suggest neither her own gratitude nor his might, she omits 202–4.

198–9 φιλότης and ἵμερος are the first two powers in Aphrodite's love-charm (216); they are not clearly personified, but cf. the formula ἵ. αἱρεῖ. Hesiod makes Desire Aphrodite's companion, and Sex, like Deception, a daughter of Night (*Theog.* 201, 224). The statement that Aphrodite subdues all gods and men was traditional (*HyAphr* 2f., 34f., cf. *Theog.* 203f.); Hesiod says this of Eros (*Theog.* 121f.), and it is applied to Night by Sleep (259), whom in his turn Here flatters as 'lord of gods and men' (233). This polar opposition is especially common, with variations, in later epos: cf. ἀθανάτους τε θεούς θνητούς τ' ἀνθρώπους (1× Hes., 2× *Hy.*, also nom., dat.); (οὐδέ τις) ἀθανάτων (οὐδὲ / τε ἰδὲ) θνητῶν ἀνθρώπων (*HyDem* 22, *Cat.* 204.104, cf. *Hy.* 14.1). Such phrases, clearly current in the hymns of Homer's own time, are not the sole elements in this episode likely to derive from hymnic or theogonic poetry: Here's request, δός, resembles the prayers which end many hymns (cf. *Hy.* 6, 10, 11, 26), and material from a cosmogony follows. For Homer's knowledge of hymns cf. 16.179–92n. δαμνᾷ, so accented, is contracted from *δαμνάε(σ)αι (from δαμνάομαι), like πειρᾷ at 21.459, 24.390. Aristarchus (in T) accented δάμνᾳ for *δάμνα(σ)αι, from δάμνημι, with a less harsh contraction (Chantraine, *GH* I 301).

200–7 Here's lie that her journey aims to reconcile the estranged 'bonds of the earth', the sea-gods Okeanos and Tethus, parodies her real intent and alludes to a threat to the cosmic order of the sort she herself now poses. It may also recall traditions that she married Zeus in a garden near Okeanos (153–353n.); but it derives, like her allusion to Kronos' punishment by Zeus,

from a theogony, one, moreover, wherein Okeanos and Tethus are the
primeval parents (201, 246), not merely the parents of all waters (as at *Theog.*
337–70, cf. 21.196f.). This differs from Hesiod, where Ouranos and Gaia
are the first divine generation, but resembles an 'Orphic' poem which Plato
cites (*Crat.* 402B):

> Ὠκεανὸς πρῶτος καλλίρροος ἦρξε γάμοιο,
> ὅς ῥα κασιγνήτην ὁμομήτορα Τηθὺν ὄπυιεν.

An old tale he retells at *Tim.* 40E makes Okeanos and Tethus children of
Sky and Earth, but parents of Kronos and Rhea. Yet at 5.898 the Titans
are 'sons of Ouranos': in this Homer agrees with Hesiod, for whom Okeanos
and Tethus are Titans like Kronos and Rhea. Now another oddity of this
episode is the importance of Night, whom even Zeus dares not offend (261).
Aristotle says some early poets made her the first being or the first ruler
(*Metaph.* 12.1071b27, 14.1091b4): in fact Night ends the 'reversed theogony'
at *Theog.* 11–20, and in the Derveni papyrus, whose Orphic cosmogony
cannot postdate *c.* 500 B.C., the first ruler Ouranos is the son of Night,
and Zeus learns from her the secrets of his rule (cols. x, vii). On these texts
see G. S. Kirk, J. E. Raven and M. Schofield, *The Presocratic Philosophers*,
2nd edn, Cambridge 1983, 13–33; Kirk deems these genealogies extra-
polated from Homer. It is simpler to suppose that the Iliadic and Orphic
theogonies both adapt a myth which made the primeval waters, perhaps
with Night as their parent, the origin of the world: so Damascius, *De Principiis*
1 319 Ruelle; O. Gruppe, *Die griechischen Culte und Mythen in ihren Beziehungen
zu den orientalischen Religionen* 1, Leipzig 1887, 614–22; J. Rudhardt, *Le Thème
de l'eau primordiale dans la mythologie grecque*, Bern 1971; West, *Orphic Poems*
116–21. Such cosmogonies prefigure Thales' idea that the earth floats on
water, which is somehow the source of all things.

Whence does this tale derive, and why does it differ from Hesiod's? There
is no reason why divergent myths should not have been current, whereby
the first separation, anthropomorphized as a quarrel, was between either
Sky and Earth, or the aquatic parents of Sky and Earth (Homer extracts
humour from the idea that, if their quarrel ends, the world will revert to
primeval chaos). Both myths were known in the Levant by the early first
millennium. The former appears in the separation of the Egyptian sky-
goddess Nut from the earth-god Keb, and in the Hittite *Song of Ullikummi.*
Moreover Hesiod's story of Ouranos' castration by Kronos, which ended
his union with Gaia, resembles the Hittite tale of Kumarbi and the Phoenician theogony preserved by Philo, which both have a generation before the
sky-god (West, *Theogony* 20–8); traces of a prior generation survive in Hesiod
(Rudhardt, *op. cit.* 52ff.).

Oriental influence on Greek myth is almost as likely in the case of Okeanos and Tethus (Lesky, *Thalatta*, Vienna 1947, 64–6, 80–5; Burkert, *Die orientalisierende Epoche* 88ff.). In the Babylonian creation-epic *Enūma Eliš* I 4, the gods' parents are 'primordial Apsū, their begetter, and creator Tiāmat, she who bore them all' (*ANET* 61). This exactly matches 201, since Apsū is the same entity as Okeanos, the fresh water which encircles the world and is the underground source of all springs and rivers (21.195–7), whereas Tiāmat personifies the salt sea, *tiāmtu*, *tāmtu* or *tēmtu* in Akkadian; their mingled waters engender the gods, including Anu, the Sky, and Ea, the Earth. This tale influenced Genesis 1, wherein the basic elements are not heaven and earth, but darkness and deep waters (*tehōm* = *Tiāmat*), which God divides into the waters above and those below by creating the firmament (Westermann, *Genesis* 26–34); the story surely reached Greece too. Burkert plausibly relates Tethus to *tāmtu*, dating the borrowing to the Ionian Renaissance, not the Late Bronze Age (in *The Greek Renaissance* 54). Okeanos' name likewise has no Indo-European etymology; its variants Ὠγην(ος) and Ὠγενός again suggest a loan-word. The idea that Alcman (frag. 5) made the first being another sea-goddess, Thetis, is exploded by G. W. Most, *CQ* 37 (1987) 1–19.

200–2 = 301–3, with ἔρχομαι for εἶμι γάρ. The formula πείρατα γαίης (2× *Od.*, *Erga* 168, *Cypria* frag. 9.10 B. = 7.10 D.) is expanded with πολυφόρβου, a traditional epithet like πουλυβότειρα; cf. γ. πολυφόρβου, *HyAp* 365, acc. 9.568, nom. *Cat.* 150.22 (Hesiod twice applies it to Demeter). γένεσις recurs only at 246 in the epos. With 202 cf. εὖ ἔτρεφεν ἠδ' ἀτίταλλε (|δεξάμενος -η), 16.191, *Od.* 19.354, *Cat.* 165.6; ἐδέξατο Γαῖα … τρεφέμεν ἀτιταλλέμεναί τε, *Theog.* 479f. This phrase always describes infants, in the last case the baby Zeus; cf. ἀτιτάλτας, 'foster-father' (Cretan). So Here too was an infant (see below). Aristarchus (Did/T) and most MSS read μ' ἐν, but the *lectio difficilior* is με (cf. 16.775–6n. and van der Valk, *Researches* II 190).

203–4 Okeanos is suitably remote for a divine refuge; Hephaistos, saved from Here's rage by Thetis, dwelt by his streams (18.395ff., cf. 295–6n.). So too Here claims to have reared Thetis at 24.59f. (cf. *Cypria* frag. 2). Zeus is usually held to have sent his bride away during the Titanomachy, a unique detail; one naturally suspects *ad hoc* invention (so Wilamowitz, *Kleine Schriften* v.2, 167). But the truth is odder. The formula in 202, and the facts that her mother Rhea, not Zeus, handed Here over to Okeanos, and that Here did not go on her own, show that she was a child at the time (cf. bT on 296). Gruppe (*op. cit.* 619f.) proposed that, in Homer's theogony, Rhea smuggled her baby away at birth to her parents so that Kronos could not swallow it, just as in Hesiod she entrusts her youngest child Zeus to her mother Gaia (*Theog.* 477ff.): cf. Orphic frag. 58, where Kronos ingests only the males. Now Here was sent away 'when Zeus overthrew Kronos', i.e. when *he* was adult; yet *she* is Kronos' eldest child (4.59). Apparently the gods whom

Kronos swallowed did not mature inside him; the weird logic of myth could require that they remain babies during this second pregnancy, and as such they could be voided forth more easily (although the Storm-God grows inside Kumarbi: *ANET* 120f.). When they are reborn, Rhea takes the infant Here away while Zeus, who was never swallowed and is therefore adult, does battle with Kronos. This also explains the discrepancy over whether Zeus is older than Poseidon (15.165–7n.): the gods born before Zeus are reborn after him, and are thus both older and younger (see *HyAphr* 22f. with F. Solmsen, *Hermes* 88 (1960) 1–13). Yet at 296 the poet says that Zeus and Here had intercourse 'in secret from their parents', presumably Rhea and Kronos; in this case they would both be mature *before* Kronos' defeat, as is also implied by the fact that the gods help Zeus against the Titans (*Theog.* 391, 617ff., 'Apollodorus' 1.2.1, surely from the Cycle). Even if the Titanomachy was a revolt *after* Zeus had deposed Kronos (Hyginus 150), the discrepancy with 295f. remains, probably because of an *ad hoc* invention there.

The MSS read Ῥείης, Aristophanes and Aristarchus Ῥείας (Did/A). Ῥείη is the usual form (3× Hes., 6× *Hy*), although Hesiod has Ῥείαν or perhaps Ῥεῖαν (*Theog.* 135 with West's n.); Ῥέη appears at *Theog.* 467, *HyDem* 459, Ῥῆ in Pherecydes of Syros (frag. 9 D.–K.), Ῥέᾳ with synizesis at 15.187. Ῥείας is surely an emendation based on the latter (cf. van der Valk, *TCO* 95). All these forms may go back to a nom. *Rēyă with a gen. in *-ās, changing from *Ῥηᾶ to Ῥέα and Ῥῆ by Ionic quantitative metathesis and contraction; Ῥείη and Ῥέη will derive by analogy from the gen. Cf. ῥεῖα, 'easily', > ῥέᾳ (13.143–4n.), or *gāyă > γέᾳ > γῆ beside γαῖα (Janko, *HHH* 234–6; Nussbaum, *Head and Horn* 49f.). The formula ἀτρυγέτοιο θαλάσσης, unique in Homer, recurs only in theogonic contexts, where it is conjoined with γαίης/γῆς (*Theog.* 413, 728, *Hy.* 22.2); the epithet describes both sea and sky, and means 'murmuring', from τρύζω (A. Leukart in *Festschrift Risch* 340–5).

205–7 = 304–6. ἄκριτα means 'unresolved', 'brought to no determination' (κρίσις): cf. ἔκριναν μέγα νεῖκος (*Od.* 18.264), διακρινώμεθα ν. (*Erga* 35) and *LfgrE* s.v.

208–10 With 208 cf. *Od.* 22.213. Opposing his predecessors' emendation κείνων γ', Aristarchus points out that κῆρ is an internal acc. (Did/AT): the best MSS rightly keep κείνω γ'. ἀνέσαιμι is from ἕζω, 'set', i.e. 'restore' (cf. *Od.* 18.265); see 13.657n. With 210 cf. φίλος (-ν) τ' ∪∪ αἰδοῖός (-ν) τε | (2× *Od.*, cf. 10.114), ἀ. (-η) τε φ. (-η) τε (18.386 = 425 = *Od.* 5.88); like 195f., this phrase derives from the type-scene of a visit, where it is an opening compliment (cf. too 1.293). It forms the climax to a repetition of the root φιλ-: if they resume φιλότης, Here will be their φίλη.

211–13 Hesiod puts 'smiles and deceit' in Aphrodite's province (*Theog.* 205); she whose smile deceives others is now deceived herself. Aphrodite naïvely accedes *because* Here sleeps in Zeus's arms: her reason befits the love-goddess's special interests, and amusingly foreshadows the result of the loan she makes! Aristarchus, following Aristophanes, athetized 213, claiming that the value of her favour is lessened if she grants it for Zeus's sake, not Here's. This would leave 212 as a one-line speech, just as the verse reappears in a like episode (*Od.* 8.358); also, Ζηνὸς γὰρ τοῦ ἀρίστου is a 'recent' phrase paralleled in *Hy.* 23 (acc.). Yet 213 must stand: it is wonderfully ironic, since Aphrodite cannot know that Here's plan is precisely to sleep in Zeus's arms (cf. 353!); in granting this favour for his sake, she is absurdly mistaken. Despite its suitability, her formula φιλομμειδὴς Ἀφροδίτη, equivalent to Διὸς θυγάτηρ Ἀ., may have been triggered by the four preceding uses of the root φιλ-: on this doublet see Janko, *Mnem.* 34 (1981) 254, and Hainsworth on *Od.* 8.303. With (Ζηνὸς) ἐν ἀγκοίνῃσιν ἰαύεις cf. *Od.* 11.261, 11.268, *HyDem.* 264; on ἰαύω see Beekes, *Laryngeals* 57, 129, and Peters, *Laryngale* 34–42.

214–17 Aphrodite's love-charm has caused much puzzlement. Oriental influence again offers a better explanation than ancient allegories (cf. Porphyry 1.194.3ff.). κεστὸς ἱμάς means a 'decorated strap', of leather, cloth or even gold; cf. πολύκεστος ἱ. (3.371), the chin-strap of Paris' helmet. κ. is not a noun, *pace* Callimachus (frag. 43.53), who is chided by Aristarchus (on 3.371); it is a verbal adj. from κεντέω, 'prick', 'stitch', not κεάζω, 'split' (Chantraine, *Dict.* s.v.). This accords with its epithet ποικίλος, often applied to dresses (5.735 etc.), but also to armour, furniture and jewellery (*HyAphr* 89); in Linear B */poikilōnux/* describes cloth. Verse 216 confirms that ornamentation is meant. The triple anaphora of ἐν recalls descriptions of Athene's aegis and Hephaistos' shields: ἐν δ' Ἔρις, ἐν δ' Ἀλκή, ἐν δὲ ... Ἰωκή (5.740); ἐν μὲν γαῖαν ἔτευξ', ἐν δ' οὐρανόν, ἐν δὲ θάλασσαν (18.483); ἐν δ' Ἔρις, ἐν δὲ Κυδοιμὸς ὁμίλεον, ἐν δ' ὀλοὴ Κήρ (18.535, cf. *Aspis* 156). θελκτήρια conveys the idea of magic (2× *Od.*); these powers are magically present in the object, like those depicted on the aegis or Herakles' shield, which function similarly, but arouse the opposite emotions.

The 'strap' is not a belt, since Aphrodite undoes it 'from her chest'; Leaf thinks it is simply a loose amulet, since she bids Here put it in her κόλπος, which he takes as the fold of her *peplos*. But Aphrodite did not carry it thus; she is surely giving directions as to how to *wear* it, like Ino at *Od.* 5.346. C. Bonner (*AJP* 70 (1949) 1–6) adduces a series of Oriental statuettes of nude goddesses of love, who wear an ornament consisting of two bands, each passing over the shoulder and under the opposite arm, and joining or crossing the other band at the cleavage between the breasts (often with a fancy boss) and at the back, forming an X or 'saltire'. Such idols are known from *c.* 3000 B.C. to A.D. 250, in Mesopotamia, Syria (Ugarit included), Iran and even India (le Comte du Mesnil du Buisson, *Le Sautoir d'Atargatis*, Leiden

1947). In the Sumerian *Descent of Inanna to the Nether World*, the love-goddess is stripped of her 'breast decoration' as of all else (*ANET* 55). This sexy brassière enters Graeco-Roman art: a fresco at Pompeii shows Venus wearing one made of pearls; cf. *LIMC* s.v. *Aphrodite*, pl. 1083 (Phanagoria, *c.* 400 B.C.). Sixth-century Cypriot mirror-handles show Aphrodite with a breast-ornament held in place by a single diagonal (*ibid.* pls. 372, 375). Whatever its origins in binding magic, such an object has a certain allure, like a garter. But, as F. E. Brenk says (*Classical Bulletin* 54 (1977) 17–20), Homer may have misunderstood it as a pectoral, such as existed in Minoan and Geometric Greece (E. Bielefeld, *Arch. Hom.* C 17f., 56f.).

Eustathius (979.61) guessed that Aphrodite wore this love-charm to Mt Ida for the judgement of Paris, a tale known to Homer (24.23–30n.). Now the next scene contains parallels with the *Cypria*, since Here's driving Paris and Helen off course to Sidon is like her driving Herakles to Kos, and her persuasion of Sleep with the promise of a bride (one of the Graces) resembles Aphrodite's persuasion of Paris; the Graces helped Aphrodite prepare (*Cypria* frag. 4f.). The plot of the *Cypria* surely helped inspire this episode. In 215 ἔνθα δέ must stand (cf. 13.21, *Od.* 21.9, *HyAphr* 59).

216–17 For Sex and Desire cf. 198–9n. ὀαριστύς, 'love-talk' (13.290–1n.), is personified nowhere else, but ὄαροι are among Aphrodite's concerns at *Theog.* 205f. With the unique πάρφασις cf. παραίφασις and -ίη (Musaeus frag. 5). The noun ought to be linked to those preceding by 'and'; the asyndeton makes 217 look like a disconnected gloss on ὀαριστύς. Aristarchus (Nic/A) took ὀ. πάρφασις as a hendiadys for 'seductive conversation', but the lack of 'and' reflects oral misunderstanding or improvisation (cf. 13.633–5n.). With ἔκλεψε νόον, 'deceived', cf. *Theog.* 613; the second hemistich recurs at 9.554. At *Od.* 15.421f. sexual experience itself is said to lead women astray.

218–23 A form of χείρ often precedes ἔπος τ' ἔφατ' ἔκ τ' ὀνόμαζε, especially in the standard verse 232 below; the addressee's name rarely follows (Hainsworth on *Od.* 5.181). τῆ, 'there', used when handing someone an object, is the instrumental of ὁ (Chantraine, *Dict.* s.v. τῆ), an archaism restricted to Homer (7×). Aphrodite confidently predicts that her talisman will work whatever Here has in mind (220 condenses 215–17). The latter may well smile at this, since vague expressions uttered by those not in the know were taken as omens, e.g. at *Od.* 2.33ff., 18.112ff. (so Aristarchus). The repetition of Here's smile stresses her eloquent silence: cf. 211–13n. Another scene ends likewise at 1.595f. (ὡς φάτο, μείδησεν δὲ θεὰ λευκώλενος Ἥρη, | μειδήσασα δέ ...), and she emits a sinister laugh at 15.101–3. In ἀπρηκτόν γε νέεσθαι, 'return unsuccessful', the verb has acquired a future sense like ἰέναι (cf. also 314–15n.).

223–4 To remove the hiatus, Aristarchus (but few good MSS) read μέσῳ, perhaps from 12.206 (Did/A; T says 'Zenodotus'). But ἑῷ resumes τεῷ (219). Hiatus before ἑός (from *sewos, Latin suus) occurs at HyDem 286 in the same phrase, and is common in this formular pattern (e.g. 11.47, Od. 4.338, 11.614, Theog. 464). It arose by analogy with * Ϝός, i.e. *swos (cf. Myc. wo-jo = /hwoio/, PY Eb 472), in paradigms like μητρὸς ἑῆς beside μητέρα ἥν; it spread because ἑός is often used after the caesura, where hiatus is common because of the *jeu de formules* – cf. the case of ἰδέ (347–8n.). T took δῶμα with Διός, assuming that Aphrodite is single and lives at her father's; but each hemistich is felt as a distinct formula.

225–79 Herē leaves for Mt Ida, but meets Sleep (Hupnos) at Lemnos *en route*, apparently by luck (231n.); yet his aid is vital to her plan, and she bribes him heavily to get it. This unlikely coincidence, the sole structural problem in this scene, is the small price Homer pays for the chance to surprise and amuse us with another display of her wiles. Zeus, like the Greeks, must not be worsted too easily; but Here's acquisition of so invincible a weapon as Aphrodite's amulet, and so mighty an ally as Sleep, gives us a powerful impression of her cunning, resolve and prospect of success. Even so she is nearly foiled, comically, by her own past trickery. When she reminds Sleep that he did her this favour before, he reminds her of its unwelcome results on that occasion, tacitly spurning the throne which she offers as a *quid pro quo*. In response she offers an even better bribe, suited both to Sleep and to her role as marriage-goddess – one of the Graces for him to wed; luckily he turns out to be in love with one of them already. The narrator's reticence leaves us wondering whether Sleep was aiming at this all along, and whether Here knew it; this all adds to the scene's charm. Sleep makes her seal her promise with a terrible oath, before she resumes her journey in his company. Edwards (*HSCP* 84 (1980) 25) detects elements of supplication, since she takes Sleep's hand (232) and his initial refusal resembles that of Zeus or Poseidon (1.511ff., 15.185ff.); but her attitude to her underling differs vastly from that of a normal suppliant.

225–30 The first leg of Here's journey takes her down the N.E. foothills of Olumpos (Pieriē) and along the Macedonian coast (Emathiē) to the 'snowy mountains of the Thracians', which are neither the Rhodope range nor Mt Pangaion behind Amphipolis (both too far N.E.), but Mt Athos itself to the S.E., whence she crosses the sea, in the same direction, to Lemnos (see Map, p. xxvi). Thence she will zigzag N.E. to Imbros, then S. down the coast of the Troad to Lekton, its S.W. tip (Strabo 13.583), now Cape Baba, before turning E. to reach Mt Ida. Had she flown in a straight line, her mileage would have been halved; her itinerary is as erratic as Poseidon's at 13.10ff. In fact she is avoiding open water, as Greek sailors did (cf. C. Fries, *RhM* 78 (1929) 54–7); the shortest island-hopping route across the N. Aegean is precisely Athos–Lemnos–Imbros (cf. E. Fränkel on Aesch. *Ag.* 285). Knowledge of such routes has affected Homer's geographical ideas. Cf. Hermes' dislike of long transoceanic flights with no cities *en route* (*Od.* 5.100–2)!

Here's motion, a cross between flying and stepping from one peak to the next, is paralleled at 13.17f. and 281–5 below (where see n.); 225 = 19.114, where (in a denser narrative) this verse expresses the whole journey. When the goddess's name need not be stated, we find instead βῆ δὲ κατ' Οὐλύμποιο καρήνων ἀΐξασα (7× Hom.). Like Hermes at *Od.* 5.50 (note the shared hemistich), Here still has her feet on the ground in Pieriē, mentioned only here in the *Iliad* and original home of the Pieres (Thuc. 2.99); cf. the Myc. fem. ethnic /Piweris/ (MY Oe 103) and name /Piweriātās/ (PY Jn 389). This is the usual first stage of divine journeys: cf. *HyAp* 216f., Πιερίην μὲν πρῶτον ἀπ' Οὐλύμποιο κατῆλθες, | Λέκτον τ' ἠμαθόεντα (Matthiae conjectured Ἠμαθίην τε, but the poet surely misremembered 225f. and 284). Emathiē, home of the Paiones (2.848–50, cf. *Suda* s.v.), once denoted the *sandy* coast of the Thermaic gulf; from ἄμαθος with metrical lengthening, it was later revived as a name for Macedon and even Thessaly. For the ἱπποπόλοι Θρῇκες see 13.4–7n. The Thracians seem further W. here than at 2.844–50, where the Paiones are furthest W., the Kikones are next, and only then come the Thracians; but Athos is called 'Thracian' at its sole other mention in early epic (Leto's wanderings between mountain-tops at *HyAp* 33), and Thracians held the coast opposite Thasos in Archilochus' day. The rhymes and assonances of 225–8, given majesty by νιφόεντα rather than σκιόεντα in 227, indicate the smoothness of Here's progress. She seems to hover over the peak of Athos (6,670 feet), when the poet tells us that her feet did not touch the ground (cf. 13.17–20n., *HyAphr* 125); thence she plunges seaward, a dramatic drop from the major landmark of the N. Aegean.

229–30 Ἀθόω is the gen. of Ἀθόως (restored at *HyAp* 33), which is for *Ἄθωος or -οος by diectasis after the vernacular had contracted it to Ἄθως; cf. Κόως (250–5n.). The rest of 229 resembles ἐς πόντον ἐδύσετο κυμαίνοντα (*Od.* 5.352 and 3× with ὑπό), whence Zenodotus and Aristophanes read ἐς (Did/A); but ἐς means 'into' and ἐπί must stand, cf. 227. Thoas' city is Murinē (bT), now Kastro, on the W. coast of Lemnos; as often in Greece today, the island and its main town are synonymous (cf. 281–5n., *Od.* 8.283). Thoas' grandson Euneos (7.467–9n.) trades in wine, metals, hides, oxen, Phoenician metalwork and slaves (23.740–9n.); this trade is attested in the Pylos tablets, since the palace had 'Lemnian' slave-women, i.e. women bought there (Ventris and Chadwick, *Documents* 410). The odd myths about Lemnos, and Hephaistos' link with it, have an unusually clear correlative in fire-ritual (Burkert, *Homo Necans*, Berkeley 1983, 71, 190–6; cf. Hainsworth on *Od.* 8.283). Despite Thoas' Greek name, Lemnos was inhabited by the Sinties (1.594), who are called ἀγριόφωνοι at *Od.* 8.294. Hellanicus said these were half-Greek, half-Thracian (*FGH* 4 F 71); a Thracian tribe called Sintoi lived on the coast opposite (Thuc. 2.98). Were they the same as the 'Pelasgians' who occupied Lemnos until *c.* 510 B.C. (Hdt. 5.26, cf. 16.233n.)? Thucydides (4.109) and Philochorus (*FGH* 328 F 100f.) call these Tyrrhenians, and inscriptions prove that an Etruscan dialect was spoken there (J. Heurgon, *CRAI* 1980, 578ff.; G. and L. Bonfante, *The Etruscan Language*, Manchester 1983, 51). Lemnian traditions of massacres may reflect several changes of population. With πόλιν θείοιο Θόαντος cf. π. θ. Μύνητος (19.296); for θ., usually at the verse-end, see p. 14 n. 19.

231 Sleep had no special business on Lemnos, which is merely a convenient spot on Here's route; he had a cult only at Troizen (Paus. 2.31.3; D. M. Jones, *CR* 63 (1949) 83–5). If pressed, the poet would have said he was going ἐπὶ κλυτὰ φῦλ' ἀνθρώπων (361), no doubt to scatter slumber like the modern 'sand-man' (cf. *Theog.* 762f.). Elsewhere Hermes puts mankind to sleep (*Od.* 24.3f.). T's plus-verse 231a, ἐρχομένῳ κατὰ φῦλα βροτῶν ἐπ' ἀπείρονα γαῖαν, absent in three of four papyri, imports an explanation where none is needed. D think Sleep frequented Hephaistos' isle to court the Grace Pasitheē, whose sister was the smith's wife (18.382f.)! Death is again said to be Sleep's brother at 16.672, *Theog.* 212 and 756ff. (κασίγνητον Θανάτοιο); their mother is Night, as Homer implies (259f.). They are often compared (11.241, *Od.* 13.80, 18.201f., Hesiod, *Erga* 116, frag. 278.6, Alcman frag. 3.62, Heraclitus frag. 21). In one way Death is weaker, as he cannot subdue the gods; hence Here calls Sleep 'lord of gods and men'. Cf. Vermeule, *Death* 145ff.; C. Ramnoux, *La Nuit et les enfants de la Nuit*, 2nd edn, Paris 1986.

233–41 As Lohmann saw (*Reden* 84n.), Here's request parodies a prayer (e.g. 1.37ff., 1.451ff., 16.233ff.), with (*a*) an honorific address, (*b*) a reminder of past favours, and (*c*) a request for present help, here preceding a promise of gratitude (*kharis*) 'all my days' (235): but before Sleep can grant her request, χάρις must be wittily transformed into the Grace (*Kharis*) Pasitheē, whom Sleep longs for 'all my days' (276)! Moreover Here's promise of a throne, described in alluring sales-talk (238–41), is too grossly materialistic for Homer's audience to fail to laugh at the frank recognition of a kind of bribery in the *do ut des* principle of Greek religion. Prayer was often parodied later (H. Kleinknecht, *Die Gebetsparodie in der Antike*, Stuttgart and Berlin 1937). The parody extends to the use of standard formulae. πάντων τε θεῶν π. τ' ἀνθρώπων is a hymnic phrase (cf. 198–9n.). Verse 234 blends parts of 16.236 and 238 (cf. 1.453, 1.455), ἠμὲν δή ποτ' ἐμὸν ἔπος ἔκλυες, ... | ἠδ' ἔτι καὶ νῦν ... The archaic ἐμὸν (ϝ)έπος is replaced by ἐμεῦ πάρος at 1.453.

235–6 Papyri and some codices read ἰδέω χάριν, versus εἰδέω χ. in the δημώδεις (Did/A) and our vulgate. Aristarchus' text χ. εἰ. removes the hiatus and synizesis; his emendation slights the digamma. εἰδέω, replacing *ϝείδω, recurs at *Od.* 16.236, Hdt. 3.140.2; a genuine Ionic form, it must be right

(Chantraine, *Morphologie historique du grec*, 2nd edn, Paris 1961, 260f.; van der Valk, *Researches* II 205f.). ἰδέω blends εἰδέω and ἴδω (Hoekstra on *Od.* 16.236). The idiom is unique in the epos (cf. 11.243, *HyAp* 153); Ζηνός is innovative too. Zenodotus' ἐπ᾽ for ὑπ᾽ (Did/A), also found in a papyrus, was opposed by his successors.

238–41 For the source of the motif of the gold banqueting-chair see 256–61n. It is to be like Zeus's at 8.442; a 'throne' is not especially honorific, as other gods and men have them. Fancy chairs existed in both Myc. (Ventris and Chadwick, *Documents* 332ff.) and Geometric times, e.g. the one inlaid with ivory, silver and glass paste from Salamis in Cyprus (V. Karageorghis in S. Laser, *Arch. Hom.* P 99–103), whose companion had legs with silver-gilt studs; cf. θρόνον ἀργυρόηλον (*Od.* 8.65, gen. 6× epos), metrically equivalent to θ. ἄφθιτον αἰεί. θρόνος is already in Myc. *to-no* = /*thornos*/ or /*thr̥nos*/. Both Myc. and later chairs came with footstools (/*thrānues*/ in Linear B), which could be inlaid with ivory or silver; these could be attached (cf. *Od.* 19.57f.), and kept one's feet off the earthen floor. The custom that men dined reclining, while women and children sat, spread from the Levant in *c.* 650 B.C. (O. Murray, *Early Greece*, Glasgow 1980, 80). For ἀμφιγυήεις see Hainsworth on *Od.* 8.300.

240–1 Aristarchus read τεύξει, a fut. with κε (Chantraine, *GH* II 225f.), not τεύξει᾽(ε); a fut., needed for this promise, is supported by ἥσει. Van Leeuwen conjectured τεύξει ϝ᾽(ε) to remove the hiatus. ὑπὸ δὲ θρῆνυν ποσὶν ἥσει (with ἧκε at *Od.* 19.57) is adapted from ὑ. δ. θρῆνυς π. ἧεν (18.390, 4× *Od.*). Once the chair arrives, Sleep *could* use it at feasts: hence the opt. ἐπισχοίης. Forms in -οίην could have arisen at any date, by analogy with athematic verbs like γνοίην, and occur both in Attic and in Sappho, e.g. λαχοίην (frag. 33). The variant -σχοιες surely comes from Attic texts that used E for η, as Alexander Cotyaeus proposed (in A). -σχοιας, likewise in papyri, also seems erroneous, *pace* Wackernagel (*SUH* 14). λιπαροὺς πόδας is also at *Od.* 17.410, cf. 186 (dat.). — After 241 'some' added αὐτὰρ ἐπὴν δὴ νῶϊ κατευνήθεντε ἴδηαι, | ἀγγεῖλαι τάδε πάντα Ποσειδάωνι ἄνακτι (in T). This is a pedantic explanation of how Sleep knows that he should tell Poseidon, as he does at 354ff. T rejects it, since, if Here told him to do so, she perjures herself at 15.41f.; but she swears only that she did not inspire Poseidon to intervene. Yet the verses, based on 15.158f. and *Od.* 4.421, are needless (Here reveals her aims at 265) and upset the structure of the speech; they fit better after 237 (Bolling, *External Evidence* 145f.). T's own idea that Sleep exceeds his orders out of gratitude to Here is subtler than the problem merits.

242 On νήδυμος, created by misdivision of (ἔχε)-ν ἥδυμος, see 2.2n., S. West on *Od.* 4.793f. ἥ. survives in Hesiod (frag. 330), Alcman and Simonides, and the formula ἥδυμον ὕπνον at *HyHerm* 241, 449. Mainland poets, aware from their vernacular of the ϝ- in ϝᾱδύς (Latin *suāvis*, Engl. *sweet*), avoided the false form; this Ionic bard did not, as 253 and 16.454 prove.

243–62 After an honorific address responding to 233, Sleep takes up Here's points in reverse order, totally ignoring the chair. The address (= 194), and innocent reference to Okeanos (cf. 201), recall the previous scene, when Here had an easier task because she could resort to lies; now she must hear an awkward truth, which raises the value of Sleep's last favour and the price of his next one. His allusion to the first sack of Troy shows that he knows why she is asking this favour, as she implies at 265.

244–8 If Sleep can subdue even Okeanos, he can clearly do the same to Zeus, as 248 confirms; this makes his refusal all the more galling for Here. On Okeanos as 'origin of all' see 200–7n.; he is imagined as the river that runs round the edge of a flat world. Hesiod thought he was wound round it like a serpent (*Theog.* 790f., with Onians, *Origins* 315ff.). Thus a Phoenician bowl from Praeneste, whose circular decoration strikingly resembles that of Akhilleus' shield, has a snake encircling the whole (K. Fittschen, *Arch. Hom.* N, pl. VIIIb, = no. E2 in G. Markoe, *Phoenician Bronze and Silver Bowls*, Berkeley 1985). Crates (frags. 32f. Mette), keen to prove Homeric geography accurate, held that Ocean is the salt sea that covers the globe (Schmidt, *Weltbild* 111–17); he adduced a very suspect plus-verse that explains πάντεσσι, namely ἀνδράσιν ἠδὲ θεοῖς, πλείστην ⟨τ'⟩ ἐπὶ γαῖαν ἵησιν (Plut. *Mor.* 938D). For αἰειγενέτης, 'whose race lives for ever', see Hoekstra on *Od.* 14.446. ποταμοῖο ῥέεθρα (also at *Od.* 6.317) belongs to the suppletive formular declension π. ῥοάων/ῥοῇσι (4×). The recent split phrase Ζηνὸς ... Κρονίονος recurs at *Od.* 11.620, beside Κρονίωνος 7× epos: the metrical variation is typical (Chantraine, *GH* I 111).

249 This v. is vexed by two problems, the sense of ΑΛΛΟΤΕΗ and the verb. We expect Sleep to say 'on another occasion your command harmed me' or '... made me do this'. The reading ἄλλοτε is supported by ἤματι τῷ at 250; moreover ἤδη με (σε, ἐ) καὶ ἄ. is a standard phrase, appearing in a related context at 1.590, cf. 20.90, 20.187, *Aspis* 359. ἄ. ᾗ will then contain ὅς standing for σός, as it may in the epos, *pace* Aristarchus (see West on *Erga* 381); since *swos survives as the reflexive possessive of all three persons in Indo-Iranian and Slavic, this usage is inherited (cf. 11.142n.). But the third foot should not conclude with a word-end; so Brugman plausibly proposed that an original Ionian psilotic text had ἄλλοτ' ἑή, which should have become ἄλλοθ' ἑή when Atticized, i.e. 'on another occasion your command ...' (cf. van der Valk, *Researches* II 625). Aristarchus (Hrd/A), followed by the OCT, sought to extract the same sense from ἄλλο τεή (for κατ' ἄλλο σή), but ἄλλο can hardly mean 'on another occasion'. Zenodotus and Ptolemy Epithetes (frag. 4 Montanari) emended to make Zeus the subject (Did/A): 'he taught me another lesson because of your command' (τεῇ ἐπίνυσσεν ἐφετμῇ). Now πινύσσω, agreed by the ancients to mean 'admonish', has a ghostlier existence than ἀπινύσσω (15.10–13n.) or πινύσκω (Simonides 508.2 etc.). Two papyri read ἐπένυσσεν, from ἐπι-νύσσω, attested later with the sense 'prick', 'stab'. As O. Szemerényi argued (*Syncope in Greek and Indo-European*, Naples 1964, 58–65), this makes sense, i.e. 'already on another occasion your command pricked me on'; this is then resumed by νῦν αὖ τοῦτο μ' ἄνωγας ἀμήχανον ἄλλο τελέσσαι (262). νύσσω is certainly metaphorical, 'urge on (with words)', in late prose (LSJ s.v. 1 2; G. W. H. Lampe, *A Patristic Greek Lexicon*, Oxford 1961, s.v. 4a). 'Prick' i.e. 'hurt' also seems possible.

250–61 Herakles' sack of Troy is mentioned at 5.640–2, where see n.; on his role in Homer see Kullmann, *Das Wirken der Götter in der Ilias*, Berlin 1956, 25–35. Zeus gives more details of his adventure at 15.26ff.: he was blown right down the Aegean while Zeus slept; the god finally returned him to Argos (for Here's persecution of her stepson see also 19.95ff.). Sleep does not say why Kos was a perilous place, let alone what Herakles did there; but 'apart from all his friends' (256) shows that shipwreck was not the danger. The poet in fact draws on an early gigantomachy or *Herakleia*; Erbse deems the whole tale invented (*Götter* 19–21), but it existed in several variants (F. Vian, *Sileno* 11 (1985) 255ff.). In Hesiod (*Cat.* 43.60ff.), Herakles fought Khalkon and Antagores, the sons of Eurupulos king of Kos; for a trivial reason (surely supplied by the weird cult-story in Plut., *Mor.* 304C–D), he sacked Kos on his return from Troy, before going on to fight the Giants at Phlegre (AT on 15.27 say 'Pallene'). Pindar twice mentions his sack of Troy, the Meropes of Kos and the giant Alkuoneus in this same order (*Nem.* 4.25–7, *Isthm.* 6.31–3). Eurupulos' wife or daughter bore him Thessalos, whose sons went to Troy – a genealogy already found at 2.678f., where see n. One of two versions in 'Apollodorus' (2.7.1) has Herakles mistaken for a pirate, injured in the battle and saved by Zeus, before going to Phlegre (cf. Pherecydes *FGH* 3 F 78, in AD).

In fact there were giants on Kos itself, as we learn from Apollodorus of Athens' *On the Gods* (*P. Köln* III 126). He quotes an anonymous local epic *Meropis*, clearly of seventh- or sixth-century date; he judges it 'post-Homeric' (νεωτέρου τινός). This told how Herakles, fighting the Meropes, would have been slain had not Athene killed his foe Asteros and flayed his impenetrable skin to use as protection in future battles; likewise she flays the giant Pallas in 'Apollodorus' 1.6.2 or the monster Aigis in Diod. 3.70 (whence her aegis). Philostratus (*Her.* 289) confirms that the Meropes were giants; Asteros must be the same as Aster(ios), a giant slain by Athene (Aristotle frag. 637). In 'Apollodorus' (1.6.1f.), Herakles is the mortal ally vital to Zeus's defeat of the giants, who were linked with Kos; cf. Zeus's foes *Coeum et Phlegraeis Oromedonta iugis* (Propertius 3.9.48) – Koios was linked with Kos (250–5n.), and Oromedon is the local mountain. Before the Greeks settled Cumae, did they identify Phlegre with the nearby volcano Nisyros, where Poseidon buried the giant Polubotes and which had a toponym Gigantea? Our tale, an *aition* for how the Dorians took Kos (E. M. Craik, *The Dorian Aegean*, London 1980, 164–6), is one of the several myths of challenges to Zeus's power alluded to by Homer in this episode (153–353n.). See further 295–6n.

250–5 Sleep does not think kindly of Herakles, avoiding his name; κεῖνος gives the generic epithet ὑπέρθυμος a pejorative nuance (cf. 5.604). ἔλεξα means 'put to sleep'; with 253 cf. 23.63. Verse 254 resembles 13.795, *Od.* 11.400, 24.110, *Hy* 7.24, 33.14, all with ἀϋτμήν or ἀέλλας instead of ἀήτας, which occurs only at the verse-end (7× epos, cf. especially 15.626, *Erga* 621). Verse 255 = 15.28. For Κόωνδ' Aristophanes' pupil Callistratus read Κόονδ' (Did/AT). Κῶς is contracted from *Κόος: cf. the Myc. name *Ko-o-ke-ne* = /*Koogenēs*/ (MY Oi 701), and the Titan Κοῖος < *Κόϊος (cf. West on *Theog.* 134). Κόως is a compromise between the two forms, with epic diectasis (cf. Ἀθόως, 229–30n.). *Κόος can always be restored (*Cat.* 43.57, 43.66, *HyAp* 42), but must not be. Κόονδ' is a conjecture depending on a theory of *metacharakterismos* (Barth, *Kallistratos* 119–32, 354).

256–61 Sleep escaped lightly, since Zeus not only flung other gods about the house, but cast them from heaven in his rage (15.23f.)! The fact that nothing actually happens to him suggests that his punishment is invented so that he can refuse Here's offer (B. K. Braswell, *CQ* 21 (1971) 22). West, quoted by Braswell, rightly thinks Sleep is based on Hephaistos: both marry one of the Graces (267–70n.), and the story is set on Lemnos, where Hephaistos landed when Zeus threw him from Olumpos for protecting Here (1.586ff.). Homer knew a variant where Here casts him out (295–6n.); cf. the punishment of Atē (19.130f.). Now the lost *Homeric Hymn to Dionysus* told how Hephaistos, angry at being cast from heaven by Here, traps her with unbreakable bonds in a chair he made, until he is induced to release her, probably in exchange for Aphrodite's hand; likewise Sleep is nearly flung from Olumpos through Here's fault, is promised a chair made by Hephaistos, and is only won over by the pledge of Pasithee's hand! R. Merkelbach identifies *P.Oxy.* 670 as from this *Hymn* (*ZPE* 12 (1973) 212–15); cf. Alcaeus frag. 349; Pindar frag. 283; Plato, *Rep.* 2.378D; *LIMC* IV.1 692–5; T. H. Carpenter, *Dionysian Imagery in Archaic Greek Art*, Oxford 1986, 13–29. This tale surely influenced the lay of Demodokos (*Od.* 8.266ff.), and may be the source of the motif of the chair here. Sleep's role has been thought to derive from the tale that Herakles overcame the giant Alkuoneus with his help, an exploit first attested on vases of *c.* 520 B.C.; the artists do not add Hupnos until later, but the way Pindar links this exploit with the Koan adventure (250–61n.) shows that there may be more truth in this than Erbse allows (*loc. cit.*).

Night is Sleep's mother (231n.); no doubt she saves him by making him invisible (cf. 5.23, *Od.* 23.372). On her importance, and why even Zeus fears her, see 200–7n. and West on *Theog.* 116. Zenodotus, Aristophanes and a papyrus read μήτειρα, which accords with the cosmogony that made her the first being. But πᾶσαι read δμ- (Did/A, *pace* T), Sleep is πανδαμάτωρ at 24.5, and the extension of the suffix -(τ)ειρα from agent-nouns is post-Homeric: cf. πρέσβειρα (*HyAphr* 32), παμμήτειρα (*Hy.* 30.1, cf. Callim. frag. *SH* 303). On why she is called θοῇ see West on *Theog.* 481; 'some' (Did/bT) read φίλη, an attempt to explain why Zeus respects her will. ῥιπτάζω (15.23–5n.), ζητέω and δμήτειρα are unique in Homer; ἄϊστος, 'unseen', is Odyssean, ἀποθύμιος Hesiodic (*Erga* 710), cf. ἀπὸ θυμοῦ ... ἔσεαι, ἐκ θ. πεσέειν (1.562f., 23.595).

263 On the poet's choice between equivalent formulae for Here see 15.92n. T say some texts substituted 1.595 + 1.361; a like substitution appears in a Ptolemaic papyrus at 8.38, but it conveys that Here is relaxed and in full control of the situation, which is less amusing.

264–6 Here's reply is heavily ironic, as her twin questions τίη ... ἦ indicate (cf. 6.55f., 15.244f., and ἦ φής at *Od.* 1.391). Thus ἀρηξέμεν, in a papyrus and early codices, is better than -γέμεν, i.e. 'Do you think Zeus will aid the Trojans in the same way (ὥς) as he was angry over Herakles, his own son?' The same variants are at 13.9. The economy and force of παιδὸς ἑοῖο make her argument irrefutable. The ancient acc. formula εὐρύοπα Ζῆν, surely 'far-thundering' not 'far-seeing' (1.498n.), recurs at 8.206, 24.331, *Theog.* 884, cf. ε. Κρονίδην (3×); this is modified into a voc. (16.241) and a nom. (28× epos). Aristophanes and Aristarchus (in Choeroboscus on Hephaestion 225.19 Consbruch), unaware that Ζῆν represents Proto-Indo-European *dyēm, thought it stands for Ζῆνα with elision at the end of the hexameter – an improbable procedure employed, in what they fancied an imitation of Homer, by Roman poets (cf. West on *Theog.* 884).

267–70 Here masterfully bids Sleep come (ἴθι) rather than asks him, as if he is already persuaded (bT). We do not hear how many Graces there are or who are their parents: cf. Callim. frags. 3–7 with scholia and Paus. 9.35.4. Hesiod makes their parents Zeus and Okeanos' daughter Eurunome (*Theog.* 907–9). Hephaistos' wife is Aglaïe, the 'youngest' (ὁπλοτάτη, 946); Homer calls her simply Kharis (18.382). Perhaps Here is their mother, unless she disposes of them in her role of marriage-goddess. They are linked with Aphrodite (*Od.* 18.194, *Cypria* frag. 4f.) or Desire (*Theog.* 64), since χάρις often meant a sexual favour. For the etymology of ὁπλότερος, originally perhaps 'young' with contrastive -τερος as in κουρότερος, see M. Wittwer, *Glotta* 47 (1969) 63f., and S. West on *Od.* 3.465; bards reinterpreted it as 'younger', creating a superlative. Aristarchus, taking it as 'younger' here, posited two sets of Graces of different ages! Verse 268 derives from genealogical epos: cf. (ἔδωκε) ... κεκλῆσθαι ἄκοιτιν, 4× Hes., *HyDem* 79 (cf. 3.138). Verse 269, an unmetrical interpolation (ἱμείρεαι) to supply a name, is based on 276; it first appears in thirteenth-century MSS. Since 270 packs in three ideas, χήρατο is a unique modification to fit in Sleep's name; for this verse-structure cf. 17.33, *Od.* 24.513, *HyAp* 61 and M. Finkelberg, *CPh* 84 (1989) 182ff.

271–9 The oath Sleep demands is one of the fullest in Homer; cf. Arend, *Scenen* 122f. In its simplest form (4× *Od.*), a request for an oath precedes ὡς ἔφαθ', ἡ δ' ... ἐπώμνυεν ὡς ἐκέλευε or the like (cf. 277f.), and then αὐτὰρ ἐπεί ῥ' ὄμοσέν (-αν) τε τελεύτησέν (-αν) τε τὸν ὅρκον (=280). Poets used three types of expansion: (*a*) giving the words of the oath, ἴστω νῦν τόδε Γαῖα for gods, or ἴ. ν. Ζεὺς (πρῶτα) for mortals, with a list of powers, followed by ἦ/μὴ μέν (Attic ἦ μήν) to introduce the thing sworn (e.g. 15.36ff.); or (*b*) putting the list of powers into the request (*HyHem* 519); or (*c*) including a sacrifice (3.245ff., 19.249ff.). This scene combines a unique version of (*a*) with (*b*): Herē's oath is given in indirect speech (she 'names' all the nether gods), yet the narrator creates variety by omitting the Stux and identifying these gods as the Titans.

To take an oath is in effect to invoke powers greater than oneself to uphold the truth of a declaration, by putting a curse upon oneself if it is false (Burkert, *Religion* 200). It is an ancient custom to touch as one swears an object embodying the power one invokes, e.g. the Bible in our courts or an altar at Athens (cf. 23.582–3n.; Càssola on *HyHerm* 460–2). The Greeks called this object a ὅρκος (cf. E. Benveniste, *Le Vocabulaire des institutions indo-européennes*, Paris 1969, ii 166–73). Thus the gods swear holding a jug of Stux-water (*Theog.* 783ff.); to put herself in contact with the Titans under the earth and sea (8.478ff.), Here must touch the earth and sea (cf. 9.568ff., *HyAp* 333ff.). A deity herself, she can invoke only older gods; why choose the Titans, her own foes and prisoners? This, coupled with her oath by the Stux, makes sense only if Homer already knew a story told in Hesiod alone (*Theog.* 383ff.). When Zeus declared war on the Titans, offering rewards to any who would join him, Stux was first to come, at her father Okeanos' suggestion; she brought her children Victory and Power, who dwell for ever with Zeus. As a reward, he made her the ὅρκος of the gods, and with reason: if Stux and her children change sides, the Titans will oust the Olympians. So Here utters the dreadful curse that, if she neglects her promise, the entire divine order is to be overturned; her plot imperils Zeus's rule.

Stux can also function as intermediary between the lower and upper worlds because her waters flow from Okeanos through the underworld up to the surface (2.755, *Theog.* 786ff.). Men often swore by springs for the same reason (West on *Theog.* 400). Stux is the water of 'Hatred' or 'Shivering'

(15.165–7n.), symbolizing the odium unleashed by perjury. Hesiod says this water sends a perjured god into a cataleptic coma, the divine equivalent of death. On mortals, of course, it has an opposite effect, as an elixir of life – or so Thetis hoped; in modern Greek folklore it has become 'the water of immortality' (West on *Theog.* 805). See further J. Bollack and R. Hiersche, *Revue des études grecques* 71 (1958) 1–41; D. Blickman, *Phoenix* 41 (1987) 350.

271–4 Sleep demands the oath in sonorous language expressive of its solemnity. The old Aeolism ἄγρει (cf. 5.765–6n.) replaces the everyday εἰ δ' ἄγε (νῦν μοι ὄμοσσον, 19.108). The obscure and sinister epithet ἀάατος recurs, scanned ∪–∪∪, at *Od.* 21.91, 22.5; cf. the equivalent phrase ἀμείλικτον Στυγὸς ὕδωρ (*HyDem* 259). From ἀ- + *ἀϝάγω (cf. ἄτη, Aeolic ἀυάτα = *ἄϝάτᾱ), it is best rendered 'inviolable'; the ancients offer 'in which there is no deceit'. ἀνάατος and ἄνᾱτος mean 'unharmed', 'harmless', 'unpunished' in later poetry and inscriptions. The hiatus after ἀ-privative and the scansion are artificial or archaic: cf. ἀάσχετος and Wyatt, *ML* 78. The usual periphrasis Στυγὸς ὕδωρ is the river's original name (West on *Theog.* 805). The weighty symmetry τῇ ἑτέρῃ … τῇ δ' ἑτέρῃ, earth and sea, is aided by the vivid epithets πουλυβότειραν and μαρμαρέην, 'shining'; the latter may be an improvisation (Page, *HHI* 229), like its metrical equivalent πορφυρέην at 16.391. Derived from μαρμαίρω, it describes the aegis, a shield-rim and the doors of the Titans' abode (17.594, 18.480, *Theog.* 811). With 274 cf. 15.225. μάρτυροι ὦσ(ι) is modified from μ. ἔστων (ἐστί, ἦσαν) at 1.338, 3.280, *Od.* 1.273, *Aspis* 20; cf. ἔστε δὲ πάντες | μ. (2.301f.). Zenodotus (Arn/A) tried everywhere to replace the *o*-stem form with μάρτυς, first attested at *Erga* 371; but see 157–8n. Shipp (*Studies* 285) deems ὦσι (also at *Od.* 24.491) Attic, but see p. 18 n. 33. Herodotus omits the initial ἐ- in some forms of the subj. of εἰμί (ὦσι is in all MSS at 2.89.1), cf. ἦσι (19.202, 3× *Od.*); the participle ὤν creeps into the epic diction from the *Odyssey* onward, usually in formular adaptations like this (Chantraine, *GH* 1 286f.; Janko, *HHH* 117, 144f.).

276 Cf. *Od.* 5.219. A Pasitheē is a Nereid, and thus Okeanos' granddaughter, at *Theog.* 246, the sort of context whence Homer could well have plucked the Grace's name.

278–9 The gods below are not called Titans elsewhere by Homer, who names only Kronos and Iapetos (8.479), but no doubt knew Hesiod's whole dozen (cf. 200–7n.). On their nature see West on *Theog.* 133. Homer perhaps connected their name with τίνω, τίσις, i.e. 'those who exact payment for divine perjury': cf. Hesiod's etymology for them at *Theog.* 209f., with West's nn. The Erinues have this role among men (3.278–9n.). ὑποταρτάριος, also at *Theog.* 851, means 'down *in* Tartaros'; nothing is lower (bT). T's variant for 278, θεὸν δ' ὀνόμηνεν ἕκαστον, goes with T's plus-verse ὤμνυε δ' ἐκ πέτρης κατ⟨αλ⟩ειβόμενον Στυγὸς ὕδωρ; this must have replaced 279, not followed it (*pace* Eustathius 985.34, cf. 15.21–2n.). But it suffices that Here 'swore as he ordered'; Homer cares more to interest us than to be pedantically correct about her oath (*pace* Bolling, *External Evidence* 147).

281–5 Herē adopts so circuitous a route (225–30n.) that a pedant in T excised Imbros by reading Λήμνοιο κατὰ μέγα ἄστυ in 281, but Lemnos and Imbros are also linked at 24.753, *HyAp* 36. The main town on each isle was homonymous with the whole: cf. 229–30n. and the easier expression 'Ἰθάκης κατὰ ἄ. (*Od.* 22.223). ἠέρα ἑσσαμένω is Hesiodic (etc., 3× *Erga*), but the ϝ- proves it an old phrase; the rest of 282 describes horses at 23.501, *Od.* 13.83 (plur.), and Aphrodite flying to Ida at *HyAphr* 67 (sing., with 68 corresponding to 283). Zeus's own arrival at Ida is related in the same verse as 283, and, in another ironic reversal, so is that of the loyal gods Iris and Apollo (8.47, 15.151). Ida merits the description 'mother of beasts': it bred wolves, lions, bears, leopards and deer (*HyAphr* 70f.), cf. 8.47–8n. — Poseidon's angry strides made the hills shake (13.18); Here and Sleep travel more gently, hardly touching the ground (cf. 228). It is a sadder world that no longer sees invisible gods' footsteps in the trembling of misty tree-tops; but this was perhaps only a blind-man's vision even then, since the recent scansion of ὑπεσείετο (σείω < *ky-), like the hiatus before ὕλη (cf. *Od.* 5.257), suggests improvisation. ἱκέσθην governs Λεκτόν as a part of the whole (so too Γάργαρον at 8.48), since Ida was held to rise from there (225–30n.).

286–8 ὄσσε is probably the subject of ἰδέσθαι, not its object (cf. 15.147); Sleep is keener not to be seen by Zeus than not to see him. Ida's mixed forests, famous in antiquity, still thrive; 'Ida' means 'forest'. Sleep chooses for his perch the tree that was then the tallest, a fir so lofty that it pierces the mist (ἀήρ) on the hillside to the clear air above. The picture is vivid and natural. But Aristarchus must have imagined the tree as gigantic, like the fir at *Od.* 5.239 (οὐρανομήκης) or Mt Taügetos at *Od.* 6.103 (περιμήκετος), since it pierces the ἀήρ to the αἰθήρ above; he took these to mean, respectively, the lower atmosphere with the clouds and the clear upper air (Schmidt, *Weltbild* 75–81). His theory, largely based on 288, was disproved by Leaf (Appendix H): ἀήρ means 'mist' or 'darkness', and αἰθήρ is the clear air, in which clouds may float, below the solid firmament (οὐρανός).

290–1 Sleep takes the form of a bird, as gods often do (13.62–5n.). Far from being 'an unknown and perhaps fabulous bird' (Thompson, *Birds* 186f.), the κύμινδις was a kind of owl familiar in Ionia, with an Anatolian name. Ida harboured many raptors (cf. 15.237), but a bird sleepy by day certainly suits Sleep best. This bird has talons (Aristoph. *Birds* 1181), and T say it is an owl (cf. schol. on *Birds* 261). Known for its call (λιγυρή), as Hipponax confirms (frag. 61), it is a mountain-dweller (ἐν ὄρεσσι), as

Aristotle agrees (*Hist. An.* 9.615b6ff.), adding that it is dark in hue, as big as a hawk, and has an Ionian name; he goes on to describe the eagle-owl, *Strix bubo*. Pollard (*Birds* 81f.) thinks this bronze-coloured owl is meant; the hawk-owl, *Strix uralensis*, is also possible. J. M. Boraston (*JHS* 31 (1911) 240f.) prefers the long-eared owl (*Asio otus*), which frequents conifers.

Why is this owl called χαλκίς by the gods but κύμινδις by men? In Hittite and Icelandic, 'divine' speech is a more elevated register of ordinary speech (J. Friedrich in *Festschrift A. Debrunner*, Bern 1954, 135–9); it seems that poets sometimes invented the 'divine' name, or called it divine to explain why there were two names, stressing their privileged knowledge (Fowler, *Phoenix* 42 (1988) 98f.). Thus Orphic frag. 91 says that the gods call the moon σελήνη, mortals μήνη; yet both terms were current, and of Indo-European origin (see also 1.403–4n.). Now Heubeck (*Kleine Schriften* 103–9) proposed that κύμινδις (or κύβινδις) was the bird's standard name, which Homer linked aurally with a girl called Kombe or Khalkis, mother of the Kouretes, after whom Euboean Khalkis was named: cf. Hecataeus, *FGH* 1 F 129; Euphorion frag. *SH* 442.4; H. Meyer, *RE* XI (1921) 1139–41 s.v. In fact Homer alludes to a tale that the girl turned into this bird. There was a bird called κόμβη or κύμβη (Chantraine, *Dict.* s.v.); a hawk-like bird appears on the earliest coins of Khalkis; Ovid mentions an avian metamorphosis of 'Combe' at Pleuron (*Met.* 7.382f.); and a Euboean local historian, Proxenus, said Khalkis, κύμινδις and Kombe were one and the same (*FGH* 425 F 1, with A. Henrichs, *Cronache Ercolanesi* 5 (1975) 17f.). This explains why we are told what the divine name is: gods alone can recognize the owl as the girl Khalkis. The allusion is witty, because Sleep disguises himself as a bird that is only disguised as a bird, and is really a person. Homer and Hesiod knew of many avian transformations, but Homer tends to gloss over them: cf. the double-named Alkuonē (halcyon)/Kleopatrē (9.561ff.), the nightingale Aëdon (*Od.* 19.578ff.) or the tale of Alkuonē and Kēüx (*Cat.* 10a.90ff., 10d). T suggest various metamorphoses, e.g. that of Harpalukē into a χαλκίς (Parthenius 13), to explain our passage.

292–353 The climactic scene of this episode elaborates the traditional story-pattern of seduction, far transcending its origin in the myth and ritual of sacred marriage (153–353n.). In typical Homeric fashion, dialogue advances the action, with brief descriptions only at the beginning and end. The couple's richly ironic conversation is symmetrically structured in both form and content; two distinct patterns provide strong defences against the ancient atheteses of 304–6 and 317–27. Formally, there is first a brief question from Zeus, then Here's false tale (11 lines), Zeus's list of his past amours (16 lines), Here's crafty objection (11 lines), and lastly Zeus's brief and impatient reply. Patterns of ring-composition cut across the changes of speaker (Lohman, *Reden* 146–8):

1. *The reason for Here's arrival* (298–311)
    (*Zeus*)   *a*   Here, why have you come from Olumpos (298)?
           b   You have no chariot and horses (299).
    (*Here*)   *c*   I am going to visit Okeanos and Tethus ... (301–6).
          b' My horses are at the foot of the mountain (307f.).
          a' I came from Olumpos to ask your permission to go (309–11).
2. *Zeus's proposition* (312–31)
    (*Zeus*)   A   Here, go later, let us bed down together in love (313f.)!
          B   Never have I felt such passion (315f.),
          C   not even when I loved Ixion's wife ... etc., etc., etc. (317–27),
          B' as the passion I now feel for you (328).
    (*Here*)   A' What an idea, to bed down together in love here (330–2)!
3. *Here's counter-proposal* (333–45)
          a   What if a god saw us and caused a scandal (333–6)?
          b   But if you wish (337),
          c   you have a chamber Hephaistos built with stout doors (338f.);
          b' let us go there, since you want to go to bed (340).
    (*Zeus*)   *a'* Here, do not fear that a god will see us; I will hide us in a cloud (341–5).

292–3 For Gargaron, where Zeus took up his station at 8.48, see *ad loc.* It is no accident that Homer calls Zeus 'cloud-gatherer' each time he names him (293, 312, 341), since he ends up dormant in one of the clouds which symbolize his power! The epithet may be a calque from Ugaritic *rkb 'rpt*, (Ba'al) 'cloud-gatherer/-rider' (West, *JHS* 108 (1988)170).

294 In arrival-scenes, the person who arrives usually *finds* the other (τὸν δ' εὗρε ...: Arend, *Scenen* 28). Instead, Zeus *sees* Here; the repetition of ἴδε stresses the departure from the norm. At last he sees, but only what Here planned he should see; he accosts her, as his standing up indicates, deeming himself the seducer rather than the seduced. Love enters through his eyes: cf. 16.182, *Cat.* 145.13, *HyAphr* 56f., West on *Theog.* 910. In ὡς δ' ἴδεν, ὥς ... the first ὥς is temporal, the second demonstrative, not exclamatory; it means 'no sooner did he see her than ...', cf. 1.512, 19.16, 20.424 (Gow on Theocritus 2.82). As Onians notes (*Origins* 420f.), love covers the sky-god's mind like a cloud (not a net, *pace* bT): cf. 3.442, ἔρως φρένας ἀμφεκάλυψε, when Paris recalls his first union with Helen, and *HyAphr* 243, ἄχος πυκινὰς φ. ἀμφικαλύπτοι, beside νέφος ἀμφεκάλυψε etc. (343, 16.350 etc.). The expansion πυκινὰς φ.(also *HyAphr* 38) aptly stresses the intelligence that is overcome (cf. 217); the epithet often describes mental concepts, e.g. πυκινὰ φρεσὶ μήδεα, not the mind itself, but cf. 15.461, *Cypria* frag. 1.3, Hes. frag. 253, *HyHerm* 538. ἔρως is found only before consonants (3.442, Hes. frag.

298), which confirms that it is a recent arrival in the epic diction, replacing Aeolic ἔρος (Chantraine, *GH* 1 211).

295-6 Zeus's secret intimacy with Here lasted three centuries (Callim. frag. 48). bT ask how they had intercourse 'in secret from their parents' if Here was reared by Okeanos and Tethus, not by Kronos and Rhea. bT's answer, that Here was adult before she was sent away to Okeanos, is not easy (203-4n.); nor can 'their parents' be Okeanos and Tethus. The motif serves as an amusing reminder that their relations are incestuous, and is transferred from an all-too-human intrigue. The thrill of secret sex is a topos (2.515,16.184, *Od.* 15.430, 22.445), and φίλους λήθοντε τοκῆας seems formular: cf. φ. λιτάνευε τ. (*Theog.* 469), λάθρα φίλων γονέων (*HyDem* 240).

Homer may have borrowed this discrepant detail from that same *désaccord* between Zeus and Here which he exploited earlier in this episode (250-61n.). He preserves decorum by making Hephaistos the child of their union (1.572, 578), but is probably suppressing the tale that they quarrelled when she bore Hephaistos on her own, and Zeus produced Athene without her (*Theog.* 924ff.). To do so Zeus seduced Metis, daughter of Okeanos and Tethus, *in secret from Here*, and then swallowed her to prevent her from bearing a son mightier than himself (cf. 15.87-8n.) or than his thunderbolt: see *Theog.* 886ff. with West's n.; 'Hesiod' frag. 343 with S. Kauer, *Die Geburt der Athena im altgriechischen Epos*, Würzburg 1959; M. Detienne and J.-P. Vernant, *Les Ruses de l'intelligence: la mètis des Grecs*, Paris 1974, 140ff. She had helped him make Kronos vomit up the other gods ('Apollodorus' 1.2.1). In a variant at *HyAp* 305-55, Here, aided by Earth and the Titans, creates Tuphōeus to challenge Zeus's power, in anger at the deformity of their joint offspring Hephaistos and at the birth of Athene (she alludes to Metis with μητίσεαι at 322, cf. 344); a similar story appears in b on 2.783. The detail, found at *HyAp* 318-20, that Here cast her lame offspring into the sea whence Thetis rescued him, recurs at 18.395-9. Now 'Apollodorus' (1.3.5f.) mentions, *between* the births of Hephaistos and Athene, the storm with which Here buffeted Herakles (cf. 250-61), Zeus's punishment of her (cf. 15.18ff.) and of Hephaistos (cf. 1.590ff.), and his seduction of Metis. These tales were clearly interrelated in Apollodorus' main source, probably Eumelus' *Titanomachy* (West, *Orphic Poems* 122-6, dates the poem far too late). Since Homer draws on so much of this material, it is possible that the tale wherein Zeus secretly seduces Metis, thereby endangering his own rule, underlies this detail, the introduction of her parents Okeanos and Tethus at 200ff., and the wider episode.

For πρώτιστον, in a papyrus and most MSS, Aristarchus read πρῶτόν περ (Did/AT), a unique phrase. πρῶτον/-ιστον are metrically useful alternatives after οἷον ὅτε (9.447, *Od.* 10.462); Nauck guessed that the variants go back to πρώτιστα with a hiatus.

298–9 Zeus's feelings are obvious; why ask where Here's chariot is, unless he hopes that she has none and will dally awhile with him? Her crafty reply that it is nearby to take her on her way (307f.) can only fuel his ardour (bT). It is comical that he asks as a matter of course where her chariot is; no mortal can drive up a mountain-peak! The metrical lengthening in κατ' Οὐλύμπου is innovative, by analogy with forms like Οὐλύμποιο, where it is needed to fit the word into hexameters (Shipp, *Studies* 40). τόδ' ἱκάνεις, a common Odyssean idiom, means 'reach this (place)', i.e. 'arrive' (LSJ s.v. ὅδε IV 2), not 'come on this errand' with an internal acc., *pace* Macleod on 24.172; it is pleonastic in 309. Verse 299 = 5.192, with ἐπιβαίης for -ην; Zenodotus, Aristophanes (Did/A) and a papyrus omit κ', a rarer construction (Chantraine, *GH* II 249).

300–6 These vv. repeat 197 + 200f. + 205–7 (where see nn.), omitting Here's request for the love-charm and her reference to Zeus's defeat of Kronos, which might arouse in him emotions unsuited to the occasion. Aristarchus, following Zenodotus (Did/AT), athetized 304–6 as redundant, since she needs no excuse to visit Okeanos now that she has the love-charm; moreover she runs the risk that Zeus might take her seriously and go with her. But bT are right that Here's tale need not lessen Zeus's desire, but is calculated to make him think of sex and restoring conjugal harmony; it also gives her an alibi for her presence on Ida to protect her later. Verses 304–6 also increase the effectiveness of 309–11: her declared purpose is so innocuous that her submissive request for leave to go seems all the more touching. At 8.477ff. Zeus said he would not care about her anger even if she went to the end of the world; now that she is going there, will he care so little? For formal objections to the athetesis see 292–353n. Nickau (*Zenodotos* 93–6) thinks Zenodotus suspected a concordance-interpolation, like the insertion of 208f. after 306 in a papyrus.

307–8 So brazen is Here that she falsifies not only her plans, but a verifiable fact – where her chariot is. The poet makes a virtue of his omission of a vehicle from this divine journey (cf. 13.10–38n.). πρυμνώρεια, for πρυμνὸν ὄρος 'the foot of the mountain', is unique in Greek; cf. its opposite ἀκρώρεια (a prose word), its synonym ὑπώρεια, the hill-town Ἀνεμώρεια and Nereid Λιμνώρεια (20.218, 2.521, 18.41). ἐπὶ τραφερήν τε καὶ ὑγρήν (*Od.* 20.98, *HyDem* 43), literally meaning 'over firm and fluid', is an underrepresented formula for 'over land and sea': τ., from τρέφω, 'make solid' (e.g. of cheese), is an archaism (Chantraine, *Dict.* s.v. τρέφω B). ὑγρή, 'sea', occurs in two other stereotyped phrases (10.27, 24.341, 3× *Od.*), cf. γλαυκή (16.33–5n.)

310–12 For the rarer μετέπειτα (4× *Od.*) Zenodotus and Aristophanes read μετόπισθε (Did/A), perhaps from 1.82, *Od.* 5.147; this variant is in a papyrus but few good codices. βαθυρρόου Ὠκεανοῖο, once *-ρόϝο', is formular (4× epos). Zeus is aptly called 'cloud-gatherer' (292–3n.): Homer could have said τὴν δ' ἡμείβετ' ἔπειτα Κρόνου πάϊς ἀγκυλομήτεω or τὴν δ' αὖτε προσέειπε πατὴρ ἀνδρῶν τε θεῶν τε.

313–28 Zeus's solicitation is a hugely distended version of Paris' (3.438–46) – a dismissal of all else in favour of intercourse, because of the burgeoning desire he feels. Paris recalls his first union with Helen; but the poet has already used this way to measure Zeus's libido (295f.), and lets the god merely allude to it at the climax of his list of past amours (327), which replaces Paris' recollection as the centre of the speech:

3.441 ἀλλ' ἄγε δὴ φιλότητι τραπείομεν εὐνηθέντε· (cf. 314)
3.442 οὐ γάρ πώ ποτέ μ' ὧδε γ' ἔρως φρένας ἀμφεκάλυψεν, (cf. 315f.)
3.443 οὐδ' ὅτε σε..., (cf. 317, 319, 321, 323, 326f.)
3.446 ὡς σέο νῦν ἔραμαι καί με γλυκὺς ἵμερος αἱρεῖ. (=328)

Zeus's roster may well offend the religious sensibilities of a Plato; it is also an odd way to prove oneself a worthy lover, *pace* the archbishop (988.27). As Aristarchus says, his brief statement at 315f. would have sufficed to signal his ardour; his list would repel Here, not attract her, and is too long-winded for the god's urgency. Hence he athetized 317–27, as had Aristophanes (Did/A). But there are formal objections to the athetesis. This speech is the centre of the exchange (292–353n.); to reduce it to five lines, when Here's false tale and counter-proposal are much longer, spoils the balance. The list is also at the mid-point of the ring-composition, where *exempla* or genealogies often occur (cf. 110–32n. and J. H. Gaisser, *HSCP* 73 (1969) 1–43). The verses are genuine, despite their omission from Plato's inexact précis at *Rep.* 3.390c.

Even so, such a roster would offend any wife; Zeus's must be especially galling to Here, who fell out with him over several of these liaisons. In fact he is made to list these amours precisely because they evoke old quarrels with Here, which he hopes are past; he means to flatter her by rating his present urge stronger than any he felt before. His tactic is gauche, since *praeteritio* mentions what it would suppress; there is also humour in the sheer length of the list, and in our impression that Zeus is running true to form. We wonder for a moment whether Here will be able to complete her mission, in the face of this new proof of his gross insensitivity, before we realize that she will perceive it as justifying her actions. As Edwards says (*HPI* 249), she cannot afford to protest for fear of ruining her plan!

The catalogue is ably constructed with *variatio*; the fine analysis by Eustathius (988.41–59) is his forte and owes little to lost scholia. ἔραμαι frames the list (317, 328); Zeus avoids repeating the verb too often, as if dimly aware that this might annoy Here. First, three mortal women with their sons receive a couplet each. Ixion's wife is unnamed; Danae is named with an epithet and patronymic; Europē is not, but her father has an epithet and she has an extra son. Next Zeus lists, in three chiastic verses, two mortals who bear him gods, Semele and Alkmene. He culminates with three goddesses in just two lines, Demeter, Leto and Here; named without offspring, each is listed more briefly than her predecessor. Zeus's ascent from mortals to deities, ending with Here herself, and his increasing brevity, give his speech the urgency that Aristarchus missed in it. The proud father also names his sons in an ascending order: Peirithoos, Perseus, Minos, Rhadamanthus, Herakles and Dionusos.

Homer could be influenced by the catalogue of Ishtar's lovers in the *Epic of Gilgamesh* VI (Burkert, *Die orientalisierende Epoche* 95). Yet Zeus's list deftly adapts traditional catalogue-poetry, and especially a standard theogonic list of his marriages, as its structure, cognates and diction prove. The Greeks traditionally organized their genealogies around women; the prime example is Hesiod's *Ehoiai*, but the *Odyssey* includes a catalogue wherein virgins seduced by gods precede the wives of mortals (11.235ff., 271ff.). Hesiod too uses this principle: at *Theog.* 886–923 and 938–44 he lists Zeus's unions with seven goddesses, starting with Metis and ending with Demeter, Mnemosune, Leto and Here, and then with nymphs or mortals, Maia, Semele and Alkmene. Like Homer, he enumerates the children, and even uses the sequence Demeter – Leto – Here, plus Semele and Alkmene; but, for the emotive purpose we have seen, Homer reverses the order of deities and mortals, and omits the deities' progeny. Both catalogues are also unique in using two-line entries (*Theog.* 938f., 943f., 1017f.): elsewhere poets need at least three verses to say who wed whom with what result. The parallels should give pause to those who deny Hesiod the end of his *Theogony*.

This list is a masterpiece of compression, only possible because both subject and verb are understood in each item, and because Homer controls the full range of genealogical formulae. The many parallels with the *Odyssey*, Hesiod and the *Hymns* prove that, far from being interpolated from a 'mainland' school of catalogue poetry, this passage derives from the same ancient oral tradition of genealogical verse (see further Kakridis, *Poetica* 5 (1972) 152–63; West, *Catalogue* 3–11). | ἥ τέκε (3×) recurs 8× Hes. With Ἰξιονίης ἀλόχοιο cf. Ἀγαμεμνονέην/Ἑκτορέην ἄλοχον, *Od.* 3.264, *Little Iliad* frag. 21.2 B. = 20.2 D. θεόφιν μήστωρ' ἀτάλαντον (318) is nom. elsewhere (4× Hom., *Cat.* 190.7). With Δανάης καλλισφύρου Ἀκρισιώνης, a fem. patronymic (Risch, *Wortbildung* 101), cf. Δανάην καλλίσφυρον (*Cat.* 129.14), κ. Ὠκεανίνην (*Theog.* 507), καλλισφύρου Εὐηνίνης (9.559), κ. Ἀργείωνης (2× *Cat.*). In 320 the scansion Περσῆᾶ before πάντων ἀριδείκετον ἀνδρῶν (cf. 11.248, *Cat.* 196.2) is a sign of strain; the formula κρατερὸν μήστωρα φόβοιο has the right metrical shape and describes Perseus at *Cat.* 129.15, but was avoided here because of 318. In the spondaic 321, τηλεκλειτοῖο

(< *-κλεϝετ-) goes with Phoinix and not κούρης, to judge by 'Ικαρίου κούρη τ. (*Od.* 19.546), Λυγκῆος γενεῆ τ. (*Aspis* 327). *Cat.* 141.13 lists Minos δίκαιόν τε 'Ραδάμανθυν; contrast the generic καὶ ἀντίθεον 'Ρ. in 322. κρατερόφρονα γείνατο παῖδα (324) recurs at *Theog.* 509, *Od.* 11.299 (catalogue, in the dual). Herakles has the particularized epithet θρασυμέμνονα at *Od.* 11.267, but is again κ. at *Aspis* 458. τέκε χάρμα βροτοῖσι (325) recurs at *HyAp* 25 (of Apollo); cf. τ. θαῦμα/πῆμα β. (*Od.* 11.287, 12.125, *Cypria* frag. 9.1 B. = 7.1 D.), χ. γονεῦσι (*Cat.* 193.19, Alkmene), χ. μέγ' ἀνθρώποισι (*Hy.* 16, Asklepios), and οἷα Διώνυσος δῶκ' ἀνδράσι χ., of wine or grapes (*Cat.* 239.1 = *Aspis* 400). καλλιπλοκάμοιο ἀνάσσης (326) is a unique combination: ἄνασσα, a *hapax* in the *Iliad*, describes Demeter at *HyDem* 75, 492; her epithets χρυσαόρου ἀγλαοδώρου (*HyDem* 4) fill the same space but begin with two consonants. Λητοῦς ἐρικυδέος (υἱός) is hymnic (*HyAp* 182, 3× *HyHerm*), entailing contraction of *Λητόος; cf. ἥβης ἑ. (11.225).

314–16 The aor. short-vowel subj. τραπείομεν, from τέρπω, occurs in other seduction-scenes with εὐνηθέντε(ς): see 3.441, *Od.* 8.292 with Hainsworth's n. περιπροχυθείς, a *hapax* in Greek, continues the image of love as a mist (294n.). Demetrius (in T), styled Ixion for ungratefully jilting Aristarchus in favour of Crates (see Fraser, *Ptolemaic Alexandria* 470f., and Barth, *Kallistratos* 82), embraced περιπλεχθείς instead, a conjecture as obnubilated as the monstrous γενέεσθαι he misbegot at 221.

317–18 Zeus's list opens inauspiciously with his passion for Ixion's wife, called Dia by οἱ νεώτεροι (schol. pap. in Erbse, *Scholia* III 556). Even if he debauched her before her wedding, his phrasing makes him sound like an adulterer. Worse yet, Ixion and Peirithoos were both notorious rapists; if the son takes after his father, this reflects badly on Zeus! Ixion tried to ravish Here (to avenge himself on Zeus?); he perforated a cloud shaped like her, engendéring the Centaurs (Pindar, *Py.* 2.21–48 with scholia); these turned the tables at Peirithoos' wedding by raping the lady guests, a tale well known to Homer (1.263–5n.). Peirithoos tried to ravish Persephone (first in 'Hesiod' frag. 280.12ff., but cf. *Od.* 11.631). He is again called 'son of Zeus' at 2.741; his name means 'very swift', with metrical lengthening of περί. Zeus allegedly took the guise of a stallion to sire him (AD on 1.263). This is but the first of the weird transformations evoked by this catalogue. Hippomorphic matings are ancient: cf. the cases of Boreas, Zephuros, Kronos and Poseidon (16.141–4, 16.149–50nn.).

319–20 Pherecydes told how Zeus took the form of a shower of gold to elude Akrisios and impregnate Danaē, who bore him Perseus (*FGH* 3 F 10); this tale, known to Hesiod (*Cat.* 135.1–5), was no doubt already current. Danaē's bronze-bound chamber with a chink in the roof and gold inside must be a fantasy based on a fabulously rich Argive tholos-tomb, with

bronze rosettes on its walls and its relieving-triangle opened by robbers. She
is kin to the three women who follow: all descend from Belos or his brother
Agenor.

321–2 The daughter of Phoinix, eponymous ancestor of the Phoenicians,
is Europeia or Europē. Hesiod (*Cat.* 140f.) told how Zeus took the shape of
a bull to trick her and carry her over the sea to Crete; the mention of her
son Minos implies this here (13.449–54n.). She bore Sarpedon too (p. 371).
More often she is Agenor's daughter, sister rather than cousin to Kadmos
('Apollodorus' 3.1.1). Rhadamanthus' name is obscure. Since he married
Alkmene (*id.* 2.4.11) before going to Elysium (*Od.* 4.564), he had Boeotian
connexions, as did his mother (West, *Catalogue* 83n., 146f.). See R. B.
Edwards, *Kadmos the Phoenician*, Amsterdam 1979. The usual epic acc. of
Μίνως is -ωα, which is in papyri but does not scan; Zenodotus, a papyrus
and the vulgate have -ω (also in Attic), with contraction. Aristarchus'
Μίνων (Did/AT) has weak MS support and is more modern, being used by
Herodotus along with a gen. Μίνω; cf. Ἄρηα/Ἄρην.

323–5 Kadmos' daughter Semele and Amphitruon's wife Alkmene both
bore (demi-)gods at Thebes. Dionusos may follow Herakles because there
is no doubt as to his divinity (cf. 6.131): Homer makes Herakles mortal at
18.117ff., but equivocates at *Od.* 11.602f. (cf. West on *Theog.* 947–55). Both
affairs gave Zeus trouble with his spouse. Homer just mentioned their
quarrel over Herakles (250–61n.). When first we hear Semele's full story,
we learn that Here caused her incineration (Eur. *Bacch.* 6–12 with Dodds'
n.); 'Apollodorus' (3.4.3) reports that she tricked Semele into asking that
Zeus woo her in the same way as he wooed Here – in a chariot of fire, as it
turned out. However, since Hesiod (frag. 217a) said Aktaion was slain for
wooing Semele, there was surely a variant wherein she was blasted for
yielding to him, as was Koronis for defiling Apollo's seed by going to bed
with a mortal; each girl's divine progeny, Dionusos and Asklepios, is saved
from the flames (Janko, *Phoenix* 38 (1984) 299–302). Semele was once an
Earth-goddess, wooed with lightning by the Sky-god: her name may mean
'Earth' in an Indo-European *satem* language, perhaps Thracian, from the
root *ghem-l-* seen in Slavic *zemlya* (cf. χαμηλός); Chantraine compares
neo-Phrygian δεως ζεμελως κε, 'to the gods of sky and earth' (*Dict.* s.v.).
Dionusos' name, once thought to have reached Greece very late, appears
in Linear B; O. Szemerényi derives it from Indo-European *Diwos-sūnus*,
'son of Zeus' (*Gnomon* 43 (1971) 665). The rarity of Homer's allusions to the
god (6.130n.) may only reflect his personal preferences, or his genre's.

326–7 Demeter's child is Persephone (*Theog.* 912f.); Leto's are Artemis
and Apollo. The tale that Here drove the pregnant Leto all over the Aegean
to prevent the birth is implied in the *Hymn to Apollo* (45ff., 95ff.), whose poet
plays it down; contrast Callim. *Hy.* 4.55ff. It was surely as familiar to Homer

as was her labour by the palm-tree on Delos (*Od.* 6.162f. with Hainsworth's n.). To mention her in the same breath as Here is thus Zeus's worst gaffe of all. Hesiod lists Here's children by Zeus as Hebe, Ares and Eileithuia (*Theog.* 922). Homer made Hephaistos their child too (295–6n.).

330–40 For the structure of Here's speech see 292–353n. Repetitions of 'bed' (331, 337, 340) frame both its halves, the latter of which is a call to action opened by ἀλλά. With the pretence of embarrassment which 330, her stock address to Zeus (6×), gains from its context, she evokes a scene just like *Od.* 8.320ff., when the gods flock to see Aphrodite snared naked in Ares' embrace – a cause of quenchless mirth. Then the all-seeing Sun spotted the adulterers trapped in the chamber Hephaistos built (8.302); now Zeus reassures Here that even the Sun will not be able to peep at them, as he refuses her coy proposal that they go to just such a chamber. He rejects this from sheer impatience for intercourse, little suspecting the havoc that would have ensued: Here would have not only lured him far from Troy, but confined him in the chamber their son fitted with a lock which she alone could open (so bT)! With 338f. cf. 166f.; the description of this lock is omitted, since it would ill serve Here's plan to mention it. Plainly the same chamber is meant, which Hephaistos built for both his parents (despite οἱ at 166 versus τοι at 338) – otherwise its existence lacks point. Thus the end of the whole episode aptly recalls its start. Homer's allusions to gods imprisoning each other are certainly comic (5.385–7, *Od.* 8.266ff.), but adapt serious motifs: Zeus now risks suffering what he made the Titans suffer. He was gaoled and perhaps emasculated in an old version of the legend of Tuphoeus ('Apollodorus' 1.6.3, surely from the Cycle, and Nonnus, *Dion.* 1.137ff.). By repeating τοι (4× in 337–40), Here stresses that it was Zeus who took the erotic initiative.

331–3 For ἐν φιλότητι ... εὐνηθῆναι cf. 314, 360, *Theog.* 380. Leaf's comma at the end of 332 rightly makes πῶς κ᾽ ἔοι the apodosis of two conditionals, the second contingent upon the first, and τὰ δὲ προπέφανται ἅπαντα a parenthesis: 'If you wish us to lie together on the peaks of Ida, where everything can be seen, how would it be, if one of the gods saw us and told the rest?' To put a stop after 332 makes this phrase an apodosis with apodotic δέ, laying too much stress on an obvious fact, to the detriment of πῶς κ᾽ ἔοι. ἔοι for εἴη may be Aeolic (Shipp, *Studies* 81).

340 κείοντες is an old desiderative or subj. of κεῖμαι with fut. sense, especially common as κακκείοντες (Chantraine, *GH* I 453); the Aeolic form εὕαδεν (p. 16) recurs at 17.647, *Od.* 16.28, 5× Hes., *Hy.* (cf. too *Cat.* 116.5). Zenodotus and Aristophanes (Did/A) prudishly read ἴομεν ... εὐνήν, 'let us go *to* bed', probably objecting to the sense 'since bed (intercourse) pleases you' (cf. 15.31–3n.); the unaccompanied acc. and parenthetic ἐπεί νύ τοι εὕαδεν would both be untypical.

342–5 Zeus wraps the lovers in a cloud at the end of the scene, just as love clouded his wits at its start (294n.). A golden cloud, suitably opaque to divine vision (cf. 13.521–5n.), is more romantic than a dark one. φάος has a twin significance, 'light' and 'sight', derived from the ancient idea of vision; we see with rays of light coming from the eye, and darkness is a mist through which such rays cannot pass (13.837n.). The Sun, the greatest eye in the cosmos, sees all (3.276–8n.; Richardson on *HyDem* 24–6). It is easy to take τό γε as object of ὄψεσθαι, but a parallel at 5.827f. shows it to be an adverbial acc., and ὅ. an explanatory inf.: 'have no fear in this regard lest anyone see'. The bad variants in three papyri come from recollection of 5.827f.

346–53 This evocative description is framed by 346 and 353 (ἀγκὰς ... παράκοιτιν – ἀ. ἄκοιτιν), although editors mark a paragraph at 352. Zeus literally, and the poet figuratively, draw a veil over the proceedings; this serves at once the plot's exigencies, the gods' privacy and the poet's usual coyness. With the cloud to cover them, the earth, unasked, throws up a carpet of spring flowers beneath the lovers, as if inspired by their divine potency and fecundated by the gleaming dew that drips down; this is a bold phrase, since we are not told outright that the dew comes from the cloud! Dew is as important as rain for the fertility of the land (*Od.* 13.245); cf. 153–353n. on the marriage of Earth and Sky as the basis for that of Here and Zeus. Nonnus (*Dion.* 7.146ff.) calls Zeus's seed ἐέρση; golden mist hides the island when Zeus weds the nymph Aigina (Pindar, *Paean* 6.137ff.). On dew's connotations of fecundity see D. Boedeker, *Descent from Heaven*, Chico 1984. Nature's reaction to the gods is integral to their function in the world, like the sea's joy at Poseidon's epiphany (13.27–31n.), the grass that grows under Aphrodite's feet as she steps ashore new-born (*Theog.* 194f.), or the ambrosia that Simoeis sprouts to pasture Here's horses (5.777); conversely, having sex in the fields enhances their fertility (West on *Theog.* 971). The idea already enters this context in Sumerian literature (S. N. Kramer, *The Sacred Marriage Rite*, Bloomington 1969, 59).

347–8 Since ποίη can denote plants in general, D may be right to say that the poet puts genus before species. Spring flowers are meant, as the hyacinth shows. 'Lotos' is not the Nile water-lily or the lotus-eaters' drug (*Od.* 9.82ff. with Heubeck's n.), but a wild fodder for horses and cows (2.776, *Od.* 4.603, *HyHerm* 107), associated with κύπειρος (galingale), from lush plains or water-meadows (12.283, 21.351). B. Herzhoff identifies it as celandine (*Hermes* 112 (1984) 257–71), but clover and trefoil are also possible; many species from diverse habitats bore this name (Theophr. *Hist. Plant.* 7.15.3). Greece has many kinds of crocus, yellow, white and purple (A. Huxley and W. Taylor, *Flowers of Greece and the Aegean*, London 1977, 154f.). The hyacinth is either *Hyacinthus orientalis*, native to the E. Aegean and ancestor of our garden variety, or a grape hyacinth of the genus *Muscari*; others suggest a scilla or iris (Hainsworth on *Od.* 6.231).

Verses 347f. are richly paralleled in post-Homeric epos, but this is owed to similarities of content, not of date. ὑάκινθος is a *hapax* in the *Iliad*. χθὼν δῖα is unique in the nom.: it appears in the acc. or dat. at 24.532, 3× Hes., *Aspis* 287, *Hy.* 30.3 (the Hymn to Earth). νεοθηλέα ποίην is another under-represented formula: cf. στεφάνους νεοθηλέας ἄνθεσι ποίης (*Theog.* 576), ἐριθηλέα ποίην (*HyHerm* 27). νεοθηλής, a metrically useful variant of ἐριθηλής (3× *Il.*, *Theog.* 30), recurs at *HyHerm* 82, *Hy.* 30.13; were these phrases traditional in Hymns to Earth? Cf. too *HyHerm* 107, λωτὸν ... ἠδ' ἐρσήεντα κύπειρον; *HyDem* 426, κρόκον ... ἠδ' ὑάκινθον; *Cypria* frag. 4.3, ἔν τε κρόκῳ ἔν τ' ὑακίνθῳ; *Hy.* 19.25f., ἐν μαλακῷ λειμῶνι τόθι κρόκος ἠδ' ὑάκινθος | ... καταμίσγεται ἄκριτα ποίη. The alternation between ἐέρση and ἐρσήεις is obscure (Peters, *Laryngale* 316n.): cf. Sanskrit *varṣám*, 'rain'. ἰδέ never had a ϝ-, as Cypriot inscriptions prove; since it usually follows the trochaic caesura, where the *jeu de formules* often causes hiatus, a hiatus may have come to seem normal to the Ionic bards. Homer treats it as if it had a ϝ- 20/32× (cf. ἑός, 223–4n.).

349–53 The required sense is that, as dignity demands, the flowers keep Zeus and Here off the ground, elevated by the softness we feel when we lie in long grass; this is best given by the vulgate's (and Aristarchus') ἔεργε. The unobvious verb inspired the old variants ἄειρε (cf. 20.325, *Od.* 8.375), ἔερπε (a graphic error) and ἵκανε (a patent conjecture, in the Chian text). Zenodotus (Did/A), no doubt to make the lovers' elevation explicit, altered 349 to end ἵν' ἀπὸ χθονὸς ἀγκαζέσθην; this may be based on 17.722, where the verb has a different sense (Düntzer, *De Zenodoti studiis* 125). He did no better at 351 with his reading (Did/T) ἀνέπιπτον instead of ἀπ-, supposedly 'dew-drops fell on (them)', perhaps a prudish attempt to remove the ambiguity mentioned above (346–53n.). στιλπνός is unique in the epos. 'Some' added after 351 δή ῥα τότ' ὀφθαλμοῖσι Διὸς χύτο νήδυμος ὕπνος, a statement of the obvious like the pedantic plus-verses after 231, 241, 278, 13.367, 13.433, 15.5, 15.78, 16.607, 16.867, all noted by T (cf. Apthorp, *MS Evidence* 41f.). πατήρ is a metrically convenient periphrasis for Zeus, used only in the nom. and when he has just been named (West on *Erga* 84); contrast Κρόνου πάϊς in 346. With 353 cf. 13.636.

354–401 Poseidon, hearing that Zeus is asleep, exhorts the Greeks, who exchange armour so that the best fighters are the best equipped. The two sides, led by Poseidon and Hektor, clash with a great din

354–401 This scene has several functions. It forms a deft transition to Aias' long-delayed duel with Hektor, who must be beaten if the Greeks are to win. It explains how the stalemate of book 13 shifts to a Trojan rout: Poseidon makes the battle turn, as the poet says at 510. The god can now lead the army openly, as he began to do at 147–52; he also reminds us about the absent Akhilleus (366–9). The troops' exchange of armour is like the arming-scene in a hero's *aristeia* – the whole army will now excel itself. This scene also lets the injured leaders implement their decision to marshal the men, when they go about the ranks exchanging pieces of armour (379–82) – the men could not do this themselves without disputes over who is better than whom. The din when the armies clash, expressed by superb similes, returns us to the exact moment when Aias' duel with Hektor was interrupted as the two sides noisily charged (13.833–7); the motif of the shout articulates the simultaneously concurrent *and* sequential scenes of these books (1–152n.). Leaf deems 363–401 interpolated, finding the exchange of armour 'partly unintelligible, partly ludicrous', and Poseidon's leadership devoid of real result (but cf. 510!); he dislikes the equation of the god and Hektor as leaders of the two sides, and the sympathetic rush of the sea, the god's element, towards the camp. Such objections will be met in their place.

354–62 Knowing of Here's success must embolden Poseidon; but 'for a little while' (358) arouses suspense by making clear that his intervention cannot last. Sleep's message is not strictly needed for the story, but certainly forms a neat transition back to it. We should not worry over how he knew to give this message (240–1n.). πρόφρων means 'with enthusiasm' (71–3n.). Ποσείδαον for -ων is the *lectio difficilior*. The hiatus in ἔτι εὕδει, paralleled at 7.217, 17.354, *Od.* 24.351, may likewise reflect improvisation; cf. μίνυνθά περ, οὔ τι μάλα δήν (3× Hom.). Verses 359f. resound with assonance of κ and η. For why Sleep is going about 'the tribes of men' (361) see 231n. — (ἐπὶ) κλυτὰ φῦλ' ἀνθρώπων | is a formula just coming into use. The *Odyssey* uses φ. ἀ. | at 3.282, 15.409 (1× Hes., 4× *Hy*.), and its extension ἐπὶ χθονὶ φ. ἀ. at 7.307 (6× Hes.); cf. *HyAp* 273, 355, 537, and 231a above. Its metrical equivalent θνητοὺς ἀνθρώπους | is confined to verses contrasting gods and men (198–9n.).

363–77 Although references to Hektor form a ring within it (364f., 375), Poseidon's speech belongs to a larger structure:

A   Exhortation of the Greeks (363–9)
B   Proposal of the exchange of armour (370–7)
B′ Proposal carried out (378–82)
A′ Poseidon leads the Greeks into battle (383–7)

We do not hear what shape the god took, but his energy ill suits his disguise as an old man at 136, and he seems to have his own superhuman form at 384–7. But Homer neither states this directly nor lets his characters remark on it; nothing must distract them – or us – from the impetus towards a swift victory for the Greeks. The god's fluent yet unformular urgings continue the themes of his previous speeches (139ff., 13.47ff., 13.95ff., 13.232ff.), i.e. slackness (364, cf. 13.95–124n., 13.234), Hektor's boastfulness and the danger he presents to the ships (364ff., cf. 13.54n.), the dispensability of Akhilleus (cf. 139ff.) and the need to boost morale by exhortation (369, cf. 13.56). As R. M. Frazer says (*Hermes* 113 (1985) 7ff.), 'he speaks as Agamemnon should have been able to speak', responding to the latter's defeatist sentiments at 42–51.

364–6 The MSS have δ' αὖτε; δὴ αὖτε is Bekker's emendation. Synizesis in δὴ αὖ(τε) is invariable in Homer (14×); the phrase conveys impatient reproof (Page, *Sappho and Alcaeus*, Oxford 1955, 13). With μεθίεμεν Poseidon tactfully includes himself in the reproach (cf. 13.114). Zenodotus read ἔλπεται, no doubt because Hektor has not overtly claimed victory; but εὔχεται fits his boastful character, as Aristarchus says, and Poseidon overstated his braggadocio before (13.54). Zenodotus made a like change at 8.526; differently Nickau, *Zenodotos* 156f.

370–7 Frazer (*loc. cit.*) sees the troops' controversial exchange of armour as a way to make them fight harder, adducing other cases where troops are so marshalled as to make them do their best (2.362–8, 4.293ff., 15.295–9). bT on 382 discern a moral point – the better the fighter, the more he deserves the protection of good armour, and the better his armour, the bolder he may be; but slackers are stripped of their good armour by their own comrades, and are thus punished for endangering the rest by being endangered themselves. The best men have the best armour at 15.616. Clearly each man supplied his own panoply, as later (Pritchett, *The Greek State at War* IV 13). The ancients never objected to the exchange of armour; 376f. was athetized for other reasons. To remove it entirely we would have to excise 370–82, which would leave 383 dangling, as Leaf admits. There is no hint that the men swapped body-armour, but it is hard to suppose that they could switch even helmets, shields and spears while the Trojan attack continued, or that this involved only slackers at the rear (contrast πάντας at 381). The lack of realism is owed to epic narrative technique. Since this scene is concurrent with the others (354–401n.), we may fancy that the armies enjoy a brief respite while the two sides form up; but cf. Glaukos' long conversation and exchange of armour with Diomedes in the midst of battle (6.230ff.), or the arming while the Trojans advance at 4.221f.

ἀσπίδες is idiomatically attracted into the nom. by the nearby relative clause, like νῆες at 75; a superlative plus ἠδὲ μέγισται is normal (e.g. *Hy.* 23.1), and with the rest of 372 cf. 15.296. But ἐσσάμενοι of wearing shields is an odd extension of its usual application to body-armour; Heyne deems it justified by the shield-strap. N-mobile is a metrical makeshift in 372f.; the article appears in 373, as at 368. It is unclear how πάναιθος, a *hapax* in Greek, denotes superior helmets; are shiny ones newer, or is the point that they are of bronze rather than leather? The longest spears are presumably best, but this too is left unsaid. With 375 cf. 13.40, 80, 15.604. The *hapax* μενέχάρμος is an improvised variation on μενεχάρμης (6× *Il.*, *Cat.* 5.3, always at the verse-end); with the rest of 376 cf. ἀμφ᾽ ὤμοισιν ἔχει σάκος (11.527), σ. ὤμῳ | (15.474, cf. 125). χείρονι φωτί (also *Od.* 11.621) is acc. at 17.149, and shares a declensional system with χείρονος (-ες) ἀνδρός (-ες). ἐν ἀσπίδι μείζονι δύτω means 'let him put on a larger shield'; (ἐν) δύω normally takes an acc., but cf. 10.254, 23.131. The oddities are not confined to 376f.; the entire proposal seems untraditional, which does not prove it interpolated.

376–7 These vv. were omitted by Zenodotus (and a papyrus) but athetized by his successors (Did/A). Aristarchus deemed it absurd that the men did not have suitable shields to start with, and saw a contradiction with 382, where the better warriors receive better armour, not larger shields, which would encumber them (cf. Arn/A on 382); he also disliked μενέχαρμος (T). But 371 shows that the biggest shields are also the best. Despite his athetesis, he preferred ἔχει, a minority reading in our MSS, to the smoother vulgate ἔχῃ (also in a papyrus). The rhyme δότω–δύτω is emphasized by the chiasmus χείρονι φωτί – ἀσπίδι μείζονι; 382 picks up this pattern (ἔδυνε ... δόσκεν).

380 = 29; Nestor is not listed because he is not wounded.

382 The elegant double polyptoton (13.130–1n.) makes the reallotment sound both natural and just; good and worse are conjoined at 1.576 = *Od.* 18.404. The old variant in *h* (χέρηϊ δὲ χείρονα δῶκεν) adds a fancy chiasmus, as in 377, but seems too sophisticated. Aristarchus (Did/AT), papyri and our vulgate rightly read δόσκεν; another papyrus has δόσκον, which gives the leaders a larger role.

383–7 Verse 383 = *Od.* 24.467, 24.500 (cf. 7.207); 378 and the first half of 384 = 133f., when the injured leaders head for battle. Frazer (*loc. cit.*) notes how the situation has changed since then: Poseidon exhorts the men as the leaders have just begun to do – a good example of the 'dual motivation' of human action (cf. p. 4). Poseidon's sword is 'like lightning' (cf. 13.242, 19.363, *Aspis* 322). Since lightning is properly Zeus's weapon (11.184), the sea-god is even now rather a fraud. His sword is so fearful (δεινόν) that from fear (δέος, the same root) no man may engage him. This excludes a duel with Hektor; it also prefigures and explains the Greek success. Leaf, thinking τῷ must refer to the sword, renders 386f. as 'it is not permitted for him (it?) to join in the battle', or '... to join in battle with it', i.e. *using* it; but μείγνυμι with χεῖρας understood, meaning 'join battle', can govern the enemy or his sword in the dat. (cf. LSJ s.v. II.1; Chantraine, *GH* II 75). Since none dares face the sword, none dares meet its owner (so Heyne). 'Fine-pointed' describes swords in the cognate phrase τανύηκες ἄορ παχέος παρὰ μηροῦ (16.473, 2× *Od.*); a variant form *ταναϝ(ο)- is fossilized in the formula τανανήκεϊ χαλκῷ (6× epos). The old phrase οὐ θέμις is no longer recognized in Myc. *o-u-te-mi* (16.803n.). | ἐν δαῖ λευγαλέῃ uniquely adapts ἐν δ. λυγρῇ (2× *Il.*, 2× *Theog.*).

388–91 Leaf objected that Poseidon and Hektor are treated as 'two equal powers', because they pull tight the rope of war (for the metaphor, frequent in these books, see 13.358–60n.). But this does not mean that they are pulling strings from on high: it is used of the two human sides at 12.436 = 15.413. They are named simply because they are leading the two armies; Hektor is built up by being opposed to the god (Heyne). ἀρήγων aptly describes the Greeks' ally Poseidon; it applies to Hektor by an easy zeugma (note also the chiasmus in 390f.). κυανοχαῖτα Ποσειδάων also begins a verse at 13.563. The repeated φαίδιμος Ἕκτωρ is a type of blemish to which an outstanding bard like Homer is less prone than we literates may expect.

392–401 The magical participation of Poseidon's element, the sea, which surges up towards the ships, increases the din from the Achaean side (bT), but may be more impressive than effective, like the god himself; for nature's reaction to gods' interventions see 346–53n. It leads us to expect stupendous strife, prefiguring the first of three negative comparisons – neither the sea nor the forest fire nor the gale is as loud as the armies' clash. Zenodotus (Arn/A), perhaps disliking how the sea at once reappears in the simile (Düntzer, *De Zenodoti studiis* 155), transposed 394f. to after 399. The whole is framed by the ideas 'Hektor', 'Trojans and Greeks' and 'armies clashing' (390–3, 400–2).

394–9 The cumulated images, familiar from e.g. 2.455ff., are especially forceful because they are packed into three couplets and held together by the overarching syntax of the negative comparison leading up to 400, where ὅσση, read by the Alexandrians but few papyri or good codices, avoids an oral anacoluthon; it may be conjectural (van der Valk, *Researches* II 194). Cf. the structure of 17.20–3: οὔτ' οὖν παρδάλιος τόσσον μένος οὔτε λέοντος | οὔτε συός ... | ὅσσον ... Nicanor, in A, keeps τόσση with a stop after 399; it is wrong to put stops after 395 and 397. Each image has the same point of comparison, noise (cf. the brief double comparison at 13.39); βοάᾳ, βρόμος, ἠπύει and βρέμεται are picked up by φωνή ... ἀϋσάντων (ὄρουσαν resumes ὀρνύμενον and ὦρετο). The balance of each distich rests on οὔτε ... τόσ(σ)ον (γε), but the second lines are deftly varied: 395 is a participial clause, 397 temporal, 399 relative. There is vivid personification: the breaker *shouts*, roused by Boreas' *painful* blast; the gale *calls out*, *roaring* in *rage* (Homer always uses χαλεπαίνω of people, 18×). The verses are rich in sound-effects (in β, μ, ν, π and ρ) and evocative epithets.

The army's din is compared to the sea at 2.209f., where κῦμα ... θαλάσσης and αἰγιαλῷ μεγάλῳ βρέμεται are like 394, 399; at 4.422–6 (very similar); and at 17.263–5, where ἠϊόνες βοόωσιν resembles βοάᾳ here (T admires both for their sound). The armies' clash is likened to that of two winds at 16.765–9, where 766 resembles 397, as does 20.491, in a simile comparing a berserker to a forest fire (cf. too 2.455f.. 15.605–9n.). Here all three images are combined, and, as bT note, heightened: a strong N. wind drives the wave ashore, the fire is at its fiercest, since it blazes up forested slopes, and the wind is not blowing freely but collides with tall oaks: θαλάσσης κῦμα, found in the plur. at *Od.* 13.88, is reversed 8× Hom. πνοιῇ Βορέω ἀλεγεινῇ adapts phrases like πνοιὴ Βορέαο | (5.697, *Od.* 10.507); Βορέα'(ο) could be restored (3× Hom.), but Βορέω is guaranteed in Hesiod (3×). πυρὸς αἰθομένοιο (9× Hom.) is again split, albeit less drastically than in 396, at 6.182, *Od.* 11.220. οὔρεος ἐν βήσσησ(ι) occurs only in similes in Homer (5×); δρυσὶν ὑψικόμοισι is formular too (5× epos, nom. and acc. included). Zenodotus' pupil Agathocles absurdly conjectured ἰξοφόροισι instead (frag. 10 Montanari, clearly from Porphyry).

396 The vulgate has ποτι where we expect 'is' (the OCT has ποτὶ); I read πότι for πρόσεστι, like ἔνι κήδεα θυμῷ for ἔνεστι (18.53), etc. Cf. the variant πέλει in *Et. Magn.* 214.36; πόθι, in a papyrus and *h*, is another attempt to emend the problem away (cf. the variants for ἔπι at *Od.* 12.209). Differently Allen, *CQ* 25 (1931) 23; Chantraine, *GH* II 131n.

402–522 Aias knocks Hektor out with a stone: he is carried off the field. In his absence, the Greeks gain the advantage and the Trojans soon flee in panic, with heavy losses

402–522 On this scene see Winter, *MNO* 122–9. Fenik finds the return to Aias' duel with Hektor, clearly imminent at 13.809ff., so abrupt that he leans to the Analytic view that 13.833–14.401 'has been inserted into an originally unified context, splitting it apart and arresting its conclusion' (*TBS* 156ff.). But the Theomachy breaks off likewise at 20.155, to be resumed at 21.383. Homeric narrative technique explains what is going on (1–152n.): but we must still ask why the poet interrupts the duel thus. This combat, awaited for most of books 13–14, is soon over, and now that it happens is de-emphasized; rather than have it cause the Trojan rout, the poet puts it first in a series of duels representing the mass battle that precipitates their flight. As Winter saw (*MNO* 124), the whole army is to win this victory, not Aias alone; Hektor's personal rout is deferred until he faces Akhilleus. Delaying the duel arouses suspense, and then subordinating it to a rush of exciting events raises more suspense: how long can the Trojans cope without Hektor? The sorry answer is soon clear. Wilamowitz (*IuH* 235f.) finds the rout at 506ff. too sudden, but in fact the Greeks have had the advantage since 440; they begin the killings, slaying three Trojans (elaborately narrated) for a loss of two of their own men (baldly told). After the first death, the fighting repeats the common pattern 'A kills B, C aims at A but slays D instead': Pouludamas kills Prothoenor, and Aias aims at him but slays Arkhelokhos (449–74); Akamas, Arkhelokhos' brother (a neat linkage), kills Promakhos, and Peneleos aims at him but slays Ilioneus (475ff.). The deaths of Arkhelokhos and Ilioneus are grisly; Friedrich well suggests that the crescendo of horror contributes to the rout (*Verwundung* 25). Yet the narration of both the *stadiē* and the ensuing rout is brisk, in contrast to the full and weighty account of the menacing Trojan gains in book 13; as Winter says (*MNO* 128f.), this matches the fact that the Greek counter-attack achieves only transient success.

402-39 Hektor's duel with Aias, albeit understated so as not to detract from the larger battle, arouses tension because, until 432, we are unsure whether he still lives, so grave is the blow he suffers (418ff.); his revival and renewed fainting (433-9) are added to remove any doubt (Winter, *MNO* 124). The duel follows the pattern where Trojan A fails to kill Greek B, and B then kills A (Fenik, *TBS* 11); thus we should sense from the start that Hektor will lose (so bT on 402). Cf. how Diomedes knocks Aineias out with a stone (5.297ff.); both victims are rescued and miraculously healed by a god. At 11.343ff. Hektor is stunned by Diomedes; he is fainter here because his wound is worse, as the narrative requires it to be. As Reinhardt says (*IuD* 209), his coma is directly consequent upon Zeus's. Aias, as usual, receives no overt divine aid; the sole mention of gods is in the ironic comparison of Hektor's fall to an oak hit by Zeus's thunderbolt (414-17n.).

402-8 Aias, his chest facing Hektor, offers a tempting target, but Hektor's spear hits the spot where the straps for his sword and shield cross over. The strap of his body-shield likewise saved Sarpedon at 12.400f. Lorimer (*HM* 182) rightly deems this event, like Aias' formula σάκος ἠΰτε πύργος, a striking reflection of the use of a tower-shield and no corslet in early Myc. warfare (15.645-52n.), as seen for example on the dagger from Shaft Grave IV depicting a lion-hunt. A sword-strap will naturally cross the right shoulder, as will that of the later round shield with central hand-grip, but that of a body-shield passes over the left, as does Aias' at 16.106f.; this type of shield, slung onto his back as at 11.545, must once have been meant. Homer never refers to Aias' corslet (Trümpy, *Fachausdrücke* 32ff.): cf. 12.400ff., when Sarpedon is hit on both the strap and the shield. Herodotus still knew of shields with straps (1.171.4), no doubt from heirlooms dedicated in temples. As Aristarchus noted, the poet does not know (or suppresses?) the tale that Aias was magically invulnerable save at one spot (cf. 16.777-867n.): found in Hesiod (frag. 250), Aeschylus (p. 207 Radt), Pindar (*Is.* 6.47f.) and Lycophron 455-61, this may go back to the *Aithiopis* (Severyns, *Cycle* 325-8). Aias is never wounded in the *Iliad*.

πρῶτος ἀκόντισε also opens duels at 13.502, 16.284. With τέτραπτο πρὸς ἰθύ οἱ cf. 13.542, ἐπὶ οἶ τετραμμένον. Papyri read πρὸς ἰθύν, i.e. 'towards his aim', with the old noun ἰθύς, 'direction', limited to Homer (Chantraine, *Dict.* s.v.); but ἰθύ can be an adv. as at 20.99, i.e. 'directly towards'. For the dat. cf. κατ' ἰθὺ γούνασι in Hippocrates (LSJ s.v. ἰθύς II 2). With οὐδ' ἀφάμαρτε supply καὶ βάλε (cf. 13.159-60n.). φασγάνου ἀργυροήλου (405) is a later adaptation, using unresolvable -ου, of the Bronze Age formulae φάσγανον ἀργυρό(ϝ)ηλον (23.807), ξίφος ἀ. (11× Hom.). The phrase τερένα χρόα traditionally describes a warrior's flesh at the mercy of a sharp spear (13.830–2n.). From χώσατο, 406f. = 22.291f., when Hektor fares yet worse, since he lacks comrades to cover his retreat. The hiatus before ἐτώσιον is caused by ϝ- (Chantraine, *Dict.* s.v. ἐτός). Eustathius (995.42) notes that ἔκφυγε is witty, since it implies that the spear left Hektor's hand of its own accord, like ποῖόν σε ἔπος φύγεν. The personification is traditional, since there is a shorter version of this phrase, ἅλιον βέλος ἔκφυγε χειρός (3×); cf. 454–7n. Verse 408, a standard one for the loser's withdrawal (13.531–3n.), likewise precedes his opponent taking a shot at him as he goes (ἀπιόντα) at 13.566, a common incident (461n.).

409–12 Telamonian Aias, punningly saved by his τελαμῶνε, hits Hektor, who is backing away from him, on the chest with one of the stones used to prop up the ships. Such props are called ἕρματα, 'cairns', at 1.486, 2.154; cf. *Erga* 624 (for ἔχμα see 13.139n.). The vivid detail conveys that they were dislodged *by* the fighting, like the helmet which a victim lost and a Greek found μαρναμένων μετὰ ποσσὶ κυλινδομένην (13.579, cf. 13.526–3n.); it also suggests how treacherous is one's foothold in such a battle. Only the strongest heroes use stones (Niens, *Struktur* 169). Verse 410 is elliptical and idiomatic. τά means '⟨one of those⟩ which', as in *Od.* 12.97, κῆτος ἃ μυρία βόσκει; the construction changes in τῶν ἓν ἀείρας (cf. 6.293, *Od.* 15.106). στῆθος βεβλήκει varies σ. βάλε (5×). His predecessors thought n-mobile should be added to pluperfects in -ει, but Aristarchus (Did/A) and the MSS oppose it here; he was inconsistent over this (van der Valk, *TCO* 142, *Researches* II 190f.). ὑπὲρ ἄντυγος means 'over the rim' of Hektor's shield (cf. 6.118).

413 A στρόμβος (from στρέφω) is anything that twirls on its axis, here a spinning-top; the short comparison leads into the simile of the falling oak, which lends its subject, Hektor, greater dignity. He gyrates and then keels over. Some thought this image describes the stone, finding it odd that a blow makes him rotate, and that a revolving warrior is likened to an oak which lies where it falls (bT). A spinning stone seems more natural, but the order of events favours applying the image to Hektor. So does the parallel at 11.147, when Agamemnon lops off a Trojan's extremities and hurls his trunk 'like a roller' into the mêlée (ὅλμον δ' ὡς ἔσσευε ...); cf. too 11.354, when the stunned Hektor ἀνέδραμε. The bizarre effect shows the blow's force; cf. Patroklos' eyes whirling in their sockets (16.792).

414–17 The oak resumes the previous image (398). A fallen warrior is often likened to a tree felled by an axe (13.178–80n.); as Krischer saw (*Konventionen* 72f.), this tree is an oak, the toughest to fell, and the thunderbolt replaces the axe to make its fall more awesome (*Aspis* 421–3 weakens the effect by making the tree an oak *or* a pine). The simile misleads us into thinking that Hektor is dead. The comparison of Aias' rock to Zeus's bolt is ironic; Aias wins because Zeus is asleep. Moreover the oak is Zeus's sacred tree (16.234–5n.); that Zeus strikes it, as he often does, is no less paradoxical than that Hektor falls on the day when Zeus promised him success. Verses 416f. put an observer into the simile to show us how fearful the oak's ruin is, stress that it is Zeus who smote it, and give us our sole hint of the Trojans' reaction to Hektor's fall – otherwise, we hear only of the Greeks' (cf. Winter, *MNO* 123).

ῥιπῆς, 'impact', is supported by papyri and parallels at 21.12 (a simile) and 12.462, when a gate shatters λᾶος ὑπὸ ῥιπῆς. A's text πληγῆς looks like an attempt to remove the jingle ῥιπῆς . . . ἐξερίπη; ῥ. is not from the same root, but poets may have imagined an etymological link. The other details increase our terror. The oak is uprooted (πρόρριζος recurs in the epos only at 11.157, in a simile); like the lightning-bolts at 8.135 and *Od.* 12.417 = 14.307, it gives off a fearsome smell of sulphur (actually ozone from the electrical discharge); the very word θέειον suggests a god's presence (16.228–30n.). ἐξ αὐτῆς is a filler, but the rest of 416 conveys the observer's fear by stating that it is not courage that possesses him (θράσος is unique in the epos, versus θάρσος 14×). Aristophanes rewrote the verse, but Aristarchus explains it aright (Did, Arn/A). ἐγγὺς ἐών brings us yet nearer to the source of dread; χαλεπός, 'hard to bear', again refers to the observer's emotions, while Διὸς μεγάλοιο κεραυνός (acc., 21.198) explains the ῥιπὴ Δ. and stresses Zeus's power.

418–20 Verse 418 is based on χαμαὶ πέσον (βάλον) ἐν κονίῃσι (4×); cf. 4.482, which introduces a tree-simile, and 7.38. The vulgate, Massaliot and Chian texts read ὦκα (Did/AT), but Aristarchus had ὠκύ, which he took as either an adv. or governed by μένος; ὠκύ never recurs thus elsewhere and is much inferior. Since Hektor made a cast at 402, the spear he drops is the second of a pair of throwing-spears. From ἀσπίς to οἱ, 419f. = 13.543f., where see n. But three papyri and MS A omit 420; this is a concordance-interpolation based on 13.544 and 13.181, which follows a tree-image. There is no need for an indication of the crash Hektor makes when he falls, since there is none in the simile.

421–4 The Greeks are heartened; their foes betray their fear only by their swift defence of their fallen leader. The enjambment θαμειὰς | αἰχμάς, also at 12.44, is not unusual since a numerical adj. is involved (13.611–13n.). The irregular scansion of τις in 423 suggests improvisation; cf. | ἀλλ' οὔ τις δύνατο Τρώων (3.451). On ποιμένα λαῶν cf. 13.598–600n.

425–6 These vv. recapitulate most of the Trojan leaders left on the field. Verse 425 lists those active in book 13; the Lycians were last seen at 12.387ff. Pouludamas led the first column jointly with Hektor (12.88ff.); he alone is prominent in trying to avert the rout. Agenor was among the leaders of the second, reappearing at 13.490, 13.598. Aineias led the fourth (13.459–61n.), the Lycians the last; comparison with 12.88ff. reveals the gravity of the Trojan losses. There is no reason to expel 426, which varies 2.876. Glaukos, shot by Teukros at 12.387, is still disabled when he next appears at 16.508; I suspect that Homer momentarily forgot his wound, although others may fancy that, like the injured Achaean chiefs, he stays on the field.

427–32 Zenodotus altered τῶν δ' ἄλλων to τῶν τ' ἄ., no doubt to remove the 'contradiction' with 424–6. ἀκήδεσεν looked odd to Aristarchus, who in one of his editions wrote -έσατ' (Did/A); but it is properly formed from the *s*-stem κῆδος (Risch, *Wortbildung* 308), and more archaic than ἀποκηδήσαντε (23.413). On ἀσπίδας εὐκύκλους see 13.712–18n. Several comrades rescue a wounded warrior at 5.663ff. (Sarpedon); from ὄφρ' onward 429–32 = 13.535–8, when Deïphobos is carted off. στενάχοντα is our first proof that Hektor still lives.

433–9 Hektor's revival and renewed fainting resemble Sarpedon's, who is taken to the oak-tree (another landmark of the plain) and has a spear drawn from his thigh, whereat he swoons (5.692–8), but at once revives; Hektor takes longer (15.9ff., 15.239ff.).

433–4 = 21.1f., 24.692f. (but 693 is spurious). This is the first mention of the ford of the Xanthos or Skamandros; the audience is assumed to know that they are the same. The Analysts asked why the space between the camp and Troy has often been crossed before with no mention of so major a barrier as a river fordable only at certain points. Leaf thought 'the poet treats his topography with the utmost freedom, according to his needs for the moment' (cf. Thornton, *Supplication* 154f.). However, Homer mentions the ford as a watering-place (24.350f.), not a barrier, save when Akhilleus drives part of the Trojan force into its deeper waters (21.3ff.). The area under the walls was bounded by the confluence of the Simoeis and the Skamandros, which flowed on the left of battle, i.e. along the E. side of the Trojan plain (13.675n.). Homer uses the topography to suit his needs, but it does not follow that his conception of it is inconsistent.

Ἷξον replaced Ἷκον when the latter seemed insufficiently marked as an aor.; C. P. Roth derives it from the analogy ὦρτο–ὦρσε, Ἷκτο–Ἷξε (*HSCP* 77 (1973) 184ff.). ἐϋρρεῖος ποταμοῖο, an old formula also at 6.508 = 15.265, is from *ἐhυρρεϝεhος, nom. *-ρεϝης; supplanted by the less anomalous ἐϋρρείτης and -ροος, the epithet recurs only at *Cat.* 13.2. On the etymology of 'Xanthos' see 20.73–4n.; for formulae for this river see 21.1–2n. For the rest of 434 see 2.741n. Zeus may be the river's father in the sense that his rain feeds it (cf. διιπετής, 16.173–5n.); Okeanos is the father of all rivers (21.196), Skamandros included (*Theog.* 345).

436–7 Splashed with water, Hektor regains consciousness (ἀμπνύνθη is read by all MSS, as also at 5.697). But he coughs up blood and faints from the pain; he is also gasping for breath (15.10, 241). He has serious internal injuries: the poet depicts the symptoms of a punctured lung or pleural effusion, which such a blow might well cause. κελαινεφές, in the same phrase at 16.667, is from *κελαινο-νεφής, 'dark-clouded', cf. ἀμφορεύς for ἀμφιφο-ρεύς. It was originally a title of Zeus, later misapplied to blood (cf. 5.796–8n. and Chantraine, *Dict.* s.v. κελαινός). Instead of ἀπέμεσσεν (in αἱ πλείους, Aristarchus and the vulgate), Zenodotus (Did/A), papyri and some good codices read the conjecture ἀπέμασσεν, 'wiped away'; both scholars clearly had MS authority. Aristarchus could adduce 15.11, where Hektor still 'vomits' blood (Arn/A *ad loc.*); no doubt Zenodotus deemed this unsuited to a hero, but it is more dramatic and physiologically apt. Since he is not known to have altered 15.11, Nickau (*Zenodotos* 193) thinks he had linguistic objections to ἀπέμεσσεν, but its 'neglected' ϝ- and -σσ- are not odd. Others emended to ἀπέσευεν, 'gushed ⟨blood⟩' (T reads †ἀπέσεσεν, but cf. 5.208). ἑζόμενος δ' ἐπὶ γοῦνα means 'kneeling', cf. πρόχνυ καθεζομένη (9.570); this was clearly an idiom (so Nic/A). 'Crouching' would be rendered 'sitting on his *legs*' (13.279–81n.).

438–9 Prompted by κελαινεφές, 438f. blend ἀμφὶ δὲ ὄσσε κελαινὴ νὺξ ἐκάλυψε (5.310 = 11.356) with νεφέλη ἑ. μέλαινα (3× Hom.); night is μ. in the nom. only here (but in other cases 14× epos). Aristarchus (Did/A) read τὼ δέ οἱ ὄσσε, to harmonize 438 with 13.616 etc., but 16.325 protects the vulgate κάδ. As at 16.106, he disliked apocope (van der Valk, *Researches* II 179f.).

440–1 A description of the Greeks' new vigour opens the five 'chain-reaction' killings that lead up to the Trojan collapse, likewise introduced by a standard couplet (506f.). The formula νόσφι κίοντα (3× Hom.) ill suits Hektor, who is carried off (cf. 11.284); hence the variant νόσφιν ἐόντα. Verse 441 = 8.252, when a brief Trojan rout begins; with 442 cf. 8.256.

442–8 Last seen at 13.701ff., Oïlean Aias does well here, since he slays the first Trojan and kills the most in the rout (520). His victim receives the standard tripartite news-item (13.170–81n.): a headline about the death, a brief but touching obituary, and the coroner's verdict of a blow to the flank, which hints that Satnios tried to flee (cf. 517, 6.64). Satnios' name, like Simoeisios' or Skamandrios' (4.474, 5.49), is related to the river where he was born (Scherer, 'Nichtgriechische Personennamen' 33); the Satnioeis flowed by Pedasos (6.34f.). His father, 'Brilliant', is a nobody dignified by the repetition of his name; Homer invents three other sons of 'Enops' – two Greeks and a Trojan (cf. 16.401–10n.). Pathetically, Satnios is born in a bucolic setting, like Simoeisios, Aineias (5.313) and Pedasos (eponym of the town?), whom νύμφη | νηῒς Ἀβαρβαρέη τέκ' ἀμύμονι Βουκολίωνι (6.21f., where see n.). Iphition too was son of a water-nymph (νύμφη τέκε νηΐς, 20.384). Since such nymphs are always localized, their sons' birthplace is always stated (Strasburger, *Kämpfer* 23).

Verse 443 blends οὔτασε δουρί | (12×) with ἔγχεϊ ὀξυόεντι (13.584–5n.).

The formular system of παρ' ὄχθας Σατνιόεντος | (cf. 6.34) includes ποτα-μοῖο/Ξάνθοιο παρ' ὄ. | (4×), π. ὄ. Σαγγαρίοιο | (3.187) and recent π. ὄχθῃσῖν Σιμόεντος (4.475). A papyrus and the vulgate rightly keep οὔτασε κὰλ (= κατὰ) λαπάρην in 447; this is also the majority reading at 517. The unique apocope, Aeolic in origin (Chantraine, *GH* 1 87f.), is frequent in compounds like καλλείπω (cf. 438–9n). οὖτα κατὰ λ., in Galen and papyri, is a normalization based on 6.64, a similar verse. ἀνετράπετο means 'fell on his back'. Verse 448 = 16.764, again describing a fight erupting over a body.

449–53 The next killing is perfunctory save for Pouludamas' boast, which begins a series of four like the set of three at 13.374–454. The Boeotians are deeply involved in this battle (476, 487, 13.685). Prothoenor is one of their leaders (2.495); his loss will be counterbalanced by that of Arkhelokhos, a man of similar rank. His father, Areïlukos, looks like an *ad hoc* invention to fit the metre, since otherwise 451f. = 13.519f., and a Trojan Areïlukos dies at 16.308; but b on 2.494f. make Areïlukos the father of Arkesilaos (slain at 15.329), uncle of Peneleos and brother of Alegenor (the father of Pro-makhos, as 503 shows, and of Klonios, who falls at 15.340). For Pouludamas' epithet-system see 13.756–9n.; he is ἐγχέσπαλος only here. This apt epithet recurs at 2.131, 15.605; πεπνυμένος occupies the same space at 18.249, when he is giving good advice. For 453 see 458–9n.

454–7 Pouludamas' vaunt is brilliantly sarcastic. He has his revenge for Aias' hit, as αὖτε, 'in turn', indicates. His javelin 'leapt not in vain from his massive hand', as if it were animate (cf. 402–8n.); this adapts e.g. αἰχμὴ ... ἄλιον στιβαρῆς ἀπὸ χειρὸς ὄρουσεν (13.504f.). He prolongs the metaphor in 456, where κόμισε χροΐ means 'took it away safely ... in his flesh!', as if the spear needs a loving home; cf. 22.286, σῷ ἐν χροῒ πᾶν κομίσαιο, also of a spear. The poet himself answers this jibe at 463, where Arkhelokhos 'takes home' Aias' javelin. Next Pouludamas wittily turns the spear into a staff for his victim to use on his way to the underworld; cf. the chiefs' use of spears at 38. σκήπτομαι, 'use a staff' (σκῆπτρον), occurs 3× *Od.*; but from Aeschylus onward σκήπτω is found with the sense 'hurl down', especially of a thunderbolt. Hence Pouludamas may also be saying, with a pun, 'I suspect that he, *struck* by it, will go down to Hades' house' – which is true, and thus all the more provoking.

458–9 = 486f., 13.417f., with different names. In each case the couplet follows A's boast, within the pattern 'A kills B, C aims at A but kills D instead' (402–522n.), just as 453 introduces vaunts at 478 and 13.413 (where see n.). The verses are designed for names shaped – ⏑⏑ – ('Αντιλόχῳ, Πηνελέῳ); the scansion Αἴαντῖ may reflect the Myc. dat. in *-ei* for this Mycenaean warrior (13.46n.). δαΐφρονι is again separated from the name at 5.181, 16.727 .

460 This v. looks like an afterthought to specify that Telamonian not Oïlean Aias is meant; the slaying-pattern (458–9n.) excludes the latter. The unusual sense of Αἴαντε in earlier stages of the tradition caused confusion over the Aiantes and Teukros (13.46n.); all three are present in this battle. The article and the form Τελαμωνιάδης (12× Hom.), a post-Myc. remodelling of Τελαμώνιος, are no reason to suspect the verse, *pace* Shipp (*Studies* 286). Standing nearest a victim gives a warrior cause to be angriest at his death, albeit less so than being his guest-friend or relative; since the poet often cites no cause at all, it is silly to complain that this one is feeble.

461–4 From ἀπιόντος 461 = 13.516, in the pattern 'A aims at B but hits C'; a retreating foe is a common target (cf. 409,13.650). With the Lesbian form ἀλεύατο contrast Ionic ἀλέασθαι (p. 16). λικριφὶς ἀΐξας, 'darting sideways', is used of a boar's oblique charge at *Od.* 19.451; cf. δοχμώ τ' ἀΐσσοντε (12.148). The adv., a *hapax* in Greek, is related to λέχριος, 'oblique' (Chantraine, *Dict.* s.v.). Antenor's sons Arkhelokhos and Akamas (476f.) helped Aineias lead the Dardanians (2.823 = 12.100); Akamas is slain at 16.342ff. Any humour in κόμισεν (454–7n.) is dispelled by the pathetic reference to the gods' plan for his death, a uniquely expressed but typical motif (e.g. 2.834, 16.693, *Od.* 18.155f.); cf. Griffin, *HLD* 42f.

465–9 The grisly detail of the death-blow hides the implausibility that a spear-cast could inflict it. Aias' spear slices through Arkhelokhos' uppermost vertebra and both tendons of his neck; his head flies off and hits the ground face down, leaving his body standing for a long moment (on beheading cf. 13.201–3n.). His head flies off in rapid dactyls; the spondees that follow suggest the terrifying pause until his legs crumple. The old formula ἀπὸ δ' ἄμφω κέρσε τένοντε describes the decapitation of Dolon, whose head falls in the dust while still speaking, and of Kuknos (10.456, *Aspis* 419); cf. 4.521, 5.307. The parallel with Dolon proves that Arkhelokhos is beheaded rather than made to turn a somersault by the force of the blow, as some commentators fancy. συνεοχμός, 'joint', a *hapax* in Greek, is an *ad hoc* alteration of *συνοχμός < συνέχω *metri gratia* (Frisk, *Kleine Schriften* 329f.). κέρσε, more archaic than Ionic κεῖρε, may be Aeolic (Risch, *Wortbildung* 249n.). Zenodotus (Did/AT) altered the datives in 469 to accusatives, but γέγωνα always takes a dat. (12× Hom.). ἐγέγωνεν is an imperf. based on the pluperf. γεγώνει (Chantraine, *Dict.* s.v.).

470–4 Aias' jibe is no less true than Pouludamas', whose taunt he caps by guessing truly that his victim belongs to Antenor's distinguished family. In this context, to pretend to praise a slain foe is to praise one's own valour. We marvel at Aias' guess – and then at the sarcasm of his question, when the poet adds 'he knew full well'! Aristophanes (Did/AT) replaces γενεήν with ῥα φυήν, but it is clear enough that Aias recognizes him from his looks; translate 'he seemed very like (him) in family', i.e. in family resemblance (Willcock). A papyrus reads κεφαλήν to meet the same difficulty. For the topos of a fair exchange of casualties see 13.446–54n.

475–8 It is the Trojans' turn to feel grief. This motif, and the fact that

Akamas is Arkhelokhos' brother (464), forms a neat transition to a reprise of the pattern 'A kills B, C aims at A but kills D instead' (402–522n.). Akamas bestrides Arkhelokhos' body to protect it; brothers often fight together (16.317–29n.). Promakhos' name looks invented, especially beside Βοιώτιον, but cf. 449–53n. His demise is swift; nothing must slow the gathering momentum of the Greek success. He was dragging the body away *by* the feet, as often occurs (13.383–5n.), not 'from under Akamas' feet'. Verse 478 recalls 453, just as 486f. recalls 458f. (where see n.).

479–85 Akamas continues Pouludamas' ironic metaphors in δεδμημένος εὕδει | ἔγχει, adapting δ. ὕπνῳ (etc., 5× Hom.); cf. *Erga* 116, θνῆσκον δ' ὥσθ' ὕ. δεδμημένοι; 11.241, κοιμήσατο χάλκεον ὕπνον. For the relation of death to sleep see 231n. He picks up several motifs from Aias' vaunt: tit for tat, φράζεσθε for φράζεο, brotherhood and the family. He caps Aias by abusing the enemy *en masse* and flaunting his victim's name, but his jibe remains personal; Peneleos replies by predicting the Greeks' safe return home (505). For ἰόμωρος and θήν see on 4.242, 13.620–5. With 'insatiable in ⟨mere⟩ boasts' cf. 7.96, where '⟨mere⟩ boasters' is an opening insult; for this sense of ἀπειλή see 20.83, *LfgrE* s.v. The n-mobile in οἴοισῖν γε betrays improvisation; with the rest of 480 cf. πόνον τ' ἐχέμεν καὶ ὀϊζύν (13.2, *Od.* 8.529), expanded from π. κ. ὀ. (cf. *Erga* 113, gen.). The fut. κατακτανέεσθε in all MSS must not be replaced by -κτεν- (Chantraine, *GH* I 449f.). ἄτιτος appears in another boast at 13.414, with ῐ as in ἄντιτος and παλίντιτος; the ῑ here is unique and etymologically unjustified, but cf. πολύτῑτος in an oracle (Herodotus 5.92.β.2). ἄτιμος, 'unpaid', as at *Od.* 16.431, is but a Renaissance conjecture. The scansion, eased by the ῑ of τίνω, is another sign of improvisation.

484–5 The vulgate runs τῷ καί κέ τις εὕχεται ἀνήρ | γνωτὸν ἐνὶ μεγάροισιν ἄρεως ἀλκτῆρα λιπέσθαι, 'hence a man may well pray that a brother be left at home to ward off war'. But in fact, when a man dies in battle, his avenger wards off the *harm* of being unrevenged; for the thought cf. *Od.* 3.196f. The text presents two problems. (i) κε never occurs with a pres. indic. MS A has κε altered to τε; this must be a Byzantine emendation, *pace* Ruijgh (τε *épique* 773f.). Eustathius and some later MSS omit κε entirely, no doubt by haplology after καί; Munro conjectured καί τίς τ'. The problem vanishes if, as I propose, εὕχεται is an old short-vowel subj. of the athematic aor. εὕγμην (cf. εὕκτο, *Thebaid* frag. 3.3). (ii) ἄρεως ἀλκτῆρες is also the vulgate at 18.213, but 18.100 has ἀρῆς ἀλκτῆρα, 'defender against harm'; the latter phrase recurs at *Aspis* 29, 128, cf. *Theog.* 657. Hence Zenodotus read ἀρῆς (Did/A); so too van der Valk, *Researches* II 586–8. This does restore the original formula, as we shall see, but fails to explain the MSS. Aristarchus read Ἄρεω in all three places, but this too is conjectural; this Ionic form, absent from the MSS, first occurs in Archilochus (frag. 18). The truth is surely as follows.

ἀρή, 'harm', of different origin from ἀρ(ϝ)ή, 'curse', is an obsolete noun fossilized in two formulae, ἀρῆς ἀλκτῆρα and ἀρὴν ∪∪ – ∪ ἀμῦναι | etc. (6× Hom.); as such it was confused with Ἄρης, who is in origin a mere personification of 'harm' (cf. 13.444n., Chantraine, *Dict.* s.vv. and Heubeck, *Die Sprache* 17 (1971) 15–22). The poet let the barely intelligible formula stand at 18.100, but here and at 18.213 he substituted Ἄρεος, a normal epic gen. of Ares, found in a few MSS; because of the substitution, it has to be scanned (uniquely) with synizesis. Ἄρεως will then be a superficial Atticism, also found as a variant at 19.47. W. Schulze takes ἄρεος as the gen. of a neuter *s*-stem ἄρος, 'harm', found in Hsch. (*Kleine Schriften*, 2nd edn, Göttingen 1966, 359n.).

489–505 Peneleos takes the grisliest reprisal yet for the death of his kinsman Promakhos (449–53n.). Akamas, a man of more words than deeds, dared not face even so mediocre a warrior as Peneleos; now Ilioneus' fate, with Peneleos' boast about it, precipitates the rout of the whole Trojan army. Ilioneus, whose name is from (W)ilios (501–5n.), appears only here, but Homer builds up his importance and makes his death more shocking by heaping up pathetic detail: his father, rich in flocks by Hermes' favour, has no other son to whom his wealth can pass. This is brutally juxtaposed with Ilioneus' ghastly death by the gouging out of an eye, normally fatal by itself (cf. 13.616f., 16.741ff.), and then decapitation (13.201–3n., cf. Peneleos' action at 16.339–41), while he spreads out both arms in a vain gesture of surrender or supplication (cf. 13.546–9n.). The common pattern of an initial hit with a spear, followed by a death-blow with a sword (cf. 20.481–3, which also ends in beheading), leads up to a worse horror: Peneleos brandishes the severed head on his spear-point, which is still in the eye-socket. As Segal remarks (*Mutilation* 23), since the impaling is by chance and the display is in the heat of battle, it does not approach the savagery of Hektor's reported threat to impale Patroklos' head (18.176f.). Yet its effect is almost as horrendous for us as it is for the Trojans, and makes their panic fully apt, even without Peneleos' claim, in his vaunt, that the Greeks will sail home safely (he does not speak of sacking Troy). J. T. Sheppard (*The Pattern of the Iliad*, London 1922, 145) thinks this scene recalls the start of this phase of the battle (13.156–205), when Meriones' spear-cast failed like Hektor's at 406, and Aias hurled Imbrios' head at Hektor.

489–91 The MSS, A included, read Πηνελέοιο (13.92n.); Leaf and Mazon rightly spurn the OCT's reading -έωο, from one very late MS. Since Phorbas' name is from φορβή, 'fodder', his pastoral connotations are no surprise. He is an invention, like Akhilleus' slave | Φόρβαντος θυγάτηρ (9.665) and Euphorbos (16.808–11n.); cf. the Phorbas related to Helios or Augeias, both keepers of herds (Hoekstra, *Epic Verse before Homer* 62f.). The diction suggests that 490f. adapts a traditional hymn to Hermes, as does

16.180ff., where Πολυμήλη | Φύλαντος θυγάτηρ bears the god a son; cf. the opening of *Hy*. 18, 'I sing of Hermes, ruler Ἀρκαδίης πολυμήλου, | ... ὃν τέκε Μαῖα | Ἄτλαντος θ. ....'. The particularized epithet π., also at 2.705, is metrically equivalent to μεγαθύμου; it hints at the father's tragedy in losing his son and heir (cf. 13.171–3n.). Hermes is already linked with flocks and herds (cf. *Od*. 14.435, Semonides frag. 20, *HyHerm* 491ff., 567ff.).

493–8 The spear-point hits Ilioneus at the base of his eye, expelling his eyeball; traversing his eye-socket and brain it emerges below his helmet through the sinew at the nape of his neck (ἰνίον, also at 5.73: not 'occiput', *pace* LSJ). The repetition of ὀφθαλμός sharpens the horror of having one's eye poked out. Peneleos slices off the head helmet and all, like Akhilleus at 20.482.

499–500 Zenodotus (Hrd/A) rightly read ὁ δὲ φὴ κώδειαν ἀνασχών, 'he, holding (it) up like a poppy ...'; the comparison befits the scarlet object. For a developed poppy-simile in a like context see 8.306–8, and cf. 17.53–8; κώδεια is next in Theophrastus. φή (or φῆ), 'like', is the instrumental of an Indo-European demonstrative otherwise lost in Greek (Chantraine, *Dict.* s.v.). Zenodotus was so keen on this rarity that, to obviate a hiatus, he read it instead of ὡς at 2.144. In reaction Aristarchus denied that Homer knew it; he read ὁ δ' ἔφη in 499, i.e. 'he said, holding (it) up (like) a poppy', athetizing 500 as an interpolation meant to supply a verb of speaking, which was felt to be missing when (ΔΕ)ΦΗ was misread as 'like'. Such interpolations did occur, but he is wrong here (van der Valk, *Researches* II 53, 444f.). φή never recurs in Homer, but is less rare than Aristarchus thought, being found before Antimachus (frag. 121) at *Cat*. 204.138, *HyHerm* 241. Moreover, πέφραδε answers by deeds the taunt φράζεσθε (482), just as κόμισε at 463 responded to 456. Aristarchus held that φράζειν never means 'say' in Homer, thus condemning 500 as pleonastic (Ap. Soph. 165.10); but it means 'show', as at 335.

501–5 Peneleos' jibe outdoes Akamas' (479–85n.). As if aware that Ilioneus is an only son, he stresses his parents' grief, an apt reprisal for the sorrow of Promakhos' wife: for the family's grief in vaunts cf. 17.27f., 21.123f. The Trojans are to take the news back home, because they will now flee! Note the parallelism πατρὶ φίλῳ – ἀνδρὶ φ.; εἰπέμεναι picks up φράζεσθε (482), and Τρῶες–Τροίης form a ring. For Alegenor see 449–53n. Both infinitives in -μεναι are epicisms rather than true Lesbian forms (Chantraine, *GH* I 489; Shipp, *Studies* 84). ἀγαυός is an Aeolic derivative of ἄγαμαι (Hainsworth on *Od*. 5.1); ἀγαυοῦ Ἰλιονῆος goes back to *-oo ϝ-, not *oι' (ϝ)-, since ἀγαυοῦ always precedes a consonant elsewhere (17× epos) and *-oo offers a better rhythm. In 505 Zenodotus and Aristophanes (Did/A) wrote ἐν for σύν; both expressions are Homeric, but σύν is standard in this formula (2.236, 16.205).

506–22 The battle enters a short phase of flight and mass slaying, quite different from the clash of two solid front lines (the *stadiē*) that has been going on since 13.126. As Latacz shows (*Kampfdarstellung* 210–13, 226ff.), mass hand-to-hand combat often leads to a rout, which consists in one side abandoning their formation to flee in chaos, and the other in pursuit making many easy killings unopposed; this hardly differs from the end of hoplite battles like that at Delion, when one seventh of the Athenian force perished. There are verbal parallels with the beginnings of other Homeric routs: 507 = 16.283, where see n.; the old variant for 506 is from 8.77. With the idiom ἔκλινε μάχην, 'turned the battle', cf. 5.37, Τρῶας δ' ἔκλιναν Δαναοί.

508–10 Thornton links this turning-point in the battle with the next invocation of the Muses (16.112f., where see n.), arguing that these frame the greatest crisis in the Greeks' fortunes (*Supplication* 42ff.). The poet invokes the Muses' help at another such transition, that from flight to the *stadiē*, when the Trojans start to resist Agamemnon's onslaught (11.218). Elsewhere he marks this transition with a question addressed as much to the Muses as to himself, ἔνθα τίνα πρῶτον, τίνα δ' ὕστατον ἐξενάριξε (5.703n.); catalogues follow, as we would expect (Strasburger, *Kämpfer* 53). On such invocations see de Jong, *Narrators* 45–53, with bibliography; she well argues that they reinforce the superlative 'who was first?', thus strengthening this focusing-device. Leaf objected that 'the turning of the battle took place really with the wounding of Hektor', but Hektor's removal did not at once cause the rout (402–522n.). As Aristarchus noted, ἀνδράγρια is a *hapax* in Greek; this fact led someone (evidently a predecessor) to athetize 508–10 (AbT). ἀ. means 'spoils', i.e. what is stripped from a slain man, just as βοάγρια means '(leather) shields', i.e. what is flayed from an ox. It is probably an Aeolic archaism, since ἀγρέω is Myc. and Aeolic, and βροτόεις, only here save in the formula ἔναρα βροτόεντα (8×), is Aeolic (Chantraine, *Dict.* s.v. βρότος). The allusion to Poseidon's activity is to 384ff. (cf. 354–401n.).

511–22 Each of the major Greek leaders still fighting receives his own mark of honour in the roster of victories. Aptly, Telamonian Aias comes first with a couplet (cf. 12.378) and an enemy chief; Antilokhos, Meriones and Teukros make two kills each; Menelaos' slaying of Huperenor is the only death described in detail ('Atreides' cannot mean Agamemnon, who is injured); Oïlean Aias kills the most. The verbs for 'kill' are deftly varied too, as Eustathius saw (1000.1); yet even these display complex systems of extension and thrift, as E. Visser shows (*Homerische Versifikationstechnik*, Frankfurt 1987). Other condensed lists of men slain in routs are 6.29–36, 15.328–42 (both with *variatio* in the verbs); elaborate examples are 5.37–84, 16.306–50. Cf. the rampage of a single hero in his *aristeia* (e.g. 16.692–7). Both kinds of catalogue often involve alliteration, here in μ and π (513–15: see Strasburger, *Kämpfer* 19). When at their sparest they are kept brief, so as not to become tedious.

Four of the victims derive, with rather typical inaccuracy, from the list at 13.790–2: Phalkes, Morus, Hippotion (there the *father* of Morus!) and

Periphetes, there named *Polu*phetes; a Greek Periphetes falls in the rout at 15.638. Another 'father' slain with his son is Ekhios at 15.339, adapted with a like inconsistency from 13.422 (see n. there and Visser, *op. cit.* 124–39). The Mysian Hurtios son of Gurtios – a rhyme redolent of *ad hoc* invention – is unknown, being absent in the Trojan Catalogue (2.858); Scherer compares Hurtakos from the Troad, Phrygian Gordios, and the pre-Greek place-names Gurtone, Oligurtos and Gortun ('Nichtgriechische Personennamen' 37). Prothoon and Mermeros, also unknown, bear transparent Greek names; the son of another 'Frightful' purveys venom at *Od.* 1.259. Huperenor is thrice an epithet in Hesiod; here he is a distinguished casualty, if we trust Menelaos' later boast that he slew a Huperenor, brother of Pouludamas and Euphorbos (17.24–8). That Menelaos killed two men of this name appears unlikely; yet his memory seems faulty when he claims that Huperenor withstood him and insulted him – conduct more suited to the *stadiē* than the rout. Aristarchus thought this might have happened here without Homer telling us about it (Arn/A *ad loc.*)! In fact Huperenor is a mere cipher, whose death is elaborated without full consistency to fit Menelaos' needs in book 17.

512 καρτερόθυμος is sing. (6× epos) save at *Theog.* 378 (acc. plur.), but is used in the gen. plur. here to avoid the Greek epithet χαλκοχιτώνων; T's variant βαρβαροφώνων comes from 2.867. The Musoi are also ἀγέρωχοι and ἀγχέμαχοι (10.430, 13.5).

517–19 For 517 see on 442–8, 13.506–9. Aristarchus saw in οὐταμένην ὠτειλήν (also at 17.86) an etymological play, supporting his theory that Homer used ὠτειλή of stab-wounds only (4.140n.); word-play is not excluded, but the theory is wrong (Heubeck on *Od.* 24.188f.). Death, and the *psuchē* (regarded as 'breath', as its etymology confirms), often follow the withdrawn spear (13.574–5n.).

521–2 Eustathius (1000.13) saw that the compliment paid to Oïlean Aias is back-handed: it is no *moral* achievement to be fastest at killing men who are fleeing (τρέω = φεύγω, cf. 13.510–15n.). When Aias' speed threatens to win him a prize, the poet makes him fall flat on his face (23.758ff.); at 16.330f. his victim has tripped, which makes his success less creditable. Whether or not Akhilleus is faster, this athletic braggart lacks his redeeming qualities (13.72n.); cf. Ares, 'swiftest of the gods' (*Od.* 8.331) but otherwise nasty. — In the phrase 'Zeus rouses them to flight' (split at 11.544), the god is invoked to explain an emotion beyond rational control: cf. 'Zeus roused them to battle' (13.794). Since he is in fact asleep, a pedant (in T) emended his name away. But the irony arouses suspense, reminding us that Zeus's slumber may end abruptly at any time; he awakens only four lines later – in the middle of a verse (cf. 1.194 for the surprise effect)! For ὅτε τε with the subj. see Ruijgh, τε *épique* 491f.

BOOK FIFTEEN

In this book, named after its opening 'the counter-attack' (παλίωξις), the poet faces the task of rapidly reversing the Greek breakthrough; to do this gradually would arouse less suspense. Yet he must also make the Trojan advance slow and painful, so as not to upset his pro-Greek audience. He must also bring the deception of Zeus to a dignified close, return Hektor to battle and keep us on tenterhooks by reminding us of Patroklos and Akhilleus. All these ends are deftly attained by a book that falls into four movements, discussed more fully in notes at the start of each; the best account of the whole is Winter, *MNO* 130–77.

In an opening *scherzo* (1–261), Zeus, now awake and undeceived, puts Here and Poseidon in their places (with amusing characterization), and sets Hektor in motion again; in so doing he reveals to Here the future course of the action. This prepares us for Akhilleus' intervention, but also advances the divine sub-plot ahead of its human counterpart (56–77n.): the quarrel among the gods is resolved in a grudging reconciliation between Zeus and Here; that among the Greeks ends only with the like reconciliation in book 19. But what a contrast between Zeus's majesty and Agamemnon's weakness! Zeus has successfully resisted another challenge to his rule; Homer repeatedly evokes his defeat of the giants and Titans (see on 18–31, 87f., 185–93), just as he alluded to threats to the god's rule in book 14 (153–353n.). Ares' wild urge to avenge his son Askalaphos, and his amusing disarmament by Athene, form a veiled commentary on the main plot: he wants to intervene, at great risk, to avenge one lost Greek; will Akhilleus refuse to intervene to avenge the many already slain, and to save the rest? Like Ares, Patroklos will be stung into action by pity (with 113f. cf. 397f.); his own rash intervention will end with his forcible disarmament by Apollo, and in the last moments of his fury he is likened to Ares (16.784ff.). Moreover Ares' grieving and vengeful desire to return to battle sets the pattern for Akhilleus. This incident also prefigures Zeus's desire to save Sarpedon (Thalmann, *Conventions* 45). Thus this *scherzo* foreshadows the tragedy to come.

In a brisk and brilliant *allegro* (262–404), Hektor, now awakened and restored to vigour (like Zeus), assists Apollo in a crushing counter-attack. The god leads a *Blitzkrieg* across the ditch and through the rampart. Thanks to Thoas' tactical advice (281–99), the Greeks retreat in decent order but with heavy losses. An ambiguous sign from Zeus (377ff.), in response to Nestor's prayer, keeps the divine background in our minds. This movement

225

ends with the Trojans at the ships and a glimpse of Patroklos' reaction: he finally leaves Eurupulos' hut to run to Akhilleus and urge him to fight (390–404). Throughout the long retardation which ensues, we know that Patroklos is on his way, just as we knew during the Trojan rout at 14.506ff. that Zeus could awaken at any moment. Then the poet did not let us wait long; now he draws out the suspense of anticipation.

Verses 405–591 must be called a *largo*. The pace slows as the armies fight before the ships, with the combat becoming hand-to-hand after 515; the Trojans gradually advance but pay a high price, losing two men for every Greek. Homer holds our attention by using all the diverse motifs of battle-narrative at his disposal – similes, vignettes of minor warriors, paired exhortations, dialogue between comrades and lists of victims.

The finale (594–746) is an *allegro con brio*. It opens with a rapid recapitulation of the *scherzo* (592–614), reminding us of Zeus's plan, but intermingles the themes of the *allegro*, since Hektor rages through the battle like the fiery war-god, driving the Achaeans back to the huts behind the first row of ships. A splendid set of similes vividly describes his rapid advance, but only one Greek falls; and from 674 the strains of the *largo* sound once more, in a renewed stalemate at the ships. But Aias' heroic resistance clearly cannot last; sooner or later, one of the Trojan fire-bearers must get through. We have already heard Nestor's entreaties in this extremity (659ff.); since he is firmly linked in our minds with Patroklos, our anxiety must centre on when the latter will reappear. When will the burning of a single ship signal to Zeus that it is time for the Greek counter-attack, as we learn at 599ff.? Must the fighting reach Akhilleus' own ships first, as the words of Zeus at 63f. (and of Akhilleus at 9.651f.) misled us into expecting? It comes as a surprise when at 16.2, with no ships yet on fire, the scene shifts to Patroklos and the work's dominant theme, Akhilleus' wrath, is finally heard in all its grandeur, while Protesilaos' ship, about which we were so worried, becomes merely another reason for the maestro to enter in person.

Much ink has been spilt as to when the rampart is broken (e.g. by Thornton, *Supplication* 157–60). Even C. H. Whitman and R. Scodel (*HSCP* 85 (1981) 9f.) assume that, although the Trojans enter its gates and surmount it at 12.469f., the references to their breaching it in book 13 (50, 87, 124, 679, 737) imply that it is undamaged, in contrast with 14.15 and 55, where Nestor sees and declares that it is ruined (τεῖχος ... κατερήριπεν). Worse yet, 345, when the Greeks pass behind it, and 384 and 395, when the Trojans swarm over it, seem to imply that it is intact, even after Apollo has wrecked it at 361ff.! Worst of all, how can anything remain for Apollo and Poseidon to erase later, when the rampart is said to have stayed intact 'as long as Troy was unsacked' (12.10ff.)? Critics think Homer nodded off, but the error is theirs. When a fortification is breached, it need not be ruined, even if it is wrecked from the defenders' viewpoint, as expressed by Nestor at 14.55; damaged in places, it may remain a barrier along the rest of its length (van Leeuwen, *Mnem.* 40 (1912) 85). Homer, as a poet, never says exactly how much of the rampart was wrecked: it would have reduced Apollo's majesty to specify that he razed only that part of it behind the causeway (358-61n.), and that the Trojans fanned out on either side. If we assume, as is reasonable, that Homer deems it partly damaged, we can see why it is sometimes a barrier, sometimes not, as need or characterization requires; Homerists too often spurn reasonable assumptions, despite Aristotle's warning (*Poet.* 1461b1ff.).

Thus there are no contradictions over the rampart, when books 13–15 are treated as a single sequential narrative; but Homer presents several scenes which can be taken as simultaneous, even though he maintains narrative continuity (see 262–404n.). Whitman and Scodel (*loc. cit.*) well argue that the various mentions of it fit into this pattern too (hence, perhaps, their deliberate vagueness): the references to its ruin at 14.15 and 14.55 make better sense if the poet 'regarded the two crossings of the wall as one. The taking of the wall is an action performed by both a god and a man, like the slaying of Patroclus in this poem, or the slaying of Achilles in tradition. But in order to accommodate the Achaean rally it is performed twice, once by Hector alone, once by Apollo alone.'

1–77 Zeus awakens and is angry at Here when he sees the Trojans in flight. She cleverly swears that Poseidon acted of his own accord. Zeus sends her to Olumpos to summon Iris and Apollo, who will reverse the rout; predicting the death of Hektor and fall of Troy, he reveals to her that his support of the Trojans is only temporary

1–13 The picture of panic flight in 1–3 adapts the phrasing of 8.343–5 to fit a Trojan rout; continuing the rapid narrative of book 14, it shows how far they fled. Crossing the rampart, presumably, they pass the line of stakes and the ditch beyond it; when it is their turn to flee, the Greeks reach first the ditch and stakes, then the rampart (344f.). The chariots that they had left beyond the ditch (12.85) form a convenient rallying-point, like the ships at 8.345. The parallels with book 8 continue, in that Hektor is described and a god pities the losing side; but there Hektor is a terrifying figure and Here pities the Greeks, whereas here Zeus awakens suddenly (14.521–2n.) to see the Trojans routed and Hektor gravely injured.

4–8 χλωροὶ ὑπαὶ δείους, reminiscent of the formula χλωρὸν δέος, recurs at 10.376 (sing.); δείους represents original *δϜέγεhος before a consonant, written ΔΕΟΣ in the first MSS (cf. p. 34 n. 61). πεφοβημένοι cannot go with ὑ. δ., *pace* Nic/A; it picks up φόβον at 14.522, and more remotely 14.506f., summing up the rout as a unit. Another ring, formed by paired mentions of Zeus and Here, encloses what Zeus sees (4–13). χρυσοθρόνου Ἥρης is a modified formula, found also at *HyAp* 305 (separated); cf. the nom. at 1.611,14.153 (separated), and the 'declension' λευκωλένου Ἥ. (3× *HyAp*). The extra verse 5a (= 2.42) is another of T's pedantic interpolations (14.349–53n.): some prude felt that Zeus ought to dress before leaping to his feet, but it is more dignified not to refer to his nakedness at all! With 6 cf. *Od.* 13.197. Verse 7 = 14.14, when Nestor sees the opposite situation; to use it here the poet departs from the usual chiasmus, adding Ἀργείους to clarify which side is routed. The spectacle, and its effect on the observer, also recall the brief account of what Poseidon sees at 13.15f. The full description amply motivates Zeus's ire.

10–13 Aristarchus (Hrd/A) took εἵατο (EATO), 'they sat', as εἵατο, supposedly equal to ἦσαν, as also at 24.84, *Od.* 20.106; he did so because of the latter verse, where the subject is inanimate. Editors falsely restore ἦατο, but cf. εἵαται (10.100), κατέαται (Hdt. 1.199.2). Hektor's shortness of breath ceases at 241 (for the phrasing cf. 16.109); his other symptoms were mentioned at 14.436f. For ἀπινύσσων, 'insensible', Aristophanes (Did/AT) read ἀπινύσκων, found nowhere else (cf. 14.249n.); ἀπινύσσω, 'be foolish', occurs 2× *Od.* The litotes 'not the weakest of the Achaeans' means the strongest, Aias. With 12f. cf. 16.431f. with n.; 'father of gods and men' brings out Zeus's power among the gods and paternal sympathy for men. δεινά (-όν) is used of scowling terribly in the same phrase at *Aspis* 445, *Hy.* 7.48: ὑπόδρα ἰδών is felt as a unit which can take an adv. For the formula see 1.148–71n.; J. P. Holoka, *TAPA* 113 (1983) 1–16.

14–77 Three speeches set in train the undoing of Here's plan. Lohmann (*Reden* 150f.) shows that they contain a ring-structure which overlaps the changes of speaker:

(*Zeus*)   A   *Accusation:* All this is your doing, Here (14f.)!

      B   *Threat:* You deserve another flogging; don't you *recall* ... (16f.)

      C   *Precedent:* ... how I punished you when ... (18–30)?

      B′   *Threat:* Let me *remind* you, so that you stop tricking me (31–3).

(*Here*)   A′   *Defence:* I swear that Poseidon's intervention was not my doing (36–44).

      d   *Proof:* I am willing to go and dissuade him (45f.).

(*Zeus*)   d′   If you are willing to agree, then he will soon yield (49–52).

      e   So go to Olumpos and fetch Iris and Apollo (52–5); they will set in motion events leading to the fall of Troy (56–71).

      d″   I shall let no other god interfere until my promise to Thetis is fulfilled (72–7).

This dialogue is climactic for the whole *Iliad*, provided that we retain 18ff. and 56–77. As often, verses athetized in antiquity lie at the centres of ring-structures. Without 56ff. the reason for the divine reconciliation, and the removal of the last divine obstacle to the fulfilment of Zeus's plan, would be left obscure. Zeus conciliates Here by magnanimity in victory; seeing his power recognized, he reveals that his support for the Trojans is a temporary stage in their eventual ruin, which she ardently desires but has in fact obstructed with her wiles. This is why she is so angry in the next scene (Erbse, *Götter* 201)! Winter regards his firm but benevolent explanation as an after-effect of the intimacy he has just enjoyed (*MNO* 131f.); paradoxically, Here's deception of Zeus leads to their reconciliation (cf. Atchity, *Homer's 'Iliad'* 109). That his anger focuses on her and not Poseidon enables the poet to restart Zeus's plan rapidly, and avoid a potentially undignified direct clash between Zeus and his brother (so Winter).

14–17 Zeus's address to Here is as convoluted as her trick; it aptly introduces his sinister statement 'I rather think that again you may be the first to profit from your troublesome scheming ...' The epic *hapax* κακό-τεχνος goes with δόλος; for ἀμήχανε see 13.726–9n. T's pedantic variant δ' Ἀχαιούς comes from 17.596. κακορραφίη ἀλεγεινή is dat. at *Od.* 12.26, cf. 2.236; it is from the metaphor κακὰ ῥάπτειν (3× Hom.). For ironic ἐπαυρίσ-κομαι cf. 1.410; ἱμάσσω is aor. subj. (cf. *Theog.* 857).

18–31 Herē's punishment, being hung in the sky with anvils on her feet, serves several poetic ends. Zeus underlines the reality of his threat by citing a precedent. Yet, precisely by giving the full story, he undercuts its force: he chastized Here for the sake of Herakles, his own son, which Hektor is not, whatever delusions of grandeur the Trojan may entertain (so Here to Sleep at 14.265f.). We also gain another perspective, with new and amusing details, on their *désaccord* over Herakles, which Sleep gave as his reason for fearing Zeus (14.250–61n.). It is almost predictable, and hence comic, that Zeus cites this same episode; like Here's crafty oath, this prolongs the humour of book 14. But real repetition is avoided (Eustathius 1003.2ff.). Also, the gods' vain tugging at the golden chain recalls how Zeus debarred them from battle at 8.5ff., an earlier stage in the present quarrel; as Aristarchus saw, Hephaistos reminded his mother of this same incident over Herakles at 1.590ff., when this quarrel began.

Leaf compares Here's torture to that of Melanthios, tied to a plank and dangled horizontally from a beam (*Od.* 22.173ff.); Willcock adduces the Roman slave manacled to a beam with heavy weights on his feet at Plautus, *Asin.* 303f. Herē was beaten too, to judge from 1.588; Zeus's threats of violence against her at 1.566f. and 8.403–5 find their climax here. Feminist critics may justly find them unfunny (K. Synodinou, *WS* 100 (1987) 13–22). The male chauvinists in Homer's audience will have been most amused by this tale's domestic aspects, but the story once had cosmic implications, even if they lie well under the surface here. The discussion below builds on Leaf and on Whitman, *HSCP* 74 (1970) 37–42, who holds that this tale recalls violence between the sky-god and earth-goddess, comparing how Zeus lashes the Earth around Tuphōeus (2.782); Zeus's lash is his lightning (13.812–16n.). In some tales Tuphoeus' mother was Here herself, who bore him out of spite against Zeus over the births of Athene and Hephaistos (14.295–6n.). Cf. too Here's binding by Hephaistos because she had cast him out (14.256–61n.).

An anvil appears in the space between heaven and earth, in a like context of binding and hurling gods headlong, at *Theog.* 717–25, when the Titans are cast 'as far below the earth as the sky is from the earth': a bronze anvil would take ten days to fall from the sky to earth, and ten days from earth to Tartaros. West thinks an anvil is chosen because heavier objects were thought to fall faster; but this does not explain the fact that 'Anvil' (Akmon) is a shadowy cosmic power. Some equated Akmon with Okeanos or his father (Callim. frag. 498 with Pfeiffer's n.); but in the *Titanomachy* (frag. 2 B.), Alcman (frag. 61) and Antimachus (frag. 44) he was Ouranos' father, and Hesychius says he *was* Ouranos (see Calame, *Alcman* 613). The Indo-European cognates of ἄκμων explain this. Its sense 'anvil' comes from 'stone', cf. Sanskrit *áśman-*, Lithuanian *akmuô*, 'stone'; but *áśman-* and Avestan *asman-* also mean 'sky', evidently via 'vault of stone'. The idea of a solid firmament was widespread (Westermann, *Genesis* 117); early man deemed the sky a stone vault, or indeed a bronze one (as Homer does), because out of it fall meteorites made of stone and metal (differently Maher, *Creation and Tradition* 85–106). T's plus-verses (21–2n.) made Here's anvils an *aition* for some μύδροι, 'lumps of metal', then shown by guides at Troy: the *omphalos* at Delphi was surely a meteorite too (West on *Theog.* 498ff.), and such stones were often deemed holy (M. P. Nilsson, *Griechische Religion*, 3rd edn, Munich 1967, 201ff.).

Thus ἄκμονες were once meteorites, regarded as thunderbolts. This is confirmed by another sense of *áśman-*, 'thunderbolt', and its Norse cognate *hamarr*, '(stone) hammer', the weapon of Thor (called *Mjǫlnir*, cf. Russian *molnja* 'lightning'). A common Eurasian folk-belief explains thunder and lightning as the fall of a thunderstone, which can be a meteorite or a prehistoric celt: thus Pythagoras was purified with a κεραυνία λίθος before entering Zeus's cave on Cretan Ida (Porphyry, *Vit. Pyth.* 17), and the Greek for a lightning-flash is now ἀστροπελέκι, 'star-axe' or (if for *ἀστραπο-) 'lightning-axe'. Cf. C. Blinkenberg, *The Thunderweapon in Religion and Folklore*, Cambridge 1911; J. Hastings (ed.), *Encyclopaedia of Religion and Ethics* xi, Edinburgh 1920, 875f.; Stith Thompson A 157.1. This belief may even explain Zeus's epithet αἰγίοχος as originally 'driver/holder of the thunderbolt', from αἴξ and (F)έχω. αἴξ also meant 'meteorite' (Aristotle, *Meteor.* 341b3); cf. the mysterious αἴξ οὐρανία mentioned by Cratinus as a source of sudden wealth (frag. 261). See further 308–11n.

The punishment of Here soon gave offence. Allegorical explanations, making Here 'air' for example, survive in D and 'Heraclitus', *Homeric Allegories* 40 (cf. Buffière *ad loc.*), Zenodotus omitted 18–31 entirely (Did/A). His motive must have been dislike of impropriety; he athetized 1.396–406, a like story of violence among the gods. Nickau thinks he excised this one because of problems over Olumpos and how Here was suspended (*Zenodotos* 206–8); cf. Apthorp, *MS Evidence* 85–7. But T's shorter version of 22–30 is highly suspect (21–2n.), and other early texts contained the whole passage, since πᾶσαι read μέμνη in 18 (Did/A).

Shipp criticizes the diction (*Studies* 287), but its oddities 'can be paralleled from late but genuine sections of the poem' (Bolling, *External Evidence* 151f.). ἦ οὐ μέμνη ὅτε recurs at 20.188, 21.396, *Od.* 24.115; cf. Shipp, *Studies* 142. To avoid a diaeresis after the second foot we should read τε κρέμω (Bentley); for the contraction cf. Shipp, *Studies* 165. ἄκμων is attested in the Myc. name /Akmonios/ (KN De 1112). The end of 20 recurs at 192 only. The formula δεσμὸν ἵηλα is otherwise Odyssean (etc., 3×), like παρασταδόν. The synizesis in ἠλάστεον, 'were upset' (cf. 12.163), is paralleled in verbs of this shape (Shipp, *Studies* 157). The formation of ῥίπτασκον (23) is 'recent', but the subj. ἵκηται after a past tense is not odd (Chantraine, *GH* I 323, II 269). γῆ is innovative for γαῖα, but Homeric (14.203–4n.). ὀδύνη is sing. in the epos only at 11.398 (plur. 25×), but this ratio holds for Greek in general (LSJ s.v.). With the scansion | τὸν σῦ ξύν (26) cf. *Od.* 1.182, *HyAp* 471. ἐπ' ἀτρύγετον πόντον modifies | π. ἐπ' ἀ. (7× *Od.*), being displaced by πέμψας. The unique scansion ῥυσάμην (29) must be an epicism influenced by ἐρύω. The contraction of *ἀϝεθ- in ἀθλήσαντα is 'late' but paralleled (Shipp, *Studies* 21).

21–2 T report that 'some' read the following verses, which must have replaced 22–30; Eustathius (1003.13) says some 'added' them (he misunderstood T similarly at 14.278f.):

πρὶν γ' ὅτε (τότε T) δὴ σ' ἀπέλυσα πεδῶν (ποδῶν T), μύδρους δ' ἐνὶ Τροίῃ
κάββαλον, ὄφρα πέλοι⟨ν⟩το καὶ ἐσ⟨σ⟩ομένοισι πυθέσθαι.

The contracted gen. πεδῶν and ending -οιτο are 'late' (see Chantraine, *GH* I 476f., for the latter); μύδρος is next in Aesch. T's other plus-verses are pedantic or prudish interpolations (14.349–51n.): did a rhapsode create these to remove what he wrongly deemed a repetition of 14.252ff., while explaining a local curiosity of the Troad?

23–5 Zeus implies that he hurled several gods from heaven; since we know only of Hephaistos (14.256–61n.), he is surely exaggerating for rhetorical effect. ῥίπτασκον (5× epos) should be either ῥίπτεσκον or ῥίψασκον; cf. ῥιπτάζω (14.257), ῥιπτάζεσκε (*HyHerm* 279). τεταγών, 'seizing him', is an isolated aor. participle corresponding to Latin *tetigi* from *tango*; it is fossilized in the phrase adapted here, ῥῖψε ποδὸς τ. ἀπὸ βηλοῦ (1.591, cf.

Little Iliad frag. 21.4 B. = 20.4 D.). βηλός, 'threshold', is from βαίνω. ὀλιγη-
πελέων, 'with little strength', recurs at 245, 2× *Od.*; cf. Chantraine, *Dict.*
s.v. The *lectio difficilior* θυμός, now in a papyrus, stands in apposition to
ὀδύνη; this gives an easier enjambment. Aristarchus (Did/AT) and some
good MSS read θυμόν, i.e. 'ceaseless grief did not leave my heart', with an
acc. of respect (van der Valk, *Researches* II 105) . For ἀζηχής see 4.433–5n.

26–8 For Herakles' exploits on Kos see 14.250–61n.: that 28 = 14.255
confirms that the same episode is meant. Herē drove him off course with
the N. wind's help, having persuaded his gales (bT wrongly think Boreas
joined her in persuading them). Βορέης ἄνεμος (etc.) is formular (4× *Od.*).
κακὰ μητιόωσα | etc. (18.312, 2× *Od.*) has other 'inflections' supplied by κ.
μηχανάασθαι etc.

31–3 Leaf thought αὖτις has no reference – why should Zeus remind
Here 'again', when he has just done so? But it means 'am I to remind you
of this ⟨by *repeating* your punishment⟩?' The double final clause at 31f. is
paralleled at *Theog.* 127f. For the vulgate ἴδης see 13.448–9n. ἦν is innovative (Chantraine, *GH* II 281f.). χραισμῇ, ironic as often, is negated as always
(e.g. 1.28), echoing in sense ἐπαύρηαι (17). Zenodotus and Aristophanes
omitted 33 (Did/A), surely because it seemed sexually explicit: cf. their
text at 14.340 (van der Valk, *Researches* II 406). But 33, in all MSS, makes
two important points. By saying 'coming from the gods', Zeus implies that
others were party to Here's plot, which provokes her denial that she made
Poseidon intervene. Also, without 33 Zeus could mean that he will punish
her for exploiting sex in general, not just for this misdeed (Apthorp, *loc. cit.*).
Leaf plausibly takes ἦν ἐμίγης as an internal acc. agreeing with εὐνή; the
unique construction seems clumsy (a sign of embarrassment?).

35 = 89, 7× *Od.*; cf. 145 below. The verse adapts masc. φωνήσας, slighting the ϝ- in ἔπεα. A papyrus has ἀμειβομένη; of the doublets καί μιν φ. ἔ.
πτερόεντα προσηύδα (54× epos) and κ. μ. ἀμειβόμενος ἔ. π. π. (4×), the
former's prevalence is owed to its greater smoothness and flexibility of
context, especially after the loss of ϝ-.

36–46 Herē's oath purposely misses the point (so Aristarchus): Poseidon
did intervene of his own accord, but this does not excuse her plot to aid him.
She is not perjured, since she never told Sleep to urge him on: Sleep did so
unasked (14.240–1n.). The poet creates the effect of collusion without its
actuality. Verses 36–8 are a standard divine oath (*Od.* 5.184–6, *HyAp* 84–6);
on such oaths see 14.271–9n. The poet avoids repeating book 14, where
Here swore in other terms and indirect speech. Her unique oath befits the
marriage-goddess, since she invokes Zeus himself and their marriage-bed,
which she would never perjure; her phrasing is more dignified than Zeus's
φιλότης τε καὶ εὐνή at 32 (so bT). Cf. how Odysseus swears by the hearth
he has come to (*Od.* 19.304). Her oath is comical because of her recent

conduct, but also flatters Zeus as a power greater than she is and reminds him of their recent intimacy! Her excuse for Poseidon is rhetorically effective because she pretends to guess (που) that he acted from pity for the Greeks, an obviously laudable motive which Zeus ought to share.

37–44 The Stux 'drips down' from a cliff (*Theog.* 786). Στυγὸς (−∪∪) ὕδωρ is moved from its normal place at the verse-end (4× epos), where the scansion ὕδωρ is usual (59×, *HyDem* 381 excepted); cf. Σ. ὕδατος (3× Hom.). ὅς in 37 agrees with its complement, not its antecedent. On κεφαλή see 16.74–7n. For κουρίδιος see on 13.626f.; Penelope even uses it to describe her house (2× *Od.*). μή with the indic. is normal in negative oaths (Chantraine, *GH* II 331). ἰότης is always dat. elsewhere (13× epos), 'by the will of …': the causal use of διά is rare and presumably recent (cf. 71; Chantraine, *GH* II 96f.). Verse 44 blends ἐπὶ νηυσὶν Ἀχαιῶν (10×) with the pattern of μυρομένους δ' ἄρα τούς γε ἰδὼν ἐλέησε Κρονίων (19.340, cf. 17.441). κτεινομένους, read by the Massaliot and Argolic texts and Aristophanes (Did/A), further heightens the Greeks' plight, but must be an 'improvement'.

45–6 Herē would advise Poseidon *too* (καί) to assent. With cool effrontery she signals her own compliance with one word, as if to deny that she ever disagreed! With the phrasing cf. τῇ δ' εἷς, ᾗ σ' ἂν ἐγώ περ ἄγω (*Erga* 208); the voc. κελαινεφές is familiar (see 14.436–7n. and Hoekstra on *Od.* 13.147). Following Zenodotus (Düntzer, *De Zenodoti studiis* 59n.), Aristarchus always advocated καὶ κειν- rather than κἀκειν-; good MSS invariably back him, but the crasis is omnipresent too (cf. 179). Since ἐκειν- was on the increase in the epic diction (Janko, *HHH* 237f.), the crasis should be correct, unless it is owed to superficial Attic influence (cf. 93–4n.).

47–55 It is one of the charms of Homer's style that we are left to wonder whether Zeus smiles because Here agrees, or because he sees through her wiles, or for both reasons. On the structure of his speech see 14–77n. ἀλλ' at 53 opens a call to action, as usual; Zeus neatly turns her profession of loyalty into a test of it. By making her go to Olumpos, he at once puts his plan into effect while remaining vigilant on Mt Ida, and avoids a direct clash with Poseidon.

49–55 Despite Aristophanes (Did/AT), some good MSS support βοῶπι, as also at 8.471, 18.357; the ῑ is original (cf. βλοσυρῶπῐς at 11.36). γλαυκῶπῑς has followed the analogy of forms in -ῐδ-. ἶσον ἐμοὶ φρονέουσα means 'sharing my opinion', cf. ῑ. ἐ. βασίλευε (9.616). Verse 52 means 'he would soon change his mind to follow your and my wish'. μεταστρέφω usually takes a direct object, e.g. at 10.107, but cf. *Od.* 2.67. Verse 53, the start of a huge paratactic sentence, blends εἰ ἐτεόν γε (8×) and ἀτρέκεως ἀγορεύσω (8× *Od.*, cf. 2.10). Verse 54 combines ἔρχεο νῦν (etc.) μετὰ φῦλα θεῶν (161, 177, 3× *HyDem*) with δεῦρο κάλεσσον (-α), 4× Hom.; cf. especially *Od.* 17.529.

T's variant κλυτὸν αὐδήν in 55 is surely from a rhapsodic text, since it is Hesiodic (*Cat.* 64.15); Apollo's Homeric epithet κλυτότοξος recurs 3× dat., cf. *Od.* 17.494.

56–77 Aristophanes and Aristarchus athetized 56–77, while Zenodotus omitted 64–77 (Did/A); T claim he did so because 64–77 resemble a Euripidean prologue (see further Nickau, *Zenodotos* 245–9). Aristarchus' reasons, however, are clear, being given in full by Arn/A and rebutted by bT. This provides a good test-case for his method in proposing an athetesis; the debate has hardly changed since antiquity (cf. Bolling, *External Evidence* 152–6).

Aristarchus objects above all that 56–77 needlessly anticipate events and are tritely composed; someone (in bT) adds that they are displeasing to Here (cf. 97). bT reply that the poet often gives summaries to comfort the philhellene audience (cf. Schadewaldt, *Iliasstudien* 111f.). Summaries of the action, sometimes looking ahead to the future, are indeed typical (13.345–60n.); the next is at 231–5. The best parallel is 8.470–6, where Zeus mocks Here's resistance by predicting the battle's course (cf. too 11.186–94). This summary is longer and looks further ahead, to the close of the *Iliad* and beyond, as well as back to its opening, as befits its place at the central turning-point of the plot. Thus Duckworth shows that books 1–14 slowly increase the audience's foreknowledge, just as the *Odyssey* gradually reveals the future until, at 16.267–307, Odysseus reveals his agenda for the rest of the epic; each poem has an extended forecast just after its mid-point (*Foreshadowing* 39). Verses 56–77 continue the series of mentions of Akhilleus and help the singer and his audience recall where he is in the tale. Also, as we saw (14–77n.), Zeus finally lets Here understand that her intrigues are in vain, since Troy will fall in the end (he tactfully omits the death of her favourite, Akhilleus). Bolling thinks the summary ruins the suspense, but Homer derives his finest effects from the agony of expectation; the more important an event, the more often the poet presents it in prospect and retrospect (de Jong, *Narrators* 85).

Aristarchus also criticizes Zeus's predictions as inaccurate: the Greeks never 'fall among Akhilleus' ships', nor does Akhilleus stir up Patroklos – the converse is true. But, as Schadewaldt showed (*Iliasstudien* 110–11nn.), Homeric summaries are often imprecise. The forecast that the fighting will reach Akhilleus' ships runs parallel to how the fighting reaches Meleagros' own chamber in Phoinix's *exemplum*, and is envisaged by Akhilleus himself (9.588, 650–2); Zeus even said Patroklos would fall among the ships (8.475f.). That we have this prospect in mind increases our agony as the battle nears the fleet. But if the Trojans had attacked Akhilleus' own ships, he could not have let Patroklos lead his men into war and abstained himself! The account of Patroklos' motivation can certainly refer to our poem, where Patroklos gives Akhilleus the idea, but the latter then urges him to hurry (16.126).

Someone (in bT) also found it odd that Zeus dooms Sarpedon here, yet pities him later (16.433ff.); but Zeus treats Hektor likewise (22.168ff.). Indeed, 'my son' (67) is emphatic and prepares us for the pathos of a father losing his son, which even Zeus must undergo. A like objection, that Troy should fall because of Here's will, not that of the co-operative Athene (as is said at 71), is also refuted by bT: Athene contrived the Wooden Horse (*Od.* 8.493).

Aristarchus' other arguments are stylistic. (i) Homer would not put Iris first at 56, since this violates chiastic sequence; but cf. e.g. 6f. (so T). (ii) The sense of ἐν ... πέσωσι in 63 is unhomeric; but cf. 11.311 (so T). (iii) παλίωξις has an unhomeric sense, 'flight', in 69, but cf. T *ad loc.* (iv) Neuter Ἴλιον (71) is unique in Homer, instead of fem. Ἴλιος (cf. 16.89–96n.); the neuter is standard later (Wackernagel, *SUH* 63). (v) πτολίπορθος (77) never describes Akhilleus, who had not sacked Troy (cf. 21.550n.); but in fact the epithet is generic and describes Akhilleus 4× *Il.* This test-case confirms that Aristarchus argues on the same basis as a modern Analyst; that he makes no appeal to MS sources for his athetesis; and that bT display a more developed literary sensibility than his (cf. p. 27 n. 33). If such was his method, can we believe that his predecessors did better?

Linguistic objections have increased since Aristarchus' day, but their cogency has not. The ending -ῃσι on sigmatic aor. subjunctives (3×) is 'recent' (Shipp, *Studies* 117). The breach of 'Wernicke's Law' in μάχην ἐς (59) is easily mended by reading εἰς for ΕΣ (Leaf, Appendix N). Shipp (*Studies* 287) dislikes the Aeolism ἀνστήσει and contracted κτενεῖ (cf. 13.285); for the vulgate πολεῖς in 66 (πολέας in *h*) see 13.732–5n. The imprecision in ἐκ τοῦ (69), over when the Greeks start to push back the Trojans, is paralleled at 1.493, ἐκ τοῖο (so Willcock). τὸ πρίν (72) means 'formerly' elsewhere (Leaf); it adapts the pattern | μὴ πρίν ... | πρίν (2.413f., 24.781 etc.), i.e. 'before then ... when', although Willcock thinks 'before then' means the same moment as ἐκ τοῦ. κάρητι (75) is a 'recent' artificial form found in the gen. 2× *Od.* (Nussbaum, *Head and Horn* 174f.), and in the same phrase at *HyDem* 466, cf. 169.

58–61 παυσάμενον is acc., not dat., because it is governed by the infin. which follows; for the verse-ending cf. *Od.* 14.153. λελάθῃ is a causal aor., 'make him forget' (Risch, *Wortbildung* 243); cf. 2.600. Hektor feels pain in his *lungs* (φρένες): cf. 16.481n.

66–8 The formula Ἰλίου προπάροιθε (also 21.104, 22.6) once contained a gen. in *-οο, since Ἴλιον scans normally when we reconstruct *Ϝιλίοο (cf. p. 15 with n. 23). Verse 68 merges the formulae Ἕκτορα δῖον and δῖος Ἀχιλλεύς; Σαρπήδονα δῖον is in 67! Homer relies heavily on stock phrases throughout this synopsis; no doubt this style was common in the Cycle, which abounded in prophecies and bald narratives – a feature of his tradition which he transcended.

69–71 For his more remote forecasts Zeus uses optatives. παλίωξις, 'counter-attack' (601, 12.71), has an opposite, προΐωξις (*Aspis* 154); on its form see Chantraine, *Dict.* s.v. πάλιν. Did/A says 'Aristarchus' read ἐκπέρσωσιν in 71, which obviates both the neuter Ἴλιον and the hiatus after αἰπύ; since this reading is not at odds with his athetesis, but offers another 'solution' to the same 'problem', we need not emend to 'Aristophanes'. διὰ βουλάς recurs 3× *Od.*, 5× Hes. (cf. 37–44n.).

72–3 Zeus repeats his prohibition of 8.7ff., but reveals that his wrath will cease when Akhilleus is honoured, i.e. when the latter renounces his own wrath (19.56ff.); Zeus turns the gods loose at 20.22ff. Thus the hero's wrath and the god's are brought back into parallel. παύσω seems inferior to the strong variant παύω read by Aristarchus (Did/AT), unless this comes from 19.67. ἐνθάδε means simply 'here at Troy'; we need not fret about the geographical imprecision.

75–7 Zeus gave his promise to Thetis (1.503ff.), but both he and Akhilleus (16.237) accept that it was made to her acting at her son's behest and on his behalf. Aristarchus' atheteses rid the hero of blame for the Greeks' defeat; but his claim (in T) that Akhilleus never prayed for their ruin begs the question (cf. 598–9, 16.236–8nn.). The hero cannot be excused so easily. If he receives no share of blame, more must attach to Zeus, which is undesirable from the poet's viewpoint; not for Homer the amoral crudities of the *Cypria*, where Zeus causes the Trojan War to lower the population (just as the Babylonian gods cause the Flood) and spawns Helen as the agent of doom. Verse 77 = 8.372, again omitted by Zenodotus and athetized by Aristarchus.

78–150 Herē goes to Olumpos to declare that resistance to Zeus is vain, yet enrages Ares by announcing the death of his son Askalaphos. Athene stops Ares from seeking revenge against Zeus. At Here's behest, Apollo and Iris go to Ida

78–150 Herē's compliance is grudging; she takes her time, and vents her frustration by urging obedience on the gods in such a way as to stir up revolt. Her provocation of Ares, and Athene's sharp warning to him, form the core of this scene; the defeat of his incipient revolt reinforces the divine obedience to come (Winter, *MNO* 133).

78–9 Cf. 168f., 236f., each followed by a simile; these repeated descriptions of divine journeys frame this whole scene and the next. The parallelism confirms that we must reject T's pedantic plus-verse 78a, Ζῆν' ὑποταρβήσασα, νόος δέ οἱ ἄλλα μενοίνα. The interpolator did not realize (as many have not) that Zeus has just given Here better cause to obey than mere terror of his might. Since T has corrupted Ζῆν' to 'Zenodotus', Bolling (*External Evidence* 156) ascribes 78a to Zenodotus of Mallos, who added 13.731 (but cf. 14.349–53n.). Verse 79 = 8.410 (spurious), 11.196. Its parallelism with 169 and 237 undermines the weak variant δ' ἐξ for δὲ κατ'. Aristarchus favoured κατά for descents from mountain-tops, but ἐξ when a god flies from Ida to Olumpos, as here (Arn/A on 11.196). T ascribe δ' ἐξ to Zenodotus, who certainly made this emendation at 169, where it breaks Aristarchus' rule (van der Valk, *Researches* II 43f.). Perhaps he proposed it wherever the verse occurred, but his successor drew distinctions.

80–3 The magical velocity of a flying god was traditionally likened to that of thought, with brief phrases like ὥς τε νόημα: so Apollo at *HyAp* 186, 448, cf. *Aspis* 222 (Perseus), Theognis 985, Thales in Diog. Laërt. 1.35. The Phaeacians' ships speed 'like a wing or a thought' at *Od.* 7.36, which, as Porphyry saw (1.129.16), combines the referent and the imagery of this passage. Similes often describe divine journeys (cf. 24.80–2n. and Scott, *Simile* 17f.); this image is apt for a horizontal journey, just as the next, Iris as hail (170), describes a vertical one (Krischer, *Konventionen* 21). But an extended comparison on this topic is paralleled only at *HyHerm* 43f., in a different context. The simile's language interacts with its setting: ἀΐσσω is often used of a god's journey (e.g. 14.225), and μεμαυῖα picks up μενοινήσειε. ἐπὶ πολλὴν | γαῖαν is a separated formula, cf. (ἰέναι) π. ἐ. γ. 3× *Od.* φρεσὶ πευκαλίμησι (14.162–5n.) is moved from the verse-end as at 20.35. εἴην, 'would I were', gives the man's wishes in a unique 'quotation'. Aristarchus (in D) took it as the opt. of εἶμι, 'go' (cf. 24.139, *Od.* 14.496); but cf. Chantraine, *GH* I 285. He also read μενοινήησι (Did/A) for the -ήσειε of nearly all MSS, a papyrus included. An opt. is odd after an aor. subj., but so is a pres. subj., especially one formed like this (Chantraine, *GH* I 77); we are surely dealing with a conjecture. *Pace* the OCT and van der Valk (*op. cit.* II 198f.), the vulgate must stand, since the poet could easily slip into the aor. opt. after εἴην.

84–6 The assembled gods are drinking as usual; cf. 4.1ff., when Zeus upsets their good cheer, or *HyAp* 2ff., when Apollo's arrival so alarms them that all leap from their seats. They do so here from eagerness to welcome the flustered Here; cf. the greetings received by Zeus, Iris and Thetis (1.533f., 23.202f., 24.100ff.), or the envoys returning from Akhilleus' hut (9.670f.). 'Zeus's house' is merely another name for Olumpos (cf. 5.398). αἰπὺν Ὄλυμπον and ἀθανάτοισι θεοῖσι are transposed from the verse-end, where they occur 3× and 38× in epos respectively. For δεικανόωντο see p. 35 n. 65. Aristarchus, followed by the OCT, rightly kept the archaism δέπασσι, unique for δεπάεσσι, and rebutted those who substituted κάλεόν τέ μιν εἰς ἓ ἕκαστος (from 23.203), or δεικανόωντ' ἐπέεσσι, an epic modernization (*Od.* 18.111, 24.410) read by Zenodotus (so b). Cf. χερσί τ' ἐδεξιόωντο (*Hy.* 6.16). δέπας, Myc. *di-pa*, once meant a vessel larger than a cup; like many words for pots it is borrowed, perhaps from Luwian *tepa* (*LfgrE* s.v.).

87–8 Herē accepts the cup of Themis, who reaches her first. Since Homer could have made her take anyone's, we must ask 'Why hers?' Themis presides at divine conclaves: hence Hesiod makes her Zeus's second wife (*Theog.* 901ff.), Zeus bids her call the gods together (20.4) and they both preside over assemblies in general (*Od.* 2.68f. with S. West's n.). An assembly is in fact called a *themis* (11.807). Her presence may also show that Right will now prevail on Olumpos (Winter, *MNO* 132f.). But her role may derive from the tales of dangers to Zeus's rule, which Homer exploits in the 'deception of Zeus' (14.153–353n.). As a Titan who sided with him (D on 318), she shares his counsels (*Hy.* 23) and protects his power. When he strove with Poseidon for Thetis' hand, it was she who warned that Thetis would bear a son mightier than his father (Pindar, *Is.* 8.30ff., with L. M. Slatkin, *TAPA* 116 (1986) 1ff.). In the *Cypria* she helped Zeus plan the Trojan War, a vital prerequisite for which was Thetis' marriage to a mortal, which Thetis underwent to please Here; the result was strife among the goddesses at Peleus' wedding-feast (so Proclus' summary and frags. 1f.). Now too Zeus and Poseidon are at odds, indirectly, over Thetis, Here is angry and there is discord at a feast. The similarities are owed to shared story-patterns; any influence is surely from the tale in the *Cypria* rather than *vice versa* (not, certainly, from the *text* of our *Cypria*). — καλλιπαρήῳ is the true spelling (Hoekstra on *Od.* 15.123). δέκτο takes the dat. of the giver, e.g. 2.186 (Chantraine, *GH* II 73f.); this athematic form appears in Myc. beside /dexato/ (KN Le 641f.). Someone thought the august Themis should not 'run' to greet Here, and read φέρουσα instead (bT); but ἀντίος ἦλθε θέων is formular (3×, especially 17.257). Themis' name is a formant in the Pylian toponym *te-mi-ti-ja/ti-mi-to-a-ke-i*; cf. 20.4–5n.

90–1 A speaker may comment on an addressee's appearance at the start of a speech, with ἔοικας at the verse-end (*Od.* 6.187, 8.166, 20.227, *HyAp* 464). Aptly, Herē looks as if she has been *routed* by Zeus (ἀτυζομένη, ἐφόβησε), as the Greeks will be. ὅς τοι ἀκοίτης underlines the humour of the marital quarrel: for the phrasing cf. 14.346. How different the effect, and how much less fitting, if Homer had said ἀγκυλομήτεω instead!

92 This v. shows how the poet's subconscious memory of his previous choice between equivalent formulae can so affect his current choice that normal formular associations are disrupted; cf the phenomenon of phrase-clustering (13.97–8n.). The weird βοῶπις πότνια Ἥρη usually follows ἔπειτα (8×, e.g. 49), whereas its equivalent θεὰ λευκώλενος Ἥ. follows finite verbs (15×, e.g. 78 = 14.277); but here the memory of θ. λ. Ἥ. at 78 surely led Homer to select the 'wrong' doublet after ἔ. The reverse occurred at 14.263, where β. π. Ἥ. is apparently chosen because it had preceded at 222 (Janko, *Mnem.* 34 (1981) 251–64). W. Beck thinks Here is 'cow-eyed' when she is at odds with Zeus or otherwise nasty (*AJP* 107 (1986) 480–8); this founders on cases like 18.239 or 20.309. Beck does show that βοῶπις is avoided where other animals appear; this confirms Hainsworth's view that the alternative arose because of 'the obscurity, or the embarrassment, of the sense of βοῶπις' (*Tradition and Invention*, ed. Fenik, Leiden 1978, 41–50). Cf. pp. 11–12 above.

93–9 Herē's speech has a double structure: (i) 'don't *ask* me, since you know how difficult *Zeus* is, but lead the *feast*'; (ii) 'you'll *hear* about *Zeus's* evil deeds, and not everyone will be glad, if anyone still *feasts* serenely' (she means Ares in particular, cf. 110). Her reticence aims to arouse curiosity.

93–4 Herē tells Themis not to ask in the words with which Zeus told *her* not to ask about his plans (1.550). 'You know for yourself' enlists Themis' own knowledge; Eustathius (1007.28–33) compares 11.653f., when Patroklos says something similar of Akhilleus, who can fault even the faultless (as Athene will say of Zeus at 137). ἐκείνου is in the MSS here and in parallels at 11.653, 18.262, *Od.* 15.212; Aristarchus (Did/A) improperly substituted κείνου (cf. 45–6n.). ἀπηνής, 'harsh', comes from *ἇνος, 'face', originally 'with the face turned away' (*LfgrE* s.v.); for the phrase cf. 23.611.

95–9 Herē takes malicious pleasure in bidding Themis begin the feast, but then spoiling it with ominous words (so Paley); ἀλλά opens her call to action. Only here does δαιτὸς ἐΐσης lack ἐδεύετο (9× Hom.); 96 adapts πᾶσι μετ' ἀθανάτοισι (3× *Il.*, *Theog.* 449). For πιφαύσκομαι, 'reveal', see 16.12–16n. With the artificial fut. κεχαρησέμεν (intrans.), based on the perf., cf. θυμὸς κεχαρήσεται (*Od.* 23.266). οὔτε βροτοῖσιν | οὔτε θεοῖς may be simply a polar expression for 'everyone', i.e. 'one which says, for greater emphasis, "neither *x* nor *y*" or "both *x* and *y*" – *y* being the opposite of *x* – where the relevant notion is only either *x* or *y*' (Macleod on 24.45, with bibliography): cf. 10.249, *Od.* 15.72f. But mortals too are concerned with the 'evil deeds' Zeus predicts, since many of them will perish; are they mentioned to allude to the real audience, who cannot remain unmoved by the song? The scansion ἔτῑ νῦν is influenced by ἔτι δ(ϝ)ήν. Contracted εὔφρων (2× *Od.*, 9× in later epos) is innovative; ἐΰφρον- and ἐϋφροσύνη occur 14× Hom., but not later (cf. p. 14 n. 19).

100–3 If a speaker breaks off and resumes, the poet indicates some odd circumstance (cf. 1.511ff., 584ff.) – here, the goddess's forced laugh, confined to her lips while she still scowls. She does not relax her μέτωπον, properly the bridge of the nose (13.615). ἰαίνω, 'warm', normally describes appeasing someone's *heart*: cf. 24.119n., and, for the drastic formular innovation, Hoekstra, *Modifications* 122. The metaphor is from wax which softens when warmed (Paley). The expression is unique; γναθμοῖσι γελώων ἀλλοτρίοισι (*Od.* 20.347) denotes the opposite kind of laughter, over which one has no control. This laugh warns us not to take at face value what Here says next; D. B. Levine (*CJ* 78 (1982) 97n.) detects 'an attempt to show self-confidence ... as she tries to cover up her defeat at Zeus's hands and preserve her dignity'. bT (on 108) think she waits to see if the gods will defend themselves against Zeus, and then bursts out in rage at their silence, but Homer had ways to say this; rather, she pauses to increase their curiosity and suspense. Verse 100 blends ἤτοι ὅ γ' ὣς εἰπὼν κατ' ἄρ' ἕζετο, used 6× in Homeric assemblies, with ἡ μὲν ἄρ' ὣς εἰποῦσ' ἀπέβη (9×). Verse 101, up to θεοί, = 1.570; for ὤχθησαν see 16.48n. Zeus's brows are the hue of lapis lazuli at 1.528 = 17.209, *Hy.* 1.13; hair is often so described (cf. κυανοχαίτης). πᾶσιν δέ is innovative (p. 9 n. 6). Does Here 'speak among them, angry at all' or 'speak among them all in anger'? A parallel at *Od.* 21.147 supports the former view; colometry, the latter.

104–12 Here overtly advises submission, but covertly stirs up revolt. Eustathius (1008.34–40) ably analyses her stinging rhetoric. By saying 'we gods are fools to be angry at Zeus', she leaves it unclear whether the gods deserve their troubles because of their wish to resist or their failure to do so effectively. By criticizing their efforts she indicts their ineptitude. Rather than acknowledge Zeus's superiority, she says that he *asserts* it; by announcing Askalaphos' death, ostensibly as a warning, she purposely provokes Ares, as his reaction shows. This is no more accidental than is Athene's role in suppressing his fury. Although Ares is Here's son (5.892f.), she and Athene hate him for supporting the Trojans (5.714ff., 832ff., 21.412ff.). This scene is foreshadowed at 13.521–5, where we were expressly told that Ares was on Olumpos, unaware as yet of his son's death. Since Here did not visit the field, how she learned of his demise is obscure; since she has come from Mt Ida, which is in the right area, Homer counts on us to assume that she knows of it. At the cost of this tiny loose end, he can develop the major theme of the gods' resentful obedience to Zeus.

104 νήπιος-comments open speeches at 21.99, *Od.* 4.371. The variant ἐριδαίνομεν ἀφρονέοντι (Did/T) destroys the ambiguity discussed above; as it introduces a hiatus, it may well be early. ἀφρονέω is unique in the epos; ἀφραδέω occurs twice, which does not support it here.

105–8 With superb feel for character, Homer makes Zeus's truly Olympian serenity (expressed by his physical apartness) the trait that really enrages Here. She tacitly confesses that her 'approach' to Zeus failed; comically, she calls the gods' methods 'either words or force' when hers was neither, but deceit, which mingles both. She is silent about his larger plan, although it fulfils her own eventual aim. Paired nouns and verbs form a chiasmus in ἢ ἔπει ἠὲ βίῃ, οὐκ ἀλεγίζει | οὐδ' ὅθεται (also at 1.180f.), κάρτεΐ τε σθένεΐ τε (17.329); note the variety of dat. endings, including -εῖ for Myc. -(*eh*)*ei*. ὅθομαι, 'worry', is rare and obsolescent (Chantraine, *Dict.* s.v.). Like Ζηνί and the contracted dat. ἔπει, φησὶν γάρ is innovative (p. 9 n. 6); for the end of 108 cf. 12.103.

109–12 Leaf and Willcock take ἔχετε as an imperative, 'accept'; but this sense is odd, ἔχω κακά at *Od.* 11.482 does not support it, and Here is too angry to urge patience without heavy irony. There must be an ellipse: 'hence you have whatever evil he sends ⟨because you do not challenge him⟩'. She maddens Ares by feigning not to be sure whether his son is dead; for her ironic ἔλπομαι, 'I expect', of present or past events, cf. e.g. 13.309. φίλτατος ἀνδρῶν is pointed, 'dearest of men (to him)'; this phrase appears on Zeus's lips when he faces the death of his own son Sarpedon (16.433). Verse 112 is needed to give Askalaphos' name; Here's addition 'whom Ares says is his ⟨son⟩' twists the knife in Ares' wound, since it casts doubt on whether he is Askalaphos' father – he *asserts* that he is, just as Zeus *asserts* his supremacy! To prove his paternity, she implies, Ares will need to take revenge on Zeus.

113–14 Slapping one's thighs signals extreme vexation and grief; cf. 12.162, 16.125, *HyDem* 245, *Meropis* frag. 3 B., Xenophon, *Cyr.* 7.3.6, Polybius 15.27.11, Plut. *Tib. Gracch.* 2, Jeremiah 31.19, Ezekiel 21.12. See further Onians, *Origins* 183f.; Lowenstam, *The Death of Patroklos*. From πεπλήγετο, 113f. = 397f., *Od.* 13.198f.; it has an antique ring, since the dual μηρώ is limited to this context, like the formula χερσὶ καταπρηνέσσ' (cf. 16.791–2n.), and the old aor. π. is replaced by πλήξατο at 16.125, *HyDem* 245, *Meropis loc. cit.* Hoekstra explains the rare elision καταπρηνέσσ' by positing that ὀλοφυρόμενος δ' ἔπος ηὔδα has ousted the archaic formula ἔ. δ' ὀλοφυδνὸν ἔειπε (3×): see *Modifications* 63–6, *SES* 50f. But, although Aristarchus and πᾶσαι (Did/A) read δ' ἔπος ηὔδα, only A and some late MSS follow the learned editions. The situation is identical at 398, *Od.* 13.199; the Alexandrians' text may come from the parallel at 12.163. They surely abandoned our vulgate δὲ προσηύδα (with its papyrus support) on the ground that it lacks an addressee in the acc., but this can be supplied from the context (cf. e.g. 5.871); so van der Valk, *Researches* II 161f. ἔπος ηὔδα occurs 12× elsewhere, but its ϝ- is never 'neglected'.

115–19 Ares is reckless, as ever, but aware of his folly; the contrast with Athene, who typifies another aspect of war, brings this out. In accord with his function, he has a morbid fascination with death, which he indulged before (5.886). ἰόντ' is surely an acc. governed by the infin., not a dat. (cf. 58–61n.). For ὁμοῦ with the dat., 'together with', see Chantraine, *GH* II 149; μετά, 'among', with a sing. noun is rare and expressive, cf. μ. στροφάλιγγι κονίης (21.503) beside ἐν αἵματι καὶ κονίῃσι (*Od.* 22.383). For Ares' sons 'Panic' and 'Rout' see on 13.299f.; since 119 is ambiguous, Antimachus deemed them his horses (frag. 37)!

121–4 Athene checks Ares' rashness because she embodies realism and a sense of responsibility (she fears for *all* the gods); so too, prompted by Here, she stopped Akhilleus from drawing his sword (1.194ff.), halted the Greeks' rush to the ships at 2.155f. (ἔνθα κεν Ἀργείοισιν ὑπέρμορα νόστος ἐτύχθη, εἰ μὴ Ἀθηναίην...), and yielded to Zeus's threats at 8.426ff. The contrafactual conditional emphasizes the gravity of the crisis; her action averts a more grievous wrath 'from Zeus against the gods' (πὰρ Διὸς ἀθανάτοισι). The rapid dactyls and *hysteron proteron* in 124 lend excitement – she is in the foyer before she rises from her chair! With 121 cf. *Od.* 4.698. In the weighty phrase χόλος καὶ μῆνις the terms are equivalent (χ. is literally 'gall'); it reappears in the gen. at *HyDem* 350, 410 (cf. 13.459–61n.). To fit in πᾶσι, Ἀθήνη replaces -αίη; the short form is moved from the verse-end (244×) only 9× Hom. (counting oblique cases), but is already in Myc. (KN V 52). διέκ, unique in the *Iliad*, occurs 12× *Od.*, 4× *Hy.*, usually with a gen. in -οιο, not contracted -ου (cf. *Od.* 21.299).

125–7 No doubt Athene disarms Ares and rebukes him simultaneously (so T). He is imagined as fully armed, in accord with his impetuous nature; since he has no arming-scene to dignify him, the stress falls on his shameful disarmament by a female. She removes his armour in standard order (cf. *Od.* 14.276f.), no doubt standing his spear in a spear-rack against a pillar (cf. *Od.* 1.128). στιβαρῆς ἀπὸ χειρός (etc.) describes arms hurling objects elsewhere (6× epos); if σ. hints that Ares resisted, it is as apt a formular usage as is θοῦρος here or at 142. Most MSS read ἐκ for ἀπό, rightly (cf. *Od.* 14.277). | ἔγχος... | χάλκεον splits χ. ἔ., cf. 22.286; for καθάπτετο see 1.582n.

128–41 As her father's daughter, Athene takes Here's speech at face value and draws out its implications: Ares has no αἰδώς – his selfish folly imperils the other gods, guilty and innocent alike. The Leipzig scholia on 128 note that she makes the same points as Here, but to opposite effect; both mention first Zeus's power, then Ares' anger and lastly Askalaphos. 'Madman' picks up 'fools'.

128–9 'Madman, deranged in wits, you are ruined; you have ears to hear in vain ...' One of Ares' traits is martial frenzy (5.717, 831, *Od.* 11.537). φρένας ἠλέ is short for φ. ἠλεέ (*Od.* 2.243, cf. 14.464). ἠλεός is related to ἠλέματος, 'vain', and perhaps ἀλάομαι, 'wander' (Chantraine, *Dict.* s.v.); the unique ἠλός may have replaced Aeolic ἄλλος, 'mad', cf. ἀλλοφρονέων (23.698). διέφθορα, an intrans. perf. like ὄλωλα, recurs in later Ionic (LSJ s.v., III).

130–4 Here returned from Zeus in a bad temper, alone; Ares would return in a worse state, bringing an angry Zeus after him! Ζηνὸς Ὀλυμπίου is a recent formula (8× epos, separated uses included); the *Iliad* has Ὀλύμπιος only in the nom. or voc., usually without Ζεύς (15×). On ἀναπλήσας, with its dead metaphor, see 4.170n. With the end of 133 cf. 12.178; words shaped ∪ – – often displace ἀχνύμενός from the verse-end. In 134 Zenodotus read θεοῖς μέγα πῆμα (cf. *Theog.* 792) for κακὸν μ. πᾶσι, read by his successors (Did/AT) and the vulgate. πᾶσι is essential to Athene's point, and the metaphor φυτεύειν governs κακόν (-ά) 6× *Od.* Zenodotus' conjecture squeezes in θεοῖς, ensuring that τοῖς ἄλλοισι could not be wrongly referred to the mortals mentioned below (Düntzer, *De Zenodoti studiis* 112f.).

135–6 Luckily for Zeus's dignity, Athene's forecast of his rage is not put to the test. Homer relegates such traditional behaviour to his characters' speeches, rather than vouch for it himself (cf. 22f., 14.256ff.): contrast the Cycle, where even Zeus dances (*Titanomachy* frag. 6 B. = 5 D.). Athene aptly applies the standard epithet ὑπέρθυμος to the Trojans (cf. 14.13–15n.). κυδοιμέω, 'throw into tumult', must be trans., not intrans. as at 11.324, its sole other appearance: θορυβέω varies likewise.

138 υἱὸς ἑῆος, 'your son', recurs at 24.422, 550, cf. παιδὸς ἑ.(1.393), ἀνδρὸς ἑ. (19.342, *Od.* 15.450), φωτὸς ἑ. (*Od.* 14.505), always in speeches. In the *Odyssey*, and perhaps at 24.422, we must read ἑῆος, 'good', adapted from *ἦϝος (*eswos*), gen. of ἐΰς: see Hainsworth on *Od.* 8.325; Beekes in *Festschrift Risch* 366f. 'Good' is clearly its original sense; but here, *pace* Aristarchus, it is used as a second-person version of the formula παιδὸς/υἱὸς ἑοῖο, 'his son' (6× epos). Bards reinterpreted ἑῆος as an equivalent of τεοῖο that conveniently begins with a vowel; verses like this or 24.422 show how this could happen. Zenodotus (Arn/AT) read ἑοῖο wherever the context demands 'your'; van der Valk (*Researches* II 72) well suggests that he is extending by conjecture the obsolescent epic use of ἑός and ὅς as a second-person possessive (14.249n.).

139–41 After abusing Ares, Athene consoles him. Her argument resembles Akhilleus' harsh but true saying to Lukaon, 'Patroklos too is dead, who is far better than you'; cf. also Here's rebuttal of Zeus's parallel wish to save Sarpedon, 'many gods' sons are fighting at Troy, so where will the process end?' (21.107, 16.448f.). Athene tactfully omits Askalaphos' name; her generalizations reduce the emotional shock of his death. She ought to refer specifically to protecting men begotten by gods. Willcock understands 'you can't protect everyone's children, even if the father is a god'; but Homer is surely using the formula πάντων ἀνθρώπων 'everyone's' where it is not fully apt (cf. 95–9n., 16.621, *HyAp* 162). Van Leeuwen wrongly emends to ἀθανάτων. βίην καὶ χεῖρας ἀμείνων mixes two formular patterns, β. ∪∪–∪ ά. (1.404, cf. 11.787) and βίη καὶ χερσί etc. (3.431, 4× Hes.). For πεφήσεται see 13.825–9n.; for athematic ῥῦσθαι cf. Myc. /wruntoi/(PY An 657) and Chantraine, *Dict.* s.v. ἔρυμαι; for the formula γενεήν τε τόκον τε see 7.127–8n.

143–5 To avoid a glaring discrepancy between public bluster and private obedience, Here calls Iris and Apollo outside to hear Zeus's message; Heyne, too charitably, thought she wants to avoid enraging the gods in general or Ares in particular. Apollo has been on Olumpos since the divine council at 8.2, save for a brief foray at 10.515ff. It is unclear whether to read θεοῖσι μετ' ἄγγελος, 'messenger among the gods' (Hrd/T), or θ. μέταγγελος; Leumann (*HW* 69) thinks the compound, attested at 23.199, *Cat.* 204.58 and *HyDem* 441, arose from phrases such as this. The former reading makes the extra point that Iris carries messages *between* gods. Fór 145 cf. 35n.

146–8 σφώ is probably elided σφῶϊ (1.574n.). Following Aristophanes (Did/A), Aristarchus athetized 147f., deeming the verses out of character – the gods would obey Zeus even if Here had not told them to, and her request would make more sense if she asked them to do what *she* wanted, not its opposite. bT do better: her unexplained order reveals her scorn, just as we angrily say 'do what you want', and her curtness confirms her displeasure. A one-line speech would be too curt even for her (Leaf).

150 The poet does not elaborate this journey because a more important one follows at 169. εἰνὶ θρόνῳ (also 8.199) reflects Myc. *ἐν θόρνῳ (Hoekstra, *Modifications* 145), unless εἰνί arose by metrical lengthening to admit words of iambic shape (cf. εἰνὶ θύρῃσι, 3× *Od.*), by analogy with phrases like εἰν ἁλί with Myc. consonantal *h*- (see p. 11). τὼ δ’ ἀΐξαντε πετέσθην adapts τὼ δ’ οὐκ ἀέκοντε π., used of a chariot-team 10× Hom.

151–280 Zeus on Ida sends Iris to Poseidon; she persuades him to withdraw. He then dispatches Apollo to revive Hektor, who recovers and re-enters the battle

151–280 These twin scenes are a fine example of events that would in reality be simultaneous but are narrated consecutively, the bards' usual device for maintaining full comprehension (cf. 14.1–152n.). There is no reason why Iris and Apollo cannot descend at the same time, although it makes better dramatic sense to dislodge Poseidon from the field before reviving Hektor (so T on 157). The same technique appears whenever Zeus sends two messengers: cf. Thetis and Iris at 24.112ff. or Athene and Hermes at *Od.* 1.84ff. and 5.28ff., where the gap between the two scenes led Homer to recapitulate the divine assembly. The plan to send two messengers is always announced in advance, to orient the audience and, no doubt, the singer himself (cf. 54ff.). Cf. Krischer, *Konventionen* 94f., 103.

151–4 The gods reach Ida in the same formular verse as had Here (151 = 14.283, with ἱκέσθην, cf. 8.47). With 152 cf. 1.498, 24.98; for εὐρύοπα cf. 14.264–8n. Zeus, still sitting in the cloud he created at 14.350, is aptly called 'cloud-gatherer'! Shipp (*Studies* 288) thinks 153 was added by someone who liked that cloud, but did not see that it had lifted by 6f., when Zeus leaps up and sees the battle. But neither Zeus nor the poet is befogged by his own creation: it evaporates when unwanted, and recondenses to clothe Zeus in majesty. θυόεις, unique in Homer, recurs 3× *HyDem*; θυήεις (6× epos), the older form, is correctly formed from the neuter θύος (cf. 13.685–8, 14.172nn.).

155–6 The litotes conveys that, far from being vexed, Zeus is pleased, and not with these gods only: their presence shows that Here obeyed him. A papyrus replaces 155 with 1.332, a concordance-variant which ineptly stresses their fear. σφωϊν is an acc. governed by ἰδών, not a dat. with ἐχολώσατο (cf. 13.326–7n.); we must not read σφωε (in late MSS), *pace* Chantraine, *GH* I 267. With 156 cf. ὧκα ἐμοῖς ἐπέεσσι πίθοντο (3× *Od.*).

158–9 Homer avoids having Iris fetch Poseidon, so that the sea-god does not confront Zeus directly (so T); she performs her task so ably that even Poseidon praises her (206f.). The first half of 158 is formular (4×); Iris' epithet aptly stresses how fast she should go. Verses 158 and 160f. remodel 54 and 57f., when Zeus announced her mission. With the epic *hapax* ψευδάγγελος cf. μετάγγελος (144), ἐτήτυμος ἄγγελος (22.438, *HyDem* 46). Etymological play and assonance enliven 159.

160–7 These vv. are repeated to Poseidon, with adjustments for the second person, at 176–83, save that 163f. is rephrased as 179f. Verbatim repetition is the usual means of conveying a message, as at 2.8ff., 8.402ff., 11.186ff. (de Jong, *Narrators* 180–92). ἀλογέω, common in Ionic prose, is unique in the epos. On the negatives in 162 and 164 see Chantraine, *GH* II 333, 336. Verse 163 = *Od.* 1.294 (φράζεσθαι ...), with an etymological play between this verb and φρήν. For ταλάσσω see 13.825–9n.

165–7 Superiority and seniority are linked, as at 2.707 and 13.355 (of Zeus). Zeus masterfully puts the argument from his superior force before that from his seniority to Poseidon; the end of his message aims to inspire not fear but respect (so bT). Aristarchus athetized 166f. as an interpolation based on what he deemed Iris' tactful invention at 182f.; he thought 166f. more suited to someone who mentions his rank out of fear, like Agamemnon at 9.160f. But Zeus also ends with soothing words at 8.407 (so T), and he is very different from Agamemnon: at 1.186f. and 9.160f. the king ends speeches with appeals to rank, not respect. In contrast with the tragic disparity between his status and his mediocrity as leader, the divine hierarchy combines rank and prowess in one person. Thus the verbal parallels between 165–7 and 1.186f. are no accident, but this time the established authority prevails; on the similarities see further Reinhardt, *IuD* 285ff. Zeus is the elder here and at 13.355; at *Od.* 13.142 and in Hesiod Poseidon is his senior. For an explanation see 14.203–4n. — On the rare ἑο cf. Chantraine, *GH* I 58; Hrd/AT, a papyrus and A offer the usual late Ionicism εὗ. Verses 166f. mean 'his heart does not shrink from deeming him equal to me, whom others dread' (cf. 182f.); for ὄθομαι see 105–8n. The original sense of στυγέω was 'shiver (from fear)'; see Chantraine, *Dict.* s.v. With 167 cf. 7.112, 8.515.

168–72 These vv. neatly adapt 78–83, altering the simile; at 8.409f. Zeus sent Iris from Ida in different phrases. The first halves of 169 and 173 recur in the next divine journey (237, 243). For Zenodotus' text in 169 see 78–9n. The hiatus before ὠκέα Ἶρις (172) arose because the poet had no alternative formula. Its internal hiatus is owed to ϝ-: Ἶρις appears as Βῖρις in Laconian dialect (Paus. 3.19.4).

170–1 Iris' plunge to Troy (more exactly, to the plain) is aptly likened to snow or hail driven by the N. wind (διέπτατο resumes πτῆται); this suppresses her gentler connotations as the 'rainbow'. Boreas is the strongest and coldest wind in Greece (cf. *Erga* 504ff.); born in the clear sky over Thrace, he sweeps down the Aegean, blowing from the clouds he amasses. His origin, and the icy weather he brings, both relate to the context: the clear sky and clouds are the realm of Zeus (cf. 154, 192), from whom Iris brings a chilling threat. Fränkel (*Gleichnisse* 33) adduces 3.222, where words painful to hear are likened to snowflakes; the poet compares missiles to snowflakes sent by Zeus or to wind-driven snow at 12.278ff., 156ff. Similes at 10.5–7 and 19.357f. juxtapose hail, snow and Zeus (cf. too 22.151f.). αἰθρηγενής is surely passive in sense, 'born in the clear sky', like most compounds in -γενής; it describes Boreas in the same verse at 19.358 (with ψυχραί), and is modified to αἰθρηγενέτης for metrical convenience at *Od.* 5.296.

173 Only here does the addressee's name and epithet follow ἀγχοῦ δ' ἱσταμένη (-ος) προσέφη (10× Hom.); this is because πόδας ὠκέα Ἶρις (4× in this speech-formula) would be clumsy after ὠ. ἾΛ. in 172, not because we need to be told who is addressed.

174–6 Iris tactfully greets Poseidon with honorific titles and calls her errand a message, not an order (so bT); cf. Hermes' tact at *Od.* 5.99ff. On κυανοχαῖτα cf. 13.562–3n. In 176 some ancient texts must have had κέλε-ταί σε for σ' ἐκέλευσε, since some good MSS read unmetrical σε κ.; like ἐκέλευε (in papyri and A), this aims at consistency with 180, where there is a variant ἄνωγε for -ει (see van der Valk, *Researches* II 167n.).

179–80 Iris makes explicit the threat Zeus hinted at in ἐπιόντα (164); since 164 transposed into the correct person would run μή (ϝ)' οὐδὲ κρατερόν περ ἐόντ' ἐπιόντα ταλάσσης, one can see why it is recomposed. καὶ κεῖνος stresses that he would come not voluntarily but as the result of provocation (so bT); Leaf detects a hyperbaton, 'he too threatened to come' standing for 'he threatened that he too would come'. In ἐναντίβιον π(τ)ολεμίξων (etc.), a fut. is found at 10.451, 20.85, a pres. at 21.477 (all with variants, as here!). Zenodotus (Did/AT) read -ίζων, Aristarchus -ίξων, which is more minatory, as it adds that Zeus will come with that intention. *Pace* the OCT, -ίζων is surely the *lectio difficilior*; van der Valk prefers it (*Researches* II 172), since the fut. is given by ἐλεύσεσθαι. The confusion goes back to early Ionic texts wherein Z resembled Ξ (cf. p. 36).

185–217 Since Poseidon refused to help Here at 8.200ff., but then intervened of his own accord, it would be odd if he yielded without protest; his claim that he has as much right as Zeus to affect events, and his threat to ensure Troy's fall (213ff.), dignify his exit.

185–93 Unable to deny that Zeus is the elder (cf. 165–7n.!), Poseidon cites their natural equality as brothers: Kronos' sons drew lots for the universe, leaving earth and Olumpos as common property. The division of a patrimony into shares agreed to be equal, which are then allocated by lot, is a system used in ancient and modern Greece (*Od.* 14.208f.; Stesichorus, '*Thebaid*' 220ff.; 'Apollodorus' 2.8.4; H. L. Levy, *TAPA* 87 (1956) 42–6; E. Friedl, *Vasilika*, New York 1962, 60–4). This cosmic division has a Babylonian antecedent (Burkert, *Die orientalisierende Epoche* 87): 'the gods had clasped hands together, had cast lots and had divided. Anu had gone up to heaven, [...] had given the earth to his subjects; [the bolt], the bar of the sea, [they had given] to Enki' (Lambert and Millard, *Atra-Ḥasīs* 43). Parallels in 'Apollodorus' (1.2.1) and the Orphica (frag. 56) prove that Homer drew this tale from an early *Titanomachy*, like other allusions in the deception of Zeus (14.153–353n.); in both texts the lottery at once follows the Titans' defeat, to which Zeus refers at 224f. Pindar adapts this idea when he says that Zeus and the gods divided the *earth* (*Ol.* 7.55). Hesiod surely knew the tale, but altered it because of his bias toward Zeus: he says *Zeus* allotted the gods their τιμαί after Kronos' overthrow (*Theog.* 73f., 881–5). 'Heraclitus' places the lottery at Sikuon (*Homeric Allegories* 41.5); Mekone, where Hesiod locates a no less important division, that of the first sacrifice by Prometheus, is an old name for Sikuon (West on *Theog.* 536)!

185–8 ὑπέροπλος, 'arrogant', recurs at 17.170 (in a similar speech-opening) and 4× Hes.; cf. Chantraine, *Dict.* s.v. ἀγαθός περ ἐών again presages disagreement at 1.131, 1.275, 19.155. The *hapax* ὁμότιμος is common in prose. Aristarchus had to insist on τ' ἐκ Κρόνου (Did/AT); a comical haplography τε Κ. (known in papyri) made Zeus Kronos' brother. Ῥέα, with synizesis and a notable ᾱ, is a recent but correct Ionic form (14.203n.): cf. τέκετο Ζεύς | (5× epos). τέκε Ῥείη, which we might have expected, lacks support. For the structure of 188 cf. 14.117; *Theog.* 850 expands its ending to ἐνέροισι καταφθιμένοισιν ἀνάσσων, cf. ἄναξ ἐνέρων Ἀϊδωνεύς (20.61, *HyDem* 357).

189–93 These vv. presuppose a flat earth and sea with Hades below and the sky above, not, as Crates held, a sphere with its S. pole in eternal night (i.e. Hades). The verses provoked much allegorizing. Critics thought 'all things have been divided' contradicts 'earth is common to all'. Hence Stesimbrotus (*FGH* 107 F 24), a fifth-century rhapsode and allegorist, read πάντ' ἃ δέδασται, 'all the things *which* have been divided', adducing the psilosis in ἐπίστιον (cf. p. 35). Crates (in A) adopted this sophism, worthy of the Derveni allegorist (identified as Stesimbrotus by Burkert, *ZPE* 62

(1986) 1–5); cf. Buffière, *Mythes* 134f. Aristarchus deemed πάντα redundant, as in 'nine in all' at 7.161 or 24.232 (cf. Porphyry 1.203.8). In fact Homer was careless with fractions and remainders, as in the notorious 'more than two-thirds of the night is past, and a third is left' (10.252f.); πάντα δέδασται (etc.) is a useful formula (6× Hom. at the verse-end), whose transposition caused a 'neglect' of ϝ- in ἕκαστος. The old perf. ἔμμορε, found in the formula ἔ. τιμῆς (etc.) at *Od.* 11.338 and 6× epos, preserves the Aeolic treatment of *-sm-(Chantraine, *GH* 1 174f.); contrast εἵμαρτο. In 192, as at 3.364, Zenodotus read οὐρανὸν αἰπύν for the formula ο. εὐρύν (45×). Aristarchus objected that α. better befits a mountain, and rightly inferred that Olumpos is attached to the earth – it would otherwise belong to Zeus alone. He was concerned to refute the view that Olumpos was in the sky (Lehrs, *De Aristarchi studiis* 164ff.; Schmidt, *Weltbild* 81–7, 101–5). Zenodotus surely altered the text to further this view, *pace* Nickau, *Zenodotos* 207n.

194 Literally 'so I shall not live by Zeus's wits', i.e. 'according to his will', an odd idiom (LSJ s.v. φρήν 4). βέομαι is a subj. from *$g^w eyH_3$-*, 'live': cf. βέη, 16.852, 24.131, and βείομαι, 22.431; Untermann, *Sprache* 145. Opposing Aristarchus, Demetrius Ixion (in D) derived it from βαίνω. βίόμεσθα at *HyAp* 528 is corrupt (Janko, *HHH* 123f.).

195–9 By saying that Zeus should stay in *his* third, Poseidon lays himself open to the retort that he should stay in his; so he adds that Zeus ought not to try to scare him (cf. 2.190), implying that he will meet his match if he does. He concludes, as had Zeus, with the topic of seniority; he is not to be bossed about like one of Zeus's children, who *must* obey him! This is not an insult to Iris, who is not Zeus's daughter (*Theog.* 266); but it fails to meet Zeus's point, which she at once raises, that he is the elder. In 197 θυγατέρεσσῖν γάρ combines a unique form with a recent use of n-mobile (p. 9 n. 6). Aristarchus and some MSS read βέλτερον, Aristophanes κάλλιον. The papyri, ancient vulgate (called οἱ εἰκαιότεροι in Did/A) and codices have κέρδιον, which is confirmed by the echo at 226 and is formular in this phrase (26× Hom.), unlike the scholars' emendations. Van der Valk (*Researches* 11 609) well suggests that they deemed κέρδιον 'unseemly when applied to the supreme god (it is too materialistic)'. So too learned editions, one of Aristarchus' included, altered κέρδιον to κάλλιον at 22.103, 22.108 (Did/AT). ἀνάγκη refers to blood-ties: cf. ἀναγκαῖοι, 'relatives'.

201–4 Iris is a perfect diplomat. Rather than advise Poseidon to agree, she asks 'Am I really to carry such a message?', reducing the issue to a matter of protocol; with 'Will you change your mind?' she appeals to his goodness, asking him to yield not as subject to king, but as younger brother to elder (cf. bT). For her apt elaboration on her message cf. how she extends Zeus's threat at 8.423f. (Erbse, *Götter* 54–6). Verses 201f. are a question; γάρ is usual in rhetorical questions casting doubt on the previous speaker's words (Denniston, *Particles* 77). φρένας is easily supplied with μεταστρέψεις (cf. 52); for the maxim see 13.115–17n. The Erinues punish breaches of respect in the family, here the violence of younger brother against elder; cf. on 9.454, 21.412.

206–8 On the structure of Poseidon's speech see 16.49–63n. He grants that Iris is right, praises her tact and excuses his anger on the ground of Zeus's tone. T say Zenodotus 'marked' 206, i.e. athetized it (for the expression cf. bT on 4.117). He perhaps found it redundant, especially given that he read εἴπη for εἰδῆ in 207 (Did/A), but we need to hear the god assent. From (μάλα) τοῦτο, 206 belongs to a system wherein κατὰ μοῖραν (2× *Od.*) can be replaced by νημερτές (3.204) or θυμαλγές (2× *Od.*) as needed. Verse 208 = 8.147, 16.52, *Od.* 18.274.

209–11 Poseidon reasserts that he is Zeus's equal, having received an equal lot. μόρος and αἶσα have their original sense 'portion' (Chantraine, *Dict.* s.vv. μείρομαι, αἶσα); neither alludes to fate or death, *pace* Porphyry 1.105.13. πεπρωμένον αἴση recurs at 16.441, 22.179, but with the developed sense of αἶσα; cf. θανάτου δέ οἱ α. πέπρωται (*Cypria* frag. 8 B. = 6 D.). The verb once meant 'allot': cf. ἔπορον, Latin *pars*, *portio*, Sanskrit *pūrtám*, 'gift'. (Ϝ)ἰσόμορος is a *hapax* in the epos for the vernacular -μοιρος, which does not scan; it is wrong to restore the Ϝ- by removing ἄν. — Verse 210 is based on a set pattern; cf. νεικείειν ∪∪ – ∪ ὀνειδείοις ἐπέεσσι (2.277); νεικείη χαλεποῖσι καθαπτόμενος ἑ. (*Erga* 332); νείκειον (etc.) ∪∪ – ∪ χολωτοῖσίν ἑ. (*Od.* 22.26, 225); νεικείεσκε χ. ἑ. (4.241). ὀνειδείοις and χολωτοῖσιν are used according to whether a consonant or vowel precedes. *Ϝέπεσσι can be restored after ὀνειδείοισι, but not after χολωτοῖσίν, where the use of Ionic n-mobile proves that the artificial Aeolism -έεσσι was so metrically useful that it continued to spread even during the Ionic phase (cf. p. 19 n. 35). Aristarchus (Did/A) wrongly altered κε to γε in 211 (Denniston, *Particles* 159). νεμεσσηθείς means 'though indignant', not 'from respect'; cf. νῦν μέν τοι ἐγὼν ὑποείξομαι αὐτὸς | χωόμενος (23.602f.).

212–17 Aristarchus called 212–17 'trite in style and thought', athetizing on three grounds: (i) it is illogical that Poseidon agrees to withdraw and then adds a threat; (ii) he knows that Zeus plans to ruin Troy in the end; (iii) someone interpolated the names of the pro-Greek gods from 20.33–6, to strengthen the opposition to Troy, but Hermes and Hephaistos have no stake in the outcome. To (i) bT reply that Poseidon adds a threat to offset his concession; his retreat is dignified because his anger is only postponed (and he never has occasion to feel it). Akhilleus follows up a concession with a threat at 1.297ff. As for (ii), only Thetis and now Here know that Zeus's plan involves temporary help for the Trojans as well as long-term willingness to see Troy fall. Poseidon is plausibly depicted as mistrustful about its future; his forecast at 14.143ff. is vague and aimed at a Greek audience. But his doubt matters less than the reminder to us of Troy's eventual fate (van der Valk, *Researches* II 426). Objection (iii) is a mere guess; Poseidon names as many gods as he can to stress his warning. The excision of 212–17 would also render νῦν μέν in 211 senseless.

For ἀγελείη see 4.128n. Ἑρμείω is a unique contraction of Ἑρμείαο, but cf. ἐϋμμελίω, Βορέω; Ἑρμέω (2× *Hy.*) represents a yet later stage (Hoekstra, *Modifications* 38, 40). AT's variant Ἡφαίστου τε καὶ Ἑρμείαο avoids this but splits the old phrase Ἡφαίστοιο ἄνακτος (2× Hom.), introducing contracted -ου. νῶϊν means 'between us two', i.e. Poseidon and Zeus: for νῶϊν of strife between two parties cf. 20.251, *Od.* 18.13, 366. For the metaphor in ἀνήκεστος cf. 5.394, 13.115n., *Theog.* 612, *Erga* 283.

218–19 The swift narration of Poseidon's exit conveys his chagrin, contrasting with his elaborate entry at 13.10ff. Its understated sequel – that the Greeks missed him – is rendered forceful and ominous by its lapidary concision: cf. the technique of κακοῦ δ' ἄρα οἱ πέλεν ἀρχή (11.604). A lesser poet would make Iris report to Zeus; the omission speeds the narrative up and implies that Zeus could follow events from the peak of Ida, an implication more impressive than a direct statement would have been. For the formulae λαὸν Ἀχαιικόν and ἥρωες Ἀχαιοί see on 13.345–60, 628–30; the repetition stresses the Greeks' loss.

220–35 Zeus, as a mature *paterfamilias*, is glad to have avoided open conflict with his brother, but leaves no doubt of the resolve with which he would have acted if necessary. He did not send Apollo, since this would have made a younger god confront an older one – exactly what Zeus dissuaded Poseidon from doing (bT); Apollo is the best god to send to Hektor, being pro-Trojan and a healer. So too Zeus sends Apollo to rescue Sarpedon's body; there are verbal parallels (with 220f., 236f., cf. 16.666f., 676f.).

223 The formula (εἰς) ἅλα δῖαν is displaced from the verse-end (11× Hom.) by the adapted phrase ἀλευάμενος χόλον αἰπύν: cf. μῆνιν ἀλευάμενος (2×), χόλος αἰνός | (22.94, cf. *HyDem* 354). αἰπύς must mean 'dangerous', like χαλεπός; it is found with other nouns of this shape (δόλος, πόνος, φόνος). For the metaphor see 13.769–73n.; it is surely evoked by the god's 'sheer' descent.

224–5 The 'lower gods' are the Titans (cf. 14.274, 279, *Theog.* 851). Does Zeus say that they *would have heard* (κε ... ἐπύθοντο), if he had fought Poseidon, or that they *have experienced* (τε ... ἐ.) battle with him (and lost!)? Editors prefer κε, with most MSS; but the sole scholium (D) and most early codices read τε, rightly (Ruijgh, τε *épique* 740). Although the din of theomachies reaches even the underworld (cf. 20.61ff., *Theog.* 681ff., 850ff.), reading κε makes 228 redundant and anticlimactic. A reference to the Titans' defeat is apt, and continues the allusions to their revolt and other dangers to his rule (185–93n.); in one version the aegis, mentioned at 229, is the weapon he used to defeat them (308–11n.). As at 5.898, Zenodotus altered (ἐ)νέρτερος to a superlative, no doubt thinking that a comparative implies that other gods are lower yet. Aristarchus refutes this (cf. 14.278–9n.): -τερος is simply contrastive (14.267–70n.). The form νέρτερος, unique in the epos but read by both scholars, has good MS support (cf. Chantraine, *Dict.* s.v. ἔνερθε).

228–30 That ὑπόειξε governs an acc. is unique, but 228 is needed to say that the struggle would have been fierce. ἀνιδρωτί, a euphemism for 'bloodless', is next in fourth-century prose. For the 'tasselled' aegis see 308–11n. τῇ goes with φοβέειν, i.e. 'rout the Greeks with it by shaking (it)': cf. 4.167.

231–5 Following Aristophanes (Did/A), Aristarchus athetized 231–5, deeming it untimely and unwelcome to Apollo for Zeus to hint that Hektor may only repel the Greeks as far as the ships; but Zeus reveals only that he will ponder what to do from then on (with κεῖθεν cf. ἐκ τοῦ at 69). Zeus seems to be addressing us as much as Apollo, to remind us that the attack on the ships (whose ships?) will mark a major turning-point, and that the Greeks will gain a respite (so Wilamowitz, *IuH* 233f.). The poet avoids repeating Zeus's full prediction (Eustathius 1014.11).

231–2 ἑκατηβόλος is used without Apollo's name (found with it 15× epos) because it is placed between two other formulae: cf. *Hy.* 9.6, where Artemis is meant, and the usage of ἕκατος (1.385, 20.71, 4× *Hy.*) or ἑκηβόλος (3× *Il.*, 5× *Hy.*). All three epithets are metrical adaptations of *ἑκᾰβόλος, 'he who shoots at will', which bards reinterpreted by association with ἑκάς as 'he who shoots from afar' (5.53–4n.). Aristarchus (Did/A), with a papyrus and a good codex, read τόφρ' for ὄφρ'; this removes a hiatus at the price of a post-Homeric usage, since τόφρα can only mean 'then', not 'while' (cf. 277–8n. and van der Valk, *Researches* II 188). τόθι is first used for ὅθι by Mimnermus frag. 11a.1, Stesichorus frag. S 8.3 and *Hy.* 19.25, τόθεν for ὅθεν by Aeschylus, and τόφρα for ὄφρα by Antimachus (frag. 3.2).

233–5 233 = 18.150 (with ἵκοντο), cf. 23.2, 24.346. The camp is imagined as facing S. towards Troy, with the sea at the rear (13.675n.). But the name 'Hellespont' proves nothing about its site: Helle was ancestor of various Macedonian tribes (16.234–5n.), and her sea was at first the N. Aegean and perhaps Propontis (cf. Hdt. 6.33 and Strabo 7 frag. 57 Jones). With ἀναπνεύσωσι πόνοιο (cf. 19.227), 'have respite from battle', cf. ἀνάπνευσις πολέμοιο (11.801 = 16.43); πόνος means 'battle' not 'pain', *pace* T.

236–43 A divine journey marked with a simile opens this scene, like the two preceding (78–9n.): the same type-scene has shared formulae at 11.195ff., when Iris obeys, flies down, finds Hektor and gives her message. Instead of οὐδ' ἄρα πατρὸς ἀνηκούστησεν Ἀπόλλων, Homer could have said οὐδ' ἀπίθησεν ἄναξ Διὸς υἱὸς Ἀ., on the model of the previous scenes; his choice seems to stress filial obedience but may simply be the standard phrase for Apollo, since 236f. (to ὀρέων) = 16.676f., when he rescues Sarpe-don's body. ἀνηκουστέω is more recent than νη- (2ϱ.14 only); νη- is from *ῃ-, 'not', contracted with the *a*-coloured laryngeal seen in ἀκούω, with ἀ-privative added to ensure that the word was felt as a negative, just as ἀνωφελής replaced Myc. /nōphelēs/(Beekes, *Laryngeals* 98ff.). Earlier poets perhaps said *ἐνηκούστησε.

237–8 Apollo is probably 'like a hawk' because of his speed, not because he takes avian shape; yet he does turn into a vulture at 7.59f. The descents of Thetis and Athene are similarly described (18.616, 19.350); cf. Poseidon's departure (13.62–5n.), but also Patroklos' charge ἴρηκι ἐοικὼς | ὠκέϊ (16.582f.). The simile is apt: Apollo will bring the Greeks the death a hawk brings fleeing pigeons or doves (bT). φασσοφόνος, a *hapax* in Homer, was later the name of a type of hawk (Thompson, *Birds* 300–2); J. M. Boraston thinks of a falcon killing rock-doves (*JHS* 31 (1911) 226f.). Cf. the similes where a dove is chased by a raptor, likewise called ἐλαφρότατος πετεηνῶν (22.139f.), or an eagle is called κάρτιστός τε καὶ ὤκιστος π. (21.253, cf. 24.293). Homer is free with such superlatives (13.365–7n.). πετεηνός is a poetic lengthened form of πετεινός (Risch, *Wortbildung* 100).

240–1 Hektor, no longer supine as at 9, is sitting up and recognizes his comrades; his symptoms of internal injury, seen at 10f. and 14.436f., are abating (in reality this would take weeks!). Here and at 21.417 ἐσαγείρατο θυμόν, 'he had regained consciousness', is superior to the imperf. read by Aristarchus but few good MSS: he must awaken before he can sit up (as often, the aor. has pluperf. force). Cf. ἐς φρένα θυμὸς ἀγέρθη (22.475, 2× *Od.*), θυμηγερέων (*Od.* 7.283). νέον means 'just (now)', as at 13.211, 24.475 etc. Chrysippus (in T) read ἀμφιγινώσκων, supposedly 'be in doubt': Aristarchus tacitly refutes him. For further cases of Chrysippus' mishandling of Homer see *SVF* iii 769ff.; Crates' methods largely continue his.

242–3 Zeus aids Hektor from afar, in tandem with Apollo; cf. how he snaps Teukros' bowstring or rouses (ἔγειρε) Hektor (461ff., 594f., 603f.). The Greek defeat is owed ultimately to Zeus, as references to him at these key moments remind us. Such divine telekinesis is less rare than Leaf thought: cf. 13.434–6n., *Od.* 24.164. It is an impressive sign of Zeus's power that Apollo finds Hektor already recovering (Eustathius 1014.35ff.). Homer surely used ἑκάεργος instead of Διὸς υἱός because Δ. preceded (cf. 252–3n.). Bards could avoid repetition: cf. on 16.297ff.

244–6 Apollo's question, to which he already knows the reply, is like Thetis' to Akhilleus at 1.362ff. (cf. 16.7–19n.). The scansion Ἕκτορ υἱὲ Πριάμοιο (also at 7.47, 11.200) is not rare (16.21n.); it adapts | – υἱὸς Π. etc. (cf. 239, 5.463f., 21.34 etc.). Democritus' reading κεῖσ' ἀλλοφρονέων (frag. 68 a 101) is a misquotation based on 23.698 (van der Valk, *Researches* ii 338f.); for ὀλιγηπελέων see 23–5n. Verse 246 = 22.337 (where see n.), cf.

16.843 (of Patroklos); with ὀλιγοδρανέων cf. δραίνω, 'be strong', at 10.96 (Chantraine, *Dict.* s.v. δράω).

247–51 Hektor alone sees the god: cf. 1.198, 24.169ff. It is an epic convention to ignore bystanders (Fenik, *TBS* 75). He is awake enough to express surprise that he still lives, and that the deity does not know what befell him. He easily recognizes a god's presence, but gods are easy to detect when they so choose (13.70–2n.); his lack of awe is typical of epic heroes, who often meet gods (Hoekstra on *Od.* 16.184f.). Parallels at 6.123 and 24.387 show that τίς δὲ σύ ἐσσι, φέριστε, θεῶν is the right punctuation; φ. is always a respectful voc. in the epos, save at 9.110. βοὴν ἀγαθός is again used with Aias, instead of with names shaped ∪∪–∪, at 17.102 (13.124–5n.). ἔπαυσε δὲ θούριδος ἀλκῆς denotes a warrior's death at 17.81; it leads naturally to Hektor's statement that he expected to die when he passed out (for ἐφάμην, 'I thought', cf. 13.83–90n.). δῶμ' Ἀΐδαο (also at *Od.* 12.21) is a useful variant of Ἀ. δόμους etc. (14× Hom.): cf. νέκυας καὶ ἀτερπέα χῶρον (*Od.* 11.94).

252–3 Aristarchus, followed by the OCT, read ἵξεσθαι (Did/A); cf. the variant at *Od.* 17.448. But ὄψεσθαι accords better with the stress on sight here (γινώσκων, ἄντην); when we faint, we are aware above all of our failing vision. Hektor, expecting to see Hades, beholds instead the unfamiliar figure of Apollo. D and Eustathius (1014.55–60) rightly take ἄϊον ἦτορ as 'I breathed out my soul'. Aristarchus equates ἄ. with ἀΐω, 'perceive' (248), comparing πληγῆς ἀΐοντες (11.532); though identical in origin (Onians, *Origins* 74f.), it must mean 'breathe' here. Cf. ψυχὴν ἐκάπυσσε (22.467), θυμὸν ἀποπνείων (4.524, 13.654, cf. *HyAp* 361f., Tyrtaeus frag. 10.24), and especially θ. ἄϊσθε (16.468, 20.403) with the aor. of the same verb, cognate with ἄημι, 'blow' (Pokorny, *IEW* 83), as is Hektor's 'panting' (ἄσθμα). θυμός (Latin *fumus*) at first meant 'breath' or 'smoke', like ψυχή or 'spirit' (Bremmer, *Soul* 56). For its alternation with ἦτορ cf. 320–2n., p. 3 n. 6 and θυμὸν/ἦ. ἀπηύρα; for the separated formula cf. φίλον ὤλεσε θ. (2×). ἄναξ ἑκάεργος Ἀπόλλων (also at 21.461) may be chosen instead of ἄ. Διὸς υἱός Ἀ. (7.23, 7.37, 16.804, 20.503) because ἑ. Ἀ. preceded (242–3n.). Yet ἄ. Δ. υἱ. Ἀ. follows 'Zeus' at 16.804, and precedes Δ. υἱέ at *Od.* 8.334f. (cf. 14.190–3n.). The doublets arose by analogy after *ϝεκάϝεργος lost its ϝ-.

254–61 Reassurances from divine visitors are a topos (24.171–4, *Od.* 4.825–8, *HyAphr* 193–5, *Hy.* 7.55, Luke 2.10), but Apollo gives Hektor good reason for courage; not only is he here to help him, but he has come at Zeus's bidding. Hektor's trust in these gods deepens his tragedy (Reinhardt, *IuD* 301). Now, in contrast with the Trojans' decision at 12.80ff., Apollo bids Hektor lead them against the ships in their chariots (where they rallied at 3 above); he promises to smooth the way, i.e. to level the ditch which had dictated their foot-slogging tactics. Zeus did not mention this, but a chariot-attack suits his order that Apollo make the Greeks flee. This makes the battle both more dramatic and more equal, since the Trojans are now a better match for the Achaeans in terms of height (so bT): they can fight from their chariots, the Greeks from the ships (386f.). Apollo does not of course relay Zeus's promise to give the Achaeans a respite (235).

254–9 ἀοσσητήρ is an old agent-noun from ἀοσσεῖν, 'help', first found in Moschus: its root *(sm̥-)sokʷ-, 'ally (together)', is seen in ὀπάων, Latin *socius* (Chantraine, *Dict.* s.v.). The second half of 255 recurs, transposed, in a like context at 21.231. Ἀπόλλωνα χρυσάορον, 'with golden sword', adapts Ἀ. χρυσάορα (*Erga* 771, *HyAp* 123); χρυσάωρ passes for metrical convenience to the o-stem declension, with a gen. in -ου (5.509, *HyAp* 395, *Hy.* 27.3) – a common shift (14.157–8n.). This odd epithet later describes Demeter (*HyDem* 4) and Artemis (in Hdt. 8.77). Wyatt takes it as 'with golden mist' (*ML* 97ff.); since Pindar uses it of Orpheus (frag. 128c.12), it is clear that, like D and bT, he already took it as 'with golden (lyre-)strap' (ἀορτήρ). The *Phoronis* (frag. 6 B. = 5 D.) called Athene δολιχάορος, which is equally odd because she uses a spear; so we learn in *P.Oxy.* 2260, surely from Apollodorus' Περὶ θεῶν (cf. 'Heraclitus', *Homeric Questions* 7.12f., with Buffière's n.). Lorimer thinks Apollo bore the epithet because his Anatolian ancestor used a sword (in *Greek Poetry and Life: Essays presented to Gilbert Murray*, Oxford 1936, 25–8); but, to the extent that he had an oriental antecedent, it was the Semitic plague-god and archer Rešef (Burkert, *Religion* 145). — The phrase αἰπεινὸν πτολίεθρον is unique beside πόλιν/Ἴλιον αἰπεινήν (etc., 6×), but has no metrical equivalent (cf. ἐΰ ναιόμενον/ἐϋκτίμενον π.). ἐποτρύνω usually takes an acc., but a dat. is used at *Od.* 10.531, *Erga* 597, and perhaps at 16.525 and in ἑτάροισιν ἐποτρύνας ἐκέλευσε (etc., 6× *Od.*). πολέεσσι is odd; does it replace πάντεσσι, to avoid an ugly cadence? Verse 259 blends νηυσὶν ἔπι γλαφυρῇσιν ἐλαυνέμεν (3×) with ἐλαύνομεν ὠκέας ἵππους (12.62, cf. 5.275), cf. ἐλαύνετε μώνυχας ἵ. (11.289, cf. 23.536).

262–404 Hektor rejoins battle, to the Greeks' alarm. On Thoas' advice, they send back the rank and file, keeping the best warriors to slow the Trojan advance. The line holds until Apollo routs them. While the Trojans strip the fallen, the Greeks pass within the rampart. The god ruins the ditch and rampart behind it; Hektor leads his men against the ships, where fierce fighting erupts. Hearing the din, Patroklos runs from Eurupulos' hut to urge Akhilleus into battle

262–404 Homer needs to restore the situation to where it was before the Greeks, inspired by Poseidon and with Hektor removed, drove the Trojans from the ships. He uses divine intervention to help the Trojans return rapidly, and with a vengeance: Apollo arranges that they bring their chariots. His choice of the brisk narrative style seen at the end of book 14 avoids a tedious repetition of their slow retreat. The battle has four stages, each shorter than the preceding, articulated by brief *speeches* of increasing importance:

262–80   Hektor returns to battle, to the Greeks' alarm
281–99   Thoas' tactical proposal
300–45   *Stadiē* in the plain, leading to a Greek rout
346–51   Hektor's exhortation
352–66   Apollo leads the Trojans through the ditch and rampart
367–89   Nestor's prayer to Zeus
379–89   The Trojans reach the ships
390–404   Patroklos' speech to Eurupulos and departure to Akhilleus

Winter (*MNO* 137) saw that the battle in the plain and rout to the rampart correspond to book 11 (also recalled by the reappearance of Nestor and then Patroklos); the easy slighting of the fortifications corresponds to their arduous penetration in book 12; and the fighting at the ships corresponds to the battles before the ships in book 13. When Patroklos sees the Trojans pouring over the rampart at 395f., the din he hears hardly differs from that heard by us at 12.471 and by Nestor at 14.1–15, since it has the same cause – the rampart is breached. Nestor needed the whole of book 13 to notice this; Patroklos takes even longer! As I argued (14.1–152n.), Homer in fact presents simultaneous scenes while preserving the impression of a sequential narrative, using the repeated motif of the din of battle to move from scene to scene. If Patroklos hears at 396 the same shout that was raised at 12.471 (so Whitman and Scodel, *HSCP* 85 (1981) 8f.), he is with Eurupulos for only 470 verses; the intervening events of books 13–15 vanish, at the risk of discrepancies over chronology and the state of the rampart (see pp. 226–7). Thus Homer has deftly constructed a narrative wherein a whole Greek rally takes place while he freezes the main action (Patroklos and Akhilleus); once the rally is over, he recapitulates the breach of the rampart to lead us back to that same point, yet lets us think that the story is advancing! For Odyssean parallels see Hoekstra on *Od.* 15.1–3.

This scene resembles others where the Greeks are routed (Fenik, *TBS* 185, 223f.). At 8.130ff. Zeus drives them back with thunderbolts; Herē asks Poseidon to help them, but he refuses on the ground that Zeus is far stronger (208ff.); this has its counterpart in Poseidon's withdrawal above. The Greeks flee to the ships, but Agamemnon prays to Zeus and is heard, just as is Nestor here (376 = 8.244; with 380 cf. 8.252). Teukros' exploits at 8.309ff. are also paralleled (445–65n.), and 367–9 = 8.345–7. At 17.593ff. Zeus terrifies the Greeks by shaking the aegis and thundering (cf. Apollo shaking the aegis and yelling at 321); they flee to the ships, but Aias prays to Zeus, who hears his prayer just as he hears Nestor's at 377f. Antilokhos takes a message to Akhilleus (17.651ff.), and the ensuing fighting allows time for his errand; he arrives at 18.2. Cf. Patroklos' mission to Akhilleus, which begins at 405 and ends at 16.2; this framework admits, of course, the elaboration of other patterns in the intervening battle. Schoeck (*Ilias und Aithiopis* 51) notes that 355–98 correspond to 645–16.125: after a Trojan attack, Nestor beseeches Zeus or the men (372ff., 661ff.), a god reacts, Aias fights at the ships and Patroklos appears, first with Eurupulos and then with Akhilleus; Patroklos first, and then Akhilleus, slap their thighs in anguish at what they see.

262 = 20.110, cf. 10.482, *Od.* 24.520; Apollo breathes into Hektor the vital strength he had almost entirely breathed out. Cf. the god's restoration of Aineias to battle or his healing of Glaukos (5.512ff., 16.527ff.). For ποιμένι λαῶν replacing a name see on 13.598ff.

263–8 = 6.506–11, where see n. Homer repeats eight major similes, all but one in the *Iliad* (Scott, *Simile* 127–40; Nickau, *Zenodotos* 106n.). Given that there are some 180 similes, repetition is rare, and this image is no less apt than in book 6. Similes often open battle-scenes; this one belongs to a pair of images marking Hektor's return to battle and the Greeks' panic thereat. Moulton (*Similes* 35) compares 16.351–67, a like turning-point, where the first image depicts the Myrmidons' attack, the second the Trojan rout. Equine similes are typical at such junctures: 22.22f. liken Akhilleus to a prize-winning horse, just after he is undeceived by Apollo, and 269 resembles 22.24 (Krischer, *Konventionen* 41–3). This image advances the narrative, since it lets the poet relate Hektor's return swiftly, and puts the spotlight on him alone; this makes the Greeks' defeat less shameful than a general Trojan victory would have been (van der Valk, *Researches* II 462f.).

Aristarchus athetized 265–8, thinking them better suited to Paris' foppish arrival from Helen's boudoir than to Hektor's resurrection from a coma. But Hektor may well exult, since he is aided by two gods (so T). Zenodotus left out 266–8 (Did/T). The view that he omitted 265, and 265 alone, rests on a false emendation: see Nickau, *Zenodotos* 118ff., who deems 266–8 interpolated from 6.509–11. However, as he admits (*op. cit.* 106), of the six similes Zenodotus shortened, all but 17.134–6 are repetitions. Van der Valk thinks he kept 265 because Hektor, like the horse, was just by a river (14.433). Hektor becomes as swift as the charioteers to whose company he runs like a stallion galloping to join its peers. Fränkel (*Gleichnisse* 77) thinks the steed's release from restraint is more apt here, although otherwise book 6 is the better context. At this instant Paris and Hektor are alike, but the larger situation underscores their difference (Bowra, *Tradition and Design* 92). Repetition inheres in the oral style; if we lacked book 6, nobody would criticize this simile. Neither context is 'original'.

269–70 With λαιψηρά ... ἐνώμα cf. 22.24; turning λ. into an adv. like κραιπνά, it neatly expands λ. δὲ γούνατ' ἑ. (2×), cf. λ. τε γοῦνα | (2×). A pedant in T read the fut. ὀτρυνέων, because, strictly speaking, Hektor must return to his men before he can exhort them. bT take ἐπεὶ θεοῦ ἔκλυεν αὐδήν as 'when he heard that it was the voice of a god', to explain Hektor's zest; but a parallel at *Od.* 2.297, when Athene has hidden her identity, shows that it means 'when he heard what the god said'.

271–6 This vigorous simile, forming a pair with the preceding, is itself resumed by 323–5: here Hektor is like a lion who scares hunters from their prey, but there he and Apollo resemble *two* beasts attacking cattle when the herdsman is away. This shift reflects the Greeks' increasing weakness (Moulton, *Similes* 69f.). The simile itself contains a progression which foreshadows events and is explicit in the *so-Satz* (277–80): the hunters chasing their quarry are like the Greeks routing the Trojans, and the lion who makes them turn is Hektor. Moulton (*Similes* 46n.) compares 11.474–81, where jackals devour a wounded stag until a lion scares them off; thus the Trojans beset the injured Odysseus until Aias frightens them off. Cf. too 3.23–6, where Menelaos sees Paris with the joy of a lion finding a dead stag or goat, even if dogs and men chase him off (272 = 3.24, almost); this prefigures Menelaos' ultimate failure. A lion driven hungry from a farm mirrors Aias' persistence and then reluctant retreat (11.548–55: 272 = 11.549).

Many details are typical. Wild goat and deer are paired at *Aspis* 407; a 'horned' deer should be male, but poets neglected this detail (cf. Slater on Aristophanes frag. 378). That the goat inhabits the rocks and the stag the forest may be supported by 13.102 (so AT). ἔλαφον κεραόν is standard in similes (3×), like κύνες τε καὶ ἀνέρες (cf. 17.65, 17.110). ἄγριον αἶγα is paralleled at 4.105f. (a digression), *Od.* 14.50. ἀγροιῶται are rustics, not specifically hunters (cf. *Od.* 16.217f.). ἠλίβατος describes πέτρη (10× epos) and lofty caves or trees (*Theog.* 483, *HyAphr* 267, *Aspis* 422): cf. αἰγίλιψ, another equally obscure epithet of πέτρη. δάσκιος, unique in the *Iliad*, occurs with ὕλη at *Od.* 5.470, 2× *Hy.*; it is a haplology for *δασύσκιος (cf. O. Szemerényi, *Glotta* 33 (1954) 260ff.). With 274 cf. 21.495, in a simile of a dove escaping a hawk by flying into some rocks; the imperf. with ἄρα conveys the predator's disappointment, a nice touch of subjective narrative. λὶς ἠϋγένειος recurs at 17.109, 18.318 (similes); the epithet surely denotes the long hairs ('feelers') round a lion's muzzle. S. West on *Od.* 4.456 thinks it is based on ἠϋκομος and means 'with fine mane'. Whiskers are a less obvious feature of a lion; but γένειον denotes facial hair, ἠϋγένειος describes whiskery Pan at *Hy.* 19.39 and εὐγένειος is so used in prose. It cannot be a form of εὐγενής: the lengthened grade ἠϋ- seems ancient (Beekes, *Laryngeals* 287ff.), cf. ἠϋζωνος (*Little Iliad* frag. 21.6 B. = 20.6 D.), -γενής (*HyAphr* 94), -θέμεθλος (*Hy.* 30.1). Did it once mean 'strong-jawed', from γένυς, 'jaw'? For ὁδός, 'way' not 'road', cf. *Od.* 10.158.

272 Aristarchus and ἅπασαι read ἐσσεύαντο (Did/A), with a good MS; at 11.549 he too read the vulgate -οντο. Van der Valk thinks he took it as an imperf. there but required an aor. here (*Researches* II 172). ἐσσευάμην is acceptable beside ἐσσύμην, cf. σεύατο (6.505), yet an imperf. seems better both times, i.e. 'they kept chasing'. Leaf (on 11.549) deems an imperf. impossible in a simile; it is surely easier when aorists follow, as here (if not at 11.549). He thinks all the thematic forms, ἐσσεύοντο included, are aorists, but cf. Chantraine, *GH* I 385, and K. Strunk, *Nasalpräsentien und Aoriste*, Heidelberg 1967, 91.

277–8 = 17.730f., with Τρῶες for Δαναοί; for 278 see 13.146–8n. Zenodotus (in T), no doubt to remove hiatus, read τείως, but εἵως can mean 'for a time' (e.g. 12.141, 13.143). Cf. his equally false τώς for ὡς at 12.75, Aristarchus' τόφρα for ὄφρα (231–2n.) and Aristophanes' τοτέ for ὀτέ at 17.178.

279–80 Does Hektor 'range' his own ranks or 'assail' the foe's? Both senses of ἐποίχομαι are known (16.155, 24.759 etc.). The former is better, since the attack only begins at 312ff. That the Greeks' θυμός sinks to their feet again shows the interchangeability of 'heart' and 'spirit' in Homer (252–3n.); cf. 10.94, 22.452, when hearts leap from the chest in fear, in one case into the mouth. Here there is an obvious allusion to running away (Leaf). For πᾶσιν δέ see p. 9 n. 6. The metrically useful form παραί was once a loc.: παρά was the acc. and πάρος the gen. of the same noun (Untermann, *Sprache* 108).

281–99 Thoas' proposal that the best warriors screen the others' retreat correctly anticipates a crushing Trojan attack. Hektor's fearsome resurrection is seen only from the Greek viewpoint (Winter, *MNO* 136ff.); Thoas expresses their collective shock (so the Leipzig scholia on 286). The first half of his speech corresponds to their dawning understanding: seeing Hektor, they infer the work first of a god, then of Zeus. Fenik (*TBS* 63f.) compares 5.590ff., when Hektor advances and Diomedes, identifying Ares as his helper, orders a retreat.

Rejecting 263–305, Leaf finds Thoas' proposal futile and untimely, 'when it would seem that every nerve should be strained to defend the wall'; how can some have retreated, when the Greeks resist ἀολλέες, are called a λαός and are likened to a herd (312–23)? But this 'inconsistency' is minor; Homer draws on standard language for the start of battle, and the best warriors are no doubt still numerous. Nor is the proposal inept; if the rampart is no longer defensible, the ships are the sole rallying-point left. Inferior troops might be too prone to panic in this crisis; an orderly retreat is better, especially with the ditch in the way (so bT on 295). The poet deftly returns the Greeks to the ships without a shameful, uncontested rout; his compromise also avoids a direct repetition of the events of the previous books. The *aristoi* save the whole army from ruin; we admire the courage of those who risk their lives to protect the rest (so Winter). Cf. Hektor's holding action at 16.362f., or how Diomedes and Odysseus screen the Greeks' escape at 11.310ff.

281-5 Thoas is a respected older figure below the first rank (cf. 19.239); Poseidon took his form to exhort Idomeneus (13.216–18n.). He does not reappear in this battle; we saw his prowess with the javelin at 4.527. Since the counsellors Nestor and Odysseus are not fighting, he is an apt substitute. The laudatory introduction merely shows that his advice will be good; cf. those at 1.68–73 (Kalkhas), 1.247–53, 9.93–5 (Nestor), 18.249–53 (Pouludamas), *Od.* 2.157–60, 2.224–8, 7.155–8, 16.394–9, 24.51–3, 24.451–3, all of which end ὅ σφιν ἐὺ φρονέων ἀγορήσατο ... (see de Jong, *Narrators* 199). The device was first designed for minor characters who have not yet appeared.

The 'best of the Aetolians' already died at 5.842f., in the person of one Periphas; liberality with superlatives is typical of heroic epic (13.365–7n.). The ascending tricolon of criteria for Thoas' excellence – javelin, *stadiē* and assembly – blends traditional contrasts between various kinds of fighting and between fighting and speaking. Thus Teukros, best with the bow, is good in the *stadiē* (13.312–14n.); Hektor knows how to fight with chariots and in the *stadiē* (7.240f.); others are 'good in assembly and at war' (*Cat.* 25.37) or 'worse at war, better in assembly' (4.400, cf. 18.106). ἐπιστάμενος takes either a dat. or a gen. (*Od.* 21.406). Verses 283f. refer to vying to make the best proposal; the Greeks always loved to compete. Thus the court-fee goes to the elder who judges best (18.508), and Nestor is told ἀγορῇ νικᾷς, γέρον, υἷας Ἀχαιῶν (2.370). Verse 284 exists to fit in the run-over verb νίκων; κοῦροι used alone is a clumsy improvisation, since it wrongly conveys that the middle-aged Thoas competes with youths. It is short for κ. Ἀχαιῶν (cf. T); the poet avoided this because of παῦροι Ἀ. in 283, but clearly had it in mind, on the pattern of 2.370.

286-93 The fact that Hektor is on his feet frames the first half of Thoas' speech, before ἀλλ' (294) opens a call to action, just as μενοινῶν ... μεμαῶτα rings its second half. Verse 286 = 13.99 etc., where see n. δ' αὖτ' ἐξαῦτις is emphatic, 'yet again' (cf. 14.364–6n.): Diomedes complains that Apollo saved Hektor likewise (11.363, where ironic ἦ θήν follows), and the god affirms that such is his practice (256f. above). In a monumental epic, Hektor must not be killed off too easily! Verse 288 blends μάλα δέ σφισιν ἔλπετο θυμός | (3×) with μένος καὶ θυμὸν ἑκάστου (11× Hom.), which is itself recent, as the neglected ϝ- and contracted gen. in -ου prove; cf. 701, ἔ. θυμὸς ἐνὶ στήθεσσιν ἑ. The hiatus in ἐρρύσατο καὶ ἐσάωσεν (290), also in ἐρύσατο κ. ἑ. (*Od.* 22.372), is avoided in ἐρύσσεται ἠδὲ σαώσει (10.44), ἐρύσατο καί μ' ἐλέησε (*Od.* 14.279). Ζηνὸς ἐρίγδουπου, with integral enjambment, innovative Ζην- and contracted -ου, derives from (Ζεὺς ...) ἐρίγδουπος πόσις Ἥρης

(7× Hom.); cf. Ζηνὸς ἐριγδούποιο (*Theog.* 41, *Hy.* 12.3),Διὸς υἱὸν ἑ. (5.672), Z. μὲν ἑ. (12.235). As we can expect of a recent creation, two equally new equivalent phrases appear elsewhere, Z. ἐριβρεμέτῳ (13.624) and Z. ἐρισθενέος (*Erga* 416). πρόμος ἵσταται means 'stands forth as champion' (πρόμαχος), cf. 7.136, 22.85; for the form cf. Τήλεμος short for Τηλέμαχος. μενοινάω normally takes an infin., but cf. *Homeric Epigram* 11.4.

294–7 Verse 294 = 14.370 (9× Hom.), just as 300 = 14.378 (14× Hom.). Surprisingly, these verses are not paired elsewhere: note that 296 is parallel to 14.371. Thoas' proposal here is as odd as was Poseidon's there. For the division πληθύς/ἄριστοι cf. 2.488f., 11.304f. ἀνώξομεν, ἐρύξομεν and στείομεν (see pp. 35–6) are aor. subj.; cf. ἀνῷξαι (*Od.* 10.531) and the fut. at *Od.* 16.404, with Risch, *Wortbildung* 345. Verse 297 means 'in case we can hold him off at first' (πρῶτον), not 'hold off him first', *pace* T. The adv. proves that a rearguard holding action is proposed.

301–5 The leaders of this action were prominent in the recent fighting, especially Aias. He, Teukros and Meges play a large part in the sequel, but the Cretans vanish until 16.342ff. Meriones and Meges are with Thoas at 19.239. Zenodotus and Aristophanes (Did/A) read Αἴαντε, but have weak MS support. Düntzer (*De Zenodoti studiis* 89f.) holds that Oïlean Aias was prominent too; but so was Menelaos, who is omitted. Cf. Αἴαντα καὶ Ἰδομενῆα (ἄνακτα) at 10.53, 10.112. Zenodotus made the same change at 12.342f. (see further p. 24 n. 23). ὑσμίνην ἤρτυνον means that they built a firm front line, cf. ἀρτύνθη δὲ μάχη (11.216), σφέας αὐτοὺς ἀρτύναντες (13.149–54n.). This holds fast until 326ff., when they are routed and 'the battle is scattered'. πληθύς also takes an article and plur. verb at 2.278 (ὣς φάσαν ἡ π.). ἐπὶ νῆας Ἀχαιῶν, usually at the verse-end (18×), is also displaced at 1.371,14.354, 24.203, 24.519.

306–7 The massed Trojan advance faces the massed Greeks, just as 306 is balanced by 312, with which cf. 5.498; 306 = 13.136, 17.262. For the formula μακρὰ βιβάς, from *βίβᾱμι, see 13.809n. As at 686 a few MSS, *h* and papyri included, have the more recent βιβῶν from βιβάω. The epos prefers nom. masc. βιβάς (7× Hom., *Aspis* 323, 2× *HyAp*), but other forms in -ω- (5× Hom.), save for βιβάντα (13.371) and προβιβῶν (*HyHerm.* 149); for some reason bards avoided the innovative forms in the nom. sing. masc. Aristarchus read -άς at 7.213, but -ῶν here with πᾶσαι (Did/A); van der Valk emends Did/A to make him consistent (*Researches* II 136n.). Zenodotus ineptly conjectured βοῶν, since Apollo 'himself shouts' at 321 (Did/AT); this is based on 2.224 (Düntzer, *op. cit.* 131f.).

308–11 Apollo alarms the foe with an appearance like Akhilleus' at 18.203ff., where Athene puts the aegis on his shoulders and a golden halo round his head; both gods then give a shout. The cloud about Apollo's shoulders suggests invisibility: this is certain at 5.186, νεφέλη εἰλυμένος ὤμους.

Yet elsewhere this is specified as a 'dark' cloud (17.551, *HyHerm* 217); at 20.150 the gods don an impenetrable force-field, ἄρρηκτον νεφέλην ὠμοῖσιν ἕσαντο.

The purpose of the aegis is equally nebulous. Fenik (*TBS* 78) likens its fearsome effect to that of Eris' πολέμοιο τέρας or Poseidon's sword (11.4, 14.385); Griffin (*HLD* 31) compares Athene's aegis at *Od.* 22.297f. I suggested above (18–31n.) that the aegis was originally a thunderbolt, whence its connexion with Zeus and Homer's treatment of it as an offensive weapon which alarms the foe when brandished. But its obvious sense is 'goatskin', and bards once imagined it as a primitive shield with a shaggy fringe: hence its unique epithet ἀμφιδάσεια (2.446–51n.). Zeus used the aegis, the hide of the goat Amaltheia, to defeat the Titans (D on 318 = *P.Oxy.* 3003). Goatskins were also used in weather-magic (see Braswell on Pindar, *Py.* 4.231, and Fowler, *Phoenix* 42 (1988) 102ff.). 'Goats' of some kind are linked with several northern thunder-gods (13.812–16n.). Yet Indo-European **aig*- means 'oak', the thunder-god's tree (Friedrich, *Trees* 132f.; Nagy in *Gedenkschrift Güntert* 113–32). αἰγίς also meant 'heartwood' and 'squall' (cf. καταιγίς). Not even Zeus's thunderbolt destroys the aegis (21.401); it symbolizes his power, although Homer no longer knew exactly why. He believed that the 'aegis-bearer' *held* it, with ἔχω (cf. 308, 318, 361 etc.), but see 13.43–5n. He also thought of it as metal like a shield: Hephaistos *forged* it for Zeus; with αἰγίδα θοῦριν cf. ἀσπίδα θ. (11.32, 20.162); with 309 cf. 12.295, of a *bronze* shield; and it is called ἐρίτιμος (361, 2.447), an epithet used of gold or tripods (9.126 = 268, *HyAp* 443).

Separate *aitia* existed for Zeus's aegis and Athene's (14.250–61n.), but none for Apollo's; since he borrows his father's (229), it is not really his own. Aristarchus thought Zeus alone possesses one and athetized Apollo's use of it at 24.20f., but cf. T on 229. For the rare use of ἐς with a final sense, 'to put men to flight', see Chantraine, *GH* II 104. ἡγήσατο λαῶν recurs at *Cat.* 234.1, cf. ἡγήτορα λ. at 20.383, 3× *Cat.*; post-Homeric epos belongs to the same oral tradition, to the last detail.

313–17 Animated weaponry enlivens this panorama of the start of battle. The aegis was called 'furious'; now arrows 'leap' (as at 470) and spears fall short 'longing to glut themselves on flesh' (cf. 13.444n.). Verses 314f. resemble 11.571f., τὰ δὲ δοῦρα θρασειάων ἀπὸ χειρῶν | ἄλλα μὲν ἐν σάκεϊ μεγάλῳ πάγεν ὄρμενα πρόσσω, and 316f. = 11.573f. This version involves repeating χρώς, but 11.570–4 repeat μεσ(σ)ηγύ. With 315 cf. 8.298. ἀρηϊθόων αἰζηῶν (also at 20.167) belongs to a system with διοτρεφέων/θαλερῶν α. (2× each); at 20.487 ἀρηΐθοος could be a name or an epithet (13.211–13n.). χρόα λευκόν replaces χ. καλόν (15× epos) only in 316 = 11.573, because flesh is traditionally thought of as vulnerable to the spear, 'white', 'tender' or 'soft', in such contexts (13.830–2n.). Does ἐπαυρεῖν, supposedly 'touch', 'graze' in such passages but 'partake of', 'enjoy' elsewhere, mean 'enjoy' here too, enhancing the personification (so Eustathius 1017.45)?

318–19 The first, long-range phase of a Homeric battle could be lengthy (Latacz, *Kampfdarstellung* 119–29); missile exchanges continue until the two lines edge so close to each other that hand-to-hand combat begins, or, rarely one side breaks and runs, as here and at 8.66–77. Such sudden panic is ascribed to divine agency – here Apollo, later Pan. Verses 318f. adapt to this context a standard couplet used to mark when the battle turns, part of an oral system deftly crafted to admit battles of varied timing and duration. If the combat begins early, we find ὄφρα μὲν ἠὼς ἦν καὶ ἀέξετο ἱερὸν ἦμαρ, | τόφρα μάλ᾽ ἀμφοτέρων βέλε᾽ ἥπτετο, πῖπτε δὲ λαός. | ἦμος δέ ... It may climax at noon ('but when the sun bestrode the middle of the sky', 8.68) or a little later ('but when the wood-cutter prepared his lunch ...', with elaboration, 11.86–9). At 16.777ff. there is stalemate from noon until the sun declines (16.777 = 8.68, but with ὄφρα μέν for ἦμος δ᾽); at *Od.* 9.56ff. battle begins early (56 = 8.66) but turns when the sun sinks (58 = 16.779). Even in their simplest forms, such passages create suspense. ἀτρέμα is unique beside -ας (8× Hom.); both forms appear later, even in prose.

320–2 The *hapax* κατ᾽ ἐνῶπα, 'in the face', modernized in εἰς ὦπα ἰδέσθαι (4× Hom.), includes ἐν governing the fossilized acc. ὦπα; κατά was added once the force of ἐν was lost. Cf. ἐνωπαδίως ἐσίδεσκεν (*Od.* 23.94). The shift of ἐν to ἐνς (εἰς) is post-Myc., being absent in Arcado-Cypriot and the Northern mainland; ἐνῶπα predates *c.* 1000 b.c. (Risch in *Language and Background* 98). The apodosis to the when-clause begins with τοῖσι δέ. With the split formula θυμὸν | ἐν στήθεσσι cf. ἦτορ | ἐν σ. (*Od.* 17.46f.). For 'bewitchment' see 12.255, 13.434–6n. Chrysippus' variant (*SVF* ii 906) φόβου δ᾽ ἐμνήσαθ᾽ ἕκαστος is linguistically innovative.

323–5 This simile develops the themes of 271–6 (where see n.). The Greeks are no longer the hunters but the prey; the 'beasts', i.e. lions, are now two instead of one, just as Apollo now helps Hektor; the night is deep and dark; the lions' attack is sudden; and the shepherd has left his flock, just as Poseidon has left the Greeks. All this heightens the terror (so bT). So does the viewpoint: since nobody is defending the sheep, the attack is seen from their angle. Conversely, when 'a lion comes upon sheep with no guardian and leaps among them with evil intent' (10.485f.), this puts us into the beast's mind so that we do not regret the dormant Thracians' deaths. For the simile's placing at this turning-point cf. 630ff., when Hektor routs the Greeks as if they were a herd of cows with a bad drover; 16.352ff., when wolves snatch lambs from the flock 'through the shepherd's folly' and the Trojans flee (with 357 cf. 322 here); and 5.136ff., when Diomedes resembles a lion attacking a flock left in the pens by a craven shepherd. Pairs of warriors are likened to pairs of lions (13.198–200n.), and two lions raid a herd at 18.579ff.

The diction, typical of similes, is formular. βοῶν ἀγελὴν ἢ πῶϋ μέγ' οἰῶν recurs at *Od.* 12.299, cf. 3.198 (a simile), 11.696; it is 'declined' into the plur. as β. ἀγελαὶ καὶ πώεα οἱ. (etc.) at 11.678, 18.528, 2× *Od.*, 2× *Cat.* (cf. Hoekstra on *Od.* 14.100f.). μελαίνης νυκτὸς ἀμολγῷ, a phrase impressive because ἀ. is so obscure (11.173n.), is modernized to μ. ν. ἐν ὥρῃ at *HyHerm* 67; cf. νύκτα μέλαιναν (9× epos, dat. 5×). In seven occurrences of νυκτὸς ἀ., all four in the *Iliad* are in similes; so are all uses of ἐλθόντ' ἐξαπίνης etc. (5.91, 9.6, 17.57). σημάντωρ, properly 'leader' (4.431, *Od.* 19.314) as in the post-Homeric formula θεῶν σημάντορι (-α) πάντων, is transferred from war to the pastoral world (Fränkel, *Gleichnisse* 60n.): cf. the μῆλα ἀσήμαντα of 10.485; the horses who lack a σημάντωρ, i.e. driver, at 8.127, or who have ἄνακτες, 'masters' (16.370–1n.); and 'shepherd of the people'.

326–42 The Greeks are not naturally 'without courage' (326), but become so now; the adj. is almost an adv. in force. The rout is ominous: we know that every Achaean to die will be one of the best (so bT). With 327 cf. 12.255, 16.730, again at the start of routs. Verse 328 = 16.306, indicating the killing usual when 'battle is scattered', i.e. one side's line breaks and the other scatters in pursuit (cf. 301–5, 14.506–22nn.). Each time, Homer moves from the general to the particular; but the casualty-list is much fuller at 16.307ff. This catalogue resembles 14.511–22, although the victims' pedigrees are more detailed – these are Greeks, after all, and elite troops. As there, the constructions and verbs for 'slay' are varied (Eustathius 1018.26ff.; Niens, *Struktur* 240–2). Again the greatest warriors, Hektor and Aineias, kill the most important victims, and prove their worth by slaying two each; ample obituaries emphasize their kills. Three lesser Trojans each fell a lesser Greek in a single couplet; Strasburger (*Kämpfer* 58ff.) compares the hierarchy of victors at 6.5ff. The final victory, Paris', is adorned with a vignette of the death-wound, which, however, reminds us that his minor victim was running away; this degrades his feat, like that of Oïlean Aias at 14.520ff. He was last seen at 13.660f. The other Trojans all took part in the recent fighting, except Polites, last seen at 13.533 (where see n.); since Pouludamas, Aineias and δῖος Agenor all appear in 14.425, Homer perhaps had that verse in mind now.

The identifiable victims are all from units in the 'mainland catalogue' (13.685ff.). Arkesilaos and Klonios were among the Boeotian leaders (2.495); two of their kinsmen have just died (14.449–53n.). The Athenian Stikhios was in Menestheus' entourage at 13.691 (cf. 13.195–7n.). Medon, 'ruler' of the Phthians, appeared in the same verses at 13.694–7, where see n. The pawns are so shadowy that their homelands are obscure. T claim that Deïokhos' descendants colonized Samos from Athens (for the traditions cf. Sakellariou, *Migration* 93ff.). Mekisteus is not Ekhios's comrade but his *son* at 13.422 (where see n.); for another such inconsistency in a rout see 14.511–22n.

330–6 The Boeotians are 'bronze-shirted' only here, but the epithet is common and probably generic: cf. Αἴαντ', Ἀργείων ἡγήτορε χαλκοχιτώνων (4.285 = 12.354). The variant καρτεροθύμων is from the previous rout (14.512). Verses 333–6 = 13.694–7; the departure from chiastic order (cf. 329–31) neatly separates the Athenian casualties.

337–8 Despite his archaic-sounding descent from Boukolos, Iasos finds no echo in Attic or other traditions; this suggests *ad hoc* invention. Wilamowitz thinks he was ancestral to a noble Attic clan like the Bouzugai or Eteoboutadai (*Homerische Untersuchungen*, Berlin 1884, 249n.). An Iasos from Orkhomenos was grandfather of Neleus' wife (*Od.* 11.281–6); Athens' links with the Pylian royal line are well attested (13.689–91n.). But the name was common: cf. the Argive Iasos, father of Io (cf. Ἴασον Ἄργος, *Od.* 18.246); the founder of (Mycenaean) Iasos in Caria; the Cypriot at *Od.* 17.443; Atalante's father (Theognis 1288); Demeter's Cretan lover Iasion/Iasios (*Od.* 5.125, *Theog.* 970); and, at Pylos, /Iwasos/ (Cn 655), the group called /Iwasoi/ in the An tablets and the /Iwasiotai/ (Cn 3). Any link with Athens is as faint as the Athenian presence in Homer generally (cf. p. 32 n. 54). Σφῆλος means 'Strong' (von Kamptz, *Personennamen* 233). καλέσκετο, here only beside καλέεσκε, is regular (Chantraine, *GH* I 322).

339 Μηκιστῆ for -ῆα is less isolated than it seems: cf. Μηκιστέως υἱός at 2.566 and 23.678, where -έος is a strong variant. Editors wrongly read -ῆος (cf. 2.565–6n.). Like Atreus, Peleus, Portheus etc., 'Mekisteus' was clearly declined -έα -έος -έϊ: cf. Τυδῆ, Ἀμαρυγκέα, Ἀχιλλεῖ, Ὀδυσεῦς (4.384, 23.630, 23.792, *Od.* 24.398). The innovation is helped by its metrical utility (cf. Shipp, *Studies* 65–8); the ending -έος is known in Chian dialect, whereas Ephesos and Miletos used -έως (Ruijgh in *Linear B* 171n.). Cf. also 660, 16.21nn.

340–2 πρώτη ἐν ὑσμίνῃ, 'in the forefront of battle' (also at 20.395), shows that Polites is among the fastest in pursuit. νείατον ὦμον means the base of the shoulder, not its top by the neck. φεύγοντ' ἐν προμάχοισι is an ironic formular adaptation of θύνοντ' ἐν π. (11.188, 203) from another context, the *aristeia*. Since champions by nature fight in front rather than flee, Deïokhos' disgrace troubled the ancients; some read πυμάτοισι, others referred προμάχοισι to the Trojans (bT). Deïokhos is hit with a spear: διαπρὸ δὲ χαλκὸν ἔλασσεν implies that this is Paris' weapon, not an arrow as at 13.662. Though he is making a rapid escape, Paris' cast overtakes him.

343–51 Luckily for the Greeks, who manage to escape as Thoas planned, the Trojans stop to strip the fallen, a normal temptation during a rout (11.755), to which they rarely get the chance to yield; hence Hektor's threats to any who do so. Nestor was less strident in a like situation (6.68–71), but Eustathius (1019.3, 21–3) rightly deems the grisly warning appropriate; cf. the threats of death for slackers or deserters at 2.357–9, 2.391–3, 12.248–50,

13.232–4, and later laws against burying traitors (Parker, *Miasma* 45). Segal thinks Hektor is overcome by the war's intoxicating savagery, in accord with his presumption towards Zeus (*Mutilation* 19f.); but all ancient generals had to deal with their men's lust for metal armour, which was both useful and valuable. The threat of being left unburied is common in vaunts over victims (11.452–4, 21.122–4, 22.335f.); Hektor makes it vivid to his men by adding that dogs will tear them *before their own city* (cf. Priam at 22.66ff.).

343–4 With 343 cf. 12.195. ἐμπλήσσω, 'dash against' an obstacle, well expresses the Greeks' panic flight hindered by their own outworks: cf. 12.72, *Od.* 22.469 (birds caught in a net) and ἐμπλήγδην, 'madly' (*Od.* 20.132). ὀρυκτή (7× with τάφρος) stands apart from its noun because 'trench and stakes' is seen as a unit, like a Roman *vallum*.

346–7 Verse 346 = 6.110, 8.172; at 6.66 ἐκέκλετο μακρὸν ἀΰσας introduces a like speech by Nestor. Does ἐ. govern 347 (as at 18.343, *Od.* 19.418), with direct speech starting abruptly in 348, or does it begin in 347 with infinitives for imperatives? Zenodotus read ἐπισσεύεσθον for -σθαι, emending the latter option into the text, but was rebuked by Aristarchus for using a dual to stand for a plur., an innovation he proposed elsewhere (13.626–7n.). It was usual not to punctuate at the end of 346: so, rightly, Nic/A, [Longinus], *On the Sublime* 27.1 and [Plutarch], *Life of Homer* 57, who cite 346ff. as an example of a shift from narrative to 'mimetic' mode. [Longinus] thinks Hektor's order, being πρέπον, is voiced by the poet himself, who then puts the grim threat into direct speech. The truth is simpler: the poet, deciding to extend the speech after he had begun in *oratio obliqua*, shifts brusquely to direct speech, as at 4.301ff., 9.684f., 23.854ff., *Od.* 1.38ff., 15.424f., *HyHerm* 523ff. For ἐὰν δ' ἔναρα βροτόεντα cf. 17.13, 14.508–10n.

348–51 ἐθέλοντα (in citations and a papyrus, but no good codices) is a concordance-variant from 2.391, 8.10; it replaces ἑτέρωθι, redundant after 'away from the ships', with a hint that Hektor will spare those with reason for absence, but he is too angry for such niceties. πυρὸς λελάχωσι, 'give him his share of fire', is a euphemism for 'burn his body' (also at 23.76, cf. 7.79f. = 22.342f.); it must be of post-Myc. date, when cremation became the rule. For the reduplicated causal aor. cf. λελάθω (58–61n.). After the fut. or subj. μητίσομαι, this subj. underlines the threat's personal tone, and the archaic fut. indic. ἐρύουσι presents as fact the result of the preceding proposition (Chantraine, *GH* II 210). For ἐρύω cf. 11.454, 22.67 (identical contexts), with Risch, *Wortbildung* 352; Aristarchus deemed it a pres. with fut. sense.

352–4 Hektor is now in his chariot, as Apollo had enjoined (258f.); warriors mount and dismount so often that it is taken for granted, especially in a rout. Cf. 8.348, where we were not told that he remounted to chase the Greeks. In his rage, he lifts his whip high to lash his horses (so bT).

κατωμαδόν means 'down from his shoulder', as in 23.500 (μάστι δ' αἰὲν ἔλαυνε κ.) and 23.431, quoted in 358–61n. For ἐπὶ στίχας *h* has κατὰ σ. from 11.91. ἐπί is best taken as '(shouting) across the ranks', not '(drove) against the (enemy) ranks', *pace* bT. Despite the 'neglected' ϝ-, ἔχον must mean 'drove': cf. *Aspis* 369, -ὸς ἐχέμεν ἐρυσάρματας ἵππους. The epithet recurs only at 16.370 (nom.), when the chariots recross the trench in the other direction (cf. Delebecque, *Cheval* 153). It may remodel *ϝερυσάρμονες (Risch, *Wortbildung* 226). It surely became obsolete when its loss of initial ϝ- made bards doubt whether it began with a vowel or a consonant; Homer uses, respectively, ἐριαύχενες -ας, 5× (or ὑψηχέες -ας, 2×), and καλλίτριχες -ας (14×).

356–7 Apollo smooths the chariots' path by kicking in the spoil-heaps either side of the ditch to make a causeway (γέφυρα), and flattening the rampart. For γεφυρόω (also at 21.245) cf. 5.87–8n. κάπετος for σκάπετος is a 'ditch' round a vineyard or a 'pit' for a grave (18.564, 24.797); cf. LSJ s.vv. Perhaps it has a derogatory sense when compared with τάφρος, to belittle the ditch as it is wrecked (Leaf): τάφροιο βαθείης does fill the same metrical position at 8.336. Zenodotus read χερσίν, making Apollo push the soil with his hands; Aristarchus replied that it is better not to make a god stoop. His kicks better reveal how easily gods can slight men's puny efforts (cf. 365). Zenodotus surely based his conjecture on 364 (Düntzer, *De Zenodoti studiis* 109), but the boy wrecks the sand-castle with his feet too.

358–61 Apollo flattens only part of the ditch, which still hinders the Trojans' retreat at 16.369ff. Yet the causeway is wide – as wide as the spear-cast of a sportsman testing his strength by throwing as far he can (cf. 16.590, quoted below). Albracht (*Kampfschilderung* I 22, II 15) estimates this as a mere 10–15 paces, but using light javelins modern athletes can cast over 250 feet; the Greeks probably equalled this (H. A. Harris, *Greek Athletes and Athletics*, London 1964, 95–7). The Trojans can pour through the gap in ranks (φαλαγγηδόν, cf. 13.126–35n.), not in a narrow column, as Eustathius saw (1020.11). The same measure of distance, ὅσον τ' ἐπὶ δουρὸς ἐρωή, describes Akhilleus' leap at 21.251. It belongs to a set of quaint expressions: ὅ. τ' ἐπὶ λᾶαν ἵησι (3.12), ὅ. τ' ἐπικίδναται ἠώς (7.451), ὅ. τ' ἐπιβᾶσα κορώνη | ἴχνος ἐποίησε (*Erga* 679f.), ὅσσον τ' ἐπὶ οὖρα πέλονται | ἡμιόνων (10.351f., cf. *Od.* 8.124). Its extension into a full simile by the addition of γίνεται, which recalls πολέμου δ' οὐ γίνετ' ἐρωή (2×), resembles ὅσση δ' αἰγανέης ῥιπὴ τανανοῖο τέτυκται, | ἥν ῥά τ' ἀνὴρ ἀφέῃ πειρώμενος ἢ ἐν ἀέθλῳ | ἠὲ καὶ ἐν πολέμῳ (16.589ff.), and ὅσσα δὲ δίσκου οὖρα κατωμαδίοιο πέλονται, | ὅν τ' αἰζηὸς ἀφῆκεν ἀνὴρ πειρώμενος ἥβης (23.431f., cf. 23.845f.); cf. too σθένεος πειρήσομαι (*Od.* 21.282), in a context of games. On similes expressing measurement see Scott, *Simile* 20–4. The subj. ᾗσι, contracted for ᾗῃ(σι), is 'recent' (Shipp, *Studies* 167); for parallels see Chantraine, *GH* I 43. The ending is properly -ησι. φαλαγγηδόν recurs in Polybius. For the aegis see 308–11n.

362–7 Only now do we realize, with a shock, what Apollo meant by his promise to smoothe the Trojans' *entire* path (261). They strained through book 12 to break the rampart; Apollo, or rather the poet, playfully does so in a few verses. The simile of a boy wrecking a sand-castle closely follows that of the athlete, heightening the contrasts between these sports and the Greeks' peril, the ease of god and the toil of man. The similes and address to Apollo (which turns out to be his *envoi*) mark the gravity of the crisis. But this image also saves Homer from showing the rampart's ruination in detail, which might be too slow for the narrative or too taxing to the imagination. He has carefully prepared us to expect the rampart to be slighted. At 7.443–64 Zeus gave Poseidon leave to wash it away and bury the shore with sand; the latter and Apollo did so after the war (12.10ff.). This idea of its vanishing into the sand surely prompted this image of a sand-castle. It now disappears from the action; it is ignored during the Trojan retreat of 16.367ff., as if Homer may conveniently forget the edifice he himself created (cf. Aristotle frag. 166 and E. Dolin, *HSCP* 87 (1983) 130). Nor are we surprised that Apollo vanishes too, now that he has kept his promise (Wilamowitz, *IuH* 238).

362–4 Similes often describe gods' wondrous deeds: Poseidon's wave wrecks a ship as a wind scatters thistledown (*Od.* 5.368f.). This one 'conveys the poet's sense of the pathos of vain human effort, and also the divine scale, on which nothing achieved or endured by men can be really serious' (Griffin, *HLD* 130); the ease of divine action is a topos (13.90n.), and the same point about human toil was made at 12.29. Moulton (*Similes* 71f.) compares Apollo's scorn for mortal affairs at 21.462ff. The image achieves its effects by both contrast and similarity. The boy's playfulness contrasts with the men's effort, his innocence of war with their martial role (cf. 2.337f., 6.467ff.), just as the previous athletic image contrasts with its military setting, although the javelin evokes it. The rampart is by the sea, like the sand-castle; just as the Greeks cause its ultimate ruin by failing to sacrifice when they build it (7.450), so the boy ruins his own work. Homer ran a risk in likening Apollo to a mere boy at such a moment (so bT), but the apt observation of the changeless patterns of children's play is a brilliant success (cf. 16.259–65n.). Other images of children describe protection by a stronger ally or odd conduct, e.g. 16.7–10 (Scott, *Simile* 74). ὅς τ' ἐπεί extends other similes at 680, 17.658, 24.42. ἄθυρμα and ἀθύρω are unique in the *Iliad*; νηπιέη means 'childishness' at 9.491 but 'folly' at 20.411, *Od.* 24.469 (on its form see S. West on *Od.* 1.297). ποσὶν καὶ χερσίν, with innovative n-mobile, uniquely adapts πόδας καὶ χεῖρας etc.

365–6 The emotive address to Apollo expresses his power (but cf. 20.150–2n.). ἤϊε is restricted to such apostrophes (20.152, *HyAp* 120); for ancient explanations of it see Hrd/A and F. Williams on Callim. *HyAp* 103. It reflects the ritual cry ἰή (*HyAp* 517) or ἰὴ ἰέ (Pindar), which became a 'voc.' ἰήϊε, whence the adj. ἰήϊος: cf. Dionusos' epithet εὔϊος from ₃the joyful whoop εὐοῖ. With κάματον καὶ ὀϊζύν cf. καμάτου καὶ ὀϊζύος (*Erga* 177), πόνος (∪∪ −) καὶ ὀϊζύς etc. (5× epos). σύγχεας picks up συνέχευε (364). φύζαν ἐνώρσας fulfils verbatim Zeus's prediction at 62; we await the next step, that the Greeks fall amid the ships ... of Akhilleus!

367–9 = 8.345–7 (starting οἱ μὲν δή), another Greek retreat under divine pressure (262–404n.). There, however, the words of the prayer are not given. The ships are the only place left where the Greeks can regroup, just as the Trojans gathered by their chariots at 3. ὥς 'thus' is awkward, since their regrouping has not begun (Leaf on 379); we must regard ἐρητύοντο as inceptive. It is wrong to end 367 with a stop, not a comma.

370 = 659, where Nestor again embodies the whole army's concern, beseeching the men to fight for their families (653–73n.). Since he is too old to fight himself, prayer is apt for him: ἔργα νέων, βουλαὶ δὲ μέσων, εὐχαὶ δὲ γερόντων (Hes. frag. 321). His reappearance leads up to Patroklos' by recalling book 11 (262–404n.). For Γερήνιος οὖρος Ἀχαιῶν see 8.80n. Verse 371 = *Od.* 9.527. χεῖρ' = χεῖρε: the Greeks raised both arms to pray.

372–6 Nestor's prayer takes the usual form: (i) an invocation, here a simple voc. rather than κλῦθι, reinforced by Ὀλύμπιε; (ii) a reminder of a past favour (introduced as often by εἴ ποτε) which is, as often, the burning of victims' fat-covered thigh-bones (cf. 1.40, 1.503, 11.773, *Od.* 4.763f., 19.366); (iii) a request for present help (with τῶν μνῆσαι cf. 22.84, *Od.* 4.765). Zeus must help if he granted that the Greeks return, when they prayed to him in Argos (i.e. in Greece, before leaving). εἴ ποτέ τις purposely understates the fact that they all prayed for this, and that, as Nestor holds, Zeus agreed; his nod makes his assent immutable (cf. 1.514, 524ff.). Verse 376 = 8.244 (not spurious?), the end of Agamemnon's prayer to Zeus, which belongs to the same narrative pattern as Nestor's (262–404n.).

ἐν Ἄργεϊ περ πολυπύρῳ is unusual, since πολύπυρος is a mid-line epithet for toponyms shaped − ∪∪ −, Bouprasion or Doulikhion (11.756, 3× *Od.*); it recurs at the verse-end at *Od.* 15.406, describing Syria (Suriē). The redundant filler περ betrays improvisation; '*even* in Argos' makes no sense, and περ cannot go with εἰ (Denniston, *Particles* 487). Homer could have used ποιήεντι instead. Aristarchus preferred οἰός and οἰῶν to ὀϊός and ὀϊῶν (Hrd/A on 3.198), and Sanskrit *ávyas* proves that οἰός is older (from *owyós*). Yet bards did evolve forms in ὀϊ- by analogy with the nom., e.g. εἰροπόκοις ὀΐεσσι for *-οισιν ὄϝισσι. Zeus is called simply Ὀλύμπιε by other gods (3× Hom.); since he is the Olympian *par excellence*, the adj. is a useful substitute for his name (1.353 etc.). The gods as a group are rarely called Ὀλύμπιοι (1.399, 20.47).

377–80 Zeus thunders in reply to Nestor, but the Trojans think the omen favours them and redouble their efforts (so T, cf. Schadewaldt, *Iliasstudien*

92). The pro-Greek audience will welcome this hint, soon amplified by Patroklos' reappearance, that the battle will turn. Nestor had to be given some sign, but Zeus could not simply assent, being bound by his promise to Thetis (so bT). There are multiple ironies: just as the Trojans cannot know that Nestor prayed to Zeus, so Nestor is unaware that his prayer may yet be answered, since Patroklos has yet to appeal to Akhilleus; nor can Nestor know that Zeus's assent involves a still greater Trojan onslaught. Cf. H. Stockinger, *Die Vorzeichen im homerischen Epos*, St Ottilien 1959, 41–3. Arn/A says Zenodotus read μέγα δ' ἔκλυε: but how can Zeus 'hear loudly'? Düntzer (*De Zenodoti studiis* 20) well argues that he read τοῦ δ' ἔ., making 377 equivalent to 16.249, 24.314 or *Od.* 20.102, and omitted 378–80, emending away the 'contradiction' over which side the omen favours. Aristarchus' rebuttal shows that he too misunderstood: Zeus heard the Greeks' prayer but was not persuaded, since he was hostile to them. Verse 380, with 'Greeks' for 'Trojans', = 14.441, 8.252, when the Greeks react to the omen Zeus sends in reply to Agamemnon's prayer (cf. 372–6n.).

381–4 This fine simile marks the climax of the Trojan onslaught and advances the narrative from the rampart to the ships. The Trojans, no longer merely by the sea like the boy at 362, are now a great wave within it, as if the ships float in a sea of attackers. The danger is like a storm, and the half-timbered rampart resembles the ship's side-wall over which the wave washes (cf. bT). The end of the simile subtly shifts to the noisy squall that whips up the waves; the squall presumably comes from Zeus, like the thunder just heard. Moulton (*Similes* 69) notes that this simile is resumed by the next, when the stalemate at the ships is likened to a shipwright's straight line (410ff.). The nautical images continue at 618ff. For other similes where the wind stirs up the waves see 4.422ff., 9.4ff., 11.297f., 11.305ff. and 14.394f.

Verse 381 blends μέγα κῦμα (17× Hom.), κ. θαλάσσης (7×) and θ. εὐρυπόροιο (*Od.* 4.432, *Naupaktia* frag. 2). *Od.* 12.2 combines the last two formulae. θ. ε. is equivalent to πολυφλοίσβοιο θ. (12× epos); this is the sole breach of the tendency to economy in the *Iliad*'s formular system for 'sea' (Page, *HHI* 227). R. Schmiel thinks π. connotes the sea-shore, ε. the sea as a path to home (*LCM* 9 (1984) 36f.). But either phrase would be apt here; context is not the main factor, but Parry's *jeu de formules*. θ. ε. arose in cases like this, when θ. is part of formulae like κῦμα θ. or θῖνα θ. (normally at the verse-end), and the poet wants to end the verse with an epithet. Since π. θ. avoids any hint of a spondaic 'verse-end' at the bucolic diaeresis, it remains standard. — τοῖχος denotes a ship's side-wall at *Od.* 12.420, that of a house elsewhere (Kurt, *Fachausdrücke* 107). καταβήσεται is surely aor. subj.; an old desiderative may underlie it (Ruijgh, τε *épique* 593). With ὑπὲρ τοίχων κ. cf. τεῖχος ὑπερκατέβησαν (13.50), just as the Trojans κατὰ τ.

ἔβαινον (cf. 13.737); they *kept coming* over the rampart and down from it towards the ships (most codices have ἔ., versus ἔβησαν in 3/5 papyri). | ἲς ἀνέμου (also at *Erga* 518) adapts ἲς ἀνέμοιο | (17.739, simile; 3× *Od.*).

385–9 The poet clumsily extends the sentence to contrast (i) the Trojan infantry scaling the rampart with their leaders driving through the breach in it, and (ii) the Trojans fighting from their chariots with the Achaeans fighting from the ships' tall sterns. To explain how such a combat can be 'at close quarters', he adds that the Greeks used long naval pikes. The image is of a sea-battle on land or chariot-battle at sea (bT). Aristarchus rightly found it striking, but thought the Trojans backed their chariots up to the ships with their horses facing Troy (449–51n.)!

386–7 The unique combat required some reshuffling of formulae. | ἔγχε-σιν ἀμφιγύοις adapts ἔ. ἀμφιγύοισιν | (13.146–8n.); cf. | δούρασι τ' ἀμφιγύοις (Eumelus frag. dub. 19 B. = 4 D.). μελαινάων ἀπὸ (ἐπὶ) νηῶν | (8× epos) is modified as at *Od.* 6.268, ν. ὅπλα μ., cf. [ν. δὲ] μ. ἐπιβαίη (*Cat.* 204.110); as a result, ὕψι is oddly placed and ἀπὸ ν. oddly conjoined with ἐπιβάντες (hence ἀποβ- in papyri).

388–9 Naval pikes with sections glued together reappear at 677f. (ξυστὸν μέγα ναύμαχον ... κολλητὸν βλήτροισι), where see n.; they were evidently used against boarders at sea or on the beach. *Pace* D. Gray (*Arch. Hom.* G 131), boarding tactics were known: the suitors take spears and shields for an ambush at sea (*Od.* 16.473f.). Bundles of spears appear at the bows or sterns of Iron Age ships (Ahlberg, *Fighting* 45f.; O. Höckmann, *Arch. Hom.* E 304f.). Pikes are also seen in the bows of the Bronze Age ships conducting armed landings in a Thera fresco and a stone rhyton from Epidauros (S. P. Morris, *AJA* 93 (1989) 525f., figs. 6–7). Aias' pike was twenty-two cubits or thirty-two feet long (678); this may be epic exaggeration, like Hektor's spear of eleven cubits (6.319 = 8.494), but the Macedonian sarissa varied from twelve to at least fourteen cubits (M. Andronikos, *BCH* 94 (1970) 102–7), the Khalubes had pikes of fifteen cubits (Xen. *Anab.* 4.7.16), and the Theran warriors have very long spears. Kurt (*Fachausdrücke* 177f.) equates the ξυστόν with the pole (κοντός) with which one pushes off a ship (*Od.* 9.487), but ξ. is a synonym for 'spear' (13.496–501n.). For κολλήεις beside -ητός, also at *Aspis* 309, see Risch, *Wortbildung* 154. στόμα means the 'point' of a weapon: this is next paralleled, with famous ambiguity, at Soph. *Ajax* 651; cf. Eur. *Suppl.* 1206; LSJ s.vv. στόμα, -όω, -ωμα; 'the great mouth of piercing war' (10.8); and κωφός, 'dull' (cf. 14.16–19n., Eur. *Or.* 1288). The spear's 'bronze-clad' tip is a unique metaphor, as if this weapon wears armour; cf. the 'bronze-helmeted' spears of 3.18, 11.43, and 13.444n.

390–404 This brief but crucial scene is placed where it arouses most suspense, at the climax of the Trojan advance and the start of the long stalemate by the ships; for this, and the motif of hearing the din, see

262–404n. Homer gives just enough detail to remind us that we last saw Patroklos in Eurupulos' hut (11.848), where he still is, and to reveal that he will indeed take Nestor's message to Akhilleus; thus 403f. adapts 11.792f. (Nestor's main point). In this crisis Homer avoids slowing down the story to explain why Patroklos dallied there, e.g. by describing his conversation or sending Iris to hurry him on; this would also have highlighted the problem that, on one level of this simultaneous *and* sequential narrative, he has stayed incredibly long with his injured comrade, like Nestor with Makhaon (14.1ff.). The lack of divine intervention also stresses his tragic responsibility for his actions; he simply hears the din. Homer sets him in motion again so that he can reach Akhilleus when the Trojans are about to burn the first ship (16.2). Just as he is stirred by the Greeks' plight after the rampart has fallen, so Akhilleus will be moved yet more by the ensuing battle for the ships. By delaying the heroes' reactions until he has portrayed each stage of the fighting, Homer makes us experience for ourselves the moral pressure to act which each must feel; by presenting Patroklos' reaction now, he builds suspense as we await that of Akhilleus himself.

391–2 τείχεος ἀμφεμάχοντο means 'they fought *for* the wall' (cf. 16.496 and Chantraine, *GH* II 88); with an acc. it would mean 'fight around'. This corresponds to the events of books 12–14 (Winter, *MNO* 147). For the split formula θοάων −∪∪ νηῶν cf. 685, 14.410, and the modernization νεῶν ∪∪−∪ θ. (17.403, 19.356). 'Hospitable' is the standard epithet in the gen. with names shaped −∪∪−∪ (13.756–9n.), despite any appeal this virtue might hold for 'kind' Patroklos.

393 Patroklos cheers Eurupulos with conversation, as well he might after operating on the latter's thigh (11.844ff.); cf. 11.643, where Nestor consoles Makhaon. Reinhardt (*IuD* 306) deems Nestor a better person to be telling anecdotes (cf. 11.643), but this is to misinterpret ἔτερπε λόγοις (for the phrase cf. *Od.* 4.239, 8.91, 23.301). T's conjecture λούων is inspired by 14.6f., where Nestor's servant will wash Makhaon after Nestor leaves. Patroklos dried the wound and stopped the bleeding (11.848); he would not please Eurupulos by soaking it now! Eurupulos' servant will continue to cheer his lord with talk (401, cf. 393). — Aristarchus noted that λόγος, like σοφίη at 412, is a *hapax* in the *Iliad*; he did not athetize the scene in consequence, unlike Wilamowitz (*IuH* 238f.) or Shipp (*Studies* 289), who dubs λόγος 'one of the most important *hapax legomena* in the *Iliad*'. Save to Alexandrian poets in search of novelty, *hapaxes* matter little, given our scant evidence for the early Greek lexicon; some Myc. words vanish until Hellenistic times. λόγος recurs at *Od.* 1.56 and 5× in Hesiod, who is not, after all, much later; see Krischer, *Konventionen* 157. It may be 'recent', but the *Iliad* has a Homeric *hapax* every nine verses (M. M. Kumpf, *Four Indices of the Homeric Hapax Legomena*, Hildesheim 1984, 206). Trust in these as a sign of interpolation is misplaced; the Chorizontes denied Homer his *Odyssey* because it *lacks* the word σοφίη (T on 412)!

394–8 ἀκήματα, in apposition to φάρμακα, is also a *hapax*. It is read by the whole paradosis save Aristarchus, who wavered (Did/AT): ἀκέσματα is the form known from Pindar onward and is etymologically expected, cf. ἀκεστός (Risch, *Wortbildung* 50). Yet ἀκήματα must stand, since it may be based on an Aeolic verb in -ημαι formed from the *s*-stem ἄκος (E.-M. Hamm, *Grammatik zu Sappho und Alkaios*, Berlin 1957,141). For Patroklos' medicines cf. 11.846ff.; for the phrasing cf. 4.191, 19.49. φάρμακον appears in Myc. (PY Un 1314). Verses 395f. = 12.143f. (with ἐνόησαν), where we must translate 'charging at the rampart'. Leaf deems 395f. crudely interpolated thence, without the requisite change of τεῖχος to νῆας. But here it means 'rushing over the rampart': this corresponds to the events of 352–66. Verses 397f. = 113f. (from πεπλήγετο), where see n.; καῖ ὤ adapts *καὶ ϝώ.

399–404 With the structure of Patroklos' speech cf. that of Nestor to Makhaon (14.1– 8n.). παρμενέμεν repeats the root for 'linger' (cf. *Od.* 9.97, 20.330); for the rest of 400 see 13.120–3n. ποτιτέρπω is unique in Greek; ποτι- conveys 'continue' (cf. Chantraine, *GH* II 131). Verses 403f. = 11.792f. (with ὀρίνω for -αις).

405–591 Both sides fight hard for the ships, the Trojans proving unable to break the Achaean line that protects them, the Greeks unable to repel the attack

405–591 This indecisive combat deftly builds suspense while Patroklos is on his way to Akhilleus; cf. the shorter delay while Antilokhos runs to Akhilleus (17.702–61). Hektor and Aias are the main figures. After an opening picture of equal battle, emphasized by a simile, Aias kills first, then Hektor (cf. 515f.). A pair of exhortations by both (484–514) divides the scene in two, with close fighting replacing missile warfare from 515; towards its end another speech by Hektor is balanced by Aias' reply (553ff.). The scene begins and ends with the deaths of cousins of Hektor, and other cousins die at 516, 543; his attack costs him dear. Although we are led to expect an equal fight, the Greeks lead by six victims to three; cf. their advantage during the deadlock of book 13 (13.540–672n.), which is recalled by the reappearance of Menelaos and Antilokhos. In the *Iliad*, 208 Trojans but only 61 Greeks are slain (C. B. Armstrong, *G&R* 16 (1969) 30f.). bT on 10.14–16 are right that 'the poet is always a philhellene', although he was surely more restrained than was traditional: for the controversy over this see de Jong, *Narrators* 250n. Vigorous speeches do much to sustain the narrative.

The nature of the combat has caused confusion. Leaf thinks it silently shifts from the Greeks fighting from the sterns as at 385–9 to a normal battle on level ground, save that at 435 a Greek falls off a ship. Winter (*MNO*

147–9) thinks 408f. predicts the close-range mêlée that actually begins at 515ff., while 415ff. matches the fighting at 385–9; Latacz, in a fine account of the whole scene (*Kampfdarstellung* 206–8), deems 385–9 an ancient depiction of chariot-warfare (!), followed by a missile battle between *promachoi* evolving, as usual, into hand-to-hand combat. Both these Unitarians feebly explain away part of the text. Perhaps Homer brought the Trojans too near the fleet for his present ends, anticipating its destruction, and quietly edges them back; but it is better to suppose that the Greeks fight both from the sterns and in a line before them (cf. 408, 494), so that they can shoot down over their own men to stop the Trojans from scurrying under the hulls with fire, as does Aias by spearing Kaletor at 419f.

405 The transitional verses at 17.700 and 18.148 use the formula πόδες φέρον to describe those in great haste (Eustathius 1022.35). Here it also seems to express a conflict between Patroklos' wish to stay and his need to go, as if his feet act of their own will: cf. 13.510–15n., on Idomeneus' reluctant retreat.

406–9 Cf. the stalemate with the Lycians at 12.417–20, when the phrasing is purposely repeated as at 416–18 below; for the repetition of ἐδύναντο cf. 22.200f. The Greeks outnumber the Trojans, whose allies redress the balance (2.122ff., 8.56, 13.739). This reminder of their greater number is meant not to hint at martial weakness, but to reassure the pro-Greek audience. There are huts behind the ships, as is clear from 478, 656; we should imagine that each contingent built its huts by its fleet, with alternating rows of each (Leaf). From the Trojan viewpoint 'the huts nor even the ships' is a *hysteron proteron*; this is a good reason to keep the vulgate οὐδέ in 409 (also in a papyrus). νέεσσι artificially combines the old Aeolic dat. with Ionic metathesis of quantity; save for 414, it recurs only in the phrases ἐπὶ πρύμνῃσι ν. and ποντοπόροισι/ὠκυπόροισι ν. (4× each). Forms in νε- are often linked with the huts, which confirms that Homer is developing a largely novel idea in the attack on the camp (Hoekstra, *Modifications* 129).

410–13 'As a line makes straight a ship's timber …'; the carpenter straightens the wood, using a string to draw a line along which he cuts it. The final panorama before we focus on individual duels is, like the previous scenes, summed up in a simile. Like the last image (381ff.), this one draws on its martial context, evoking the peaceful building of the ships now facing destruction; Athene stands in the background, as does Zeus in the narrative. Similes depict ship-timbers at all stages of production (13.389–91n.). The poet moves from negative ('neither side could') to positive, as at 618ff., when two nautical similes, even more closely juxtaposed, depict the attack on the fleet, or 12.421ff., when paired images describe an equal fight: men with yardsticks dispute a boundary, and a woman with a balance (σταθμός) weighs wool (413 = 12.436). Leaf thinks the equality of the battle 'is symbolized by the equal straining of the "ropes" by which the two armies are moved' (this is how he takes the metaphor in 413); yet 'the point to be illustrated is the equality of two strains, while the simile gives only the intensity of one', i.e. of the carpenter's line. But in 413 the battle-line is pulled taut like a *single* rope, with neither side yielding at any point (cf. 13.358–6on.). The simile illustrates this exactly; the poet admires the straight edge, hard to achieve with simple tools.

D gloss στάθμη as 'a carpenter's tool, also called κατευθυντηρία; with this wood is kept straight. It is a thin string smeared with a red or black pigment.' The pigment served to transfer the straight line onto the plank when the string was twanged. The στάθμη could be confused with the line it left, or with the κανών, 'ruler': see Pearson on Soph. frags. 330, 474 P. It reappears in the phrase ἐπὶ στάθμην ἴθυνε, of carpenters (5× *Od.*, especially 5.245): cf. Theognis 805. ἐξιθύνω recurs in Hippocrates. δαήμων (23.671, 3× *Od.*) is a pointed epithet: δαΐφρων could have replaced it. The gen. with οἶδα is normal: cf. *Od.* 5.250, ἐΰ εἰδὼς τεκτοσυνάων (Chantraine, *GH* II 55f.). As at 1.385, the transposition of the verse-end formula ἐ. εἰ. etc. entails contraction of ἐΰ (p. 14 n. 19). σοφίη, sole instance of this root in Homer (393n.), next occurs at *Erga* 649, of poetic skill, but is used in archaic verse of arts like riding or helmsmanship (see West *ad loc.*). Stesichorus spoke of the σοφία of the carpenter Epeios (frag. S 89.7f.); cf. the Cyclic tag σοφὸς ἤραρε τέκτων ('Homer' frag. 2 D.). Athene imparted this skill (cf. 5.6of., *Od.* 6.233f., 8.493, *Erga* 430, *HyAphr* 12f.); ὑποθημοσύνῃσιν Ἀθήνης recurs at *Od.* 16.233.

414–15 Verse 414 was at 12.175 (with πύλῃσι for νέεσσι); μάχην ἐμά-χοντο recurs at 673, cf. 18.533, *Od.* 9.54. Polyptoton and etymological play make 414 an effective focusing device, showing that similar combats are erupting all along the front line. Hektor swiftly engages Aias. ἄντα, 'against', governs a gen. (cf. 16.621); ἐείσατο derives from (ϝ)ίεμαι not ἐ(ϝ)ίσκω, cf. Ὀδυσῆος ἐείσατο κυδαλίμοιο (*Od.* 22.89). Homer does not say whose ship is involved. Pausanias (10.14.2) thought it was Protesilaos', cf. 704ff.; yet at 685ff. Aias leaps from ship to ship, and the proximity of Teukros' hut at 478ff. suggests that his own ship is meant. As Willcock says, oral poets can be vague at first and specific later, as in Zeus's forecasts.

416–18 These vv. restate the impasse with more economy and balance than did 406–9. Three infinitives depend on δύναντο, and the repeated ὁ τόν is brief in the extreme; Hektor's identity is shown by reminders of his aim, 'to burn the ships', and of the fact that a god brought him near, which makes him harder to repel (cf. 21.93). Cf. the stalemate at 22.200f., οὔτ' ἄρ' ὁ τὸν δύναται ὑποφεύγειν οὔθ' ὁ διώκειν, | ὣς ὁ τὸν οὐ δύνατο μάρψαι ποσίν, οὐδ' ὃς ἀλύξαι. Verse 418 is also like the impasse at 12.419f., οὔτε ... ἐδύναντο | τείχεος ἂψ ὤσασθαι, ἐπεὶ τὰ πρῶτα πέλασθεν; the preceding battle there resembles the sequel here, since Aias and Teukros are involved (cf. Winter, *MNO* 152–4). Hektor's contest with Aias over a single ship (416) prefigures 704ff. Aristarchus conjectured νῆα in 417, for consistency with 416 (Did/A); but νῆας is better, since Hektor aims to burn the whole fleet (cf. 8.182, 235, 12.198, 14.47, 16.82, all with νῆας). νῆα enters a few later MSS from the scholia. Conversely, some MSS have unmetrical νῆας in 420 (so T and a papyrus).

419–21 Like Priam, Klutios was Laomedon's son (525–43n.); so *his* son is Hektor's cousin (422). It is no accident that, when Hektor and Aias next slay each others' followers, Aias kills a Laomedon son of Antenor (516f.). Most of the Trojan elders listed at 3.146–8 lose sons in 419–591, as if Homer based his casualties on them (Fenik, *Homer and the Nibelungenlied* 186). Kaletor, like Kalesios (6.18), would be an apt name for a herald (cf. 638–52n.). Borne by a Greek at 13.541, it recurs as an epithet for a herald in the phrase κήρυκα καλήτορα (24.577), where in fact Homer has surely forgotten Idaios' name (24.325, 470) and calls him Kaletor; at 24.701 he calls him Astubootes! Aias is φαίδιμος 6×, Hektor 29×; the epithet is generic, cf. φ. Ἄτλας (*Cat.* 169.3). κατὰ στῆθος βάλε δουρί (11.108) also precedes δούπησεν δὲ πεσών at 13.186f., where see n. The poet can be inventive in the second hemistich, where 'his armour clattered about him' is often replaced by 'the spear quivered in his heart', 'he hit the ground with his forehead', 'great grief seized the Greeks' etc. Here 'the torch fell from his hand' recalls the threat to the ships; this phrase too belongs to a substitution-system, cf. τόξον δέ οἱ ἔκπεσε χειρός (also with δέπας, σκῦτος, νεκρός, σκῆπτρον). On δαλός see 13.319–20n.

422–5 Hektor's exhortation is introduced as at 484f. (with the traditional ἐνόησεν for εἶδεν): 424f. = 485f., cf. 11.284–7. His speeches frame Aias' dialogue with Teukros. Just as he sees Kaletor fall in the dust before the ship, so he makes Lukophron fall in the dust from the ship (434f.), a tit-for-tat killing. Homer calls Kaletor 'his cousin' to show us Hektor's viewpoint (de Jong, *Narrators* 103). Terms expressing kinship often have this aim (e.g. 13.207, 14.156, 20.419, 21.469); for like effects in Hebrew tales see R. Alter, *The Art of Biblical Narrative*, New York 1981, 7, 180.

426–8 Hektor's order not to yield precedes the usual call to save the corpse. μή πω means 'not at all'; 'not yet' would be absurd. πω preserves its former identity with πως, as at e.g. 1.124 (where the Alexandrians emended to που), 3.306 (*pace* the n. there), 12.270: cf. οὕτω(ς), ὥστε/ὧτε (Alcman), and ὡς used of both time and manner. μάχης goes with χάζεσθε. στεῖνος denotes the narrow gap between either the ships and the chariots (bT) or the ships and the rampart, as at 8.476 (Eustathius 1023.40); at 12.66 it means that between the rampart and the ditch. Verse 428 = 16.500; νεῶν ἐν ἀγῶνι maintains the original sense of ἀγών, 'gathering' (cf. 16.239, 19.42 and 24.141, ἐν νηῶν ἀγύρει), whence derives its post-Homeric sense 'contest'

(*LfgrE* s.v.). The innovation νεῶν results from adaptation in the preceding hemistich of phrases like τεύχεα συλήσας (Hoekstra, *Modifications* 127f.); so too πεσόντα νεός in 423 modifies πεσὼν νηός.

429–35 It is common to slay someone other than one's target (13.183–4n.). Lukophron's death follows the usual schema (biography, death-wound), save that the initial death-notice is omitted to build suspense, producing an oral anacoluthon (ὁ δ᾽ ἔπειτα . . . τόν ῥ᾽ ἔβαλε, cf. 11.122ff., 13.424–54n., 16.401–4, 16.463–5, 17.306–9, 17.610ff.). The full pathos of his no doubt fictitious story is reserved for Aias' speech (438f.): the Aiantes honoured their θεράπων 'like their parents', i.e. he was a generation older. Phoinix too was exiled for murder and honoured as a θεράπων by those who took him in; cf. Patroklos or Medon, slain at 332 (13.694–7n.). With Lukophron's name cf. Lukomedes: the wolf's cleverness was proverbial. His father Mastor has a related name, 'Tracker' (von Kamptz, *Personennamen* 250); the wise Halitherses aptly receives the same patronym (*Od.* 2.158).

431–2 Kuthera, off Cape Maleia (*Od.* 9.81), is not in the *Catalogue of Ships*, like many isles; it is unclear who held it. Sparta took it from Argos in the sixth century; Andron (*FGH* 10 F 11) guessed from *Od.* 4.514ff. that Aigisthos lived there! Autolukos gave a helmet he stole in Boeotia to a Kutheran, who gave it to a Cretan (10.266ff.), but why Lukophron fled to Aias at Salamis is obscure. T's emendation Κυθήρριον is an attempt to explain this: Kutherros was an Attic deme (van der Valk, *Researches* I 455f.).

Kuthera, a major entrepôt between Bronze Age Crete and the mainland, appears in a tribute-list (really an itinerary) of Amenhotep III, along with Amnisos, Phaistos, Kudonia, Mukenai, Thebes, Messene (?), Nauplia, Knossos and Luktos in the lands of the Cretans (*Kftiw*) and Danaans (*Tny*): see Coldstream and Huxley, *Kythéra*, London 1972, 33; Stella, *Tradizione micenea* 170; W. Helck in H.-G. Buchholz, ed., *Ägaische Bronzezeit*, Darmstadt 1987, 218f.; S. Wachsmann, *Aegeans in the Theban Tombs*, Louvain 1987, 95f. The slaves at Pylos included 'women from Kuthera', no doubt bought at a market there, like those from Lemnos (14.229–30n.), Miletos, Knidos, Chios and Assuwa (Chadwick in *Studies E. L. Bennett*, Salamanca 1988, 91). Phoenicians founded the island's cult of Aphrodite (Hdt. 1.105.3). They surely came for the purple dye boiled from the sea-snail *Murex brandaris* for which they, and Kuthera, were famous (P. Cartledge, *Sparta and Lakonia*, London 1979, 122f.); on their presence in the Aegean see 23.740–9nn. Aphrodite's cult-image was armed, which accords with her descent from the war-goddess Astarte (Frazer on Paus. 3.23.1). Hesiod derives her epithet Κυθέρεια from 'holy' Κύθηρα, implying that her cult there antedates that on Cyprus (*Theog.* 192ff.). Homer may have this in mind when he calls Kuthera ζάθεα, but this adj. can describe places that are not especially holy, e.g. Nisa or Pherai; ἱερός is used with equal licence (e.g. 2.625, 4.378n.).

436–9 436 = 466 (with Τεῦκρος), a significant repetition since 436 lacks other parallels. For πέπον, rare with a name in the voc. (5.109, 16.492, *Aspis* 350, cf. *Od.* 9.447), see 13.120–3n. Aias' iteration νῶϊν–νῶϊ stresses Teukros' share in their mutual loss. ἔνδον ἐόντα conveys that Lukophron came to join their household (13.363n.). The topos of a young stranger granted the same honour as one's sons, as at 9.481ff. (cf. 13.170–81n.), exalts that person without demeaning one's family. Here 'parents' replaces 'children' to suit Lukophron's age. Zenodotus conjectured τέκεσσιν (Arn/A); no doubt he thought a retainer must be junior to his lord, comparing 551, 5.71.

440–1 Hektor is μεγάθυμος only here: the epithet, generic before names shaped ∪ – – | (4×), is moved from its usual place. Aias is reproachful; with ποῦ νύ τοι ἰοί cf. π. τοι τόξον (5.171), π. τοι ἀπειλαί (13.219, 20.83), all in dialogues where X chides Y for not fighting, Y explains, and X persuades him to enter battle (13.206–45n.). Here Teukros' exploits interrupt this pattern, postponing Y's explanation and X's reply to 467ff. Arrows are again 'swift to kill' at *Od.* 22.75: elsewhere ὠκύμορος means 'swift to die' (1.417 etc.). Apollo likewise gave Pandaros and Herakles their bows (2.827, *Cat.* 33.29), yet Pandaros obtained his bow for himself (4.105ff.). Aristarchus saw this as figurative, i.e. the god gave Teukros his *skill*; no doubt he thought Apollo should not help his foes, the Greeks. But Apollo can give archers both their bows and their skill, just as the Muses gave Hesiod and Archilochus both their equipment and their talent (cf. West on *Theog.* 22–34). The bow is useless without the skill, and *vice versa*. For 'gifts of the gods' see 4.320, 9.37–9, 13.727ff., *Od.* 8.167f.; S. R. van der Mije, *Mnem.* 40 (1987) 241–67. Teukros already made good use of his bow in this battle (13.177–8n.): Geometric vases depict archers mainly as defenders of ships (Ahlberg, *Fighting* 107).

443–4 Cf. *Od.* 21.11f., 59f., up to the Iliadic *hapax* ἰοδόκος. The epos had an elastic formular system for bows, using sing. and plur. forms: καμπύλα/ἀγκύλα τόξα, παλίντονα τ. (8.266, *Hy.* 27.16), τ. π. (10.459), τόξον ἔΰξοον. Teukros' swift volley proves him a good archer. The synizesis in βέλεα is paralleled in σάκεα (4.113), στήθεα (11.282) and several words at the verse-end (Chantraine, *GH* 1 56); full contraction is seen in τεύχη, τεμένη, αἰνοπαθῆ (7.207, *Od.* 11.185, 18.201).

445–65 Teukros' exploits resemble 8.309–29 (Fenik, *TBS* 227), when he kills Hektor's driver (for whom Hektor finds a substitute) but fails to kill Hektor, who hurls a stone that snaps his bowstring; here he kills Pouludamas' driver (whom Pouludamas replaces), but misses Hektor when Zeus snaps his bowstring. There are verbal similarities (452 = 8.314; with 458, 465 cf. 8.309, 329). See further 262–404n.

445–51 The victim's usual biography is replaced by the pathetic detail that Kleitos was slain *because* (explanatory asyndeton) he was having trouble with his horses, *since* (γάρ) he had steered into the worst fighting to please Hektor. Kleitos looks like an invention, cf. Klutios (419): two minor characters are called Peisenor (*Od.* 1.429, 2.38). The choice between ἀγλαὸς υἱός and ἄλκιμος υ., formulae also found in the acc., is affected by the father's name: names in -έος and -ίου precede ἄλκιμος 15/21× in the epos, whereas those in -ονος and -οροs precede ἀγλαὸς 25/36×, ἄλκιμος never. On Pouludamas' epithets see 13.756–9n.

449–51 Pouludamas is not far from his chariot, as 454 implies; Kleitos dies for his folly in driving towards the thickest mêlée, where Hektor is, rather than staying near his leader, as drivers should (see on 13.383ff.). He is hit from behind, presumably because he had turned his chariot round in order to move to another sector of the battle. Pouludamas bids the substitute driver stay close and watch him (456f.) – this calamity must not recur! Aristarchus athetized 449–51 on two grounds. (i) Verses 449f. recur at 17.291f., where they describe an ally who fights 'to please Hektor and the Trojans'; this ill suits a Trojan fighting for himself and his father. But a Trojan can surely wish to help Hektor and the Trojans win; thus at 744f. Trojans act χάριν Ἕκτορος. (ii) Kleitos cannot be hit from behind if he is driving forwards. In his book *On the camp* (13.681n.) Aristarchus retracted this objection, arguing that the Trojans backed their chariots towards the sterns, with the drivers facing Troy and the warriors facing the foe, protecting their drivers' backs with their shields (cf. bT on 385–7). Aristophanes emended this 'problem' away by reading πρόσθε for ὄπισθε (Did/T)! In one of his editions Aristarchus had the majority reading ἱεμένῳ (Did/A), an error after οἱ; ἱεμένων arouses pathos (differently van der Valk, *Researches* II 117). Arrows are πολύστονοι only here; cf. βέλεα στονόεντα (5× epos), στονόεντες ὀϊστοί (2× *Od.*). For the wounds they inflict see on 11.375ff.

452–60 For the pathetic detail of empty chariots rattling about the battlefield cf. 16.377–9n. Trojans named Astunoos die at 5.144, *Little Iliad* frag. 13 B. = 14 D.; the unknown Protiaon is based on the archaism προτί. Note the etymological play σχεδὸν ἴσχειν (456). Teukros would indeed have stopped Hektor from fighting, had he slain him! Aristophanes, missing the understatement, read ἔπαυσε μάχην (Did/A), which is in few MSS; ἔ. μάχης, in Zenodotus and the vulgate, is the expected phrase, cf. 15, 250, 17.81. βαλὼν ἐξείλετο θυμόν 'conjugates' β. ἐκ θ. ἔλοιτο etc. (4×).

461–70 Zeus acts from afar, by means obscure and terrifying, to make Teukros' bowstring break and save Hektor. On such interventions cf. 13.434–6n. and de Jong, *Narrators* 70f.; thus Athene deflects Pandaros' arrow, Apollo makes Teukros miss Hektor and Zeus saves Sarpedon from Teukros' shot (4.127ff., 8.311, 12.400–3). We call these accidents, but bards had little idea of chance and no word for it; every event is willed by a god, even if there is also an obvious human cause (see pp. 3–7). Unlike his characters, the poet knows which god is at work. Teukros, finding the event unexpected and unwelcome, blames a *daimon* (468), which connotes sudden, malevolent interference; the more objective Aias speaks of a *theos* (473); Hektor, utterly confident, ascribes it to Zeus (489ff.), but has to add that his interventions are easily detected (see Erbse, *Götter* 259ff., especially 267; de Jong, *Narrators* 157–9).

461–5 Διòς πυκινòν νόον splits the formula Δ. ν. (αἰγιόχοιο), as at 16.688, 17.176; π. enters from phrases like π. ἔπος (4×), μήδεα πυκνά (3.202), cf. Ζηνòς πυκινόφρονα βουλήν (*HyHerm* 538). εὖχος means not 'prayer' here – Hektor has not prayed – but 'glory'. It belongs to the same substitution-system as κῦδος, i.e. εὖχος ἔδωκε/ἀρέσθαι/ὀρέξῃ etc. (Muellner, EYXOMAI 108ff.); cf. κ. ὑπέρτερον (3×) beside ὑ. εὖχος (11.290). The verb once meant 'declare': cf. Latin *fāri* beside *fāma*. For ἐὖστρεφής, here of a bow-string, see 13.599n.; the material would be ox-sinew (4.122). ἐὖστρεπτος describes leather halyards at *Od.* 15.291. A. A. Parry (*Blameless Aegisthus* 100) asked why the bow is 'blameless', since all other epithets of bows denote physical qualities; but this gives the mishap an apt emphasis (de Jong, *Narrators* 157–9). τῷ in 464 denotes Hektor, and ἐρύοντι goes with οἱ; the repeated οἱ stresses Teukros' lost control over his weapon. ἰòς χαλκοβαρής recurs at *Od.* 21.423; χ. otherwise describes μελίη (3× Hom., cf. 11.96) or δόρυ (*Od.* 11.532), cf. ὀϊστòς | ὀξυβελής (4.126).

467–70 Teukros' reaction resumes the rebuke-pattern (440–1n.). He shudders, as had Aias when he urged him to use his bow (436–9n.); Teukros refers back to this as 'our plan of battle'. From πάγχυ, 467 = 16.120, where a like setback befalls Aias himself: Hektor lops the end off his pike; Aias shudders, recognizing Zeus's action, and retreats. For the metaphor ἐπì ... κείρειν, 'curtail', cf. διακείρειν at 8.8. Teukros reveals his growing alarm by proceeding backwards from the fact that a god has dashed the bow from his hand via its broken string to the fact that he had fitted a new one that morning, knowing that many arrows would 'leap' from it (cf. 313–17n.). νεόστροφον, a *hapax* in Greek, and the Homeric *hapax* πρώϊον both make this clear. ἐὖστροφον (in Did/A), an easy error after 463, is a genuine form (13.599n.); but, as Eustathius saw (1025.43–5), Teukros' speech carefully varies the preceding narrative. No doubt to remove the 'problem' that a new string snaps, Zenodotus read πρώην (better πρώην), 'two days ago' (cf. 2.303); Aristarchus wavered (Did/A), but in Arn/A well replies that Teukros' string broke during the rout the day before (8.328), so he would just have fitted a new one that morning.

472–5 Aias bids Teukros arm for close combat: he is good at this too (cf. 13.313f.). Aias' call to action, which begins at once with ἀλλά, is calm and calming. A god has 'set at naught' Teukros' bow (cf. 366), not 'broken' it, and 'grudges' it to the Greeks (cf. 23.865), instead of 'hates us' or the like:

supply βιόν with both verbs. Verse 472 adapts the phrase βιὸς καὶ ταρφέες ἰοί (11.387, *Od.* 22.246). Leaf thinks 473 may be interpolated to supply an infin. to go with ἔα, like 20.312 or 24.558, both spurious; but ἐάω often governs a runover infin., especially κεῖσθαι (5.684f., 5.847f., 8.125f., 19.8f.). Teukros must take in his hands a spear, and a shield on his shoulder: note the chiasmus and zeugma. The epithet 'long' (4× Hom.) shows the spear's virtue: a naval pike is not meant.

476–7 'May they not take the ships without effort, even if they defeat us' (δαμασσάμενοι is middle). Cf. 8.512, μὴ μὰν ἀσπουδεί γε νεῶν ἐπίβαιεν ἕκηλοι, or 22.304. 'The wish is perhaps tinged with an asseverative force, and "I swear they shan't" lurks beneath "may they never"' (Denniston, *Particles* 332). Leaf implausibly discerns a concessive opt., 'though they may take the ships, at least it surely must not be without effort'. ἀσπουδεί is an old loc.; A's spelling -δί is wrong (Risch, *Kleine Schriften* 167–75).

478 The scansion ὁ δὲ τ- is caused by the bard recollecting 442, ὣς φάθ', ὁ δὲ ξ-, since the rest of 442 is remodelled in 483, framing this brief arming-scene; ὁ δ' αὖ, a 'correction' *metri gratia*, is in no MS prior to Eustathius. On the huts' location see 406–9n.

479–82 These vv. resemble *Od.* 22.122–5, when Odysseus, out of arrows, dons those parts of the panoply not used by archers (cf. 13.714f.), in the standard order – shield, helmet and spears; a like scene at *Aspis* 135f. reverses the spear and helmet. These versions of the arming type-scene (3.330–8n.) omit the greaves, corslet and sword, because archers already wear them. Thus 479 condenses 3.334f. = 16.135f. = 19.372f., to exclude the sword (for τετραθέλυμνον see 13.130–1n.); 480f. = 3.336f., 16.137f., *Od.* 22.123f., but 481, absent in papyri and most good codices, is clearly a concordance-interpolation. Verse 482 recurs at *Od.* 1.99, 15.551 and 20.127 in another type-scene, that of a civilian dressing and going out (carrying a spear was still necessary, cf. Thuc. 1.5.3ff.); at 10.135 and 14.12 it is used of Nestor, who is really a non-combatant. A warrior usually takes two spears or one 'which fits his palm' (16.130–9n.).

Wilamowitz (*IuH* 241) asks why Teukros arms at all, when he achieves nothing and never reappears. Winter (*MNO* 152) well replies that his arming leads up to the close combat at 515ff.; his *aristeia* must have its arming-scene, but this is placed at its end because, as an archer, he needs no panoply. Also, this scene undercuts Hektor's exhortation, since we already know that Teukros is still in the fight; our last view of him is of his confident return to battle.

483–4 For 483 see 478n. and cf. *Od.* 22.99, 112, again in the context of arming an archer. εἶδεν Τεύκρου β- is innovative (cf. 422–5n., 16.818).

485–514 Fenik (*TBS* 90f.) shows that Hektor's exhortation parallels two sequences where a Greek retreats and is seen by Hektor, who boasts that

Zeus is aiding the Trojans (8.172ff., 11.284ff.); each time the opening verses resemble 484–7 (cf. too 424f., 17.183–5). His speech, and Aias' equally fine reply, both aim to make the men engage at close quarters, forming a dense line; as Latacz proved in *Kampfdarstellung*, this is the usual purpose of such speeches. Thus ἀγχιμαχηταί and ἀολλέες on Hektor's lips are matched by αὐτοσχεδίῃ on Aias', and by the latter's thesis that it is better to decide the issue at once by coming to grips, than to endure slow attrition by a weaker foe (510ff.). This change in tactics explains why we hear of stab-wounds as well as missile-wounds in the ensuing battle. The balance between the speeches, of similar length, is maintained in the poet's summary of each (500 = 514).

486–99 ἀλλά at 494 bisects the speech, as often. Lohmann discovered the ring-structure in 486–94 (*Reden* 67n.): a central maxim at 490–2 is framed by references to Zeus's aid, with exhortations on either side forming a preamble (486–8) and call to action (494ff.) respectively. Mentions of the ships at the beginning (488), middle (494) and end reinforce this pattern: the last two frame Hektor's call to die gloriously to save one's country, family, house and property. We are often reminded that the Trojans are defending their wives and children (8.57, 10.422, 17.223, 21.587); Nestor bids the Greeks recall their 'children, wives, property and parents' at 663. As Winter saw (*MNO* 155), Aias matches Hektor's trust in Zeus by restating the Greeks' natural superiority (518); both leaders understand their own strengths, since both themes persist during this battle.

489 Διόθεν, also at 24.194, 24.561, arose by analogy with *o*-stems, as did πατρόθεν, ἀλόθεν or λειμωνόθεν; such forms are common later. For the original form of the suffix cf. Arcadian θύσθεν, 'outside', from θυρ- (M. Lejeune, *Les Adverbes grecs en -θεν*, Bordeaux 1939, 59, 104). Cf. the spread of -όφι to κοτυληδονόφῑν (*Od.* 5.433). βλαφθέντα means 'sent off course', 'hindered' (cf. 647, 16.331), not 'damaged', because Hektor refers to the arrows, not the bow; he knows that these are no longer coming at him, but cannot see the bowstring snap. βλάπτω, often used of gods (22.15n.), first means 'harm' in Hesiod (*LfgrE* s.v.).

490–3 For several reasons, the poet makes Hektor think of Zeus rather than Apollo, who aided him at 355ff. Hektor has trusted in Zeus's support ever since 11.200ff.; Apollo has dropped from view because stress must now fall on the plan of Zeus in action; and, as Hektor says, Zeus ultimately grants victory or defeat: cf. 20.242f., Ζεὺς δ' ἀρετὴν ἄνδρεσσιν ὀφέλλει τε μινύθει τε, | ὅππως κεν ἐθέλῃσι, and 17.176–8 (cf. 16.688–90n.). It can be hard to detect a god or know his mind (13.72n., *Erga* 483f.). Hektor blends the formula ῥεῖα δ' ἀρίγνωτος etc. (4× *Od.*) with the hymnic theme of how easily a god can humble or exalt, give or take away; cf. *Erga* 6, ῥεῖα δ' ἀρίζηλον μινύθει καὶ ἄδηλον ἀέξει, or *Theog.* 442f. with West's nn. After stating the antithesis in a distich, he applies it to the Greeks and Trojans in a single verse; the forceful chiasmus ἐγγυαλίξῃ – μινύθῃ – μινύθει – ἀρήγει and the varied constructions lead up to the emphatic ἄμμι δ' ἀρήγει.

ἐγγυαλίζω is from a root γυ-, '(curved) hand', seen in ἐγγύς, 'at hand', ἐγγύη, 'pledge', μεσηγύ, 'between (the hands)', ὑπόγυος, 'present' (see 13.146–8n. and Nussbaum, *Head and Horn* 59f.). The innovative synizesis in ἠμὲν ὁτέοισῑν (with n-mobile making position) is paralleled in the sing. at 664,12.428 (cf. Shipp, *Studies* 80); Leaf, misinterpreting Hrd/A, invents a variant ὅτοισιν. For κῦδος ὑπέρτερον see 461–5n. The variant μινύθῃσι is an error by anticipation of οὐκ ἐθέλῃσι, which forms a single idea, 'refuses' (otherwise we would expect μή).

494–9 Lycurgus (330 B.C.) quotes these stirring verses from memory or a rhapsodic text (*In Leocr.* 103); his departures from the vulgate are all inferior. His διαμπερές removes the call to close combat conveyed by ἀολλέες (485–514n.); his νήπια τέκνα (cf. 5.480, 17.223) conveys the vulnerability of orphans, but the loftier παῖδες ὀπίσσω stresses the continuity of the warrior's family (cf. bT); *Od.* 14.64 supports οἶκος καὶ κλῆρος (he reverses the nouns); his ἵκωνται for οἴχωνται imports the Greek viewpoint. Note the ample doublets βλήμενος ἠὲ τυπείς (for the difference cf. 13.288–9n.) and θάνατον καὶ πότμον, which exalts death as something fated: cf. θ. τε μόρον τε, θ. κ. κῆρα(ς), θάνατος καὶ μοῖρα and 16.684–7n. The repetition τεθνάτω – τεθνάμεν, in emphatic runover position (cf. 3.102, 22.365), is matched by 'safe' and 'unharmed' in the emotive list of wife, children, home and property (cf. Callinus frag. 1.7). Verse 499 = 7.460; Eustathius (1026.62) queried the redundancy of 'be gone with their ships' – how else can the Greeks depart? But this is not a clumsy misuse of a standard verse, but sets up Aias' reply that they cannot *walk* home without the ships (504f.). Hektor's demand that they go is more reasonable than his actions, which give them no option but to fight to the end; we are meant to notice the discrepancy.

Patriotism for one's *polis* is certainly present in Homer (Greenhalgh, *Historia* 21 (1972) 528–37); at 24.500 Priam says Hektor died 'fighting for his fatherland'. Lohmann (*Reden* 119n., 168n.), denying this, thinks οὔ οἱ ... τεθνάμεν (496f.) is interpolated from Tyrtaeus, along with 12.243. This is to reverse the truth, as Latacz shows (*Kampfdarstellung* 1–10, 232ff.). ὑμέων is normal (7.159, 3× *Od.*, 4× *Hy.*), beside ὑμείων with metrical lengthening (4× Hom.); it will not scan otherwise. Cf. ἡμέων, ἡμείων (10×, 4×), and p. 8 n. 2. κλῆρος with the sense 'property' evolved from the 'lot' used to share out the patrimony among the heirs (185–93n.). This sense is 'late' (2× *Od.*, 3× Hes.); many Greeks derived it from a supposed primordial allotment of land (so D). ἀκήρατος, 'untouched', is from κηραίνω, as at *Od.* 17.532; it denotes 'unsullied' water at 24.303. Its etymology is disputed (see *LfgrE* and Chantraine, *Dict.* s.v.).

500–1 Despite ἑκάστου with 'neglected' ϝ- (as at 505) and contracted -ου, 500 is formular (9×); with 501 cf. 13.489 (Aineias).

502–13 Aias is a blunt and forceful orator, asking whether the Greeks think they can walk home, if Hektor takes the ships – he is urging *his* men to fight, not to dance! As Hektor cited Zeus's aid as a source of hope, so Aias appeals to the Greeks' sense of shame at losing to an inferior foe (513). He does not even mention flight; only later (563f.) does he invoke the fact that more are slain in a rout than when men stand firm. By unmasking Hektor's intent, he shows that they have no choice but to fight: Hektor aims not to repatriate them but to annihilate them by burning the ships (494–9n.). Events have already proved this true (419f.); Hektor's own words do so at 557f. Hence Aias rightly urges that they avoid lengthy attrition and come to grips at once, when their superiority will be most telling. Ring-composition structures the speech (Lohmann, *Reden* 20). Appeals mentioning the ships and the choice of death or salvation mark its opening and close. Then follow two scornful questions about the ships (cf. 735f., 5.465f.), and two statements about fighting; Aias raises and dispels any illusions his men may have. He shifts the emphasis from feet, with which we walk or dance (or flee!), to hands, with which we fight (510). Hektor's speech flowed smoothly: Aias' asyndeta convey the urgency of the crisis.

502–6 On the rallying-cry αἰδώς see 13.95,120–3n. 'Now it is *sure* that we perish or ...'; for this sense of ἄρκιος cf. 2.393 and Chantraine, *Dict.* s.v. ἀρκέω. With the phrasing of 502f. cf. 1.117, 17.227f. Verse 504 resembles 11.315, which has εἴ κεν for ἤν (contracted from εἰ ἄν). Since ἤν, standard in Herodotus, is not rare in Homer, it must stand, *pace* Chantraine, *GH* II 281f.; contraction entered the epos fastest in small words used with the most fluidity. ἐμβαδόν recurs in Pausanias; cf. the joke to visitors to Ithake, 'I don't suppose you came on foot' (*Od.* 1.173 and 2×). Verse 505 adapts ἤν/πρὶν πατρίδα γαῖαν ἵκεσθαι etc. (14× *Od.*); to admit ἵξεσθαι, ἕκαστος ousts the verb from the verse-end, as its 'neglected' ϝ- confirms. π. γ. ἵκεσθαι itself extends π. γ. | (78×). Verse 506 blends ὄτρυνε δὲ λαὸν ἅπαντα (16.501, 17.559) with ὀτρύνοντος ἄκουσαν (2× *Od.*, cf. 199).

508–10 Dance and massed battle are opposite poles of group activity, just as sex and duels are antithetic forms of intimacy (on the comparison of war to sex see 13.290–1n.). Thus Aphrodite says Paris looks as if he is going to a dance rather than coming from battle; Hektor boasts that he knows how 'to dance in War'; Aineias mocks Meriones, who eluded his spear, by calling him a tumbler; Patroklos taunts a victim for somersaulting like a dancer; and Priam praises his sons' skill at dancing – they are useless in battle (3.392ff., 7.241, 16.617, 16.745, 24.261)! This polarity perhaps led to the interpolation of 13.731. νόος καὶ μῆτις is formular: cf. 7.447 (acc.), *Od.* 19.326 (acc., separated), 'Homer' frag. 11 D. ἤ after τοῦδε is pleonastic but aids comprehension. With αὐτοσχεδίη supply μάχη: bT's variant -ίην, an adverb, is the usual form (12.192, 17.294, *Od.* 11.536, cf. σχεδίην at 5.830), but that does not prove it right.

511–12 'Better *either* to perish once for all *or* to survive, *than* to suffer thus in vain for a long time . . .' (so Aristarchus, Nicanor). Ancient readers were confused by the two senses of ἤ and the asyndeton usual with βέλτερον: cf. 14.81, 18.302, 22.129 (β. αὖτ' ἔριδι ξυνελαυνέμεν ὅττι τάχιστα), *Erga* 365. ἕνα χρόνον is a unique idiom for 'once for all': cf. χρόνον meaning '(for) a while' (LSJ s.v., 3a), and βούλομ' ἅπαξ . . . ἀπὸ θυμὸν ὀλέσσαι, | ἢ δηθὰ στρεύγεσθαι ἐὼν ἐν νήσῳ ἐρήμη (*Od.* 12.350f.). στρεύγομαι, 'be distressed', next in Timotheus, may come from an Indo-European word for 'wear away' (Chantraine, *Dict.* s.v.); Aristarchus glossed it στραγγίζεσθαι, 'be squeezed' drop by drop (στράγξ) 'and perish slowly', perhaps comparing στραγ(γ)εύομαι, 'loiter'.

515–91 The close-range killing (405–591n.) begins with the alternation Greek–Trojan–Greek, with participants of high rank; this pattern is rare in disjointed lists (Strasburger, *Kämpfer* 62). Contrast e.g. 6.29–36, where all the dead are Trojans. The list soon becomes a chain, where each death causes the next (520ff.): Meges, seeing his follower fall, slays a Trojan in revenge; Dolops attacks Meges as he strips the body, but is speared; Melanippos advances to avenge him, but is speared by Antilokhos. The leisurely narrative conveys the deadlock: elaboration stresses how Meges is saved by his corslet, while antithetical speeches by Hektor, Aias and Menelaos mark the importance of Melanippos' death (545–91n.).

515–17 It passes belief that Hektor slays *two* Phocian leaders called Skhedios – the son of Iphitos (2.518) at 17.306, and Perimedes' son here. Only by renaming Skhedios' father did Homer avoid killing the same man twice, a crime he committed elsewhere (13.643–59n.). Aristarchus held as usual that this is merely a case of two men with the same name. T record another evasion: if we alter 'Phocians' to 'Athenians', and 'Stikhios' to 'Skhedios' at 13.195, the problem vanishes – but so does the text (cf. Zenodotus' conjecture at *Od.* 3.307). Kullmann (*Quellen* 122f.) thinks Homer erred because in pre-Homeric saga Skhedios was not slain: traces of his *nostos* survive in later sources. Laodamas is one of Antenor's sons, who are readily invented for cannon-fodder: of the eleven in the *Iliad*, seven die. Homer reshuffles the same onomastic elements to create the Antenorids Laodokos and Iphidamas (4.87, 11.221); he already had Antenor's father Laomedon in mind (419–21, 525–43nn.). Minor Odyssean personages are called Laodamas and Perimedes, which was an everyday Myc. name. For Laodamas' unique title 'leader of the infantry' cf. 5.743–4n.; πρυλέες hardly means πρόμαχοι, who have no specific leader. He surely receives this title simply to put him on a par with the Greek victims listed either side, since the poet could give his unit no geographical name. πρύλις once meant a 'war-dance', whence πρυλέες came to mean simply 'warriors' (cf. 508–10n. and Trümpy, *Fachausdrücke* 179).

518–19 The Epean leader Otos is unknown; a namesake is son of Aloeus (cf. 13.478–80n.). He is from Kullene, the port of Elis opposite Meges' island realm (not Mt Kullene in Arcadia, 2.603); Meges' father Phuleus, at odds with Augeias for not paying Herakles, led a group of Epeans from Elis to Doulikhion (13.685–8n.), and Otos may have joined this exodus. Kullene, on the N. side of Cape Khelonatas below the Myc. citadel probably called Hurmine (2.615–17n.), is now Killini/Glarentza, once Angevin capital of the Morea; Middle Helladic sherds are known and Myc. occupation is likely. The port appears in a tale about the early Arcadian king Pompos (Paus. 8.5.8). See J. Servais, *BCH* 85 (1961) 123–61 and 88 (1964) 9–50; differently J. A. Richmond, *CQ* 18 (1968) 195–7. Verse 519 blends the patterns of 5.534, Αἰνείω ἕταρον μεγαθύμου, and μεγαθύμων ἀρχὸς Ἀβάντων (2×).

520–4 Short clauses with constant changes of subject express the rapid events of 520–4; contrast the flowing periods and parentheses of 525–34. In a typical case of dual causation, Pouludamas evades Meges' spear-thrust because he recoils *and* Apollo protects him (cf. 5.662, 8.311, 13.554f.). Leaf thinks this implies that Pouludamas was a seer: cf. his understanding of omens and ability to see 'past and future' (12.217ff., 18.250). His father was allegedly a priest from Delphi (D on 12.231)! ὕπαιθα, 6× *Il.* only, means 'out from under', < ὑπαί + -θ(ε)ν: cf. 21.255f. The hiatus in Πάνθου υἱόν (also 17.9, 17.59) comes from *Πανθόο' (see p. 18 n. 34). Kroismos is a unique name, perhaps Asiatic (cf. Kroisos). For the formulae of 523f. cf. 16.593–9n.; the latter half of 524 recurs at 6.28, 22.368, as one of many sequels to δούπησεν δὲ πεσών (cf. on 419–21, 539–44). ἐσύλα is an inceptive imperf., cf. 17.60.

525–43 Dolops matches Meges' onrush and his blow (525, 528 replicate 520, 523), but not his success; he sustains a wound like Kroismos', and is stripped likewise (with 540–5 cf. 520–4). It is typical that Meges is attacked while stripping a victim, rare that he hits back (13.383–401n.). A Dolops son of Klutos dies at 11.302 (cf. Dolopion at 5.77); the name is no doubt related to the Dolopes, an obscure Thessalian tribe (9.484). This Dolops is Hektor's cousin, since Priam, Lampos, Klutios(!) and Hiketaon are all sons of Laomedon (cf. 3.146f, where Panthoos also appears, and 20.237f.); Klutios lost a son earlier (419–21n.), and Hiketaon's son dies next (576f.). Again Homer just avoids killing the same man twice (515–17n.).

Dolops' lineage is neatly crafted, with an outer ring formed by αἰχμῆς ἐῢ εἰδώς – ἐῢ εἰδότα θούριδος ἀλκῆς, an inner ring of sonorous patronymics, and his father Lampos at the centre reinforcing the assonance. His fine pedigree stands in pathetic contrast to the sequel. First we hear that the corslet which saves Meges' life was *his* father's, and a more useful inheritance it is (this is framed by ἤρκεσε θώρηξ – ἤρκεσ' ὄλεθρον); next we see Dolops docked of his pretensions (Meges shears off his crest) and cheated of his hopes by Menelaos' spear, the weapon with which Dolops is supposedly so skilled. His lack of success and continuing expectation of it characterize him as a fool like Peisandros, also slain by Menelaos (with 539 cf. 13.609). With the latter's intervention cf. how Adamas smites Antilokhos' shield but is hit by Meriones, or how Harpalion dies (with 528f. cf. 13.561f., 646f.).

526 The patronymic Λαμπετίδης is oddly derived from Λάμπος. Leaf deems Λάμπος a *Kurzform* of Λάμπετος: both names are historically attested. Lampos was an equine name (8.185, *Od.* 23.246), Lampetos was a hero from Lesbos (Ap. Rhod. frag. 12 Powell) and Lampetiē was the Sun's daughter (*Od.* 12.132). But long and short forms of names rarely denote the same person (16.11n.). Homer gives the name 'Lampos' to make clear that it is not 'Lampetos' (Eustathius 1030.22). Λαμπετίδης is formed *metri gratia*, since *Λαμπίδης scans – ∪ –; cf. λαμπετόωντι (1.104 = *Od.* 4.662), an epic adaptation of the dual λάμπετον comparable to εὐχετόωντο, ἐρχατόωντο or ναιετάω (Leumann, *HW* 178–87). Many patronymics are altered to fit the metre, e.g. Δευκαλίδης (Janko, *Glotta* 65 (1987) 71). Dolops' incapacity belies the variant φέρτατου ἀνδρῶν, which T explain away as '(best) of his own *sons*'; this shows how the old reading φ. υἱόν arose. φέρτατος ἀ. is the best text: it is easy to introduce an acc. to bring εἰδότα closer to its noun, but in this context Lampos needs to be glorified, not his son.

530–4 The corslet's story stresses its value as a life-saver, and that of the institutions of *xenia* and inheritance by which Phuleus has secured his son's safety: the noble aims of the otherwise unknown Euphetes are fulfilled, and 534 subtly presents the event from Phuleus' viewpoint (οἱ ... παιδός). The poet gives, as usual, a brief detail of the object (its γύαλοι) and an account of how it entered the family. Cf. the histories of Apollo's aegis, Agamemnon's sceptre, Areïthoos' club, Meriones' boar's-tusk helmet, Akhilleus' spear or Odysseus' bow (309f., 2.101ff., 7.138ff., 10.266ff., 16.144f., *Od.* 21.13–38). Like Meriones' helmet, a corslet 'fitted with plates' must be a Myc. heirloom. The Dendra corslet has two large plates of bronze front and back, with extra ones to guard the neck, shoulders and belly; in the Pylos Sh tablets, corslets have twenty big and ten small /*opaworta*/, i.e. plates 'attached' to a cloth or leather backing, as in the Dendra specimen (Ventris and Chadwick, *Documents* 376f.). Plates from true scale-corslets appear at Mycenae only during LHIIIC, later than in Anatolia, the Levant or Cyprus. The Late Geometric corslet from Argos, consisting of two well-shaped bronze plates, proves that such armour was made in Homer's day, but Meges clearly wears an heirloom validated by its history and craftsmanship. Cf. on 5.99f. and H. W. Catling, *Arch. Hom.* ε 77–117.

531 One Ephurē was in Thessaly (13.301–3n.), another *was* Corinth (6.152–3n.), but this Ephure must be in Elis. It is surely Phuleus' place of origin, and thus forms another reference to his move from Elis (518–19n.), explaining, for any who have forgotten, why Otos of Kullene in Elis was among his officers. Hippias of Elis knew of Elean Ephura (*FGH* 6 F 12); from Strabo 8.338f. we deduce that Demetrius of Scepsis located it at or near Oinoē, 120 stades S.E. of Elis town, and equated the Selleeis river with the Ladon (cf. D and T, with Crates in D on 11.741). Demetrius adds that Herakles captured his bride Astuokheia at this Ephure (2.659, almost identical with 531); there too lived Agamede, venomous daughter of Elean Augeias (11.739ff.), and Odysseus got his poisons (*Od.* 1.259ff., 2.328f.). There is no need to assume that Homer knew of the Thesprotian Ephura, later Kikhuros, which appears in Pindar (*Nem.* 7.37) and Thuc. 1.46.4; 'Apollodorus' (2.7.6) and Diodorus (4.36.1) say Herakles won his bride at this Ephura, but call her father, whom he slew, Phulas or Phuleus. Like his pupil Apollodorus (see *FGH* 244 F 179–81 with Jacoby's nn.), Aristarchus thought Homer mentioned the Selleeis to show that he meant Thesprotian Ephure; both scholars linked the name with the Selloi (16.234–5n.), but it could just as well be cognate with Sellasia in Laconia or the Messenian river Sellas. Another Selleeis was near Arisbe in the Troad (2.838f.), yet its eponymous hero Arisbas belongs in Crete or Boeotia, where there were other places called Arisbe (cf. 13.363n., Hes. frag. 257, *Suda* s.v.)!

533–4 ἀλεωρή, found in the same phrase at 12.57, remained current in Ionic. ἤρκει, in a papyrus but few good codices, comes from 13.440; the aor., needed here, is supported by 529 (cf. 13.371, 397 and the formula ἤρκεσε λυγρὸν ὄλεθρον, 20.288–91n.). Someone in T deemed 534 redundant after 529; antiquity never liked ring-composition.

535–6 The noun κύμβαχος surely denotes the '(curved) plate' of a helmet. κ. recurs only at 5.585f., where it is an adj. describing a driver falling 'head-first' (ἔκπεσε δίφρου | κ. ἐν κονίῃσι), Like Callimachus (frag. 195.29), Homer perhaps linked that usage of it with κὔβιστάω, 'tumble (head-first)', since another driver falls from his vehicle 'like a tumbler' (16.742–5). Both senses are surely related to κύμβη, 'pot', 'head' (cf. Latin *testa* > French *tête*), κυμβητιάω, 'hurl headlong', and other words for curved objects like κύμβος, 'hollow', κύμβαλον, 'cymbal', κυφή, 'head' and κῦφός, 'stooping', with a root of non-Proto-Indo-European form **khu(m)bh-* (yet cf. Sanskrit *kumbháḥ*, Irish *cum*, 'vase'). Its suffix can be Greek, cf. στόμαχος, οὐριαχός. Leumann (*HW* 231–3) deems the noun original, the adj. a poetic misunderstanding: comparing the phrases ὕπτιος ἐν κονίῃσι | κάππεσεν (3×), κ. ἐν κονίῃσι (538, cf. helmets at 12.23) and ἐξεκυλίσθη | πρηνὴς ἐν κ. (a driver at 6.42f.), he thinks Homer used it as a fancy substitute for πρηνής at 5.586. O. Szemerényi (*Die Sprache* 11 (1965) 1–6) detects an Eastern loan-word, comparing

Hittite *kupaḫi-*, Hebrew (Philistine?) *qōbaʿ*, 'helmet'; Hoekstra takes it as 'crest-holder' (*Modifications* 98). For the epithets for helmet and spear see on 13.584f., 13.712–18.

537–8 The crest which Meges lops off the helmet itself (αὐτοῦ) is of horsehair, cf. λόφον ἱππιοχαίτην (6.469); crests of various types were used in both Myc. and Geometric times, but their large role in the formular system for helmets must be old. There is pathos when the newly dyed plume falls in the dust: cf. the befouling of Akhilleus' crest or of his horses' manes, or of the lovely hair of the dead Euphorbos and Hektor (see on 16.794ff.). Sea-purple, the fastest known dye, was precious (cf. 431–2n. and R. J. Forbes, *Studies in Ancient Technology* IV, Leiden 1956, 114–22); in Homer it is used on cloth, leather and ivory.

539–45 It is Dolops who still hopes to win, not Meges, despite the rapid shift of reference in 540 (οἱ = Meges). Having darted forward to make his thrust (529), he ought to retreat to safety, but is fool enough not to (for the irony cf. 525–43n.). He is no doubt turned sideways to face Meges, and thus fails to see Menelaos approach behind his back from the other side (for εὐράξ see 11.251n.): ὄπισθεν cannot mean 'behind his shield' (Leaf), since he sinks face-down, and a fugitive was hit 'in the shoulder from behind' at 341. — As usual, the good MSS rightly have unmetrical ἕως and ἤλπετο with contraction over a lost ϝ- (cf. 701 and p. 17f.). On the variant ἦλθ' ἐπαμύντωρ see 13.383–5n. For the demonic spear of 542f. cf. 5.661, 13.444n. ἐλιάσθη was used differently at 520. ἐεισάσθην is from ἵεμαι, 'be eager', not ἔΐσκω, 'suppose,' 'decide', despite Aristarchus' doubts: verbs connoting eagerness often take a fut. inf. (Chantraine, *GH* II 310). χαλκήρης, formular of arrows, spears and helmets (535), describes τεύχεα only here, in a drastic remodelling of the formula ἀπ' ὤμων τεύχε' ἐσύλα (524 above – another echo of those verses).

545–91 This scene begins and ends with attempts to strip a Trojan corpse. Its structure depends on twin antitheses between the opposing leaders Hektor and Aias and between the speeches of reproach, with an elaborated death for Melanippos; Hektor picks him out for rebuke as a relative of the slain Dolops. His reproach is balanced both by Aias' exhortation to the troops in general and by Menelaos' rebuke of Antilokhos in particular (since Menelaos slew Dolops, he has a right to talk). The insertion of these speeches transforms the expected tripartite narrative of Melanippos' death, since his death-notice is omitted, his biography is at 547ff., and his death-wound is described only at 576f.; lest his sad story be forgotten, he is addressed with an apostrophe at 582. The Greeks close ranks in reaction to Aias' speech, but Zeus rouses the Trojans (565ff.); this foreshadows their repulse of Antilokhos and the account of the god's plans (589ff.), thus introducing the next scene. Wilamowitz (*IuH* 241, 517n.) thought this one encompasses too much; in excising 560–7, he did not see how these verses heighten the crisis, remind us of the ships and lead up to the next scene (cf. Winter, *MNO* 159f.).

545–6 κασίγνητοι include cousins here – an Ionic usage (Hdt. 1.171.6); cf. the synonymic phrases κ. τε ἔται τε (etc., 3×), ἔ. καὶ ἀνεψιοί (9.464). When ἀδελφεός became the usual word for 'brother', the Ionians gave κ. a wider sense (cf. the fate of φρατήρ); some dialects kept it as 'brother' (Bowra, *JHS* 54 (1934) 65). Leumann (*HW* 307) derives Herodotus' usage from Homer, but both reflect a shifting vernacular. ἐνένιπε is a reduplicated aor. of ἐνίπτω/ἐνίσσω, hardly less odd than ἠνίπαπε (2.245 etc.); unique at the verse-end, it recurs 14× Hom., 8× as at 552.

547–51 Melanippos too is Hektor's cousin (525–43n.). From Perkotē on the Hellespont (2.837–9n.), he may well be invented, *pace* Schoeck, *Ilias und Aithiopis* 127f. As Fenik saw (*TBS* 147f.), three 'other' Melanippoi end lists of persons – two Trojan victims and a Nestorid (8.276, 16.695, 19.240); the name is used simply to fill up catalogues. It is rare enough that a speaker is described (281–5n.), let alone an addressee who does not reply. In fact 547–51, framed by ἐνένιπεν, turn out to be Melanippos' obituary (545–91n.); his pastoral life in peacetime, his renown among the Trojans and Priam's respect for him all evoke pathos. The audience, knowing the conventions, will have expected the worst. Other Homeric princes supervise cattle (5.313, 11.106, 14.445, *HyAphr* 76ff.). | ἴφθιμος is a rare epithet with names shaped ∪∪ – (∪), e.g. Μενέλαον (17.554). ὄφρα is used like ἕως, 'for a while' (277–8n.). On εἰλίποδας βοῦς see 6.424n.; with the alliteration (and etymological play!) in β. | βόσκε cf. 21.448, βοῦς βουκολέεσκες. Verses 549–51 = 13.174–6, where see n.; 551, absent in two papyri, may be lost by accident, but is surely a concordance-interpolation.

553–9 Hektor appeals to Melanippos' αἰδώς at seeing their cousin slain and, worse, the enemy handling his armour: ἐντρέπομαι, 'pay heed' (cf. *Od.* 1.59f.), is but a step from its modern sense 'feel shame'. Aias will exhort the Greeks in like terms. For the cognate theme of slackness (μεθήσομεν) cf. 13.95ff. Hektor's call for close combat deepens the sense of crisis (ἀποσταδόν is a *hapax* in Greek, cf. ἀποσταδά, *Od.* 6.143), confirming Aias' claim that he plans to fight to the death (502–13n.) – it is kill or be killed (cf. 12.172). Note the harsh assonances of 557f., and the forceful combination 'lofty Troy from top to bottom' (also at 13.772f.); so intent is he on slaughter that he leaves us to supply the necessary changes of subject. ἀνεψιοῦ κταμένοιο reflects *-ῐόο κτ-, with -ῐ- lengthened to preserve the Dark Age formula: cf. ἀδελφειοῦ κτ- for *-εόο κτ- (5.21) and p. 15 with n. 23. Verse 559 = 11.472, 16.632, again after rebukes.

561–4 =5.529–32 (Agamemnon speaking), save that 5.529 ends καὶ ἄλκιμον ἦτορ ἔλεσθε, whereas 561 = 661 below. This change makes 562 redundant: absent in two papyri and a few good codices, it must be a concordance-interpolation, *pace* van der Valk (*Researches* II 517–19). Aias means that more die when the ranks break and men flee than when they stand firm (cf. Tyrtaeus frag. 11.11–14); this was just as true of Geometric as of later battles (14.506–22n.). Aristarchus rightly left δ' out to make 563 more emphatic (Did/A); it is in nearly all MSS.

567 A 'brazen fence' is a line of armed men; cf. 4.299. The metaphor recurs in 'fence of teeth', 'fence against spears' (a shield, 646, cf. 5.316) and 'fence of the Achaeans' (Aias, 3×, and Akhilleus at 1.284).

568–71 Verse 568 recalls 560, as if to show that both speeches answer Hektor's. Menelaos is depicted as Antilokhos' friend (Willcock in *Mélanges Delebecque* 479ff.). Antilokhos saves his life; he sends him to bring Akhilleus bad news; and he rejoices at Antilokhos' concession in their quarrel, owning his debt to him (5.561ff., 17.685ff., 23.596ff.). A. Parry, noting that Menelaos is unusually aware of his own middle age, finds his reference to Antilokhos' youth condescending (*HSCP* 76 (1972) 18). But 'no Achaean is younger or swifter' is a hyperbaton for 'no young Achaean is swifter' (Heyne): Antilokhos 'beat all the young men at running' (23.756), yet does not win the race. His speed will be needed for the attack. With the phrasing cf. νεώτερός εἰμι | σεῖο (Antilokhos to Menelaos, 23.587f.); οὔ τις σεῖο βροτῶν ὀλοώτερος ἄλλος (23.439, Menelaos to Antilokhos); and 10.165, *Od.* 3.111f., 10.552f., *Erga* 445. The rare parenthesis ὡς σύ comes from the phrase-structure of ὡς σὺ κελεύεις (7× Hom.). For εἰ opening a wish, here amounting to a polite request, see Chantraine, *GH* II 214.

573–5 = 4.496–8, from καί; Antilokhos looks about, to check that nobody leaps out to cast at him in his exposed position before the front rank (bT), but the Trojans 'back away' (ὑπὸ ... κεκάδοντο). This is not from χάζομαι, but cognate with the aor. active at 11.334 and fut. at *Od.* 21.153, 21.170 ('deprive of'), cf. ἐκεκήδει, 'had withdrawn' (Hsch.). The hunter's successful shot (581) may imply that Antilokhos casts at Melanippos, as if he heard Hektor's exhortation, and not at random; the same question arises at 16.284ff.

576–8 On Melanippos see 547–51n.; he is coming to join the fight, as Hektor ordered (556). For the phrase υἱὸν ὑπέρθυμον ⏑⏑ – – | cf. 4.365; it is nom. at 5.376, *Od.* 3.448, and reshaped as | υἱὸν ὑπερθύμου ⏑⏑ – ⏑⏑ at 5.77, 8.120, where the contracted gen. betrays innovation. πολεμόνδε means 'to battle': cf. ἱέμενον π. βάλε στῆθος παρὰ μαζόν and νισόμενον π. κατὰ σ. β. δουρί (8.313, 13.186). Verse 578 = 13.187; its absence in three of four papyri and some codices, like the existence of a variant 'darkness covered his eyes', prove it a concordance-interpolation like 5.42, to make clear that the blow is fatal.

579–91 Antilokhos' rush forward and wise retreat, the pathos of his victim's fall and the mounting fury of the Trojan attack are conveyed, first, by a fine pair of similes that convert him from a hound fetching a slain fawn into a lion retreating before a crowd can gather; second, by the address to Melanippos which the similes frame; and by the Trojans' progress, in the continuing series of animal images, from being like a fawn, which evokes timidity (13.102–4n.), to resembling men driving off lions (588), lions themselves (592) and then a lion scattering cows (630ff.). These images herald and then frame the next scene, a Greek rout (Moulton, *Similes* 69f.).

579–81 Antilokhos leaps out as had Meges and Dolops (520, 525); the hunting-dog symbolizes his obedience to Menelaos' behest. Melanippos' body is likened, ignobly, to a dead fawn. A like image describes the Trojans trying to snatch Patroklos' body, but their failure is conveyed by how the simile ends, not by a second image (17.725ff.): ἴθυσαν δὲ κύνεσσιν ἐοικότες, οἵ τ' ἐπὶ κάπρῳ | βλημένῳ ἀΐξωσι πρὸ κούρων θηρητήρων ... The dog starts the fawn from its den (cf. 22.190). τόν is governed by βαλών, since τυγχάνω takes a gen. (cf. 23.726).

582–5 An apostrophe to so minor a hero as Melanippos is unique; its emotive tone evokes his sad biography (547–51n.). It is often applied to Menelaos, whose name gravitates to the same metrical slot (see 4.127, 13.602–3nn.). μενεχάρμης, 3× of Antilokhos, adorns other names shaped − ∪∪ − (11.122, 303); though generic, the epithet is apt. With 584 cf. 17.257; 585 appears with Aineias' name at 5.571.

586–8 This simile resembles the scene on Akhilleus' shield where lions raid a herd of cattle defended by drovers and dogs (18.579ff.); this reflects the realities of life in Ionia. As if to authenticate the Nemean lion, lion-bones are known from Mycenaean Tiryns and Keos; lions roamed Macedonia throughout antiquity and Turkey until the sixteenth century A.D. (Hdt. 7.125f.; B. Helly, *REA* 70 (1968) 275–82; P. Warren, *JHS* 109 (1979) 123n.; J. Boessneck and A. von den Driesch, *Archäologischer Anzeiger* 1981, 257f.). The lion is the θήρ *par excellence*. At 11.546ff. Aias retreats θηρὶ ἐοικώς (cf. 3.449); a full simile two verses later likens him to a lion driven by men and dogs from a farmyard full of cattle. Here the expansion θ. κακὸν ῥέξαντι ἑ. turns the usual brief image into the start of a full simile. Leaf takes κ. simply as 'harm', but Eustathius (1031.63) thinks the lion flees as if it knew it has done 'evil'; Virgil made this explicit in his adaptation at *Aen.* 11.809ff., where a wolf is *conscius audacis facti*. Touches of 'subjective narrative' from the animals' viewpoint enter other similes (323–5n.); Moulton (*Similes* 114) compares 24.42f., where a lion βίη καὶ ἀγήνορι θυμῷ | εἴξας εἶσ' ἐπὶ μῆλα βροτῶν ἵνα δαῖτα λάβῃσι, 'as if the lion may be conceived as having better instincts, which would sometimes restrain him' – he knows he should keep to wild prey and not eat mutton for 'dinner' (cf. p. 23 n. 20). Zenodotus read οἱ αὐτῷ for βόεσσι; this removes the indication that the dog or cowherd is defending the herd, which is why they are offered as alternatives. He surely disliked the word-play βούκολον – βόεσσι (cf. 547–51n.). Aristarchus rightly objected that οἱ αὐτῷ is too distant from ἀολλισθήμεναι.

589–90 =8.158f., from ἐπί; the Trojans rain weapons at Antilokhos' back as he runs to his own lines. Verse 591 = 11.595 (spurious?), 17.114.

592–746 In accord with Zeus's plan, Hektor drives the Greeks from the first row of ships: Aias leaps from ship to ship fending off the enemy with a pike. Hektor finally grasps the stern of Protesilaos' vessel and calls for fire; Aias, driven back to the centre of the ship, keeps killing Trojans as they bring up blazing torches

592–746 Hektor wins his greatest victory – greater than his defeat of Patroklos – with agonizing effort; even at 746 he has yet to set any ship aflame, and his final triumph at 16.112 is undercut by our knowledge that Patroklos is about to counter-attack. The Greeks, still naturally the stronger, are beaten only by his supreme effort with Zeus's backing (Winter, *MNO* 161). The more the god and the man are united for the moment, the more their ultimate goals diverge, as Homer reminds us by summarizing Zeus's compliance with Thetis' prayer and foreshadowing Hektor's death (596ff., 610ff.; so Reinhardt, *IuD* 304f.). These interventions in the poet's *persona* frame a graphic depiction of Hektor gone berserk (605–9), giving his frightful assault a context tragic for both him and the Greeks; the elaboration of past and future deepens and extends the crisis. The narrative advances through three splendid similes. At first the Greeks resist as a cliff resists the waves; then Hektor attacks them as a wave swamps a ship, whose crew expects death; finally they flee like cows before a lion (this recalls the lion-image at 592, framing the whole of 592–630). Like this lion, Hektor kills but one of them, Periphetes; references to their terror frame his elaborate death (637, 652). Thus plot-summary and similes, not battle-narrative, convey the collapse of their line before the ships.

Verse 653 opens a new phase: 653–16.125 correspond to 355–404 (see 262–404n.). Panoramic descriptions frame Nestor's plea; the Greeks stand firm behind the first row of ships, and Athene lifts the mist from their eyes so they can see the full extent of the peril. Then the focus shifts to Aias and Hektor; similes glorify both (674ff.). An account of both sides' hopes and fears leads up to Hektor grasping Protesilaos' ship; 704 and 716 frame an overview of the contest for it. Aias reacts to Hektor's call for fire with an exhortation, and the scene ends in deadlock. Homer uses a striking variety of means, especially the alternation of panorama and close-up, to heighten the grandeur and suspense, with little change in the impasse since 416ff., where Aias and Hektor first contest a single ship, and Aias first kills a Trojan carrying fire. Fenik (*TBS* 178) compares 592–638 and 696–715 with the retreat at 17.722–61 (five similes but no individual duels), or the pursuit of

Hektor at 22.137–207, with its similes, surrealist general narrative and descriptive digressions.

592–614 Summaries of the past and future are typical (13.345–60n.); this one is unique in that it frames a depiction of Hektor, but it resembles Zeus's forecast at 56ff. in its wide temporal perspective, from Thetis' request to Hektor's death. Its initial mention of Zeus's commands (593) is clarified only to a limited and tantalizing degree. We hear not that the Greeks will fall amid Akhilleus' ships (as at 63f.), but that the Trojans will set fire to the fleet, and that a burning ship is Zeus's signal for the counter-attack (597f.). It is sublime that Homer makes Zeus part of the audience (bT on 599f.); we can infer that the god shares our anxiety. In contrast to 64ff., we hear nothing of Patroklos or Sarpedon; to listeners who cannot read and reread the text, their reappearance will thus seem a surprise that is somehow also expected. As bT saw, Homer's forecast of a change in the Greeks' fortunes comforts an audience fretful at their losses, as does his description of Thetis' request as 'immoderate'; by heralding a counter-attack, he makes his hearers eager for something they would normally hate to see, a ship ablaze; and by announcing Hektor's doom he gives him our sympathy. Ancient readers were 'tortured' with suspense here: on bT's fine understanding of foreshadowing see Duckworth, *AJP* 52 (1931) 320–38.

592–5 This lion-simile is one of a set (579–91n.); the same image extends into a second verse at 5.782f. = 7.256f. λείουσιν for λέ- (22.262) obeys the rule that words shaped ∪ – – and starting with a group of consonants can lengthen the first syllable; λ- is treated as a cluster (Chantraine, *GH* I 101f.). Διὸς δ' ἐτέλειον ἐφετμάς is part of a substitution-system: cf. Δ. δ' ἀλίτωμαι ἑ. (24.570, cf. 586), Δ. δ' ἐτελείετο βουλή (1.5, *Od.* 11.297, *Cypria* frag. 1.7), Δ. δ' ἐξείρετο βουλήν, Δ. δ' ἀλεώμεθα/ὠπίζετο μῆνιν. With 594f. cf. 12.254f., 22.18.

596–604 Like 13.345–60, this summary is delimited by repetition, here of 'Priam's son Hektor' and 'give glory' (596f., 602–4). Three references fix our gaze on the ships – fire cast upon them, Zeus waiting to see a ship burn, the Trojans driven from them. Hektor and Thetis at one side, Trojans and Danaans at the other, frame Zeus in the middle; we gain privileged access to his eyes and ominous thoughts (599–603, cf. 17.198–209). The whole is splendidly adorned with vivid epithets.

596 = 12.174; the sentence is extended with | Πριαμίδῃ, separated from Ἕκτορι (cf. 13.157 = 803): contrast 604 etc. πῦρ | ... ἀκάματον is another split formula. Homer sought grandeur by using both the paired formulae for fire, ἀ./θεσπιδαὲς πῦρ | (9× and 8× respectively), and in successive verses at 21.341f.): cf. ἔμβαλον ἀ. π. | (16.122), | ἐμβάλοι αἰθόμενον δαλόν (13.320). For a like case see 704–6n. On θεσπιδαής see Chantraine, *Dict.* s.v. θεσπέσιος.

598–9 Many are shocked that the poet endorses Agamemnon's ruthlessness towards the Trojans at 6.62 (αἴσιμα παρειπών), and now condemns Thetis' request to Zeus (1.503ff.) as ἐξαίσιος, the opposite of αἴσιμος: it was 'immoderate' and thus wrong. De Jong thinks her request is seen through Zeus's eyes (*Narrators* 139); it 'shows that Zeus's patience with Achilles' intransigence is sorely tried' (Thornton, *Supplication* 52n.). So too Agamemnon's advice at 6.62 could be 'right' from Menelaos' viewpoint. But we may so admire the fine characterization of Akhilleus as to forget that he may be in the wrong; in rejecting the embassy, and in asking Zeus (via Thetis) to ruin his own side, Akhilleus may arguably be considered traitorous. Zeus's reluctance to agree warns us that the morality of his request is not clear-cut (cf. 75–7n.). ἐξαίσιος is unique in the *Iliad* (cf. *Od.* 4.690, 17.577, in speeches). ἐμβάλοι is in a papyrus, but -η should be kept (cf. Chantraine, *GH* II 269); the subj. makes setting the ships ablaze a more vivid fact than the fulfilment of Thetis' prayer, which is in the opt. The form Θέτιος, found in quotations and *h*, is in Pindar; Homer has dat. Θέτῑ (18.407), acc. Θέτιν, but gen. Θέτιδος (4× each). ἐπικρήνειε is contracted from -κρηη- (Chantraine, *Dict.* s.v. κραιαίνω).

601–4 All MSS have ἔμελλε. Did/AT says Aristophanes read μέλλε; even he removed some augments (p. 25f. nn. 27, 30), but the name should probably be 'Aristarchus'. For παλίωξις see 69–71n. κῦδος ὀρέξειν picks up 596, whence the variant ὀρέξαι. The poet shifts νηυσὶν ἐπὶ γλαφυρῇσι, 12× at the start of the verse (and before ἔγειρ- at 8.531 = 18.304), to the second hemistich (cf. 8.180), extending it by replacing νηυσί with νήεσσι; the same modification appears with κορωνίσι (3×) and θοῇσι (12.112, 13.320), both found 12× with νηυσί. With 604 cf. 14.375: μάλα περ μεμαῶτα, 3× at the verse-end, is displaced by a phrase shaped ∪ − −, a frequent adaptation (cf. 651, 13.317); in the nom. it becomes μάλα περ μενεαίνων (617, *Od.* 5.341). As if aware that the words are related, Homer moves from μεμαώς to μαίνετο. That Zeus urges on Hektor, who is eager anyway, typifies dual divine and human motivation (cf. 13.46n.).

605–9 Hektor is frenzied like Ares or a forest fire; we see his foam-flecked mouth, fiery eyes and flashing helmet. His frenzy appears elsewhere (8.355, 12.462–6, 13.53n., 21.5). Others go berserk too, e.g. Diomedes and his spear (5.185, 6.101, 8.111, 16.75). Such warriors are often likened to Ares (cf. 8.348f.), one of whose traits is madness (128–9n.). Rather than expand this comparison, as at 13.298ff., the poet adds another, the forest fire, with enough detail to convey that the fire is fierce, because it has plenty of fuel and can burn up the slopes (a terrible, unforgettable sight); this too is a traditional image (14.394–9n.). The simile's continuation means that Ares rages 'in the mountains' and the fire is personified; the fusion of war-god and fire is apt amid the roar of the narrative. bT think the verses also evoke a wild beast: the foam at Hektor's mouth resembles 20.168 (a lion) or *Aspis* 389f. (a boar with blazing eyes), but burning eyes are a normal sign of battle-madness (8.349, 12.466, of Hektor).

ἐγχέσπαλος is a rare epithet (2.131, 14.449); its twin, δουρίκλυτος, starts with a consonant. The under-represented formula ὀλοὸν πῦρ is reversed at 13.629, gen. at *Od.* 12.68. βαθείης τάρφεσιν ὕλης (in a simile at 5.555) has become βαθέης to admit ἐν; cf. β. at 5.142, 21.213, always at the caesura, and the 'declension' βαθέην . . . ὕλην at 16.766 (Hoekstra, *Modifications* 119). This Ionic innovation appears in Herodotus; cf. Homeric ὠκέα for -εῖα, πλέων for πλείων, κέαται for κείαται (Chantraine, *GH* i 73). τάρφεα, 'thicket', confirms the etymological link of ταρφύς with τρέφω (Chantraine, *Dict.* s.v.). ἀφλοισμός, 'foam', also in Euphorion and Aetolian dialect (so D), may be cognate with φλοῖσβος from φλοιδ-, 'swell', 'bubble' (Chantraine, *Dict.* s.vv. φλίω, φλοῖσβος; cf. *bloat*). βλοσυρός, 'fierce', is especially associated with the face (3× *Il.*, 4× *Aspis*); it means 'hairy' in Phocylides (frag. 2), which fits its use with eyebrows here (cf. on 7.212f., 11.36). For the forceful enjambments cf. 647f. and τὼ δέ οἱ ὄσσε | λαμπέσθην (19.365f.); here σμερδαλέον describes the helmet's sinister glitter, cf. 13.805. Aristonicus (in AT on 21.5) notes that one might have marked 21.5 to support μαινομένοιο here, since 'some' read μαρν-, which is in fact in almost all MSS; *ergo* Aristarchus read μαιν-, which looks like a conjecture inspired by 605.

610–14 The foreshadowing of Hektor's death is typical and effective (592–614n.). A warrior's short life is a standard pathetic motif (1.352, 1.505, 4.478 = 17.302, 21.84f.); Hektor is exalted by Zeus to contrast tellingly with his death, as at 16.799f., where he wins Akhilleus' helmet *because* his doom is nigh (Schadewaldt, *Iliasstudien* 107). Both passages belong to a crescendo of allusions to his death (68, 17.201ff., 18.96, 18.133); see Duckworth, *Foreshadowing* 53f., 6of. Aristarchus athetized 610–14, which Zenodotus had omitted (T), on three grounds: (i) 'of Hektor' is redundant, since we know he is meant; (ii) 610–14 interrupt the vigorous narrative of his attack; (iii) 610 repeats 603f. in a way typical of the Cycle. bT also object that 'from heaven' is odd, because Zeus is on Mt Ida (but heaven is his sphere of control); Leaf dislikes μοῦνον ἐόντα (but Hektor *is* picked out for glory), and how Athene 'carries out the work of fate' in 613 (but she is the goddess of Greek victory, cf. 71, 22.214ff.). The athetesis spoils the ring-structure of 592–614 (592–746n.). μόρσιμον ἦμαρ (also *Od.* 10.175) forms a pair with αἴσιμον ἦ. (5× epos); it is more dignified than its metrical equivalent νηλέες ἦ. would have been. As it is a synonym for 'death', ἐπόρνυμι can govern it (cf. *Od.* 7.271). Παλλάς has been linked with Semitic *ba'alat* = πότνια (see Hainsworth on *Od.* 6.328), but appears as Myc. *Qa-ra₂* (TH Of 37–8).

615–17 Hektor attacks where the enemy is strongest, as if from pride: did Homer know the military principle that the whole line will break if worsted at its strongest point? στίχας ἀνδρῶν, 14× at the verse-end, is displaced as at 12.47 (a lion-simile). 'Not even so' is apt, since μάλα περ μενεαίνων (cf. 604) signals his special effort.

618–36 Rather than extend his tower-image for the firmness of the Greek ranks (cf. 13.126–35n., and for ἀρηρότες cf. 13.800, 16.212–14), Homer adduces another stone object, a cliff; this begins the set of three related similes which advance the narrative to the rout at 636 (592–746n.). Sets of similes may depict the same event (14.394–400) or successive ones, e.g. the pairs at 11.548ff., 16.482ff., or the series at 17.725–59 (Scott, *Simile* 113f.); the technique marks a climax. The idea of reversal and the nautical content, apt for a battle by the ships, unite the first two similes. The second and third both shift from Hektor at the start to his foes at the end: so Winter (*MNO* 162), who notes that the second gives their inner reaction to him (fear), the third their external reaction (flight).

618–22 Similes often depict resistance: cf. the Greeks as static clouds (5.522ff.), warriors as oaks (12.132ff.), Aias as a ridge blocking a torrent (17.747ff.) or Odysseus 'firm as a rock' (*Od.* 17.463). But cognate images can serve other ends: the army's din is like winds and waves lashing a rock, Hektor lops off heads as a squall whips up spray, or the ranks advance as a gale drives waves shoreward (2.394ff., 11.305ff., 13.795ff.). For ἠλίβατος see 271–6n. For 620 see 14.16–19n.; λιγέων ἀνέμων and κύματά τε τροφόεντα recur at *Od.* 3.289f. (a shipwreck), cf. τρόφι κῦμα (11.307, simile). τροφόεις is a metrically useful creation like φαιδιμόεις (13.685–8n.), based on the original sense of τρέφω, 'make big'; Herodotus still uses τρόφις for 'big', 'adult' (4.9.4). As if aware of the etymology, Homer says κῦμα ... ἀνεμοτρεφές at 624f. Aristarchus read τροφέοντο at *Od.* 3.290, and there is a variant τροφέοντα here, but the late and rare τροφέω is transitive. The well-fed waves 'belch' at the rock; the metaphor recurs at *Od.* 5.403, 438 (a wave 'spits' spray at 4.426). Aristarchus (Did/A) preferred the vulgate αὐτήν to ἀκτῇ, a conjecture made when αὐτήν had weakened in force and was felt to be unbearably flat (contrast van der Valk, *Researches* II 118f.). Verse 622 = 5.527, after another wind-simile; the variant ἐξ ἁλός· ὡς Δαναοί, also spurned by him, is another effort to reinforce the end of the image, this time by ensuring that αὐτήν is not its last word.

623–9 Hektor's armour blazes: cf. that of Diomedes or Akhilleus (5.4, 19.374ff., 22.134f.). He now attacks the line at every point, not just its strongest (cf. 616): πάντοθεν goes with ἔνθορε, not λαμπόμενος. Just as Homer shifted from tower to rock, so now, rather than develop a fire-image, he likens Hektor's onset to a wave swamping a ship. In this context of burning the fleet, fire naturally evokes a nautical simile, especially after the previous image: the Greeks are turned from a solid rock into sailors on a fragile craft that is, as bT note, barely seen amid the storm. Just as wind, cloud and waves collaborate to terrify the crew, so Hektor with Zeus's support alarms the Greeks; but we may not see their panic without a hint of their final salvation – the sailors 'just escape death' (cf. the foreshadowing in the simile at 16.753). This image amplifies that at 381–4, where see n.; cf. 9.4–7 (9.8 = 629), 11.297f., 11.305ff. Like the previous image, it shares a verb with the narrative, so that we cannot miss the progression: cf. μένει ... μένον (620, 622), ἐν δ' ἔπεσε ... ἐν νηῒ πέσησι (624). Likewise θυμός (629) resumes φρένα (627), which enters the next simile in ὀλοόφρων (630). ὑπαὶ νεφέων ἀνεμοτρεφές explains λάβρον: the wind and clouds 'feed' the waves, unless ὑ. ν. means 'touching the clouds', cf. 16.375 (Chantraine, *GH* II 141f.). ἀ. describes a spear at 11.256, where see n. δεινός leads up to its cognate δειδιότες, implying that the noise terrifies the sailors. With ὑπὲκ θανάτοιο cf. 20.300, Hesiod frag. 307.1.

626 The ship is hidden *by* spray, like the coast at *Od.* 5.403; ἄχνη, read by Zenodotus (Did/AT) and nearly all MSS, is nonsensical. It is harder to choose between δεινὸς ἀήτη, an odd agreement, and δ. ἀήτης, an odd noun-formation. Aristarchus, followed only by A, read δ. ἀήτη, adducing κλυτὸς Ἱπποδάμεια (2.742, cf. *Od.* 5.422). ἀήτη(ς) governs a fem. adj. at *Erga* 645, 675 (in the modification Νότοιό τε δεινᾶς ἀήτας), plus 4× in Sappho and other lyric, but is masc. in Hellenistic verse. At *Od.* 4.567 the vulgate has Ζεφύροιο λιγὺ πνείοντας ἀήτας, but Aristarchus read πνείοντος. Van der Valk (*Researches* II 176f.) thinks he emends both times, but Risch (*Wortbildung* 34) is right that the fem. is older and ἀήτη the *lectio difficilior*. δεινή was surely avoided for euphony; cf. θερμὸς ἀϋτμή (*HyHerm* 110), ἡδὺς ἀ. (*Od.* 12.369), θῆλυς ἀϋτή (*Od.* 6.122). Callimachus makes the best comment with his joke θῆλυς ἀήτης (frag. 110.53). The scansion δὲ δ(ϝ)εινός is innovative.

630–6 This simile, the last in its set (592–746n.), likens Hektor's attack to a lion raiding cattle. The elaboration is grand, the similarities and contrasts telling: the lone victim is like the single warrior who falls and the cows stampede like the Greeks. Eustathius (1034.45ff.) notes how Homer ends the simile with them, but returns to Hektor slaying a single victim, as if to unify the double point of comparison. On similes where the flocks of foolish or absent rustics are raided with impunity see 323–5n.; for lions see on 586–8 (they attack ἐν πρώτῃσι βόεσσι at 18.579). At 11.172ff. the Trojans flee like cows before a lion, who kills one; cf. 5.161f., 16.487ff., 17.61ff. ὀλοόφρων lets us see the lion's mental fury; the adj. also describes a snake and a boar (2.723, 17.21), as well as evildoers like Aietes (3× *Od.*). οὔ πω (= πως) σάφα εἰδώς conveys the drover's despair over what to do. Note the etymological play νέμονται – νομεύς and assonance in -ῃσι.

631 = 4.483 (a poplar simile, with ἥ ... πεφύκει); swamp and water-meadow is the best land for cattle in Greece, and a 'large' marsh is needed

for so big a herd. ἕλικος βοός declines the formula ἕλικας βοῦς (etc., 16×
epos), as at *Od.* 12.355 (nom. plur., separated), 22.292 (gen. plur.); for the
epithet see S. West on *Od.* 1.92. φοναί, 'carnage' at 10.521 and in tragedy,
means 'carcase' here, not 'place of slaughter', *pace* bT. ὑστάτιος (also at
8.353) is modified *metri gratia* from ὕστατος, like Hellenistic poets' μεσσάτιος
for -τος: cf. πύματόν τε καὶ ὕστατον (3×); πρῶτόν τε καὶ ὕ. (etc., 4×
epos); τίνα π., τίνα δ' ὕ. ἐξενάριξε (etc., 3×); τί π. τοι ἔπειτα, τί δ' ὑστάτιον
καταλέξω (*Od.* 9.14). ὁμοστίχαει is also innovative; Bekker proposed ὁμοῦ
στιχάει (for ΟΜΟΣ-), comparing ἅμ' ἐστιχόωντο βόεσσιν at 18.577, but this
leaves the odd active ending. This is the sole Iliadic verb in ὁμο-, but cf.
Odyssean ὁμηγυρίζομαι, ὁμοφρονέω and the variant ὁμοτροχόωντα for ἅμα
τρ- at *Od.* 15.451. It presupposes an adj. *ὁμόστιξ.

637 Constant reminders that Hektor and Zeus are working together exalt
the hero and stress the risk to the Greeks (cf. 596, 603, 610, 694). D gloss
the epic *hapax* θεσπεσίως 'divinely', which is how the bards took it; from the
root *θεσ- of θεός, plus *s(e)kʷ-, 'say' as in ἄ-σπετος, ἔννεπε, it once meant
'divinely inspired', cf. θέσφατος.

638–52 Periphetes' death, anticipated in the simile, follows the usual
pattern of announcement (638), biography (639–43, recapitulated after the
typical excursus on his father, cf. 526f., 16.328f.), and manner of death
(644ff.). He may be an *ad hoc* invention, like Euphetes or the Trojan
Poluphetes = Periphetes (532, 13.789–94n.); his name suits a herald's son,
cf. the herald Periphas (419–21, 17.322–6nn.). His father Kopreus comes
from sagas about Herakles, on which Homer drew above (25ff.). Eurustheus
employed Kopreus son of Pelops as a herald to take his orders to Herakles,
since he was too timid to go in person, like Agamemnon *vis-à-vis* Akhilleus
at 1.320ff. ('Apollodorus' 2.5.1). Herakles was traditionally linked with a
Kopreus: in the *Thebaid* (frag. 8 B. = 6 D.) he received the horse Arion from
a Boeotian king Kopreus (cf. *Cat.* 70.29). Kopreus' name, borne by several
Myc. and later Greeks, is less malodorous than it might seem: it is from
κόπρος in its extended sense 'cow-yard' and merely means 'farmer' (for
manuring cf. *Od.* 17.299). Did the conjunction of a herald's name with the
bovine simile waft Kopreus into the poet's mind? Homer certainly smelt
opprobrium in his service to Eurustheus (see 8.363n.), since he takes care to
build Periphetes up, calling him good at everything and even that rarity in
the heroic world, a son better than his father. Even if he dies to pay for his
father's sins, like Phereklos (5.59ff.), his end is pathetic, since he 'gives
Hektor glory' by the merest chance, betrayed by the clatter of his helmet
(with 644 cf. 491, 12.437): it is no credit to Hektor that he kills his victim
only because the latter trips up. Periphetes dies near his comrades, who
cannot help him despite their grief – a tragic version, surely, of 23.774f.,
where Oïlean Aias nose-dives on some cow-muck (*kopros*) and loses the race,

to the onlookers' delight: Kopreus' son is a good runner too! Another warrior dies when he trips at 16.330ff.

639–43 ἄνακτος qualifies Eurustheus at *Hy.* 15.5 also, hinting at his rule over Herakles; the 'neglect' of ϝ- is no argument against it. The variant ἀέθλων, in three of four papyri but few codices, surely derives from 8.363 or 19.133, and was introduced as being less polite to Eurustheus and more precise in specifying Herakles' labours as the orders Kopreus used to bring. For ἀγγελίης, 'messenger', see 13.251–3n.; Zenodotus emended it away by reading ἀγγελίην, but Aristarchus objects that this leaves οἴχνεσκε dangling. For periphrastic proper-name formulae cf. 13.246–8n.; with Ἡρακληείη cf. Myc. */Etewoklewehios/* (PY Aq 64). Such forms help bards use metrically tricky names in -κλέης. For an acc. of respect coordinated with an infin., as in 642, cf. 1.258; the combination of martial and conciliar virtues is best (13.726–9n.).

645–52 Only Periphetes is called a 'Mycenaean' in the epos, but it is by chance that his ancient body-shield is of a type we call Mycenaean; Hektor's oxhide shield is imagined likewise at 6.117f., where its rim taps his heels and neck as he walks (see *ad loc.*). Periphetes catches his foot in his shield-rim and falls on his back; that he is stabbed in the chest makes his death seem less ignoble. Verse 650 uniquely adapts μεταφρένῳ ἐν δόρυ πῆξε (etc., 5×), as if the poet is aware of turning him over by this unique mishap. He seems to wear no corslet; the use of a body-shield without one is an Early Myc. reminiscence (cf. on 11.545, 14.402–8). ἀσπίς does not denote only the later round shield (13.158n.).

The unique πάλτο, glossed ἐνεπλάκει, 'was entangled', by D, is an unrecognized aor. middle of the rare Ionic verb *παλέω, 'be disabled', 'be wrecked', which functioned like a passive of βλάπτω: cf. παλήσειε, 'suffer loss' (Hdt. 8.21) and πεπαλμένος· βεβλαμμένος in Hsch. It may be related to πάλη, 'wrestling' (once 'entanglement'?), παλεύω, 'decoy' (once 'entrap'?). Leumann derives πάλτο from a misdivision of ἔπ-αλτο from ἄλλομαι, 'leap' (*HW* 60–4), but it is resumed by βλαφθείς, 'entangled', in 647 (cf. 6.39). The *lectio difficilior* ποδηνεκέ'(α) is read by Ap. Soph. and MS Ve¹. The adj. should agree with ἀσπίς, not ἕρκος; cf. δέρμα λέοντος ... ποδηνεκές (10.24f.), ἔ. ἀκόντων (4.137, with 567n.). Its root is ἐνεκ- in its intrans. sense, 'extend' (cf. διηνεκής, ἐνεγκεῖν). With 647f. cf. 608f. The latter half of 649 = 442 only. Verse 651 blends ἀχνύμενός περ ἑταίρου (3×) with οὔ τι δυνήσομαι ἀ. π. | χραισμεῖν (1.588f., cf. 241f.); adaptation proceeds, as often (601–4n.), by the addition of a word shaped ∪ – – at the verse-end. 'They feared Hektor' picks up 628 and 637, rounding off this section.

653–73 The battle's course is clear, but has caused dispute. The Greeks retreat via the gaps within the first row of ships, chased by the Trojans (τοὶ δ' ἐπέχυντο), and make a stand at the huts behind it. Homer exactly delimits how far they retreat in the rout of 636ff., using his usual technique of alternation between detailed incidents and general scenes (see Winter, *MNO* 164–7). The next scene contrives further to delay their total withdrawal from the first row of ships – Aias leaps from ship to ship with his pike. When Porphyry (1.207.14) asks why the Trojans do not burn the first ships they reach, he misunderstands the situation. Critics have also disliked how Athene supports Nestor's exhortation by lifting the mist from the soldiers' eyes, but the passage follows the pattern (262–404n.) where the Greeks flee, a Greek prays and a god answers, once by lifting the mist (for Aias, 17.645ff.): 653–71 resemble 343–78 above, where the men flee, Nestor prays and Zeus replies with thunder. Verse 659 = 370; Nestor's tone is yet more urgent now.

653–4 'They came within the ships, and the ends of those ships confined them which were drawn up first', i.e. furthest inland: at 14.75 the same phrase ὅσαι πρῶται εἰρύατο denotes, with an easily intelligible reversal of viewpoint, the ships nearest the sea. εἰσωποί has been taken as 'within sight of' the ships (cf. D, bT), but this interpretation (popular among Analysts) is impossible; the Trojans have been near the ships since 385. Leaf rightly holds that -ωπός has lost its force, as in ἐνώπια, 'inside (walls)', at 8.435, στεινωπός for στεινός (23.427) or Euripidean ἐξώπιος, 'outside'. For the enjambment ἄκραι | νῆες cf. 12.51f., 17.264f., 13.611–13n.; ἄ. is not a synonym for πρῶται, but predicative.

656 A papyrus, some early codices and *h* read the innovative form πρωτέων; Crates cited 656 with this text to refute the heresy that there were only two rows of ships (in bT on 14.31f., whose unclear wording led Lehrs, *De Aristarchi studiis* 222, to ascribe this heresy to Crates). Indeed, Akhilleus' ships were five rows deep (16.173–5n.). But the vulgate προτέρων, in two papyri, is surely the *lectio difficilior* and gave rise to the theory of two rows of ships; πρωτέων is a conjecture after πρῶται in 654, meant to confirm that there were many rows (van der Valk, *Researches* II 87). But προτέρων does not disprove the latter view: it means only '(the ships) that were in front'. On the proximity of the huts see 409n.

657–8 The Greeks feel too much shame before each other, and too much fear for the ships, to give up; to these emotions Nestor will add shame and fear for their families. For αἰδώς cf. 13.120–3n.; for both feelings together cf. Macleod on 24.435, Richardson on *HyDem* 190 and *Cypria* frag. 18 B. = 24 D. For the artificial form ὁμόκλεον see 12.59n.

660 Old Nestor aptly adjures the men by their parents. ὑπέρ means not 'in place of', *pace* Nic/A, but 'in the name of', as usual: cf. 22.338, λίσσομ' ὑπὲρ ... τοκήων; 24.466f.; *HyAphr* 131, πρὸς Ζηνὸς γουνάζομαι ἠδὲ τ. Innovative τοκέων (juxtaposed with -ήων at 663) recurs at 21.587, in another rhetorical reminder of one's family; cf. contracted ἱππεῖς (11.151) and names in -εύς -έος (339n.). τεκέων is a Byzantine 'correction'. γουνοῦμαι is metaphorical, cf. *Od.* 6.149.

661-6 Nestor begins with a standard verse (661 = 561), but varies Aias' theme of shame by specifying that the Greeks should feel it toward their families. On such appeals see 494–9n.; for an appeal to absent kin cf. *Od.* 11.66f. The unusual thought that their parents might be dead is expressed with the novel forms ὅτεῳ (490–3n.) and κατατεθνήκασι (cf. Shipp, *Studies* 112). Leaf rejects 664 as an afterthought added because many warriors must be orphans after so long at Troy; but at his age Nestor would be well aware of mortality. καί, not ἠδέ, again resumes ἠμέν at 670, *Erga* 339. For τρωπᾶσθε cf. 11.568 and p. 17.

668-73 As if responding to Nestor, Athene scatters the mist from the Greeks' eyes on both the side of the ships and that of the battle, so that all, fighters and slackers alike, can see the peril (Winter, *MNO* 166f.). Divine mist is a traditional dramatic effect: see 5.127–30n. and Kakridis, *Homer Revisited* 89–103, with parallels from modern Greek folk-song. Athene lifts the mist from Diomedes' eyes so that he can tell gods from men (5.127f.); Poseidon befogs Akhilleus' vision so Aineias can escape (20.321ff.). Gods send general darkness to help one side (5.506ff., 21.6f.) or to honour the dead (16.567f.). The best parallel is when Zeus pours gloom on the battle and lifts it in reply to Aias' prayer (17.269f., 643ff.). Aristarchus athetized 668–73 because no mist was mentioned before, and Zeus's threats should deter Athene from interfering (8.5ff.); but Zeus conceded to her this sort of non-physical intervention at 8.36ff. (Erbse, *Götter* 151). — For ὁμοίιος cf. 13.358n.; on Hektor as βοὴν ἀγαθός cf. 13.124–5n. Leaf deems the division of the Greeks into those fighting by the ships and those hanging back (cf. 13.738, 14.132) at odds with 655f. and 675, where, he thinks, they are not fighting at all; but ἀφέστασαν means simply 'stood back'. Only some had been fighting, but now all have retreated to form a new front line.

674-703 A brilliant device extends the suspense: Aias holds off the whole Trojan army by leaping from ship to ship with a huge naval pike. Similes pick out him and Hektor, leading into another panorama.

674-6 The generic epithet μεγαλήτορι, also used of Aias at 17.166 (gen.) and 626 (acc.), stresses his courage; for the scansion Αἴαντῑ see 14.458–9n. ἤνδανε is contracted from *ἐϝα-, but *ἄνδανε must not be restored (see p. 17). ἴκρια, originally 'supports', 'scaffolding', are the raised half-decks seen at the prow and stern of Geometric ships: see D. Gray, *Arch. Hom.* G 99, with the figures at G 61, and Kurt, *Fachausdrücke* 128ff. Homer mentions the front deck at *Od.* 12.229f. only; the rear deck could hold both the helmsman and the dormant Odysseus (*Od.* 13.73ff.). For βιβάσθων see 13.809n.

677-8 For Aias' pike see 388–9n.; it is made of sections glued together with pins through the joints. The unique βλῆτρον is often taken to be a 'clamp' or metal band *round* the joints; but it occurred in other contexts, and meant something driven in like a peg or wedge (cf. D, Ap. Soph. and Hsch. s.v.). Greeks still use it with the sense 'bolt', 'peg' (Chantraine, *Dict.* s.v.

βάλλω); it may have a Myc. cognate (Ventris and Chadwick, *Documents* 504). With δυωκαιεικοσίπηχυ cf. -ίμετρον (23.264); this number is handy in hexameters (2.748, *Od.* 9.241, 10.208).

679–84 As Fränkel explains (*Gleichnisse* 79f.), the retainer must select four horses at the stud-farm and bring them to town; rather than yoke his team, he harnesses them together and rides each in turn, to avoid overtiring any one horse or just to show off, changing mount as they gallop, to the amazement of wayfarers on the road. Does he leap to the ground and run beside his steeds, a trick practised by the ἀναβάται (Paus. 5.9.2)? Or does he ride bareback standing up, leaping from horse to horse without slipping (ά-σφαλές) like a Roman *desultor* or a circus *artiste*? This is more exciting and more apt; Aias is too high up to leap to the ground before he vaults onto the next ship. Ships are called 'horses of the sea' at *Od.* 4.708; a ship's steady speed is likened to a quadriga's (ἀσφαλέως ... ἔμπεδον, *Od.* 13.86, cf. 13.141–2n.). But these ships are static, whereas the horses are galloping; as if aware of this and wishing to prove his image apt, Homer calls the ships 'swift' in 685, reminding us of their true nature.

Homer rarely refers to riding: Odysseus rides a ship's timber 'like a race-horse' (κέλης) at *Od.* 5.371; he and Diomedes ride stolen horses at 10.499f., 10.513, 10.529; Adrastos fled Thebes on his steed Arion in a like emergency (*Thebaid* frag. 7 B. = 6 D.). κελητίζω is unique in the epos. Aristarchus guessed that Homer knew of riding but avoided it for his heroes, just as he eschewed trumpets, boiled meat, fish or quadrigas (cf. 16.407–8n. and Schmidt, *Weltbild* 231ff.). Archaeology confirms this: cf. J. K. Anderson, *Ancient Greek Horsemanship*, Berkeley 1961, 10ff.; J. Wiesner, *Arch. Hom.* F 110ff.; Crouwel, *Chariots* 45ff.; Greenhalgh, *Warfare* 53ff. Depictions of riders and Centaurs appear in LHIIIB–C; a LHIIIB sherd may show a warrior standing on a horse and guiding it with reins (*ibid.* 44–6). Myths about the Centaurs and Pegasos may reflect awe at this new and magical skill, practised with no saddle or stirrups. But if these four horses are meant for a single chariot, the simile has a Late Geometric background. The lack of quadrigas until then, proved by archaeology, confirms that Homer avoids them as an anachronism, although they creep in at 5.271, 8.185, 11.699, 23.171, *Od.* 13.81 (cf. 16.152–4n.). — The city is big, so it can support many horses and a highway (this evokes Ionia); the road is populous to give the rider an audience. λαοφόρος is next in Herodotus (λεω-). πολέες τέ ἑ θηήσαντο is formular (cf. *Od.* 8.17, *Erga* 482), as is ἀνέρες ἠδὲ γυναῖκες (3× epos).

680 D and all MSS read συναγείρεται, i.e. 'he gathers together four horses out of many'. From bT and the second-century A.D. Atticist Philemon (in Porphyry 1.287.14ff.) all editors accept συναείρεται, 'harnesses together'; cf. συνήορος, 'joined together', συνωρίς, 'pair', παρήορος, 'trace-horse' and σὺν δ' ἤειρεν ἱμᾶσι, 'harnessed them together' (10.499). Porphyry rightly objects that 'gathers' makes good sense, since the horseman has to choose and herd together the steeds he wants. Indeed 'four *out of many*' is odd with 'harnesses', which must be a clever conjecture. Now Philemon, claiming that Homer's text is often corrupt, calls -αγείρεται 'dull and very stupid' and proposes 'harnesses', adducing 10.499. Since he continues with an argument for Aristophanes' conjecture ὧς at 21.127, the latter may be the source of *both* emendations. Erbse assigns -αείρεται to Aristarchus, avowing that Aristophanes' textual reasoning never survives at length (*Beiträge zur Überlieferung der Iliasscholien*, Munich 1960, 20–22, 30); but this misses Aristophanes' textual arguments over *Od.* 4.336 (in the schol. on 339), Alcaeus frag. 359 and Anacreon frag. 408 (frags. 367, 378 Slater), plus the fact that these conjectures all concern animals, in which he took great interest. Cf. van der Valk, *Researches* II 620. — πίσυρας reflects *k^weturns, cf. Sanskrit *catúraḥ*; this is an Aeolism used for metrical convenience, since its closest cognate is Lesbian πέσ(σ)υρες, with πε- < *k^we-. The -ι-, constant in Homer in both nom. and acc. (6×), may be a development within the *Kunstsprache*, perhaps by assimilation to Ionic -ü- in the next syllable (Hainsworth on *Od.* 5.70), unless it reflects a zero-grade or the Myc. shift of *e* to *i* next to a labial, as in the relation of *πενυτός to πινυτός, *qe-to* to πίθος (cf. Householder and Nagy, *Greek* 65f.).

685–9 ἴκρια ... μακρὰ βιβάς forms a ring with 676. Aias' shouts (687 = 732) introduce the Trojans' ὅμαδος, '(noisy) throng', which in turn introduces the simile about the traditionally noisy waterfowl (cf. 2.459ff.). On θοάων — ∪∪ νήων see 391–2n.; for βιβάς see 306–7n. Verse 687 = 732; σμερδνός (also at 5.742) and σμερδαλέος, 'terrible' (painful?), are cognate with English *smart* (Chantraine, *Dict.* s.v.). Τρώων ∪∪ — πύκα θωρηκτάων recurs at 739, cf. 12.317. Adding π. is a neat way to extend a phrase: cf. (π.) ποιητοῖο. After 689 'some' (so T) read 22.459 = *Od.* 11.515, 'but he kept running far forward, yielding to none in his might' – a feeble explanation of 'he no longer stayed amid the throng', anticipating the simile.

690–2 An attacking warrior is often likened to an eagle or hawk chasing birds or other prey (16.582f., 17.460, 21.252f, 22.308–10); eagles were especially partial to geese (*Od.* 15.161, 19.543). Geese, cranes and swans still feed together in water-meadows like the delta where the Greek camp was (cf. the related simile at 2.459ff.). The 'long-necked' birds evoke the ships' thin curved prows and sterns (cf. 716–17n.); Geometric vase-painters often put such a bird by the ends of a ship, as if to make just this comparison (see D. Gray, *Arch. Hom.* G pls. VI–IX). Again a simile probably has a Geometric background, although LHIIIC vase-painters certainly knew the Sea-Peoples' bird-headed ships (Bouzek, *Aegean* 177–80, 202f.). αἴθων also describes bulls, lions, oxen, horses, cauldrons, hunger and iron; it means 'tawny' (S. West on *Od.* 1.184), but Homer exploits its etymology 'fiery' here, when Hektor is bringing fire to the ships as the eagle brings death to the birds. Cf. Hektor's horses Aithon and Lampos at 8.185 (names surely borrowed from the steeds of Helios, cf. *Titanomachy* frag. 7 B. = 4 D.). ἔθνος is used of winged creatures (2.87–93n.). ὄρνις can be fem. (9.323f., 14.290), but πετεηνός has fem. endings elsewhere; the poet surely changed the gender of ὅ. to fit in the metrically useful βοσκομενάων (for blatant cases of this see *Theog.* 910, *Aspis* 7, where Hesiod treats βλέφαρον as fem.). The euphonious 692 (= 2.460) continues the assonances in -ων: δουλιχόδειρος is unique.

693–5 Homer does not identify the ship as Protesilaos' until 705, as if by a sudden inspiration; yet see 704–6n. The 'recent' formula νεὸς κυανοπρώροιο (also 8× *Od.*) is modified at the caesura from νηὸς κ. (2× *Il.*, 3× elsewhere): see Hoekstra, *Modifications* 125f., and cf. νεὸς ... ποντοπόροιο (704), adapted from νηὸς ... π. (5× epos). Aristarchus' text ὦσεν (Did/A, cf. bT), in few MSS, makes more vivid (or indeed grotesque) the image of Zeus's 'long arm'. But the vulgate ὦρσεν (in a papyrus) smooths this metaphor for Zeus's power and is apt: cf. 4.439 and 9.419f., where χεῖρα ἑὴν ὑπερέσχε express his protection of Troy (wrongly Erbse, *Götter* 220). At 1.97 the MSS read λοιμοῖο βαρείας χεῖρας ἀφέξει (cf. 1.89, 21.548), but Aristarchus had Δαναοῖσιν ἀεικέα λοιγὸν ἀπώσει! A. K. Gross (*Gymn.* 77 (1970) 365–75) cites Near Eastern parallels for the 'hand of god'.

696–8 δριμύς, 'fierce', originally 'acrid', is also metaphorical at 11.270, 18.222, *Od.* 24.319, *Aspis* 457; μάχην δριμεῖαν is a Hesiodic formula (3×). αὖτις refers to the renewed fighting 'by the ships' after the retreat of 655, not to 385ff. Fresh warriors have more strength (16.44f.). Direct appeals to the listener are rare and dramatic: see 14.58f., 17.366n. and de Jong, *Narrators* 54ff. For φημί meaning 'think' cf. 700, 13.83–90n. Tyrannio (Hrd/A) accented ἀντέσθαι, rightly: all forms of this verb are explicable as aorists (*LfgrE* s.v.).

699–703 A parenthesis gives both sides' thoughts as at 17.412–23 (with n.), where direct speech reveals their equal determination, or 13.89, where the poet lets us see the Greeks' despair; cf. too summaries of the action on the divine plane like 596ff. For 701 see on 286–93, 539–45. ἐφέστασαν ἀλλήλοισιν forms a ring with 697f., but denotes the closeness of men on the same side at 13.133 = 16.217.

704–6 Hektor's grasping of the stern, heightened at 716f., frames the struggle for Protesilaos' ship, emphasized by her three epithets. Homer marked her for destruction at 13.681–3, by saying that the rampart was lowest near her (this chimes ill with any idea of a wide berm between rampart and ships). She is almost superfluous; since her captain is dead, her loss cannot disgrace him (cf. bT). The allusion to his death in 706, of which 2.699ff. is a more openly emotional version, gains its force from understatement (cf. Griffin, *HLD* 109); 'failure to return' is a traditional pathetic

motif (T's variant ἀφίκετο is from the otherwise identical 13.645). On νεὸς
... ποντοπόροιο see 693–5n. ποντόπορος/ὠκύαλος νηῦς | are complemen-
tary formulae (4× and 2× *Od.*, never *Il.*); Homer had the pair in mind
when he added ὠκυάλου, just as he exploited the pair ἀκάματον/θεσπιδαὲς
πῦρ (596n.). ὠ. is usually taken as 'swiftly leaping', from ἅλλομαι, but
Homer linked it with ἅλς, i.e. 'swift at sea', since he includes it, with
Ἀγχίαλος and Ἀμφίαλος, among the nautical names at *Od.* 8.111ff. He may
even be right: cf. πρωτόαλος· πρωτόπλους (Hsch.).

709–12 The list of weapons enhances the importance of this moment (cf.
bT). So too Archilochus predicts that the Euboeans will not fight for long
at a distance with bows and slings, but will soon come to close quarters with
swords (frag. 3). Both passages reflect the normal evolution of contemporary
battles from long-range to hand-to-hand combat (16.772–5n.). The rare
ἀϊκή, 'rush', is from the root of ἀΐσσω, with ῑ *metri gratia*: Apollonius Rhodius
(4.820) treats it as a consonant-stem, no doubt comparing κορυθ-, πολυ-άϊξ.
ἀμφὶς μένον means 'endured on either side'; οὐδ' ἔτ' is better than οὐδέ τ'
(Ruijgh, τε *épique* 706). οἱ γ' denotes both sides, but ἕνα θυμὸν ἔχοντες
(16.219, 17.267, *Od.* 3.128) means that *each side* is 'of one mind'. Lorimer
thinks only the attackers would wield axes, whereas the Greeks would use
swords and spears (*HM* 305f.); but the defenders of the ships at Marathon
used axes (716–17n.). The mention of swords is needed to introduce 713f.,
as Dionysius Thrax noted (Arn/A) in refuting Aristarchus' athetesis of 712.
His mentor had claimed that 712 is 'ordinary' and does not maintain the
battle's peculiarity, since warriors always use swords and spears. The verse
never recurs in exactly this form (cf. 13.146–8n.).

713–15 For the vivid detail of weapons dropped underfoot cf. 13.578f.;
the ground traditionally flows with blood in the mêlée (cf. 4.451 = 8.65,
17.360f., 20.494). Verse 713 expands | φάσγανα κωπήεντα (in a Cyclic verse
in the *Contest of Homer and Hesiod* 126), cf. ξίφει − ∪∪ κωπήεντι (2×). The
swords have dark hilts (bT), bound no doubt with leather, cf. μελάνδετον
ἄορ at *Aspis* 221. Some took the epithet as 'iron-bound', but it may well be
of Bronze Age origin; χαλκόδετος is in Linear B. Luxury Myc. hilts had silver
or gold rivets and ivory or horn decoration (2.45n.; S. Foltiny, *Arch. Hom.* E
238f.). The 'dark' hilts and earth evoke the colour of the blood. For Aristarchus' text πέσον see 13.616–19n. He argued that the swords fall to the
ground when axes lop through warriors' shoulders or wrists. Erbse wrongly
deems 'wrists' absurd and emends to 'straps'; but it does not follow from
Aristarchus' athetesis of 712 that he thought swords were not in use. The
swords can fall 'from their hands' when violent blows knock them away.
Had Homer meant that severed limbs were everywhere, he could have said
so; yet we cannot exclude an understatement of this idea.

716–17 οὐχί, which is tragic and Attic, recurs in the epos only at 16.762

(in the same hemistich), versus οὐκί 10×; but the inherited suffix -χί may already appear in Myc. *o-u-ki* (Chantraine, *Dict.* s.v. οὐ). Zenodotus read οὐκ ἐμεθίει to emend it away (Arn/AT, cf. p. 24); forms like ἐκαθέζετο or ἐκάθευδε, which he read at 1.68, 611 and *Od.* 6.1, exist in later Ionic (ἐκάθητο, *Hy.* 7.14; ἐμετίετο, Hdt. 1.12). Another 'remedy' was οὔ τι (schol. Ap. Rhod. 1.1089, from Didymus; *h* at 16.762). The ἄφλαστον Hektor grasps, a *hapax* in the epos, is the carved stern-post, later ἀκροστόλιον (so Apollodorus, *FGH* 244 F 240). This appears as a forward-curving 'horn' in pictures of Geometric ships (cf. 690–2n.); it was some seven feet off the ground (J. S. Morrison and R. T. Williams, *Greek Oared Ships*, Cambridge 1968, 47). These posts are called ἄκρα κόρυμβα at 9.241. While grasping the ἄφλαστα of a departing enemy ship at Marathon, as the Greeks called for fire to burn the Persian fleet, Aeschylus' brother had his arm severed by an axe (Hdt. 6.114).

718–25 Hektor's jubilant call for fire marks a new development – Aias' retreat from the poop-deck; his boasts of god-given success ring his speech (cf. Winter, *MNO* 169). But his words also show his folly, to which he alludes unwittingly at 724f. We know that the ships did not arrive against the gods' will; nor was it the 'cowardice' of the Trojan elders that kept Hektor and his men from the camp in the past, but fear of Akhilleus, as we hear from the gods and Akhilleus himself (13.105–6n.), although Pouludamas displays such caution at 12.216ff., 18.254ff. Willcock deems Hektor's claim an *ad hoc* invention (*HSCP* 81 (1977) 48). — οἴσετε is an imper. of the mixed aor. in σ with thematic endings, like βήσετο, ἄξετε (Risch, *Wortbildung* 250). These began as desideratives (C. P. Roth, *Glotta* 48 (1970) 155–63, 52 (1974) 1–10). ἀϋτή means 'battle', not 'war-cry': in reaction the Trojans redouble their efforts (726), not their shouts. πάντων ἄξιον means '(a day) worth all (the rest)'. With 722 cf. 14.51. ἰσχανόω is a metrically useful modification of ἰσχ(άν)ω, like ἐρυκανόω from ἐρυκ(άν)ω etc. (Risch, *op. cit.* 321f.); only here is ἐρητύομαι middle, not passive. For βλάπτω cf. 489n. With 725 cf. 16.690 = 17.178 (again describing Zeus).

727 = 16.102, enclosing within this ring Aias' retreat and speech, which balances Hektor's, and Patroklos' plea to Akhilleus; 16.102–11 resumes the situation seen here.

728–30 Aias retreats slightly, and only for the best reason (cf. on 699ff.): he expects to die if he stays (for the phrase cf. 4.12, *Od.* 20.21). The 'seven-foot bench' is a wide cross-bench amidships (so Ap. Soph. 88.15), which bonded the central ribs of the hull to prevent the ship from breaking her back and to support the mast, like the μεσόδμη at *Od.* 2.424 (D. Gray, *Arch. Hom.* G 99; S. Marinatos, *ibid.* 151). Seven feet is the right width for a penteconter: Greek feet were 11.5–13 inches long (West on *Erga* 423). A rower's bench, ζυγόν elsewhere in Homer, is later termed θρανίον; this θρῆνυς must be called 'seven-foot' because the other benches were much shorter and did not straddle the ship. Aias presumably retreats by stepping from bench to bench: there was no half-deck above the rowers, as their vulnerability to Scylla proves (*Od.* 12.245f.). Since θρῆνυς also meant 'footstool' and originally 'support' in general (cf. Chantraine, *Dict.* s.v. θρόνος), Morrison and Williams (*op. cit.* 48f.) and Kurt (*Fachausdrücke* 119ff.) aver that it is a stout beam across the stern, projecting each side outside the hull below and forward of the helmsman's seat, on which he could put his feet (his seat could not itself be seven feet wide). This makes Aias retreat only a step, not far enough to blunt the force of the missiles hurled at him. Leaf imagines a 'bridge' between the fore and after decks, seven feet above the floor of the hold. For the form ἑπταπόδης (also at *Erga* 424) cf. ὀκτα-, τρι-, Οἰδι-πόδης (Hesiod). δεδοκημένος, from the root of δέκομαι and δοκέω ('expect' > 'think'), means 'watching' (cf. δοκεύω); resumed by δεδεγμένος at 745, it recurs at *Aspis* 214 and in Hellenistic verse.

732 = 687, but now introduces Aias' full reply to Hektor's speech. After a standard opening (733 occurs 4×, 734 7×, but not together), twice calling the men φίλοι, he poses two rhetorical questions, answers them with two couplets (one negative and one positive), and draws the obvious conclusion, in a verse of gnomic concision, that salvation lies in strength. As usual, he is blunt, brief and effective, including himself within the paraenesis. For exhortations based on twin rhetorical questions cf. 504ff. (Aias), 5.464–9.

735–6 'Do we think there are some allies behind us, or some wall better ⟨than this⟩?', i.e. than the defence they now have. ἄρειον is not for Ἀρήϊον (see 4.407n.).

737–40 Hektor lamented that he had been penned in the city (722f.); the Greeks feel the lack of just such a city, since the one nearby is hostile. I prefer Aristarchus' τι (Did/AT, with a few good MSS) to the vulgate τις, an easy dittography. ἑτεραλκέα δῆμον means 'a people with other strength' to turn the battle: cf. ἑ. νίκην (16.358–63n.), and for the phrasing 17.330. With 739 cf. 685–9n. πόντῳ κεκλιμένοι is an odd idiom: cf. 16.67f., where the Greeks ῥηγμῖνι θαλάσσης | κεκλίαται, or λίμνῃ κεκλιμένος (5.709), of a man 'living by a lake'. The ancients linked the forms with κλείω, i.e. 'cut off', 'surround' (Porphyry 1.209f.), but they are from κλίνω, as is clear from how islands ἁλὶ κεκλίαται (*Od.* 4.608) and a shore is εἰς ἅλα κεκλιμένη (*Od.* 13.235, cf. *HyAp* 24). Bards misunderstood islands or shores 'sloping' into the sea as 'lying' by it (P. Janni, *Quaderni Urbinati di Cultura Classica* 3 (1967) 7–25); cf. κλειτύς, Latin *clīvus*, 'slope'. The sense may be pejorative, like that of ἥμεθα: 'lying' and 'sitting' are postures better suited to 'luxury' than war.

741 At 508 Aias told the Greeks they were at a battle, not a dance; now he says their salvation is in their arms, not in μειλιχίη. This too alludes to sensuality: 'luxury' appears with 'pleasure' and 'sex' among Aphrodite's interests at *Theog.* 206. To gloss it 'supplication' (Hsch.) creates an unwanted reminder of surrender. Aristarchus, taking it as 'mildness' or 'sloth', rightly read μειλιχίη (with several good MSS) and took πολέμοιο with φόως. Dionysius Thrax, reading -ίη, punctuated after φ. to produce the forceful maxim 'there is no mildness in war' (D and Nic/A), like οὐχ ἕδος ἐστί, 'there is no time to sit' (11.648); cf. van der Valk, *Researches* II 194f. For 'light' as a metaphor for salvation see on 16.297ff.

742–6 For ὀξυόεις see 13.584–5n. πυρὶ κηλείῳ uniquely varies π. κηλέῳ (8×), yet -εῳ is the newer form. κηλείῳ has replaced *κηϝαλέος, cf. Aeolic καυαλέος in Hesychius (Chantraine, *Dict.* s.v.); -εί- is by metrical lengthening. The contraction recurs in περίκηλος, 'combustible' (2× *Od.*); the frequency of κηλέω is odd, but cf. that of νεῶν for νηῶν. The use of χάριν as a preposition, foreshadowed here only in Homer, is next approached at *Erga* 709 (cf. Semonides frag. 7.104); for the phrase 'a favour *to* Hektor' cf. 449, 5.211. The reading ἔγχεϊ μακρῷ (8× Hom.) is preferable, since 745 resumes 730; ὀξέϊ χαλκῷ (36×) is used more often because it can apply to swords as well. With 745 cf. 21.402. Aias' success in killing twelve Trojan fire-bearers amplifies his slaying of Kaletor at longer range (419f.). Twelve is a standard epic number (cf. 18.230, 336); but more Trojans run up continually, and sooner or later one will get through.

BOOK SIXTEEN

Patroklos' presence defines and dominates book 16, whence its title *Patrokleia*. The poet must save the ships from Hektor's assault. We know that Patroklos is *en route* to Akhilleus, and hopes to persuade him to rejoin the war (15.390ff.); we now expect the hero simply to agree, even though Zeus's forecast that his own ships would come under attack is still unfulfilled (15.56–77n.). But Homer has grander plans, which lead his hero to disaster. Although moved by Patroklos' passionate speech, Akhilleus is too concerned over losing face to join the fighting himself with no personal apology from Agamemnon. The Greek leaders ought by now to be here, offering restitution in person – but clearly cannot, if they are as badly wounded as Patroklos says. So Akhilleus tries to buy time for another, humbler embassy by accepting the compromise proposed by Nestor (11.794ff.), and advanced by Patroklos as if his own idea, that he send Patroklos in his own place at the head of his men. He can thus assuage his guilt (not unmixed with *Schadenfreude*) that the Greeks are imperilled because of his refusal the night before to end the quarrel when he had the chance, even though that entailed terms he found intolerable – and when the concessions he made, tacitly retracting his threat to sail home, went unnoticed after his initial outburst. Torn between anger and pity, he now accepts the compromise which he should have rejected, after rejecting the compromise he ought to have welcomed. He is consistently and plausibly characterized as brusquely hiding his pity for Patroklos and the Greeks, and as willing to shift his ground but loth to admit it (7–10, 72–3nn.).

Thornton (*Supplication* 123) notes that, by his continued refusal to fight, Akhilleus brings about the intervention of the Prayers, who, when scorned, supplicate Zeus to send Atē (9.502ff.): Patroklos' death is the punishment for his intransigence. Yet, with the moral ambiguity that makes the *Iliad* a great tragic poem, it can also be seen as the result of a set of misunderstandings. In Phoinix' paradigm of Meleagros (9.529–99), the angry warrior refuses to help until his own chamber comes under attack, when his wife Kleopatre persuades him to do so; by waiting so long, he forfeits the gifts he has been offered to make him end his strike. But Akhilleus acts as if Meleagros had sent out his own closest *philos*, Kleo-patre (= Patro-klos; on this equivalence see 9.561–3n.). Akhilleus excuses his own refusal on the ground that the war has yet to reach his own ships (61ff.). His acceptance of this half-measure is logical enough, but fraught, as he senses, with a double risk: should Patroklos do too well, Akhilleus would lose the glory he might have won himself; should things go awry, he could lose his friend. Akhilleus' culpability in endangering him is reduced by Patroklos' neglect of his command not to advance too far – even if that order was given for the wrong reason; Patroklos' responsibility for the idea is lessened by the fact that Nestor first proposed it, and that both act for the best possible motive. Patroklos was perhaps stirred by Nestor's tale of his own exploits, but his real wish is to rouse Akhilleus, as he told Eurupulos (15.402ff.). The plan misfires badly; all the protagonists are somehow to blame – Akhilleus, Agamemnon, Nestor, Patroklos and even Odysseus, who misreported Akhilleus' reaction to the Embassy as totally obdurate. Akhilleus' silence (save for the reminder at 237) about the fact that he did in fact pray for the Greeks' ruin helps us sympathize with him as he makes a hard choice. In short, we have a tragic *hamartia* of the kind so well analysed by Aristotle in the *Poetics* (so Redfield, *Nature and Culture* 91–8; cf. R. Scodel, *CPh* 84 (1989) 91–9). The opening scene, and Akhilleus' secret prayer to Zeus, brilliantly depict the psychology of a fierce, proud but not basically unreasonable hero.

By having him accept this compromise, Homer forges the vital link between Akhilleus' wrath and Hektor's death: his wrath causes Patroklos' death, which he must then avenge. Without this link we would have first, a tale of angry withdrawal and restitution, a traditional pattern (cf. 13.459–61n.); and second, a tale of revenge, an expansion of the traditional incident in battle where A kills B and C kills A to avenge his comrade or relative, as in the story of Memnon (see below). The effect of merely juxtaposing these two simple tales is seen in the dull and episodic narrative of Dictys of Crete, where Akhilleus' wrath ends *before* Hektor ambushes Patroklos and Akhilleus kills him in revenge. It is unlikely that this reflects the traditional story as Homer received it; yet cf. Allen, *Transmission* 177ff., and Lord, *Singer* 158ff. Akhilleus' fateful and largely unexpected compromise is in any case the linchpin holding the poem's two halves together.

To this compromise Homer adds another twist: Patroklos will wear Akhilleus' armour (130–54n.). This is an innovation which the poet has not fully harmonized with the tradition. At the end of the *Iliad* Akhilleus owns *two* divine panoplies, one each for Aias and Odysseus; the story of their strife over his armour must be older, and betrays the innovation. In folktale, whence the motif comes, his armour was impenetrable – hence Apollo must strip it from Patroklos before he can be slain; but Homer suppresses its magical properties, and his inconsistency over whether Patroklos' body still wears the armour may reflect unease about them (777–867n.). Again, earlier songs probably used the theme of armour as disguise, protecting its wearer by scaring the enemy, as Nestor proposes to Patroklos. But this idea is not developed: the Trojans are at first alarmed, but Sarpedon is soon asking who this warrior is, and Glaukos knows it is Patroklos (280, 423, 543). There is good reason for this: disguise in battle contradicts the heroic ethos, since one's glory depends on recognition by others (cf. Reinhardt, *IuD* 316–19); and it would be bathetic for Hektor to kill Patroklos and only then find that his victim was not Akhilleus (Edwards, *HPI* 255)!

The risks of introducing the divine armour are vastly outweighed by the gains, most evident later. The panoply visibly identifies Patroklos as Akhilleus' substitute; his inability to use Akhilleus' spear underlines his inadequacy in Akhilleus' role. When Apollo strips his armour off and he stands helpless in the battle, we again see his frailty, and that of all mortals confronted by the divine. When Hektor dons it he makes visible his presumption and fatal overconfidence; he is no more worthy to wear it than is Patroklos. Its loss brings disgrace on Akhilleus, giving him further cause for rage; but he cannot fight without armour, so there is a delay while Hephaistos forges a new set. This gives Homer the chance to depict Akhilleus' shield, retarding the plot so that the next climax, his duel with Hektor, is not too soon after Patroklos' death. The poem's structure is based on advances and retardations: books 1, 9, 16, 22 and 24 are the main advances, but the rest slow down the action, giving it 'magnitude', in Aristotle's term. Finally, when Hektor is at Akhilleus' mercy, the fact that he wears this armour dooms his plea that his body be spared mutilation. On the armour see further the Introduction to book 18, where it is argued that this theme comes from the tale of Memnon (see below).

Whitman well analyses the ring-structure of book 16 (*HHT* 281f.). Balanced scenes with dialogue depict Patroklos' despatch and death respectively (see on 1–100, 101–277, 777–867). These scenes frame two battles, by the ships and by the wall of Troy (278–418, 684–776). These battles, in turn, frame this book's central episode, the duel with Sarpedon and its aftermath, which begins and ends with scenes on Olumpos (419–683n.). The fighting is analysed by Fenik, *TBS* 190–218.

A glimpse of the failing defence of the fleet by his cousin Aias reinforces Akhilleus' decision: in a short but powerful scene, the Trojans at last ignite a ship (101–24). Lengthy preliminaries, including a list of the Myrmidons' leaders, show the importance of their return to war. The tragic outcome of Patroklos' *aristeia* is foreshadowed in his arming (130–54) and Akhilleus' prayer (220–56). Patroklos' arrival heartens the other Greeks, causing a general success; his personal *aristeia* begins when he kills so many of the routed enemy that he attracts Sarpedon's notice. Since Sarpedon is the leading Trojan ally, a son of Zeus and second in importance only to Hektor (as book 12 established), killing him proves Patroklos a worthy second to Akhilleus, but also contributes to his death. Swept away by this success, he forgets Akhilleus' warning; moreover, if Zeus cannot save his own beloved son, he will certainly not stop Apollo from intervening against the man who slew him. Formally, Sarpedon's death prefigures both Patroklos' and Hektor's. Patroklos kills Sarpedon's driver and then Hektor's; Zeus ponders saving both Sarpedon and Hektor. All three heroes speak after the fatal blow, their opponents win their armour, their bodies face the threat or reality of mutilation, and there are long battles for Sarpedon's and Patroklos' corpses. The supernatural removal of Sarpedon's body to Lycia meets the needs of local cult, but above all raises for the first time the theme of proper burial. These parallels underline the causal nexus linking the three major deaths in the poem with the yet greater one outside it, Akhilleus', which must soon follow Hektor's.

Perilously elated, Patroklos drives the Trojans back until Apollo intervenes to stop him from taking Troy. Since Homer warns us of his death, we await the fatal blow; but he prolongs our agony by delaying this by means of a duel with Hektor and a fight over a body, this time that of Hektor's driver (684–776). Apollo's final intervention against Patroklos is the most terrifying scene in the *Iliad*; as well as sympathizing with a man stripped defenceless by a god, we admire Patroklos for defying Hektor with his dying breath. His prophecy and death prefigure those of Hektor in book 22 (830–63n.). The fact that Euphorbos first wounds Patroklos lowers Hektor's stature, but this can be built up later; what matters now is to make us feel Patroklos' loss as keenly as if we ourselves were Akhilleus (Owen, *The Story of the Iliad* 155). Book 16 amply achieves this by combining scenes of great psychological depth with a martial narrative of superb clarity and power, articulated by many of Homer's finest similes; accelerating to a final climax, it dies away as Patroklos' life ebbs. But there is no true closure; the poet makes clear that Patroklos is right to predict that Akhilleus will slay Hektor. Our sympathy now shifts to both these adversaries until the poet makes us see, with the vision which Akhilleus so painfully acquires, that even our deadliest foes are human beings too.

Neo-analytic scholars have placed almost beyond doubt the theory that Patroklos' *aristeia* and death are based on those of Akhilleus himself. According to the *Aithiopis*, Akhilleus slew the Ethiopian hero Memnon to avenge the death of his friend Antilokhos, but was then killed at the Scaean Gate by Apollo and Paris, having ignored a warning from Thetis. Antilokhos died when Nestor's trace-horse was slain: this incident is drawn upon at 470–5 (where see n.). Patroklos' death resembles Antilokhos', since Akhilleus avenges both, but it also prefigures his leader's. Like Akhilleus, Patroklos is hit from behind near the Scaean Gate by Apollo and Euphorbos, who is an invention based on Paris (777–867n.); Hektor's role in the tale is secondary – he too was created to replace Paris, who was once the leading Trojan warrior, able to vanquish even Akhilleus (Severyns, *Homère* 83f.).

Zeus's son Sarpedon resembles Memnon, a major Trojan ally and the son of a deity, Eos (*Theog.* 984f.); as the son of Priam's brother Tithonos (20.237), Memnon is Hektor's cousin. Sarpedon's role is invented: traditionally, he lived much earlier and was slain by Tlepolemos (419–683n.). He is heroized, but Memnon (with the profligate generosity of the Cyclic tradition) is immortalized. The motif of Sleep and Death transporting Sarpedon's body perhaps belonged to Memnon, whose mother Dawn might naturally have such beings at her service; it is apt for her to wash her son's body, less so when Apollo bathes Sarpedon's (666–83n.). Before Memnon's death, Zeus weighed his fate against Akhilleus'; the motif of Zeus's scales, alluded to here (658n.), is developed before Hektor's death (22.209ff.). Thetis prophesied to Akhilleus that his own death would follow Memnon's: he joined the fray only when Memnon killed his friend Antilokhos. The motif of such a warning appears here (49–50n.), and is developed when Akhilleus decides to kill Hektor; Thetis' interview with her son to warn him about Memnon underlies not only 18.70–126, but also Akhilleus' warning to Patroklos (83–100n.) and even his simile at 7–10. Thus the theory that a '*Memnonis*' lies behind the *Iliad* explains much in book 16. But neither the *Iliad* nor any part of it need postdate the version of the story recorded in the *Aithiopis*; Homer knew a mass of traditional tales, many first attested in sources far later than the Cycle. Nor does this background diminish his achievement; if this story was indeed a major source of his inspiration, we are all the better placed to see his skill in adapting it. See further the Introduction to book 18.

Patroklos is often deemed Homer's own creation (von Scheliha, *Patroklos* 236–51; Erbse, *Hermes* 111 (1983) 1–15). But he first enters as 'son of Menoitios' (1.307), as if he is well known already; he has some old epithets (20n.), and appears in the legendary background of Akhilleus' family (168–97n.). Menoitios was in Phthia when his son left for Troy, as if he too belonged there (11.765–90); this is at odds with Patroklos' Locrian origin (18.324–7, 23.85f.), but cf. 13.694–7n. The *Cypria* told how Patroklos sold Lykaon on Lemnos (cf. 21.40), and perhaps how Telephos wounded him and Akhilleus healed him: cf. the cup by Sosias, *c.* 500 B.C. (*LIMC* s.v. Achilleus, pl. 468), and Pindar, *Ol.* 9.70ff. See further Kullmann, *Quellen* 44f. Now Hesiod made Menoitios Peleus' brother (*Cat.* 212a), and perhaps included Patroklos among Helen's suitors, since Akhilleus was too young (cf. 'Apollodorus' 3.10.9); the fourth–century writer Philocrates said Patroklos was Akhilleus' nephew (*FGH* 601 F 1). Akhilleus calls Patroklos a Myrmidon at 18.10. He once avenged a kinsman, not a friend; but Homer suppresses any blood-ties. There is good reason to think that he greatly enhanced Patroklos' importance for Akhilleus and for the *Iliad*, remodelling his role to match that of Akhilleus' other friend Antilokhos (E. Howald, *Der*

Dichter der Ilias, Zurich 1946, 63ff.). Homer explicitly says that the latter was second to Patroklos in Akhilleus' heart: Patroklos' ashes were mixed with Akhilleus', whereas Antilokhos' were not (*Od.* 24.76ff.). Incidentally, this especially obvious revision of the tradition supports my view (first reached on linguistic grounds) that the same poet composed both epics much as we have them; only a bard who had already created an *Iliad* wherein the two heroes were to be buried together (23.83ff.), with a Patroklos who played a far larger role than before, would have troubled to endorse this version of the story and deny the other. Epics based on the theme of heroic friendship, like the *Chanson de Roland*, are rare. In pre-Homeric tradition, as von Scheliha says (*Patroklos* 283ff.), Akhilleus was better known for erotic exploits than friendship. Perhaps this theme was inspired by the tale of the half-divine Gilgamesh and his friend Enkidu, who dies in his stead (on the similarities see Lord, *Singer* 197); David and Jonathan swapped clothing and weapons to mark their amity (1 Samuel 18.4). For Akhilleus' later history as a character see King, *Achilles*.

1–100 Patroklos begs Akhilleus to intervene to save the ships, or at least to send him in his stead. Akhilleus, still refusing to fight himself, bids him borrow his armour, lead the Myrmidons to battle and return when he has driven the Trojans from the ships

1–100 Akhilleus sent Patroklos to ask after the wounded Makhaon (11.599ff.) – a sign of concern for the Greeks after his rejection of the Embassy, as Nestor realized (11.656). Patroklos' errand was overtaken by his meeting with Nestor (644ff.), who urged him at least to propose the compromise he now advances (794–803). He runs back to persuade Akhilleus, but stops *en route* to tend Eurupolos (814ff.), only leaving his hut at 15.390ff. His journey takes the rest of book 15; Homer makes him arrive just before the first ship is ignited, so that by then the suspense has already shifted to the counter-attack. This also allows his conversation with Akhilleus to be more relaxed than it could have been were a ship already ablaze. Save for an opening simile and the foreshadowing of Patroklos' death at 46f., the whole scene consists of dialogue – Akhilleus' brusque and ironic inquiry, Patroklos' passionate charge that he is pitiless towards the Greeks and his acceptance of Patroklos' compromise, based on a typical vacillation between continuing concern for his honour and an unstated wish to save them from ruin (cf. Wilamowitz, *IuH* 119f.); he bids Patroklos do only the minimum necessary. On this scene cf. Schadewaldt, *Iliasstudien* 128–30; von Scheliha, *Patroklos* 257–9; Owen, *The Story of the Iliad* 146–55; D. E. Eichholz, *AJP* 74 (1953) 137–48; E. W. Williams, *CQ* 51 (1957) 103–8; Whitman, *HHT* 196ff.; Lesky, *Gesammelte Schriften* 72–80. For a trenchantly Analytic view see Page, *HHI* 305ff. On the place of this scene in the structure formed by 15.653–16.125, and how it corresponds to 15.355ff., see 15.262–404n.; for structural parallels between 1–324 and 18.1–242 see R. M. Frazer, *Hermes* 117 (1989) 381–90.

1–3 The transitional line 1 is not paralleled exactly. Such verses often begin books (bT cite books 9, 12, 18, 23 and *Od.* 6, 7), but the book-divisions are owed to editors, not to Homer. Patroklos' entry motivated the book-division, which has a certain logic, but there is a full continuity as usual (above all at 102ff.). The ship is Protesilaos' (15.704–6n.). The imperfect παρίστατο makes Patroklos' arrival coincide with the fighting: Leaf renders it 'was coming up'. π. ποιμένι λαῶν recurs at 5.570, 19.251; Akhilleus receives this generic epithet only here. Homer could have said παρίστατο δάκρυα λείβων (cf. 6.405), but preferred the expansion δ. θερμὰ χέων (etc., 6× Hom.), which next describes Antilokhos and Akhilleus himself weeping for Patroklos (18.17, 235). 'Hot tears' contrast beautifully with the chill rivulet to which they are compared.

3–4 = 9.14f., from χέων, where the simile describes Agamemnon's grief and humiliation at the Greek defeat, symbolized by the watch-fires at 8.554ff. (cf. the fire at 15.744); it introduced the Embassy. Moulton thinks we are meant to contrast Patroklos' selfless motivation here (*Similes* 103f., cf. V. di Benedetto, *RFIC* 115 (1987) 273ff.). Well may Patroklos weep at what he has heard and seen; Phoinix already wept for the ships the day before (9.433, cf. T). But this simile leads up to further imagery. It is a spring's nature to pour forth water, which suggests that tears are the natural response; it was not improper for a hero to weep, save from fear or physical pain (S. West on *Od.* 2.81). Yet it is as surprising to see a tough warrior weep as to see water pour from a cliff (Fränkel, *Gleichnisse* 21); thus Akhilleus chides Patroklos' tears, calling them girlish and babyish (7f.). In reply Patroklos likens him to a son of the sea and cliffs for his harshness (34f.); Eustathius saw this connexion (1043.11ff., cf. T on 7). Schoeck (*Ilias und Aithiopis* 89) remarks that, in book 16, Akhilleus will play the role taken by his mother in the *Memnonis* – that of spectator; thus he equates himself with the mother in the simile. Water is usually 'dark' (cf. μέλαν ὕδωρ, 7× epos); does it reflect Patroklos' mood (de Jong, *Narrators* 126n.)? I imagine it as flowing down the grey limestone typical of Greece, against which rivulets look like black streaks.

5 = 23.534, cf. 11.814 (of Patroklos). Akhilleus' pity, which redeems him in the end, leads him to disaster here. ᾤκτιρε, the rarer verb in Homer, is equivalent in shape and sense to ἐλέησε. Aristarchus read θάμβησε instead, claiming that Akhilleus would not have jested in his questions to Patroklos if he had pitied him (Did/T). This misjudgement removes the central theme of pity from this central scene of the *Iliad*, and confirms that Aristarchus could emend on improper grounds (θ. is in no MS).

7–19 Willcock calls Akhilleus' speech 'a delicate combination of friend-ship and irony'; Edwards (*HPI* 257) compares the 'aggressive impatience' with which he affected not to know the real reason why Athene had come, and ironically advanced another (1.202ff.). Faced with a Patroklos too overcome to speak, he mocks his tears with a friendly rebuke. Ironic questions form the kernel of his speech – 'Have you or I bad news from home?' – to which he himself gives a negative reply; thus he ends, naturally, with the question that gives the true answer – 'Do you grieve for the Greeks?' It is standard epic technique to ask 'Is it *x* or *y*?' when it is in fact neither, e.g. 1.65, 93f.: 'Is Apollo angry over a vow or a hecatomb?' ... 'He is angry about neither a vow nor a hecatomb, but ...'; 6.378–86, 'Has she gone to visit *x*, *y*, or *z*?' ... 'No, she has not gone to visit *x*, *y*, or *z*, but ...'; *Od.* 2.30–45, 'Has someone had news, or ...?' ... 'I have had no news, nor ..., but ...' This focusing device stresses the true reason; Akhilleus' inclusion of that reason, after discounting other possibilities, shows that he knows it and dislikes that knowledge. The device comes from folk-poetry and is typical of oral traditions, e.g. modern Greek (γιατί δακρύζεις ...; | μήνα πεινᾶς, μήνα διψᾶς, μὴν ἔχεις κακὴ μάνα; | – Μήτε πεινῶ, μήτε διψῶ, μήτ' ἔχω κακὴ μάνα ...). Ours is a sophisticated example, being within one speech: contrast 50–2, which answer 36–8 in a variant of this pattern (see Kakridis, *Homeric Researches* 108–20; Macleod, *Iliad XXIV* 41).

7–10 Akhilleus 'utters more similes than any character' (Moulton, *Similes* 100): cf. 59, 9.323, 9.385, 9.648, 18.109f., 21.282, 22.262. This is 'a fully intended aspect of his characterization', which Moulton links with his singing to the lyre at 9.186ff.; Homer gives him the acute perceptions of a bard – imagery is the proof of poetic genius (Aristotle, *Poet.* 1459a7). Moulton also shows that the motif of parent and child pervades the similes describing Akhilleus and Patroklos, starting at 9.323, when Akhilleus likens himself to a mother bird bringing food to its young: cf. 17.4, 17.133, 18.56f., 18.318, 23.222. He is usually cast in the protective parental role, Patroklos in that of the protected party. It is all the more ominous when Patroklos is sent out to protect the Greeks; Akhilleus will blame himself for failing to protect him. Figuratively, Patroklos is clasping Akhilleus' knees in supplica-tion, just as the toddler grabs her mother's skirts; she has to run to keep up with her busy mother (bT). Homer closely observes children's behaviour, like Astuanax' fear of his father's helmet (6.467ff.) or the boy with the sand-castle (15.362ff.); cf. ἠύτε κούρη | νήπιος (2.872f.). νηπίη evokes its original sense *infans*; it is a baby-talk form of νηπύτιος, from ἠπύω, 'speak'. Akhilleus alludes to Patroklos' inability to speak through his tears (7 and 11 form a ring); the poet soon calls Patroklos νήπιος in its other sense, 'fool', for what he says (46).

Since Akhilleus weeps over Briseis (1.348), but chides Patroklos for weep-ing at such terrible events, bT infer that he is brusque on purpose, to deter

Patroklos from his request (cf. his allusion to the Greeks' transgression at 18, and Patroklos' reply μὴ νεμέσα); people who are harsh see those who are reasonable as womanish, and the latter deem the former savage, cf. 35 (based on Aristotle's ethics, this may reflect his *Homeric Questions*). We may indeed imagine that Akhilleus gruffly steels himself to resist by reminding himself that the Greeks are in the wrong and that the only death which should move him is one in his own family. For δεδάκρυμαι, 'be tearful', cf. 22.491, *Od.* 20.204; Chantraine, *GH* II 197. εἰανοῦ is a unique metrical lengthening of ἑανός, 'dress' (14.180n.). ὄφρ' ἀνέληται, '*until* she is picked up', stresses the child's insistence.

11 Πάτροκλος is the short form of Πατροκλέης, a metrically convenient variation; cf. Ἰφικλέης/-κλος, Ἐχεκλέης/-κλος. *Kurzformen* keep only the initial consonant(s) of the second part of the compound name, e.g. Τηλέμαχος/Τήλεμος (von Kamptz, *Personennamen* 3–13). They rarely denote the same person. Akhilleus' driver Alkimedon is also called Alkimos, perhaps to avoid a jingle with Automedon, at 19.392 etc. (but cf. 193–7n.); the same man is called Diokles/-klos at *HyDem* 153, 474–8. On formulae for weeping see 3.142n.; for δάκρυον cf. 14.157–8n.; for εἴβω see S. West on *Od.* 4.153.

12–16 'Have you news for the Myrmidons or for me, or have you heard a message from Phthia ⟨that concerns you⟩ alone?' This interpretation is confirmed by the chiastic order of the persons mentioned next – Menoitios, Patroklos' father; Peleus, Akhilleus' father; and lastly the Greeks, who, by the logic of the chiasmus, concern the Myrmidons in general. Akhilleus can envisage nothing worse than losing his old father far off over the sea (cf. 19.321–5, 24.486ff., 24.507ff.) – he does not imagine the loss of Patroklos at all. For πιφαύσκομαι, 'proclaim', cf. 21.99, *Od.* 2.32; it is cognate with φά(ϝ)ος, φαίνω and φημί (Chantraine, *Dict.* s.v. φάε). Eustathius (1042.27ff.) noted the *variatio* ζώειν φασί ... ζώει, like that in βέβληται – οὔτασται – β. at 25–7. On τεθνηώς/-ειώς see p. 36 with n. 66.

19 = 1.363, cf. 18.74, in dialogues where Akhilleus tells Thetis that he has lost (respectively) Briseis and Patroklos. The verse follows τέκνον, τί κλαίεις; τί δέ σε φρένας ἵκετο πένθος; (cf. 7), and precedes τὴν δὲ βαρύ στενάχων προσέφη (cf. 20). Demeter addresses a variant of it to Persephone at *HyDem* 394, where τέκνον precedes; it was surely typical of parent–child interviews – an apt resonance here.

20 The poet applies the rare apostrophe especially to Menelaos and Patroklos, unusually sympathetic figures (13.602–3n.). It is used of Patroklos 8×, always in book 16; its greater frequency near the end confirms that it is emotive as well as metrically convenient. Such addresses fall into a sort of formular pattern (4.127n.). With προσέφης, Πατρόκλεες ἱππεῦ (3×) cf. π., Εὔμαιε συβῶτα (15× *Od.*); ἱππεύς is not voc. elsewhere, but cf. ἱππότα, ἱππηλάτα and other fossilized vocatives used as nominatives (13.562–3n.). Patroklos' old epithets ἱππεύς and ἱπποκέλευθος (126–9n.)

support the view, argued above (pp. 313–14), that he was a traditional figure who has been built up in the *Iliad* or just before, by a poet sympathetic to such loyal, sensible and altruistic characters as receive apostrophe (cf. Page, *HHI* 286; Hoekstra, *Modifications* 139). The MSS have Πατρόκλεις; editors restore -κλεες, since the oldest texts must have had -ΚΛΕΣ, but the contraction cannot be removed at 693, 859, unless we were to scan Πᾱτρὄκλεες, cf. Πᾱτρὄκλε̄ at 19.287 and 554–5n. M. Baltes thinks the variation of 20 at 744 and 843, with ἐπικερτομέων and ὀλιγοδρανέων replacing βαρὺ στενάχων, marks the stages of Patroklos' *aristeia* – pity for the Greeks, overconfidence and death (*A&A* 29 (1983) 47f.).

21–45 Patroklos' speech, well analysed by Lohmann (*Reden* 275), falls into three parts. The first and third repeat the opening and close of Nestor's speech in book 11, like a repeated messenger-speech (cf. de Jong, *Narrators* 180–5); but Patroklos does not admit that he is relaying a message, replacing Nestor's central *exemplum* of his youthful exploits with a passionate denunciation of Akhilleus:

A 21–9   The Greeks' plight (24–7 = 11.659–62; 23f. and 28f. form a ring)
B 29–35   Akhilleus' pitilessness (29 and 35 form a ring)
C 36–45   Patroklos' request (= 11.794–803)

Lohmann thinks 29–35 continue the theme of Akhilleus' savagery broached by Aias at 9.628ff. and 636ff., as if Patroklos must combine Aias' friendly yet severe rebuke with Nestor's practical advice before Akhilleus can be moved; parallels between Akhilleus' replies to Aias and to Patroklos confirm this (49–63n.). Patroklos is persuasive (cf. bT). After an emollient opening, where he begs indulgence not for his tears but for his request, he elevates Akhilleus by listing the wounded leaders who have failed to save the Greeks, but at the same time aims to shock him with their number: as if from tact, he names Agamemnon neither first nor last, but does not omit him entirely. Then, as if upset by his own list, he rebukes Akhilleus in terms as harsh as any Aias used: doctors can tend the wounded, but he is incurable (29); posterity will not gain from his valour if he does not save the Greeks; he may claim to care for Peleus, but his parents were the sea and cliffs, so harsh is his mind. This leads naturally to Patroklos' request, via the thought that Akhilleus may be holding back because of some prophecy: as bT say (on 41), this imputes cowardice to him, but Patroklos at once adds a reminder of his superiority – he could rout the enemy just by appearing to them, as he does at 18.215ff.

21 = 19.216, *Od.* 11.478 (spurious). Editors print Πηλῆος υἱέ, i.e. υῐέ (so too 1.489, cf. on 13.275–8, 15.244–6); but -ῆος is in only a few late MSS each time. The rest of the paradosis has -έως or -έος. Since | – ∪∪ Πηλέος υἱέ (etc.) is found 6×, -έος should stand (cf. 15.339n.). Verse 22 = 10.145, when Nestor apologizes for waking Odysseus; with 29 cf. 10.167, from the latter's grumpy reply. The word-play Ἀχιλεῦ – Ἀχαιῶν – ἄχος reflects the etymology of Akhilleus' name (173–8, 818–22nn.).

23–7 = 11.658–62 (where see nn.), from ἄριστοι onward; Patroklos replaces Nestor's opening words with Eurupulos' formulation, which he heard at 11.825. Nestor began 'Why does Akhilleus grieve for the Achaeans? – he knows nothing of the suffering that has arisen', and described the woundings that occurred in book 11, ending with the doctor Makhaon, ostensible cause of Patroklos' mission; but the latter mentions instead the doctors' power to heal. Patroklos' omission is apt, since Makhaon was a mere pretext: Akhilleus was concerned as to how the Greeks were faring (1–100n.). Eustathius (1044.7) thinks Patroklos purposely misrepresents the wounded leaders as being out of action, when in fact they have been exhorting the men (14.134ff., 379f.); but Patroklos cannot know this because he has been in Eurupulos' hut acting as a doctor, in an effort to help as best he can without fighting. Hence he describes the latter's wound in detail at 27 (= 11.662, probably spurious).

28–31 πολυφάρμακος also describes the witch Kirke (*Od.* 10.276, Hes. frag. 302.15). ἀμήχανος, 'impossible to deal with' (13.726n.), has overtones of 'incurable' here (R. P. Martin, *Healing, Sacrifice and Battle*, Innsbruck 1983, 30). γ' οὖν, here with the restrictive sense of Attic γοῦν, recurs in the epos only at 5.258 (Denniston, *Particles* 448). Akhilleus stores up his bile like a precious wine: the metaphor in φυλάσσω is rare. Aristarchus equated χόλος and μῆνις (cf. *HyDem* 350, 410), but see 13.459–61n. αἰναρέτη is the voc., like Ἀτρείδη or ὑψαγόρη, of an adj. in -ης, glossed by Aristarchus as ἐπὶ κακῷ τὴν ἀρετὴν ἔχων; if so, it is an oxymoron like δυσαριστοτόκεια (18.54), mixing praise and blame in one word. For the compound cf. αἰνο-παθής, -μορος, -παρις (Alcman), -γαμος -λεκτρος -πάτηρ (Aesch.). But if Ainarete, 'praised for valour', not Enare(t)e, was a name (that of Aiolos' wife), the word might be a sarcastic compliment. The conjecture αἴν· ἀρετῆς, rejected by Aristarchus, is in no MS; nor can one read αἴν' ἀρετῆς, 'cursed in your valour', *pace* Leaf. Nestor ended his *exemplum* with the thought that others will not gain from Akhilleus' valour (11.763, οἷος τῆς ἀρετῆς ἀπονήσεται), adding that he too would suffer if the army perished; Patroklos means that posterity (ὀψίγονοι) learns from ancestral examples (cf. 3.353). Note the urgent asyndeta in 31–3.

33–5 For the old notion that mankind sprang from trees, rocks or earth cf. *Od.* 19.163, *Cat.* 234, Asius frag. 8, *PMG* 985 (surely by Pindar), West on *Erga* 145, *Theog.* 35, 187 and 563, where μελίαι means 'men'; the Myrmidons came from ants (*Cat.* 205). Patroklos blends with this the idea that the elements are unfeeling and harsh; this is already undercut by the simile of the weeping rock (3f.). Telemakhos calls Penelope's heart harder than stone (*Od.* 23.103, cf. 4.293, 5.191); Apollo likens Akhilleus' savagery to a lion's

(24.41ff.). Cf. τοο πέτρας καὶ πολίας θαλάσσας τέκνον (Alcaeus frag. 359), in a riddle about a limpet! The sea and cliffs evoke the habitats of Akhilleus' parents (so T), in a 'reversal of personification' (Edwards, *HPI* 257). The sea-goddess Thetis turned into water in her shape-changing struggle to resist Peleus' advances (Sophocles frag. 150; cf. Frazer, Appendix x). Folk-etymology linked Peleus with Mt Pelion, where his nuptials took place and Kheiron reared Akhilleus (141–4n.). In fact Πηλεύς is from not Πᾱλίον but Aeolic πῆλε = τῆλε (cf. Myc. *Qe-re-wa* = Τηλέας), like Φηρεύς for Θηρεύς (J. L. Perpillou, *Les Substantifs grecs en -εύς*, Paris 1973, 183); yet Homer may have compared Ἀλωεύς < Ἀλώϊον, Ὀϊλεύς < *Ϝίλιος. At 142–4 he also relates 'Peleus' to πῆλαι, 'shake'; bards are not limited to a single etymology, and later poets linked Peleus with πηλός. With the phrasing and thought cf. 203f., σχέτλιε Πηλέος υἱέ, χόλῳ ἄρα σ' ἔτρεφε μήτηρ, | νηλεές (Akhilleus quoting Myrmidon complaints), and 18.331f.

γλαυκή describes the sea only here in Homer, but is the name of a sea-nymph at 18.39 and *Theog.* 244 (with Thetis in the same verse); cf. Hesiod's Γλαυκονόμη 'Dweller in the γλαυκή', his *kenning* for the sea, γλαυκὴν δυσπέμφελον (*Theog.* 256, 440), and the like use of ὑγρή (14.307–8n.). Page (*HHI* 229) censures γλαυκή, claiming that we expect πολιή ... θάλασσα (4× Hom. in acc., gen.); but here π. would suggest old age, and in other contexts γ. might have metrical advantages. Glaukos is a Myc. and later name; the adj. means 'blue-' or 'grey-(eyed)'. P. G. Maxwell-Stuart notes that such eyes can seem sinister to dark-eyed races (*Studies in Greek Colour Terminology* I, γλαυκός, Leiden 1981, 108ff., 124ff.); thus γλαυκιόω means 'glare' (20.172), and blue averts the evil eye among the Greeks and Arabs. ἀπηνής, 'harsh', is Akhilleus' term for Agamemnon (1.340), cf. 15.94, 23.484, 611, *Od.* 18.381. For ὅτι, 'because', Aristarchus (in T) read ὅτε, 'since', a needless change lacking MS support.

36–45 These vv. repeat 11.794–803 (where see nn.), with adaptations for the second person. πρόες ὥχ', ἅμα δ' ἄλλον λαὸν ὄπασσον (cf. 18.452) is for προέτω, ἅμα δ' ἄλλος λαὸς ἐπέσθω (elision at the caesura replaces hiatus!); in 39, innovative ἤν που replaces αἴ κεν (cf. 8.282), and 40 wholly remodels 11.798. Verses 41–3 recur (adapted) at 18.199ff., when Iris asks Akhilleus to appear at the trench (but 201 may be spurious). On the armour see above pp. 310–11. Patroklos' request is modestly phrased, but Akhilleus still deems it needful to warn him against pressing the Trojans too hard.

46–8 The poet stresses Patroklos' blindness in seeking his own death-warrant: he is νήπιος not, as Akhilleus charged, for weeping (7–10n.), but in a more tragic way. The pathos is yet greater than at 11.604, where his innocent emergence from his hut to answer Akhilleus' call elicited the poet's remark 'that was the beginning of evil for him'. νήπιος-comments refer to present ignorance (ν., οὐδ' ἐνόησεν, e.g. 22.445f.) or future suffering, e.g. ν., οὐδ' ἄρ' ἔμελλε ... ἂψ ἀπονοστήσειν (12.113ff.) or νήπιοι, οὐδ' ἄρ' ἔμελλον ἀναιμωτί γε νέεσθαι (17.497); for μέγα νήπιος cf. *Od.* 9.44, 3× *Erga* (see further 684–91n. and de Jong, *Narrators* 86f.). λίτεσθαι is a pres. infin. (cf. *Hy.* 16.5), not an aor.; the 'parallel' λιτοίμην at *Od.* 14.406 is illusory (read ἀλιτοίμην). Yet, for the nuance of destiny needed here, a fut. would be better (cf. Chantraine, *GH* II 308f.); the poet has clumsily adapted the formular system θάνατον καὶ κῆρα μέλαιναν etc. (684–7n.) for the sake of the etymological play λισσόμενος – λίτεσθαι. This oddity led to a variant λιπέσθαι; Leaf rejects 46f. With οἵ αὐτῷ cf. *Erga* 265 and *Cat.* 10a.62 (‖ ἵν δ᾽ α. θανάτου ταμίης). J. Audiat takes ὀχθήσας as 'irritated' (*REA* 49 (1947) 41–57); S. Scully (*TAPA* 114 (1984) 20ff.) thinks it evokes Akhilleus' semi-divine status, but cf. 17.18, *Od.* 15.325!

49–100 Lohmann (*Reden* 60–4) well analyses Akhilleus' reply into three parts, each to be discussed *ad loc.*:

A 49–63 Akhilleus explains his continuing absence from battle.
B 64–82 He gives Patroklos his permission.
C 83–100 He explains why Patroklos must not exceed his orders.

Akhilleus' abrupt shifts from topic to topic mirror his character; but the structure is in fact carefully controlled. 'The whole speech in its present form, with its alternations of penitence and passion, is as perfectly conceived and perfectly executed as any other literary piece in existence' (Leaf). The frequency of periodic and integral enjambment reflects Akhilleus' passion (Kirk, *YCS* 20 (1966) 129). Ancient objections were mostly against 89f. and 93–100; the Analysts attack 69–79 and 84–6, or argue that 60f. and 84–6 presuppose an *Iliad* without book 9.

49–63 Lohmann (*Reden* 274f.) shows that the first part of Akhilleus' speech falls into three parts, forming a reprise of his reply to his cousin Aias at 9.644ff.:

A Patroklos, I do not refrain from battle because of a prophecy (49–51).	A Aias, your words please me (9.644f.).
B But pain reaches my heart at how Agamemnon has treated me like a dishonoured refugee (52–9).	B But my heart swells with anger at how Agamemnon has treated me like a dishonoured refugee (9.646–8).
C But let bygones be bygones. I said that I would not end my anger until the battle reached my ships . . . (60–3)	C But tell the Greeks that I will not end my anger until the battle reaches my ships (9.649–55).

Poseidon's speech at 15.206–17 has a like structure (52 = 208); he acknowledges what was said, restates his grievance and yields with a threat. Akhilleus' threat not to intervene until his ships are attacked is in fact a concession in book 9 – at least he is not sailing home; here too it tacitly introduces another concession, but also explains why he himself will not yet fight. Just as he hides his pity for the Greeks, so he does not admit that Patroklos has moved him, but implies that it is unnatural to be angry for ever (60f.), as if his own nature, not his regard for Patroklos, is the cause of his yielding (Eustathius 1046.3). His restatement of his grudge, even though Patroklos knows it, is in character too. Patroklos spoke as if he did not know the cause, when he asked whether he was holding back because of a prophecy (so bT): hence Akhilleus' protest ὢ μοι (49), although he is also pained at the hard choice he must make. Lohmann (*Reden* 60n.) remarks on his rising emotion; he starts with a negative priamel and generalities (50–4) to focus on the Greeks and Agamemnon (with passionate asyndeton at 55f.), until he reins in his anger at 60f.

49–50 For a speech opening ὢ μοι ... οἷον ἔειπες cf. 8.152, when Nestor scorns Diomedes' fear of being mocked for cowardice (52 = 8.147); with other addressees the verse may begin ὢ πόποι instead (7.455, *Od.* 13.140). διογενές is a generic voc. used 5× of Patroklos, and also of Laertiades, Telamonios, Meleagros or no name at all (9.106, *Od.* 10.443). Akhilleus denies that he has heard of any prophecy, rephrasing 36f. in a variant of the traditional device 'Is it *x* or *y*?', 'No, it is not *x* or *y* but *z*' (7–19n.). Were this not a tragic epic, he would surely seek prophetic advice; his denial accords with his anguished recollection – too late – of Thetis' prediction that the best of the Myrmidons would die before him (18.9ff.). He is not allowed to recall this here, nor do the listeners yet know of it; Homer gives his characters only such knowledge as suits the dramatic needs of the moment, and keeps their motivation on a human level, in contrast to the Epic Cycle. Willcock sees *ad hoc* invention here (*HSCP* 81 (1977) 49); bT think Akhilleus refers to 9.410–16, where he said that Thetis told him he has two fates – an early but glorious death at Troy, or a long but inglorious life. But this detail, like so much in book 16 (pp. 312–13), surely derives from the tale of Akhilleus' own death. In the *Aithiopis*, Thetis predicts to her son τὰ κατὰ τὸν Μέμνονα (Proclus); as Welcker saw, she must have warned him that his death would ensue if he slew Memnon (cf. 18.95–6n.; Schoeck, *Ilias und Aithiopis* 87). Such a prophecy is only hinted at here: Homer postpones the full revelation until 18.96. Akhilleus' denial matches our knowledge: until 17.408f. we never hear that Thetis told him of Zeus's plan – as Reinhardt says (*IuD* 34), such a scene would have made us ask why he is not warned about Patroklos' fate. Aristarchus altered ἦν to εἰ (in no MS) to make his knowledge of a prophecy explicit, deeming it more in character if he knows of one but ignores it (Did/AbT). But cf. οὔτε θεοπροπίης ἐμπάζομαι (-ζόμεθ') ἦν (τινα) at *Od.* 1.415, 2.201.

52–5 These vv. are marked off by repetition of αἰνὸν ἄχος, with anticipatory τόδε and retrospective τό. Verse 52 = 8.147, 15.208, *Od.* 18.274;

like Poseidon at 15.185ff., Akhilleus complains that an equal has trespassed on his rights. Aristarchus altered δή to τις (Did/T), again no doubt trying to make him be more explicit; but ὁππότε (κεν) δή occurs 12×, cf. 62. The article in τὸν ὅμοιον is a 'late' usage, cf. ὡς αἰεὶ τ. ὅ. ἄγει θεὸς ὡς τ. ὅ. (*Od.* 17.218). For ἀμέρσαι, 'rob', cf. 13.339–44n. ὅ τε, 'since', should probably be read ὅτε (Ruijgh, τε *épique* 810–23), as the following subj. confirms (Chantraine, *GH* II 286); by someone who κράτεϊ προβεβήκῃ, Akhilleus means a man with more status, like Agamemnon (cf. 6.125f., *Aspis* 354f.). With πάθον ἄλγεα θυμῷ cf. 18.397, *Od.* 13.263; Akhilleus used it of his thankless martial toil (9.321).

56–9 With Akhilleus' summary of his humiliation cf. 9.367f.; Thetis repeats it (18.444f.), omitting the emotive verses 57 and 59. He remarks at 9.343 that Briseis was δουρικτητή, stressing his toil and his right to profit by it (9.325ff.). Her town of origin is Lurnessos at 2.690, but Pedasos in the *Cypria* (frag. 27 B. = 21 D.); yet her name links her with Brisa on Lesbos (Erbse, *Hermes* 111 (1983) 2). κτεάτισσα, 'acquired' (4× *Od.*, Eumelus frag. 3 B. = 2 D.), is an epic innovation based on the plur. κτέατα. The archaism εὐτείχεα is remodelled to -εον at 1.129 and 5× to avoid hiatus (Meister, *Kunstsprache* 16); even so, the scansion πόλῑν suggests innovation (cf. 69). Verse 58 means that Agamemnon was personally to blame for removing Briseis, not that he fetched her himself (1.185n.): note the contrast between the active ἔξελον and middle ἕλετο. ἂψ (= Latin *abs*) stresses his high-handedness – the booty had already been distributed (*LfgrE* s.v. B 1c).

59 = 9.648, where Akhilleus likens himself to a refugee (for the poor treatment of refugees cf. Tyrtaeus frag. 10.3ff.). Here we must supply με, in the double-acc. construction usual with verbs of removal: Agamemnon 'took her back ⟨from me⟩, as if ⟨I were⟩ a dishonoured migrant'. So Aristarchus, no doubt refuting the conjecture offered by Rhianus and the Marseilles text, who have μετανάστιν (next in Philo) denoting Briseis (Did/bT). The harsh ellipse may point up the irony that Akhilleus' woes are trivial compared to those which war inflicts on such captives. ἀτίμητος and μετανάστης next recur in prose, but cf. Myc. /metaktitai/ (PY An 610).

60–1 'But let us leave these matters in the past. It is, after all, impossible to be furiously angry ...' Verse 60 = 18.112, 19.65 (ending with ἀχνύμενοί περ), as Akhilleus renounces his wrath more and more publicly. ἐάσομεν is aor. subj.; the plur. associates him with all who feel likewise (V. Bers, *Greek Poetic Syntax in the Classical Age*, New Haven 1984, 49). Since τέτυκται approximates to 'is', προτετύχθαι means 'to exist in the past' (πρό). ἀ-σπερχές is from σπέρχομαι, 'hurry', 'be hasty (in temper)', with ἀ-intensive; cf. the torrent Σπερχειός and ἀ. μενεαίνω (4.32 etc.). It does not mean 'unceasingly', *pace* D. The imperf. with ἄρα signals an unexpected outcome: cf. 33, 23.670 (Chantraine, *GH* II 192).

61–3 ἔφην is often taken to refer to 9.650–5, where Akhilleus said he would not end his wrath until the war reached his ships (so T, cf. p. 234); but Aristarchus well remarks that it means 'I intended', with the implication that this was always his plan (cf. 13.83–90n.; Page, *HHI* 329n.). He omits his former stipulation (9.653) that the ships must be ablaze – another sign of weakening resolve. μηνιθμός, from μηνίω, recurs in Greek only at 202 and 282 (cf. 13.459–61n.). After οὐ πρίν we expect πρίν, 'I will not desist ... until' (cf. 9.650f.), but 'until' is replaced by 'but when'; this makes Akhilleus' promise to fight more definite, at the price of convoluted syntax. ἀϋτή τε πτόλεμός τε is formular (etc., 3× epos).

64–82 Lohmann (*Reden* 60–3) skilfully detects another ring-structure here, which undermines the Analysts' objections to 69–79 or 74–9:

A 64–5 Arm and lead the Myrmidons to war.
B 66–70 The Trojans have penned in the Argives by the shore.
C 71–7 For I am absent (because of Agamemnon's attitude), Diomedes is absent to repel disaster, and Agamemnon's orders are unheard.
B′ 77–9 But the Trojans, urged on by Hektor, are defeating the Achaeans.
A′ 80–2 So attack, to stop them from burning the ships.

Repetitions of 'ships' and ἐπικρατέως (67, 81) reinforce the ring; so does section C, with its symmetrical references to Agamemnon. The lack of Akhilleus' helmet, Diomedes' spear and Agamemnon's orders makes the disaster vivid; Akhilleus' elaboration of this picture evokes a man torn between *Schadenfreude* at his enemy's discomfiture and alarm at the crisis he has caused. Aristarchus thinks he mentions Diomedes because he had heard of the latter's bold sayings against him (9.698ff.), but T adduce his *aristeia*.

64–5 τύνη (6× *Il.*, 3× Hes.) is an emphatic form of σύ, once τύ as in Doric. The same suffix, in Laconian τούνη, ἐγώνη (Hsch.) and Boeotian τύνει, τούν, survives in modern Cypriot (ἐ)σούνη, ἐγώνη, Pontic ἐτούνε and Euboean (Kimi) τούνη (Shipp, *Vocabulary* 542f.); like τεός for σός or ἑός for ὅς, it must be an archaism, not a Dorism, *pace* West, *JHS* 108 (1988) 167f. At *Theog.* 36 it signals a like transition; West (*ad loc.*) notes its peremptory tone, also audible at 19.10. The generic epithet φιλοπτολέμοισι (10×) again describes the Myrmidons at 23.129; gen. at 17.224, it precedes the caesura at 90, 17.194.

66–9 εἰ δή implies a fact, not a hypothesis: 'since now'. Someone (in D, bT) read ᾖ δή, so that Akhilleus bids Patroklos attack where the fighting is densest. Frequent integral enjambment reinforces our sense that he utters an unstoppable torrent of words (cf. 9.335ff.). Repeated βέβηκε links the metaphors κυάνεον Τρώων νέφος and Τ. πόλις. A cloud is often dark blue, and may 'bestride' a peak, cf. νεφέλη δέ μιν ἀμφιβέβηκε | κυανέη (*Od.* 12.74f.); but a mass of birds or troops is called a 'cloud' (4.274n.), the ranks are κυάνεαι at 4.282, a 'cloud' of death or grief may cover one (345–50n.) and there is a 'cloud' of war at 17.243. The epithet brings out the metaphor's sinister connotations (cf. Moulton, *CPh* 74 (1979) 290). It is resumed by the cloud-simile at 297ff., when the fire is dispelled from the ships (so T). πόλις is a metaphor for the townsfolk as at *Erga* 240; the scansion πόλῖς suggests adaptation of the formula Τρώων τε π. καὶ νῆες Ἀχαιῶν (20.60, 2× acc.). ἐπικρατέως, also at 23.863 and in Hesiod, contrasts with the cloud-image, recalling the violence it betokens. On κεκλίαται see 15.737–40n.

70–1 For θάρσυνος see on 13.821–3. The 'forehead' of Akhilleus' helmet is its front; the metaphor, common later, is barely felt (LSJ s.v. II). A mere glint from it would rout the Trojans (cf. 18.203ff.), who would soon fill the torrent-beds with corpses; like 2.860f., this may refer forward to the massacre by the river at 21.1ff. In Homer's day the plain (whatever its extent) was crossed by channels which were dry in summer, as is still the case. ἔναυλος recurs only at 21.283, 312 with the sense 'torrent-bed', < αὐλός: so Aristarchus (Did/A), who evidently rejected a variant ἐπαύλους, 'sheep-folds' (cf. *Od.* 23.358). Dionysius Thrax glossed it 'hollows' (schol. pap. on 21.283). At *Theog.* 129 and 4× *Hy.* it denotes deities' 'haunts', < αὐλή.

72–3 '... if Agamemnon had kindly feelings towards me'. Akhilleus refers to his misconduct in book 1 and general attitude (Schadewaldt, *Iliasstudien* 129f.); the rights and wrongs of his own refusal of the Embassy are irrelevant. But kindness is the last quality to be expected of Agamemnon (cf. e.g. 6.55ff.). Page (*HHI* 308f.) thinks the poet of 72f., 84ff. and 11.607ff. knew nothing of the Embassy, but, on the easiest reading of the text (and given Akhilleus' tacit shifts of position in book 9, which Page misses), Akhilleus is hoping for another, humbler approach, and seeks to buy time for it (M. Lynn-George, *Epos*, London 1988, 168f.). Even if Page were right to claim (against Schadewaldt) that Akhilleus renounced the gifts for ever at 9.378ff., it does not follow that he cannot make concessions when his temper cools and the situation alters (cf. Kirk, *Songs* 214f.; O. Tsagarakis, *Hermes* 99 (1971) 257–69). He is prepared to shift his ground but loth to say so (cf. Aristotle frag. 168 and Eustathius 1046.57f.). His frustration, and awareness of what he could achieve were he reconciled, flashes out again; on his implication that only in his absence do the Trojans dare venture out see 13.105–6n. στρατός has, as often, its original sense 'camp' (Chantraine, *Dict.* s.v.); 'army' evolved from this, like the use of πόλις for 'citizens' at 69.

74–7 With 74f. cf. Diomedes' boast that his δόρυ μαίνεται ἐν παλάμῃσι (8.111); for the 'personified' spear see 13.444n. For the abl.-gen. with λοιγὸν ἀμῦναι instead of the usual dat. cf. 80, 21.539. Akhilleus does not extend the parallelism of οὐ γὰρ Τυδείδεω – οὐδέ πω Ἀτρείδεω (with innovative

325

genitives) to include their activities: aptly from his viewpoint, Agamemnon does not wield a spear but only barks orders. ὀπὸς ἔκλυον αὐδήσαντος blends (ϝ)ὀ. ἔ. (22.451) with ἔ. αὐ. (etc.), 4× epos; the phrase is old (Hoekstra, *Modifications* 74n.). With Ἀτρείδεω ... αὐ. cf. Ἕκτορος ... κελεύοντος (77f.). Leaf, comparing ἤϋσεν ὅσον κεφαλὴ χάδε φωτός (11.462), thinks the phrase 'hateful head' is used because the head is the origin of the voice; but 'head' .is an idiomatic synecdoche for 'person', e.g. 8.281 (Τεῦκρε, φίλη κ.), 11.55, 15.39, 17.242, 18.82 (ἶσον ἐμῇ κεφαλῇ), 18.114 (φίλης κεφαλῆς = Patroklos), 21.336, 23.94. Later too it can have a good or bad sense, as in Demosthenes' ἡ μιαρὰ καὶ ἀναιδὴς αὕτη κεφαλή (LSJ s.v. 2). For ἀνδροφόνοιο see 716–20n.

78–9 These vv. seem clumsy and untraditional: the contraction in νικῶντες is irresolvable. We must supply ὄψ, 'voice', from 76. Hektor's voice 'bursts out all round': the metaphor recurs in περὶ δέ σφισιν ἄγνυτο ἠχώ (*Aspis* 279, 348); βρονταὶ περιερρήγνυντο (Plut. *Crass.* 19); κατερρήγνυτο πᾶς ὁ τόπος ὑπὸ τοῦ κρότου (Polybius 15.32.9). The phrase is usually taken to mean that the sound 'goes all round' (Ap. Soph. 130.24); Leaf derives it from waves on a beach. The Trojans 'fill' the plain with shouting (*LfgrE* s.v. ἔχω II 7).

80–1 'But even so' refers back to Akhilleus' reasons for not aiding the Greeks, which he last mentioned at 72f.; this transition is not too abrupt for him, since his injured pride is never far from his thoughts. The construction πυρὸς ... νῆας ἐνιπρήσωσι (6×), rather than πυρί, recurs at 9.242 etc. (Chantraine, *GH* II 52).

83–100 Lohmann (*Reden* 63f.) shows that another ring-structure shapes the third and last part of this speech, Akhilleus' advice to Patroklos, which is marked off by 83. His analysis constitutes a strong defence against ancient and modern atheteses, and runs roughly thus:

A *Introduction*: Do as I command, to win for me honour and recompense (83–6).

B *Warning*: a Drive them from the ships and come back (87).
          b But if Zeus gives you glory (87f.),
          c do not wish to fight the Trojans alone (89f.),
          d lest you reduce my honour (90).
          c' Do not lead an attack on Troy (91f.),
          b' lest a god, Apollo, intervene (93f.).
          a' But turn back when you have driven them from the ships (95f.).

A' *Wish*:   If only we two could sack Troy alone (97–100)!

This impossible wish is linked with the introduction by means of the idea of shared honour; Akhilleus wishes he could share the glory of sacking Troy with Patroklos alone, yet sharing his honour is just what he refuses to do.

By refusing to fight, he risks winning no glory at all. The theme of re-compense also recalls the start of his speech, viz. the slight he suffered (52ff.). Patroklos' disregard for his warning is based on how Akhilleus himself ignored Thetis' prediction and assaulted Troy, with fatal results (Whitman, *HHT* 201).

83–8 Replacing a traditional verse like ἄλλο δέ τοι ἐρέω, σὺ δὲ σύνθεο καί μευ ἄκουσον, 83 (with an irresolvable gen. in -ου) insists on obedience – Akhilleus puts the 'completion' or 'fulfilment' of his words into Patroklos' mind; for the phrase cf. 630, 9.56, 9.625, 19.107, 20.369. His foreboding is of course fulfilled, not his orders, as the poet says at 685ff. Eustathius (1047.6ff.) notes the poetic justice that, just as he neglected Phoinix's advice, so Patroklos ignores his. Although he spurned Agamemnon's attempt to buy him off (9.378ff.), he is still anxious not to miss restitution from the Greeks. Some (in bT) thought he sinks to Agamemnon's level of greed and lust by mentioning the gifts and concubine, and is jealous lest Patroklos win glory which should be his; but in the heroic world no warrior can be glorious without due recognition from his society.

περικαλλέα κούρην recurs at *Cat.* 193.11. ἀποναίω is stilted, as it means literally to 'settle' someone elsewhere, cf. the middle at 2.629, *Od.* 15.254, and μετανάστης. The unreliable Morgan papyrus reads ἀποδάσσωσιν; this is no better than its ἀναπρήσωσι at 82. Note the n-mobile preceding a consonant, an innovative trait (p. 9 n. 6). The formula ἐρίγδουπος πόσις Ἥρης is preferred to Ὀλύμπιος ἀστεροπητής because it is used in prayers or wishes (13.149–54n.).

89–96 As Aristarchus tells us, Zenodotus replaced 89–96 with

μή σύ γ' ἀγαλλόμενος πολέμῳ καὶ δηϊοτῆτι (cf. 91)
Τρῶας ἐναιρόμενος προτὶ Ἴλιον αἰπὺ δίεσθαι (cf. 92),
μή σ' ἀπογυμνωθέντα λάβῃ κορυθαίολος Ἕκτωρ (cf. 93–6).

His motives were mixed. He surely omitted 89f. and rewrote 91 because it seemed improper for Akhilleus to say that Patroklos' success would reduce his honour (so van der Valk, *Researches* II 22), not because it is inept for him to forbid Patroklos to fight alone, when he is sending him out to do just that (*pace* Nickau, *Zenodotos* 226f.). But 89f. are needed to express Akhilleus' aim (so Aristarchus). His abrupt orders leave 'the Trojans' to be supplied with ἐλάσας in 87 and 'the Myrmidons' with ἡγεμονεύειν at 92 (unless the verb is used absolutely), whereas Zenodotus' smoother αἰπὺ δίεσθαι lets us supply Τρῶας from earlier in the verse; but the conjecture, perhaps based on 12.276, is betrayed by the neuter Ἴλιον, found only at 15.71 but introduced by Zenodotus at 18.174 also (differently Hoekstra, *Mnem.* 31 (1978) 15ff.).

Aristarchus castigates the replacement verse for 93–6 as 'ordinary in style and sense'. T quotes it with ἀπομουνωθέντα, but -γυμνωθέντα (cf. *Od.* 10.301) is guaranteed by Dionysius Thrax (in T), who said that Zenodotus should have put δάκῃ for λάβῃ; a homoerotic joke is unexpected from this austere grammarian. Zenodotus surely wished to remove the repetition of 87 in 93–6 (required by the ring-structure), and to evoke Patroklos' death stripped of his armour (793ff., 815). His rewriting makes Akhilleus' warning too vague. Nickau thinks it reflects recension, since changes of reading as well as omissions are involved; Bolling (*External Evidence* 159ff.) and Wilamowitz (*IuH* 120f.) share this *petitio principii*.

95–6 For τρωπᾶσθαι see p. 17; τροπάασθαι is original here, being read by Apollodorus, Hrd/A and the vulgate. τοὺς δ' ἔτ' ἐᾶν is better than the variant τούσδε δ' ἐᾶν; so Ruijgh (τε *épique* 700), who thinks it may overlie τοὺς δ' ἐάαν, like τόνδε δ' ἔασκε for τὸν δ' ἐάασκε (24.17), or μηδὲ ἐᾶν for μηδ' ἐάαν (*Od.* 10.536). But contracted ἐᾶν is attested (15.347).

97–100 Exasperated by all this folly and the absence from fighting it entails, Akhilleus wishes that both sides could perish so that he and Patroklos might alone sack Troy. Wilamowitz (*IuH* 122) notes the irony that neither hero will see Troy fall, as Apollo declares at 707ff. Akhilleus' wish expresses the contradiction in his position: he still wants glory yet would reject the heroic society which can alone confer it (cf. King, *Achilles* 35f.). Like his prayer at 237, his wish serves as an oblique reminder that he did curse the Greek army, and underlines the moral ambiguity of his stance. The impossibility of his wish, and his knowledge that it is impossible (explicit at 17.406f.), is signalled by 97, which opens other such wishes (2.371, 4.288, *Od.* 7.311), especially longings for one's lost youth (7.132, 2× *Od.*); cf. 13.825–9n. Von Scheliha (*Patroklos* 259f.) compares how, before his fall, Hektor fantasizes about making peace with Akhilleus (22.111ff.). Yet sacking a city single-handed is a typical heroic feat: Diomedes ends a speech by saying that he and Sthenelos will take Troy alone, if need be (9.46ff.), 'one of many ways in which Diomede corresponds to Achilles and stands in for him in the earlier part of the *Iliad*' (Macleod, *Iliad XXIV* 25n.). Kakridis (*Gymn.* 78 (1971) 509f.) thinks Homer had in mind the earlier sack of Troy by Herakles and Telamon, although the poet never mentions the latter's role in it; cf. too Peleus' sack of Iolkos (Pindar, *Nem.* 3.34).

Heroic friendship is a firm bond; Homer never states that Akhilleus and Patroklos are lovers, but could be suppressing some such tale (cf. 11.786n. and K. J. Dover, *Greek Homosexuality*, London 1978, 194ff.). 'Let everyone perish but us' is paralleled as an erotic motif in modern folk-song (Kakridis, *loc. cit.*). Recalling their explicit portrayal as lovers in Aeschylus' *Myrmidons* and later, Zenodotus and Aristarchus (in T) athetized 97–100 as the work of an interpolator with this view of their relationship. Plutarch too objected (*Mor.* 25E). T cite other criticisms – the wish is childish, the Myrmidons had done nothing to merit it, and sacking a city with no defenders is no great feat. But as far as Akhilleus is concerned, the enemy, and the Greeks who allowed his humiliation, can both go to the devil (cf. 1.410); he is sending Patroklos only because his friend wishes it (cf. bT). Thornton sees only 'an outburst of rage and merciless hatred' (*Supplication* 133f.), but the poet leaves us free to interpret his harsh posture as intended to conceal, from Patroklos and perhaps from himself, real concern about the disaster.

Some inferred from Athene's inclusion in 97 that Homer was Athenian (13.195–7n.), but these gods were so widely worshipped that this standard verse was surely developed for audiences of mixed origins; Aeolic αἲ γάρ confirms its antiquity. Aristarchus perhaps objected to νῶϊν as nom. (cf. T), but the form has parallels (13.326–7n.). ἐκδῦμεν is an opt. with *-υι- contracted to -ῦ-, like δαίνῦτο at 24.665 (Chantraine, *GH* I 51). With 100 cf. Hoekstra on *Od.* 13.388 (Τροίης λύομεν λιπαρὰ κρήδεμνα); the breaching of the citadel's ring of walls is compared to a captive woman's headdress being torn off (on the nature of 'head-binders' see 14.184n.). Similarly Thebes' ring of towers is likened to a diadem (στεφάνη) in the epithet ἐϋστέφανος (19.99, *Theog.* 978 with West's n.); cf. the metaphor πολίων κατέλυσε κάρηνα (2.117). ἱερά replaces traditional λιπαρά here, no doubt because of phrases like Τροίης ἱερὸν πτολίεθρον (*Od.* 1.2).

101–277 The Trojans set fire to a ship. Akhilleus bids Patroklos arm; he takes Akhilleus' whole panoply save the hero's great spear, and his driver Automedon harnesses the divine horses. Akhilleus exhorts his men, whose leaders are listed. Returning to his hut, he prays to Zeus that Patroklos will drive the Trojans from the ships and return safely. Patroklos leads the Myrmidons into battle

101–277 In a masterly use of overlapping scenes to maintain suspense, the firing of the first ship, anxiously awaited for so long (15.592–746n.), becomes merely an exciting prelude (dignified, certainly, by an appeal to the Muses) to Patroklos' arming and other preliminaries; these are duly elaborated in anticipation of the major events to come. We learn the names and pedigree of Akhilleus' horses, see his troops thirst for war like wolves, meet their five leaders, and watch them close ranks in impressive array; in his solemn prayer Akhilleus reveals his concern for Patroklos, acknowledges that Zeus has granted his original request in book 1 and asks for continued favour. The foreshadowing of Patroklos' doom continues (46f., 140ff., 250–2). The pattern of simile, preparation and exhortation or, in the second case, prayer, appears thrice, each time more briefly (156ff., 212ff., 259ff.); in the first case a long catalogue is interposed.

101–24 This brief but crucial scene concludes what has now become the sub-plot, just as the vignette at 15.390–405 reintroduced Patroklos and prepared for the shift away from the battle at the ships as the centre of the action. It is ringed by the transitional verses 101 and 124, and by references to Aias' withdrawal (102, 122) and Zeus's will that the Trojans win (103, 121). It at first recapitulates Aias' gradual retreat, vividly depicted at 15.727–46 (102 = 15.727), where the stress fell on his endurance; here it falls on the terrible bombardment he is under. His suffering symbolizes that of the whole army, innocent victim of Akhilleus' wrath. At the scene's mid-point Homer deepens the crisis by asking the Muses to tell how the first ship burned, but even now Aias' defeat brings no disgrace; Hektor merely lops off the tip of the pike with which his foe has been fending the Trojans off, and Aias retreats out of range, beaten as much by Zeus's will as by his foes. For Zeus's role in this disaster see 15.242n.; Protesilaos' burning ship marks the end of his support for Hektor (15.597ff.). The single Greek, driven back by many Trojans, is in a typical situation and never gets hurt (13.550–9n.); but Hektor's failure to harm Aias is telling, like his defeat by him while Zeus sleeps at 14.402ff. – he is not even given the honour of being first to set a ship ablaze. This is Homer's response to the difficult task he undertook – to persuade his partisan audience to accept the Greeks' defeat.

102–8 The line-internal stops in 102–7 evoke the constant bombardment (Kirk, *YCS* 20 (1966) 132). So does the chiastic repetition, βελέεσσι – βάλλοντες – βαλλομένη – βάλλετο – βελέεσσι, which is spoilt by the variant τύπτετο (Arn/A) for βάλλετο; in no MS, this must be a conjecture to remove repetition, like that at 14.177. Since 104f. are so quoted by Aristarchus (Did/A), τ. was surely Aristophanes' text (differently van der Valk, *Researches* II 175f.). Aristarchus rejected it because it confounds his distinction between hitting at long and at short range (13.288–9n.).

104–6 Kirk (*art. cit.* 110) thinks the complex 'violent' enjambment of 104f. may reflect 'literate intervention', but parallels exist (13.611–12n.), and 104f. adapt traditional material like 13.805, ἀμφὶ δέ οἱ κροτάφοισι φαεινὴ σείετο πήληξ; 15.608f., ἀ. δὲ π. | σμερδαλέον κ. τινάσσετο; 647f., ἀ. δὲ π. | σ. κονάβησε περὶ κροτάφοισι. The wide separation of δεινήν from its noun is paralleled at *Aspis* 226f., δεινὴ δὲ π. κ. ἄνακτος | κεῖτ' Ἄϊδος κυνέη; this creates the elegant pattern δεινήν – φαεινή – πήληξ – καναχήν (the gap led to the obvious error δεινή). For the idiom κ. ἔχε, 'made a din', cf. 794, *HyAp* 185, Tyrtaeus frag. 19.20, Semonides frag. 7.20. Aristarchus' καὶ φάλαρα for κὰπ φ. (so all MSS, papyri included) is plainly a conjecture; he deemed βάλλετο δ' αἰεί a parenthesis (Arn, Nic/A), i.e. '(Aias) was constantly being hit', but '(the helmet) was constantly hit (on its plates)' makes better sense. For the apocope cf. κὰπ πεδίον (2×), κὰδ δ-, κὰλ λαπάρην (14.438–9, 14.442–8nn.). φάλαρα (unique in Homer), often taken as metal bosses or disks on a leather helmet, are best explained as the metal plates of which the helmet is made, like φάλοι (see on 5.743f., 13.132f.). The innovative contraction of ἐϋ- in εὐποίητος recurs at *Od.* 13.369, *HyAp* 265, *Aspis* 64, always neut. plur. (contrast ἐΰπ. at 636, 5.466 and 5× epos); cf. the modifications εὐξέστῳ, εὐεργέος, εὐκτίμενος, εὔσκοπος (402, 743, *HyAp* 36, *HyAphr* 262) and p. 14 n. 19.

106–11 Aias 'was weary in his left shoulder, always holding steady his dappled shield ...' The Trojans fail to 'shake (the shield) around him by pressing (it) with missiles', i.e. to knock it away from him to expose his body. He may be imagined as using an early Myc. oxhide body-shield with the hair left on the outside, hence 'dappled' (cf. 7.222); but this epithet was reinterpreted as 'glittering' and adapted to the ζωστήρ (4.215). The Theran ship-fresco depicts dappled tower-shields (S. P. Morris, *AJA* 93 (1989) 525, fig. 6); the figure-of-eight shields in frescoes at Knossos are dappled too. A strap passed over the left shoulder supported such shields (14.402–8n.). Whatever his shield's shape, it is rightly imagined as very heavy; earlier he had bearers to support it when he needed a pause from 'toil and sweat' (13.710f.), but he has no rest now. With 109 cf. 15.10; κὰδ δέ οἱ ἱδρὼς | πάντοθεν ἐκ μελέων πολὺς ἔρρεεν elaborates phrasing like 23.688f., ἔ. δ' ἱ. | πάντοθεν ἐκ μ., and *Od.* 11.599f., κατὰ δ' ἱ. | ἔ. ἐκ μ. For the metaphor 'evil was set upon evil' cf. 19.290, δέχεται κακὸν ἐκ κακοῦ αἰεί; for the polyptoton cf. κακὸς κακὸν ἡγηλάζει (*Od.* 17.217), φέρουσα κακῷ κακόν (*HyAp* 354) and 13.130–1n.

112–13 The Muses are invoked at other turning-points, 11.218 and 14.508, where the same formular verse as 112 appears (also at 2.484, cf. *Theog.* 114, *Cat.* 1.14). Marked by asyndeton, this is often held to signal a great crisis. Here Zeus waits to see a ship burn as the signal for the Trojan tide to ebb (15.599f.), but even this event is largely symbolic now that we know Patroklos will intervene. The Muses are usually asked for information, and a catalogue often ensues as if in reply (cf. 14.508–10n.); but here, instead of 'who first ...', 'how first ...' follows. This is a rare but traditional variant: thus most of the *Hymns* begin 'Sing of X, who ...', but *Hy.* 7 opens 'I shall recall Dionusos, *how* he ...' As W. W. Minton says (*TAPA* 91 (1960) 300), this 'invocation stands out with a kind of impersonal detachment, suggesting ... the working of some independent force on the firing of the ships', namely Zeus's will. This pause in the action contrasts with the welter of events in 114–24, which are so heavily enjambed that the scene ends in mid-verse.

114–18 Aias' spear is called 'ashen' not 'brazen' because emphasis falls on its wooden shaft (13.597n.), which Hektor severs behind the socket (καυλός) of the spearhead (αἰχμή, in its original sense): see on 313–15, 13.162. *Pace* R. M. Frazer (*CPh* 78 (1983) 127–30), Homer may have forgotten that Aias was using a huge pike (15.676ff.), since Hektor stands 'near' him to strike: the references to Aias' spear at 15.730, 742 and 745 were ambiguous. With Hektor's great slashing-sword, ἄορι μεγάλῳ, cf. ξίφεϊ μ. etc. (5×) and 13.577n. Aristarchus held that he cuts only part-way through the shaft, and that the spearhead drops off when Aias shakes the whole weapon; thus 'he sheared it right through' is a summary of the entire event, which is then told in detail. But, however unlikely it is that Hektor could lop off a spearhead in one blow, heroes must be allowed such exploits. Homer narrates this one with a superb slow-motion effect (cf. 13.434–6n.). For the long instant between the blow and Aias' realization of what it has achieved, he wields his weapon just as before (αὔτως), unaware that it is useless: τὸ μέν contrasts the blunted shaft (κόλον δόρυ) with its tip, which falls far below his perch on the ship until it clatters on the ground, alerting him to what has happened (for the significant sound-effect cf. 794f., 13.526–30n., *Od.* 18.397). κόλος, 'docked', properly of an animal with its horns cut off, is unique in the epos (cf. κ. μάχη, the old title of book 8); κολούω is used metaphorically to mean 'cut off short' (20.370, 2× *Od.*).

119–21 Aias now suffers the fate that befell his brother at 15.461ff., when Zeus snapped his bowstring: 120 resembles 15.467, whence the variant κείρει rejected by Aristarchus (Did/A). Like Teukros, Aias shivers when he recognizes divine intervention cutting off his options as sharply as Hektor cut off his spearhead (Eustathius 1049.24 noted the witty metaphor). κατὰ θυμὸν ἀμύμονα recurs 2× *Od.*, but 'blameless' never appears with other cases of θυμός; it is adapted from verses like κ. θυμὸν ἀμύμονος Αἰγίσθοιο (*Od.* 1.29, cf. 4.187). ῥίγησεν can govern ἔργα and need not be parenthetical: cf. ῥ. πόλεμον (5.351). With 121 cf. 7.21, 12.67f.

122–4 Aias' retreat frames the scene (cf. 101–24n.); the ship's stern can now be set ablaze. For the phrasing cf. 15.597f. and φλογὶ ... ἀσβέστῳ (17.88f.); ἄ. has no separate fem. elsewhere. ἀμφέπω, 'attend on', is metaphorical as at 18.348, γαστρὴν τρίποδος πῦρ ἄμφεπε.

124–5 For the rapid shift of scene at the bucolic diaeresis cf. 15.405 and Zeus's rude awakening at 15.4. Akhilleus slaps his thighs in alarm, as had Patroklos (15.397); the scene is structurally parallel (15.262–404n.). For his gesture and the innovative form πληξάμενος see on 15.113f.

126–9 Akhilleus' role is as active as he thinks the situation allows; he will gather the troops while Patroklos arms (cf. Wilamowitz, *IuH* 123n.). In this crisis he need not say that the panoply is his. His orders ὄρσεο and δύσεο frame their cause (the blazing ships) and their aim (to save them); his multiple asyndeta (Nic/A) and end-stopped verses (Kirk, *YCS* 20 (1966) 124) convey urgency (cf. 22.41–3n.). Verse 128 is a separate sentence, not subordinate to 126 with 127 parenthetical (so Nic/A; *contra*, Chantraine, *GH* II 353).

At this solemn moment he blends διογενὲς Πατρόκλεις (49–50n.) with Π. ἱπποκέλευθε (584, 839). ἱ. must mean 'charioteer', like ἱππεῦ (20n.); cf. Chantraine, *Dict.* s.v. κέλευθος, and ἵπποισι κέλευθον ... λειανέω (15.26of.).

ἰωήν, which means 'roaring blast' at 4.276, 11.308 (both with hiatus) and 'sound' elsewhere, is read by Aristarchus (as I infer from Did/A), Apion, who glossed it 'flame' (Neitzel 311), a papyrus and some good codices. A lost ϝ- surely caused the hiatus; A. Athanassakis links ἰωή with (ϝ)ίεμαι (*AJP* 89 (1968) 77–82). On how it means both 'sound' and 'blast' see Onians, *Origins* 69. The Marseilles text (Did/A) and vulgate read ἐρωήν, 'rush', elsewhere used of spears. Since this never has any sign of initial ϝ-, it surely arose via the haplography ΔΗΙΟΙ⟨ΟΙ⟩ΩΗΝ (differently van der Valk, *Researches* II 8f.). — On the innovative scansion δῇοιο or δῆῖοιο see Chantraine, *GH* I 107. οὐκέτι φυκτὰ πέλωνται is impersonal, 'there is no escape' (see on 14.96ff.). The middle δύσεο is used when τεύχεα δύω (etc.) is moved from the verse-end, as at *Aspis* 108. The subj. ἀγείρω is a virtual fut., but takes κε, 'in that case', because it follows an imper. (Chantraine, *GH* II 211): Akhilleus' action depends on Patroklos' readiness to arm. After 129 a few MSS add a verse based on 39, no doubt to make explicit the hero's sympathy for the Greeks; absent in papyri, it is redundant after 128.

130–54 Major arming-scenes also open the *aristeiai* of Paris, Agamemnon and Akhilleus. The basic sequence is always greaves, corslet, sword, helmet and spear (for full discussion see on 3.330–8, 11.15ff., 19.356ff.); many verses are standard, which must have been relaxing for both poet and audience after the drama which preceded. For a later version of this type-scene see *Aspis* 122–38; many of the same verses recur, despite two centuries' evolution of the oral tradition. Homer includes three telling modifications: first, the traditional extra verse about the corslet consists of a reminder that it is not Patroklos' but Akhilleus' (134), just as Paris borrowed Lukaon's (3.333) and Herakles wore Athene's (*Aspis* 125ff.); second, the poet adds that Patroklos cannot wield Akhilleus' great spear (141–4 = 19.389–91); and he adds a scene where Automedon yokes Akhilleus' immortal steeds, attaching a mortal trace-horse which the hero won as booty (cf. 19.392ff.). These details hint at Patroklos' unfitness for his task (both horse and hero are slain), and stress his inferiority to Akhilleus. Both the divine armour and the horses will be defiled in the dust (795ff., 17.439f.). Krischer (*Konventionen* 29) thinks the hero's armour ominously fails to glitter, but cf. 134, 279. J. I. Armstrong (*AJP* 79 (1958) 346f.) notes that the smoothness of 130–9, which follow the standard pattern, makes the distinctive 140ff. all the more effective in presaging Patroklos' tragic limitations (cf. Reinhardt, *IuD* 310–16).

Homer probably invented the idea that the armour was a gift to Peleus upon his marriage; originally, Thetis brought it to Akhilleus when he left for Troy (see the Introduction to book 18, and 19.12–13n.). The poet also says the gods or specifically Poseidon gave Peleus the horses (867, 23.277f.), although he does not call them wedding-gifts (867a below is spurious). The scholia to Pindar (*Py.* 3.167 Drachmann) say Poseidon gave horses, but

Hephaistos a dagger; in the Akastos tale, Peleus already had a knife made by Hephaistos (*Cat.* 209 with schol. on Pindar, *Nem.* 4.95 Drachmann). In the *Cypria* 'the gods gathered on Pelion for Peleus' wedding with Thetis; they brought Peleus gifts at the banquet, and Kheiron cut a flourishing ash-tree and gave it as a spear; they say that Athene polished it and Hephaistos assembled it' (frag. 3, = AD on 140). Pindar surely innovated when he made Peleus cut his spear himself (*Nem.* 3.33). Akhilleus used it to wound Telephos. After his death it went to Neoptolemos; the *Little Iliad* (frag. 5) said it had a gold ring to bind the socket to the shaft, and a double point. This strange weapon clearly had a long prehistory before the *Iliad* (Kullmann, *Quellen* 232–6).

W. R. Paton (*CR* 26 (1912) 1–4) brilliantly discerned behind this a traditional story where Peleus received three magical gifts, a standard folk-tale motif: impenetrable armour, a spear which returns to its master and divine horses (cf. Stith Thompson D 1381.3.3, 1840; D 1428.2; B 184.1.1). This is why Patroklos must be stripped of the armour before he can be killed (793ff.); Akhilleus must have it replaced (Patroklos' own suit would clearly fit him!); he has to find an unprotected part of Hektor's body to kill him (22.321ff.), and is himself slain when Paris shoots him in his unprotected heel, a tale known to Homer (777–867n.). The poet does not spell this out, in accord with his rationalizing genius (cf. p. 1 n. 2), just as he makes a god return Akhilleus' spear to him when it misses, rather than have it come back by magic (20.322ff., 22.276ff.). His armour rendered the hero indispensable; hence the strife over it after his death, a tale older than our *Iliad* (see pp. 310–11). For similar arguments see Ph. J. Kakridis, *Hermes* 89 (1961) 288–97.

130–9 With 130 cf. 7.206, where one verse encapsulates Aias' arming, and 19.364; ἐδύσετο νώροπα χαλκόν is part of the same formular system (2.578, 11.16, both of Agamemnon). All four major arming-scenes share 131–3 and 135f., save that 11.29–40 expand on the sword and shield; the corslet is elaborated upon in all the scenes save 19.371. Verses 137f. appear in Paris' arming, but also in Teukros' and Odysseus' (15.479–82n.); 137 = *Aspis* 136. Homer could have continued with εἵλετο δ' ἄλκιμα δοῦρε δύω κεκορυθμένα χαλκῷ (11.43 = *Od.* 22.125), or εἵ. δ' ἄλκιμον ἔγχος ὅ οἱ παλάμηφιν ἀρήρει (3.338 = *Od.* 17.4), but mixes both verses; the unique result contrasts Patroklos' twin spears (an armament of Geometric date) with Akhilleus' single great (Myc.?) spear, leading up to the point that Patroklos cannot use that weapon, which does *not* 'fit his palm'.

134–5 A shield is ποικίλος at 10.149; armour is often ποικίλα χαλκῷ, as if made of leather with bronze rivets, like some LHIIIC corslets (Bouzek, *Aegean* 110). ἀστερόεις elsewhere describes the sky and Hephaistos' house (18.370). Leaf compares a cauldron called ἀνθεμόεις, 'adorned with rosettes'

(23.885), but H. W. Catling prefers to take the epithet as 'gleaming' (*Arch. Hom.* E 76); the images in Akhilleus' arming-scene support this (19.362ff.). The formula ποδώκεος Αἰακίδαο (10× Hom.) belongs to the same set as ποδώκεα (-ϊ) Πηλεΐωνα (-ι); poets seem not to worry that Aiakos was Akhilleus' *grand*father. Αἰακίδης describes Peleus 3× *Il.*, 2× Hes., and Aiakos' descendants generally 2× Hes.; metrical utility encouraged its extension to Akhilleus. T's variant κακῶν βελέων ἀλεωρήν (cf. 15.533) is an obvious attempt to emend away the 'problem' that Patroklos takes exactly Akhilleus' size in corslets; Aristophanes parodies this (Cyclic?) phrase at *Wasps* 615 (cf. Bolling, *External Evidence* 161f., and van der Valk, *Researches* II 80f.). Since Hephaistos forges Akhilleus no sword in book 18, T infer that Patroklos took his own, but Homer commits a small oversight there (cf. on 791ff.).

141–4 = 19.388–91, where see n. for the motif of an object that only one man can wield (Stith Thompson D 1651.1.1); this stresses Akhilleus' strength. Megaclides (fourth century B.C.) read 140–4 (so A); hence Zenodotus' athetesis of 140 and omission of 141–4 (Arn/A) is likely to rest not on MS evidence (*pace* Nickau, *Zenodotos* 74f.), but on his dislike of repeated passages. Conversely Aristarchus obelized 19.388–91, claiming that the verses are needed here to explain why Patroklos does not take the spear. Leaf thought Homer should describe it only when it is being taken! It would indeed be awkward if Akhilleus' most distinctive equipment were lost; but Homer wishes to foreshadow Patroklos' failure (101–277n.).

On the legends about this spear see 130–54n. It is made of ash simply because this flexible wood was the usual and best material, as in the traditional epithets εΰμμελίης, μείλινος; just as δόρυ, once 'tree', came to mean 'spear', so did μελίη, both regarding Akhilleus' weapon (8× in books 20–22) and at 2.543, 3× *Od.*, *Aspis* 420. The *Iliad's* habit of using μελίη for Akhilleus' spear is owed merely to the formula Πηλιάδα μελίην (4×, nom. at 20.277), whose scansion confirms its age (cf. ἐΰμμελίης); differently R. S. Shannon, *The Arms of Achilles and Homeric Compositional Technique*, Leiden 1975, 32ff. Homer plays on the meaning of Πηλιάς, offering as cognates πῆλαι, Πηλίον and no doubt Πηλεύς; its true origin is surely Πηλίον (cf. 33–5n.). Like Athene's spear (5.746 = 8.390 = *Od.* 1.100), Akhilleus' is 'heavy, long and strong'; when the same phrase describes Patroklos' spear (802), it emphasizes the strength of Apollo who shatters it, but may also reflect a slip by Homer, implying that Patroklos has Akhilleus' spear (cf. Bannert, *WS* 18 (1984) 27–35 and *Formen des Wiederholens* 159–67).

Save for Kheiron's role in teaching medicine (4.219, 11.832), which fits his name (from χείρ), Homer ignores the 'justest of the Centaurs'; Hesiod says he dwelt on Pelion (as Homer implies) and raised Medeios, Iason, Akhilleus and Aktaion (*Theog.* 1001, *Cat.* 40.2, 204.87ff., *P.Oxy.* 2509 with Janko, *Phoenix* 38 (1984) 301). Kheiron rears Akhilleus in seventh-century art (*LIMC* s.v. Achilleus, pl. 21); cf. 203–6n. In the *Titanomachy* Kronos became a stallion to sire this hybrid (frag. 10 B. = 9 D.); Homer as usual quietly ignores such tales (but cf. 149–50!). Von Scheliha (*Patroklos* 222ff.) well suggests that he invented Phoinix to replace Akhilleus' rearing by Kheiron after Thetis abandoned her baby (cf. Kullmann, *Quellen* 371). Also, by suppressing Kheiron in favour of Peleus, Homer is able to reinforce the leitmotif of the aged father, vital to the whole poem (13.658–9n.).

Aristarchus (Did/AT) wavered between τάμε, which fits the *Cypria*'s tale of Kheiron felling the ash, and πόρε, which alliterates in *p*-. Good codices read πόρε here but τάμε at 19.390, yet papyri offer the reverse. πόρε is formular, as in πατρὶ φίλῳ ἔπορον (17.196), π. φίλα φρονέων πόρε Χείρων (4.219); the two verses surely had different verbs, a typically oral variation which Aristarchus tried to standardize. He read ἐν κορυφῇς both times (Did/A), but this lacks MS support (cf. 13.10–12n.). Note the Aeolisms ἔμμεναι ἡρώεσσι.

145–8 The ring ἵππους δ' Αὐτομέδοντα – Αὐτομέδων ... ἶ. introduces Automedon son of Diores (17.429), who is first seen, with his superiors, at 9.209. Both honour him most after each other (cf. 24.574f.). As third in command, he serves as Patroklos' driver, just as Patroklos is Akhilleus'; so too Kebriones, Hektor's charioteer, himself has a driver, as does Meriones (12.91f., 17.610). After Patroklos' death he and Alkimos again yoke the divine horses (19.392); perhaps present at Akhilleus' death (864–7n.), he became Neoptolemos' charioteer (Virgil, *Aen.* 2.477). ὁμοκλή means 'order' here, not the enemy's 'shouting' (*pace* LSJ s.v.): cool obedience is a driver's main virtue. The scansion ζευγνῦμεν (contrast 15.120) is an improvisation, like διδοῦναι (= -ō-) at 24.425: elsewhere ἄνωγα (etc.) always follows an infin. in -σθαι. For ῥηξήνωρ see 13.322–5n.

149–50 Xanthos and Balios are 'Bay' and 'Dapple'; for other horses called 'Bay' cf. 8.185, Alcman frag. 25, Stesichorus frag. 178 (with Podargā). 'Podargē' probably means 'White-foot', not 'Swift-foot': her foal Xanthos is πόδας αἰόλος (19.404), and Podargos, a hipponym at 8.185 and 23.295, is the name of a lumbering ox on Knossos tablet Ch 899. Zenodotus, taking ἅρπυια as her name, read πόδαργος; Aristarchus refutes this by citing 19.400. ἅ., 'storm-wind', is a title, like νηῒς Ἀβαρβαρέη (6.22).

These, the best horses at Troy (2.770), 'used to fly with the breezes' because both their parents are winds; Xanthos' boast that they run ἅμα πνοιῇ Ζεφύροιο (19.415) means that they are as fast as their father. Zephuros clearly took equine form, like Kheiron's father (141–4n.); Boreas adopts this shape to cover Erikhthonios' mares (20.223ff., cf. 14.317–18n.). It was widely held that the wind could impregnate oestrous mares (Aristotle, *Hist. An.* 6.572a14ff.; Varro, *De Re Rustica* 2.1.19; Virgil, *Georg.* 3.271ff.). Equine pedigrees were traditional: cf. those of Aineias' steeds (5.265–72) and of

Arion, sired by Poseidon in the shape of a horse (*Thebaid* frag. 8 B. = 6 D., with Janko, *CQ* 36 (1986) 51–5). The Harpuiai, 'snatchers', personify the gales' demonic force, as comparison of *Od.* 1.241 and 20.77 with 4.727 and 20.66 shows; Hesiod calls them Aello and Okupete, αἵ ῥ' ἀνέμων πνοιῇσι ... ἅμ' ἕπονται (*Theog.* 267f., cf. *Cat.* 155). Atalantē runs 'like a *harpuia*' (*Cat.* 76.18). The form Ἀρέπυιαι, in a vase-inscription and a gloss, may link them with the verb ἀνηρε(ί)ψαντο, but see Hoekstra on *Od.* 14.368–71. For the Myc. and later cults of the winds see Heubeck on *Od.* 10.1–79.

152–4 The trace-horse Pedasos exists mainly to give Sarpedon a major victim. He forms a sad contrast to the immortal pair; Sarpedon will kill him in Patroklos' stead, as if to symbolize the latter's mortality (466ff.). The fact that Akhilleus won him from Eëtion's city Thebe, with Khruseis and other booty (6.395–7n.), may enhance the pathos, but above all reminds us of the hero's glory. Literary and archaeological evidence confirms that Pedasos is a recent addition to the story (cf. J. Wiesner, *Arch. Hom.* F 20–3, 90, 99). Heroic chariots usually have two horses (one has three at *Od.* 4.590); chariots with three horses and then four, invented in the Levant in the ninth century, reach Greece and Etruria by the eighth (Greenhalgh, *Warfare* 27f.; 15.679–84n.). Trace-horses are rare, anachronistic and dispensable in Homer; only these horses die in the fighting (8.87–91n.). At 8.80ff. a dead trace-horse disables Nestor's chariot; he tries to save himself by cutting the traces with his sword, like Automedon below (472ff.). The extra horse was not yoked, but was controlled by traces (παρηορίαι) passed through a ring in the yoke (470–5n.); παρήορος means 'harnessed alongside' (15.680n.), but reinterpretations at 7.156 and 23.603 show that the word was poorly understood (see *ad loc.*). Pedasos is not a spare, as he is the only mortal steed. Delebecque (*Cheval* 98–102) deems trace-horses a poetic fiction, to get two-horse chariots into dangerous but not fatal crises: such a horse could not pull and would ruin the steering. But there clearly was a transitional stage in the evolution of the quadriga, which was effectively a two-horse chariot with a trace-horse on either side. Dionysius of Halicarnassus (*Ant. Rom.* 7.73.2) records that the three-horse vehicle survived in Roman ritual.

A Trojan warrior and a local town are called Pedasos (6.21–2n.); cf. Hittite Pitassa and later toponyms (13.171–3n.). Since Homer at once refers to another such town, Thebe, the name was perhaps evoked by this rather than by the similar-sounding Pēgasos (first at *Theog.* 281), unless it is from πηδάω, 'leap' (von Kamptz, *Personennamen* 155). No other Homeric horse is 'blameless'; see further 13.641–2n.

155–6 Akhilleus tours the huts telling his men to arm; mentions of this frame the wolf-simile, just as allusions to the harangue which he finally delivers at 200 frame the list of his officers (168–97). θωρήσσω is causal, 'make to arm', as at 2.11; T's conjecture κόσμησεν, 'marshal', suits the open field, not the huts (cf. Fränkel, *Gleichnisse* 73). σὺν τεύχεσι is added as in the phrase σ. τ. θωρηχθέντες (6×), which precedes ῥώοντ᾽ at 11.49 (the same verb is delayed here until 166). Zenodotus read πάντῃ (Did/A), perhaps comparing 1.384, 6.81.

156–63 This simile, expanded to suit the gravity of the moment, is one of Homer's best; on the larger structure here see 101–277n. Some deem it too independent of the narrative and unsuitable in detail (e.g. Scott, *Simile* 54n., 61n.); Fränkel's fine discussion refutes this (*loc. cit.*). Attacking warriors are often briefly compared to wolves, as at 4.471, 11.72 (cf. names like Areïlukos); wolves prey on deer in a comparison at 13.103; and the Greeks attack like wolves snatching lambs or kids at 352ff. Given the wolf's reputation for sneak attacks, this image may reflect the unexpectedness of the Myrmidons' onslaught (cf. Schnapp-Gourbeillon, *Lions* 50–2). As often, this simile serves to advance the narrative. At 155f. the Myrmidons, hungry for battle after long abstinence, are arming for war, and at 164ff. their leaders (and plainly they too) rush to assemble; so too the wolves hungrily feast on a stag and then rush down to drink. For this technique cf. 15.271ff. (a stag hunted by dogs) and especially 11.474ff., where jackals chase and eat a wounded stag until a lion suddenly appears (there are close verbal parallels). Repeated words and ideas create a pleasing symmetry: the wolves' fierce and carnivorous nature appears at 157 and 162f.; the gore round their snouts reddens 159 and 162; αἵματι φοινόν – μελανύδρου – μέλαν ὕδωρ – φόνον αἵματος form a chiasmus. Epithets paint a vivid picture: the wolves lap the dark water's surface with their narrow tongues, staining it with the gore they belch forth (cf. the Kuklops' bloody vomit at *Od.* 9.373f.). The stag is 'big' so that it can feed them all. Leaf objects that a glutted wolf is cowardly, 'in a pack' is inept in a comparison that covers the leaders only, and troops should not be sated *before* battle begins. But zoological imprecision does not justify athetesis (cf. on 13.198ff.). The simile includes the men; the shift to their leaders at 163 serves to introduce the catalogue. The wolves' meal anticipates the battle, which is likened to a feast elsewhere (e.g. *Cat.* 206); a meal often precedes a battle, and this simile may replace one (19.145–237n.).

The innovative use of n-mobile before a consonant (3×) is, as often, associated with integral enjambment (p. 9 n. 6). For ὠμοφάγος cf. 11.479 (simile), *HyAphr* 124; with the end of 157 cf 4.245 (simile). δάπτω is used specifically of animals, like German *fressen* (5.858n.). With αἵματι φοινόν cf. αἵ. φοινικόεις (23.717, *Aspis* 194), φοίνιον αἷμα (*Od.* 18.97), φοινήεις (12.202) and δαφοινός; φοινός recurs at *HyAp* 362 and in Hellenistic verse. Homer deemed it cognate with φόνος (cf. 162), but see Chantraine, *Dict.* s.v. For φόνος, 'gore', cf. 10.298, 24.610, and LSJ s.v.; αἵματος is gen. of material. The 'declension' κρήνης μελανύδρου | (also 21.257, simile) entails a contracted gen. sing.; the formula occurs in other cases (4× epos), and recalls the very different image at 3f. For ἄτρομος cf. 5.126. *Pace* Aristarchus, περιστένεται stands for -στένει (*Hy*. 19.21, cf. Oppian, *Hal*. 5.209); the wolf's belly 'growls' like the lion's heart at 20.169. The middle replaces the active *metri gratia* (cf. Meister, *Kunstsprache* 31). A lion's γαστήρ bids it attack at *Od*. 6.133 (simile). φοινός, ἀγεληδόν, λάπτω and περιστένομαι are Homeric *hapax legomena*.

161 Zenodotus read λάψαντες, i.e. 'they come from the spring *after drinking*' instead of 'they come *to drink* from the spring'. Aristarchus, claiming that the word-order misled him, rightly objects that this spoils the effect. Fränkel (*loc. cit.*) notes that the fut., very rare in a simile, is protected by 13.493, where sheep go to drink *after* pasture (cf. *Od*. 10.159f., when a stag visits a spring *after* feeding); also, the wolves would lose their goal had they already drunk – our last view of them would be of aimless motion. They are fiercer *before* they drink (van der Valk, *Researches* II 61). The future scene of their drinking is so detailed that we see it as present (it is admired by 'Demetrius', *On Style* 220, cf. 94); so too we will soon see the troops glutted with war.

164–7 The vv. frame the simile (155–6n.). Verse 165 = 17.388; the idea that θεράπων is cognate with Hittite *tarpašša-/tarpan(alli)-*, 'ritual substitute', is implausible, *pace* e.g. Nagy, *BA* 292. With 167 cf. 2.554, where see n.; on ἀσπιδιώτης cf. Risch, *Wortbildung* 35f.

168–97 Catalogues stress the importance of an impending attack, as in the Catalogue of Ships (2.484ff.), where similes precede, as here; cf. too the marshalling at 4.250ff., 11.56ff. Akhilleus has fifty ships, as at 2.685, and 2,500 men; his army has five units, each with its own leader. Homer and his audience probably assumed that contingents have a set of subordinate officers: cf. H. van Wees, *CQ* 36 (1986) 285–303. The Boeotian and Pylian forces both have five leaders (2.494f., 4.295f.); one leader per ten ships is the usual ratio (Latacz, *Kampfdarstellung* 60). In the list at 12.86ff. the Trojans are divided into five battalions, each with more than one leader; the last three entries are the fullest. Here they grow briefer; despite the details about Menesthios, Eudoros and Peisandros, none reappears.

In fact this catalogue is a well-disguised remodelling of a standard Myrmidon muster-list headed by Akhilleus and his erstwhile kinsman Patroklos, whom Homer did not invent (see pp. 313–14). Menesthios, son of Peleus' daughter Poludorē and a river-god, has replaced Akhilleus, son of Peleus and a sea-goddess, who likewise abandoned her baby in the traditional tale (Schoeck, *Ilias und Aithiopis* 54); at 21.184ff. Akhilleus boasts that his own descent is better than that of a son of a river. A Polumelē, here the mother of Eudoros, is linked with Peleus' family elsewhere, either as Aktor's daughter and Peleus' first wife (Pindar frag. 48), or as Peleus' daughter who married Aktor's son Menoitios to bear him Patroklos (Philocrates, *FGH* 601 F 1); or else Peleus begot Akhilleus by *Philo*melē, daughter of Aktor (Daïmachus, *FGH* 65 F 2)! The names could be *ad hoc* inventions, as they are common (another Polumele is at *Cat.* 38); but since these tales seem too early and complex to derive from Homer, the poet has surely based Ekhe*kles*, son of Aktor, and his bride Polumele on Patroklos (-*kles*), grandson of Aktor (14) and son, presumably, of Polumele. Patroklos eliminates his *Doppelgänger*, now a Trojan named Ekhe*klos*, at 694 (cf. 570–80n.). My theory is confirmed when Peisandros, the third leader listed, is called 'best spearman *after Patroklos*' (195).

168–72 The list's preamble, in ring-form (168, 172), stresses Akhilleus' power over his men, contrasting the many and the one. It was traditional to tally up items which contain fifty of something else, using the phrase ἐν δὲ ἑκάστη (-ῳ): thus Helios' seven herds contain fifty animals each (one for each day of the year), twelve sties each hold fifty pigs, and nine gatherings have 500 men in each (*Od.* 12.129f., 14.13ff., 3.7); cf. also 2.123ff., Hes. frag. 304. In a Cyclic passage quoted at *Certamen* 143ff., the army at Troy had fifty hearths each with fifty spits, each spit roasted fifty morsels, and there were 900 men per morsel! A crew of fifty who both rowed and fought was normal for a ship of Homer's era, a 'penteconter' (cf. 2.719, *Od.* 10.203–9). Crews of twenty are also known (*Od.* 4.669): cf. D. Gray, *Arch. Hom.* G 108f. Aristarchus (in T), thinking it odd that Akhilleus has but fifty when the Boeotians had 120, proposed that only the rowers are meant; but the latter figure must be a hyperbolic compliment to the Boeotians, supposedly 6,000 strong (2.509–10n.). Thucydides (1.10.4) and Dionysius Thrax (frag. 59 Linke) deemed 120 and 50 the maximum and minimum.

Most good MSS offer ἐν δ' ἄρ' ἑκάστη, despite ἐν δὲ ἑ. 4× elsewhere; 'neglect' of ϝ- in a typical oral variation is no reason to reject the vulgate (ἐν δ' ἄρ(α) occurs in this place 27× epos). κληῖδες are not 'benches' but the thole-pins (later σκαλμοί) to which the oars are tied with leather thongs (*Od.* 8.37, 53; D. Gray, *op. cit.* 98). With 172 cf. *Theog.* 403, αὐτὸς δὲ μέγα κρατεῖ ἠδὲ ἀνάσσει, which 'maintains' the ϝ-, and 1.288, where it is 'neglected'; *ἐϝάνασσε must not be restored (cf. 572, 10.33, 2× *Od.*, 2× *Cat.*).

173–8 Another invented Menesthios appears at 7.9; the name is short for -sthenes, like Menestheus, -sthes, -sthos or -sthō (von Kamptz, *Personennamen* 209). The Sperkheios, Akhilleus' local river (23.142), debouches by modern Lamia; it is 'tireless' because it flows even in summer (cf. 60–1n.). Other rivers have human offspring at 5.544ff., 21.157 (cf. *Od.* 11.238ff.). Menesthios' mother Poludorē is aptly named after the gifts she will win (178), like Alphesiboia or Polumele; cf. the naming of Pandorē (*Erga* 80–2) or the formula ἄλοχος πολύδωρος (3×). Eudoros below is named for the gifts his mother would attract (190). Typically, Aristarchus deemed Poludorē's father not our Peleus but an unknown namesake; otherwise Homer would have called her Akhilleus' sister (Zenodotus, in T, renamed her Kleodorē, probably because she had this name in Hesiod, *Cat.* 213). Yet Odysseus' sister appears but once (*Od.* 15.363). Poludorē is surely a child of Peleus' first marriage, which Homer suppresses in favour of his union with Thetis; Akhilleus must remain, for him, an isolated figure. Her mother was Antigone, granddaughter of Aktor (cf. 189!), in Pherecydes (*FGH* 3 F 61) and 'Apollodorus' (3.13.1–4), or, according to Thessalian writers (in T), Eurudike, Aktor's daughter, or Laodameia. Other girls named Poludorē have local links: one bore Druops to the Peneios or Sperkheios river (Pherecydes, *FGH* 3 F 8, and Nicander frag. 41); another, alias Laodameia (!), was Protesilaos' bride (*Cypria* frag. 26 B. = 18 D.). Behind them all stands the fruitful Thessalian earth-goddess Pandora or Anesidora, ancestress of mankind (see West on *Erga* 81), especially if Peleus was popularly linked with πηλός, 'mud' (33–5n.); Pandora was ἐκ πηλοπλάστου σπέρματος θνητὴ γυνή (Aesch. frag. 369).

Bōros son of Periēres opens another vista of legend. Hesiod (*Cat.* 10a.27) knew of a Perieres son of Aiolos; Hellanicus (*FGH* 4 F 125) makes a Boros the father of a Penthilos, descendant of the Aiolid Neleus and ancestor of the Neleid leaders of Athens and of the Ionian migration (cf. Paus. 2.18.8). Hardly by chance, a tribe called Βωρεῖς, whose eponymous ancestor will be Βῶρος, existed at Ephesos, Miletos and the Samian colony Perinthos (Sakellariou, *Migration* 73f., 256ff.; von Kamptz, *Personennamen* 322). An allusion to the Neleids would flatter audiences in those cities (cf. 13.689–91n.); Aeolic Lesbos would applaud one to the Penthilids who ruled there until *c.* 610 B.C., and would welcome a relationship to Akhilleus (his name, 'grief to the people', means the same as Penthilos and his female *Doppelgänger* Penthesileia, whom he kills, cf. Nagy, *BA* 70n.). A Maeonian Boros appears at 5.44. Περιήρης is from *Fῆρ-, 'favour' (14.130–2n.).

173–5 Elsewhere *στίξ means a 'line' (φάλαγξ) of warriors, from στείχω (Latacz, *Kampfdarstellung* 48f., 60–2). But the sing. recurs only at 20.362, and H. van Wees (*CQ* 36 (1986) 293) thinks 'column' would make better sense. In fact *στίξ must mean a line *of ships* here; hence their number, fifty, is given (Latacz). The ships are drawn up in five lines of ten, with one leader per decade. For ἴα see p. 17 n. 28. αἰολοθώρηξ, also at 4.489, is equivalent to ὄρχαμος ἀνδρῶν, ὄζος Ἄρηος or (F)ἰσόθεος φώς; did Homer have Menesthios' *Aiolid* descent in mind? Note the assonance in the four-word 174. διιπετέος ποταμοῖο, a fossilized formula used 8× in the epos, is usually taken as 'river fallen *from* Zeus', who may be the father of rivers because his rain begets them (so T): see Strabo 1.36 and Porphyry 1.213.6ff. *διFειπετής entails an Arcado-Cypriot use of the Myc. dat. ΔιFεί as an abl. (cf. p. 11 n. 10); the spelling διει-, invoked by Risch to support this view (*Wortbildung*

220), rests on the poor authority of Zenodorus, a scholar cited by Porphyry (Erbse, *Lexica Graeca Minora*, Hildesheim 1965, 253ff.). Whatever its sense, it was soon reinterpreted. *HyAphr* 4 applies it to birds 'flying in the sky' (from πέτομαι); Alcman alters it to διαιπετής, of a star 'falling through' the sky (frag. 3.67); others took it as 'radiant' or 'translucent' (e.g. Eur. *Ba.* 1267, *Rh.* 43). See also 17.263n., S. West on *Od.* 4.477. Aristophanes, Aristarchus (Did/A) and some MSS read ὄν in 175, as is usual with τέκε; a papyrus and the vulgate have a *lectio difficilior* τόν, with asyndeton (cf. *Cat.* 25.20).

176–8 The collocation of woman and god, vividly expressing their union, is a standard device in catalogues: cf. θεὰ βροτῷ εὐνηθεῖσα (2.821), West on *Theog.* 380. ἐπίκλησιν, elsewhere in the formula ἑ. καλέεσκε (etc.), 'gave as a nickname' (7×, counting 7.138), here means 'in name', as at *HyAp* 386; Poludorē's marriage reconciles propriety with the welcome inclusion of a god in the family, just as Herakles was Zeus's son in fact but Amphitruon's in name, Poseidon's sons the Aktorione were formally Aktor's (*Cat.* 17) or Jesus was nominally Joseph's. The suitor gave the bride's father gifts to win his consent (13.365–7n.); for the formula cf. 190, *Od.* 19.529, *Cat.* 198.10. For υἷι (Hrd/AT) papyri read υἱεῖ, a recent form also at the verse-end in *Od.* 14.435, *Cat.* 217.2. Brandreth held, not implausibly, that ὅς ῥ' has replaced ὅς ϝ(ε), which gives 178 a direct object; ἀναφανδόν is *hapax legomenon*.

179–92 Menesthios and Eudoros are doublets (Heubeck, *Kleine Schriften* 119f.); cf. 168–97n. Like Poludorē, Polumelē has a bastard son by a god; she too is married off for wealthy gifts, but this time the baby is reared by the grandfather, not the step-parent as at 175ff. or 5.70f. She too is καλή; like Peisandros (193), her son ἀρήϊος ἡγεμόνευε. But Homer deftly varies the pattern by adapting hymnic material. Eustathius (1053.54) saw that he aptly links Polumele and swift Eudoros with Hermes, god of flocks, swift runner and giver of good things. In fact he draws on the proem of a *Hymn to Hermes* like those in our *Homeric Hymns* (4, 18): 'sing, Muse, of Hermes ... ruler of Arcadia *rich in sheep*, whom Maia, *Atlas' daughter* (Ἄτλαντος θυγάτηρ, cf. 181) bore ... in secret ... and *brought to daylight*' (εἴς τε φόως ἄγαγεν, cf. 188). Ἀρκαδίης πολυμήλου is turned into Ἀργεάδην Πολύμηλον at 417; here too the epithet may have become a name. Eileithuia brings Apollo 'forth to the light' (πρὸ φόωσδε) in a hymn glorifying his birth (*HyAp* 115–19); cf. 19.118, in a like context. For Homer's knowledge of hymns cf. 14.198–9, 14.347–8, 14.489–91nn. The details are typical. Hermes espies Polumele at a dance in honour of Artemis, the quintessential virgin, just as he snatches another girl from another such festival (*HyAphr* 118ff., where 118 resembles 183 here); at dances well-born girls escaped their usual seclusion and looked as lovely as Artemis herself (*Od.* 6.151–7). To see her sufficed to fire his ardour (cf. 14.294n.). He sneaks into her room to debauch her secretly, like

Ares and Astuokhe (2.514f., cf. 184 here); women dwelt above to keep them from harm (on the risks of letting one's wife live downstairs cf. Lysias 1.6ff.).

179–81 Aristarchus noted that ἑτέρης is for δευτέρης, which would not scan; that παρθένιος means 'born of a (supposed) virgin' – as in Pindar, *Ol.* 6.31, and the παρθενίαι, bastard sons of Spartan mothers who settled Taras (this ambiguity of παρθένος begot the Christian myth of a virgin birth); and that χορῷ καλή goes together, 'lovely in the dance', like καλλίχορος. As Homer explains, Hermes fell in love with Polumele at a dance; she did not give birth at one! κρατὺς Ἀργεϊφόντης (9× epos, here only *Il.*) is the first of several ornate formulae for gods, which help make 181–8 stately and numinous; their very obscurity would evoke awe at the limits of ordinary knowledge and the scope of the bard's. Aristotle called this important effect τὸ ξενικόν (*Poet.* 1458a21); cf. Parry, *MHV* 240–50. The epithet-system for Hermes, though ancient, is not fully represented in the tradition before the *Hymn to Hermes* (Janko, *HHH* 21ff.). The bards took Ἀργεϊφόντης as 'slayer of Argos', since ἀνδρεϊφόντης is based on it (S. West on *Od.* 1.37ff.).

183 This v. was athetized because Hermes should have shown Artemis more respect (so T)! O. S. Due (*C&M* 26 (1965) 1–9) explains both her epithets (cf. 20.70–1n.). Her noisy hobbies, listed at *HyAphr* 18f. and *Hy.* 27, motivate κελαδεινή; the ancients rightly refer this to the din of the hunt. ἠλακάτη already meant 'spindle' in Myc., since the tablets mention /ālaka-teiai/, 'spinning-women': Homer interpreted χρυσηλάκατος thus at *Od.* 4.122, since at 131 he gives Helen an impractically heavy golden distaff (see S. West *ad loc.*). But the wholly undomesticated virgin-goddess is no spinster. In accord with her epithet ἰοχέαιρα or her golden bow at *Hy.* 27.5, D and bT rightly suggest 'with golden arrows'. Indeed ἠλακάτη first meant the giant reed *Arundo donax*, apt for the shafts of both arrows and distaffs; this sense is first in Theophrastus (LSJ s.v.), but cf. πολυηλάκατος, 'reedy' (Aesch. frag. 8). Arrows were made of 'reed-cane' at Ugarit (*ANET* 151) and in Bactria (Hdt. 7.64).

185–7 Aristarchus saw that ἀκάκητα is a fossilized voc. used as a nom. (cf. 13.562–3n.). It recurs at *Od.* 24.10, *Cat.* 137.1 (with Ἑρμάων, a Peloponnesian form) and *Theog.* 614 (of Prometheus, another herald and fire-god). Like Callimachus (*Hy.* 3.143), Eratosthenes derived it from Mt Akakesion in Arcadia, where some said Hermes was reared (Paus. 8.36.10). In reply Apollodorus (echoing Aristarchus?), vainly denying that divine epithets can relate to cult-places, upheld a derivation from ἀ- and κακός, comparing δῶτορ ἐάων (*FGH* 244 F 353); cf. ἀκάκᾱς (Aesch., *Pers.* 855). No doubt Homer took it thus. The epithet is surely prior to the title Akakesios and derives from the Bronze Age Peloponnese, just as ἐριούνης is based on an old Arcado-Cypriot root οὐν-, 'run', and Κυλλήνιος is from Hermes' other birthplace, Mt Kullene. πόρεν δέ is innovative (Hoekstra,

Modifications 89n.); ἀγλαὸν υἱόν follows a father's name everywhere else (etc., 35×). Verse 186 = *Od.* 3.112 (nom.), 4.202, with Antilokhos' name instead – a striking coincidence given the parallels between him, Patroklos and Eudoros (cf. 168–97n. and pp. 313–14). θείειν is for *θεϝεμεν or -εhεν. For Eileithuia see 11.270n., J. Russo on *Od.* 19.188; μογοσ-τόκος, 'giving birth ⟨only⟩ to pains', is based on the acc. plur. *μόγους, cf. δικασ-πόλος (Risch, *Wortbildung* 220).

188–92 πρὸ φόωσδε, read by Zenodotus and most MSS, has hymnic parallels (179–92n.). Like Aristophanes (Did/A), Aristarchus read φώωσδε, no doubt deeming πρό redundant; he let πρό stand at 19.118, since Eurustheus was born prematurely. But πρό means simply 'forth', and φόωσδε is a false conjecture (van der Valk, *Researches* II 73). Once the vernacular had contracted φάος to φῶς, bards said φόως when metre allowed (p. 17); φῶς first enters the epos at *Cat.* 204.150, *HyHerm* 402. The ancients never understood the cause of diectasis (cf. their conjectures at 13.191, 14.255). Note the (pre-Homeric) formular innovation ἠελίου (ϝ)ίδεν αὐγάς beside ὑπ᾽ α. ἠελίοιο (4× *Od.*): cf. | α. τ᾽ ἠελίου (*HyDem* 35). Mother and baby go their separate ways in the leisurely catalogue-style wherein Homer was fully fluent (14.313–28n.): with 189 cf. 7.38, 23.837, *Cat.* 16.9, 252.6; with 190 cf. 22.472, *Od.* 11.282, 15.238, *Cat.* 26.37, 43.21; with 191 cf. 14.200–2n. Phulas rears the child like his own son: cf. 5.70f., *Cat.* 180.2.

193–7 Peisandros is introduced like Eudoros (179), but far more briefly. For Trojans of this name see 13.601–42n. A Peisandros led Aiolian settlers to Lesbos with Orestes (Pindar, *Nem.* 11.33); this name too had resonances for Aeolic audiences. Maimalos' name may come from μαιμάω (von Kamptz, *Personennamen* 245); Myc. *Ma-ma-ro* (PY Cn 655) can equally stand for |*Marmaros*|. Patroklos is meant in 195. Phoinix needs no description (cf. 9.168n. and his life-story at 9.447ff.); he is next seen at 19.311 (cf. 17.555). The epithets ἱππηλάτα and ἱππότα often adorn aged heroes or those of a prior generation, as if by a folk-memory of early Myc. chariot-fighting (cf. 808–11, 4.301–9nn.). Alkimedon, also called Alkimos, becomes Automedon's driver when the latter takes command (17.467n.). On the two forms of his name see 11n.; I think Homer simply invented and then reinvented him as a doublet of Automedon (cf. the case of Idaios/Kaletor, 15.419–21n.). Another Laerkes is at *Od.* 3.425; for the formation 'defender of the people' cf. Laertes.

198–9 Akhilleus 'set them all in order with their leaders, choosing well'; this completes the marshalling he began at 164–7, framing the whole catalogue.

199–209 Akhilleus is stern: κρατερὸν δ᾽ ἐπὶ μῦθον ἔτελλε denotes threats at 1.25, 326 and 379, cf. 8.29, 9.431. His tone again conceals the concession he is making. On the surface, he is reacting to his men's threats to sail home, insubordination which no leader can allow; thus 205 closely resembles 2.236, where Thersites urged the Greeks to sail away. Yet his past toleration of such grumbles shows his mildness (so bT): cf. Thersites' taunt at his forbearance towards Agamemnon (2.241f.). Both complaints point out that this quarrel hinders victory, imply that he was wronged by the king (the Myrmidons reproach him only for keeping *them* from battle), and note his capacity for anger, excessive or, in Thersites' view, deficient. He is Thersites' opposite and mortal enemy (Nagy, *BA* 259–62, 279), yet both Thersites and the Myrmidons parody his reaction to Agamemnon (Thalmann, *TAPA* 118 (1988) 19ff.); he too threatened to sail home (9.356ff.), and has since 'forgotten his threats' (cf. 200).

Lohmann (*Reden* 21) detected a concentric ring-structure in his speech. His quotation of his men's complaint forms its core, framed by mentions of χόλος; he bids them fight in an outer ring, of three verses each time, reinforced by the repetition λελαθέσθω ... Τρώεσσι – Τ. μαχέσθω. They now have what they wanted – war. Exhorting them to be consistent and seize their chance is effective, whatever light it sheds on Akhilleus' own inconsistency in refusing to lead to war those whom he once threatened to lead home.

200–2 Reminders of past threats are a typical provocation: cf. 7.96, 13.219f., 14.479, 20.83. A prohibition with a third-person aor. imperative recurs only at *Od.* 16.301 (Chantraine, *GH* II 231). For the jerky rhythm at the end of 201 cf. 6.477, 13.175, 13.454. For ὑπό with an acc. expressing duration cf. 22.102 and Powell, *Lexicon to Herodotus* s.v. A II 2.

203–6 Akhilleus knows how to dramatize others' views as well as his own; the powerful image of his mother rearing him on bile, not milk, shows his sensitivity to Patroklos' charge that he was born savage (33ff.). Does Homer wittily allude to the tradition that Kheiron fed him on the guts and marrow of savage beasts ('Apollodorus' 3.13.6)? We did not hear of his men's complaints before, but could infer them from his own longing for war and their restiveness (1.492, 2.773ff.). So too we hear of the army's anger at Agamemnon only from Poseidon and the king himself (13.107–14n.); for self-reproach put into others' mouths cf. 22.107 (Hektor). σχέτλιε, often in the middle of a speech (e.g. *Od.* 4.729, 9.351, 13.293), opens *oratio recta* only here: it once meant 'obstinate', < *σχέ-θλιος (Chantraine, *Dict.* s.v.). χόλος, here alone literally 'bile', has an exact Avestan cognate (cf. English *yellow*, *gold*); elsewhere, save perhaps at 9.646, χολή supplants it in this sense.

207–9 μ' is for με not μοι, since βάζω takes an acc. (9.58f., *Erga* 186). Crates' follower Hermias (Hrd/A) and papyri read ταῦθ' ἄμ', wrongly anticipating θάμ'; cf. the variant at *Od.* 4.686. Aristarchus' typical deletion of the augment in ἐβάζετε (Did/A) has, typically, no MS support (cf. p. 26 n. 30); before νῦν δέ the past tense needs to be well marked. With 207f. cf.

11.734, 12.416. ἕης is an artificial form for ἧς, by analogy with ὅου (from *ὅο) and the possessive ἑός/ὅς; cf. ἑέ for ἑ (2×) and ἕεις for εἷς at *Theog.* 145, also at the caesura. ἐράασθε too looks improvised (cf. ἐράεσκε at *Cat.* 30.32): athematic ἔραμαι is older. τις means effectively 'each', cf. 200, 2.381ff.

210–56 These vv. form the second occurrence of the thrice-repeated pattern of simile, preparation and speech, on which the preliminaries to this battle are based (101–277n.). Thus 210 = 275, which closes the third instance of this pattern. Akhilleus' visits to his hut delimit his prayer: with 221 cf. 254; 257f. pick up 218–20.

211–17 The troops are close-packed, in both directions, like stones in a wall tight enough to exclude the wind, though the house be lofty. The builder of such a wall resembles Akhilleus, whose order has a like effect: repetitions of ἀραρίσκω and πυκ(ι)νός stress this. Verse 213 = 23.713, in a simile of a builder. Dense formations are likened to a tower or fence at 13.152 and 15.567 (cf. 13.126–35n.); 215–17 were used at 13.131–3 to describe how the Greeks close ranks to halt a Trojan charge with the weight of their armour. Conversely, the impact of this solid mass will break the Trojan line. With 214 cf. *Od.* 19.32. The aor. ἄραρον is intrans. only here and at *Od.* 4.777, perhaps by analogy with perfect forms like ἀραρυῖα, in a verb obsolete in the vernacular; for the reverse process see *Erga* 431 and the variant at *Od.* 5.248 (cf. *LfgrE* s.v.). 'The same loss of feeling for *trans.* ἤραρον produced the sigmatic ἦρσα' (Shipp, *Studies* 291); ἄρθεν at 211 is unique. For ὀμφαλόεις see 13.190–4n. Verses 214f. form a chiasmus, helmets – shields – shields – helmets.

218–20 Patroklos and Automedon stand out from the mass, as if seen through Akhilleus' eyes; Patroklos' reappearance aptly leads into the next scene. The variant θωρήσσεσθον, perhaps inspired by 12.421, has no better support than ἀφίκεσθον at 13.613 (where see n.).

220–32 Having given Patroklos all the practical help he can, Akhilleus resorts to prayer. His elaborate preparation underlines the importance of this moment; his libation is 'a regular cult act transformed into a pure expression of emotion' (Griffin, *HLD* 17f.). He keeps a gold cup, dedicated to this sole purpose, in a chest brought from home, as was Nestor's gold cup (11.632ff.). Peleus used such a cup for libations to Zeus (11.774); this was surely the function of the gold cups given to various gods in Pylos tablet Tn 316. 'Nor do we fail to see the pathos of Thetis, the careful mother, packing for her doomed son the human comforts of warm clothes; these garments are worth mentioning because the poet relies on his audience to understand that they are the vehicles of profound emotion' (Griffin).

Aristarchus noted that Homer makes Thetis stay with Peleus until her son is adult, whereas later poets (οἱ νεώτεροι) made her leave her baby when it was twelve days old, no doubt because Peleus thwarted her efforts to immortalize it (see Ap. Rhod. 4.869ff. with Vian's n.; Richardson on *HyDem* 237ff.; Frazer on 'Apollodorus' 3.13.6, with Appendix x; cf. 'Hes.' frag. 300). Her abandonment of Peleus was traditional, since it motivates Kheiron's role in raising Akhilleus (cf. *Cypria* frag. dub. 35 B.; Severyns, *Cycle* 254–61; Jouan, *Chants Cypriens* 89–91). Since Homer knew of Kheiron, as of Peleus' first marriage (141–4, 173–8nn.), he surely knew of Thetis' 'divorce' too, despite Aristarchus' denial (so van Leeuwen, *Commentationes Homericae* 109–19; von Scheliha, *Patroklos* 240). By quietly contradicting this story Homer, as usual, makes the mermaid's son less weird than had the folktale (see further Severyns, *Homère* 86–95).

221–4 Clothes and valuables were stored in chests (24.228ff., *Od.* 13.10f.). ἀνεμοσκεπής, unique in Greek, is formed like ἀνεμοτρεφής: cf. χλαῖναν ... ἀλεξάνεμον (*Od.* 14.529), σκέπας ... ἀνέμοιο (4× *Od.*), and 213 above! τάπητες are rugs used to cover furniture or for bedding (9.200, 10.156 etc.). οὖλος, 'curly', 'thick', is a standard epithet for cloaks (24.646, 6× *Od.*), but rugs too are made of wool (*Od.* 4.124). In 223 Zenodotus and Aristophanes (Did/AT) read ἰόντι, with a hiatus, for ἄγεσθαι, perhaps to enhance the pathos of Akhilleus' departure or to prevent ἄγω from governing an inanimate object, as does happen in Homer, despite Aristarchus' dogma (Lehrs, *De Aristarchi studiis* 137f.): yet the latter kept ἄγεσθαι, no doubt as a metaphor from animate entities (cf. Arn/A on 11.632).

225–7 The syntax makes us expect 'nor did anyone else, either man or god, drink from this cup', like οὐδέ τις ἄλλος | ἤδεεν οὔτε θεῶν οὔτε ... ἀνθρώπων (18.403f., cf. *Od.* 9.520f.); but no Olympian can sip a libation, hence the anacoluthon at 227. On the rationale for the rite see Burkert, *Structure and History in Greek Mythology and Ritual*, Berkeley 1979, 41–3. The irrevocable gift of part of one's drink, the simplest type of offering, often precedes prayers before a journey: cf. *Od.* 13.38ff., 15.147ff., 15.258, Pindar *Py.* 4.193ff., Thuc. 6.32. The most telling parallel is how, before leaving for the Greek camp, Priam washes a cup and prays to Zeus for a safe return (with 24.306f. cf. 231f. here!); see on 24.281ff. Aristarchus' reading ὅτι μή, 'except' (Did/A), a common idiom in Herodotus and later, has no Homeric parallel; ὅτε μή is supported by 13.319, 14.248 etc., and σπένδεσκε is easily supplied.

228–30 Sulphur was a holy substance; its name θέειον was linked with θεός (Plut. *Mor.* 665c), its smell with the thunderbolt (14.414–17n.). Its volcanic origin increased its mystery: Greeks could find it on Melos, Nisyros or Lipari. See R. J. Forbes, *Arch. Hom.* κ 10; Parker, *Miasma* 227f. Odysseus fumigates his blood-stained palace with it (*Od.* 22.481ff.); such cleansing is both physical and religious, like the hand-washing. Priam libates to Zeus after rinsing his hands (24.302ff.); Hektor refuses to do so with bloody

hands (6.258ff., with runover | πρῶτον, ἔπειτα as here). The scansion | τό
ῥα is paralleled at 22.307, *Od.* 22.327 (ὅ ῥ'). Apollonius Rhodius used the
spelling τόρρα (1.769, 3.37 with scholia); Aristarchus avoids it (Did/AT).
Papyri offer another 'solution', τόν ῥα.

231–2 = 24.306f., to εἰσανιδών; the rare statement that the addressee is
listening arouses suspense and shows the occasion's importance (cf. 8.4, 492).
Like other Homeric houses, Akhilleus' hut is imagined to have an enclosed
yard with an altar of Zeus; the god's ear is best caught in the open, by calling
up into the sky (cf. Peleus' prayer to him αὐλῆς ἐν χόρτῳ, 11.774). ἕρκεϊ
implies his title Herkeios, guardian of the home. Odysseus' yard had an altar
of Zeus Herkeios where one could seek asylum (*Od.* 22.334ff., 379); Priam
was slain by his own such altar (*Sack of Troy* in Proclus and *Little Iliad* frag.
16 B. = 17 D., in overlapping narratives; Virgil, *Aen.* 2.512ff., 550ff.). See
further Jebb on Soph. *Ant.* 487. Greek prayer is an act of drawing attention
to oneself, not of submission: cf. the twin sense of εὔχομαι, 'pray' and 'boast'
(13.54n.). οὐρανὸν εἰσανιδών, with a 'neglected' ϝ, may adapt ο. εἰσανιών
(7.423, *Theog.* 761); Δία is innovative too (14.157–8n.). τερπικέραυνος,
'rejoicing in the thunderbolt', should be *τερψι-; hence Nagy derives it from
*perkʷi-peraunos, 'striking with the thunderbolt', with metathesis (*Gedenkschrift Güntert* 128).

233–48 Akhilleus' prayer, the most solemn in Homer, follows the usual
structure of invocation (233–5), claim for attention (236–8) and request
(239ff.), as seen at e.g. 1.451ff. (cf. 14.233–41n.). The invocation is long
and weighty: ἄνα, 'lord', is a rare religious archaism (3.351, *HyAp* 179, 526,
lyric, tragedy). Akhilleus' claim that Zeus has honoured him and hurt the
Greeks exactly echoes Khruses' at 1.453: but he fails to end their woes as
Khruses ended the plague, because he will not intervene himself. Thus his
wrath and Khruses' now diverge, with grim results for him. Lowenstam
(*Death of Patroklos* 109f.) likens his double wish – for glory, and for Patroklos'
safe return – to his own 'choice of fates' at 9.410ff.; neither hero's life may
be both glorious and long.

233 Akhilleus prays to Zeus of Dodonē, which lies far from Phthia over
the Pindos range below Mt Tomaros, twelve miles S. W. of modern Yannina.
Dodone rivalled Delphi in claiming to be the oldest oracle (9.404–5n., Hdt.
2.52). This matches the archaeological evidence; dedications are known
from the eighth century onward. The site has a long prehistory (H. W.
Parke, *The Oracles of Zeus*, Oxford 1967, 95ff.) and a non-Greek name,
like other places in -ōnē and -ēnē (perhaps both from -ānā). Akhilleus has links
with Epirus: in the *Nostoi* his son returned from Troy overland to Epirus,
not to Phthia. As we saw (231–2n.), he is praying to Zeus Herkeios, the god
symbolic of home and one's deepest roots: Athenian youths being admitted
to citizenship were asked where their cult of Zeus Herkeios was, along with

their ancestral tombs (Aristotle, *Ath. Pol.* 55.3). Thus Homer derives Peleus' family from Dodone.

Even more oddly, Homer seems to explain 'Pelasgian' by saying that the Helloi live there. Hesiod frag. 319, Δωδώνην φηγόν τε, Πελασγῶν ἕδρανον, explodes bT's conjectures Πελαργικέ or -αστικέ. Aristotle says the ancient land of Hellas was around Dodone, 'for the Selloi dwelt there and those who were once called Graikoi and now Hellenes' (*Meteor.* 1.352b1). The odd fact that Hellenes occupy Phthia and *Pelasgian* Argos (2.529–30, 2.681nn.) is paralleled at Dodone. The Pelasgoi were a prehistoric tribe in parts of Greece and the N.E. Aegean, regarded as indigenous (*Cat.* 160, Asius frag. 8, Aesch. *Suppl.* 250ff.) and speaking an alien tongue (14.230n., *Od.* 19.175ff., Hdt. 1.57f.). D say Pelasgians settled at Dodone when driven from Boeotia by Aeolians from Arne in Phthiotis; Herodotus (1.56) contrasts the settled Pelasgians with the Hellenes who moved from Phthia to the Pindos and then returned as Dorians (cf. the Dorian name 'Pindar'). This passage proves that Homer knew of some such movement (Severyns, *Homère* 88). Links between the Aeolic and N. W. Greek dialects confirm that the peoples of Thessaly and Epirus were akin (see pp. 15–16).

Many tried to make Akhilleus invoke a more local deity, just as Pandaros invokes Lycian Apollo or Priam Idaean Zeus (4.101, 24.308), by positing a Thessalian Dodone: so we learn from Steph. Byz. s.v. A local writer, Suidas (fourth-century), read Φηγωναῖε, claiming that Zeus had a cult under that title at Skotoussa, whence the oracle moved to Epirus (*FGH* 602 F 11, cf. Cineas, *FGH* 603 F 2). Others read Βωδωναῖε, from Perrhaebian Bodonē (cf. Apollodorus, *FGH* 244 F 189), a town perhaps imagined by analogy with Aeolic 'Belphoi' for 'Delphi' (from *G^w-). But Homer places Zeus's oracular oak in Thesprotia (*Od.* 14.327f. = 19.296f.), and puts Dodone in Gouneus' realm at 2.749–51, again calling it 'wintry'; the site is some 1,600 feet up and exposed to the N. Zenodotus (in T) altered δυσχειμέρου to πολυπίδακος, either because he deemed this adj. more fitting (cf. Callim. frag. 630 with van der Valk, *Researches* II 64), or (better) because he accepted Suidas' alleged Thessalian Dodone here, since he too read Φηγωναῖε (Steph. Byz. *loc. cit.*). τηλόθι ναίων adapts Zeus's epithet αἰθέρι ν. (5× epos, in a prayer at 2.412).

234–5 'Around you dwell the Helloi your interpreters, with unwashed feet, sleepers on the ground.' Since early Dodone had a holy oak but no temple (Parke, *op. cit.* 116f.), Zeus was believed to dwell in the oak itself; Hesiod perhaps said that he ναίει δ' ἐν πυθμένι φηγοῦ (*Cat.* 240.8; ναῖον MSS). The oak is also implied by 'interpreters'; in early tales it could speak for itself, like the Dodonaean plank in the Argo (Aesch. frag. 20, Ap. Rhod. 1.527), and not through doves or dove-priestesses (women replaced men in this role by classical times: Parke, *op. cit.* 55, 75). The sky-god was widely linked with the oak in pagan Europe (Frazer, *The Golden Bough*, 3rd edn, London 1911–13, II 356ff., cf. p. 261 above), but rarely in Greece: cf. the 'oak of Zeus' (5.693, 7.60) and his title ἔνδενδρος (Hsch. s.v.).

The priests' weird customs must be taboos, not mere signs of backwardness; W. Pötscher (*Mnem.* 19 (1966) 143–5) thinks they drew strength from the earth as does an oak. Alexander Aetolus (in AD) claims they were descended from Tyrrhenians and followed ancestral custom: for the equation Pelasgians = Tyrrhenians (Etruscans) see 14.230n. Their practices recur among the Romans and the pagan Prussians. The Flamen Dialis had to sleep with mud smeared on the feet of his bed, and might not pass three nights elsewhere (Aulus Gellius 10.15); this was surely a substitute for sleeping on the earth itself. The priest of Potrimpo, a god who dwelt in the holy oak at Romove, had to pass three nights on bare earth before sacrificing to him; the Prussians held that gods lived in tall oaks, which might give enquirers audible answers. See Frazer, *op. cit.* II 43, with *CR* 2 (1888) 322; H. M. Chadwick, *Journal of the Anthropological Institute* 3 (1900) 22–44.

Does ΣΕΛΛΟΙ mean Σελλοί or σ᾽ Ἑλλοί? Aristarchus argued for 'Selloi' like the river Selléeis, which he wrongly located in Epirus (15.531n.); Sophocles (*Trach.* 1167) and Aristotle (*Meteor.* 1.352b1) speak of Selloi. Callimachus knew both forms (frags. 23.3, 675, cf. Strabo 7.328), but the (H)elloi have Pindar's support (frag. 59.3). Their Thessalian ancestor, Hellos the wood-cutter, founded the shrine (bT, D); Hesiod calls its environs (H)ellopiē (*Cat.* 240). Apollodorus' claim (*FGH* 244 F 198) that the locals derived this name from the nearby marshes (ἕλη) supports the *H-*. Lesky (*WS* 46 (1927/8) 48–67, 107–29) rightly upholds 'Helloi', adducing Hellotis, a title of Europē (who, some said, founded Dodone); Hella, a name of the shrine (Hsch. s.v.); Helle, ancestress of some Macedonian tribes; and Hellenes, with the N. W. Greek ethnic suffix -ᾶνες. G. Restelli implausibly deems 'Selloi' an archaism for 'Helloi' (*RIL* 104 (1970) 3–18, 537–90). The sonorous repetition of ναίω evokes Zeus's local title 'Naïos' (probably from νάω, 'flow', of rain); cf. the rain-god Zeus *Hellanios* on Myrmidon Aigina, and further D. Evans in G. Larson (ed.), *Myth in Indo-European Antiquity*, Berkeley 1974, 99–130. For the internal correption in χαμαιεῦναι cf. χαμαιευνάδες (2× *Od.*) and later χάμευνα/-η, with 13.275–8n. ἀνιπτόποδες recurs as a name for temple prostitutes of Zeus in Roman Lydia (cf. Montanari, *RIL* 110 (1976) 202–11).

236–8 = 1.453–5, where Khruses replaces ἐμὸν ἔπος, an old phrase in a old verse (cf. 14.234), with contracted ἐμεῦ πάρος. The claim on the god's attention may be either past worship or the favours he has granted; the epos is rich in expressions for it (Nickau, *Ζenodotos* 81n.). Like Khruses (233–48n.), Akhilleus aptly cites the god's fulfilment of his prayer for a Greek defeat, which Thetis conveyed to Zeus at 1.500ff. The Alexandrians

rejected so unpatriotic a prayer. Zenodotus omitted 237, which his successors obelized (Did/T); Aristarchus, believing 237 to come from 1.454, held
that the hero never prayed thus, but was honoured because of Thetis'
request and mentions past favours generally. This cannot excuse Akhilleus
from responsibility (15.75–7n.); Bolling (*External Evidence* 164f.) and Nickau
defend the athetesis, but miss 18.74–8, where Thetis says her son prayed for
a Greek defeat. τιμήσας should be accented as a participle, not a second
person aor. sing., *pace* 1.451–6n. ἴψαο (*ἴπτομαι), 'harm', is cognate with
ἰάπτω, which has reduplicated the initial laryngeal (Beekes, *Laryngeals* 129).

239–41 On ἀγών, 'gathering', cf. 15.426–8n. For πόλεσῖν see 326–9n.;
the latter half of 240 = 23.60, *Od.* 11.495. With 241 cf. κῦδος ἄμ' ἔψεται
(4.415), κ. ὀπάζειν; εὐρύοπα, originally acc., is voc. only here and at *Hy.*
23.4 (14.264–6n.).

242–8 '... so that Hektor will learn whether Patroklos knows how to fight
on his own, or his unspeakable hands rage (only) then, when I enter the
battle (with him)'. If this contradicts Akhilleus' order, implicit at 83ff. and
overt at 18.13f., that Patroklos is not to fight Hektor, the contradiction lies
in his own position (Ferrari, *Oralità* 38f.). Cf. 8.110f., ὄφρα καὶ Ἕκτωρ |
εἴσεται εἰ καὶ ἐμὸν δόρυ μαίνεται ἐν παλάμησι: for ὅ. with a fut. in final clauses
cf. *Od.* 17.6 and Chantraine, *GH* II 273. Verses 244f. again allude to Akhilleus' refusal, and wish, to fight; it is an ironic result of his refusal that he
never fights beside Patroklos again. Since he knows how well Patroklos fights
when with him, he uses the factual indic. μαίνονται beside the more hypothetical subj. ἐπίστηται. Aristarchus rejected Zenodotus' indic. ἐπιστέαται,
claiming that all such endings in -αται are plur. But some bards falsely
extended them to the sing.: most MSS read θεὰ κεχαροίατο at *Od.* 3.438, all
have νόμος βεβλήαται ᾠδῆς at *HyAp* 20, and Hellenistic poets followed
suit (cf. Pfeiffer on Callim. frag. 497). Zenodotus' reading, like his πεποιέαται at 6.56, is an over-eager extension of such forms (van der Valk, *Researches*
II 47). For ἄαπτος see on 13.317f.; for the abl.-gen. ναῦφι cf. 281, 2.794 and
13.588–90n. μάχην ἐνοπήν τε is part of a synonymic system for 'battle', cf.
251, 12.35, 20.18. ἀσκηθής, perhaps an exact cognate of 'unscathed', survived in Aetolian (so T) and Arcadian. For ἀγχέμαχος cf. 13.4–7n.

249–52 The old verse 249 concludes the related prayer at 24.314, cf.
1.457 (Priam, Khruses). We catch our breath at 'Zeus heard him', which
means that the god agrees; but the poet adds, with devastating concision,
that he agrees only in part. The order of Akhilleus' requests followed that
of Patroklos' sortie and return; the repetition of this sequence stresses Zeus's
refusal to let him return safely. To refuse, he 'nods upward' with that toss
of the head and raising of the eyebrows (*Od.* 9.468) still used by the Greeks;
likewise they still 'nod down' to agree. As at 9.681, Aristarchus (Did/A)
wavered between σάον and σόον. The epic forms in σο- arose by diectasis

when the vernacular had contracted *σάϝος to σῶς, just as φόως replaced *φάϝος after it became φῶς (188–92n.); the MSS rightly read σόον.

253–6 Akhilleus' return to his hut frames his prayer, forming a ring with 220ff. The statement that he re-emerged because he still wished to watch the battle lets us infer the mingled longing and concern which he must feel; with 256 cf. 4.65, 5.379.

257–77 This is the third, last, and briefest of the preliminary scenes built on the same pattern of simile and exhortation (101–277n.). The Myrmidons charge the Trojans twice, which frames the scene (258, 276); the simile and exhortation are simultaneous (cf. 14.1–152n.). The poet stresses their high morale (258, 266), which Patroklos' speech augments. Chantraine (*Dict.* s.v. στείχω) takes ἔστιχον in 258, unique in Homer, as aor. not imperf., rejecting as erroneous the pres. στίχω (Hsch., MSS of Hdt.).

259–65 Just as the Myrmidons were like a wolf-pack (156ff.), so they now resemble wasps. Again their number is not the main point of comparison, but their mood (264–6) and movement (with 259 cf. 267); ἐξεχέοντο does not imply a chaotic mob (Latacz, *Kampfdarstellung* 252ff.). Swarms of insects describe hordes of warriors at 641ff., 2.87ff., 2.469ff.; at 17.570ff. a hero stands firm with the bravery and persistence of a blood-sucking fly. The image of 12.167–70 is no less psychological: two soldiers stand fast like wasps or bees which 'make their homes by a steep path, ... face the hunters and defend their children' (cf. 261, 265). Other similes evoke animals' dogged courage in guarding their brood, e.g. 17.4ff., 17.133ff., *Od.* 20.14f.; Homer often grants them emotions which many wrongly deem exclusive to humans. These wasps have a home (not a nest), brave hearts and children to defend: cf. the 'brave-hearted' wolves or lions of 157, 17.111, 20.169.

Wasps' irritability was a topos (M. Davies and J. Kathirithamby, *Greek Insects*, Oxford 1986, 75f.). Provoked by boys' repeated teasing, they bravely beset any wayfarer who chances to brush against their nest, built no doubt in a tall sage-bush; so too the Myrmidons, their ferocity increased by long abstinence since the leaders' quarrel, attack the Trojans who are, in this, innocent outsiders, since their assault has not touched Akhilleus' own ships (cf. 61–3n.). Both the provocation and the bravery are needed here (Krischer, *Konventionen* 46f.). Some hold that 260–2 contains a 'double recension', and that the simile fits better if the wasps are unprovoked. This is refuted by Kakridis (*Homer Revisited* 138–40) and M. Marcovich (*AJP* 83 (1962) 288–91), who admit to Balkan boyhoods amusingly misspent in making trouble for others by teasing wasps' nests. Homer knowingly describes this game (cf. 15.362–4, the sand-castle simile). Eustathius (1059.10) saw wit in the wasps' roadside animosity: at 6.15 a man 'who lived by the road' gave hospitality to all comers. On the free modal syntax, typical of similes, see Chantraine, *GH* II 355.

261 This v. explains in chiastic order the rare words ἔθω, 'be wont' (9.540, cf. εἴωθα), ἐριδμαίνω (next in Hellenistic verse, cf. Risch, *Wortbildung* 290) and εἰνόδιος (*Cat.* 23.26, cf. 6.15). Homer explains other compounds of his at 737, 1.238, 2.212, 5.63, 5.88, 8.527, 9.124, 24.488, *Od.* 1.299, 2.65, 5.67: cf. L. P. Rank, *Etymologiseering en verwante Verschijnselen bij Homerus*, Assen 1951, 74–84. The repetition also mimics the boys' repeated teasing, as may the assonance in -οντ-. Following Aristophanes (Did/A), Aristarchus athetized 261 as redundant, adding that κερτομεῖν properly describes words, not deeds; but it can mean 'tease' non-verbally, e.g. Eur. *Helen* 619 (J. Jackson, *Marginalia Scaenica*, Oxford 1955, 26). He, ἅπασαι and some good codices keep ἔχοντας; the easy error -οντες is in papyri (cf. van der Valk, *Researches* II 195).

262–5 For runover νηπίαχος cf. 2.337f., a simile contrasting soldiers with boys innocent of war. The old third plural τιθεῖσι is for -εντι, retained in Doric (Chantraine, *GH* I 298): its subject is the boys, not the wasps. ἄνθρωπος is rarely used with another noun, in contrast to ἀνὴρ χαλκεύς etc.: cf. ὁδιτάων ἀνθρώπων (*Od.* 13.123) and Schwyzer, *Grammatik* II 614. Verse 265 buzzes with alliteration in π, σ and τ. For its typically oral syntax cf. 20.166, ἀγρόμενοι πᾶς δῆμος: the phrase ἄλκιμον ἦτορ ἔχοντες eases the shift to the sing. (Chantraine, *GH* II 15).

266–77 Patroklos' speech, tactically effective, is strategically ruinous (8.172ff. is verbally similar). He invokes the men's loyalty to Akhilleus, the best leader of the best troops, as Glaukos grants in the same words (17.164f.). But this underlines the inconsistencies that Akhilleus is not leading them, and that fighting to give him honour will hardly make Agamemnon admit that he dishonoured him (cf. 84ff.). Patroklos does not, and cannot, tell his men not to fight too hard or too long: Akhilleus' compromise is thus doomed to fail. With 267 cf. *Epigonoi* frag. dub. 7 B.; 268 blends ἑτάροισιν ἐκέκλετο (4×) with ἑ. μακρὸν ἀΰσας (9×). Verse 270, found 7×, as usual follows a whole-line address (4× ending in ἀγχιμαχηταί, cf. ἀγχέμαχοι at 272 with 13.4–7n.). From ὅς, 271f. = 17.164f., each time with the ellipse 'Akhilleus who is best ... and ⟨so are⟩ his retainers'; Seleucus athetized 272 (in T). Verses 273f. = 1.411f., Akhilleus ending a speech with a threat; ἄτη, originally 'satiety' like κόρος, evolves into 'folly', 'delusion' and 'ruin' (see on 19.85ff.). Verse 275 = 210 (see 210–56n.). Verses 276f. = 2.333f., from ἀμφί; all the Greeks cheer, not the Myrmidons only.

278–418 Unnerved by Patroklos' appearance, the Trojans are driven from the ships and flee across the ditch with heavy losses

278–418 The Trojans, though alarmed by the arrival of a figure they take for Akhilleus (281f.), resist for a while (301–5n.); Patroklos and eight other

Greeks make an unbroken series of kills, until they can bear no more (351–7n.). Hektor at first stands fast to protect his men, then flees by chariot, chased by Patroklos (364–93), who storms unchallenged over the plain, making fourteen kills in succession (394ff.). Fenik (*TBS* 9f., 191f.) well compares how Diomedes' *aristeia* starts during a battle (5.1–94). Both heroes unnerve the enemy with an initial kill; then other leaders take turns, a simile sums up the effect, a rout, and each wreaks havoc until he meets an obstacle – there Pandaros' arrow, here Sarpedon (see further 306–57n.). The Greeks seem to need only the stimulus of Patroklos' first kill to succeed in repelling the Trojans; again Homer takes pains to mitigate their defeat. The narrative is swift but full; wolf- and weather-similes mark its key stages (297ff., 352ff., 364f., 384ff.), reminding us of Zeus's role in bringing the cloud of war upon the ships. A parallel narrative is 15.312–66, where the Trojans and Apollo rout the Greeks: cf. too 11.1–283.

278–92 Verses 278–83 are a glance back at the Trojans during the Myrmidons' charge, and 284–92 describe Patroklos' action during that charge, before 293ff. state its results (Latacz, *Kampfdarstellung* 251). The Trojans take Patroklos for Akhilleus and Automedon for Patroklos, 'glittering in their armour' (cf. 13.331, 801): gleaming armour is a traditional detail early in an *aristeia* (cf. 130–54n.), but their natural supposition that Akhilleus is fighting, because he has ended his wrath (true) and been reconciled (false), proves that we are meant to recall the exchange of armour (see further pp. 310–11).

280–3 πᾶσιν ὀρίνθη θυμός denotes panic (5.29, 18.223f.). With ἐλπόμενοι it is easy to supply 'the Trojans' (so Aristarchus). Zenodotus (in T) read -μεναι to agree with φάλαγγες; cf. his 'corrections' at 1.251, 2.626. The rest of 281 = 8.474 (in Zeus's first prophecy of Patroklos' death); ναῦφι is abl.-gen. (242–8n.). Anger is imagined as a burden to be cast off, as at 9.517. Verse 283 = 14.507 (*Od.* 22.43 is spurious), and sounds traditional (Hoekstra, *Modifications* 74n.); the Trojans do not flee immediately, but pick out escape-routes. Aristarchus admired how their alarm precedes their flight (T), and Aristotle called this 'the most terrible of Homer's verses' (frag. 130); 'each' puts us into the mind of a warrior in a moment of mortal fear.

284–92 Eustathius (1060.15) saw wit in the death of 'Fire-spear' when the threat to the ships is averted. Patroklos' success is typical (Fenik, *TBS* 192). As usual we hear who kills first in a new phase of battle (cf. 13.170n.): 284 blends πρῶτος ἀκόντισε (13.502, 14.402, in duels) with ἀ. δουρὶ φαεινῷ (14×, thrice, as here, before | καὶ βάλε, cf. 13.159–61n.). He casts into the ranks, seemingly at random (cf. 15.573–5n.); the hero of an *aristeia* often attacks the densest mass (with 285 cf. 5.8, 11.148, 15.448), here by Protesilaos' ship (15.704–6n.). Naturally, Patroklos hits a leader; that his victim is an ally prepares for Sarpedon's fate. Puraikhmes' death typifies Beye's tripartite pattern of basic statement, biography of the victim and account of the wound (13.170–81n.). His fall is standard (with 289f. cf. 4.522, 13.548, *Od.* 18.398), as is his men's panic at their leader's demise: the Epeans flee at 11.744ff. when they see fall ἡγεμόν' ἱππήων, ὃς ἀριστεύεσκε μάχεσθαι (cf. 292), and the Paiones flee at the death of 'the excellent' Asteropaios (21.205ff., cf. 6.5ff.), who takes Puraikhmes' place (21.155f.). At 17.351 another Paeonian 'was the best fighter' after Asteropaios. In the heroic world the king always fights best, with the problematic exception of Aga-memnon leading his unique coalition of armies.

287–90 With 287f. cf. 2.848f. with nn., Πυραίχμης ἄγε Παίονας ἀγκυλο-τόξους | τηλόθεν ... ῥέοντος (as 288). The Paiones are ἀγκυλότοξοι at 10.428 also, where the *Maiones* are ἱπποκορυσταί (431); they are 'equippers of chariots' here and at 21.205. This equivalent epithet is generic (cf. 2.1 = 24.667), but Mimnermus says the Paiones raised horses (frag. 17). Juvenal (3.69) lists Amudon among real places in the Aegean; Strabo equates it with a fort called Abudon which the Macedonians razed (7 frags. 20, 23). N. G. L. Hammond places it at Vardaroftsa on the E. bank of the Axios near its mouth (*A History of Macedonia* i, Oxford 1972, 176f., 296, 432). A Paeonian is called Mudon at 21.209. — As part of Aristarchus' war on augments (see p. 26 n. 30), in which he was reacting against Zenodotus (15.716–17n.), he read ἀμφὶ φόβηθεν (Did/A); papyri and most codices have ἀμφε-. He also altered ἀνεκυμβαλίαζον and ὑπεσείετο (379, 14.285).

293–6 Protesilaos' ship, ablaze since 123, is still only half-burnt; we glimpse the smoking hulk as the battle surges by it, a vivid symbol of Trojan failure. The phrase αἰθόμενον πῦρ arose by analogy with πυρὸς αἰθομένοιο; it breaches the tendency to formular economy, which is no reason to accept A's variant ἀκάματον πῦρ (9× elsewhere). Conversely Hesiod uses both πυρὸς μένος ἀκαμάτοιο and π. μ. αἰθομένοιο (*Theog.* 563, 324); cf. G. P. Edwards, *The Language of Hesiod* 62. ἡμιδαής, formed like θεσπιδαής (Risch, *Wortbildung* 81), recurs in Hellenistic verse. Verse 296 = 12.471; Leaf deletes it, disliking the repetition of ὅμαδος. But 12.470 ends Δαναοὶ δ' ἐφόβηθεν, a phrase which Homer has divided between 294 and 295, anticipating his use of ὅμαδος in the process; a similar anticipation in 298 suggests his excitement here (cf. 301–5n.).

297–300 Moulton (*Similes* 33f.) shows that this is the first of a trio of storm-images which reflect the shift in the battle (364f., 384ff.); Zeus's presence in all three hints that his plan caused this shift. Cf. too Whitman, *HHT* 150ff.; V. di Benedetto, *RFIC* 115 (1987) 267f. 'The sudden gleam of new hope is magnificently compared to a sudden burst of light through clouds hanging over a mountain peak, as though a cleft were opened into the very depths of heaven' (Leaf). 'Light' is a metaphor for salvation (Braswell on Pindar, *Py.* 4.270): cf. 39, 15.741 or Aias' prayer to Zeus for light, the granting of which presages success (17.645ff.). Also, a 'cloud' is a common metaphor for a crowd of warriors (66–9n.); do the ships' high sterns evoke mountain-tops (15.690–2, 717nn.)? Homer had a range of cloud-similes for different occasions. At 5.522ff. warriors stand firm like windless clouds which Zeus sets upon a peak; here Zeus moves the cloud a little and the foe gives ground; at 11.305ff. he scatters the clouds with a gale, just as Hektor routs a mass of men.

Verse 297 = *Aspis* 374; cf. *Od.* 9.481, *Hy.* 33.4. With 298 cf. πυκινὸν νέφος (5.751 = 8.395). στεροπηγερέτα, a unique makeshift to avoid the usual epithet νεφεληγερέτα after νεφέλην, is gauche: Zeus gathers clouds, not lightning, and here he is clearing a cloud away. So too Homer avoids πόδας ὠκύς in 23.168, μεγάθυμος Ἀχιλλεὺς | ἐς πόδας (F. M. Combellack, *CPh* 71 (1976) 54); cf. 15.242–3n. The cloud evoked 'cloud-gatherer' in his mind, or indeed represents an anticipation of it; he forgot that the rarer phrase Ζεὺς τερπικέραυνος (4×) would also fit here. A poet using writing could easily have avoided this oddity. Parry (*MHV* 187f.) rightly denied that στεροπηγερέτα is meant to suit its setting: Eustathius' idea (1060.44ff.) that the mountain is lit by *lightning*, the wrong image in this hopeful context, shows the risk of such an approach. Verses 299f. = 8.557f., in the star-simile describing Trojan watch-fires; Moulton detects 'an echo which nicely under-lines the reversal of that earlier high point of Trojan confidence', and may be right even if the couplet is traditional, as parallels at *HyAp* 22f. and 144f. suggest (πᾶσαι δὲ σκοπιαὶ ∪∪ — καὶ πρώονες ἄκροι | ὑψηλῶν ὀρέων). πρώονες is by diectasis for πρήονες after the Ionic vernacular had contracted it to πρῶνες via *πρέωνες.

301–5 As Nestor foresaw (11.800), the Greeks can now 'catch their breath' and redouble their efforts. At 283, 290f. and 294f. a rout seemed imminent, but now we hear that the Trojans still resist. bT think more losses are needed to make them flee, especially after such an offensive. But the poet hesitates over this rout, giving signs of it at 306, 308, 313–15, 331 and 342f.; he has surely anticipated it in his excitement (293–6n.). ἐρωή is in the same phrase at 17.761 (cf. 13.776, 17.422); Chantraine (*Dict.* s.v.) well argues that it first meant 'departure', 'swift motion', which evolved into both 'escape' or 'respite' and 'rush'. From Τρῶες, 303 = 6.73, 17.319. The unique προτροπάδην recurs in prose.

306–57 The breaking of the Trojan ranks implies a rout (cf. 17.285), but see 301–5n. Cf. the serial killings in routs at 15.328ff. (much condensed, since the dead are Greeks – 328 = 306 here) and at 5.37ff. (see 278–418n. with Strasburger, *Kämpfer* 63ff.). The participants are alike: in book 5, Agamemnon, Idomeneus, Menelaos, Meriones, Meges and Eurupulos; here, Patroklos, Menelaos, Meges, four others and both Cretans (warriors prominent in books 13–15). Both scenes end with a generalizing verse (351, 5.84), and begin by saying who killed first (with 306f. cf. 5.37f.); this duplicates 284. Patroklos, who has already killed once, is in Agamemnon's place because the latter is injured (so Strasburger); 358f. explain the omission of Aias – he is facing Hektor. Book 16 has fewer pitiful anecdotes but more grim wounds: our shock at these makes the Trojans' panic more convincing (for this technique see on 14.489ff.). Eustathius (1061.33ff.) notes the variety of injuries and phrases for death; simple and complex slayings tend to alternate, but motifs are often adapted from one to the next. The style is fluent and traditional, with few oddities of diction.

307–10 Areïlukos is hit while turning to flee, as often occurs (5.40, 12.428); a Greek has the same name (14.449–53n.). Nicanor (in A) noted that one can put a stop after 307, with ἕλεν supplied; 308 then starts a new sentence, cf. *Od.* 4.220. ἔγχεϊ ὀξυόεντι, found 9× at the verse-end, is transposed as at *Od.* 19.33; for its sense cf. 13.584–5n. With 310f. cf. 413f., 579f., 21.118.

311–12 Thoas dies facing his foe Menelaos, last seen at 15.540–68 with Meges and Antilokhos. Thoas' name is common, but was perhaps suggested by how the Greek Thoas appears with Meges and Nestor's sons (13.92f., 19.238f.). Verse 312 = 400. For his wound, when he carelessly *exposes* his chest behind his shield, cf. 4.468; γυμνωθείς also has this sense at 12.389, *Aspis* 418, 460 (regarding an arm, neck and thigh). This usage may date back to early Myc. times, when warriors lacked corslets and relied on body-shields (15.645–52n.).

313–15 Phuleus' son Meges gets his blow in first, cf. 322, 23.805; (ἔγχεϊ) ὀρέγομαι, 'reach', comes to mean 'hit'. 'Amphiklos' is short for *-kles* (11n.); both forms are in inscriptions. He dies not only facing the Greeks, but attacking. Like Areïlukos, he is hit in the thigh: πρυμνὸν σκέλος means the top of the leg, just as π. βραχίονα is the arm by the shoulder (323, 13.532). Death would soon follow the severing of his femoral artery; the rending of his *gluteus maximus*, which is indeed the thickest muscle in the body, would not itself cause it. Fenik (*TBS* 196) thinks this wound implies a shameful blow *from behind*, as if he were fleeing, another hint of a rout (301–5n.). Cf. 13.545ff., when Antilokhos hits Thoon μεταστρεφθέντα δοκεύσας. Aristophanes emended the problem away by reading ὑφορμηθέντα (not found in the epos), supposed to mean 'withdrawing' (Did/bT). The word σκέλος, unique in the epos, hints that Thoas merits contempt (cf. the use of δέρμα at 340f.). It is a vulgar synonym for πούς, related to σκολιός, 'crooked', Latin *scelus*; later verse (save comedy) continues to avoid it unless an *animal's* leg is meant, and it often enters pejorative contexts (e.g. in discussing trousers). LSJ miss this: contrast Hsch. s.v. It describes the 'legs' of a tripod at Pylos (Ta 641). μυών recurs at 324 and in Hellenistic verse. ἔγχεος αἰχμή (20.416), parallel to δουρὸς ἀκωκή (323 and 7×), preserves the original sense of αἰχμή: cf. Myc. /enkhessi-qe aixmans/, 'points for spears' (PY Jn 829).

317–29 Nestor's sons slay two comrades of Sarpedon, which makes us expect their lord's intervention. Maris' wound recalls Amphiklos' in detail and phrasing, but 'a unique combination of familiar details' neatly avoids the monotony of a fourth unconnected killing (Fenik, *TBS* 196). The death of two brothers is typical (5.148ff., 5.152ff., 5.159f. etc.), even when one tries to avenge the other (11.221–63, 11.426ff.); two Greeks slay a warrior and driver at 5.576ff., 11.320ff., 11.328ff.; the more prominent Greek kills first (Antilokhos and Thrasumedes are still together at 17.378); the scene ends with a pathetic comment on the fraternal deaths (cf. 5.559ff., 11.262f.) and the motif of the bereft father, common when brothers die together. Many fight as a team, especially as warrior and driver (C. A. Trypanis, *RhM* 106 (1963) 289–97). But this is the only time when two brothers kill another such pair, and when, in such a duel, a man dies trying to avenge his brother: the outcome signals the Greeks' superiority (contrast the tragic duel of the Dioskouroi and Apharetidai in the *Cypria*).

Amisōdaros and his sons bear real Anatolian names (Scherer, 'Nicht-griechische Personennamen' 41–3): cf. Ἰσεμενδαρος (Caria), Πιξεδαρος (Lycia), Πιξωδαρος (both areas), Ουαδαρος (Pisidia), names in -*da-ro* in the Knossos tablets, and perhaps Pandaros and the town Amisos on the Euxine. Xenomedes of Ceos (*FGH* 442 F 3, fifth century) said Amisodaros was the ruler of Caria (not Lycia) whose daughter married Bellerophon; the fact that he 'reared' the Khimaira does indeed imply this. Thus his sons are Bellerophon's brothers-in-law and Sarpedon's uncles (6.197): the chronological problem proves that Homer has redated Sarpedon (pp. 371–3). The king, unnamed at 6.172ff., was called Amphianax by Pherecydes (*FGH* 3 F 170) and probably Iobates by Hesiod (*Cat.* 43a.88); both place him in Lycia. Clearly this king was traditionally anonymous, which is why Homer could give him a local name.

'Atumnios' resembles the Carian name Tumnes, Lycian Α/Ερμεδυμνος and the border-towns Tumnos and Tumnessos; a Paphlagonian bears the name at 5.581 (in a similar slaying). In legend this and cognate names are linked with both Sarpedon and Apollo, who are related in other ways too (p. 372). Sarpedon quarrelled with his brother Minos over a beloved boy called Miletos or Atumnios, who was the son of Apollo or Zeus ('Apollodorus' 3.1.2); he founded his Lycian realm and Miletos as a result (cf. Hdt. 1.173 and S. Marinatos, *RA* 34 (1949) 11–18). The Gortynians worshipped an *Adymnus*, brother of Europa (Solinus 11.9); an Atumnios was Apollo's lost beloved, bewept in Crete (Nonnus, *Dion.* 11.131, 258, 19.183f.). A Cretan called (*A*)*thumbros*, akin to Sarpedon, settled and was honoured in Caria (*Etym. Magn.* 44.17ff.); cf. Apollo *Thumbraios*, *Thumbra* etc. in the Troad. Clement of Rome (*Homilies* 5.15) says Apollo was the lover of *Tumnaios*' son Brankhos, founder of the oracle at Didyma. The Minoan colony found at

Miletos confirms the links between Crete and S. W. Anatolia; this passage must reflect local saga, like Sarpedon's duel with the Rhodian Tlepolemos (p. 371), since Atumnios is slain by an ancestor of the Neleids who finally ruled Miletos, replacing the Carians (see 2.867f.; Hdt. 1.146; 'Apollodorus' 3.1.2; Sakellariou, *Migration* 362ff.). Bryce (*The Lycians* 33) well argues that the saga arose in the Bronze Age in the area round Miletos, whence the Lukka later migrated to Lycia. That Cretans and then Mycenaeans settled in Miletos, which must equal Hittite Millawata, is certain (K. B. Gödeken in French and Wardle, *Prehistory* 307–15). On the historical background see further 6.168–70n. The notion of Sarpedon's beloved dying in battle, which helps provoke his intervention, anticipates the effect of Patroklos' death on Akhilleus: cf. that of Antilokhos' death in the *Memnonis* (see p. 312). The name Maris is like Greek Maron and Mares, but appears in Hittite and later Anatolian tongues; Homer's knowledge of Anatolian names confirms his East Ionian origin.

317–25 For the typically oral apposition and anacoluthon in 317f. cf. οἱ δὲ δύω σκόπελοι, ὁ μέν ... τὸν δ' ἕτερον (*Od.* 12.73ff.). αὐτοσχεδά is unique for -όν (8×), cf. ἀμφαδά/-όν. Thrasumedes, seen in this battle only here (cf. 14.10), again has the generic epithet ἀντίθεος at *Od.* 3.414, but is αἰχμητής at *Cat.* 35.10. In a neat variation on Meges' blow (314–16), he severs at the equivalent place an arm instead of a leg. ἄφαρ, 'quickly' (cf. ἄφνω, 'suddenly'), sounds odd at the end of a clause: cf. θοῶς at 5.533 (*LfgrE* s.v.). The spear 'rent the top of the arm from the muscles' which join it to the shoulder, and '*utterly* smashed the bone' (for this sense of ἄχρις see 4.522n.). Verse 325 echoes 316: κατὰ δέ uniquely replaces τὸν δέ (11× in this phrase).

326–9 Duals stress the pathos of the brothers' last journey together. Erebos, Night's daughter (*Theog.* 123), is the subterranean 'darkness' where the dead dwell (*Od.* 11.564, 20.356); the phrasing is unusual and thus powerful. ἀκοντιστής is next at *Od.* 18.262. For the Khimaira, and its separated epithet ἀμαιμάκετος, 'raging' (from μαιμάσσω), see 6.179–83n. and A. Leukart in *Festschrift Risch* 344. πόλεσῖν is innovative (Hoekstra, *Modifications* 73n.).

330–4 The unknown Kleoboulos dies because he 'tripped' in the rout (βλαφθείς, 15.489n.): cf. Periphetes, who trips in the rout at 15.645ff., or the Trojans caught and slain when their horses stumble or get out of control (6.37ff., 11.127ff.). In this rapid narrative the poet does not let him beg for his life; in any case such pleas, always made by Trojans, all fail in the *Iliad* (cf. 6.45n.). Typically, his mishap undercuts Oïlean Aias' achievement (cf. 14.521–2n.); Meriones' success at 342f. is more impressive. In a common *hysteron proteron*, the salient fact of the killing comes first, the blow second: contrast 11.240, ἄορι πλῆξ' αὐχένα, λῦσε δὲ γυῖα. From ξίφει, 332–4 =

20.476–8, with ἤλασε for αὐχένα: the victim is one Ekhe*klos*, the context another slaying-catalogue. The heating of the sword by hot blood up to its hilt shows that it was buried in Kleoboulos' neck; this deep slash into the neck recurs in the next killing (339f.). For κωπήεις see 15.713–15n. With 333f. cf. 5.82f. (in another *androktasia*), *Little Iliad* frag. 21.4f. B. = 20.4f. D.; μοῖρα κραταιή (11× epos) is based on the original fem. *κραταιά of κρατύς (cf. Πλάταια from πλατύς), whence the epos formed κραταιός (Risch, *Wortbildung* 74).

335–41 At 14.488ff. Peneleos missed Antenor's son Akamas (14.461–4n.), but beheaded another Trojan; now Meriones slays Akamas, and Peneleos beheads the unknown Lukon. The pattern 'A misses B, B misses A, A kills B with a sword' is adapted to an attack with simultaneous spear-casts like those at 5.655ff., 21.161ff. Initial misses occur with a simultaneous charge at 462ff., 13.604ff. and 22.248–330, Hektor's duel with Akhilleus. This duel ends with a horrific spectacle like 13.616ff., where see n.

335–6 The warriors' failed spear-casts appear in a flash-back (framed by συνέδραμον) to explain why they charge at each other (so bT); note the contrast 'spears' – 'swords'. Repetition of ideas is basic to traditional oral narrative, extending from double clauses, as seen in 336 or 'when they had sworn and concluded the oath', through paired nouns like 'death and doom' down to noun–epithet formulae themselves, where the epithet, by expressing an essential quality of the object, as it were expands the noun: for Irish and Greek examples see K. O'Nolan, *CQ* 28 (1978) 23ff., with H. A. Paraskevaïdes, *The Use of Synonyms in Homeric Formulaic Diction*, Amsterdam 1984.

338–40 Like Menelaos' at 3.362f., Lukon's sword shatters on one of the plates of his foe's helmet. Verse 338 blends ἱππόκομοι κόρυθες (216 = 13.132) with κόρυθος φάλον ἤλασεν (13.614), introducing a contracted gen. in -ου in the process; for φάλος see 13.132–3n. Editors read καυλόν, deeming καλόν, in most good MSS, a corruption after φάλον. But καυλός never means 'hilt' elsewhere (13.162n.), and the enjambment καλὸν | φάσγανον is paralleled (13.611–12n.). φ. and ξίφος were already synonyms for 'sword' in Myc.; swords were not kept distinct from daggers (cf. S. Foltiny, *Arch. Hom.* E 232–4). With 340 cf. 21.117f., πᾶν δέ οἱ εἴσω | δῦ ξ.; the entire *width* of the sword sank into Lukon's neck, since θείνω is used of slashing, not stabbing (Trümpy, *Fachausdrücke* 97ff.).

340–1 'Only his hide held fast, but his head dangled', i.e. only a flap of skin held it. Cf. the warrior hit in the chest whose head lolls like a rain-sodden poppy (8.306). ἔσχεθε is intrans. (cf. 12.461, 13.608). δέρμα, from δέρω, 'flay', has a vulgar nuance like σκέλος at 314 above; the epos uses it 17× for an animal's hide, but applies it to skin only when Athene turns Odysseus into a shrivelled old gaffer (*Od.* 13.431). It finally displaced χρώς ('complex-ion' > 'skin' > 'flesh'). The pejorative touch is meant to amuse the poet's pro-Greek audience. With παρηέρθη, from παραείρω, 'hang beside', cf. παρήορος (152–4n.). ὑπέλυντο δὲ γυῖα extends λύντο δ. γ. (2×), cf. (ὑπέ)λυσε δ. γ.

342–4 Cowardly at 14.488, Akamas now tries to flee, but Meriones, who often kills in routs (5.59ff., 14.514), is too fast for him (cf. 13.249–50n.). κιχείς is the participle of *κίχημι, 'reach', cognate with Engl. 'go'; it was replaced by κιχάνω (Chantraine, *Dict.* s.v.). The rare formula ποσὶ καρπα-λίμοισι recurs at *HyHerm* 225, *Nostoi* frag. 11 B. = 8 D.; cf. πόδεσσί (τε) κ. (809, reversed at 22.166). Verses 343f. = 5.46f., but with στυγερὸς δ' ἄρα μιν σκότος εἷλε· κατὰ δ' ὀφθαλμῶν κέχυτ' ἀχλύς is at 5.696, cf. 20.421.

345–50 Erumas' vivid death should scare us as well as the Trojans. The spear of Idomeneus (last seen at 15.301) enters his mouth to traverse the base of his brain and stick out at the back, emptying his mouth of teeth and filling his eyes with blood; he vainly blows the blood from his nose and mouth, gaping as he gasps for breath. Wounds involving teeth are inflicted at 5.72ff. (from behind), 290ff. (from an angle), 17.617ff. (from the side). Von Kamptz (*Personennamen* 193) derives Erumas from ἐρυ-, 'protect', cf. Erulaos (411), Erumelos; T's variant 'Orumas' is an attempt to emend away the 'problem' that, through an oversight by the poet, *another* Erumas dies at 415! Yet the pre-Greek toponym Erumanthos appears with an *O*- at Pylos (Cn 3), cf. E/Orkhomenos. The runover verb νύξε repeats 343; the rest of 346 = *Od.* 10.162. Save for the formula ὀστέα λευκά, the powerfully assonantal description has few parallels (for a list of head-wounds see 11.95–6n.). ἀνὰ στόμα καὶ κατὰ ῥῖνας neatly expands (ἀν) σ. τε ῥ. τε (3×); the 'black cloud of death' recurs at *Od.* 4.180, with θανάτοιο for the innova-tive θανάτου δέ (for the metaphor cf. 17.591, 20.417f.).

351–7 Verse 351 rounds off the slaying-catalogue: cf. 306 and the end of the Catalogue of Ships (2.760). A simile sums it up, but also opens a new phase, Trojan flight. Moulton (*Similes* 35) compares the sequence, again with similes, at 15.262–80; finding Hektor's brief holding action intrusive, Fenik (*TBS* 193f.) athetizes 358–63, but it is no accident that Thoas pro-poses a like action at 15.281ff., where see n.

352–5 The Greeks fall upon the Trojans like wolves upon lambs, a standard image (cf. 4.471, 8.131, 11.72, 13.102f., 22.263f.); the Myrmidons were likened to wolves at 156–63, where see n. (a single hero is instead compared to a lion or boar). Sheep and goats, often pastured together in Greece, are collectively μῆλα, perhaps cognate with *small* (i.e. 'small ani-mals'); cf. 10.485f. The shift of gender in μήλων ... αἵ, as if ὄϊες preceded, is paralleled in reverse at 5.137–40; it may add pathos – they are *mothers*, deprived of their children by the foolish shepherd who let them scatter. The bad herdsmanship, often to blame for such losses (15.323–5n.), evokes Hektor's folly. ἐπέχραον, 'beset' (also 356, *Od.* 2.50), is related to ζαχρηής (13.682–4n.); for σίντης see 20.165n.

356–7 These vv. form a chiastic antithesis, based on μνήσασθε/λάθοντο δὲ θούριδος ἀλκῆς (7×, 15.322, cf. 602). Warriors scream most in the rout, when most casualties occur (14.506–22n.): the pursuers yell too (cf. Artemis' epithet κελαδεινή, 183n.). δυσκέλαδος describes Envy at *Erga* 196 and the Erinues' song at Aesch. *Seven* 867.

358–63 Aias still opposes Hektor, who is now the one under fire (contrast 114ff.); for Hektor's holding action see 351–7n. Aias is called 'the great', as in 'great Telamonian Aias' (12×), to distinguish him from Oïlean Aias, who is 'smaller' and 'swift' (2.528f., 10.110). The unique article in ὁ μέγας signals an innovative adaptation of Αἴας τε μ. (9.169), Αἴαντα μέγαν (2×). For (Ϝ)ιδρείη see 7.197–9n.; Hektor brags of his skill with his 'oxhide' at 7.237ff. (for 'oxhide shield' cf. 13.159–61n.). A neat chiasmus includes δοῦπον ἀκόντων (11.364 = 20.451): the whistle of arrows conveys their speed, the thud of javelins their weight (so bT). Hektor 'watches for' these sounds: note the synaesthesia (cf. 13.837n.). σκέπτομαι (also at 17.652), a metathesis of *σπεκγ- (Latin *specio*), is used in Ionic prose but replaced by σκοπέω in Attic. For ἐτεραλκέα νίκην, 'victory with help from others', later reinterpreted as 'victory for the losing side', see 15.737–40n. and A. Casabona, *Annales de la Faculté des Lettres d'Aix* 43 (1967) 1–11 (differently 7.26–7n.). The imperfect σάω (also at 21.238, imperative 2× *Od.*) is from athematic *σάωμι, not *σαόω (> ἐσάωσα): Chantraine (*GH* I 307) adduces the second person σάως in Alcaeus frag. 313.

364–93 Many find the simile difficult, and the ditch a deeper obstacle than did the Trojans; Leaf excised 364–71. It is bad enough that the rampart is ignored (cf. 15.362–7n.), worse that the ditch lets Hektor's chariot pass yet stops the Trojan masses, who (Leaf assumes) are on foot; the situation was reversed, he thinks, at 12.61ff., when they left their vehicles on their side of it. But Homer at once clarifies why the ditch now stops them – their chariots are smashed in it (370f.): on its military purpose see 12.65–6n. Since Apollo erased a part of it to let the Trojans cross in their chariots (15.358f.), we may infer that Hektor flees through that gap, whereas his men run foul of it elsewhere (Albracht, *Kampfschilderung* II 14f.). But Homer wanted to contrast his withdrawal with his laborious advance. To make it more inglorious, Hektor must abandon his men: the ditch offers an easy way to arrange this and to fulfil Pouludamas' warning that they would retreat in chaos by the paths they had taken to advance (12.225ff.). Verses 364–93 also shift attention from Hektor's past clash with Aias to his future duel with Patroklos, who already seeks him out (382f.). They display a neat ring-structure (Thalmann, *Conventions* 17f.):

A 364-7 The Trojans flee (weather-simile with λαῖλαψ)
B 367f. Hektor flees (Ἕκτορα δ' ἵπποι | ἔκφερον ὠκύποδες)
C 368-71 The Trojans' chariots break in the trench
D 372f. Patroklos pursues (| Πάτροκλος δ' ...)
E 373-6 The Trojans choke the paths in flight
D' 377f. Patroklos makes for the densest mêlée (| Πάτροκλος δ' ...)
C' 378f. The Trojans' chariots are in chaos
B' 380-3 Hektor flees, chased by Patroklos (τὸν δ' ἔκφερον ὠκέες ἵπποι)
A' 384-93 The Trojans flee (weather-simile with λαῖλαψ)

364-5 'As when a cloud enters the sky from Olumpos, after bright air, when Zeus extends a squall ...' The cloud starts on Zeus's mountain-top and moves off the peak just as the Trojans are driven off the ships, the image of 297ff.; but now Zeus is blowing up a storm, as in the next simile (384ff.). Thus the storm evolves as the Greek assault, backed by Zeus, gains force (cf. 297-300n.). *Pace* Chantraine (*GH* II 99), αἰθέρος ἐκ δίης means simply *'after* clear weather', ἐξ εὐδίας; cf. καύματος ἔξ, 'after heat' (5.865, in a cognate simile), ἐκ νυκτῶν, 'after dark' (*Od.* 12.286), ἐκ δὲ αἰθρίης τε καὶ νηνεμίης συνδραμεῖν ἐξαπίνης νέφεα (Hdt. 1.87.2, cf. 7.188.2) and LSJ s.v. ἐκ II 2. For the phrase cf. *Od.* 19.540, *HyDem* 70: δῖα is aptly formed from **diw-*, '(bright) sky', 'Zeus'. Many, taking ἐκ as 'out of', complain that the cloud cannot come both 'from Olumpos' and 'out of the air', but cf. Leaf's Appendix H. Ancient comments ('αἰθήρ may stand for ἀήρ', Nic/A) reflect Aristarchus' false belief that the αἰθήρ could not contain clouds (14.286-8n.).

366-9 The Trojans flee from the ships and recross the ditch (364-93n.). From γένετο, 366 = 12.144, 15.396 (cf. 373, 4.456). ἵπποι | – ∪∪ ὠκύποδες (etc.) is a split formula found 4×: cf. ἵππων | ὠκυπόδων (etc.), ἵ. ὠ. (etc.), 6× each, and ὠ. ∪∪ ἵ. (2× epos) – the phrase is unusually flexible. σὺν τεύχεσι implies that the horses managed to bear Hektor away despite his heavy armour. For λαὸν | Τρωϊκόν cf. 17.724, 21.296.

370-1 The Trojan failure to cross the trench contrasts with Patroklos' success (380). Their chariot-poles snap at the weak point behind the yoke (ἐν πρώτῳ ῥυμῷ) when the horses try to climb the side of the ditch; this leaves the pair free to run (cf. 6.40, 23.393). For technical details see Crouwel, *Chariots* 93-6. On the expanded formula ἐρυσάρματες ⟨ὠκέες⟩ ἵπποι see 15.352-4n. After πολλοί the dual ἄξαντ' is odd; many chariots break, so we need a plur. denoting many pairs. This could be a dual replacing a plur., a usage possible at 1.567, 3.279 and 9.182ff., certain at *HyAp* 487 and recognized by Zenodotus; for Ionic bards' problems with dual verbs see 13.346n. But the hemistich surely comes from contexts like 6.40, where it denotes one chariot and pair; cf. 17.387, where παλάσσετο μαρναμένοιιν describes two armies but is derived from duels between two men. For the 'neglect' of ϝ- cf. 507, where λίπον ἅρματ' ἀνάκτων denotes a single vehicle (cf. 13.533–9n.); the ἄνακτες are the horses' 'masters' (cf. 15.323–5n., *Od.* 10.216 and the name 'Hipponax').

372–6 With σφεδανόν, 'violently' (3×), cf. σφόδρα; with 373 cf. 367, 783. The Trojans scatter and fill the paths over the plain, raising dust-clouds that recall the cloud-similes. Paths are notoriously dusty (13.335); dust is the usual atmosphere of a retreat, especially by chariot. ἀέλλη (from ἄημι) means a 'swirl' of it; dust is likened to a θύελλα at 23.366. A nom. in -ᾰ appears at *HyAphr* 208 and in Alcaeus (ἄυελλα), but Hesychius' entry ἀείλη shows that the form in -η is not merely a unique epicism based on the oblique cases. The dust rises *up to* the clouds: the MSS read ὑπαί in this phrase (15.625, 23.874), not ὑπό (νέφος is not from *sn-*). For τανύοντο see 23.323–5n., for μῶνυξ 5.236n. The first half of 376 = 12.74, whence A's variant here; but other parallels protect the vulgate (45 = 11.803, 14.146).

377–9 Patroklos heads for the most chaotic sector, where he can do most damage. ἔχε is from ϝέχω, 'drive' (13.326–7n.). ἀνακυμβαλιάζω, a *hapax* in Greek, is obscure. The context suggests that it means 'overturn', a cause of the Trojans' falling from their vehicles, or 'rattle', its result; it may be cognate with κύμβαχος, 'headlong', or κύμβαλον, 'cymbal' (cf. 15.535–6n.). Both renderings are ancient (Hsch. s.v.). Chariots overturn at 23.436f., and rattle away empty in routs (11.160, 15.453); *LfgrE* s.v. think 'overturn' would require a middle verb, but the incident may be parallel to 6.37ff., where a Trojan is flung out face down when his chariot-pole snaps (cf. 371). At 11.534 a vehicle drives over corpses.

380–3 The shift from the Trojans' chariots back to Patroklos' becomes clear only at 382; 381, absent in a papyrus and most early codices, is interpolated from 867 to show whose vehicle is meant (866 = 383!). This shift looks like an improvisation to introduce the heroic feat of leaping the ditch, which Hektor vainly boasted his chariot could do (8.179). Perhaps Homer momentarily forgot that at 370 he had made the Trojan chariots fall foul of the trench, and then adds 382 to explain that he means Patroklos'. Delebecque imagines a confusion with horseback riding (*Cheval* 77f.). Other signs of clumsiness are the chiasmus of ὠκέες ἵπποι and ἵεσθαι with different referents, and the need to supply ἵεσθαι with κέκλετο (cf. 22.206). βαλέειν δέ ἑ ἵετο θυμός (8.301, 310, cf. 13.386f.) is reshaped as κ. θ., | ἵ. γὰρ β.

384–93 A fine storm-simile brings to a climax the set of cloud-images describing the intensifying Trojan rout (297ff., 364–5nn.). A rout is likened to a rain-fed river in flood at a like stage in Diomedes' *aristeia* (Fenik, *TBS* 20, on 5.87ff.); cf. 5.597ff., 11.492ff. Images of torrents often depict noise (4.452–5). This one has burst the usual banks of an extended simile to flood nine verses; in a standard oral technique, its paratactic construction loosens as it sweeps on (Scott, *Simile* 155f.). Zeus's λαῖλαψ (365) has now hit the earth; the torrents do fearful harm as they rush seaward, 'groaning loudly'. Noise is the explicit point of comparison, since the Trojan mares 'groan loudly' as they flee; 391 rhymes with 393, but στενάχω is no mere metaphor for their neighing – it signals their grief and pain. The implicit point of comparison, however, is controversial. The Trojans rush *from* the sea, not *to* it; they suffer as they go, rather than do harm; but they too are driven by Zeus, just as Hektor charged like a rock dislodged by Zeus's rain (13.137ff.). The storm shows Zeus's wrath at men's crooked judgements; this is stated in three verses, too many for a redundant detail. Van der Valk (*Researches* II 475n.) and Moulton (*Similes* 35–8) compare 21.522–4, where a Trojan rout is likened to a city destroyed because of the gods' anger; here the Trojans are linked with wrongdoing, and the poet comes near to an open justification of Troy's fall, all the more persuasive because we are left to infer it for ourselves.

The *Iliad*'s tragic vision emphasizes the amoral gods of myth, but we sometimes glimpse 'an underlying conviction that these powers are on the side of right and justice' (G. M. Calhoun in *Companion* 449; cf. Lloyd-Jones, *Justice of Zeus* 1ff.). In such contexts 'Zeus' and 'the gods' are rarely distinct. Cf. Zeus's interest in the Abioi as paragons of justice, Menelaos' faith that Zeus Xenios must punish the Trojans, the muted criticism of Paris' morality, or the gods' wrath over an unburied body (13.4–7, 13.620–39, 13.660–72nn., 22.358). The *Odyssey*, for its own poetic ends, is more overtly optimistic, both in its main plot and in detail: gods travel incognito to watch human conduct (17.485–7), abhor evil acts but honour justice (14.83f.), and grant the righteous and pious king a flourishing realm (19.109–14, with the classic statement by Hesiod at *Erga* 225–47 and West's n. *ad loc.*). Conversely, the injustice of a few can ruin a whole society (*Erga* 240).

The Hesiodic parallels and rarity of references to such beliefs in the *Iliad*, where Zeus cares above all for guests and suppliants, have led many to suspect this simile. Dodds (*The Greeks and the Irrational* 32) termed it 'a reflex of later conditions, which, by an inadvertence common in Homer, has been allowed to slip into a simile'; H. Munding detects a sententious 'Hesiodic' interpolation (*Philologus* 105 (1961) 161–77, refuted by L. Bertelli, *Atti dell'Accademia delle Scienze a Torino, Classe di Scienze morali* 101 (1966/7) 371–93); Leaf deleted 387f., claiming that they spoil the simile's balance. But, as Griffin says (*HLD* 41), this image is less isolated than it seems: when Zeus grieves for his son he sends bloody rain (459), when he plans a grim battle he thunders all night (7.478), and when angry he lashes the earth until she groans (2.781–3). I doubt the old view that the *Iliad*, *Odyssey* and *Erga* reflect successive stages in the evolution of the idea of justice, and of Zeus's concern for it (E. A. Havelock, *The Greek Concept of Justice*, Cambridge, Mass. 1978, 214f.). Linguistic data prove Homer prior to Hesiod (see pp. 13f.), but in traditional societies concepts change slowly; bards chose from the common stock those ideas suited to their current poetic ends. We forget at our peril how few of their songs survive.

384–5 The heavy rhythm κελαινὴ βέβριθε χθών varies γαῖα μέλαινα; cf. κελαινῇ ... αἴη (*Aspis* 153) and also κ. λαίλαπι ἶσος (11.747). The water, not the clouds, weighs down the earth: cf. κουφίζουσαν ἄρουραν of dry tilth (*Erga* 463). Elsewhere the earth is heavy with crops, gold or people (*HyDem* 472f., *HyAp* 135f., *Cypria* frag. 1). Rainfall weighs heavily (ἐπιβρίσῃ) in the related simile at 5.91, cf. 12.286. Greece receives a third of its rain in November and December alone; cf. Διὸς ὄμβρῳ | πολλῷ ὀπωρινῷ (*Erga* 676f., cf. 674). χέει ὕδωρ recurs at 4 = 9.15 (simile).

386–8 The hiatus after δή, kept in many good MSS, is protected by 6.306, 10.536 etc. κοτεσσάμενος χαλεπήνῃ recurs at *Od.* 5.147 (of Zeus), 19.83. The rest is paralleled in Hesiod: cf. *Theog.* 85, διακρίνοντα θέμιστας; *Erga* 221, σκολιῆς δὲ δίκης κρίνωσι θ.; 251, θεῶν ὄπιν οὐκ ἀλέγοντες; and personified 'Justice' is expelled at 220ff. (cf. 256ff.), unless this merely means that the 'case' (δίκη) is refused and the plaintiff forcibly driven away (Havelock, *op. cit.* 136f.; for this sense cf. *Erga* 39 etc.). Homer too uses personification, as in the Litai (9.502ff.), but 388 is too vague to prove it here. Oral precedents (θέμιστες) formed the basis for decision by judges whose duty it was to pick (κρίνειν) the right ones and decide accordingly; thus δίκαι and θέμιστες are equated at *Od.* 9.215, cf. *Theog.* 235f. On the sense and etymology of δίκη see further 18.497–508n., *LfgrE* s.v., Richardson on *HyDem* 152, Hoekstra on *Od.* 14.59. M. Gagarin (*CPh* 68 (1973) 86) takes it as 'legal process' here and at *Od.* 14.84; M. W. Dickie (*CPh* 73 (1978) 91–101) defends the usual view that it means 'justice', but we cannot exclude 'case' here. Properly, the king, elders or others agreed upon by the parties decide (18.497ff.); here they impose a bad ruling by force, heedless of the gods who watch over human conduct (Griffin, *HLD* 179ff.). In the *Iliad* the gods more readily gain amusement from this than punish sinners, but the latter idea is ancient: the formula 'gaze of the gods', θεῶν ὄπις, already connotes 'punishment' (as also at *Od.* 14.88, 20.215 and 3× *Erga*).

389–92 Two couplets, rich in assonance (especially at the verse-ends), state the same basic idea. First come the rivers flowing in spate, then the torrents eroding the slopes and last, implicit in the first couplet but overt in the second, the harm they do to the terraced fields on which humans subsist (the simile at 5.87ff. also stresses this). Soil erosion, placed last for emphasis, is a fit requital for our maltreatment of nature; it was far advanced by Plato's time (*Critias* 111c–d). ποταμοὶ πλήθουσι ῥέοντες is paralleled at 4.452, 5.87, 11.492, *Od.* 19.207 (similes). The torrents aptly 'cut away' the hills: the same verb described the Trojans scattered in rout (374). κλῖτύς has replaced κλειτύς, perhaps by analogy with κλίνω (Wackernagel, *SUH* 74f.). The sea is πορφύρεος only here (yet cf. 14.16–19n.), but the epithet often describes a wave; this may be an *ad hoc* adaptation like ἅλα μαρμαρέην (14.271–4n.), cf. ἁλιπόρφυρος (*Od.*, Alcman). For the earth or sea 'groaning' see 2.95, 2.781–4, 24.79, *Theog.* 843, 858. The unique ἐπὶ κάρ means 'headlong' (cf. Latin *praeceps*): cf. ἀνὰ κάρ in Hippocrates, glossed εἰς τὸ ἄνω μέρος by Galen (19.79 Kühn). Aristarchus took κάρ as short for κάρα; the same form appears as a loc. in Old Hittite *kit-kar*, '(here) at the head'. Nussbaum (*Head and Horn* 75ff., 261ff.) shows that it is an adverbialized relic, a loc. or perhaps acc. in origin, which has become one word like πρόχνυ from πρός + γόνυ (cf. Peters, *Laryngale* 234). μινύθω is intrans. (cf. 17.738, *Erga* 409). ἔργ' ἀνθρώπων (19.131, *Od.* 6.259) means 'fields', especially the laboriously constructed terraces so ubiquitous in Greece.

394–8 The carnage which ends this phase of Patroklos' *aristeia* (278–418n.) starts with a reminder that he is still obeying his orders (83ff.) by blocking the Trojans' front ranks from their retreat and driving them back upon the ships: cf. the tactics used at 10.363f., 21.1ff. (Akhilleus). This device also lets Patroklos rout the foe again, fatally extending his foray (Krischer, *Konventionen* 29). He exacts that requital for prior Greek losses which Pouludamas had feared (13.745f.): on this usage of ποινή cf. 13.658–9n. The killing-ground is between Troy to the S.E., the ships to the N. and the Skamandros to the E. (13.675n.); the need to cross the river to reach the city is not mentioned, perhaps because it was not a serious obstacle (14.433–4n.). τείχεος ὑψηλοῖο means the Greek rampart at 512, 12.388, but the Trojan wall, as here, at 702, 21.540. ἐπικείρω, 'cut off', was metaphorical at 120; misunderstanding of it gave rise to a variant ἐπέκυρσε. παλιμπετές recurs in *Od.* 5.27 and Hellenistic poets. πόληος … ἐπιβαινέμεν, 'enter the city' (cf. *Od.* 6.262), is so phrased because early towns were on elevated sites (cf. Thuc. 1.7.1).

399–418 This catalogue of Patroklos' victims is an expanded version of the massacres, consisting largely of lists of names, caused by minor warriors elsewhere: cf. 693–5 (Patroklos), and Teukros at 8.274–7, Leonteus at 12.188–94, both summed up by the same verse as 418. Here the structure is that X falls first (399), Y second (402), then Z (411) and then *nine* others (415–17). The narrative speeds up with the death-rate; the victims, all unknown, bear Greek names, but Sarpedon's reaction shows that many are Lycians.

399–400 Pronoos is facing Patroklos, who has turned about (394–8n.), but dies because he exposes his chest behind his shield (400 = 312). Eustathius (1067.6) saw word-play in that Πρό-νοος falls πρῶτος. The name may be related to Thestor, 'seer', the next victim, who is his driver. Oddly enough, a Pronoos slew the seer Alkmaion ('Apollodorus' 3.7.6), who had a son called Amphoteros (cf. 415); this Arcadian saga might also be evoked by the names 'Erumas' (415) and Ἀργεάδην Πολύμηλον (417), cf. Erumanthos (345–50n.) and Ἀρκαδίην πολύμηλον (179–92n.). At 12.394 Sarpedon kills an Alkmaon son of Thestor! δουρὶ φαεινῷ (also at 409), λῦσε δὲ γυῖα and δεύτερον ὁρμηθείς recur in the reverse situation at 465–7, when Patroklos first slays the driver and then engages Sarpedon.

401–10 The unique introduction of a new victim after δούπησεν δὲ πεσών may signal Patroklos' speed, like the oral anacoluthon in 402, where the verb is delayed until the sentence has restarted at 404; Ferrari (*Oralità* 40) discerns a break in an oral poet's verbal flow, rapidly corrected (cf. 15.429–35n.). Enops, who begets much cannon-fodder for both sides (14.442–8n.), is soon reforged back into an epithet for bronze (407–8n.). Thestor's death is typical. He crouches in his chariot, no doubt too scared to try to turn it round; cf. how one driver is too alarmed at his leader's death to turn his vehicle, another is hit and releases the reins, and two Trojans drop them in panic (13.394ff., 5.580ff., 11.122ff.). This last parallel begins with a like anacoluthon, when biographical detail interrupts the killing. Patroklos spears Thestor in the mouth and yanks him forward over the rail; he dies gaping like a fish hauled ashore by hook and line, a grotesque, apt and unflattering image. So too Patroklos mocks Kebriones, who falls from Hektor's chariot, by likening him to a diver, and Peneleos raises the severed head of a Trojan whom he had speared in the eye (746ff., 14.498f.). Erumas, whose name is reused at 415, received a like blow to the mouth at 345, where see n.

402–6 For ἐϋξέστῳ ἐνὶ δίφρῳ see 17.464–5n.: here εὐ- is irresolvable (cf. 104–6n.). The hiatus before ἠῒχθησαν is anomalous, unlike that before (F)αλείς; αὐτοῦ has its weakened anaphoric sense (Chantraine, *GH* II 157). The vulgate has ἕλκε in 406, but εἷλκε in 409 as usual (save at 18.581); Alexandrian poets kept the latter usage. Aristarchus (Did/AT) read ἕλκε (cf. p. 26 n. 30), but augmented forms are better, being closer to the bards' vernacular; early texts had simply ΕΛΚΕ (see pp. 33–4).

407–8 Supply εἷλκε from the main clause. Caught fish epitomize pathetic helplessness (5.487, *Od.* 10.124, 22.384). Angling, rarely mentioned by Homer, is practised only as a last resort (*Od.* 4.368f., 12.330ff.); this oddity of the heroes' diets, already noticed by Plato (*Rep.* 3.404B) and Eubulus (frag. 118), was used as an argument by the Chorizontes. Aristarchus well replied that eating fish – or vegetables – was simply deemed unheroic: see Arn/A on 747; 15.679–84n.; Schmidt, *Weltbild* 182–7; Montanari, *Studi Classici e Orientali* 25 (1976) 325–31. The blessings of a wealthy realm include plentiful fish (*Od.* 19.113); fishing enters the everyday world of the similes at 24.80–2, when Iris dives into the sea like a weighted fish-hook, and *Od.* 12.251–4, when Scylla hauls men ashore just as an angler, fishing from a point with rod and baited hook, hauls fish from the sea (literally θύραζε, 'outdoors', with a dead metaphor, as here). This image is no less grisly. The angler is using a rod, which corresponds to Patroklos' spear, and a flaxen line with a bronze hook; he sits on a jutting rock because the catch is best there (προβλής occurs in a simile at 2.396 and 3× *Od.*).

The ancients debated why this fish is called ἱερός (cf. Pfeiffer on Callim. frag. 378). Hellenistic poets identified it as the λεῦκος or as the κάλλιχθυς, also called ἀνθίας and χρύσοφρυς (dorado). Clitarchus equated the latter with the πομπίλος (cf. A. W. Mair on Oppian, *Hal.* 1.185), which was called 'holy' ('Epimenides', *FGH* 457 F 22, cf. Dionysius Iambus and others in Ath. 7.282A–284E): he claimed it was so called because it escorted ships to port (*ibid.*). Aristotle, who is not discussing Homer, offers a like report about the ἀνθίας: since, when it is present, sponge-divers do not fear to dive, they call it 'holy' (*Hist. An.* 9.620b33). Oppian applies this story to the κάλλιχθυς, also called καλλιώνυμος (*Hal.* 5.627ff.). Hence this fish may be meant: see Thompson, *A Glossary of Greek Fishes*, London 1947, s.vv. Homer's next marine simile concerns a diver (742ff.).

Aristarchus denied that any specific fish is intended, claiming that ἱερός means merely 'well-fed' and so 'big', just as a holy ox grows fat by grazing freely! Since ἱερός is cognate with Sanskrit *iṣiráḥ*, 'strong', a sense sometimes still seen in Homer (e.g. 10.56, 24.681, or ἱερὸν μένος), the fish may be 'vigorous' or 'active' (see J. T. Hooker, ΙΕΡΟΣ *in Early Greek*, Innsbruck 1980; S. West, J. Russo on *Od.* 1.2, 18.60). Otherwise ἱερός is merely a metrically useful filler, as at 17.464, ἱερῷ ἐνὶ δίφρῳ (where see n.). Leaf thought it is 'holy' because the early Greeks had a taboo against fish: but the taboos amassed by Frazer (on Paus. 7.22.4) relate mainly to the Levant and Egypt. ἤνοπι χαλκῷ describes cauldrons at 18.349 = *Od.* 10.360. The obscure ἦνοψ once began with F- (cf. 401); it clearly means 'bright', and is an archaism obsolescent beside αἴθοπι (12× epos of armour).

411–14 For Erulaos' name see 345–50n. Patroklos must be on foot to grab a stone (cf. 734, and παραστάς in 404): Homer takes for granted that he often mounts and dismounts in rapid pursuit, save when he jumps down to fight Sarpedon and Hektor (427, 733). With the latter half of 411 cf. 511, 12.388, 20.288 (all with ἐπεσσύμενον, not -ος); 412 = 20.387 (cf. 20.475). From κεφαλήν, 412–14 = 578–80 (with νεκρῷ for γαίη), describing the next minor casualty. On 414 see 13.541–4n.

415–18 Patroklos kills as many Trojans as all the preceding warriors together (311–50). Lists of victims' names almost always precede a hostile intervention, often resulting from divine help: cf. 692ff., where such a catalogue heralds Apollo's intervention, or 5.677, 5.703, 8.273, 11.299, 21.209. Such lists contain seven or nine names; more would be tedious, and for the enemy not to react would be implausible (Fenik, *TBS* 68, 120).

Erumas is reused from 345, Ekhios from 15.339. Aristarchus distinguished Amphoteros from ἀμφότερος by altering the accent, a dubious expedient (Hrd/A); for the name, common in Ionic inscriptions (Fraser and Matthews, *Names* s.v.), see on 399f. Epaltes and Ekhios evoke sinister beasts, Ekhios the snake, Epaltes the owl, like Ephialtes (13.422, 13.478–80nn.). Tlepolemos, presumably a Lycian, is surely based on the Tlepolemos slain by the Lycian Sarpedon (see below). Damastorides is a handy patronymic reused 4× *Od.* Like Ipheus, Puris is unknown: cf. Lycian *Puresi* and *Purihimeti* = Πυριματις (L. Zgusta, *Kleinasiatische Personennamen*, Prague 1964, 437), Πυρις in Thasian inscriptions (Fraser and Matthews, *Names* s.v.) and *Pu-ri* at Knossos (B 799 etc.). Euhippos and Polumelos have similar meanings and are both used as epithets (see on 399f.): ἐΰιππος is at *Cat.* 150.21, *HyAp* 210, but Ἐΰ- cannot be restored here (cf. 104–6n.). Names in -ιππος are post-Myc.: see P. H. Ilievski in *Res Mycenaeae* 210. The historical Argeadai were a Macedonian clan with a name based on Ἄργος. For 418 see on 399f.

419–683 Sarpedon intervenes. Zeus, to avert his son's doom, suggests wafting him away alive, but Here persuades him to have Sleep and Death rescue his body. Sarpedon kills Patroklos' trace-horse, but is slain by Patroklos. A fierce fight erupts, until the Greeks strip Sarpedon of his armour. Zeus sends Apollo, Sleep and Death to convey his body to Lycia for burial

419–683 This episode, prepared for at 317–29 and predicted by Zeus at 15.67, neatly achieves several important effects (Wilamowitz, *IuH* 135ff.; Reinhardt, *IuD* 341ff.). Patroklos' exploit is needed to make him push his success too far and neglect Akhilleus' warning; by slaying Sarpedon, second in rank to Hektor and the only son of a god on the Trojan side (Aineias excepted), Patroklos shows himself a worthy deputy to Akhilleus. With Sarpedon we also find the fate of the slain man's body and armour becoming a major question. Patroklos wins the armour but not the body, the same outcome as in his own case; it is ironic that Sarpedon's panoply becomes a prize in Patroklos' funeral games (23.798ff.). Since Hektor does not kill Patroklos explicitly to avenge Sarpedon, there is no direct anticipation of Hektor's own death. Yet Zeus makes Hektor his agent in avenging his son (649), and by killing Sarpedon Patroklos gives Zeus no choice but to kill him. The whole *Patrokleia* has a symmetrical structure, with Sarpedon's death (preceded by that of his charioteer), then the fight over Sarpedon's body, then the death of Hektor's driver Kebriones, a fight over *his* body, and Patroklos' death (to be followed by the fight over *his* corpse). Wilamowitz excised 432–58, 491*b*–503*a* and 508–658, but such cuts ruin the balance of the narrative, with its anticipation of Kebriones' fall and Hektor's own intervention. The episode is in ring-form (M. E. Clark and W. D. E.

Coulson, *MH* 35 (1978) 65ff.):

Sarpedon has been built up as a powerful and sympathetic figure. He slew Herakles' Rhodian son Tlepolemos and breached the Greek battlements (5.628ff., 12.307ff.); his true awareness of *noblesse oblige* in his speech to Glaukos (12.310ff.) makes his fall all the more tragic. As head of the Trojan allies (12.101), he is loyal to Hektor but unafraid to rebuke him; his status in the army, closely analogous to Akhilleus', is one reason why Homer made him Patroklos' greatest victim.

As the only son of Zeus before Troy, Sarpedon is too prominent to be the poet's invention. Now his fate is adumbrated when Tlepolemos deals him a grave wound, but 'his father still warded ruin from him', and 'it was not fated' for him to die (5.662, 5.674f.); he begs Hektor to save his body from the foe and to let him die in Troy, if he may never return to Lycia (684ff.), but his appeal falls flat, since his wound is not fatal. Homer already had his death and transfer to Lycia in mind, and knew a local saga wherein Tlepolemos slew *him* in Lycia (so M. Valleton, *De Iliadis fontibus et compositione*, Leiden 1915, 126); cf. the Milesian saga behind the death of Sarpedon's beloved Atumnios (317–29n.). There was a tradition that Tlepolemos survived: like Askalaphos, he takes part in the battle against Penthesileia in Dictys 4.2; [Aristotle], *Mir. Ausc.* 107, says he finally went to Italy. The poet warns his hearers to revise their expectations, by saying that Sarpedon is *not yet* fated to die (cf. 12.402f.). In Hesiod, the Sarpedon who fought at Troy is a son of Zeus and Europē, and thus Minos' brother (*Cat.* 140f., cf. Aesch. frag. 99, Hellanicus *FGH* 4 F 94, [Eur.] *Rhesus* 29); Sarpedon's comrade Glaukos has the same name as Minos' son. Homer surely introduced Sarpedon from an earlier era so that Patroklos could kill a god's son (so Severyns, *Homère* 82f., and E. Howald, *MH* 8 (1951) 111ff.); the fact that Sarpedon's comrades include the sons of Amisodaros, his own grandfather, confirms the anachronism (317–29n.)! Homer evaded the problem by renaming the hero's mother Laodameia (6.199); for this device cf. 13.694–7n. Others posited a homonymous grandfather and grandson (Diodorus 5.79.3), or made Sarpedon live three generations ('Apollodorus' 3.1.2, probably from *Cat.* 140.20)!

Since Homer wishes to give Sarpedon respect like that which he shows for the Aineiadai, no doubt because his cousin Glaukos was ancestor to ruling families in Ionia (508–31n.), his body is spirited to Lycia. This motif could be traditional, but may come from the *Memnonis*, where Memnon's mother Eos obtained immortality for her son; in Quintus of Smyrna (2.550–92) the winds bear his body away, but in a vase of *c.* 480 B.C. the bearers are Eos, Sleep and Death (*LIMC* s.v. Eos, no. 320). The *Aithiopis* also made Thetis snatch Akhilleus from the pyre and take him to the White Isle. In Sarpedon's case his foe Here insists that he must not be immortalized, but proposes the rescue of his corpse. H. Pestalozzi (*Die Achilleis als Quelle der Ilias*, Zurich 1945, 14), Schadewaldt (*Welt* 155–202) and Kullmann (*Quellen* 34) deduce that his death is based on Memnon's: cf. pp. 312f. for the close parallels between the two tales. Fenik suspects that the resemblances are multiforms of typical elements, in which no version is basic (*TBS* 231–40), but the similarities are too great for coincidence (so Clark and Coulson, *art. cit.*; L. M. Slatkin, *TAPA* 116 (1986) 2ff.).

Sarpedon's background suggests that he was once a non-Greek god (cf. H. E. Zwicker, *RE* IIA (1921) 35–47). His name was borrowed into Greek as Σαρπᾱδων, before the Ionic sound-shift of ᾱ to η; it appears in Lycian as *zrppudeine* (Bryce, *The Lycians* 26f.), cf. the Lycian name Σερποδις (von Kamptz, *Personennamen* 313). Demes were named after him at Tlos and Xanthos (Bryce, *loc. cit.*); his cult at Xanthos no doubt centred on his supposed tomb (Appian, *Bell. Civ.* 4.78, with Nagy in C. A. Rubino and C. W. Shelmerdine, edd., *Approaches to Homer*, Austin 1983, 194ff.). A Cilician hill named after him had a shrine of Apollo Sarpedonios and Artemis Sarpedonia with an oracle (Strabo 14.676, Diodorus 32.10.2); Hermippus of Berytus reports a dream-oracle of his in the Troad (Tertullian, *De Anima* 46.11). Hills, headlands and islands were linked with him, as with Apollo (cf. *HyAp* 30–44): the Gorgons' isle was called 'Sarpedon' (*Cypria* frag. 32 B. = 26 D., cf. Stesichorus frag. 183), as was a windy headland in Thrace (Simonides frag. 534, Pherecydes *FGH* 3 F 145, Aesch. *Suppl.* 869ff., Hdt. 7.58, Ap. Rhod. 1.211ff. with schol.), where a brute named Sarpedon lived until Herakles slew him ('Apollodorus' 2.5.9; Tlepolemos is Herakles' *son*). Since, in Cretan/Lycian legend, either Apollo or Sarpedon loved Atumnios (317–29n.), Apollo Sarpedonios may be a syncretism based on a Cretan and Anatolian god akin to 'Lycian' Apollo (so L. Preller, *Griechische Mythologie* II, Berlin 1875, 133); hence, perhaps, the role of Sarpedon's brother Apollo in sending him to Lycia. Popular etymology probably linked his name with the winds via the Harpuiai, 'snatchers' (149–50n.): Vermeule compares the Harpy-Tomb at Xanthos, on which harpies bear away the dead, adding 'it is not too surprising that Homer makes Sarpedon the object of the only big snatch in the *Iliad*, though he transformed the carriers from lady birds to Sleep and Death, to match the more familiar configurations of epic mortality' (*Death* 169).

I conclude that Homer or a predecessor made Sarpedon die at Troy because that was where a great Asiatic warrior had to die, just as the *Nibelungenlied* falsely synchronizes Attila and Theoderic (cf. Bowra, *Tradition and Design* 157f.); but, needing to return his body to Lycia as local cult required, the poet adapted the tale of Memnon's death. In his *Sack of Troy* Stesichorus transferred the motif to Hekabe, whom Apollo conveyed to Lycia, no doubt because Hektor was Apollo's son (frags. 198, 224); Ἑκάβη is from the god's epithet *ἑκᾱβόλος (716–20n.).

419–21 The rare adj. ἀμιτροχίτων, 'with unbelted tunic' (cf. Aristotle frag. 584 and Nonnus, *Dion.* 48.507), attests an unknown peculiarity of Lycian everyday attire; Homer could have said ἐϋκνημῖδας. Cf. αἰολομίτρης (5.707), the epithets denoting the special hairstyles of the Abantes and Thracians (2.542, 4.533), and Ἰάονες ἑλκεχίτωνες (13.685). If the μίτρη meant the metal plate which guarded the belly (4.137–8n.), we would need to take χιτών as metaphorical with no sign that the 'tunic' is of metal, as in χαλκοχίτων. Hesiod uses μίτρη of ladies' girdles (*Cat.* 1.4); it also came to mean a woman's headband (Calame on Alcman frag. 1.67f.). With 420 cf. 434, 452. Verse 421 is like 12.408; καθαπτόμενος is used absolutely as at *Od.* 2.39, 24.393 (cf. 1.582n.), and the datives go with κέκλετο.

422–5 Sarpedon's protreptic is powerful: 422 contains three distinct ideas. For appeals to αἰδώς see 13.120–3n. θοοὶ ἔστε is an order: his men must do their best because he will set an example (ἀντήσω γὰρ ἐγώ ...). θοός, originally 'sharp', means 'keen', 'swift ⟨in battle⟩' (494, 5.536, 5.571, 15.585); cf. θοόω, 'sharpen'. Sarpedon knows only that his opponent is not Akhilleus; the theme of tricking the enemy with the hero's armour receives little emphasis (see pp. 310–11). Verses 424f. = 5.175f. (where see n.), at the same point in Diomedes' *aristeia*, when Aineias bids Pandaros shoot *whoever* is doing the damage. Thus a typical detail may be adapted to fit Patroklos' 'disguise'.

426 = 4.419, and occurs 6× with αὐτίκα/Ἕκτωρ δ'. With 427 cf. ἑτέρω-θεν ἀφ' ἵππων ἆλτο χαμᾶζε at 733 and 755, where it precedes a simile likening Patroklos and Hektor to lions (cf. the raptors here); it is altered, with contracted δίφρου, to admit ἐπεὶ (ϝ)ἴδεν, so that its content balances 419 + 426. Homer neglects to say that Patroklos had remounted (411–14n.).

428–30 The well-matched warriors are likened to two great birds of prey, αἰγυπιοί (13.531–3n.). This begins a set of similes describing Patroklos, which lengthen as the climax nears: he defeats Sarpedon as a lion overcomes a bull and chases the foe as a hawk chases birds; he and Hektor are like rival lions, and Hektor defeats him as a lion worsts a boar (487, 582, 756, 823). M. Baltes analyses the thematic development (*A&A* 29 (1983) 36–48); he notes that similes where animals of the same species fight never recur, and deems the lions a deliberate heightening of the raptors. Sarpedon is

Patroklos' first adversary of equal calibre; thus the weapons of both birds (talons and beaks) are mentioned to show the mutual danger, whereas at 489, where he is likened to a victorious lion and his foe to a bull, only the lion's claws appear. The birds fight on a high cliff, just as the warriors excel the rest in valour. The simile also advances the duel, so that it can form a background for the divine scene (Krischer, *Konventionen* 64): the overt point of comparison is the din the warriors make while charging. κλάζω, the same verb as κεκλήγοντες, can describe both birds and warriors (Silk, *Interaction* 16).

428 = *Od.* 22.302, the start of a simile depicting the attack on the suitors; 428f. = *Aspis* 405f., where duellists charge each other (430 = *Aspis* 412). γαμψώνυχος replaces -ῶνυξ in prose. Most MSS and lexica rightly offer ἀγκυλοχεῖλαι, 'with hooked beaks', in all three passages plus *Od.* 19.538 (αἰετὸς ἀγκυλοχείλης), not the minority reading -χῆλαι, 'with hooked claws'. -χείλ- was written -ΧΕΛ- in both Attic and Ionic script (p. 33), since χεῖλος is from *χελ-ν- or *χελ-σ- (Chantraine, *Dict.* s.v.). F. Bechtel deems -χεῖλαι a misreading of -χῆλαι when written in Attic script: the formation is wrong for χεῖλος (-χειλεῖς is expected), and -χήλης was in Aristophanes' text of Homer, since βυρσαίετος ἀγκυλοχείλης at *Knights* 197 (so most MSS), in a parody of an oracle, is explained at 204f. as τί δ᾽ ἀγκυλοχήλης ἐστίν; ... ὅτι ἀγκύλαις ταῖς χερσὶν ἁρπάζων φέρει (*Lexilogus zu Homer*, Halle 1914, 7). -χῆλαι is certainly right at *Batrachomyomachia* 294, when it describes crabs with claws (van der Valk, *Researches* II 632). But Eustathius (1068.50) already noted the resultant tautology with γαμψῶνυξ; poets do use χεῖλος of a bird's beak (Eur. *Ion* 1199, Oppian *Hal.* 3.247). Aristophanes surely deforms -χείλης to make his pun (so *LfgrE* s.v. and Shipp, *Studies* 121; differently C. Russo on *Aspis* 405f.).

430 Aristarchus and some good MSS keep the Aeolic perf. participle κεκλήγοντες. -ῶτες was read by his other edition and αἱ πλείους (Did/AT), i.e. most of the emended texts (so too at *Od.* 14.30); other good MSS have unmetrical -ότες here and at 12.125 (cf. van der Valk, *op. cit.* II 5f.). The Aeolism survived in the plur. because of its scansion (8× epos, often with -ῶτες as a variant); in the sing. all MSS confirm that bards had replaced -ων with the metrically equivalent -ώς (9× epos). See Wathelet, *Traits* 324–9, and, for like variants, 13.59–61n.; on how Aeolisms persist for metrical reasons cf. pp. 16ff.

431–61 A divine scene interrupts the duel, which resumes exactly where it left off (462 echoes 430). Fenik (*TBS* 202) compares how, at 20.290–317 and 22.167–87, major duels are interrupted by dialogues where one god asks another about his plan to save one of the combatants (from ἔειπες, 440–3 = 22.178–81, concerning Hektor). Herē lets Poseidon rescue Aineias, but dissuades Zeus here: cf. how Poseidon dissuades her in the brief exchange at 8.200ff. Sudden shifts of scene to Olumpos also occur at 4.1, 18.356, *Od.* 13.125, 24.472.

The contemplative, pitying Zeus is familiar: cf. 644ff., 17.198ff., 17.441ff., 18.356ff. (another dialogue with Here). Zeus's pity for Sarpedon dignifies both opponents and arouses the suspense of anticipation (cf. bT). Sarpedon's death is foreshadowed several times (above, p. 371); when Zeus predicts it to Here at 15.67, his words 'my son' already betray his anguish. Even the king of the gods must share the lot of the bereaved fathers whose grief is a leitmotif in the poem. His protest against fate does not prove that he can reverse it, although Here implies this; the question of relative power, though posed, is left unanswered. His words reveal his feelings: Here's reply upholds the order of the Homeric cosmos, and indeed that of the plot – although her death-sentence on her stepson does have the air of a jealous wife's vendetta; when Poseidon wants to save Aineias she raises no objection (20.310ff.)! The purpose is dramatic, not theological: nothing ever happens beyond fate in the *Iliad* (see p. 5). Nor may Sarpedon gain heroic status without death, in Homer's tragic vision; contrast the *Aithiopis'* handling of Memnon and Akhilleus. As Eustathius notes (1069.23ff.), Homer neatly evades a dilemma: if Zeus saves Sarpedon, the story fails, for then Thetis could save Akhilleus, as Here hints; but if Zeus does nothing, he looks implausibly feeble; so he must yield to a higher power. See further pp. 4ff. and Erbse, *Götter* 287f.

Zenodotus omitted the whole dialogue (so T); περιγράφει (Arn/A) could mean that he only athetized 432–58 with a large bracket, but a parallel in Arn/A on 2.156–69 points to omission (Nickau, *Zenodotos* 10f.). Plato had attacked the portrayal of Zeus feeling pity (*Rep.* 3.388c, misquoting 433f. with αἲ αἴ); Zenodotus' rationale was more trivial – Here was last on Olumpos (15.150), yet Zeus is on Ida (Arn/A). Similarly he altered 666 and left out 677 to make clear that Zeus calls to Apollo from Ida (!); he added 17.456a to take Zeus to Olumpos, and athetized 17.545f. because it implies that he is still on Ida (cf. p. 23 n. 19). Nickau takes his changes seriously (*op. cit.* 140–54). Aristarchus well replied that Here returned to Ida κατὰ τὸ σιωπώμενον, i.e. the poet did not bother to narrate her return, any more than Apollo's (cf. Arn/A on 666) or Iris' at 15.218f. Yet oral poets can err on such details. Perhaps Homer imagined both gods in their usual place, as at 22.167ff., or had in mind Thetis' supplication of Zeus on Olumpos when her son fought Memnon (Schoeck, *Ilias und Aithiopis* 59f.).

431–2 With 431 cf. 15.12. The more popular πατὴρ (δ') ἀνδρῶν τε θεῶν τε (36× epos) is replaced by its metrical equivalent Κρόνου πάϊς ἀγκυλομήτεω (8× *Il.* only), which everywhere else follows aorists in -κε (ἧκε, δῶκε, θῆκε); it surely came to mind because of ἀγκυλοχεῖλαι at 428 (cf. 15.10–13n.)! Despite its contraction of -αο to -εω (replacing Lesbian -ᾱ?), it sounds archaic and might be expected to drop out of use, like βοῶπις πότνια Ἥρη. Verse 432 resembles 18.356, *Hy*. 12.3: the traditional phrase reflects Here's twin claims to respect (cf. 4.58ff.).

433–9 Here sarcastically called Askalaphos 'dearest of men' when she told Ares of his son's death (15.111). Verses 434 and 438 adapt 420, framing the speech and giving Sarpedon's death more weight than his rescue, especially since the latter option is in second place; Here will reverse this sequence. Verse 435 is a unique version of the theme of pondering (cf. 13.455–8n.): δίχθα recurs at *Od*. 1.23, *Hy*. 22.4, φρεσὶν ὁρμαίνοντι (etc.) at 10.4, 2× *Od*. For the apt δακρυοέσσης (instead of κυδιανείρης) see 13.765–9n. Λυκίης ... πίονι δήμῳ recurs at 514, 673, 683, cf. 455. δῆμος is extended from 'people' to a place where people live. Verse 439 = 4.25, 8.462, 14.330 (439f. = 1.551f., 18.360f.).

441–3 = 22.179–81, when Athene dissuades Zeus from saving Hektor; the repetition may link his death with Sarpedon's (Thalmann, *Conventions* 46). The defiant 443 = 4.29, 22.181, both times at the end of rebukes. The word-play θνητός – θάνατος makes mortals' deaths seem inevitable. For πεπρωμένον αἴσῃ ... ἐξαναλῦσαι see on 15.209–11, 22.180; ἐ. depends on the idea of fate as a cord or thread (cf. Onians, *Origins* 382–9). On δυσηχής see 2.686n.; Thetis longs to hide her son from θανάτοιο δυσηχέος (18.464).

444–9 As often, 'I'll tell you something else' introduces a clearer statement of consequences, not a new point: cf. 1.297 or 4.39, where Zeus tells Here 'if you insist on my city being sacked, I'll sack yours'. Athene dissuaded Ares from avenging his son by saying that it would be hard to protect all gods' mortal offspring (15.140f.). In fact few sons of gods are at Troy: Menesthios, Eudoros, Ialmenos, Askalaphos, Podaleirios, Makhaon, Sarpedon, Aineias and Akhilleus. ζών, in Aristarchus (Did/A) but few good MSS, is contracted from *ζωϝός as at 5.887, Hdt. 1.194.3; Archilochus used ζοός (frags. 133, 145.7). The vulgate ζωόν has a unique and harsh synizesis (cf. van der Valk, *Researches* II 197f.). The repeated suffix in ὄνδε δόμονδε neatly declines οἶο δόμοιο (Hoekstra on *Od*. 14.424); cf. Myc. *do-de* (14.173n.) and possessives like ἡμέτερόνδε. ὃν φίλον υἱόν is in this place at 6.474, but 5× at the verse-end. Bards never say ἀπ' αἰνῆς δηϊοτῆτος for ἀπὸ κρατερῆς ὑσμίνης (cf. 645, 18.243, 13.206–9n.). Verse 448 adapts the mobile formula (περὶ) ἄστυ μέγα Πριάμοιο (ἄνακτος), found 8× Hom.: cf. *Od*. 5.106, ἄ. π. Π. μάχοντο. With the end of 449 cf. 8.449 (Zeus warning Here and Athene); τοῖσιν denotes the gods.

450–5 Here's concession is not one which saves her stepson. Aristarchus (Did/A) and some good MSS read φίλος, which looks like a learned 'improvement'. φίλον is flatter but more formular: cf. εἴ πού τοι φ. ἐστί (etc., 6× Hom.); καί τ. φ. ἔπλετο θυμῷ (etc., 9× epos). So too at 23.548 most good MSS read εἰ δέ μιν οἰκτίρεις καί τοι φ. ἔ. θ., but he and πᾶσαι have φίλος.

With the rest of 450 cf. 22.169 (of Hektor); with 451f. cf. 420, 21.207f. ἐπεί can take a subj. without ἄν (Chantraine, *GH* II 256); ἐπήν is a modernizing minority variant (13.284–7n.). ψυχή and αἰών are functional equivalents, since 453 blends λίποι α. (5.685, *Od.* 7.224) and ψ. λ. (*Od.* 18.91), cf. λίπε θυμός (2×); just as ψ. and θ. once meant 'breath' (481n.), so αἰών was 'vital force' (Bremmer, *Soul* 15f.). With 454f. cf. 671–3; Sleep and Death are twins (672, 14.231n.). πέμπειν goes with Θάνατον, φέρειν with μιν; the word-order reflects the ancient tendency to put enclitics as early as possible in the clause. For νήδυμος see 14.242n. εὐρείης (-η) is a generic epithet for fem. toponyms shaped ∪∪− (cf. 433–9n.).

456–7 = 674f. ταρχύω, 'bury', is surely unrelated to ταρῑχεύω, 'pickle' (7.85n.), or to Hittite *tarḫ*-, 'conquer' (via 'deify'), cf. the Luwian god *Tarḫund*- (*pace* Chantraine, *Dict.* s.v.). See also Hoekstra, *Modifications* 142f. For (F)ἔτης, 'kinsman', see on 6.239, 15.545f. Sarpedon's brothers, otherwise unknown (AbT on 674), are in fact Minos and Rhadamanthus (above, p. 371)! On the custom of crowning a tumulus with a gravestone see 13.437n.

458–61 The sequel (666ff.), as well as the bloody rain, shows Zeus's sorrowful obedience (458 = 4.68). He creates other such portents: at 11.53f. he sends ἔερσας αἵματι μυδαλέας, because he is about to hurl many brave men into Hades; at *Aspis* 384f. he casts down bloody drops to give his son a sign for battle (κὰδ δ' ἄρ' ἀπ' οὐρανόθεν ψιάδας βάλεν αἱματοέσσας). The motif seems traditional. Bloody rain was a common portent at Rome (e.g. Livy 24.10.7, 39.46.5 etc.), but not in Greece (cf. Pritchett, *The Greek State at War* III 91ff.). The rain may be a fantasy, but I have seen in Greece and even, once, in England, showers which deposited a red dust, wafted, the meteorologists said, from Saharan sandstorms. ψιάς is cognate with ψίζομαι, ἔψιδε, 'weep', Engl. *spit*. αἱματόεις, usually at the verse-end, is displaced by κατέχευεν ἔραζε, cf. χεῦεν ἔ. (4× Hom.). The pathos in 'his dear son' shows us Zeus's viewpoint; 'death far away' is a common pathetic motif (539, 18.99f., *Od.* 2.365, cf. 1.30, 24.541). So too Thetis weeps for her son ὅς οἱ ἔμελλε | φθίσεσθ' ἐν Τροίη ἐριβώλακι, τηλόθι πάτρης (24.85f.). ἐ. is a generic epithet for toponyms shaped (−)∪∪−; to end 461 with βωτιανείρη or μητέρι μήλων (1.155, 11.222) would have yielded less pathos.

462–507 The charge now over (462 resumes 430), the duel begins; after such weighty preliminaries it is suitably long and complex, yet largely consists of familiar elements (Fenik, *TBS* 203ff.). It falls into two rounds, 462–75 and 476–507.

462–75 In round one, both warriors' spear-casts hit other targets – Sarpedon's charioteer and Patroklos' trace-horse. Although many a driver is slain by a cast aimed at his leader (737, 8.119, 8.312, 15.430), and both warriors may fail on the first cast (11.232ff., 13.604ff., 22.273ff.) or miss entirely (335ff., 21.161ff.), 'this is the only combat in the poem where both

... manage to kill somebody or something else instead' (Fenik, *loc. cit.*). This shows how perilous the duel is for both parties, but the fact that Sarpedon kills only a horse adumbrates his inferiority; so does the way Homer says that he missed, but omits to say that Patroklos missed too (cf. 13.506–9n.). Thalmann thinks Patroklos aimed at the driver (*Conventions* 46), but Sarpedon is the foe he must fear.

463–5 'Thrasumelos', in a few good MSS, is an old and sheepish error. Not all compound names need make sense (von Kamptz, *Personennamen* 10); but Philomelos, Polumelos and Eumelos do, whereas 'Bold-sheep' is laughable. Nicanor, a papyrus and the vulgate rightly read 'Thrasudemos'. The error arose when copyists' eyes strayed from -ΔΗΜΟΝ to (Α)ΛΛΗΛΟΙ- in 462; this also created -ΜΗΔΟΝ, which Byzantine scribes altered to -μήδην. ἀγακλειτόν, here only acc. sing., is a generic epithet equivalent to ὑπέρθυμον (3× Hom.) and ἀρηΐφιλον (7×, usually of Menelaos): it is gen. 3× epos, plur. 3× and fem. 9×. ἠῢς θεράπων (also at 653) recurs 4× as θ. ἐΰς. τόν in 465 resumes the construction after the parenthesis; cf. the resumptive ὁ in 467 and 15.429–35n. For νείαιρα see 5.537–40n.

467–9 'The commentators' (Did/T) read δεύτερον ὁρμηθείς as at 402, in a typical attempt to standardize the irregularities of this oral dictated text; some good MSS agree, but the old vulgate was δεύτερος. Homer was inconsistent: the MSS have δεύτερον ὄρνυτο χαλκῷ at 3.349 but δεύτερος at 17.45 (otherwise the same verse), cf. ὕστερος ὅ. χ. (479 = 5.17).

οὔτασεν, 'stabbed', is the wrong verb, since Sarpedon too cast his spear. I suspect a simple error by the poet, who was perhaps distracted by resumptive ὁ δέ, which normally marks a change of grammatical subject: cf. 21.68 and the odd use of τύπτω at 13.571. Philemon (*c.* 200 B.C.?) read ἤλασεν instead. Aristarchus merely noted the problem: Did/A should be emended to read 'no doubt ⟨no⟩ reading was current (μήποτε γραφή τις ⟨οὐκ⟩ ἐφέρετο) in which Homer maintained his usual expression; for Aristarchus would not have left it as incorrigible'. But T say Aristarchus made drastic changes, inserting 153f. after 467: ὁ δὲ Πήδασον ἀγλαὸν ἵππον | [153f.] | τὸν βάλε δεξιὸν ὦμον. Such rewriting departs from his normal caution (see pp. 26f.); A. Roemer is surely right (*RhM* 66 (1911) 352f.) that 'Aristarchus' is an error for 'Aristophanes', who certainly favoured rewritings of 10.349 and *Od.* 2.51 involving extra verses. The interpolator wished to allude to Akhilleus and make clear that Pedasos is the mortal horse, as well as to remove οὔτασεν. — Pedasos 'crashed down' (ἔβραχε, cf. 5.859), 'gasping out his life' (θυμὸν ἄϊσθων, cf. 15.252–3n.). Verse 469 = *Od.* 10.163, 19.454, cf. *Od.* 18.98; μακών suits only animals and the comical Iros.

470–5 On why Patroklos has a trace-horse, and the archaeological background, see 152–4n. Pedasos' fall imperils the chariot by alarming the other two horses, entangling the reins and putting strain on the yoke, which creaks (κρίκε, from κρίζω) as if about to snap the pole to which it was attached (24.27off.); this was the greatest danger to a chariot (370–1n.). J. Wiesner (*Arch. Hom.* F 21) thinks Pedasos was fastened to the horse beside him by a harness, which Automedon severs to save the situation; but the traces surely passed through rings or hooks ('terrets') on the yoke. Priam's waggon, with a team of four, certainly had these (οἴηκες, 24.269); depicted on Myc. vases, they are found on the Geometric chariot excavated at Salamis (cf. Wiesner, *op. cit.* 56, 71, and Crouwel, *Chariots* 108f.). Thus Automedon rushes up and hews the traces away *from the yoke* with one blow, like Nestor at 8.87f.; the reins straighten the horses up (cf. 23.324). ῥυτῆρες, 'reins', are next at Soph. *O.C.* 900; cf. *Aspis* 308 (ῥυτά).

The theory that the *Iliad* draws on the tale of Memnon (pp. 312f.) rests partly on this scene. Pindar (*Py.* 6.28–39) tells how, in the battle against Memnon, Nestor's chariot was disabled when Paris shot one of his horses; Antilokhos died to save his father. This must derive from Cyclic epic. In a striking parallel at 8.8off., Paris shoots Nestor's trace-horse; the old man, hewing at the traces, is saved from Hektor only by Diomedes (cf. Willcock in *Mélanges Delebecque* 482f.; Mühlestein, *Namenstudien* 47ff.). A dead trace-horse is an obsolescent traditional motif, since the phrase κεῖτο παρήορος is famously misused at 7.156. Note the urgent asyndeta in 472f. Verse 473 = *Od.* 10.439, 11.231, cf. 14.383–7n.; when the subject must be given, Homer says ξίφος ὀξὺ ἐρυσσάμενος παρὰ μηροῦ (5×).

476–507 The duel's second round completes a chiasmus, since Sarpedon now casts first; the familiar pattern it follows often constitutes a whole combat. Trojan P throws at Greek Q and misses, whereat Q kills P; cf. 5.16–18, repeated here with Patroklos replacing Diomedes (478–80; 462 = 5.14). Sarpedon's fall is likened to that of a tree, his death-struggle to that of a bull, two standard images. He dies like the poem's other great casualties, Patroklos and Hektor (502–5n.); like them, he is given a last speech. But, rather than address his foe, he asks Glaukos to save his body from spoliation, just as at 5.684ff. he asked this of Hektor (cf. p. 371); this avoids having him face the unwanted question of who is wearing Akhilleus' armour (Edwards, *HPI* 262).

476–80 Verses 476f. resume 462 and 466 (ἀπήμβροτε δουρὶ φαεινῷ recurs nowhere else); θυμοβόρος, a standard epithet of strife, is in the same formula at 7.301, 20.253, modified at 7.210, 19.58. Eustathius (1071.43) liked the pattern ἀ. – οὐδ' ἔβαλ' – οὐχ ἅλιον βέλος – ἀλλ' ἔβαλ'.

481 Sarpedon is hit 'where the lungs are shut in around the dense heart', an anatomically correct description. As Onians argues (*Origins* 26ff.), φρένες are the lungs, into which the θυμός (once 'breath') gathers as one revives (22.475, cf. 15.252–3n.); they were deemed the seat of the intelligence because of the breath they contain. They are not, as is often held, the diaphragm, which, being taut muscle attached all round, would not come out with the spear (504); it is incredible that so many men should be hit in the diaphragm, but only one in the lungs (4.528). Cf. too the sense of μετάφρενον, 'back'. See also Bremmer, *Soul* 62; *contra*, S. Laser, *Arch. Hom.* s 43–6, citing *Od.* 9.301, ὅθι φρένες ἧπαρ ἔχουσι, and S. D. Sullivan, *Psychological Activity in Homer*, Ottawa 1988, 178–80. A pulmonary wound explains Sarpedon's noisy breathing (βεβρυχώς, 486); cf. that of Asios, whose throat is pierced (13.388–93), and Virgil, *Aen.* 4.689, where *infixum stridit sub pectore vulnus* 'expresses the whistling sound with which breath escapes from a pierced lung' (J. W. Mackail *ad loc.*). Verse 660 may mean that Sarpedon was hit in the heart, which is in the same area. Even if the spear missed his heart, it is a miracle of poetic licence that he can still speak (cf. Hektor at 22.327ff.). The puzzling form ἔρχαται is used as an aspirated perf. of (ϝ)έργω, 'enclose', i.e. ἐεργμέναι εἰσί (Hoekstra on *Od.* 14.73); on it is based ἐρχατόωντο (*Od.* 14.15). It may be from the root *sergh-* seen in ἔρχατος, 'enclosure' (cf. 14.122–5n.). ἀμφ' ἀδινὸν κῆρ is metaphorical at *Od.* 19.516; κῆρ has a physical sense only here and perhaps at 14.139f. ἀδινός, 'dense' in time or space, describes droves of sheep, incessant sobs and here a beating heart (*LfgrE* s.v.).

482–6 = 13.389–93, where see nn.; Sarpedon's chariot is immobilized, so it is just as apt for him as it was for Asios to fall before it. There is no reason to suspect this simile, since the next image depicts a later stage in his fall: paired similes are common at critical moments (15.618–36n.). It is soon Patroklos' turn to resemble a log (17.744).

487–9 Warriors, especially leaders, often die like bulls (13.570–3n.): cf. too αἱματόεις ὥς τίς τε λέων κατὰ ταῦρον ἐδηδώς (17.542), and the everyday scene where lions catch a bull from the herd (18.579ff., cf. 15.586–8n.). This simile is heightened and reversed at 823ff., where Patroklos becomes a boar worsted by the lion Hektor (so Moulton, *Similes* 105); it also heightens the bird-simile at 428ff., as Baltes saw (428–30n.). The bull has dignity even in death, since it 'groans' (στενάχων) like a warrior (contrast μακών, 467–9n.); μεγάθυμος endows it with heroic courage. αἴθων often describes lions, but horses and oxen are αἴθωνες μεγάλοι at 2.839, *Od.* 18.372. The variant ἐπ' for ἐν, avoided by Aristarchus, αἱ πλείους (Did/AT) and many early codices, may come from 6.424; van der Valk thinks it better represents the bull as head of his herd (*Researches* II 99n.).

490–1 Sarpedon speaks only with effort. The concrete sense of ὑπό, 'at Patroklos' hands' (cf. 489), is still felt with κτεινόμενος (698–701n.). Aristarchus took μενέαινε as 'fainted' or 'was angry', but it means 'struggled (mentally)' as at 15.104 (A. W. H. Adkins, *JHS* 89 (1969) 17f.); the phrase is improvised from (κατα)κτάμεναι μ. (8× Hom., cf. *Od.* 20.315). The rest of 491 recurs at 23.178 = 24.591, in addresses to the dead Patroklos.

492–501 Even as he dies Sarpedon is vigorous, direct and mindful of the heroic code. Verses 492–4 form a chiastic preamble: compliment (πολεμιστά) – νῦν – νῦν – compliment, '*if* you are θοός' (the usual adj. with πολεμιστής, cf. 422–5n.). From νῦν, 492f. = 22.268f. (Akhilleus to Hektor); 493 = 5.602. His last wishes, again in three verses, are carried out exactly (495–7, to ἔπειτα, = 532–4, with ὤτρυνεν). His use of his own name at 496 may be pathetic but is certainly proud and defiant: cf. 833, 7.75 (Hektor), 1.240, 19.151 (Akhilleus), 8.22 (Zeus), 11.761 (Nestor). Aristarchus thinks he is quoting the orders Glaukos must give his men (cf. 533). His warning that his cousin will otherwise incur disgrace fills a further three verses: with 498 cf. 17.556, Athene urging Menelaos to save Patroklos' body; 501 = 17.559, the call to action that ends Athene's speech.

With 'a soldier among *men*' (492) cf. ἐσθλὸν ἐόντα μετ' ἀνδράσιν (13.461); μ. ἀ. has the same force at 557, 11.762, 15.611, *Od.* 19.315. T's conjecture πάρος for πέπον is from 557 (cf. Nic/A *ad loc.*). bT's θρασύς (494) emends away the oxymoron in ἐελδέσθω πόλεμος κακός (cf. πόλεμον θρασύν, 10.28 = *Od.* 4.146); but κ. is a standard epithet, as apt as at *Od.* 22.152. ἤματα πάντα διαμπερές (499) recurs, describing disgrace, at *HyAphr* 248; this pleonastic formula is found reversed 3× in epos. Verse 500 = 15.428, where see n.; 'at the fleet' is less apt here, but, as Willcock notes, Patroklos drove the Trojans back towards the ships (395). bT accent νέων to remove this 'problem'! For ἔχομαι, 'hold fast', cf. 9.235.

502–5 The same distinctive verse, 502, ends the last words and the lives of the poem's three major casualties (= 855, 22.361); both its half-lines are traditional, since they occur elsewhere and reflect the Ϝ- in εἰπόντα (5.553, *Od.* 5.313). The 'end that is death' covers Sarpedon's eyes and nose, i.e. he ceases to see and breathe. We next hear why: Patroklos steadies his victim with his heel (13.616–19n.) and pulls out the spear, which drags out his lungs (481n.) and with them his life (were φρένες abstract, 505 would be repetitious). Death often follows the weapon's removal (13.574f., 14.518f., both *ending* with 'darkness covered his eyes'); the motif is modified when it is the turn of Patroklos and Hektor to die (862f., 22.367). The neat zeugma of 505 is apt: the soul is imagined as breath which escapes through the wound (481n.). Aristarchus (Did/T) and nearly all MSS read unmetrical ποτί in 504; προτί is a facile normalization of the rough-hewn text. His ἔχοντο (cf. 501) lacks MS support. On the split formula ἔγχεος ... αἰχμήν cf. 313–15n.

506–7 Sarpedon's steeds may be 'snorting' because they resist Myrmidon control – cf. 4.227n., *HyHerm* 118 (of cows); but there is no metrically equivalent epithet for horses. ἐπεὶ λίπον ἅρματ' ἀνάκτων is a misused half-line, found above at 371. Here the chariot-pole did not snap, so the horses cannot have left the vehicle; since Homer had such an accident in mind at 470, he has made a minor slip. Zenodotus (Arn, Did/A) and a few good MSS keep λίπον: most adopt Aristarchus' impossible emendation λίπεν, supposedly an aor. pass. third plur. (van der Valk, *Researches* II 74f.).

508–31 Glaukos, shot in the arm by Teukros (12.387ff.), was still fighting at 14.426 where, I suspect, Homer had forgotten his wound; here too Sarpedon did not mention it. In answer to his prayer, Apollo miraculously heals him; his joy at this balances his initial grief that he cannot help his cousin (508f., 530f.). Glaukos is a sympathetic figure, no doubt because leading Ionian families deemed him their ancestor (Hdt. 1.147). Aias slew him in the fight over Akhilleus' body: see 'Apollodorus', *Epit.* 5.4; *LIMC* s.v. Achilleus, pl. 850 (Chalcidian vase, *c.* 540 B.C.). In Quintus of Smyrna (4.4–12) Apollo and the winds take his body to Lycia. Being Lycian, he prays to Lycian Apollo, like Pandaros (4.119). Prayer is often answered at once (8.236ff., 15.372ff., 17.645ff.); Homer always rewards the just and pious who resort to it. Cf. especially 5.115ff., where Diomedes, shot in the shoulder, prays to Athene and receives a burst of energy which enables him to fight on. Van der Valk (*Researches* II 432) suggests that, for nationalistic reasons, Homer avoids having the Trojans pray for victory (save at 6.311, where their prayer is refused), and reintroduces Glaukos' wound so that he can ask for healing instead; Apollo's response unobtrusively grants them a success (cf. his healing of Hektor at 15.239ff.).

510–13 Glaukos squeezes his arm, no doubt trying to stop the bleeding (cf. 518f.) and relieve the pain (cf. *Erga* 497). E. W. Williams (*G&R* 6 (1959) 148) diagnoses a lesion to its median nerve, which would cause pain in both hand and shoulder and paralyse the flexor muscles of hand and wrist; but this requires taking χείρ as 'hand' not 'arm' at 517. Unemphatic αὐτόν (510) is recent, like contracted αὐτοῦ in 519. For the idiom ἕλκος, ὃ δή μιν ... βάλεν ἰῷ cf. 5.361, 5.795; 511f. rephrase his original wounding at 12.388, ἰῷ ἐπεσσύμενον βάλε τείχεος ὑψηλοῖο. On ἀρή, 'harm', see 14.484–5n. The first half of 513 recurs only at *Od.* 7.330, but the 'observed' F- proves it ancient; for ἑκηβόλος, 'far-shooter', see 5.53–4n.

514–26 Glaukos' urgent prayer adapts the usual form (14.233–41n.): (*a*) he invokes Apollo with κλῦθι and notes his power to hear wherever he is; (*b*) he replaces the reminder of past favour with an account of his wound and the resultant risk to Sarpedon, reproaching Zeus for not protecting his son; (*c*) he blends his request, in a diminishing tricolon of imperatives (including δός as often), with a call to action (ἀλλά, 523). The centre of his speech, based on the exhortation-pattern, is delimited by repetition of ἕλκος ... τόδε καρτερόν (517, 523).

514–16 To make a prayer work, one must state where the god is and the name by which he prefers to be called (E. Norden, *Agnostos Theos*, Leipzig 1913, 144ff.); he must have no excuse for not listening. Like Aeschylus at *Agam.* 160ff., Homer piously adapts this traditional pattern to convey a nobler theology: wherever the god is, he hears a man in trouble. κλῦθι ἄναξ for the usual κ. (μεῦ) recurs at *Od.* 5.445, where too ἄ. is repeated in the request with which the prayer closes, in a reminder of its honorific opening. εἴς (better accented εἶς) is an Ionic replacement of Aeolic ἐσσί, via non-Homeric εἶ with -ς added by analogy. εἶς, normal in Herodotus, is tending to oust ἐσσ' and ἐσσί from the epic diction: it occurs 4× *Il.* but 16× *Od.* (beside ἐσσί 33× each), always before a vowel save at *Od.* 17.388. ἤ, from elided ἠέ = *ἠϝέ (cf. Latin -*ve*), has a 'neglected' -ϝ- in a rare correption before ἐνί (cf. 21.576n.). Aristarchus rightly kept πάντοσ' ἀκούειν, an idiom based on the archaic idea of hearing as a power going out from the ear (633–4n.); Zenodotus (Did/A) read πάντ' ἐσακούειν. ἀκούω and κλύω can take a dat. (cf. 531), by analogy with verbs of obeying (Chantraine, *GH* II 70); differently M. Meier-Brügger in *Festschrift Risch* 346–53. For κῆδος ἱκάνει see 13.463–7n.; note the etymological play.

518–19 When Agamemnon stops bleeding, pain racks him (11.267ff.); contrast 529 below. The epithet-system for 'pains' is flexible, since heroic song is full of them; they can be χαλεπῇσι, κακῇσι, βαρεῖαι, ὀξεῖαι, μελαινάων or κακῶν, in varied permutations. ἐλήλαται, 'is pierced', is also used in the middle (4.135). τερσῆναι is from the old intrans. aor. of τέρσομαι, not trans. ἐτέρσηνα (529); intransitives like ἔβην or ἔστην are the origin of the aor. pass. in -(θ)ην. βαρύθω recurs in the epos only at *Erga* 215.

521–6 With 521f. cf. 24.384, 5.683. For ᾧ παιδὶ ἀμύνει Aristarchus, supplying περί, read οὗ παιδὸς ἀ.; this effort to emend away a hiatus is in no good MS (with the hiatus cf. 17.196). ἀ. never takes a gen., since Τρῶας must be supplied at 13.109f. (cf. van der Valk, *Researches* II 162f.). For the dat. cf. 265 and 512, versus Ζεὺς κῆρας ἄμυνε | παιδὸς ἑοῦ (12.402f.). κοιμάω is metaphorical for lulling winds or waves at 12.281, *Od.* 12.169. Verse 525 resembles Λυκίοισιν ἐκέκλετο (3×); from ἀμφί, 526 = 565. Disyllabic νέκυι, here in a declension of the formula νεκύων κατατεθνειώτων (8× Hom., acc. *Od.* 22.448), recurs at 24.108, cf. πληθυῖ etc.; on these recent forms (4× *Il.*, 8× *Od.*) cf. Chantraine, *GH* I 50.

527–34 Verse 527 = 1.43, 457; with 528f. cf. 11.812f.; the end of 529 blends μένος δέ οἱ ἐν φρεσὶ θῆκε (21.145), μ. ἔμβαλ' Ἀθήνη (10.366) and (ἵμερον) ἔμβαλε θυμῷ. Verse 530 adapts ἔγνω ᾗσιν ἐνὶ φ. φώνησέν τε (3×); γήθησέν τε never recurs at the verse-end. Verse 531 forms a ring with 527. For the dat. with ἀκούω cf. 514–16n.; εὐξαμένοιο reverts to the usual construction seen in 1.453. With 532–4 cf. 495–7.

534–61 Glaukos wisely seeks help before defending Sarpedon's body himself; the narrative flows smoothly towards a new climax. 'Almost all of the action from 16.538 to the end of book 17 is sustained by a sixfold (counting 17.483, a sevenfold) repetition of the same pattern of Trojan rebuke (or consultation), charge and repulse. Moreover this sixfold repetition occurs, with only one exception (16.721), in connexion with a fight over the body of a fallen warrior. The exception, the rebuke at 16.721, leads to the fight in which Kebriones dies and over whose body a vicious battle develops' (Fenik, *TBS* 205, cf. 49ff.). This pattern, found also at 5.471ff. and 11.523ff. (rebukes by Sarpedon and Kebriones), consists of:

1. Greek success (462–538, 555–683, 17.1–69, 17.128–39, 17.274–318, 17.375–581)
2. Glaukos/Apollo rebukes Hektor/Aineias (538ff., 721, 17.70, 17.140, 17.319, 17.582)
3. Hektor charges (548ff., 726, 17.87, 17.233, 17.333, 17.591)
4. The Greeks, Aias and Patroklos/Menelaos included, rally (555ff., 733, 17.89, 17.237, 17.356, 17.626)
4a. Darkness falls on the battle (567f., 17.268, 17.366, 17.643, cf. 5.506f., 12.252ff.)
5. The Greeks halt or repulse the Trojans (555–683 (elaborated), 780, 17.128–39, 17.274–318, 17.375–581, 17.651ff.)

534–6 On Glaukos' stride see 13.809n. He seeks the main Trojan leaders, last seen at 15.521, 15.340 and 15.332 respectively, but chiefly Hektor, who shares the epithet χαλκοκορυστήν (654, 15.221, dat. 5×) with his allies Sarpedon and Memnon (6.199, *Theog.* 984). Mühlestein thinks it was originally Memnon's (*Namenstudien* 182). The Greek equivalent is θυμολέοντα (Akhilleus, Herakles); ποιμένα λαῶν is truly generic.

538–47 Glaukos tells Hektor that *Patroklos* slew Sarpedon, ending the motif of the Trojans' deception by Akhilleus' armour (pp. 310–11). Lohmann (*Reden* 124f.) saw that his speech is matched by that of Patroklos to the Aiantes (just as these leaders stand in a parallel relationship). Both open with the exhortation 'resist' (538–40, 556f.), announce Sarpedon's fall (541–3, 558f., both starting forcefully with 'there lies dead' in asyndeton) and end with a call to action introduced by ἀλλά (544–7, 559–61). Glaukos bids the Trojans save the body from being stripped and mutilated because of the Myrmidons' rage over the Greek losses at the ships (a neat reminder of their recent success); Patroklos urges his men to mangle and strip the corpse, and kill its defenders (so Glaukos' fears are real). The same tripartite structure shapes the rebuke at 5.464–9, with asyndetic κεῖται opening its central section. ἐγχείησιν (547) resumes ἔγχεϊ (543), stressing the idea of killing in revenge, which will soon become as major a theme as stripping armour and maltreating bodies (see Segal, *Mutilation* 19f.).

538–40 That the allies do all the fighting is a topos of Lycian rebukes to Hektor (5.472ff., 17.142ff.); cf. Akhilleus' complaint about Agamemnon (1.165ff., 9.321ff.). Fenik guesses that their ill-feeling against the Trojans was traditional (*TBS* 171). Sarpedon used the tragic motif of dying far from home in rebukes at 5.478ff., 686ff.; the poet applied it to him at 460f., where see n. θυμόν is the object of ἀποφθινύθουσι, not a limiting acc.; it means 'lose their lives'.

541–7 Asyndeton gives bad news maximum impact, as at 18.20, cf. 22.386. Sarpedon protected Lycia by just judgements (δίκαι) as well as martial prowess (cf. *HyDem* 153); the two desiderata for a king are to avert civil strife and prevent foreign attack. σθένεϊ ᾧ scanned ∪∪ − − reflects *swos, if not also the Myc. dat. in -*ei*: such phrases survive 5× Hom. On the syntax of ὑπό cf. 490–1 n. χάλκεος Ἄρης is metaphorical nowhere else (5×). The second half of 544 is formular (cf. 2.223, *Od.* 1.119, 4.158). Verse 547 means not 'we ⟨Lycians⟩ slew', but 'we ⟨Trojans and allies⟩ slew', as in the parallel at 21.135.

548–53 Glaukos' speech could not fail: the Trojans are grief-stricken (cf. 17.83 etc.), and anger fuels their ardour. The mention of Sarpedon's role in defending Troy gives their viewpoint. As at *Od.* 11.588, we should read κατ' ἄκρηθεν not κατὰ κρῆθεν, *pace* Aristarchus (Hrd/A). This phrase is a variant of κατ' ἄκρης (5× Hom.), 'from the top down', 'utterly'; later bards re-interpreted it as κατὰ κρῆθεν, 'from the head down' (*Theog.* 574, *Cat.* 23a.23, *HyDem* 182, cf. ἀπὸ κ. at *Cat.* 195.14 = *Aspis* 7), by a false analogy with κρή-δεμνον (Leumann, *HW* 57f.; Nussbaum, *Head and Horn* 74f.). ἄσχετον, οὐκ ἐπιεικτόν means 'irresistible, invincible', from (ϝ)είκω, 'yield'; cf. μένος ἄ. (etc., 6× epos), μ. . . . ἀάσχετον, οὐκ ἐ. (5.892, cf. 8.32, *Od.* 19.493). ἕρμα, literally a 'stone' or a 'prop' for a ship (1.486), is metaphorically a 'support', cf. ἕ. πόληος ἀπέκταμεν (*Od.* 23.121); this usage is our first hint of the 'ship of state' image in Alcaeus (cf. Archilochus frags. 105f.). Cf. metaphorical ἔρεισμα (Pindar, *Ol.* 2.6; Soph. *O.C.* 58). The first half of 551 = 2.578; the rest is a standard description of fallen heroes (5×). With 552 cf. 12.106.

554–5 Patroklos' address to the Aiantes is explained more by the standard rebuke-pattern (534–62n.) than by the fighting to come, where they do not appear (cf. 563–644n.); 555 = 13.46 (where see n.), and looks traditional. With 554 cf. the periphrasis Πυλαιμένεος λάσιον κῆρ (2.851); heroic hearts are 'shaggy' because they are in, or *are*, their chests (1.188f.). For the vulgate Μενοιτιάδαο Πατροκλῆος some good MSS say -δεω Πάτρο-. Homer uses so-called 'Attic correption' before -τρ- only from metrical necessity, except in φαρέτρης (8.323, normally ∪ − −) and Ὀτρυντεύς (20.383–9): cf. Chantraine, *GH* 1 108. Here he is adapting the formula Πατρόκλοιο Μενοιτιάδαο; we might expect to find a gen. in -εῳ as at 18.93, but the MSS show that he chose this vulgar innovation instead. It is commonest in Hipponax and comedy (W. S. Allen, *Vox Graeca*, 3rd edn, Cambridge 1987, 106–10); 6.479, where the formula καί ποτέ τις εἴπῃσι precedes πᾶτρός, proves that Homer used it in emergency (the variant εἴποι πᾶτρός emends it away). Cf. 20n.

556–62 This speech closely matches Glaukos' in structure and content (538–47n.). bT ask why Patroklos, so mild in peace, voices the brutal wish to mangle Sarpedon's body. This sets up this motif as a major theme, first adumbrated by Glaukos; it also justifies in advance the fate of Patroklos' armour and peril to his corpse. He is swept away by the savagery of war, like any other warrior at this stage in it – or in the poem: contrast how Akhilleus once honoured Eëtion's body (6.416ff.). μετ' ἀνδράσιν is a compliment, as at 492. ἀρείους (2× *Od.*), replacing the old comparative plur. /*aryohes*/ (KN L 7409), agrees with οἷοι; contraction, as in the masc. acc. sing. ἀρείω (10.237, *Od.* 3.250), enabled bards to decline the standard verse-ending καὶ ἀρείων (-ον). From ὅς, 558 = 12.438, where it describes Hektor; the novel sigmatic aor. of ἅλλομαι confirms that the rampart is an innovation (Hoekstra, *Modifications* 129n.). Since Sarpedon was not the first to enter the Greek camp, Eratosthenes' mentor Lysanias took ἐσήλατο as 'shook (the rampart)', Aristarchus as 'leapt onto' (Hrd/A). Rhianus' εὖ in 559 (Did/A) removes the use of εἰ with the opt. for 'if only', a typically reckless conjecture (cf. van der Valk, *TCO* 108). Verse 562 = 15.565.

563–644 Panoramas frame the deadlock over Sarpedon's body (569–632), which comprises four combats. The greater warriors kill first: Hektor and Glaukos slay a Myrmidon each, while Trojans fall to Patroklos and Meriones, who then exchanges spears and insults with Aineias. Meriones takes Aias' place (554–5n.) because Patroklos can more aptly command a junior warrior. Fenik (*TBS* 206) compares 17.262ff.; both sides stiffen the fight for Patroklos' body, a panorama includes Zeus casting darkness on the battle, the Trojans drive back the Greeks (274 = 569 here), and the first man to die is hauling the body away (289, cf. 577 here). This is but the closest of many parallels (534–62n.).

563 This v. resembles ἑτέρωθεν ἐκαρτύναντο φάλαγγας (3× epos). Verse 564 modifies Τρῶες καὶ Λύκιοι καὶ Δάρδανοι ἀγχιμαχηταί (6×) to form a chiasmus, since the Myrmidons and Lycians are *de facto* the main ally on each side (hence Patroklos kills Sarpedon). For συμβάλλω, 'meet (to fight)', cf. 21.578, *LfgrE* s.v. βάλλω III 1e. With 566 cf. δεινὸν ἀϋσάντων (14.401), μέγα δ' ἔβραχε (5.838), βράχε τεύχεα (3× epos) and τ. φωτῶν (23.15).

567–8 The murk ('night') which Zeus sheds over the battle has its usual place in this rebuke-pattern (534–62n.). It reflects his grief as well as the brutal fighting to come; in the gloom Night's children, Sleep and Death, can remove his son's body unnoticed (666–83n.). The gods can also clear the air when they choose (15.668–73n.). ὀλοή often describes νύξ (22.102, *Od.* 11.19, 2× *Theog.*); as if relaying Zeus's thoughts, the poet neatly relates the 'horrible' murk to the 'horrible' toil to come. νύκτα θοήν, cf. θ. διὰ ν. (4×), would have been less apt. κρατερῇ ὑσμίνῃ (12× Hom.) follows ἐνί everywhere else. For the dat. with περί expressing what one fights over see Chantraine, *GH* II 127.

570–80 The first casualty is the most elaborate; the triple schema of announcement (570f.), biography (571–6) and death-blow is usual (13.170–81n.). The announcement is in the passive because the effect of this slaying matters more than the slayer (O. Tsagarakis, *Form and Content in Homer*, Wiesbaden 1982, 131). The same death-blow felled the last minor victim: from κεφαλήν, 578–80 = 412–14! Eustathius (1076.23) likens Epeigeus' name to the river Sperkheios, since both connote haste; cf. Myc. *E-pe-ke-u* (PY Jn 431). His father Agakles is but a glorified epithet: cf. ἀγακλῆος Πριάμοιο/Μενελάου (738, 23.529, also 2× voc.), and the next Myrmidon to die, wealthy Βαθυκλῆα μεγάθυμον (594). These names recall the two Myrmidon leaders introduced at 173ff., never to reappear: one is a son of Sperkheios, the other a stepson of *wealthy* Ekhe*kles*. If Homer invented those figures, as I argued (168–97n.), he might well reinvent them now, when he needs prominent Myrmidon victims.

570–4 For the litotes 'far from the worst' cf. 15.11 (Aias), *Od.* 4.199 (Antilokhos). Do we fear for a moment that Patroklos is dead? Like Akhilleus' other retainers, Phoinix and Patroklos himself (9.478ff., 23.85ff.), Epeigeus escaped a vendetta by fleeing to Peleus. Strasburger deems him a doublet of Patroklos, prefiguring his fall (*Kämpfer* 30); cf. R. Schlunk, *AJP* 97 (1976) 202ff. Fenik objects that the audience has yet to hear of Patroklos' past (*TBS* 206f.). Exile is a common motif, often invented, yet Homer probably did have Patroklos in mind here, if the hero was really from Phthia (see pp. 313f.). Now bT say Boudeion was a town in Phthiotis named after one Boudeios, but rightly add that, in this case, Epeigeus flees to the king of his own land, contrary to custom (for a like illogicality in an invented story of exile see 13.694–7n.). So they posit a Boeotian city named after Erginos' mother Boudeia. But Boudeia was also a Thessalian title of Athene and a city in Thessalian Magnesia (Steph. Byz. s.v., cf. D). The claim that Boudeion was in Phthia, usually spurned as a bad guess, is surely true, since 573 is an afterthought added to include the pathetic motif of exile: 'he ruled Boudeion before, but then fled to Peleus'. In all eleven such cases in Homer we never hear that the refugee was himself a king; Phoinix gained his rank from Peleus. Oidipous did not quit his realm after killing his father (*Od.* 11.275); it is fear of vendetta, not blood-guilt, that banishes heroes. The clumsiness of τὸ πρίν, ἀτὰρ τότε, which denotes the narrative's present time at *Od.* 4.518 and *HyDem* 451, confirms that 573 is an afterthought.

Homer treats Peleus and Thetis as still together, contrary to tradition (220–32n.). The formula ἐῦ ναιομένῳ, declined into the dat. only here, usually precedes a word for 'town', but the space is taken by ἤνασσε (cf.

168–72n.). Θέτις ἀργυρόπεζα (11× epos, plus 3× reversed) is acc. only here, an innovative trait; Hesiod often declines formulae for gods similarly (West, *Theogony* p. 79).

576 = *Od.* 14.71, cf. 5.551, *Od.* 2.18, 11.169; the formula Ἴλιον εἰς ἐΰπωλον is limited to the context of leaving for war (cf. Δαρδανίην ἐ. |, *Little Iliad* frag. 28 B. = 1 D.). Warriors often perish trying to drag a body away (13.526–39n.). For 578–80 see 411–14n.

581–5 Patroklos reacts to Epeigeus' death just as Glaukos and the Trojans reacted to Sarpedon's (cf. ἄχος γένετο and βάν δ' ἰθύς at 508, 552). The psychological momentum of war sweeps him along; the inexorable cycle of death and revenge pauses only with Hektor's ransom. Mentions of his feelings for his comrade at 581 and 585 form a ring; within this 582 and 584f. (ἴθυσεν . . . ἰθύς) frame the central image of a hawk. Verses 584f. extend to unequalled length the emotive apostrophe which the poet applies to Patroklos elsewhere (20n.). This device retains our sympathy for the hero; noble motives underlie both sides' escalating savagery.

582–3 The poet's choice of simile is free: ἴθυσεν δὲ διὰ προμάχων precedes a boar-image at 17.281, which is at the same point in this rebuke-pattern, since 569 + 588 = 17.274 + 316. Patroklos and Sarpedon were likened to raptors at 428f.; the hawk epitomizes deadly speed (cf. 15.237f. with n.). Eagles chase big birds like geese (15.690–2n.), hawks smaller ones: cf. especially 17.755ff., where the Greeks flee as a flock of starlings or jackdaws flees a falcon. The jackdaw (*Corvus monedula*) was proverbially gregarious (Thompson, *Birds* 156f.). It is unknown why starlings (*Sturnus vulgaris* or *S. roseus*) are called ψῆρας here but ψαρῶν at 17.755. Chantraine posits *ψήρα *ψῆρα *ψᾱρός, ascribing ψᾱρῶν to metrical lengthening (*Dict.* s.v.); but the survival of ψᾱρ not *ψήρ in later Greek suggests that ψῆρας is artificial (Shipp, *Vocabulary* 579). Thompson (*Birds* 335) plausibly links the word with *sparrow*: cf. σπαράσιον, ψαρίς, 'sparrow' (Hsch.) and Pokorny, *IEW* 991.

586–7 Sthenelaos is unknown (cf. Sthenelos); on his father's name, known in inscriptions, see von Kamptz, *Personennamen* 103. Tendons, even in the neck, can be plur. as well as dual, cf. 17.290, *Od.* 3.449 versus 10.456, 14.466.

588–92 The Trojans fall *back* as far as the spear-cast of one who throws *forward* as hard as he can: the image is conceived from the Greek viewpoint. Verses 588 and 592 form a ring, and 592 reverses 569. Verse 588 = 17.316 (see 582–3n.) and 4.505, again after a revenge-killing. Similes often express measurement. This one is paralleled at 15.358f., where see n.; πειρώμενος means 'trying his strength'. An αἰγανέη is a light javelin used in hunting and sport (2.774, *Od.* 4.626 = 17.168). The poetic τανα(ϝ)ός next occurs at *HyDem* 454 and Aristeas frag. 4 B. = 2 D., where it certainly means 'long', not 'slender'; cf. αἰγανέας δολιχαύλους (*Od.* 9.156, with Heubeck's n.). ἀφέη is a rare innovative aor. subj. with a short vowel: contrast ἀφήῃ etc. (Shipp, *Studies* 30). The second half of 591 recurs at 18.220 (simile); its gen. in -έων proves it more recent than θάνατος χύτο θυμοραϊστής (580, cf. 13.541–4n.). The scansion Τρῶες ὦσαντο reflects a lost ϝ-, cf. ἔωσα.

593–9 A warrior may turn when chased, but nowhere else kills his pursuer at once (Fenik, *TBS* 207f.). Glaukos' sudden blow, just when his foe caught him up, halts the Trojan rout: he proves himself worthy to succeed Sarpedon as Λυκίων ἀγὸς ἀσπιστάων. Both this killing and the next (603–7) follow Beye's tripartite pattern and put the focus on the unknown victim's father. Bathukles is invented, like Agakles (570–80n.), but his father Khalkon bears a name from Glaukos' own family. Hesiod (*Cat.* 43a.53ff.) makes Sisuphos' son Glaukos the putative father both of Eurupulos, father of the Khalkon who fought Herakles on Kos (14.250–61n.), and of Bellerophon, our Glaukos' grandfather (6.155ff.). Homer mentioned killing a cousin just above, at 573! A duel between a Koan and a Lycian may well reflect local saga (for parallels see 317–29n.). Yet the Koans had a Thessalian connexion: Eurupulos' grandson was called Thessalos. Such associations helped oral poets invent minor warriors, but are hard to prove; as Prodicus said (in T, omitted by Diels–Kranz), Khalkon and his son may simply be named from their wealth! The motif of the victim's father living a good life at home arouses pathos.

Hellas means a region in central Greece, including Peleus' realm (2.529–30n.). ὄλβῳ τε πλούτῳ τε recurs at 24.536, of Peleus himself, and *Od.* 14.206 (also, adapted, at *Erga* 637 and 2× *Hy.*). On pairs of synonyms cf. 335–6n.; the rest of 596 occurs at 194, in the Myrmidon catalogue which this passage reflects. στῆθος μέσον οὔτασε δουρί always precedes δούπησεν δὲ πεσών (15.523, 13.438, where *three* verses intervene). With 598 cf. 5.65, where pursuer slays victim.

600–2 ἀολλέες as usual marks a rally, and rout changes into a standing fight (*stadiē*); with 602 cf. 356–7n., μένος χειρῶν ἰθὺς φέρον (5.506) and ἰ. φέρεται μένει (20.172); ἰ. is often separated from the gen. it governs, e.g. at 24.471.

603–32 The new phase of battle opens with a typical killing by Meriones, last seen at 342, who replaces Aias in this rebuke-pattern (563–644n.). His victim is the sole casualty in this scene, which shows that the Greeks have the advantage. In a curious duel, he dodges Aineias' spear, the Dardan mocks him as a clever dancer, he replies in kind and Patroklos rebukes him for wasting time on words when deeds are wanted. Rather than renew the duel he follows Patroklos elsewhere, 'no doubt leaving Aineias gaping in astonishment' (Fenik, *TBS* 208). This overstates the difficulty; the jibes afford light relief in a grim narrative (so Eustathius 1078.12). Willcock has seen that both men are depicted elsewhere as talkative when embarrassment or anxiety would be natural – Meriones upon meeting his chief Idomeneus behind the lines, when the humour is obvious, and Aineias when faced with Akhilleus (13.246ff., 20.176ff.). This abortive duel is paralleled at 13.502ff., when Aineias missed Idomeneus (610 = 13.503), and 17.526–9 (= 610–13); these are characters whom Homer cannot kill off.

603–7 This slaying resembles the last (593–9n.). ἔνθ' αὖ marks the new phase of battle, since the phrase (Τρώων) ἕλεν ἄνδρα (κορυστήν) is limited to this context (4.457, 8.256, cf. 306 = 15.328); at 5.541 ἔνθ' αὖτ' Αἰνείας Δαναῶν ἕλεν ἄνδρας ἀρίστους conveys that the Trojans are resisting, like the Greeks here. Laogonos and Onetor are handy names used elsewhere (20.460, *Od.* 3.282): /onātēres/, 'beneficiaries', held land at Pylos (each has an /onāton/, 'benefice'), but the bards knew little of the complex Myc. society whose baser glories they celebrate. θρασὺν υἱόν may replace φίλον υἱ. for variatio after 595; someone in T conjectured φ., since Laogonos did nothing to merit the title 'bold'. Several priests' sons die, all but one Trojans (13.663–70n.); the motif arouses pathos. For 606f. see on 13.671f., a priest's son slain in a like way; cf. too 5.78. For Idaean Zeus cf. 24.290f., 308. The god had cults on both Trojan and Cretan Ida (A. B. Cook, *Zeus* II 932ff., 949ff.); Dictaean Zeus was worshipped at Knossos (Fp 1), where Idaios was a man's name (*I-da-i-jo*, K 875). Perhaps local Cretan saga lies in the background: cf. how Idomeneus kills 'Phaistos' (5.43) and 13.363n. T say 'some' texts added after 607 Μηριόνης δ' ἀνέπαλτο, φίλον δέ οἱ ἦτορ ἰάνθη (cf. *Od.* 4.840), 'which is why Aineias mocks him' (617f.); but Meriones' agility at 611 suffices to provoke the jibe. For other pedantic interpolations in T see 14.349–53n.

609–13 For 609 see on 13.156–8; for 610 see on 13.183–4. Note the chiasmus δόρυ χάλκεον – χ. ἔγχος. Verses 610–13 = 17.526–9. The separate halves of 612 are modified at 17.437 and 13.443; in a variant of the topos of a spear quivering in the ground, 613 = 13.444, where see n. Aristarchus omitted 613 in one edition (Did/A), perhaps recognizing a concordance-interpolation from 17.529; in the other he marked the verse as insoluble with the ἄλογος, probably shaped '|'. Since this is our sole evidence that he used this sign in editing Homer, Lehrs emended to ὄβελος; but see Erbse, *Scholia ad loc.*, and Didymus' note on Alcaeus frag. 117b.40. Eustathius (1921.56) says Aristarchus used another rare sign, the χ, in athetizing *Od.* 22.144f.; see further Fowler, *Lyric* 119.

614–15 These vv. are interpolated from 13.504f., repeating 612; this addition, once a marginal parallel, postdates Eustathius.

617–19 War and dance are opposite social activities; to call a warrior a fine dancer is a good insult (see on 745–50, 15.508–10), worsened no doubt by the Cretans' fame, modern and ancient, as dancers (so T and Ath. 5.180F–181B). The dancers on Akhilleus' shield are Cretans (18.590ff.); the

Cretan Kouretes allegedly invented the martial πυρρίχη (see further P. Warren, *BSA* 79 (1984) 307–23). ὀρχηστής recurs in the epos only at 24.261 (versus -τήρ 2×). Verse 619 = 13.254 (where see n.), but with δουρίκλυτος for πεπνύμενος.

620–6 Meriones' jibe caps Aineias' in both form and content. Thus χαλεπόν σε καὶ ἴφθιμόν περ ἐόντα is the antithesis of τάχα κέν σε καὶ ὀρχηστήν π. ἐ. (the alteration of χαλεπόν σοι into χ. σε, by attraction from the following acc. and infin. as at *Od.* 23.81f., increases the parallelism); σβέσσαι μένος answers κατέπαυσε (for the metaphor cf. 9.678), and εἰ καὶ ἐγώ σε βάλοιμι caps εἴ σ' ἔβαλόν περ. Verse 624 blends κρατερός περ ἐών (4×) with χερσὶ πεποιθώς (-α, 2× *Od.*); 625, save for δοίης, = 5.654, 11.445, always ending vaunts (note the antithesis εὖχος – ψυχήν). For ἐνένιπε see 15.545–6n.; with 626 and 628 cf. *Od.* 18.326, ἐ. ὀνειδείοις ἐπέεσσι.

627–32 It is comical that Patroklos scolds Meriones for scolding Aineias, especially since he hurls such a jibe himself at 745ff. He is polite but insistent: with 627 cf. *Od.* 17.381 (Eumaios to Antinoos), and for πέπον see 13.120–3n. With his understated threat and rare use of πάρος cf. π. τοι δαίμονα δώσω (8.166), πρὶν καί τινα γαῖα καθέξει (*Od.* 13.427, 15.31). Verse 630 is a pithy chiastic maxim (cf. 15.741) based on the standard contrast between war and counsel (2.202, 9.53f., 13.726–9n.). τέλος πολέμοιο occurs at 3.291; supply τ. with ἐπέων (cf. 83–8n.). Verse 632 = 11.472, 15.559, again after rebukes.

633–44 These vv. offer a tableau of the entire deadlocked battle, ending the set of individual combats which began at 569. A perfect pair of similes frame a picture of Sarpedon's corpse mangled beyond recognition; thus the focus shifts back to his body and its fate. The woodcutters' hewing and the falling trees symbolize his and others' deaths: he fell 'like a tall tree' (482f.). The flies swarming round the milk-pails are a hint of the decay awaiting the dead. The images ostensibly depict the battle's noise and density respectively.

633–4 τῶν denotes the two armies, which, though unmentioned, form the constant and readily recalled backdrop to the particular combats; cf. 17.755, where τῶν is clarified only after the simile. As Aristarchus noted, the sonorous phrase ὀρυμαγδὸς ὀρώρει can apply to both the woodcutters and the armies (it describes armies 5× *Il.* and at *Aspis* 401). The sound echoes far *because* it is in the glens. As often in the similes, this detail implies an observer; in fact both we and Zeus are watching. Leaf compares 4.455, τῶν δέ τε τηλόσε δοῦπον ἐν οὔρεσιν ἔκλυε ποιμήν (where the din of battle is described, as here), and explains ἕκαθεν thus: '"hearing" (ἀκουή) being regarded as a power going out from the ear, the hearer hears *to* a distance, his hearing comes to the source of sound *from* a distance'. Cf. too πάντοσ' ἀκούειν or πεύθετο γὰρ Κύπρονδε μέγα κλέος (515, 11.21); this archaic concept of hearing was based on that of sight (13.837n.). Unaware of this belief, Aristophanes (Did/AT) read ἀϋτή for ἀκουή (unique in the *Iliad*).

ὀρώρει, Aristarchus' text, is a pluperf. used as a pres., cf. γεγωνεῖν or ὀρώρεται (13.269–71n.); Nicanor and a few MSS read ὄρωρεν, an effort to remove the 'anomaly'. Bekker proposed ὀρώρη (cf. van der Valk, *Researches* II 634), but γίνεται supports an indic. Found in Myc. (PY Vn 10), δρυτόμος retains the original sense of δρῦς, exact cognate of *tree*: cf. 11.86f., δ. περ ἀνήρ ... | οὔρεος ἐν βήσσῃσι (οὔ. ἐν β. occurs 5× Hom., only in similes). For the probable elision of -ησι before (ϝ)έκαθεν cf. 2.456f., οὔ. ἐν κορυφῇς, ἔ. δέ τε φαίνεται αὐγή, | ὡς τῶν ... (contrast 13.179, a tree-simile); in a further innovation βήσσῃς precedes consonants at 766, *Erga* 510.

635–7 δοῦπος as usual echoes the noise of a collision; since it rises sky-ward, it is natural that we soon see Zeus's reaction. 'From the broad earth' shows that Homer already has in mind the perspective of a god gazing down; the fly-image at 641ff. is also seen from above (Fränkel, *Gleichnisse* 36n., 71). χθονὸς εὐρυοδείης recurs 3× *Od.*, 8× Hes., *Hy.*; Shipp notes its 'late' distribu-tion (*Studies* 121f.). It is adapted from *εὐρύοδος by analogy with feminines in -εια (cf. S. West on *Od.* 3.453): for the sense cf. χθονὸς εὐρέος (Asius frag. 13.3), χθὼν εὐρυάγυια (*HyDem* 16), εὐρεῖα χ. and θαλάσσης εὐρυπόροιο. Aristarchus thought 636 'would have been better' without the τ' after βοῶν, so that the leather belongs to the shields and is not distinct from them (read ἄμεινον ⟨ἂν⟩ εἶχε in Did/A); his idea entered a few MSS. Oxhide was also used in armour and belts, so there is no real problem. Verse 636 adapts the old formula (ϝ)ρινοῖσι βοῶν, 'shields' (12.263, 13.406), as the contracted gen. ῥινοῦ proves; cf. Myc. *wi-ri-no* (PY Ub 1318). Xenophon uses βοῦς alone for 'oxhide' (*Anab.* 5.4.12), an old and colloquial idiom: cf. 7.238 and the name Boupalos = σακέσπαλος. Those who read ῥινῶν τε βοῶν (Did/A), no doubt dropping τ', were trying to emend it away. Verse 637 = 14.26 (of noise); see 13.146–8n.

638–40 The mangling, albeit accidental, of Sarpedon's body anticipates the potential mutilation of Patroklos' and actual savaging of Hektor's. It arouses pathos that 'not even a clever man' would have recognized Sarpe-don; cf. the corpses at 7.424 (Griffin, *HLD* 84, 137). This also facilitates his body's removal (666–83n.). The topos of a hypothetical observer of the battle (13.126–8n.) again leads up to Zeus looking on. Aristarchus (Nic/A) emended Σαρπήδονα δῖον, the reading of αἱ κοιναί and our MSS, to the dat. (cf. his change at 668). This yields 'not even one acquainted with Sarpedon would have recognized ⟨him⟩', which solves the 'problem' of how the imagined observer could identify him without having seen him before; but such a person can *ex hypothesi* know anything! φράδμων is next in an oracle (φράδμονος ἀνδρός, Hdt. 3.57); cf. Φραδμονίδης (8.257). Akhilleus' helmet is likewise befouled with 'blood and dust' at 796; the phrase recurs at 15.118, *Od.* 22.383. With 640 cf. | ἐς πόδας ἐκ κεφαλῆς (18.353, 23.169);

Homer also applies the dead metaphor εἴλυτο, 'was wrapped', to snow, sand and sea-spray.

641–4 'They fought round the corpse' frames the simile. Its *Vergleichspunkt* is not explicit, but every detail is apt: the flies are many, persistent and noisy, like the warriors; milk slops everywhere, like the blood. The image also works by contrast. The pastoral detail that milk is most copious in spring clashes poignantly with the martial context; milk is an innocent liquid and the flies seem harmless, but Homer knew that they cause decay (19.24–31). Near Eastern epic even likened gods swarming round a sacrifice to flies (Lambert and Millard, *Atra-Ḥasīs* 99, cf. 95–7). For other insect-similes see 259–65n.; 2.469–71 is especially close (643 = 471). With ἐνιβρομέωσι cf. ἱστίῳ ἐμβρέμεται (15.627). περιγλαγής, 'full of milk', is unique in Greek; the variants ἐΰ- and πολυ- are misquotations (van der Valk, *Researches* II 78). γλάγος (for *γλάκος) is an ancient word limited to poetry (cf. γλακτοφάγος, 13.6): see Chantraine, *Dict.* s.v. γάλα. πέλλα recurs in Hipponax and Theocritus; wooden bowls are meant (cf. Pindar frag. 104b.5).

644–83 Homer breaks the deadlock with a compromise: the Greeks win Sarpedon's armour, but Zeus has his body rescued. A larger concern now eclipses Sarpedon's fate: Zeus ponders *when* (not *whether*) his son's killer must die. He grants Patroklos a great but lethal favour – a last foray to Troy, which takes the hero so far from the ships that Akhilleus knows nothing of his fate (so Eustathius 1080.5). Scenes of divine deliberation and action (644–55, 666–83) frame the start of this foray and stress its importance. Poseidon's rescue of Aineias is split into two such scenes (20.112–55, 291–339).

644–51 Zeus keeps his gaze fixed on the battle, as if taught by his error at 13.3 (the phrasing is alike). For pondering-scenes, of which this is a normal example, see 13.455–8n.; 652 = 13.458 etc. The second option is given briefly (651) because it is stated in full when Zeus selects it, whereas Homer readies us for Patroklos' death and the loss of his armour by describing that eventuality in detail; clearly the respite is but fleeting. As usual when summarizing action, past or future, the poet relies on standard epithets and formulae (cf. 15.66–8n.).

645–8 The formula ὄσσε φαεινώ (13.1–3n.) ousts ἀπὸ κρατερῆς ὑσμίνης (etc.) from the verse-end, where it occurs 35× (648 included). The contraction in ὅρα betrays a conjugation of the phrase-pattern ἴδον φράσσαντό τε θυμῷ (*Od.* 24.391), ὁρόων ἐφράζετο (*HyAphr* 84, cf. *HyDem* 313, *HyAp* 415). For ἀμφί, 'concerning', with the dat. see Chantraine, *GH* II 88.

650–1 The 'vivid' subj. preceding the 'more remote' opt. seems odd: ὀφέλλειεν expresses the option Zeus chooses. As at 14.162–5 (where see n.), verbal moods subtly convey a character's emotion: in his anger and grief Zeus's first thought is to destroy his son's killer, not let him continue. So too he thinks of Patroklos as simply κεῖνος (cf. 13.746, 14.250, 18.257), but gives Sarpedon and Hektor honorific epithets (648f.); and he vindictively formulates the alternative as 'making more men suffer', not 'giving Patroklos more honour'. But he controls his feelings; the poet later says 'he did not hate *even* Patroklos' (17.270). The subject of ὀφέλλειεν may be Patroklos or Zeus; a parallel at *Od.* 2.334 supports Patroklos. For πόνον αἰπύν see on 13.769–73, 17.364–5.

653–7 Instead of an infin., ὄφρα with the opt. is used, as if Zeus had pondered *how* to attain this end rather than *what* to do. Verse 655 blends hemistichs seen at 45 and 5.691, causing the innovative synizesis πολέων at the caesura (Hoekstra, *Modifications* 118). A papyrus and most good codices read ἀναλκίδα θυμὸν ἐνῆκεν, cf. 691 and ἀ. θ. (355), θάρσος ... ἐ. (17.570, cf. 20.80); θυμόν is resumed by ἦτορ in 660. The variant ἀ. φύζαν (ἐνῶρσεν), perhaps from 15.62, emends away the typically oral repetition of θυμόν (cf. 709f.): differently van der Valk, *Researches* II 105f. ἔτραπε governs δίφρον or ἵππους understood, as at 8.157, 257; an intrans. would be unparalleled.

658 Hektor suddenly senses that the tide of battle has turned; cf. Aias' recognition of Zeus's agency at 119ff., or how Zeus makes him flee at 11.544. For the scales in which Zeus weighs both sides to decide a combat, see on 8.69–72, 19.221–4, 22.208–13 (cf. Theognis 157). Clark and Coulson (*MH* 35 (1978) 65ff.) rightly hold that this motif reflects the weighing of souls in the tale of Memnon's death, on which Sarpedon's is based (see p. 313): this is first depicted on vases of *c.* 540 B.C. (*LIMC* s.v. Achilleus, no. 799). The rapid allusion proves the idea traditional; a figure holding scales on a LHIIIA 1 crater from Enkomi may be a god (but cf. E. T. Vermeule and V. Karageorghis, *Mycenaean Pictorial Vase Painting*, Cambridge, Mass., 1982, 14f.). The unique phrase Διὸς ἱρὰ τάλαντα, probably an under-represented formula (supply ῥέποντα), is as old as the Dark Age, since ἱρός is Aeolic (see p. 17 n. 28).

659–62 Since the Trojans are routed, the Lycians flee too. The verses are difficult, because Homer wavers between explaining why the whole army fled (because of Hektor's panic) and why the Lycians did (because of Sarpedon's fall): they 'all' flee when they see their king βεβλαμμένον ἦτορ and lying in a heap of bodies. If 'all' means 'the Lycians' and the 'king' is Sarpedon, who was indeed hit in the chest (481), why is 'harmed in his heart' so weak an expression for 'dead', how can they see him if he is buried under corpses, and why do they react to his death only now and not at 532, when Glaukos told them of it? But if 'all' means 'the whole army' and the 'king' is Hektor, this explains βεβλαμμένον and motivates the general rout – all flee when they see that Zeus has 'harmed Hektor's heart', i.e. made him panic (cf. 656 and βλάπτειν φρένας at 15.724, *Od.* 14.178); yet how can Hektor be lying amid corpses? A. Cheyns (*AC* 48 (1979) 601–10) defends the variant βεβλημένον, but this must be a Byzantine emendation; van der

Valk (*Researches* II 579f.) is right that, were it correct, most good MSS would not offer either the *lectio difficilior* βεβλαμμένον (now in a papyrus) or δεδαϊγμένον, which is surely a conjecture based on 17.535f. (cf. *Od.* 13.320). Wilamowitz accepts δ. as proof of his theory that 659ff. once followed 507 (*IuH* 139f.); Leaf similarly rejects 505–658. Paley kept β., as applying to Hektor's panic, and deleted 661f. The problem does lie in a conflation of versions, but the Analysts mistook its cause – an oral poet's brief hesitation, to which the ambiguity of 'all' contributed; Homer needed to re-establish his focus on Sarpedon's corpse, a minor issue, perhaps, but one which had to be settled. For the point of saying that many others *had fallen* (κάππεσον) on top of the body see 666–83n. ἄγυρις is a rare Aeolism (contrast Myc. *a-ko-ra*). For the traditional metaphor of Zeus pulling taut the rope of war see on 13.358–60; does the ring-structure formed by 658 and 662 suggest that it once denoted the *cord* by which he suspended his scales?

663–5 Just as Hektor will strip Patroklos and give his armour to his comrades to take to Troy (17.125–31), so Patroklos joins his men in stripping Sarpedon (*pace* Fenik, *TBS* 15); with the plural in 663 cf. 19.412, Τρῶες ἀπ' ὤμοιιν Πατρόκλου τεύχε' ἕλοντο. Retainers often take spoils back to base (5.25f., 13.640f., 17.193f.). μέν hints that the armour's fate may be sealed but the body's is not: hence Zeus intervenes. (ἔντεα . . .) χάλκεα μαρμαίροντα is formular (18.131, 23.27); cf. χρύσεα μ. (13.22), ἔ. μ. (12.195), ἔντεσι μαρμαίροντας (279, cf. 13.801).

666–83 Note the poet's sleight of hand: Sarpedon's body must be visible so that it can be stripped, but it is mangled unrecognizably (638–40n.) and buried in corpses (661f.) so that its removal in the murk (567) is neither discreditable to the Greeks nor too obvious, since any reaction to this marvel would detract from the vital matter of Patroklos' attack. Not even Glaukos knows that it was spirited away (17.150f.). On the cultic necessity of Sarpedon's removal to Lycia, and his links with Apollo, see pp. 372f. Zeus tacitly acts on Here's proposal (671–5 adapts 454–7); the detail of his behest hints at his paternal concern. As at 15.220ff., Apollo obeys his father without demur (with 220f., 236 cf. 666f., 676f.); had his errand aided the Greeks, Athene would have run it.

Zenodotus deemed it improper for Apollo to cleanse a body (Did/AT on 667f.), but the god cares for Hektor's at 23.188ff., 24.18ff.; for like actions by other gods see Nickau, *Zenodotos* 211. The humbler task of being pall-bearers is left to Sleep and Death (see further Barrett on Eur. *Hipp.* 1437–9). Schadewaldt (*Welt* 160, 165f.) derives these details from the *Memnonis*, where perhaps Dawn herself cleansed her son's body to give it to Sleep and Death – a rite more aptly performed by a mother than by Apollo. The extent of Zenodotus' athetesis is unclear, but he surely rejected 666–83. He also rewrote 666 as καὶ τότ' ἄρ' ἐξ Ἴδης προσέφη Ζεὺς ὃν φίλον υἱόν and omitted 677 entirely (Arn/A). As Aristarchus alleges, this is a typical attempt to remove a supposed topographical inconcinnity: Apollo, last heard of on the plain (15.365f.), has not explicitly returned to Ida, so Zenodotus made Zeus call to him thence (cf. 431–61n.)!

667–8 The speech is less polished than the narrative. ἐκ βελέων is a clumsy afterthought to fit in the idea of bearing the body out of range of the missiles that might mar it further; cf. 18.152, ἐκ β. ἐρύσαντο νέκυν. At 678 the initial cleansing is smoothly omitted, and ἀείρας governs ἐκ β. Σαρπήδονα. The variant μελέων reflects confusion of minuscule β and μ. Aristarchus (Did/A) read Σαρπήδονι, but verbs of cleansing can take a double acc. (10.572, 18.345); cf. his change at 638.

669–73 These vv. are adapted from the imperative to the third person preterite at 679–83: κάτθεσαν ἐν Λυκίης ... δήμῳ (683) is again smoother than innovative θήσουσῖν Λ. ... δ. (673), but note λοῦσεν, χρῖσεν (679f.). θήσουσ' ἐν is a correction to supply ἐν, like Aristarchus' insertion of ἐν in 775. Both halves of 669 are formular. Anointing always follows washing, as in the formula λοῦσαν καὶ χρῖσαν ἐλαίῳ; ambrosia is the gods' equivalent of oil, and Aphrodite uses 'immortal oil' to protect Hektor's corpse (23.186f., cf. 14.170–1n.). The chiasmus in 670 and the etymological plays ἀμβροσίη ... ἄμβροτα, (ϝ)εἵματα (ϝ)έσσον and πέμπε ... πομποῖσιν give 670f. a musical flow. Immortal clothes are reserved for those who are to be heroized (the dead Akhilleus, *Od.* 24.59) or for gods (*Od.* 7.260, *Hy.* 6.6). That the brothers Sleep and Death (14.231n.) are twins, a unique idea, merely stresses their affinity. The lack of further details deepens the beauty and mystery of this scene; Sarpedon is borne away in a death as gentle as sleep, just as Odysseus is taken home in a sleep as heavy as death (*Od.*13.80). Having tragically deprived one of his most sympathetic characters, Zeus, of his only son at Troy, Homer lets him redress the balance with this sublime and touching sign of favour.

674–5 = 456f., but this prediction has no counterpart in the sequel; as usual, the poet refrains from confirming that his tale validates current beliefs or cult-practices. We are none the less expected to know that the Lycians did give Sarpedon a heroic tomb (p. 372). The idea of the *aition* is already latent in Homer; examples in the *Hymns* show that it was traditional. A papyrus omits 675, perhaps from homoeoteleuton.

679–83 These vv. adapt 669–73, where see n.

684–776 Perilously elated by success, Patroklos drives the Trojans back to the wall of Troy, where Apollo warns him that he cannot take the city. The god urges Hektor against him, but Patroklos kills Hektor's charioteer Kebriones; a fierce fight arises over his body

684–776 Patroklos' ruinous overconfidence, born of his triumph over Sarpedon, grows yet greater now that the Greeks have won the Lycian's armour. Homer repeats the pattern wherein a Trojan rout ends when

Patroklos meets an obstacle (Sarpedon, the wall of Troy); this precedes a rebuke, a major duel and a fight over a corpse leading to a Trojan repulse (cf. 395–665). This pattern is basic to books 16–17 (534–61n.). But last time, Patroklos slew his opponent's driver and went on to kill his opponent and win his armour; now he slays a driver but must fight just to strip his victim. This creates another pattern, since the battles over Sarpedon, Kebriones and Patroklos himself have different results: the Greeks win Sarpedon's panoply but not his body, Kebriones' corpse fully armed, but Patroklos' body stripped bare. The repetition puts emphasis on this last and most important outcome. Patroklos' triple assault on Troy, halted the fourth time by Apollo, is based on the typical motif 'thrice ... but the fourth time'; this recurs at his death, when he thrice enters the fray but is then met by Apollo (784ff.). Fenik (*TBS* 209f.) thinks his duel with Hektor (731ff.) becomes a fight over Kebriones' corpse because of pressure from the standard scene where a driver is slain and a fight erupts over a body. But a more 'literary' explanation exists. A duel with Hektor arouses great suspense, and is inevitable. Since Patroklos cannot kill Hektor, the poet lets him kill Kebriones instead: Kebriones is, as it were, Hektor's substitute, just as Patroklos is Akhilleus'. The duel ends – after Patroklos wins the body, brightening his glory, and Apollo and Euphorbos intervene, dimming Hektor's – with the death-blow Hektor strikes at 818ff. For a full linguistic commentary on 684–867 see Untermann, *Sprache*.

684–91 The poet lets us glimpse Patroklos' state of mind as he plunges him, and us, back into battle, reminding us that he will be led to disaster by disobeying Akhilleus' order to return after saving the ships (87ff.). This is another case of dual motivation: his foolish delusion is his own responsibility but also part of Zeus's inexorable plan (Strasburger, *Kämpfer* 57n.). Fenik (*TBS* 211f.) compares how Hektor becomes too dizzy with victory to heed the warnings; like Patroklos (653ff.), he is granted an extra meed of glory before his death (17.206ff.). Summaries of the general situation can introduce an *aristeia* (13.345–60n.); for νήπιος-comments foreboding doom cf. 46–8n., 2.873–5, 18.310–11.

684–7 Patroklos attacks on foot, bidding Automedon *follow*: this is easily supplied after κελεύσας (cf. 13.361, 20.351). μέγ' ἀάσθη does not connote a moral lapse: the same terms describe the fatal error of leaving one's chariot too far behind (11.340). The phrasing δὲ (ϝ)έπος Πηληϊάδαο φύλαξεν is old, but -δέῳ ἐφ- is in some good MSS. ὑπέκφυγε κῆρα κακὴν μέλανος θανάτοιο belongs to a flexible formular system where the epithets are used with either noun: cf. κῆρες μ. θ., 2.834 = 11.332; ὑ. κῆρα μέλαιναν, 5.22; (ἐκφυγέειν) θάνατόν τε κακὸν καὶ κῆρα (μ.), 3×; κακὰς ... κῆρας, 2×. The added gen. of definition extends the system further: cf. μοῖρ' ... μέλανος θανάτοιο, θ. κακὸν τέλος (*Od.* 17.326, 24.124).

688–90 = 17.176–8 (Hektor speaking). Antithetical maxims about how easily a god can do this or that are rare in the poet's own *persona* (20.265f. only). For the thought cf. 22.18f., *Erga* 5f. and 13.90n.; Zeus gives or removes success as he chooses (15.490–3n.). The Hellenistic nom. κρείσσω for -ων, rejected by Aristarchus, may come from Zenodotus, who read such forms at 1.80, 1.249, 3.71, 3.92 and 7.114 (cf. p. 24 and Wackernagel, *SUH* 73). In both 688 and 17.176 most MSS say 'Zeus's mind is mightier *than a man's*' (ἠέ περ ἀνδρός). The weak variants ἀνδρῶν here and αἰγιόχοιο at 17.176 are conjectures to make it clear that ὅς in the next verse refers to Διός, not ἀνδρός; Homer '*ought* to have said' ἀνδρῶν according to T, who may para-phrase Aristarchus (cf. the wording of Arn/A on 17.178). But 689f., omitted in papyri and some good codices, are a concordance-interpolation from 17.177f., unless the omission arose in error (both 689 and 691 open ὅς ... καί). Van der Valk defends 689f. because its stress on Zeus's power makes Patroklos' fate more tragic (*Researches* II 27–9). Shipp (*Studies* 292) objects that φοβεῖ (with contraction) means 'terrify'; but the sense is 'Zeus *makes* a man *flee* ...', but at another time (ὁτὲ δ') urges him to fight.' There are numerous parallels for indefinite ὁτέ (Shipp, *Studies* 198); Aristophanes emended it to τοτέ in 17.178. ἐποτρύνῃσι is a conjecture that mends the metre: some good MSS have ἐποτρύνει, and the true text is -ει μαχέσ⟨ασ⟩θαι. The same haplography crept in at 17.178, 20.171.

691 Editors read ἀνῆκεν, 'urged on', but ἐνῆκεν (in a papyrus but few good codices) is better: Zeus 'put spirit into' Patroklos (cf. 653–7n.). The usual construction for ἀνίημι is Σαρπηδόνα θυμὸς ἀνῆκε (12.307).

692–7 In an emotive adaptation of the standard opening of slaying-catalogues, the poet addresses Patroklos himself, not the Muse (cf. 14.508–10n.), and reminds us that this is his last foray, since 'the gods called him to his death' (cf. Hektor's realization of this at 22.297). Zenodotus extended the address to Patroklos impossibly far by reading ἕλες in 697 (Arn/A). With 692 cf. *Od.* 9.14; the antithesis between first and last is traditional (15.630–6n.). Lists of nine or so victims in *aristeiai* always provoke a foe to react (415–18n.), here Apollo; asyndeta signal the beginning and end, and even the names are standard. Two massacres open with the same verse as 692 (5.703, 11.299), name Hektor in another verse (as 693 names Patroklos), and add three lines of victims' names: with 694 cf. 11.301, (Ἀσαῖον) μὲν πρῶτα καὶ Αὐτόνοον καί ... A rampage by Teukros starts ἔνθα τίνα πρῶτον ... (Ἄδραστον) μὲν πρῶτα καί ..., ending καὶ Μελάνιππον (8.273–6). In one by Aias, the first verse closes with Δόρυκλον, the last with ἠδὲ Πυλάρτην (11.489–91): cf. Ἔχεκλον ... ἠδὲ Π. here. At 20.472–4 Akhilleus slays another Moulios and another Ekheklos! Quests for meaning in such lists are clearly vain.

The dead all bear Greek names. Three are *Kurzformen*: Ἔχεκλος < -κλέης (189), Πέριμος < -μήδης (15.515), Ἔλασος < -σιππος (cf. Δάμασος from

-σιππος). There were Myceneans named Adrāstos (in the adj. /*Adrāstios*/),
Perimos, Megās (gen. *Me-ka-o*, PY Na 571) and Pulartās (13.413–16n.). For
other Trojans called Adrestos and Melanippos see on 6.37ff., 13.663–70,
15.547–51. Epistor, 'Expert', is contracted from ἐπι(Ϝ)ίστωρ (*Od.* 21.26).
Neoptolemos perhaps slew an Elasos in the *Little Iliad* (frag. 14 D.); another
founded an Attic clan, the Elasidai (*SIG* 926). Moulios, the name of an
Epean and a herald (11.739, *Od.* 18.423), is surely cognate not with μῶλος
but with Meriones' father Mŏlos, the Mŏlione and historically attested
Mŏlon, from μολεῖν with metrical lengthening (von Kamptz, *Personennamen*
245f.). With φύγαδε μνώοντο, 'turned their thoughts to flight', cf. the
proleptic expression φόβονδ' ἀγόρευε (5.252); φύγαδε, a root-noun fossilized
in this acc. form, is confined to the *Iliad* (Risch, *Wortbildung* 6).

698–711 Patroklos would have taken Troy but for Apollo. He nearly
outdoes Akhilleus' impossible wish that they capture it together, which
followed his warning not to assail the city lest Apollo intervene (91ff.);
indeed the god tells Patroklos that neither warrior may sack it. Leaf rejects
698–711, claiming that the attack on Troy is unexpected (but cf. 91ff.!)
and at odds with Hektor's attitude at 713ff.; but Hektor ponders whether to
call his men inside, the right way to defend the walls. We hold our breath
when Apollo thrice thrusts Patroklos back, expecting a fatal blow the fourth
time, a typical motif (702ff.): but the poet prolongs the fighting, with
agonizing suspense, until he repeats this motif at 784ff. Such siege-poetry
certainly goes back to Myc. times (see on 12.107ff. and S. P. Morris, *AJA*
93 (1989) 511–35).

698–701 Apollo saves Troy by urging Hektor on. In Akhilleus' *aristeia*
the Greeks would have taken Troy had the god not inspired Agenor to stand
fast (21.544f. = 698 + 700, to Ἀπόλλων); cf. 17.319ff., where he exhorts
Aineias, and 13.723ff. Patroklos, clad in his leader's armour, prefigures his
actions: as we shall see, his death is based on how Apollo and Paris slew
Akhilleus during an assault on Troy (777–867n.). Akhilleus died at the
Scaean Gate (22.360n., cf. *Aithiopis* testimonium 9 B. = 3 D.), where Hektor
is found at 712, and where, according to Thetis at 18.453, this battle is taking
place! In Quintus of Smyrna (3.26–82) Apollo gives Akhilleus a like warning
at this gate, beginning with χάζεο (40, cf. 707 here), just before he shoots
him in the heel; so this motif too may derive from the tale of Akhilleus' death.
Verse 699 = 11.180, with Ἀτρείδεω for Πατρόκλου, in a similar context –
Agamemnon storms towards the wall of Troy, until Zeus intervenes.

ὑψίπυλος also describes Thebes (6.416). ὑπὸ χερσί usually goes with
passive verbs, notably δαμῆναι, but can be used with actives of like meaning
(Chantraine, *GH* II 140f.). An ugly word-end after the second foot betrays
that Ἀπόλλων Φοῖβος remodels Φ. Ἀ. | (51× epos), as in 20.68, 21.515, 545,
Hes. frag. 307. ἐΰδμητος describes towers in the acc. and gen. plur. (3×),

as well as walls, altars and cities: its declension into the sing. entails a contracted gen. in -ου, as in ἀφ' ὑψηλοῦ πύργου, θείου ἐπὶ π. (12.386, 21.526). The antithesis in 701 blends a phrase like 373, Τρωσὶ κακὰ φρονέων, with Τρώεσσιν ἀρήγων (etc.); cf. too ὀλοόφρων.

702–6 Bards like to contrast 'thrice ... thrice', whether in one verse (23.817, *Od.* 9.361) or more (8.169f., 11.462f., 18.155–7, 18.228f., *Od.* 11.206f.); they also like 'thrice ... but the fourth time', as at 13.20, 22.165 + 208 (with a vast parenthesis), *Erga* 596 and *Aspis* 362f. (cf. 'for nine days ... on the tenth'). This complex variant blends both patterns, as at 21.176f. and *Od.* 21.125–8; its closest cognates are scenes where Apollo repels a Greek's assault at 784–7, 5.436–9 + 443f. (Diomedes), 20.445–8 (Akhilleus). All these begin τρὶς μὲν ἔπειτ' ἐπόρουσε, with τρὶς δ' in the next verse, and then ἀλλ' ὅτε δὴ τὸ τέταρτον ἐπέσσυτο δαίμονι ἶσος (but 20.447 is spurious): then this standard comparison of hero to god collides with the harsh reality of divine superiority. These scenes end δεινὰ δ' ὁμόκλησας προσέφη ἑκάεργος Ἀπόλλων (706, 5.439), or ... ἔπεα πτερόεντα προσηύδα (20.448), whence the variant here, which is surely meant to remove the repetition of Ἀ. (cf. van der Valk, *Researches* II 164f.). Moreover 5.437 runs τρὶς δέ οἱ ἐστύφελιξε φαεινὴν ἀσπίδ' Ἀ. (cf. 703f. here), and Apollo's reproof to Diomedes begins like 707 (φράζεο Τυδεΐδη καὶ χάζεο, 5.440) and has a like effect: 5.443f. = 710f., save that it has 'Diomedes' for 'Patroklos' and τυτθόν for πολλόν. There is no hope of establishing priority; these scenes all draw on the same traditional pattern (cf. 5.436–9n.).

The 'elbow' of the wall must be the angle between the enceinte and the tower on which Apollo stands: it means 'corner' in Hdt. (1.180). Huge, projecting, rectangular towers defended the gates of Troy (C. W. Blegen in *Companion* 375f.). Some detect a memory of the wall of Troy VI, which rises at a slope of one in three until it meets, at an 'elbow', its vertical upper half (Lorimer, *HM* 433). Both these features were probably still visible in Homer's day, but there is no proof that either inspired the poet: Ionian cities of his time likewise used bastions to protect the gates (H. Drerup, *Arch. Hom.* O 100–3). Patroklos' lack of a scaling-ladder may be a heroic exaggeration. βῆ is displaced from the start of 702 because of the need to begin the verse with τρίς; so too Πάτροκλος displaced τρίς in 703. νύσσω, normally 'prick', means 'nudge' as at *Od.* 14.485; Apollo need only touch Patroklos' shield to send him tumbling down.

707–9 Athene ends a speech to Herakles with a like warning: ἄψ δ' ἀναχάσσασθαι, ἐπεὶ οὔ νύ τοι αἴσιμόν ἐστιν | οὔθ' ἵππους ἑλέειν οὔτε κλυτὰ τεύχεα τοῖο (*Aspis* 336f.); cf. 5.440ff., cited above. In 707 Aristarchus read πω for τοι (Did/A); few MSS support this. ἐστι is often omitted with αἶσα. With 708 cf. 21.584. The unique form πέρθαι, 'be sacked', is from not πέρθεσθαι but *πέρθ-σθαι, being an old athematic aor. middle infin. (with passive force), like δέχθαι beside ἐδέγμην/ἐδεξάμην (Risch, *Wortbildung* 236); contrast Chantraine, *GH* 1 384. The variant πέρσαι is worthless. ὅ(ς) περ σέο πολλὸν ἀμείνων is formular (7.114); Akhilleus uses this phrase no less frankly when he bids Lukaon expect no mercy – even Patroklos died, a better man by far (21.107).

710–11 Zenodotus read τυτθόν for πολλόν as at 5.443 (cf. 702–6n.), at once excising the typically oral repetition of π. and standardizing a typical oral variation: others imported π. at 5.443 (Did/T). Aristarchus replied that Diomedes had Athene's words to hearten him, whereas Patroklos has heard Akhilleus' warning and withdraws further. Most MSS offer ἀλευόμενος in 711 but -άμενος at 5.444. Aristarchus standardized ἀνέρι εἰσάμενος to ἀ. εἰδόμενος in 716, comparing the aor. in 720; in this phrase the MSS have a pres. here and at *HyAp* 449, but an aor. at 17.73 and 21.213, where Aristarchus wavered. Bards cared little about either variation.

712–15 The Scaean Gate is nearest to the battle (3.145n.) and will be the aptly ill-omened site of Akhilleus' death (698–701n.). A god again settles a character's doubts at 1.188ff., 10.503ff. Σκαιῇσι πύλῃσι is moved from its usual place at the verse-end (4× epos) with elision before the old verb (ϝ)ἔχε, 'drove' (13.326–7n.); for the formula μώνυχας ἵππους cf. 5.236n. Homer no doubt took ἔχε as 'halted' and linked μῶνυξ with μοῦνος, if he pondered the matter. δίζω, 'doubt', recurs only in an oracle (Hdt. 1.65); like ἐν δοιῇ (9.230) or *doubt*, it is cognate with 'two', i.e. 'be in two minds'. Verse 715 blends ὡς ἄρα (or ὧδε δέ) οἱ φρονέοντι (δοάσσετο), 9× Hom., with the pattern (– ∪∪ – ∪∪)-οντι παρίστατο (-αι).

716–20 Within a ring formed by 715f. and 720 (cf. 710–11n.), we hear that Apollo takes the shape of Asios, who is neatly described as an uncle, brother and son, to emphasize his kinship with Hektor; this ensures that Hektor will listen. So too the god becomes Hektor's *xenos*, Phainops *son of Asios*, to exhort him at 17.582ff., and changes shape to exhort Aineias (17.322ff., 20.79ff.). Verse 720 = 20.82 (17.326 and 585 are spurious); with 716 and 726 cf. 17.73, 82, in another Apolline rebuke to Hektor. Like Phainops, 'Asios son of Dumas' is invented to replace the slain Asios son of Hurtakos (13.383–401n.). Of obscure origin, 'Dumas' is merely another handy name: Athene takes the shape of a daughter of a Dumas at *Od.* 6.22, just as Apollo becomes a Mentes (17.73), another of her *personae* (*Od.* 1.105)! No wonder Tiberius liked to quiz scholars about Hekabe's mother (Suet. *Tib.* 70), when even her father was obscure: elsewhere he is the Thracian king Kisseus (Eur., *Hec.* 3 with schol.) or the Sangarios itself (Pherecydes, *FGH* 3 F 136)! This, the main river of Bithynia which debouches E. of the Bosporus, is still called the Sakarya; Priam mentions it at 3.187, and Hesiod lists it among N. W. Anatolian rivers (*Theog.* 344). If the Hittites knew it as the Seḥiriya (Stella, *Tradizione micenea* 193), it was within their borders.

μήτρως means 'mother's brother' as at 2.662. Hektor receives the generic epithet ἱπποδάμοιο 5× in the *Iliad* only. Its metrical equivalent ἀνδροφόνοιο describes him 12× (*Cat.* 141.29 included), but also the brutes Ares (4.441 (spurious), *Aithiopis* frag. 1 B. = frag. spur. D., *Aspis* 98), Lukoorgos (6.134) and Poluphemos (a variant at *Od.* 10.200). ἀ. is surely borrowed from Ares, as is ὄβριμος (differently R. Sacks, *The Traditional Phrase in Homer*, Leiden 1987, 152–75). The scansion -τὸς Ἑκάβης reflects a lost ϝ-; cf. 6.293, 24.193 and Corinthian ϝακαβα. The name is short for *'ϝεκᾶβόλος; ἐκηβόλος has metrical lengthening (Chantraine, *Dict.* s.v.). On the bardic form ἐεισάμενος from εἴδομαι see Ruijgh in *Studies Chadwick* 539ff.; Untermann, *Sprache* 62.

722–5 There is irony in the disguised god's humble profession of inferiority to Hektor, and pious wish that Apollo grant him success; he soon inflicts on Patroklos the ruin of which he warns Hektor. On threats to slackers see 13.232–4n.; this one, couched in a powerful antithesis, resembles in phrasing 1.186, *Od.* 21.372–4. Characters admit inferiority at 19.217, 20.434 (Odysseus and Hektor to Akhilleus). Verse 724 = 732, with αὐτὰρ ὁ for ἀλλ' ἄγε: rebukes are usually obeyed without delay or demur. κρατερώνυχας ἵππους recurs at 5.329, *Od.* 21.30 (separated); μώνυχας ἵ. was used at 712. For divine horses Homer uses χρυσάμπυκας instead (4×). With 725 cf. 7.81, Hektor speaking.

726–32 Verse 726 = 17.82, 13.239 (cf. 716–20n.); it forms a ring with 728f., since Apollo re-enters the mass twice, while 727f. and 732 form a second ring, since Hektor twice directs his horses. The first ring frames Hektor's brother and driver Kebriones (appointed to that post at 8.318f., and last seen at 13.790), who is at the centre of the ensuing combat. The second frames the fact that Apollo grants the Trojans glory, which fulfils the god's wish at 725 and increases our concern that Hektor will at once kill Patroklos. Fenik (*TBS* 215) thinks the disarray Apollo causes among the Greeks has no visible effect and is soon forgotten; but this is a sinister preparation for his actions at 788ff. With the aor. infin. πεπληγέμεν supply 'with whips' (cf. 23.363). With 728–30 cf. 11.537–9, 12.255, 15.326f.

733–50 Patroklos' duel with Hektor opens typically enough with the slaying of a charioteer with a cast that misses his leader, just as he hit Sarpedon's driver, albeit with a spear not a stone (462–75n.). He scores this major success before Hektor can even dismount: he jumps down at 733, Hektor only at 755, a similar verse (and Hektor has no choice, since his chariot is disabled!). Worse yet for the Trojans, they are given no reply to his vaunt (745ff.). This unexpected victory delays his last encounter with Hektor, turning their duel into a fight for Kebriones' body (684–776n.); cf. 8.118f., where Diomedes kills Hektor's driver (with 739 cf. 121) and Hektor withdraws to find another. Akhilleus' duel with Hektor is similarly interrupted: they first fight over Poludoros' body (20.419ff.), and next meet at 22.131 (Fenik, *TBS* 213f., 221f.). As befits a lesser hero, Patroklos' final duel is not delayed nearly so long.

Kebriones' fall is related in a full style with vivid detail and powerful suspense. Patroklos has his spear in his left hand, saving it to use later (his shield must be supported by its baldric). He grabs a stone: we see its shine and jagged edge. His cast is not in vain – he hits Hektor's . . . driver, Priam's bastard son (what a *coup*!). After this blend of headline and biography comes the usual coroner's report. The stone hits Kebriones between his eyes, which fall out and land by his feet; *he* falls out and lands on his head! Complaints over his eyes' absurd trajectory, especially when conjoined with his own, miss the wit, which begins before Patroklos' jest and overrides naturalistic concerns. But this is Patroklos' – and our – last laugh, as the fearsome *peripeteia* nears.

735–6 Untermann (*Sprache* 71f.) notes that the stone is oddly small (cf. 4.518n.). Homer probably wanted Patroklos to use a larger one (he braces himself to hurl it), but had to give the unique detail that he holds it in one hand, because the hero had only one hand free, holding his spear in the other. Yet even a pebble can shatter one's forehead: it happened to Goliath (1 Samuel 17). Verse 735 forms a ring with ὀξέϊ λᾶϊ at 739; cf. μαρμάρῳ ὀκριόεντι (βαλών), used without πέτρῳ at 12.380, *Od.* 9.499. The 'neglect' of ϝ- in οἱ is rare but Homeric (13.561n.); it arose by adaptation at the caesura of the pattern ὅς/ἅ/τήν οἱ περί (*Od.* 2.116, 21.54 etc.).

736 The scholia and MSS read οὐδὲ δὴν ἅζετο φωτός, 'he did not long stand in awe of the man'; Eustathius, followed by a few late MSS, ignores ἅ. and reads χάζετο. Leaf deems this a bad conjecture; or it could be a slip after λάζετο in 734. Yet it has merit. χάζομαι often takes a gen., but ἅζομαι always takes an acc. (and φῶτα would scan). Also, cf. 11.539f., where Hektor, with Kebriones as driver, charges into the fray: ἐν δὲ κυδοιμὸν | ἧκε κακὸν Δαναοῖσι (cf. 729f.), μίνυνθα δὲ χάζετο δουρός, 'not for long did he back away from (their) spear(s)'. But P. von der Mühll (*Ausgewählte kleine Schriften*, Basel 1976, 399) keeps ἅζετο, proposing that, as sometimes elsewhere, δήν here means 'far (from)'.

737–9 Bastard sons of Priam die at 4.499, 11.102, 490; Kebriones' name is from Kebren, an Aeolic town in the Troad with a native name (cf. 'Ilioneus'). ἁλιόω is rare, but cf. οὐχ ἅλιον βέλος ἧκε (4.498, 15.575); note the etymological play β. βάλε. ἡνιοχεύς (4×) is a metrically useful variant of ἡνίοχος, like πατροφονεύς for -φόνος at *Od.* 1.299f. (Meister, *Kunstsprache* 173f.); there, as here, Homer at once explains the term (ὅ οἱ πατέρα . . . ἔκτα), cf. 261n. Another driver of Hektor's, aptly named Eniopeus, dies ἵππων ἡνί᾽ ἔχοντα and falls from his chariot (8.121). The poetic neuter ἡνία beside fem. ἡνίαι (Myc. /āniai/) also arose *metri gratia* (Chantraine, *Dict.*

s.v.). Both ἀγακλῆος (570–80n.) and Priam's metrically equivalent epithet ἐϋμμελίω (4.47 = 4.165 = 6.449) seem to be generic; in other cases ἐ. adorns other heroes. With ὀξέϊ λᾶϊ cf. ὁ. χαλκῷ (37×), ὁ. δουρί (11×, including 11.95, μετώπιον ὁ. δ.); μ. never recurs in this sense. On the declension of λᾶας see Untermann, *Sprache* 75.

740–4 Kebriones apparently performs a backwards somersault, following the impetus of the blow to his forehead; Homer conjoins with this another freakish event, the excussion of his eyeballs (cf. 13.616–17n.). σύνελεν, 'destroyed', unparalleled in this sense until imperial prose (LSJ s.v. συναιρέω II), may be colloquial: one expects συνέλασσεν. As at *Od.* 22.4, αὐτοῦ πρόσθε ποδῶν means '*there* before (his) feet'. The idea of crushed bones forms the link with the ensuing diver-image: cf. 12.384–6, σὺν δ' ὀστέ' ἄραξε | ... κεφαλῆς· ὁ δ' ἄρ' ἀρνευτῆρι ἐοικὼς | κάππεσ' ἀφ' ὑψηλοῦ πύργου, λίπε δ' ὀστέα θυμός (= *Od.* 12.412–14, with 414 adapted to suit a ship). This brief comparison is traditional: thus a fresco from Mycenae shows a warrior falling backwards off a building, probably with both arms out straight like a diver (Stella, *Tradizione micenea* Tav. xliv). Recent contractions and synizesis show that κάππεσ' ἀπ' εὐεργέος δίφρου adapts ἐϋεργέος ἔκπεσε δ. (5.585 = 13.399); on contracted εὐ- see 104–6n. ἀρνευτήρ means 'diver' as at Aratus 656 and in Hsch. s.v., not 'acrobat' (κυβιστητήρ) as Ap. Soph. glosses it (43.17), misled by how Patroklos likens Kebriones to an acrobat before developing this marine image (modern lexica are confused too). At 406ff., conversely, a man hooked from a chariot on a spear-point is likened to a fish yanked from the sea. For 744 see 20n.

745–50 With the cruel mockery typical of vaunts (e.g. 21.54ff.) and used by the poet in his own *persona* at 406ff. and 742, Patroklos praises Kebriones for his somersault, just as Aineias praised Meriones for 'dancing' out of the way of his spear (617–19n.). Since Patroklos says the Trojans *too* have acrobats (750), his jest is a riposte to Aineias, whom he is imagined to have overheard. Acrobats lead dancers at 18.605f. = *Od.* 4.18f.; the leaders of Greek dances still perform lively gyrations while the rest of the line does the basic steps. Patroklos frames within this jibe (745, 749f.) a striking development of the poet's diver-image (742) in the style of an extended simile (cf. Moulton, *CPh* 74 (1979) 287). Kebriones' antics on land (ἐν πεδίῳ) show how good a diver he would make at sea too (καὶ ἐν πόντῳ), so good that he could dive even in rough weather; let him put his talent to use – by fetching up sea-food! The apparent irrelevance increases the humour, until Patroklos explains by adding 'leaping off a ship'. This wretched occupation makes a good insult, since it is unheroic (407–8n.); diving for octopuses is implied by a simile at *Od.* 5.432f. The two images, and the link with Aineias' joke, were explained by W. E. D. Downes, *CR* 20 (1906) 147f. Many think Patroklos' jest proves him deluded (e.g. Reinhardt, *IuD* 347f.), but what is tragic is his unawareness that he will soon perish too. κυβιστάω, 'somersault', is from κύβος, 'dice' (Untermann, *Sprache* 79).

747–8 τήθεα are not oysters, but clearly the same as the τήθυον, 'sea-squirt'; *τῆθυ later shifted to the *o*-stem declension (cf. 14.157–8n.). This ascidian is classified among ὄστρεα ('molluscs') by Aristotle (H. Bonitz, *Index Aristotelicus*, Berlin 1870, s.v.). The adult sea-squirt adheres to a rock, its sack-like body swathed in a leathery integument. Pliny calls these tunicate molluscs *tethea*, attesting that they were eaten (*H. N.* 32.93, 117). In time of want the Greeks ate much that disgusts well-fed stomachs: Hesiod mentions eating mallow and asphodel (*Erga* 41, with West's n.). Kebriones must 'grope' in the depths for this humble and noisome fare: διφάω, 'seek', can have this sense (Ap. Soph. 59.14; West on *Erga* 374). With δυσπέμφελος, 'rough', supply πόντος (cf. *Theog.* 440, *Erga* 618); this is its primary sense (cf. πομφόλυξ, 'bubble'). Zenodotus read δυσπέμφελοι εἶεν, i.e. 'even if they were surly', clearly deeming it impossible that 'many' would like this food! His emendation is based on *Erga* 722, where Hesiod uses δυσπέμφελος to mean 'surly' (so Aristarchus in Arn/AT).

751–76 A grand panorama depicts the long struggle for Kebriones' body. Patroklos' ill-fated valour is compared to that of a lion whose courage causes his death; his equal duel with Hektor is likened to two lions fighting. Then the focus widens to include its background, the armies colliding like rival winds crashing into a forest; myriad missiles fly to and fro over the body, but Kebriones lies in the dust unaware even of his essential skill, horsemanship. We leave 'the tremendous but frozen turbulence . . . for the sudden still vision of the single man in the eye of the storm who has left it all behind' (A. Parry in Parry, *MHV* liii).

751–3 Patroklos, likened to a lion at 487–9, leaps forth like a lion heroically wounded in the chest: the foreshadowing of his doom, already announced at 685ff., is unmistakable (M. Baltes, *A&A* 29 (1983) 41). Cf. the adumbration of Akhilleus' revenge in the lion-cub simile at 18.318ff. Lions are slain by men defending sheepfolds in similes at 5.556ff., 12.305f.; wounded lions are fiercer (5.136ff., 20.164ff.). The beast 'slain by his own valour' may be a traditional motif, since it enters in a lion-or-boar simile describing Hektor at 12.46 (ἀγηνορίη δέ μιν ἔκτα): but Hektor too will die in this way, as Andromakhe said (6.407). Another image is similarly introduced by αἰετοῦ οἴματ' ἔχων (21.252); οἶμα and οἰμάω, 'spring forward', are used only of predators (see further Chantraine, *Dict.* s.v.). ἐπὶ Κεβριόνῃ frames this image, just as περὶ Κεβριόναο frames the next (756–9).

754–5 The address to Patroklos is emotive (cf. 692f., 744). Hektor's leap matches his; 755 also recalls 733, where Patroklos dismounted. Now they will fight on equal terms, as the ensuing simile confirms. μεμαώς is squeezed into the space filled by χαμᾶζε in 733 (cf. ἆλτ' ἐπί οἱ μεμαώς, 21.174). The

-ᾰ- (from *-ῃ-, cf. μέμονα) is lengthened by analogy with μεμᾱότε(ς), where metrical lengthening is warranted by the usual criteria: cf. ᾱνήρ at 12.382 after ᾱνέρι etc. (Chantraine, *GH* 1 100).

756–8 This image expands the usual brief comparison of warriors to lions (7.256, 15.592); see Fränkel, *Gleichnisse* 62. Pairs of fighters are likened to pairs of lions at 5.554ff., 10.297 and 13.198ff., where, as here, the beasts' conduct fits the narrative but not their real habits; lions neither co-operate in carrying a carcase nor fight over one, even if hungry. Lions also duel over a body in a simile at *Aspis* 402–4, cf. 405ff. Hunger makes them fiercer (cf. 3.23–6, 18.162). Warring animals are of the same species when the combat is equal (bT on 823), as in the vulture-image describing Sarpedon and Patroklos (428f.); when it is unequal, a stronger beast fights a weaker one, as at 487–9 (Patroklos as lion, Sarpedon as bull) or 823–6 (Hektor as lion, Patroklos as boar). The nine dual forms in 756–9 stress that the opponents are evenly matched; the dead doe stands for Kebriones, insignificant even when alive, yet his body is vital to the comparison, as its frame emphasizes. These images form a series wherein this one heightens the vulture-simile (Baltes, *art. cit.* 40f.): μεγάλα κλάζοντε μάχωνται (429) is replaced by μέγα φρονέοντε μάχεσθον; cf. in the next lion-simile (824) ὄρεος κορυφῇσι μ. φ. μ. (the formula ὄ. κ. also enters the simile of two lions at 5.554). Just as at 482ff., a tree-simile is nearby. Baltes thinks the lions duel 'in the peaks' because the two warriors far excel the rest in valour.

756 δηρινθήτην is odd: save for δηρινθῆναι, derived hence by Apollonius Rhodius (2.16), no form of δηριάομαι contains -ν-. Homer could have said δηριάασθον or -ίσαντο (12.421, *Od.* 8.76). Risch adduces ἀμπνύ(ν)θη (*Wortbildung* 336), and some MSS emend the ν away, but I believe that the true text is δῆριν θήτην, adapted from the phrase δῆριν ἔθεντο | (17.158, epigram in Dem. *De Cor.* 289, Euphorion frag. 98.2, anon. in *SH* 928.6). The older form is θέτην, but the short vowel of dual and plur. root-aorists is often altered by analogy, e.g. βήτην beside βάτην (Chantraine, *GH* 1 378); θήτην presupposes the lost sing. *ἔθην, just as -βλήτην (*Od.* 21.15) is from *ἔβλην. Everyone has been misled by the texts' lack of word-division, combined with the extreme rarity of a word-end after a fifth-foot spondee (see Meister, *Kunstsprache* 7f., and West, *Greek Metre*, Oxford 1982, 37n.).

761 = 13.501, again in a major duel; 764 = 14.448, again in a fight for a body. Corpses are dragged by the head (cf. 3.369, 13.188), by the feet (13.383–5n.) or by both ends in both directions, as here (cf. 17.389ff.). Verse 762 resembles 15.716, where see n.: like the n-mobile in ἔχεν π-, the gen. κεφαλῆφιν is innovative (it is ablatival elsewhere).

765–9 A splendid five-verse simile introduces five lines describing the 'precarious balance of violent forces in battle' (A. Parry, *loc. cit.*). Their equality is shown by how the winds compete as equals, as the duals and the repetition of 'each other' indicate. Fränkel (*Gleichnisse* 37) thinks both the winds and the woods they shake stand for the two armies, in a failed attempt to depict the battle's reciprocity; Baltes (*art. cit.* 42f.) equates the winds with the duellists and the forest with their men, just as the lone tree at 482ff. stands for a single warrior. This is too subtle. At 9.4ff. two winds stir up the sea; this expresses the Greeks' alarm, but one cannot equate the winds with their leaders. The image follows the pattern wherein a natural force hits field, forest or sea, and the simile's last clause describes the visible or audible effect (cf. 633–4n., 2.148, 2.210, 7.64 etc.). The winds are personified; the idea that they play with one another recurs at *Od.* 5.331f. The density of the woods magnifies their impact (bT). The 'sharp-pointed' boughs that the trees hurl at each other evoke the missiles flying to and fro at 772ff. τανυηκής describes only swords elsewhere (14.383–7n.); Aristarchus glossed it simply 'slender' (ταναός), treating -ηκής as senseless, but it is a fine example of interaction between a simile's diction and its context. Both the ash and the cornelian cherry (*Cornus mas*) were used for spears (141–4n., *HyHerm* 460). ἠχῆ θεσπεσίη (9× Hom.) often enters panoramic tableaux of battle.

Εὖρός τε Νότος τε is formular (2.145 (simile), 2× *Od.*). βήσσης βαθέην, perhaps with an etymological play, is linguistically recent: it blends the formulae οὔρεος ἐν βήσσῃσι and βαθείην ... ὕλην, where original βαθεῖαν is itself remodelled after the gen. βαθείης (Untermann, *Sprache* 90): see on 633f., 15.605–9. Most sources until Eustathius have the error πολεμιζέμεν. τανύφλοιος is obscure. The bark of the cornelian cherry is not especially thin, although it does peel when the tree ages: LSJ propose 'with long-stretched bark', i.e. 'tall', but this tree is no taller than *c.* 22 feet! Later poets use the epithet of the poplar, fir and wild fig. D suggest 'fibrous', Leaf 'with fine, smooth bark', which is best (so R. Meiggs, *Trees and Timber in the Ancient World*, Oxford 1982, 111). With 769 cf. 13.283; note the lack of a verb. The fractured hiatus before (ϝ)αγνυμενάων forms the climax to a whole set of sound-effects, in a sentence that runs from 765 to 771.

770–1 = 11.70f. This old couplet belongs to a larger pattern, since it opens the panorama of massed missile-fighting framed by 777ff. (where see n.), which resembles 11.84ff. The repetition of 'each other' picks up 765 and 768. How the arrows 'leap' (773) resumes how the armies 'leap' at each other, and Kebriones is 'forgetful of his horsemanship' (776) just as neither side 'remembered' about fleeing.

772–5 With the Trojans regrouped outside the city wall, the battle enters its usual opening stage of long-range combat, while the leaders fight between the lines as πρόμαχοι; the armies do not fight hand to hand until 17.262ff. (Latacz, *Kampfdarstellung* 118ff., 124f.). The description, framed by Κεβριόνην ἀμφ' ... ἀμφ' αὐτόν, is heightened by anaphora of πολλά, the half-rhyme -εντες ... -όντες and the sheer multiplication of kinds of missile (cf. 15.709–12n.). ὀξέα δοῦρα occurs 6× Hom. in other metrical positions (cf. 5.619, 11.44): 3.135 has ἔγχεα μακρά with the same verb. Arrows are often 'feathered', like words (4.117n., 5.171, 20.68); for ἀπὸ νευρῆφι see 13.584–5n. As usual, Aristarchus (Did/A) preferred the plur. ἐστυφέλιξαν with a neuter plur. subject (cf. 13.616–19n.): the sing. is worse attested here.

775–6 These vv. have long been admired (751–76n.). The distich is too grand to have been invented for Kebriones (so Schadewaldt, *Welt* 168), who was likened to a diver and a dead deer; Griffin is wrong to cavil if this aesthetic judgement becomes a means of 'inquiry into Origins' (*HLD* 106n.). The couplet's origin is hardly less clear than is the pathos which its adaptation to this context arouses: like other details of Patroklos' death, it derives from that of Akhilleus (see pp. 312f.), to whom Homer applies two variants of it, as Kakridis saw (*Homeric Researches* 85ff.). At 18.26f. Akhilleus has heard that Patroklos is slain: αὐτὸς δ' ἐν κονίῃσι μέγας μεγαλωστὶ τανυσθεὶς | κεῖτο. The Nereids soon bewail him as if he too is already dead. A yet closer parallel at *Od.* 24.39f. decides the case: the Greeks saved Akhilleus' body, μαρνάμενοι περὶ σεῖο· σὺ δὲ στροφάλιγγι κονίης | κεῖσο μέγας μεγαλωστί, λελασμένος ἱπποσυνάων. Then the Nereids weep by his corpse, as happened in the *Aithiopis*. The closing phrase fits both the charioteer Kebriones and Akhilleus: every leader must excel as both driver and spearman, like Euphorbos or Hektor (809, 11.503), and the fact that Akhilleus has the best horses implies that he can handle them with commensurate skill (2.769f.). Willcock thinks the couplet was created for the charioteer heroes of yore like ἱππότα Νέστωρ; but the phrasing is not especially old (Heubeck on *Od.* 24.39f.). As at *Od.* 24.39, the vulgate is δὲ στροφάλιγγι; Aristarchus (Did/A) read δ' ἐν σ., a facile emendation (cf. on 669–73, 14.200–2). σ. κονίης recurs at 21.503, preceded by μετά; cf. στροφαλίζω (*Od.* 18.315), related to στρέφω like (ἐν)τροπαλίζω to τρέπω (Risch, *Wortbildung* 300). The artificial phrase μέγας μεγαλωστί is an emphatic repetition like οἰόθεν οἶος or αἰνόθεν αἰνῶς; μεγαλωστί is an isolated form based on μεγάλως (Risch, *Kleine Schriften* 171).

777–867 The Greeks manage to win Kebriones' body, but Apollo smites Patroklos, stripping off his armour and dazing him; then Euphorbos wounds him in the back, and Hektor stabs him in the belly. In reply to Hektor's taunt that he failed to obey Akhilleus' orders and kill him, the dying Patroklos defiantly predicts that Hektor himself will soon be slain by Akhilleus

777–867 Patroklos' death is extraordinary. Why does Apollo knock Akhilleus' armour from his body, leaving him helpless and dazed? Why is he first hit in the back? Why does Homer dim Hektor's glory by giving the first wound to Euphorbos, a hero of whom we have never heard, and whom

Menelaos at once dispatches (17.9ff.)? Why is it later implied that Patroklos' body still wears its armour (17.13, 17.125, 17.205)? It is too easy to guess, with Leaf, that this scene replaces one where Hektor alone slew Patroklos, or to reject 793–804 because it implies the exchange of armour (so P. von der Mühll, *Kritisches Hypomnema zur Ilias*, Basel 1952, 252). The literary effects of these details are clear (cf. Reinhardt, *IuD* 319ff.); but only traditions behind the *Iliad*, especially those about Akhilleus' own death, can explain their precise configuration.

First, the armour. Edwards (*HPI* 264) notes that its removal reminds us that 'divine armour is not proper for Patroklos, who has no divine ancestry'; disarmed, he is tragically helpless before Apollo's sinister power. It is less shameful that a god strips off his armour than if Hektor does so (bT on 793ff.). The scene foreshadows Akhilleus' own death, when his helmet rolls in the dust (794–800n.); the poet had Akhilleus' death in mind (775–6n.). But a major reason for Apollo's action must be that Akhilleus' armour was originally impenetrable (130–54n.); Patroklos is invincible until he is disarmed. The folk-tale idea of a god stripping him (Stith Thompson D 1403.3), necessary once Homer decided to clothe him in this armour, perhaps seemed too bizarre for the poet's taste; hence the narrative soon reverts to the usual pattern where a body wears its armour until it is stripped.

Second, the detail that Euphorbos hit the disarmed Patroklos with a spear hurled at the small of his back and then fled (806–7n.) resembles Hagen's cowardly blow at *Nibelungenlied* xvf. Hagen steals Siegfried's armour and kills him in just that same spot where alone he is vulnerable, since the dragon's blood which made the rest of his body impervious to steel was not smeared between his shoulders; Hagen then runs away. Again Homer suppresses any magical aspect, simply omitting to explain; he does not even state that Patroklos' back is turned towards the enemy, although we may fancy that Apollo's blow made him spin round (the fact that his eyes whirl round is based on this, cf. 791–2n.). The nature of this blow is suggestive of a pre-existent legend. The most obvious parallel is the tale of Akhilleus' invulnerability save at his heel, where Apollo and Paris shot him: see 'Apollodorus', *Epit.* 5.3 with Frazer's n.; *LIMC* s.v. Achilleus, pl. 850 (Chalcidian vase, *c.* 540). On the vase Paris apparently shot Akhilleus in the shoulder, and Apollo shot him in the heel (Schoeck, *Ilias und Aithiopis* 130). Proclus omits to say whether Akhilleus was shot *in the heel* in the *Aithiopis*, but this surely happened; the incident inspired how Paris shoots Diomedes in the heel at 11.369ff. (on Diomedes as Akhilleus' substitute see on 97ff.). The legend that Thetis dipped her baby in the Stux to make him invulnerable, holding him by the ankle, is first in Hyginus 107 and Statius (*Ach.* 1.269f.), but seems ancient (cf. 'Hesiod' frag. 300). Cf. too the invulnerability of Aias (14.402–8n.) and Stith Thompson z 311.

Thirdly, Euphorbos is not invented solely to dim Hektor's glory (E. Bethe, *Homer* I, Leipzig 1914, 318) or to offer an immediate model for Akhilleus' revenge upon him (Strasburger, *Kämpfer* 35), although both effects suit the poem's design. Homer based Euphorbos on Akhilleus' slayer, Paris, as Mühlestein proved (808–11n.). Both Patroklos and Akhilleus die by the Scaean Gate (698–701n.) through the joint action of Apollo and a Trojan (19.416f., 21.277f., 22.359f., *Aithiopis* in Proclus' epitome). Like Paris, Euphorbos strikes from afar. We shall see that he is Paris' double: both are nobles, herdsmen, excellent at games, handsome and foes of Menelaos.

777 This v. blends the standard line ὄφρα μὲν ἠὼς ἦν καὶ ἀέξετο ἱερὸν ἦμαρ (8.66, 11.84, *Od.* 9.56) with ἦμος δ᾽ ἠέλιος μέσον οὐρανὸν ἀμφιβεβήκει (8.68, *Od.* 4.400). The former always precedes the same line as 778, save at *Od.* 9.56ff., where 58f. = 779f. (to δή); the tradition has a full set of phrases for battles at various times (15.318–19n.). There was good reason to vary the pattern shared with 11.84ff. (770–1n.): 11.84 describes an earlier hour, towards noon; to have repeated it unchanged would have produced two noons in the same day. The action of 11.90–16.776 all takes place in 'the middle of the day', which the epos divides into three parts, ἠὼς ἢ δείλη ἢ μέσον ἦμαρ (21.111). It is now afternoon; the fight for Patroklos' body lasts until sunset (18.241). It is absurd to cavil that too much happens for the time available. Homer exploits 'the splendid symbolism of the sun's descent heralding the final hour of Patroklos' (Fenik, *TBS* 216). It is all the more unexpected that this hour sees the Greeks win – we had foreseen disaster. The poet creates tension with this traditional device, and then uses another to introduce Apollo (784–6n.), deftly piling up standard motifs.

779 It was usual to loose the oxen from ploughing when the day was two-thirds gone, so that they could graze and renew their stamina: cf. Aristoph. *Birds* 1499f., where βουλυτός is 'a little after noon' (also Aratus 825, Ap. Rhod. 3.1340–2). Later authors took it as 'evening' (LSJ s.v.). Frazer (*CR* 2 (1888) 260f.) noted that German *Morgen* can mean a measure of land (0.6–0.9 acres), i.e. a day's ploughing; in ancient Wales too ploughing ceased at noon. Typically, Hesiod stresses the need to begin at dawn, but omits to say that one must not use the same team all day (*Erga* 578–81, with West's nn.). ἦμος has an Aeolic psilosis: with ἦμος – τῆμος cf. ὅτε – τότε etc.

780–3 That they prevail 'beyond what was fated' is the ultimate accolade for Patroklos and the Greeks: nothing else in the *Iliad* happens ὑπὲρ αἶσαν. Contrast 6.487 and the moral outlook of the *Odyssey* (pp. 5f.). We know this cannot last. The usual pattern is typified by 17.319, 'they would have taken Troy even beyond what was fated by Zeus (καὶ ὑ. Διὸς α.), had not Apollo . . .' To take the phrase as merely 'beyond expectation' (Erbse, *Götter* 291f.) spoils the hyperbole. The generic epithet ἥρωα is again separated from the name at 22.298; note ἔρυσσαν with 'observed' ϝ-. Τρωσὶ κακὰ φρονέων occurred at 373, when Patroklos first entered the fray.

784–6 For Apollo's intervention Homer uses the motif of a man's triple assault repulsed the fourth time by a god, as at 702–6 (where see n.). Apollo's warning then should have sufficed, but it was already too late. Hostile intervention often follows a list of victims' names (415–18n.); here Patroklos' victims are nameless, but he kills twenty-seven, nine at each swoop – an unparalleled feat, although twelve Trojans perish at Akhilleus' yell (18.230). Like the Greeks' success, this is clearly 'beyond fate'; Homer reserves such feats for extraordinary moments, thus honouring Patroklos and making his fall into helplessness all the more precipitous and terrifying. The old formula θοῷ ἀτάλαντος Ἄρηϊ (13.295–7n.), inspired perhaps by anticipation of δαίμονι ἶσος, reinforces the equation of hero to god – an equation which a real god can cancel in a second, as Apollo at once proves. The choice of Ares may not be purely mechanical, since Patroklos is filled with a frenzy like Ares' (cf. p. 225). For σμερδαλέα ἰάχων see 5.302–4n.; Untermann, *Sprache* 100f.

787–90 The sudden address to Patroklos 'indicates one who sympathizes; "for you, Patroklos", for the person who was so beloved by Akhilleus, who would go to any lengths to save the Greeks, who patiently put up with Nestor, who affectionately healed Eurupulos, who wept for the Greeks and persuaded the stubborn Akhilleus, who made the foray succeed at the risk of his own life – by relating all this to the apostrophe, one can see the emotive element in it' (bT, cf. 20n.). Verse 787 resembles 7.104, ἔνθα κέ τοι Μενέλαε φάνη βιότοιο τελευτή (he arms to face Hektor). It is sinister that Apollo 'meets' Patroklos, who could not avoid him because the god was 'wrapped in mist', i.e. invisible; a reprise of 'he met him' frames this explanation. ἄντομαι need not denote enmity (cf. 22.203, *HyDem* 52), but implies a face-to-face encounter. The emphatic runover adj. δεινός, separated from its noun and preceding a stop, recurs only at 22.133f., Πηλιάδα μελίην ... | δεινήν, an equally electrifying scene. With 790 cf. ἠέρι καὶ νεφέλη κεκαλυμμέναι (2× *Od.*), κ. ἠ. πολλῆ | (etc., 7× epos).

791–804 Finally the blow falls; yet Apollo hits Patroklos not with an arrow but merely 'with down-turned hand'. For the contrast between effortless divine action and its drastic effects cf. 703f., 845f., 15.361f. The immediate impact is physical, not mental (contrast 805f.): Patroklos' eyes whirl round, his armour flies off piecemeal and his spear shatters. We saw this 'slow-motion' technique at 13.434ff., where Poseidon paralyses Alkathoos so that Idomeneus can kill him. A plethora of stately epithets (the spear has five) slows the narrative further. First, Akhilleus' helmet is knocked off and dust befouls its crest. The poet dwells on this moving detail as if it stands for the hero's own head lying in the dust (794–800n.). Before, this was not allowed to occur; but now Zeus has granted that Hektor don the helmet. As bT saw, Homer softens the shock of this first announcement that Hektor will wear the panoply by adding that his doom is near, even before Patroklos says so (852–4). This digression stresses the armour's importance; the poet can now hurry past the more bizarre aspects of Patroklos' disarmament – as Eustathius says (1087.36f.), one could lose a helmet by accident. Patroklos loses his spear, shield and corslet; we do not hear of his greaves or sword (cf. 134–5n.). In other disarming-scenes the sequence is helmet, shield and spear (15.125f., *Od.* 14.276f.); but here Homer reverses the sequence of an arming-scene, i.e. corslet, shield, helmet and spear, save that the helmet comes first.

791–2 Apollo slaps Patroklos' 'back and broad shoulders'; this formular phrase (cf. 2.265f., 23.380, *Od.* 8.528) must be a hendiadys for his back *between* the shoulders, where Euphorbos wounds him at 806f. (the phrasing is similar). It is as if Apollo's blow is a metastasis, as well as essential precursor, of Euphorbos' (note the phrasing of 816). χειρὶ καταπρηνεῖ, often taken as 'with down-turned hand', means 'with the flat of the hand' here: the god's palm must face sideways (cf. Untermann, *Sprache* 104f.). The formula recurs with ἐλάσαι at *Od.* 13.164, when Poseidon turns a ship into a rock, and *HyAp* 333, when Here beats her palms on the earth to invoke chthonic powers. It is used in the plur. at *Od.* 19.467 and of slapping one's thighs (15.113–14n.). The metrical makeshift πλῆξεν δέ and contraction in καταπρηνεῖ are innovative traits; the dual εὐρέε τ' ὤμω enables τ' to be fitted in, cf. εὐρέας ὤμους (6× epos). στρεφεδίνηθεν is a bold and evocative compound inspired by μετάφρενον nearby (cf. 777–867n.), which formulae associate with the idea of turning round (e.g. στρεφθέντι μεταφρένῳ, 5.40). Its sole parallels are Aeschylus' στροφοδινοῦνται and τροχοδινεῖται δ' ὄμμαθ' ἐλίγδην (*Ag.* 51, *Pr.* 882); Risch (*Wortbildung* 181) derives it from *στρεφεδινής, but it may well be an *ad hoc* creation. Elsewhere eyes that turn indicate good vision (17.679f., *HyHerm* 45).

794–800 These vv. develop two standard motifs – fallen objects rolling noisily on the battlefield (13.526–30n.), and human hair or horsehair crests fouled in the dust (Fenik, *TBS* 163). Thus Akhilleus' horses mourn Patroklos, fouling their manes (17.439f.); Dolops' crest falls in the dust, before Menelaos kills him with a spear-cast at his shoulder from behind (15.537f.); blood fouls Euphorbos' lovely hair (17.51f.) and Akhilleus defiles his 'head and fair face' with dust in mourning (18.23f.). The most telling parallel or indeed echo is 22.401–4, when Akhilleus drags Hektor's body behind his chariot: ἀμφὶ δὲ χαῖται | κυάνεαι πίτναντο, κάρη δ' ἅπαν ἐν κονίῃσι | κεῖτο πάρος χαρίεν· τότε δὲ Ζεὺς δυσμενέεσσι | δῶκεν ἀεικίσσασθαι. The pathetic contrast between past beauty and Zeus's present willingness to let it be disfigured is also exploited here (Griffin, *HLD* 134–7). Like Patroklos',

Hektor's body is pierced more than once; his head re-enacts the fate of Akhilleus' helmet (cf. Thalmann, *Conventions* 48).

794–5 Dactylic rhythm, alliterating κ, ν, π and χ and geminated π and σ mimic the helmet bouncing away under the horses' hooves. For καναχὴν ἔχε see on 104–6; for αὐλῶπις τρυφάλεια see 13.526–30n. ἔθειρα once began with ϝ-: cf. *Od.* 16.176 (*pace* Aristarchus), *HyAphr* 228, *Hy.* 7.4. For 'befoul with blood' or 'dust' cf. 4.146, 23.732; 'blood and dust' is formular (638–40n.). ἱππόκομος describes κόρυς (338–40n.) and τρυφάλεια (12.339). θείοιο recurs in this position only at 10.315; it alludes to Akhilleus' divine parentage – he alone can wear divine armour with impunity (Thalmann, *Conventions* 46). κάρη χαρίεν τε μέτωπον belongs to a loose formular system, cf. κ. . . . χ. (22.402f.), κ. ∪∪ – ∪ μέτωπα (*Od.* 6.107), χ. ∪∪ – ∪ πρόσωπον (18.24, *Hy.* 31.12), χαρίεντι μετώπῳ (Aristeas frag. 6 B. = 2 D.).

801–2 οἱ denotes Patroklos, last mentioned at 793; we soon gather that the parenthesis is over. 'Some' (Did/A) emended πᾶν to τῷ, but Aristarchus explained that πᾶν means the 'whole' spear, not 'every' spear; cf. 3.367, where Menelaos complains that Zeus smashed his sword. Since the formula βριθὺ μέγα στιβαρόν describes only Athene's spear and Akhilleus', the poet may have lapsed into thinking that Patroklos has his leader's weapon (141–4n.). A unique adaptation of δοῦρε δύω κεκορυθμένα χαλκῷ (3.18, 11.43, *Od.* 22.125, in arming-scenes) prolongs the cumulation of epithets; the omission of χ. is awkward.

803 For the baldric see 14.402–8n. τερμιόεις, used of tunics at *Od.* 19.242 and *Erga* 537, appears in Myc. as *te-mi-dwe* = /*termidwens*/, an epithet of wheels, probably 'with tyres'. The ending -όεις remodels this form, just as φοινικόεις with anomalous ῑ has replaced *φοινῑκ-ϝεις while continuing its metrical shape (Risch, *Wortbildung* 152n.). The root is τέρμις, glossed πούς by Hesychius; this occurs on tablet KN V 280 in the phrase *to-pe-za o-u-ki-te-mi*, 'a table, (with) no τέρμις' (Ventris and Chadwick, *Documents* 476). The ancients took the adj. to mean 'down to the feet', but 'edged' better fits our evidence, since shields, tunics, wheels and tables can all have special edges: cf. the elaborate *border* (a binding of dyed leather thongs?) on the wheel in the Tiryns fresco of ladies driving (J. Wiesner, *Arch. Hom.* F Abb. 8). C. Picard (*RA* 46 (1955) 68–71) thinks the shield had a leather fringe (cf. the LHIIIC Warrior Vase from Mycenae). Bards may well have reinterpreted this archaism, which Zenodotus perhaps sought to introduce at 3.334 also.

804–5 Unless Homer's phrasing simply follows the mention of Zeus at 799, his choice of ἄναξ Διὸς υἱός Ἀπόλλων instead of ἄ. ἑκάεργος Ἀ. (15.252–3n.) stresses that Zeus stands behind his son's action, as Patroklos says at 845. When Apollo 'looses' Patroklos' corslet, 'confusion' seizes his mind and his knees are 'loosed': cf. ὑπέλυσε . . . φαίδιμα γυῖα, of killing (6.27), and πέδησε δὲ φ. γ., of Alkathoos' divinely caused paralysis (13.435).

For ἄτη see 266–77n. Apollo strips Patroklos of all defences, physical and mental, but does not interfere directly with his mind, as did Poseidon in Alkathoos' case. Cf. instead the topos of charioteers scared out of their wits (401–10n.). Patroklos is at first swept away by his exploits, then stunned by Apollo's blow, but never insane; even now, Homer upholds his dignity.

806–7 Euphorbos' cowardly hit is in the same spot as Apollo's, with verbal parallels (791–2n.); neither is fatal. The effect is to stress that the god aids Euphorbos, not Hektor; as when Athene helps Akhilleus slay Hektor, such aid glorifies its recipient. The poet blends στῆ δὲ ταφών (24.360) with στῆ δ' ὄπιθεν (2×), as at 11.545, and then μετάφρενον ὀξέϊ δουρί (20.488) with μεταφρένῳ ἐν δόρυ πῆξεν | ὤμων μεσσηγύς (3×, cf. *Od.* 22.92f.). Oddly, we have not heard that Patroklos' back is turned to the enemy (cf. 777–867n.). To avoid a 'contradiction' Zenodotus read σχεδὸν οὔτασε, but Aristarchus rightly objects that 812 confirms σχεδόθεν βάλε (as do 819, 17.15). σχεδόν is used eisewhere with verbs of thrusting, not casting, but ἔβαλε σ. ἐλθών (17.600) shows that 'hit at close range' makes good sense (Lehrs, *De Aristarchi studiis* 59f.). A thrust would be the true counterpart of Apollo's blow, yet Paris shoots Akhilleus.

808–11 As Mühlestein shows (*Namenstudien* 78–89), Euphorbos is based on Paris, his role on that of Paris in Akhilleus' death (777–867n.). This is clear not only from his good looks (17.51f.), Menelaos' enmity to him and the special favour Apollo grants 'the best of the Trojans' (17.80), but also from analysis of his background. T ask how he can be a Dardan if his father Panthoos is a Trojan elder (3.146ff.). Now 'Euphorbos' is a pastoral name; the Achilles-painter calls the shepherd who saves the baby Oidipous 'Euphorbos' (Seneca, *Oed.* 840ff., calls him Phorbas), and Dardanians live on Ida (2.819ff., 20.215ff.), where herds were pastured (11.105f., 21.448f., *HyAphr* 53ff.). Now Euripides' *Alexandros* told how Paris was exposed and reared as a shepherd on Ida; he returned to Troy, triumphed incognito in games there and was recognized by his parents (a tale perhaps in the *Cypria*, cf. Jouan, *Chants Cypriens* 135–7). Thus Paris too was both a Dardan and a noble Trojan. Homer surely knew this story, since he at once describes Euphorbos' prowess in *games*, another way in which he resembles Paris.

Verses 808–11 are a biographical digression to uphold Patroklos' honour by glorifying the unknown Euphorbos (so T); Patroklos has just slain twenty-seven men (785), so he knocks down twenty (cf. 843–7n.). But when and how did he 'dislodge twenty men from their chariots' (for the expression cf. 5.163f.)? Spear-throwing, chariotry and running all have athletic as well as martial uses (with 808f. cf. 2.530, 11.503, 14.124f., 23.289); the son of Πάν-θοος is suitably swift. Aristarchus wavered between a martial and an athletic interpretation. Did/A says he read τότε (also in a papyrus); this means that Euphorbos first came to war on this day and slew twenty men.

But the topos of the Trojan late-comer is normally used to arouse pathos, not to explain why we never heard of someone before (13.361–82n.). Moreover, Aristarchus also read our vulgate ποτε: Arn/A, with the lemma ποτε, records his note 'it was a custom among the ancients to joust from chariots with blunted lances, and to upset them from their vehicles'. Dionysius Thrax objects that Euphorbos' exploit was 'not for practice, but he slew them when he first contended and first joined the war' (read πρῶτον ἀγωνιῶν). However, the Mycenaeans did use war-chariots for races and jousts, a risky sport of which traces survive in the myths of Euenos, Pelops and Kuknos: see Janko, *CQ* 36 (1986) 58; Vermeule, *PCPS* 33 (1987) 141; E. Rystedt in French and Wardle, *Prehistory* 437–42. ποτε reflects Euphorbos' prehistory as Paris; it must not be emended away, *pace* van der Valk, *Researches* 1 563–5.

ἡλικίη means 'his (young) age-mates', as in ὁμηλικίην ἐκέκαστο (13.431, *Od.* 2.158). For the gen. with διδασκόμενος cf. 21.487, πολέμοιο δαήμεναι. Pythagoras proved metempsychosis by recognizing Euphorbos' shield, on show at Didyma, as once his own (Diog. Laërt. 8.1.4f.); perhaps he liked Euphorbos' name for its hint of dietary restraint.

812–17 The emotive apostrophe marks another stage in Patroklos' demise (cf. 787). Even now Euphorbos is too wary of his unarmed foe to do more than snatch his spear from the wound and retreat to the ranks (like Meriones at 13.528–33), before Patroklos withdraws too; this increases our respect for Patroklos' valour (so bT). A bolder man would run up and deliver a fatal blow (cf. e.g. 4.524); the second half of 813 describes a retreat at 11.354. The choice of δόρυ μείλινον rather than δ. χάλκεον (814) stresses the spear's shaft, which Euphorbos grabs (13.597n.). — Patroklos is in a tunic, not naked (*LfgrE* s.v. γυμνός). Thus Hektor says Akhilleus would kill him γυμνός 'like a woman, once I take off my armour' (22.124f.) – men always carried arms (15.479–82n.). Warriors wore tunics under their corslets (841, 3.359). For δουρὶ δαμασθείς (etc., 10×) without ὑπό cf. 22.246; the Leipzig scholia note that δ. can mean 'wounded', and need not contradict οὐδ' ἐδάμασσ' at 813 ('did not kill'). Verse 817 mainly describes warriors who are disabled or will be slain (Fenik, *TBS* 140). ἐχάζετο and ἀναχαζόμενον must be conative: Patroklos *tries* to retreat. Had he gone any distance, he would have left his armour behind; yet his body is later with the armour, if not in it (777–867n.).

818–22 Warriors often attack discomfited foes trying to withdraw (e.g. 11.447, 13.516, 13.566f., 13.648,14.408f.). The neat chiasmus in 819 sums up and inverts 816f.; its first hemistich is adapted, aptly enough, to Euphorbos' death (17.47, duly followed by δούπησεν δὲ πεσών). The scansion εἶδεν Πατροκλῆα μεγάθυμον is a makeshift; elsewhere this name–epithet phrase fills the space from the fem. caesura, as in Βαθυ-/Διο-/'Επι-/'Οϊ-κλῆα μ. As usual (14/16×), ἀγχίμολον is linked with ἐλθεῖν; this reflects its etymology (ἄγχι + μολεῖν). The blow to Patroklos' lower flank is typical: cf. 5.857, 11.381, *Od.* 22.294f. When he falls, we think him dead (823–6n.); but he remains sitting up until 863. Since his death is based on Akhilleus', it may be no accident that his fall 'grieved the Achaean host': Akhilleus' name is from ἄχος + λαός (Palmer, *The Greek Language* 37f.). ἤκαχε is a root-aor. more ancient than ἀκάχησα or ἀκαχίζω; this sequel to δούπησεν δὲ πεσών never recurs (cf. 15.419–21n.).

823–6 A fine simile, framed by λέων ἐβιήσατο χάρμη and λ. ἐδάμασσε βίηφιν, marks Hektor's victory. The aorists show that the combat is already decided: the lion, naturally stronger than the boar, has won. When Hektor's contest with Patroklos was equal, they were likened to two warring lions (756–8n.). Fränkel (*Gleichnisse* 62) deems this duel almost as unrealistic as the battle between massed lions and boars at *Aspis* 168–77. But many duels between lions and boars appear in archaic art (Russo, *Scutum* 11f., 24, and Scott, *Simile* 181 with pl. 2); Aesop tells how a lion fights a boar over a spring, until they see vultures waiting for one of them to fall (338 Perry). Aristotle reports that lions will run from a hostile boar (*Hist. An.* 9.630a2); a view so widely held will have seemed natural to the audience. Homer depicts the greatest unequal duel he knew of in the natural world, heightening the image of a lion killing a bull for Patroklos slaying Sarpedon (487–9n.). The series of animal similes extends to 17.20ff. The following analysis draws on M. Baltes, *A&A* 29 (1983) 44ff.

The image recalls the last lion-simile (756–8), where both halves of 824 appear. Thus it sums up both the long, hard fight for Kebriones' body (represented by the disputed spring) and the fatal blow (the frame stresses this, as we saw). Both animals are fierce (duals put them on the same level), the spring is tiny and both are thirsty (hunger spurred them on last time). The lion has no epithet, but the beaten boar is 'tireless', an epithet reserved for the sun and the Sperkheios; this evokes the hitherto unbeaten Patroklos. Its panting proves it still alive: this conveys the length of the recent struggle (πολλὰ δέ τ' ἀσθμαίνοντα is echoed by πολέας πεφνόντα in 827), and is our sole hint that Patroklos still lives. His fall at 822 and the summary of his foray, now ended in death, at 827ff. mislead us into thinking him dead (for this effect cf. 14.402–39n.); his reply at 843ff. comes as a shock – we thought Hektor was boasting over a corpse.

825 The survival of πῖδαξ, from πιδάω, 'gush', in Ionic prose and modern Greek shows that it was in Homer's vernacular, and is not a poetic fossil; as Mark Edwards suggests to me, the poet links it with πιέμεν, which may even be the true etymology. He certainly plays on ἀμφί and ἄμφω. ἀμφί with the gen. recurs at *Od.* 8.267, *Aspis* 402, *HyHerm* 172; a gen. is usual with ἀμφιμάχομαι. πιέμεν (2× *Od.*) displays metrical lengthening to avoid ∪∪∪; it has ῐ elsewhere (*Od.* 18.3, *HyDem* 209).

827–9 πεφνόντα is the aor. of θείνω, 'smite', 'kill', parallel to Sanskrit *jaghnant-* from *hánti*, 'smites'; the root is *$g^{w}hen$-, cf. Latin *de-fendo*, Hittite *kuenzi*. ἀπηύρα, with its participle ἀπούρας (< ἀπο + *ϝρᾱ-), fut. ἀπουρήσουσι and sigmatic aor. ἀπό(ϝ)ερσε, is an equally isolated archaism (cf. σχεδὸν ἄορι θυμὸν ἀπηύρα, 2×). The variant ἀγόρευε comes from 21.121, 21.427, which have προσηύδα as a variant.

830–63 Hektor's boast reveals his self-delusion; Patroklos' defiant reply lays this bare, his own folly forgotten in the clear vision brought by approaching death (Reinhardt, *IuD* 323–5). By saying that Apollo disarmed him – something he cannot know without mantic powers, since the god was invisible – he proves to us his veracity in predicting Hektor's death, already foreshadowed by the poet at 800; this is confirmed by how he dies before Hektor can gainsay him. The play on illusion and reality gives the scene a tragic aspect (so Lohmann, *Reden* 115–17): Hektor, the apparent winner, hears that he is in fact the loser, a neat *peripeteia* (but he suffers no *anagnorisis* until 22.296). I give the essence of Lohmann's analysis below:

	Hektor's vaunt		*Patroklos' reply*
I	*Hektor's victory* (830–6)	I	*Hektor's victory* (844–50)
a	*Illusion*: You expected to sack Troy, *fool*.	a	Boast away.
		b	Zeus and Apollo gave you victory.
b	*Hektor's role*: But I defend the Trojans.	c	I could have slain twenty men like you.
		b′	Apollo and Euphorbos killed me.
a′	*Reality*: Vultures will eat you.	a′	You are only my third killer!
II	*Akhilleus and Hektor's death* (837–42)	II	*Akhilleus and Hektor's death* (851–4)
a	Akhilleus didn't help you,	a	Akhilleus will soon kill you.
b	saying 'Don't return to the *hollow ships* without killing Hektor',		
a′	and persuaded you, *fool*.		

Other patterns cut across these correspondences. Hektor mocks Patroklos' folly at 833 and 842; Patroklos' closing prediction answers his false claim that vultures will eat him. Hektor's delusion is clearest when, in order to hurt Patroklos and mock Akhilleus, he imagines what Akhilleus said upon sending him forth, portraying the hero as a cowardly, bloodthirsty deceiver who duped his friend. The direct speech in which he casts Akhilleus' words, and which aims at greater rhetorical effect, in fact subverts their validity, since we ourselves heard them (83–96): Akhilleus never persuaded Patroklos, but warned him against Apollo, and, as he later claims (18.14), against Hektor too (but cf. 242–8n.). Patroklos does not rebut this, explain that his own success swept him away or try to justify the fact that Akhilleus was not there to defend him (Akhilleus will reproach himself for this at 18.98f.); fiercely loyal to his friend, he parries jibe with jibe in the best tradition of warriors' taunts. Hektor learns nothing, replying that he may kill Akhilleus rather than vice versa. He discovers the truth only in book 22, where his dialogue with the victorious Akhilleus runs parallel to this scene in both language and themes. Akhilleus' opening vaunt at 22.331–6 resembles Hektor's here (again I follow Lohmann, *Reden* 159–61, cf. 22.330–67n.):

a *Illusion*: Hektor, you expected to be safe after killing Patroklos, you *fool*.
b *Akhilleus' role*: But I was left by the *hollow ships* to avenge him.
c *Reality*: It is you that will be torn by dogs and birds, but him the Greeks will bury.

This vaunt is not based on delusion; Hektor cannot dispute Akhilleus' prediction, since the latter can treat his body however he wishes. When Hektor replies, 'feebly' like Patroklos at 843, he begs his foe to return it to Troy, but Akhilleus rejects his plea (thus their exchange is two speeches longer than this one). The similarities increase as the dialogue ends: Hektor predicts Akhilleus' death, and dies in the same verses as Patroklos (855–8, up to προσηύδα, = 22.361–4); the victor replies, although his victim is already dead, and pulls his spear from the body. Hektor's vain hope of victory contrasts with Akhilleus' clear-eyed acceptance of death 'whenever the gods will it' (cf. Thalmann, *Conventions* 46f.). Thus book 22 heightens and elaborates this death-scene, which itself heightens and elaborates Sarpedon's (476–507n.).

830–1 ἔφησθα, as often (13.83–90n.), means 'you said (to yourself)', 'thought': cf. the start of Akhilleus' taunt to Hektor (22.331), ἀτάρ που ἔφης. Hektor's hesitant tone, conveyed by the thrice-repeated που, is a sham: he is sure he is right. In fact Patroklos did come close to taking Troy (698ff.); even in this Hektor misses the mark. Bekker conjectured κεραϊξέμεν for the -ϊζέμεν of all sources; a fut. is unavoidable, especially in view of ἄξειν (832). This corruption goes back to confusion between zeta (Ⅰ) and xi (Ⅎ) in early East Ionic script (see p. 36 n. 70). On ἀμός see p. 8 n. 2. For ἐλεύθερον ἦμαρ ἀπούρας cf. 6.455n., 20.193; the echo ἤ. ἀναγκαῖον (836) frames the first half of Hektor's speech, stressing his claim that vultures will devour Patroklos.

833–4 νήπιε opens a verse in the middle of a speech at 18.295, 22.333 (cf. 2.38n.). Eustathius (1089.23–6) notes that, from pride, Hektor uses his own name (cf. 492–501n.), just as he imagines Akhilleus calling him ἀνδροφόνος

(840, cf. 716–20n.). His steeds race to battle, literally 'stretch out with their feet': cf. 375 (τανύοντο ... ἵπποι), where the Trojans' horses flee in panic. That his team led the rout (367f.) gives the lie to this boast. ὀρωρέχαται is from ὀρέγω.

836–8 Hektor's shocking threat to feed Patroklos to the vultures forms the centre of his speech; lapidary concision gives it emphasis (he paints a gorier picture to Aias at 13.831f.). This vital theme appeared when Glaukos worried that the Greeks might abuse Sarpedon's body, as Patroklos enjoined (538–47n.); it intensifies in book 17. For γῦπες ἔδονται cf. 4.237, 18.271, 22.42. ἆ δειλέ conveys sympathy, real or fake; it can open a speech or a new section of one (e.g. 11.441, 11.452, 11.816). ἐσθλὸς ἐών is concessive, almost 'although he is able to (help)': cf. 11.665. The antithesis μένων ... ἰόντι hints that Akhilleus hung back from cowardice.

839–42 The voc. ensures that we know that Hektor is quoting Akhilleus' words. He gives his foe a bloodthirsty imagination: so too Agamemnon prays to 'rip Hektor's tunic about his chest, tattered by the bronze' (2.416f.). Like ῥωγαλέον there, αἱματόεντα is proleptic. The oxymoron in φρένας ἄφρονι πεῖθε adds that Akhilleus duped Patroklos; the same hemistich described Athene's suasion of Pandaros at 4.104.

843–54 On the structure of Patroklos' reply see 830–63n. 'He is not terrified by death, the severity of his pain or the lack of anyone to help him, but is still full of defiance and taunts Hektor rather than supplicates him, claiming victory even after his decease' (bT). Aptly, he dies with Akhilleus' name on his lips.

843–7 For 843 cf. 15.244–6n. The combination ἤδη νῦν, 'now indeed', reflects the origin of ἤδη as ἤ δή (Chantraine, *Dict.* s.v.). The ease of divine action is a topos (13.90n.). Many Analysts reject 846 because it refers to the removal of Patroklos' armour, but it is needed to contrast the gods' easy action with Hektor's paltry deed (Reinhardt, *IuD* 323–5). τοιοῦτοι means 'such (as you)', with a harsh ellipsis. Since Patroklos defeated Sarpedon and has just slain twenty-seven men (785), his jibe that he could have slain twenty Hektors on the spot reflects his valour as well as his defiance. 'Twenty' is a randomly large number (13.260–1n.).

849–50 The involvement of Zeus, fate (μοῖρα), Apollo and Euphorbos in Patroklos' death increases his stature and reduces Hektor's (bT). How can Hektor be his 'third' killer after all these? Aristarchus rightly thought Patroklos counts only those who laid hands upon him. Now Zeus and Apollo in 845, and fate and Apollo here, form a kind of hendiadys, since both pairs take the sing. verbs ἔδωκε and ἔκτανεν (so Leaf): cf. 'Hesiod' frag. 280.2, [ἀλλά με μοῖρ' ὀλο]ὴ καὶ Λητοῦς ὤλεσε[ν υἱός], where Meleagros refers to his death in battle at Apollo's hands (cf. *Cat.* 25.12f.). The ring formed by 845 and 849 confirms that Zeus and fate are equated; these are two ways to explain the same event – it can occur because Zeus (or 'the gods') decide it, or because it is simply one's portion in life (on Zeus's relation to fate see pp. 4ff.). Zeus ultimately grants victory or defeat (15.490–3n.). Apollo occupies a lower rung on the same ladder of causation; by striking Patroklos he is responsible for his death, yet he acts for Zeus (cf. 650–1n.). Mortals' actions are on the bottom rung, occurring at the same time as, and in parallel with, divine action; thus Thetis and Xanthos say Apollo slew Patroklos and gave Hektor glory (18.454–6, 19.413f.). On this 'dual motivation' of events see pp. 3f. The formula (Διὸς καὶ) Λητοῦς υἱός (etc.) recurs 2× Hes., 3× *Hy.*, and is adapted to Λ. ἀγλαὸς/ἐρικυδέος υἱ. (etc., 6× *Hy.*). Its sole Homeric recurrence is also in modified form, | Λ. καὶ Διὸς υἱ. (1.9), where *Λητόος cannot be restored. The original sense of (ἐξ-)εναρίζω, 'strip' (cf. ἔναρα), is apt here, where the focus is on the armour; ἐναίρω has lost this sense. Stripping the armour was so usual that it became synonymous with killing. The present tense stands for an immediate future: cf. 8.541, 9.261, 24.110, *Od.* 20.156.

852–4 Dying was held to bring precognition: so Xenophon, *Cyr.* 8.7.21; Plato, *Apol.* 39c; Aristotle frag. 10; Artemon of Miletus in AT; Cicero, *De Divinatione* 1.63 with Pease's n.; Genesis 49. The like belief that dying swans sing from foreknowledge of their death appears in Aeschylus (*Ag.* 1444f.) and Plato (*Phaedo* 84E). From δηρόν, 852f. = 24.131f. (Thetis to Akhilleus). On θήν see 13.620–5n.; for βέη, 'you will live', cf. 15.194n. Death and fate, treated almost as synonyms (cf. 335–6n.), are personified by the verb: cf. μοῖρα παρεστήκη θανάτοιο (*HyAphr* 269). παρέστηκεν is innovative; for the formula (θάνατος καὶ) μ. κραταιή see 330–4n. Aristarchus took δαμέντ' as dat. after τοι (Did/A); the acc. would be a *constructio ad sensum*. With the rest of 854 cf. Ἀχιλῆος ἀμύμονος (2×), ἀ. Αἰακίδαο (140).

855–8 = 22.361–4, up to προσηύδα (but 363 is spurious); 855 = 502, where see n. Homer or a recent predecessor reserved 855 for the deaths of his greatest heroes; its repetition stresses the uniquely important link between the deaths of Sarpedon, Patroklos and Hektor. Verses 856f. contain two notable archaisms, but the whole couplet cannot go back to Bronze Age poetry; even καί is post-Myc., and bardic diction was always a complex patchwork. (i) ῥέθεα, here 'limbs', meant 'face' in Aeolic (so Aristarchus). Tragic and Alexandrian poets use it for 'face' (Pfeiffer on Callim. frag. 67.13); ῥεθομάλιδας, 'apple-cheeked', is 'Aeolic' (D on 22.68), and ῥέθος is in Sappho (frag. 22.3). Dionysius Thrax (in AbT *ad loc.*) took it as 'face', since we expire through our mouth and nose. This was no doubt its original sense (Leaf adduces the two meanings of Latin *os*), but Ionian bards reinterpreted it as 'limbs': cf. ῥεθέων ἐκ θυμὸν ἕληται (22.68); ἐκ μελέων θυμὸς πτάτο (23.880); θ. ᾤχετ' ἀπὸ μ. (2×, cf. 7.131, *Od.* 15.354). See Leumann, *HW* 218–22; Chantraine, *Dict.* s.v.

(ii) The scansion of ἀνδροτῆτα as ∪∪ – ∪ goes back to a Myc. or even earlier form *anr̥tāta (cf. Sanskrit nr̥ṣu = ἀνδράσιν), as Wathelet showed, comparing the Aeolisms ἀβροτάξομεν and ἀβρότη (p. 11). The ancient scansion also survives at 24.6, where μένος ἠΰ looks equally old. The sense must be 'manhood' or 'vigour', like μένος, not 'courage' (ἠνορέη). The conjecture ἀδροτῆτα, 'vigour', read by Plato and Plutarch, fails to explain the vulgate. Ἄϊδόσδε βεβήκει recurs 2× *Od*. For τεθνειῶτα see pp. 35f.

859–63 With his usual confident scorn for omens (13.821–3n.), Hektor is unshaken. But his reply falls flat: since Patroklos is already dead, he loses even the satisfaction of extracting his soul along with the spear (contrast Patroklos killing Sarpedon at 505, but cf. Akhilleus at 22.364). Akhilleus' reaction to prophecies of his death is more fatalistic (see 830–63n., 18.98ff., 19.420ff.). Verse 861 echoes 848; but Hektor does not say ἐμῷ ὑπὸ δουρὶ δαμείς, since ἑ. ὑ. δ. τυπεὶς ἀπὸ θυμὸν ὀλέσσῃ (etc.) traditionally ends speeches (11.433, 12.250, 18.92). It is clumsily adapted here: φθήῃ governs τ. and ὀλέσσαι is a complementary infin., i.e. 'may first be stabbed by my spear so as to lose his life'. To remove his spear, Hektor callously steadies the body with his heel, shoving the sitting Patroklos onto his back as he pulls it out. 'Brazen spear' aptly stresses the spear's point (cf. *Od*. 10.164f.), not its shaft as 'ashen spear' would have done (13.597n.). For λάξ see 5.620n.

864–7 Horses are often part of the spoils: cf. the winning of Sarpedon's or Asios' (506f., 13.400f.). Hektor longs to win Akhilleus' divine pair, but they elude him just as he earlier eluded Patroklos (866 = 383); his greed gives Menelaos the chance to defend Patroklos' body and armour (17.1ff., 75–8). Nor has he slain Patroklos' charioteer, whose escape prepares for his brave resistance at 17.429–542 and prefigures Akhilleus' return. Automedon's introduction as *Akhilleus'* driver signals his importance (he was last mentioned at 684); Eustathius (1090.46) remarks that it is as if Akhilleus had already promoted him to Patroklos' post, the usual system when one's leader was slain (145–8n.). Since a verse like 865 twice describes Patroklos (165, 17.388), whose death is based on Akhilleus', Automedon's designation as the latter's driver supports Kullmann's guess (*Quellen* 133f.) that Automedon was traditionally present at *Akhilleus'* death; he was certainly at Antilokhos' (*LIMC* s.v. Achilleus no. 811: a Corinthian vase, *c*. 560), on which Patroklos' death is also based (see p. 312).

867 = 381 (spurious). The gods gave Peleus the horses when he married Thetis (130–54n.); to make this explicit someone (in T) added 867a, ἤματι τῷ ὅτε γῆμε Θέτιν λιπαροκρήδεμνον, clearly on the model of 18.85 (the latter half of 84 = 867). Cf. T's other pedantic interpolations (14.349–53n.). λ. may be of rhapsodic origin; isolated in Homer (18.382), this epithet is popular later (*Od*. 12.133a, *Cypria* frag. 5.3, *Cat*. 244.17, 3× *HyDem*). As usual the next book runs on with almost no break.

INDEX

For the rules governing the transliteration of Greek names see vol. I, x. An index of Greek words will appear at the end of vol. VI.

423

Index

Akkadian, 121, 182, 206
Akmon, 230
Akrisios, 203
Aktaion, 204, 335
Aktor, 70, 134, 339–40, 341, 342
Alastor, 100
Albracht, F., 62, 266, 362
Alcaeus, 22, 44, 47, 57, 80, 139, 144, 192,
303, 320, 362, 364, 385, 390
Alcmaeonis, 122, 164
Alcman, 153, 161, 182, 188, 189, 230, 319,
336, 342, 367
Alegenor, 218, 222
Alexander Aetolus, 350
Alexandrian poets, 14, 271; scholars, xi, 20,
22–8, *and see* Aristarchus, Aristophanes,
Zenodotus
Alexion, 71
Alkathoos, 93, 100, 101, 102, 103, 105, 106,
109, 128, 164, 413–14
Alkimakhe, 134
Alkimedon, Alkimos, 317, 336, 344
Alkinoos, 38
Alkmaion, 367–8
Alkmene, 202, 204
Alkuone, 197
Alkuoneus, 191, 192
allegory, 168, 184, 231, 247
Allen, T. W., 20, 21, 22, 212, 310; W. S.,
385
allies, 273, 371, 384, 386
alliteration, 46, 47, 112, 144, 153, 159, 166,
176, 223, 289, 336, 353, 413; *see also*
sound-effect
Aloni, A., 31
Alpers, K., 21
alphabet, *see* manuscripts, script, writing
allusion: internal, 111, 162, 229; to myths,
169, 179, 180, 190, 192, 197, 199, 203,
205, 225, 247, 250
Alōeus, 285
Alphesiboia, 340
Alter, R., 275
Althaia, 164
Amaltheia, 261
Amazons, 121
ambrosia, 174, 396
ambush, 82
Ameis, K. F., 167
Amenhotep III, 276
Amisodaros, 358, 371
Ammonius, 25
Amnisos, 276
Amphiaraos, 128–9
Amphiklos, 357
Amphimakhos, 41, 67, 70, 72, 73, 74, 132

Amphios, 128
Amphitruon, 70, 204, 342
Amphoteros, 368, 370
Amudon, 355
anachronism, 42, 302, 313, 358, 371,
373
anacoluthon, 71, 101, 118, 211, 276, 347,
353, 359, 368
Anacreon, 24, 57, 303
anagnorisis, 417
Analysts, 40, 41, 55, 65, 129, 132, 216, 235,
314, 321, 395, 419
anaphora, 136, 142, 184, 407
Anatolia: customs of, 65; lions in, 291;
Mycenaeans and, 19, 359, 371; weaponry
of, 121, 286; *see also* Hittites, loan-words,
Lycians, names
anatomy, 114, 126, *and see* wounds
anax, 118, 364, *and see* king
anchor-stones, 158
Andersen, Ø., 33, 162, 164
Andraimon, 164
androktasia, see killings
Andromakhe, 178, 405
Andron, 276
Andronikos, M., 102, 270
anecdotes, see *exempla*
anger, 105–6, 160, 242, 319; of gods, 365,
366; metaphors for, 319, 354; as motive
for killing, 40, 72, 98, 219, 385, 388; *see
also* Akhilleus, withdrawal
animals, 116, 238–9, 364; Aristophanes on,
165, 303; emotions of, 257, 262, 291, 297,
352, 361–2, 365; and slang, 357, 360; *see
also* Aristarchus, Aristotle, metamorphoses, similes, zoological accuracy
animism, *see* personification
Ankhises, 93, 99, 100, 101, 106, 170
answering-formulae, 201, 232
ant, 319
Antagores, 191
Antenor, 101, 219, 275, 284
anthropomorphism, 1, 179, 181
Antilokhos, 40, 54, 97, 108, 114, 223, 256,
272, 284, 288, 290, 292, 357; in *Aithiopis*,
312, 421; and Akhilleus, 312–14, 315,
359; epithets of, 98, 291; and Nestor, 115,
126, 312, 379; in *Od.*, 313–14; and
Patroklos, 313–14, 344, 421
Antimachus, xxv, 26, 36, 50, 222, 230, 241,
251
Antinoos, 96
antithesis, 81, 129, 138, 282, 362, 391,
397–8, 400, 402, 419
Anu, 247
anvil, 229–30

425

Index

mulberry, 177

Munding, H., 365

murex, 276

murder, *see* manslaughter

Murinē, 187

Musaeus, 31

Muses, 147, 223, 329, 330, 331

music, musician, 8, 28, 125

Muški, 42

Musoi, 42, 143, 224

mutilation, *see* corpses

Mycenaean, xxv, 9–13, 14, 15–19, 116, 118, 119, 130, 135, 139, 152, 262, 303, 306, 386, 395, 403; dative, 130, 240, 341, 385; formulae, 10–12, 214; *h*, 10, 11, 244; patronymics, 299, 399; syllabic *r*, 11, 159, 244, 421; toponyms, 94, 238, 276; verbs, 17, 238, 243; vocabulary, 271, 323, 343, 391, 413; *see also* Knossos, Linear B, names, Pylos, Thebes

Mycenaeans: and Anatolia, 19, 359, 371; chariots of, 113, 152, 344, 413, 415; corslets, 286; cults, 115, 337; and Egypt, 14, 276; epics of, 10–12, 13, 15, 16–18, 19, 48, 214, 399, 420; festivals, 171; figurines, 177; furniture, 189, 413; games, 415; gods, 85, 115, 394; land-tenure, 165, 390; mercenaries of, 133, 140; myths, 19, 129, 218, 291, 359, 371, 415; slave-trade, 187, 276; spears, 64, 334; tombs, 10, 14, 136, 177, 203, 213; warfare, 19, 129, 136, 213, 270, 344, 359, 371, 404; weaponry, 10–11, 13, 218; *see also* clothing, fresco, helmet, names, shield, sword

Myrmidons, 313, 317, 319, 324, 353, 354, 384, 386, 387; leaders of, 339–44; resent Akhilleus, 156, 320, 344–5; similes for, 338, 352–3

Mysians, *see* Musoi

myths, xi, 1, 164, 169, 170; expurgation of, *see* suppression; Babylonian, 182, 202, 236, 247, 314, 393; Egyptian, 181; Germanic, 50, 145, 230, 373, 409; Hittite, 121, 181, 183; Indic, 174; Myc., *see* Mycenaeans; Phoenician, 181, 198

n-mobile, 9, 19, 64, 88, 91, 144, 168, 209, 214, 220, 240, 248, 258, 267, 280, 282, 359, 406, 415, 420; before digamma, 19, 249; as Ionic remedy, 113, 139; in runover verb, 9, 49, 59, 119, 167, 327, 338, 343, 396, 412

Nagler, M. N., 178

Nagy, G., 8, 9, 10, 11, 16, 17, 94, 106, 261, 303, 339, 341, 345, 348, 372

Naiads, 217

nameless characters, 74, 96, 100, 119, 166, 358, 411

names, Aeolic, 19, 320; Anatolian, 95, 143, 285, 358, 359, 370, 372, 401; of barbarians, 68, 70, 367; based on rivers, 217; bovine, 51, 135, 336; characters with two, 134, 143, 197, 317, 371; chthonic, 100; from epithets, *see* epithet; equine, 304, 336; from functions, 96–7, 143, 275, 298, 305, 399; glossed by poet, 42; homonyms, 284, 340–1, 371; invented, 22, 42, 96–7, 99, 101, 134, 218, 220, 221, 224, 284, 289, 298, 370, 371, 387, 389, 401, 414; of isles, 44, 187; lists of, *see* lists; Minoan, 358; misremembered by poet, 134, 142, 143, 224, 344, 387; Myc., 14, 68, 71, 85, 94, 95, 99, 100, 104, 108, 135, 165, 187, 192, 231, 284, 298, 320, 344, 370, 387, 399; Prodicus on, 389; reused, 370, 401; short form of, 286, 317, 340, 398; too terrible to utter, 137, 192, 393; tribal, 42, 187; used of oneself, 381, 418–19

narratology, xi, *and see* point of view

nature, 45, 206, 211, 365–6

Naupaktia, 42, 134, 269

Nauplia, 276

navel-stone, 230

necessity, 164

neck, *see* wounds

necklace, 177

negative, 245, 282; adjectives, 252; comparisons, 211

Neitzel, H., 87

Neleidai, Neleus, 19, 31, 70, 115, 134, 264, 341, 359

Nemean lion, 291

nemesis, 58–9, 159, 249

Neo-Analysis, xi, 312

Neoptolemos, 334, 336, 348, 399

nēpios-comment, 240, 320, 397, 418

Nereids, 195, 200, 320, 408

Nestor, 31, 33, 134, 156, 210, 228; and Agamemnon, 152, 153, 154, 156; age of, 73, 77; and Antilokhos, 115, 126, 312, 379; chariot of, 271; and Diomedes, 162, 163; and Makhaon, 149–50, 151, 152, 255, 271, 272; and Odysseus, 318–19; and Patroklos, 4, 150, 226, 255, 256, 268, 271, 309, 310, 314, 318, 319; prayer of, 225, 255, 256, 268–9, 300; and rampart, 157, 226–7; shield of, 99, 152; sons of, 357–8; spear of, 152, 280; speeches by, 151, 157, 259, 264, 292, 300–1, 319, 322; on Zeus, 156

neuter plural, 122, 403, 408

Index

Othrus, Mt, 94
Otos, 108, 285, 287
Ouranos, see Sky
overdetermination, see double motivation
overlengthening, 43
Ovid, 108, 197
Owen, E. T., 41, 312, 314
owl, 108, 196–7
oxen, 51, 135–6, 187, 291, 297–8, 336, 340, 410; see also leather
oxymoron, 142, 319, 381, 419

Page, D. L., xi, 133, 209, 269, 314, 318, 320, 324, 325
pain, 117, 383
painting, see fresco, vase-painting
Paiones, 117, 187, 355
Paley, F. A., 239, 395
Pallas, 191, 295
Pallene, 191
Palmer, L. R., 8, 15, 16, 44, 416
Palmus, 143
Pamphylian, 88
Pan, 257, 262
Panathenaea, 30–1, 37
Pandaros, 93, 96, 121, 277, 349, 358
Pandora, 169, 170, 173, 340, 341
panhellenism, 8
panic, see fear, rout
panorama, 40, 88–9, 90, 167, 273, 292, 300, 304, 386, 391, 405, 407–8
panther, 56
Panthoos, 140, 285, 414
Paphlagonians, 126, 358
papyri, xii, xxv, 20, 21, 25, 327 and passim; Ptolemaic, 22, 23, 28, 36, 193
paradigms, see exempla
Paraskevaïdes, H. A., 360
Paris, 109, 116, 121, 141, 256, 333, 379, 414–15; and Akhilleus, 127, 312, 334, 409–10, 414; and Aphrodite, 3, 283; and Hektor, 130, 141, 142; and Helen, 3, 4, 170, 198, 201; hypocrisy of, 40, 127; Judgement of, 27, 124, 169, 173, 175, 185; killings by, 73, 113, 127, 263, 264; and Menelaos, 5, 120, 127; weapons of, 118, 264
Parke, H. W., 348, 349
Parker, R., 265, 347
paroemiac, 10
Parry, A., 120, 290, 405; A. A., 84, 125, 279; M., xi, 9, 13, 16, 18, 20, 45, 54, 64, 112, 343, 356
Parthenius, 197
particle, 17, 52, 81, 123, 249, 268, 280, 319

pasai, 26, 109, 110, 135, 163, 193, 231, 241, 257, 260, 353, 376
Pasitheē, 188, 195
Pasquali, G., 20, 21, 23
pathos, 4, 6, 40, 67–8, 93, 129, 278, 285, 392; and gods, 2, 4, 42, 90, 267, 411; in similes, 69, 267, 361, 393; sources of: apostrophe, 317–18, 412, bereft father, 67–8, 126, 127, 128, 221, 235, 336, 358, 375, 377, 389, brevity of life, 295, brothers' deaths, 358, choice, 4, compliments, 101, 289, death far away, 75, 377, 384–5, 389, death of priest's sons, 128, 390, exile, 164, 276, 387, failure to return, 304–5, 346, 347, fate, 6, foreknowledge, 128, hair in dust, 288, 412, helplessness, 53, 101, 368, late arrival at Troy, 93, 143, 415, lost beauty, 412, lost tranquillity, 67, 289, pastoral setting, 217, 289, unawareness, 111–12, 130, 320, 405, 408, understatement, 304, useless wealth, 68, 128, 221, 222, widow's grief, 67, 100
Paton, W. R., 334
patrimony, division of, 247, 282
patriotism, 282
Patroklos, 276, 313–14, 317–18, 339–40, 386; on Agamemnon, 318; and Aiantes, 384, 385, 386; and Akhilleus, see Akhilleus; and Akhilleus' armour, 310–11, 333–5, 353, 373, 386, 397, 408–9, 411–13, 415; on Akhilleus, 239, 315, 353; runs to Akhilleus, 226, 256, 271, 272, 273, 309; and Antilokhos, 313–14, 344, 421; apostrophe to, 120, 317–18, 388, 398, 405, 411, 415; like Ares, 225, 411; aristeia of, 311, 312, 318, 353–4, 356–7, 364, 367; arming of, 332–3; ashes of, 314; assaults Troy, 399–400; charioteer of, 336, 421; corpse of, 72, 221, 386, 392, 397; death of, 97, 234, 304–13, 328, 329, 337, 370, 381, 405, 408–21; as Akhilleus' deputy, 78, 309, 311, 370; disobedience of, 310, 311, 312, 327, 370, 393, 397, 417; epithets for, 271, 317–18; funeral games of, 370; as healer, 272; and homosexuality, 328; intervention of, 234, 255, 269; and Kebriones, 397, 402–5; killings by, 354–5, 368, 369–70, 412; and Kleopatre, 309; and Lukaon, 313; mental state of, 386, 396, 404, 412, 414; and Meriones, 386, 389, 391; feels pity, 225, 271, 315; poet on, 320; and Sarpedon, 310–11, 337, 370–4, 377–95, 419; similes for, 315, 316, 373–4, 416; speeches by, 283, 318–20, 353, 386, 391, 404–5,

Index